Southern Living

COOKBOOK
Classics

Compiled and edited by
Jean Wickstrom Liles

Oxmoor House

Library of Congress Control Number: 00-135378
ISBN: 0-8487-2468-2

Printed in the United States of America
Second printing 2001

Editor-in-Chief: Nancy Fitzpatrick Wyatt
Editorial Director, Special Interest Publications:
    Ann H. Harvey
Senior Foods Editor: Susan Carlisle Payne
Senior Editor, Copy and Homes:
    Olivia Kindig Wells
Art Director: James Boone

Menu and Recipe Consultant: Jean Wickstrom Liles
Assistant Editor: Kelly Hooper Troiano
Copy Editors: Keri Bradford Anderson, Donna Baldone,
    Jacqueline Giovanelli, Jane Phares,
    Catherine Ritter Scholl
Editorial Assistants: Heather Averett, Julie A. Cole,
    Valorie J. Cooper, Jane Lorberau, Suzanne Powell
Designers: Melissa Jones Clark, Rita Yerby
Photographers: Ralph Anderson, Jim Bathie,
    Tina Cornett, J. Savage Gibson, Sylvia Martin,
    Charles Walton IV
Photo Stylists: Kay E. Clarke, Virginia R. Cravens,
    Ashley Johnson, Leslie Byars Simpson,
    Ashley J. Wyatt
Director, Production and Distribution: Phillip Lee
Books Production Manager: Theresa L. Beste
Associate Production Managers: John Charles Gardner,
    Vanessa Cobbs Richardson
Production Coordinator: Marianne Jordan Wilson
Production Assistants: Faye Porter Bonner,
    Valerie L. Heard

Cover: *Asian Pork Salad, page 798*

WE'RE HERE FOR YOU!

We at Oxmoor House are dedicated to serving you with reliable information that expands your imagination and enriches your life. We welcome your comments and suggestions. Please write us at:

Oxmoor House, Inc.
Editor, *Southern Living*® *Cookbook Classics*
2100 Lakeshore Drive
Birmingham, AL 35209

To order additional publications,
call 1-205-877-6560.

We Want Your FAVORITE RECIPES!

Southern Living cooks are the best cooks of all, and we want your secrets! Please send your favorite original recipes for main dishes, desserts, and everything in between, along with any hands-on tips and a sentence about why you like each recipe. We can't guarantee we'll print them in a cookbook, but if we do, we'll send you $20 and a free copy of the cookbook. Send each recipe on a separate page with your name, address, and daytime phone number to:

Cookbook Recipes
Oxmoor House
2100 Lakeshore Drive
Birmingham, AL 35209

Contents

Southern Living

ALL-TIME FAVORITE

30-MINUTE
MEALS

Contents

Make It . . . Quick and Easy

Even with today's fast-paced schedules it's possible to have quick, easy, *and* delicious meals on the table in 30 minutes. Many of our recipes have a short ingredient list and may use quality convenience products in a unique way. These recipes, along with our TimeSaver tips, are designed for speed. While your hands-on preparation shouldn't exceed 30 minutes, note that most menus contain one or more make-ahead recipes. These are designated by the diamond symbol (◆) in the menu.

Organize Your Kitchen

Arrange food, equipment, and utensils in your pantry and cabinets for easy access and quick cooking.

• **Stock** your pantry with staple items. Group similar items together, and rotate older items to the front to use first. Keep as many labels as possible in plain sight for at-a-glance inventory.

• **Alphabetize** spices on a turntable or rack for speedy identification.

• **Use** plastic drawer dividers to organize kitchen drawers. Keep small measuring items together, and separate small utensils from large utensils.

• **Keep** knives sharpened and in a safe, convenient holder.

• **Keep** a cutting board on the counter near the sink to save food preparation time.

• **Store** aluminum foil, plastic wrap, and food storage bags in a drawer near your work area.

• **Use** decorative jars near the cooktop and mixing center to store the following items: wooden spoons, plastic scrapers, metal spatulas, tongs, whisks, long-handled cooking spoons and forks, kitchen shears, and a ladle.

• **Hang** pot holders next to the oven, cooktop, and microwave oven. Keep a trivet on the counter near the oven for hot containers.

• **Use** stackable canisters for flour, sugar, and coffee to save space. Keep a dry measuring cup in each canister to use as a handy scoop and measure.

Shortcut Strategies

Use these shortcuts to streamline your time.

• **Read** all the recipes in the menu and assemble all the ingredients and equipment.

• **Make** a game plan. First start with make-aheads; then plan the portion of the meal that involves more total time than active time—such as cooking the rice.

• **Plan** for leftovers by fixing a large quantity or simply doubling a recipe; freeze or refrigerate the remainder so you will have a heat-and-eat meal to serve another day.

• **Measure** dry ingredients before moist ones to minimize cleanup. Before measuring honey and other sticky ingredients, rinse the measure with hot water; then the honey will slide right out.

• **Chop** an ingredient only once, even if it's called for in two recipes in the menu. Divide the ingredients into appropriate portions.

• **Chop** dry ingredients such as breadcrumbs or nuts in a food processor first. Then chop or shred moist or wet foods without washing the workbowl.

• **Use** a food processor to chop, slice, or shred several ingredients consecutively or together without washing the workbowl if the ingredients will later be combined.

• **Chop** and freeze ½-cup portions of green pepper, onion, and parsley in zip-top freezer bags, or purchase prepackaged frozen chopped onion and green pepper. When you have extra time, prepare dry breadcrumbs, shredded cheese, and toasted nuts to freeze.

• **Buy** ingredients in closest-to-usable form. Choose such items as skinned and boned chicken breasts, peeled shrimp, and shredded cheese. Select bags of precut produce at your super-market, or purchase ready-pre-pared ingredients at the salad bar.

• **When** slicing vegetables like carrots, green onions, or celery, slice 3 or 4 pieces at a time.

• **Cut** vegetables into small pieces or thin slices to cook faster.

• **To** peel a tomato or peach, dip the fruit into boiling water for 15 to 30 seconds; the skin will slip off easily.

• **Shape** patties for burgers in a flash. Shape ground meat into a log, partially freeze, and cut into slices of preferred thickness.

• **Buy** precut packaged meat for stir-frying. Or to slice your own, first partially freeze the meat; then slice it across the grain into thin strips.

• **Substitute** an equal amount of ready-to-serve chicken broth for homemade chicken stock.

• **Use** refrigerated or fresh pasta. It cooks faster than dried. Boil-in-bag rice takes half the time of regular rice to cook.

• **Cook** extra quantities of rice and pasta; freeze in individual or family-size portions up to 6 months. Microwave to thaw.

• **Add** pasta to boiling water in small batches. A few drops of oil added to the water prevents pasta from sticking together.

Put Equipment to Use

Utilize kitchen gadgets and equipment to maximize your time and trim minutes off daily meal preparations.

• **Use** two sets of measuring cups and spoons so you can measure consecutive ingredients without washing or wiping out the measure repeatedly.

• **Use** two cutting boards to hold separately chopped ingredients; this will keep you from having to transfer the items to another container.

• **Chop** canned tomatoes right in the can with kitchen shears.

• **Use** a salad spinner to rinse and dry vegetables.

• **Keep** a swivel-bladed vegetable peeler handy for tasks other than peeling vegetables. Use it to shred a small amount of cheese, remove strings from celery stalks, or make quick chocolate curls.

• **Use** a pastry blender to slice hard-cooked eggs and butter or

to mash avocados for chunky guacamole.

• **Use** nonstick cookware and bakeware for easy cleanup.

• **Place** a metal colander upside down over the skillet when frying or sautéing; this will prevent splatters while allowing steam to escape.

• **Use** a pizza cutter to cut dough or to cut day-old bread into cubes for croutons—it's faster than a knife.

• **When** baking or roasting, remember to preheat the oven before preparing the recipe; if you forget, it will take the oven about 20 minutes to reach the specified temperature.

• **Avoid** splatters with your electric mixer by punching holes in a paper plate; insert beaters, and keep the surface of the plate even with the top of the bowl.

• **Use** a meat mallet to tenderize and flatten meat.

• **Use** a microwave oven for thawing foods quickly or for shortcuts such as softening butter and melting chocolate.

• **To** make cracker crumbs or cookie crumbs without a food processor, place crackers or cookies in a heavy-duty, zip-top plastic bag; roll with a rolling pin or pound with a meat mallet.

Microwave Shortcuts Save Time

These techniques are quicker to do in the microwave than in the conventional oven and yield good results.

COOKING BACON—Cook at HIGH

1 slice	1 to 2 minutes
4 slices	3½ to 4½ minutes
6 slices	5 to 7 minutes

Place bacon on a microwave-safe rack in a 12- x 8- x 2-inch baking dish; cover with paper towels. Microwave at HIGH until bacon is crisp. Drain bacon.

MELTING BUTTER OR MARGARINE—Cook at HIGH

1 to 2 tablespoons	35 to 45 seconds
¼ to ½ cup	1 minute
¾ cup	1 to 1½ minutes
1 cup	1½ to 2 minutes

Place butter in a microwave-safe glass measure; microwave at HIGH until melted.

SOFTENING BUTTER OR MARGARINE—Cook at LOW (10% power)

1 to 2 tablespoons	15 to 30 seconds
¼ to ½ cup	1 to 1¼ minutes
1 cup	1½ to 1¾ minutes

Place butter in a microwave-safe measure or plate; microwave at LOW until softened.

MELTING CHOCOLATE—Cook at MEDIUM (50% power)

1 to 2 squares	1½ to 2 minutes
4 to 5 squares	2 to 2½ minutes
½ to 1 cup morsels	2 to 3 minutes
1½ cups morsels	3 to 3½ minutes

Place chocolate in a small bowl; microwave at MEDIUM until melted, stirring once.

TOASTING NUTS—Cook at HIGH

¼ cup chopped nuts	3 minutes
½ cup chopped nuts	3½ minutes
1 cup chopped nuts	4 to 5 minutes

Spread nuts on a pieplate. Microwave at HIGH until toasted; stir at 2-minute intervals.

MICRO-BAKED POTATOES—Cook at HIGH

1 medium (6 to 7 ounces)	4 to 6 minutes
2 medium	7 to 8 minutes
4 medium	12 to 14 minutes

Rinse potatoes; prick several times with a fork. Arrange potatoes at least 1 inch apart. (If more than 2 potatoes, arrange them in a circle.) Microwave at HIGH until done, turning and rearranging potatoes once. Let stand 5 minutes before serving.

Handy Substitutions

Needed Ingredient	Substitute
Baking Products:	
1 cup self-rising flour	1 cup all-purpose flour, 1 teaspoon baking powder, plus $\frac{1}{2}$ teaspoon salt
1 cup cake flour	1 cup sifted all-purpose flour minus 2 tablespoons
1 cup all-purpose flour	1 cup cake flour plus 2 tablespoons
1 cup powdered sugar	1 cup sugar plus 1 tablespoon cornstarch (processed in food processor)
1 cup honey	$1\frac{1}{4}$ cups sugar plus $\frac{1}{4}$ cup water
1 cup light corn syrup	1 cup sugar plus $\frac{1}{4}$ cup water
1 teaspoon baking powder	$\frac{1}{4}$ teaspoon baking soda plus $\frac{1}{2}$ teaspoon cream of tartar
1 tablespoon cornstarch (for thickening)	2 tablespoons all-purpose flour
1 tablespoon tapioca	$1\frac{1}{2}$ tablespoons all-purpose flour
1 (1-ounce) square unsweetened chocolate	3 tablespoons cocoa plus 1 tablespoon butter or margarine
Dairy Products:	
2 large eggs	3 small eggs
1 cup milk	$\frac{1}{2}$ cup evaporated milk plus $\frac{1}{2}$ cup water
1 cup whipping cream	$\frac{3}{4}$ cup milk plus $\frac{1}{3}$ cup melted butter (for baking only; will not whip)
1 cup plain yogurt	1 cup buttermilk
1 cup sour cream	1 cup yogurt plus 3 tablespoons melted butter or 1 cup yogurt plus 1 tablespoon cornstarch
Vegetable Products:	
1 pound fresh mushrooms, sliced	1 (8-ounce) can sliced mushrooms, drained, or 3 ounces dried
1 medium onion, chopped	1 tablespoon instant minced onion or 1 tablespoon onion powder
3 tablespoons chopped sweet red or green pepper	1 tablespoon dried pepper flakes or 2 tablespoons chopped pimiento
3 tablespoons chopped shallots	2 tablespoons chopped onion plus 1 tablespoon chopped garlic
Seasoning Products:	
1 tablespoon chopped fresh herbs	1 teaspoon dried herbs or $\frac{1}{4}$ teaspoon powdered herbs
1 clove garlic	$\frac{1}{8}$ teaspoon garlic powder or $\frac{1}{8}$ teaspoon minced dried garlic
1 tablespoon chopped chives	1 tablespoon chopped green onion tops
1 tablespoon grated fresh gingerroot or candied ginger	$\frac{1}{8}$ teaspoon ground ginger
1 tablespoon grated fresh horseradish	2 tablespoons prepared horseradish
1 tablespoon dried orange peel	$1\frac{1}{2}$ teaspoons orange extract or 1 tablespoon grated orange rind
1 (1-inch) vanilla bean	1 teaspoon vanilla extract
1 teaspoon garlic salt	$\frac{1}{8}$ teaspoon garlic powder plus $\frac{7}{8}$ teaspoon salt
1 teaspoon ground allspice	$\frac{1}{2}$ teaspoon ground cinnamon plus $\frac{1}{2}$ teaspoon ground cloves
1 teaspoon apple pie spice	$\frac{1}{2}$ teaspoon ground cinnamon, $\frac{1}{4}$ teaspoon ground nutmeg, $\frac{1}{8}$ teaspoon ground cardamom
1 teaspoon pumpkin pie spice	$\frac{1}{2}$ teaspoon ground cinnamon, $\frac{1}{4}$ teaspoon ground ginger, $\frac{1}{8}$ teaspoon ground allspice, $\frac{1}{8}$ teaspoon ground nutmeg
Miscellaneous Products:	
$\frac{1}{4}$ cup Marsala	$\frac{1}{4}$ cup dry white wine plus 1 teaspoon brandy
1 tablespoon brandy	$\frac{1}{4}$ teaspoon brandy extract plus 1 tablespoon water
$\frac{1}{2}$ cup balsamic vinegar	$\frac{1}{2}$ cup red wine vinegar (slight flavor difference)
1 cup tomato juice	$\frac{1}{2}$ cup tomato sauce plus $\frac{1}{2}$ cup water
2 cups tomato sauce	$\frac{3}{4}$ cup tomato paste plus 1 cup water
1 cup tomato sauce	$\frac{3}{8}$ cup tomato paste plus $\frac{1}{2}$ cup water

What's for Supper?

Some nights supper has to be ready fast. These quick-fix recipes call for only a few ingredients and will help you get food on the table in a flash.

Soft Beef Tacos, Grilled Chicken, Golden Chops with Vegetables

Boiled Shrimp with Zippy Red Sauce, Sweet-and-Sour Chicken Nuggets, Sautéed Peppers

Oven-Fried Chicken Chimichangas, Broccoli-Shrimp Stuffed Potatoes, Pasta Salad

Caesar's Fish, Pecan-Crusted Turkey Cutlets, Sweet-and-Sour Shrimp

Beef with Red Wine Marinade (page 14)

Soft Beef Tacos

Supper Olé

Soft Beef Tacos • Cantaloupe Salad • ◆ Chocolate Cream Cheese Pie

Soft Beef Tacos

1 pound ground beef
1 small onion, minced
2 cloves garlic, minced
½ green pepper, chopped
1 jalapeño pepper, seeded and minced
1 cup water
1 teaspoon ground cumin
1 teaspoon chili powder
½ teaspoon dried oregano
¼ teaspoon salt
⅛ teaspoon pepper
8 (7-inch) flour tortillas
2 cups shredded lettuce
2 tomatoes, chopped
1 cup (4 ounces) shredded Cheddar cheese
1 (8-ounce) carton guacamole
Commercial taco or picante sauce

Cook first 5 ingredients in a large skillet until meat is browned, stirring to crumble; drain well. Stir in water and next 5 ingredients; bring to a boil. Cover, reduce heat, and simmer over low heat 20 minutes, stirring occasionally. Uncover and cook 5 minutes.

Wrap tortillas securely in aluminum foil; bake at 350° for 10 minutes or until thoroughly heated.

Spoon equal amounts of meat mixture lengthwise down center of each tortilla. Top with lettuce, tomato, cheese, guacamole, and desired amount of taco sauce. Fold bottom third of tortillas over filling. Fold sides of tortillas in toward center, leaving top open. Secure with wooden picks, if necessary. Serve with additional taco sauce, if desired. **Yield: 4 servings.**

Cantaloupe Salad

½ cup mayonnaise
3 tablespoons frozen orange juice concentrate, thawed and undiluted
1 small cantaloupe, chilled
Leaf lettuce
1⅓ cups seedless green grapes, divided

Combine mayonnaise and orange juice concentrate, mixing well; set aside.

Cut cantaloupe into 4 sections; remove seeds, and peel. Place cantaloupe sections on lettuce leaves; spoon ⅓ cup grapes over and around each section. Drizzle with mayonnaise mixture. **Yield: 4 servings.**

Chocolate Cream Cheese Pie

1 (8-ounce) package cream cheese, softened
¾ cup sifted powdered sugar
¼ cup cocoa
1 (8-ounce) carton frozen whipped topping, thawed
1 (6-ounce) chocolate-flavored crumb crust
½ cup coarsely chopped pecans

Combine first 3 ingredients in a mixing bowl; beat at medium speed of an electric mixer until soft and creamy. Add whipped topping, folding until smooth. Spread over crumb crust, and sprinkle with pecans. Chill at least 4 hours. **Yield: one 9-inch pie.**

Sunset Supper
(pictured on page 11)

SERVES 6

◆ Beef with Red Wine Marinade • Leafy green salad • Tomato wedges
Parslied Garlic Bread • ◆ No-Bake Banana Pudding

Beef with Red Wine Marinade

1 (1½-pound) top round steak or flank steak
1 cup red wine
¼ cup soy sauce
¼ cup vegetable oil
1 teaspoon seasoned salt
1 teaspoon pepper
1 teaspoon dried oregano
1 teaspoon garlic juice

Place steak in a heavy-duty, zip-top plastic bag. Combine wine and remaining ingredients in a 2-cup glass measuring cup; stir well. Pour marinade over steak. Seal and chill 8 hours, turning occasionally.

Remove steak from marinade; grill, covered with grill lid, over medium coals (300° to 350°) 7 to 9 minutes on each side or to desired degree of doneness. To serve, slice steak across grain into thin slices. **Yield: 6 servings.**

Parslied Garlic Bread

1 (16-ounce) loaf French bread
¼ cup butter or margarine, softened
1 clove garlic, crushed
¼ cup chopped fresh parsley

Cut bread into 1-inch slices, cutting to, but not through, bottom crust. Combine butter, garlic, and parsley; spread between slices and on top of bread. Wrap in heavy-duty aluminum foil.

Grill bread over medium coals (300° to 350°), turning frequently, 10 to 15 minutes or until thoroughly heated. **Yield: 8 servings.**

No-Bake Banana Pudding

2 (3.4-ounce) packages vanilla instant pudding mix
1 (8-ounce) carton sour cream
3½ cups milk
Vanilla wafers
3 large bananas
1 (8-ounce) carton frozen whipped topping, thawed

Combine first 3 ingredients in a large bowl; beat at low speed of an electric mixer 2 minutes or until thickened.

Line bottom and sides of a 3-quart bowl with vanilla wafers. Slice 1 banana, and layer over wafers. Spoon one-third of pudding mixture over banana. Repeat layers two more times. Cover and chill. Spread whipped topping over pudding just before serving. **Yield: 10 servings.**

TimeSavers

• To chop parsley, place in a glass measuring cup and snip with kitchen shears.
• Preheat gas grill 20 minutes or light charcoal 30 minutes before grilling beef and bread.

South of the Border

SERVES 4

Oven-Fried Chicken Chimichangas • Sunny Fruit Salad • Orange sherbet

Oven-Fried Chicken Chimichangas

3 (5-ounce) cans white chicken, drained and
   flaked
1 (4.5-ounce) can chopped green chiles,
   drained
1 cup (4 ounces) shredded Monterey Jack
   cheese
½ cup sliced green onions
8 (9-inch) flour tortillas
Vegetable oil
Shredded lettuce, salsa or picante sauce,
   sour cream

Combine first 4 ingredients; set aside. Wrap tortillas in damp paper towels; microwave at HIGH 15 seconds or until hot. Brush both sides of tortillas, one at a time, with vegetable oil (keep remaining tortillas warm).

Place a scant ½ cup chicken mixture just below center of each tortilla. Fold in left and right sides of tortilla to partially enclose filling. Fold up bottom edge of tortilla; fold into a rectangle, and secure with a wooden pick. Repeat with remaining tortillas and chicken mixture.

Place filled tortillas on a lightly greased baking sheet. Bake at 425° for 10 minutes or until crisp and lightly browned. Serve with shredded lettuce, salsa, and sour cream. **Yield: 4 servings.**

Oven-Fried Chicken Chimichangas

Sunny Fruit Salad

½ cup plain yogurt
2 tablespoons honey
1 teaspoon lemon juice
Pinch of grated nutmeg
1 cup orange sections
2 large bananas, peeled and cut into ½-inch
   slices
3 kiwifruit, peeled and cut into ½-inch slices
Lettuce leaves

Combine first 4 ingredients in a medium bowl. Add fruit, and toss gently. Serve on lettuce leaves. **Yield: 4 servings.**

What's for Supper?   15

Sweet-and-Sour Special

SERVES 4
Sweet-and-Sour Chicken Nuggets • ◆ Cranberry Oriental • Sesame Bread Twists
Fortune cookies

Sweet-and-Sour Chicken Nuggets

1 (12-ounce) package frozen breaded chicken
   nuggets
1 cup water
1 cup uncooked instant rice
1 (16-ounce) can apricot halves, drained
1 (6-ounce) package frozen snow pea pods
¾ cup commercial sweet-and-sour sauce

Cook chicken according to package directions.
Set aside.
   Bring water to a boil in a small saucepan; add
rice. Cover and remove from heat. Let rice stand
5 minutes.
   Combine apricot halves, snow peas, and
sweet-and-sour sauce in a medium saucepan;
cook over medium heat until thoroughly heated.
Stir in chicken nuggets. Spoon rice onto a serving
plate, and arrange chicken mixture evenly over
rice. **Yield: 4 servings.**

Cranberry Oriental

1 (16-ounce) can whole-berry cranberry sauce
1 (8-ounce) can crushed pineapple, drained
1 teaspoon lemon juice
1 (8-ounce) carton sour cream
Lettuce leaves

   Combine first 4 ingredients; stir until blended.
Pour mixture into an 8½- x 4½- x 3-inch loaf-
pan, and freeze until firm. Cut into 1-inch slices.
Serve on lettuce leaves. **Yield: 8 servings.**

Sesame Bread Twists

1 (8-ounce) can refrigerator crescent
   dinner rolls
1 large egg
⅓ cup sesame seeds

   Unroll dough, and separate into 4 rectangles.
Press 2 rectangles together end to end, making 1
long rectangle. Cut each long rectangle lengthwise into 6 strips.
   Beat egg lightly with a fork in a pieplate; set
aside. Sprinkle sesame seeds onto a 15- x 12-
inch piece of wax paper. Twist each strip of
dough several times; dip in egg, and roll in
sesame seeds.
   Place strips 1 inch apart on a greased baking
sheet. Bake at 400° for 8 to 10 minutes or until
golden brown. **Yield: 1 dozen.**

TimeSavers

• Use leftover rice or prepare instant
or quick-cooking rice to serve with
chicken nuggets. One cup uncooked
instant rice equals 2 cups cooked.
• Make Cranberry Oriental ahead
and freeze in a loafpan or as individual salads in paper-lined muffin
pans. When frozen, transfer salads
to a freezer bag to use as needed.

Sweet-and-Sour Chicken Nuggets

Grilled Chicken

Grill-a-Meal

SERVES 4

Grilled Chicken • Lemony Corn on the Cob • Grilled Zucchini Fans
Sliced tomatoes • French bread • Pound Cake with Strawberry-Banana Topping

Grilled Chicken

½ cup white vinegar
½ cup balsamic vinegar
½ cup water
1 teaspoon chili powder
½ teaspoon dried oregano
½ teaspoon freshly ground black pepper
1 bay leaf
4 skinned and boned chicken breast halves

Combine first 7 ingredients in a heavy-duty, zip-top plastic bag. Add chicken, and marinate 20 minutes in refrigerator; remove chicken from marinade, reserving marinade. Bring marinade to a boil; discard bay leaf.

Grill chicken, covered with grill lid, over medium coals (300° to 350°) 6 minutes on each side, basting twice with marinade. **Yield: 4 servings.**

Lemony Corn on the Cob

¼ cup butter or margarine, softened
½ to 1 teaspoon lemon-pepper seasoning
4 ears fresh corn

Combine butter and lemon-pepper seasoning; spread on corn, and place each ear on a piece of heavy-duty aluminum foil. Roll foil lengthwise around each ear, and twist foil at each end.

Grill corn, covered with grill lid, over medium coals (300° to 350°) 20 minutes, turning after 10 minutes. **Yield: 4 servings.**

Grilled Zucchini Fans

3 tablespoons olive oil
¼ teaspoon garlic powder
4 small zucchini, cut into fans

Combine olive oil and garlic powder. Cut each zucchini into lengthwise slices, leaving slices attached on stem end. Fan slices out, and place on grill; brush zucchini with olive oil mixture.

Grill zucchini, covered with grill lid, over medium coals (300° to 350°) 5 minutes on each side, basting once with olive oil mixture. **Yield: 4 servings.**

Pound Cake with Strawberry-Banana Topping

2 tablespoons butter or margarine
2 tablespoons brown sugar
2 tablespoons lemon juice
¼ cup light rum
3 medium bananas, sliced
6 fresh strawberries, cut in half
Commercial pound cake

Melt butter in a skillet on grill. Add sugar, lemon juice, and rum; stir well. Cook, stirring constantly, until sugar dissolves (2 to 3 minutes). Add bananas and strawberries, and cook until bananas are soft but not mushy (about 2 minutes). Serve over pound cake. **Yield: 4 servings.**

Note: Strawberry-Banana Topping may be served over vanilla ice cream.

Special-Occasion Dinner

SERVES 4

Pecan-Crusted Turkey Cutlets • Quick-cooking rice mix • Sautéed Peppers
◆ Microwave Chocolate Pie • White wine

Pecan-Crusted Turkey Cutlets

¾ cup dry breadcrumbs
½ cup finely chopped pecans
½ teaspoon dried sage
¼ teaspoon salt
¼ teaspoon pepper
1 egg white, lightly beaten
1 tablespoon water
4 (4-ounce) turkey breast cutlets
Butter-flavored cooking spray

Combine first 5 ingredients in a shallow dish; set aside.

Combine egg white and water. Dip turkey cutlets in egg mixture; coat with breadcrumb mixture. Place on a baking sheet coated with cooking spray. Coat cutlets with cooking spray.

Bake at 350° for 12 minutes or until juices run clear when cut with a knife. **Yield: 4 servings.**

TimeSavers

• For packaged rice mixes, choose from long grain and wild rice, brown rice, and regular rice mixtures.
• Buy sliced peppers at a salad bar for Sautéed Peppers. Red, yellow, and green peppers make it a colorful dish, but you can use one or any combination of peppers.
• Prepare pie ahead. To save time, substitute 2 cups frozen whipped topping, thawed, for whipped cream.

Sautéed Peppers

1 yellow pepper, seeded and cut into thin strips
1 red pepper, seeded and cut into thin strips
1½ tablespoons olive oil
2 teaspoons balsamic or red wine vinegar
⅛ teaspoon garlic salt
1 teaspoon parsley flakes

Cook peppers in hot oil in a large skillet over high heat, stirring often, 6 minutes or until edges of peppers are lightly browned.

Reduce heat to medium; stir in vinegar, garlic salt, and parsley flakes. Cook 3 minutes, stirring often.

Serve immediately. **Yield: 4 servings.**

Microwave Chocolate Pie

2 cups miniature marshmallows
1 cup milk chocolate morsels
1 cup milk
1 (1-ounce) square unsweetened chocolate
1 cup whipping cream, whipped
1 (6-ounce) chocolate-flavored crumb crust

Combine first 4 ingredients in a 2-quart glass mixing bowl. Microwave at HIGH 4 to 5 minutes, stirring once. Cool.

Fold in whipped cream, and pour mixture into chocolate crust. Freeze until firm. **Yield: one (9-inch) pie.**

Pecan-Crusted Turkey Cutlets

Festive Family Supper

SERVES 6

◆ Grilled Marinated Pork Tenderloin • Julienne Squash • French bread
Fudge Pie • Iced tea

Grilled Marinated Pork Tenderloin

2 (¾-pound) pork tenderloins
1 (8-ounce) bottle Italian salad dressing
Garnishes: cherry tomato halves, fresh parsley
     sprigs

   Place pork tenderloins in a heavy-duty, zip-top plastic bag. Pour dressing over tenderloins; seal and chill 8 hours.
   Remove tenderloins from marinade. Insert meat thermometer into tenderloins, being careful not to touch fat. Grill tenderloins, covered with grill lid, over medium-hot coals (350° to 400°) 12 to 15 minutes or until thermometer registers 160°, turning them once. Garnish, if desired.
Yield: 6 servings.

Fudge Pie

1 cup sugar
¼ cup all-purpose flour
¼ cup cocoa
½ cup butter or margarine, melted
2 large eggs, beaten
¼ teaspoon vanilla extract
½ cup chopped pecans
1 unbaked 9-inch pastry shell
Ice cream (optional)

   Combine first 6 ingredients; stir well. Stir in pecans. Pour mixture into pastry shell. Bake at 350° for 25 minutes or until a wooden pick inserted in center comes out clean. Serve with ice cream, if desired. **Yield: one 9-inch pie.**

Julienne Squash

1½ tablespoons vegetable oil
1½ tablespoons lemon juice
1½ tablespoons white vinegar
1 teaspoon salt-free herb-and-spice blend
⅛ teaspoon garlic salt
2 yellow squash
2 large zucchini

   Combine first 5 ingredients. Stir well; set aside.
   Cut yellow squash and zucchini into very thin strips. Arrange on a steaming rack, and place over boiling water; cover and steam 4 minutes.
   Place vegetables in a bowl. Pour sauce over vegetables; toss gently to coat. **Yield: 6 servings.**

TimeSavers

• Marinate pork tenderloins in a heavy-duty, zip-top plastic bag for easy clean-up.
• Use a meat thermometer to test pork's doneness. Cutting the meat to see if it's still pink lets the juices run out.

Golden Chops with Vegetables

6 (½-inch-thick) pork chops (about 2¼
　　pounds)
1 (10¾-ounce) can golden mushroom soup,
　　undiluted
¼ cup water
½ teaspoon rubbed sage
1 cup sliced carrot
½ cup chopped onion
1 medium-size green pepper, cut into strips

Brown pork chops in a large nonstick skillet;
remove pork chops and drain. Combine soup,
water, and sage in skillet; add carrot and onion.

Arrange pork chops over soup mixture; cover
and simmer over medium heat 15 minutes, stirring and rearranging pork chops once. Add green
pepper; cover and cook 10 additional minutes.
Yield: 6 servings.

Golden Chops with Vegetables

Soufflé Potatoes

2⅔ cups mashed potato mix
1 large egg, beaten
1 (2.8-ounce) can French-fried onions
¼ teaspoon salt
½ cup (2 ounces) shredded Cheddar cheese

Prepare mashed potato mix according to
package directions. Add egg, onions, and salt,
stirring until blended.

Spoon mixture into a greased 2-quart baking
dish; sprinkle with cheese. Bake, uncovered, at
350° for 5 minutes. **Yield: 6 to 8 servings.**

Quick Fruit Cobbler

1 (21-ounce) can cherry or blueberry pie filling
1 (8-ounce) can unsweetened crushed
　　pineapple, drained
1 (9-ounce) package yellow cake mix
⅓ cup butter or margarine, melted

Spoon pie filling into a lightly greased 8-inch
square baking dish. Spoon pineapple over pie filling.

Sprinkle cake mix evenly over pineapple.
Drizzle butter over cake mix. Bake at 425° for 20
to 22 minutes. **Yield: 6 to 8 servings.**

Breaded Grouper Fillets

Just for Two

SERVES 2

Breaded Grouper Fillets • Green Beans with Mushrooms
Deli coleslaw in pepper cups • Chocolate-Mint Sundaes

Breaded Grouper Fillets

½ cup nutlike cereal nuggets
2 tablespoons chopped fresh parsley
½ teaspoon dried rosemary
¼ teaspoon salt
2 (4-ounce) grouper fillets
⅓ cup low-fat plain yogurt
Garnish: lemon slices

Combine first 4 ingredients in a shallow dish; mix well. Brush fillets with yogurt on all sides; coat with cereal mixture. Place fillets in a 9-inch pieplate.

Microwave fillets at HIGH 1½ minutes; give dish a half-turn. Microwave 1½ to 2 minutes or until fish flakes easily when tested with a fork. Let stand 5 minutes. Garnish, if desired. **Yield: 2 servings.**

Green Beans with Mushrooms

1 tablespoon minced onion
1 tablespoon vegetable oil
1 (8-ounce) can cut green beans, drained
1 tablespoon diced pimiento
1 teaspoon chopped fresh parsley
1 (4-ounce) can sliced mushrooms, drained
⅛ teaspoon salt
⅛ teaspoon pepper

Cook onion in hot oil in a medium skillet until transparent. Stir in beans and remaining ingredients; cover and cook over medium heat 10 minutes or until thoroughly heated. **Yield: 2 servings.**

Chocolate-Mint Sundaes

6 chocolate-covered mint patties
1 tablespoon milk
Vanilla ice cream

Combine mint patties and milk in a 1-cup glass measure. Cover with heavy-duty plastic wrap, and microwave at MEDIUM (50% power) 45 seconds or until patties melt. Serve warm over ice cream. **Yield: 2 servings.**

TimeSavers

• Chop parsley all at once for grouper and green beans.
• Buy the coleslaw at the deli to get a headstart on this menu. If fresh tomatoes are available, serve slaw in tomato cups rather than pepper cups.

Catch-of-the-Day

SERVES 4

Caesar's Fish • Quick Potatoes • Tossed salad
Pineapple Soda

Caesar's Fish

Quick Potatoes

1 tablespoon olive oil
1 large onion, chopped
2 cloves garlic, minced
½ cup chopped sweet red pepper
½ teaspoon salt
¼ teaspoon pepper
¼ teaspoon hot sauce
3 cups unpeeled cubed potato
2 tablespoons butter or margarine

Heat olive oil in a 10-inch cast-iron skillet. Add onion and garlic; cook over medium heat, stirring constantly, until tender. Stir in red pepper and next 3 ingredients; cook 2 minutes, stirring constantly. Add potato and butter, stirring well.

Bake in skillet at 400° for 20 to 30 minutes. **Yield: 4 servings.**

Caesar's Fish

1 pound flounder fillets
½ cup golden Caesar salad dressing
1 cup round buttery cracker crumbs
½ cup (2 ounces) shredded Cheddar cheese

Arrange fillets in a single layer in a lightly greased 13- x 9- x 2-inch baking dish. Drizzle Caesar dressing over fillets; sprinkle cracker crumbs over top of fillets.

Bake fillets at 400° for 10 minutes; top with cheese, and bake 5 additional minutes or until fish flakes easily when tested with a fork. **Yield: 4 servings.**

Pineapple Soda

1 (8-ounce) can unsweetened crushed
    pineapple, undrained
2 tablespoons milk
1 pint vanilla ice cream
1 cup club soda

Combine first 3 ingredients in container of an electric blender; blend until smooth. Stir in club soda. Serve immediately. **Yield: 3½ cups.**

Shortcut Supper

SERVES 2

Broccoli-Shrimp Stuffed Potatoes • Layered Fruit Salad
Pita Crisps • Commercial cookies

Broccoli-Shrimp Stuffed Potatoes

2 large baking potatoes (about 1¼ pounds)
⅓ cup loaf process cheese spread
2 tablespoons milk
1 cup fresh broccoli flowerets
1 (6-ounce) can shrimp, drained and rinsed
1 green onion, chopped

Scrub potatoes; prick several times with a fork. Place potatoes 1 inch apart on a microwave-safe rack or paper towel.

Microwave potatoes at HIGH 10 to 13 minutes, turning and rearranging once; let stand 2 minutes. Cut an X to within ½ inch of bottom of each potato. Squeeze potatoes from opposite sides and opposite ends to open; fluff with a fork.

Combine cheese spread and milk in a heavy saucepan; cook over low heat until cheese melts, stirring often. Remove from heat, and set aside.

Place broccoli in a 9-inch pieplate; cover and microwave at HIGH 2 to 3 minutes or until tender. Arrange broccoli and shrimp in potatoes. Spoon cheese sauce over potatoes, and sprinkle with green onions. **Yield: 2 servings.**

Broccoli-Shrimp Stuffed Potatoes

one-fourth of sour cream. Top with half of pineapple and one-fourth of sour cream. Repeat procedure with remaining ingredients. **Yield: 2 servings.**

Pita Crisps

1 (6-inch) whole wheat pita bread round
1 tablespoon butter or margarine, melted

Split pita round to yield 2 flat discs. Cut each disc into 4 triangles; brush each triangle with melted butter.

Place triangles on paper towels in microwave. Microwave at HIGH 20 seconds or until edges curl.

Let stand to cool. **Yield: 2 servings.**

Layered Fruit Salad

½ cup sliced strawberries
¼ cup sliced banana
¼ cup sour cream
½ cup pineapple chunks

Layer half each of strawberries and banana in a small serving dish; lightly spread fruit with

Family-Pleasing Shrimp

SERVES 4

Sweet-and-Sour Shrimp • Mandarin Orange-Lettuce Salad • ◆ Pineapple Pie

Sweet-and-Sour Shrimp

1 tablespoon vegetable oil
¼ cup chopped sweet red pepper
¼ cup sliced green onions
1 clove garlic, minced
1 pound peeled, medium-size fresh shrimp
⅓ cup red plum jam
2 tablespoons dry white wine
2 tablespoons white vinegar
2 tablespoons cocktail sauce
2 tablespoons chutney
½ teaspoon salt
¼ teaspoon dried crushed red pepper
¼ pound fresh snow pea pods
Hot cooked rice

Combine first 4 ingredients in a 1½-quart baking dish. Microwave at HIGH, uncovered, 2 to 3 minutes or until vegetables are tender; stir mixture at 1-minute intervals.

Add shrimp, and cover with heavy-duty plastic wrap; fold back a small edge of wrap to allow steam to escape. Microwave at MEDIUM (50% power) 8 to 10 minutes or until shrimp are opaque and firm, stirring at 3-minute intervals. Drain.

Combine jam and next 6 ingredients; stir well. Pour over shrimp, and stir gently. Cover and microwave at HIGH 1 to 1½ minutes or until sauce is heated. Add snow peas, and stir gently. Cover and microwave at HIGH 2 to 2½ minutes or until snow peas are crisp-tender. Let stand, covered, 1 to 2 minutes. Serve over cooked rice. **Yield: 4 servings.**

Mandarin Orange-Lettuce Salad

1 (16-ounce) package mixed lettuces
1 (11-ounce) can mandarin oranges, chilled and drained
⅓ cup golden raisins
1 (2-ounce) package cashew nuts, toasted (⅓ cup)
½ cup commercial Italian or sweet-and-sour salad dressing

Combine first 4 ingredients in a large bowl. Just before serving, pour dressing over salad and toss. **Yield: 4 servings.**

Pineapple Pie

1 (14-ounce) can sweetened condensed milk
½ cup lemon juice
1 (20-ounce) can crushed pineapple, drained
1 (8-ounce) carton frozen whipped topping, thawed
1 (9-ounce) graham cracker crust

Combine condensed milk and lemon juice; stir well. Fold in pineapple and whipped topping. Spoon mixture into crust. Chill. **Yield: one 9-inch pie.**

TimeSavers

• Purchase a package of mixed lettuces or keep torn salad greens in the refrigerator for a quick salad.
• Chill mandarin oranges a day ahead for salad.

Sweet-and-Sour Shrimp

Shrimp Boat Feast

SERVES 6

Boiled Shrimp with Zippy Red Sauce • Pasta Salad
Onion-Cheese French Bread • Fresh fruit

Boiled Shrimp with Zippy Red Sauce

Pasta Salad

4 cups uncooked rotini
1 medium zucchini, sliced
2 carrots, peeled and sliced
½ sweet red pepper, cut into thin strips
1 cup broccoli flowerets
1 (6-ounce) can sliced ripe olives
1 (8-ounce) bottle Italian salad dressing

Cook rotini according to package directions; drain. Rinse pasta with cold water and drain.

Combine pasta and remaining ingredients, tossing well. Serve immediately or, if desired, chill. **Yield: 6 to 8 servings.**

Boiled Shrimp with Zippy Red Sauce

1 cup chili sauce
1 cup ketchup
2 tablespoons prepared horseradish
2 tablespoons picante sauce
3 tablespoons lemon juice
2 tablespoons Worcestershire sauce
1 teaspoon onion powder
1 teaspoon garlic powder
3 pounds unpeeled, large boiled shrimp

Combine first 8 ingredients, stirring well. Cover and chill at least 2 hours. Serve with boiled shrimp. **Yield: 6 servings.**

Onion-Cheese French Bread

¼ cup butter or margarine, softened
¾ cup (3 ounces) shredded Cheddar cheese
½ cup mayonnaise
¼ cup chopped green onions
1 (16-ounce) loaf French bread

Combine first 4 ingredients in a small bowl; mix well.

Slice bread in half lengthwise. Spread cheese mixture on bread. Broil 6 inches from heat (with electric oven door partially opened) 2 minutes or until bubbly. **Yield: 8 servings.**

All-in-One-Dish

Consider an easy approach to meal planning on hectic days.
Our collection of all-in-one-dish combinations may be just what
you need to simplify meal preparation and cleanup.

Szechuan Noodle Toss, Chicken and Vegetables, Shrimp Dee-Lish

Kielbasa-Vegetable Dinner, Linguine with Clam Sauce, Fish-and-Potato Platter

Lime-Ginger Beef Stir-Fry, Stir-Fry Beef and Asparagus, Sausage Ratatouille

Pork Marsala, Shrimp and Tortellini, Easy Red Beans and Rice

Turkey Sauté (page 36)

Quick Oriental Fix

SERVES 6

Szechuan Noodle Toss • Salad Mandarin
Breadsticks • Caramel Surprise

Szechuan Noodle Toss

Szechuan Noodle Toss

1 (8-ounce) package thin spaghetti
2 large sweet red peppers, cut into very thin strips
4 green onions, cut into 1-inch pieces
1 clove garlic, crushed
¼ cup sesame oil, divided
1 (10-ounce) package fresh, trimmed spinach, torn into bite-size pieces
2 cups cubed cooked chicken
1 (8-ounce) can sliced water chestnuts, drained
¼ cup soy sauce
2 tablespoons rice vinegar
1½ teaspoons dried crushed red pepper
1 tablespoon minced fresh gingerroot

Cook spaghetti according to package directions; drain. Rinse with cold water; drain. Place spaghetti in a large bowl; set aside.

Cook red pepper, green onions, and garlic in 2 tablespoons hot sesame oil in a large skillet, stirring constantly, 2 minutes. Stir in spinach; cover and cook over medium heat 3 minutes or until spinach wilts. Remove from heat; cool.

Spoon spinach mixture over pasta. Add chicken and water chestnuts.

Combine remaining 2 tablespoons sesame oil, soy sauce, and remaining ingredients; stir well. Pour over pasta, tossing gently to coat. **Yield: 6 servings.**

Salad Mandarin

1 medium head Bibb or Boston lettuce, torn
1 (11-ounce) can mandarin oranges, chilled and drained
½ medium avocado, peeled and thinly sliced
½ cup coarsely chopped pecans, toasted
2 green onions, thinly sliced
Freshly ground pepper to taste
⅓ cup commercial Italian dressing

Combine first 6 ingredients in a medium bowl. Add Italian dressing, tossing gently. **Yield: 6 servings.**

Caramel Surprise

1 quart vanilla ice cream
4 (1½-ounce) English toffee-flavored candy bars, frozen and crushed
¼ cup plus 2 tablespoons Kahlúa or other coffee-flavored liqueur

Spoon alternate layers of ice cream and crushed candy into 6 parfait glasses. Top each with 1 tablespoon Kahlúa. **Yield: 6 servings.**

TimeSavers

• Use leftover cooked chicken or buy cooked chicken from the deli for the noodle toss.
• Purchase prewashed spinach, if available.
• Assemble dessert ahead of time and freeze; top with Kahlúa at serving time.

Skillet Dinner

SERVES 2

Chicken and Vegetables • Cheesy Pita Triangles
◆ Individual Pots de Crème

Chicken and Vegetables

Chicken and Vegetables

2 carrots, scraped and sliced
¼ cup chopped onion
1 to 2 tablespoons vegetable oil
2 skinned and boned chicken breast halves,
   cut into ¼-inch strips
¼ teaspoon dried basil
¼ teaspoon garlic powder
⅛ teaspoon salt
⅛ teaspoon pepper
¼ cup chicken broth
2 tablespoons white wine
1 (6-ounce) package frozen snow pea pods,
   thawed and drained
1 medium tomato, cut into 8 pieces
⅓ cup minced fresh parsley

Cook carrot and onion in 1 tablespoon hot oil
in a large skillet over medium heat, stirring constantly, until crisp-tender. Remove vegetables
from skillet, reserving pan drippings.

Add chicken to skillet; sprinkle with basil,
garlic powder, salt, and pepper. Cook chicken 3
minutes on each side or until browned, adding 1
tablespoon oil if needed. Add reserved vegetables, chicken broth, and wine.

Cover, reduce heat, and simmer 10 minutes.
Stir in snow peas, tomato, and parsley; cook until
thoroughly heated. **Yield: 2 servings.**

TimeSavers

• Save time and nutrients by leaving peel on tomato. Substitute
cherry tomatoes, if desired.
• Press thawed snow peas between
paper towels to speed draining.
• Use kitchen shears to cut pita
bread into triangles.

Cheesy Pita Triangles

1 (8-inch) white or whole wheat pita bread
   round
¼ cup (1 ounce) shredded Swiss cheese

Cut pita bread round into 6 triangles; sprinkle
Swiss cheese inside each triangle, and place on a
baking sheet.

Bake at 350° for 10 minutes. Serve immediately. **Yield: 2 servings.**

Individual Pots de Crème

½ (4-ounce) package sweet baking chocolate
2 tablespoons egg substitute
2 teaspoons sugar
¼ cup whipping cream
¼ teaspoon vanilla extract
Garnish: whipped cream

Melt chocolate in a heavy saucepan over low
heat. Combine egg substitute, sugar, and whipping cream; gradually stir into melted chocolate.

Cook over low heat, stirring constantly, 5
minutes or until thickened. Remove from heat;
stir in vanilla.

Spoon mixture into individual serving containers. Cover and chill at least 3 hours. Garnish,
if desired. **Yield: 2 servings.**

Spotlight Turkey Tonight
(pictured on page 31)
SERVES 4
Turkey Sauté • Buttered rice • ◆ Tomato-Herb Salad • Chocolate-Mint Dessert

Turkey Sauté

2 teaspoons cornstarch
2 tablespoons soy sauce
¼ cup water
1 teaspoon sugar
1 clove garlic, minced
½ teaspoon grated fresh gingerroot
2 tablespoons vegetable oil
1 pound turkey breast cutlets, cut into
    bite-size pieces
1 (6-ounce) package frozen snow pea pods,
    thawed
1 (8-ounce) can sliced water chestnuts,
    drained
½ small sweet red pepper, sliced

Combine first 4 ingredients; set aside. Cook garlic and gingerroot in hot oil in a large heavy skillet until tender.

Add turkey, and cook, stirring constantly, 3 minutes or until lightly browned. Add snow peas, water chestnuts, and red pepper slices; cook 1 minute, stirring constantly. Add soy sauce mixture, and cook 2 minutes or until thickened.
Yield: 4 servings.

TimeSavers

• Press thawed snow peas between paper towels to remove excess water.
• Allow tomatoes time to marinate for best flavor.
• Use bakery or deli brownies as the base for dessert.

Tomato-Herb Salad

3 small tomatoes, sliced
2 tablespoons vegetable oil
2 tablespoons white wine vinegar
½ teaspoon salt
¼ teaspoon pepper
2 tablespoons chopped fresh chives
Lettuce leaves

Arrange tomato in a 13- x 9- x 2-inch dish.
Combine oil and next 3 ingredients in a jar; cover tightly, and shake vigorously. Pour dressing over tomato. Sprinkle with chives. Cover and chill at least 2 hours. Serve on lettuce leaves.
Yield: 4 servings.

Chocolate-Mint Dessert

1 (5.5-ounce) can chocolate syrup
2 tablespoons green crème de menthe
Brownies
Vanilla or chocolate-mint ice cream

Combine chocolate syrup and crème de menthe, stirring well. Serve warm or cold over brownies topped with ice cream. Yield: about ⅔ cup sauce.

Lime-Ginger Beef Stir-Fry

1 (1-pound) top loin steak
¼ teaspoon freshly ground pepper
½ teaspoon grated lime rind
¼ cup lime juice
1 tablespoon sugar
2 tablespoons dry sherry
2 teaspoons soy sauce
1 teaspoon grated fresh gingerroot
1 clove garlic, minced
1 tablespoon safflower or vegetable oil
2 green onions, cut into 2-inch lengths
1 large carrot, cut into 1½-inch strips
1 sweet red pepper, cut into 1½-inch strips
1 tablespoon cornstarch
¼ cup water
Hot cooked rice
Garnish: lime slices

Lime-Ginger Beef Stir-Fry

Slice steak diagonally across grain into thin strips; sprinkle with pepper, and set aside.

Combine lime rind and next 6 ingredients; set lime mixture aside.

Pour oil around top of preheated wok, coating sides; heat at medium-high (375°) for 1 minute. Add steak; stir-fry 2 to 3 minutes. Add vegetables; stir-fry 2 to 3 minutes. Add lime mixture, and stir-fry until mixture boils.

Combine cornstarch and water; stir into vegetables and bring to a boil, stirring constantly. Cook, stirring constantly, 1 minute. Serve over rice. Garnish, if desired. **Yield: 4 servings.**

Cantaloupe Cooler Salad

3 cups cubed cantaloupe
Lettuce leaves
½ small onion, thinly sliced and separated
    into rings
6 slices bacon, cooked and crumbled
Commercial poppy seed dressing

Arrange cantaloupe on lettuce leaves. Top with onion and crumbled bacon. Drizzle dressing over salad. **Yield: 4 servings.**

Stir-Fry Beef and Asparagus

Dinner from a Wok

SERVES 4

Stir-Fry Beef and Asparagus • Quick Cheese and Mushroom Salad
Crusty rolls • ◆ Decadent Mud Pie

Stir-Fry Beef and Asparagus

1 pound boneless sirloin steak
1 tablespoon cornstarch, divided
3 tablespoons dry sherry, divided
3 tablespoons soy sauce, divided
1½ tablespoons vegetable oil
1 pound fresh asparagus, cut diagonally into
    1-inch lengths
3 tablespoons beef broth
Hot cooked rice

Slice steak diagonally across grain into thin strips; place in a shallow dish.

Combine 2 teaspoons cornstarch, 2 tablespoons sherry, and 2 tablespoons soy sauce; pour over steak, and marinate 10 minutes. Remove steak from marinade.

Pour oil around top of preheated wok, coating sides; heat at medium high (375°) for 2 minutes. Add steak; stir-fry 4 minutes. Remove steak from wok. Add asparagus and beef broth. Bring to a boil; cover, reduce heat, and simmer 3 minutes.

Combine remaining 1 teaspoon cornstarch, 1 tablespoon sherry, and 1 tablespoon soy sauce. Add cornstarch mixture and steak to wok; bring to a boil. Cook, stirring constantly, 1 minute. Serve over rice. **Yield: 4 servings.**

Quick Cheese and Mushroom Salad

2 cups torn Bibb lettuce
2 cups torn iceberg lettuce
6 slices bacon, cooked and crumbled
¼ pound sliced fresh mushrooms
⅓ cup grated Parmesan cheese
¾ cup (3 ounces) shredded Swiss cheese
Commercial creamy Italian salad dressing

Combine all ingredients, except dressing; toss gently. Serve with dressing. **Yield: 4 servings.**

Decadent Mud Pie

½ gallon coffee ice cream, softened
1 (9-inch) graham cracker crust
1 (11.75-ounce) jar hot fudge sauce, heated
Commercial whipped topping
Slivered almonds, toasted

Spread ice cream evenly over crust; cover and freeze until firm. To serve, place pie slice on serving plate; spoon hot fudge sauce over each slice. Dollop with whipped topping, and sprinkle with toasted almonds. Serve immediately. **Yield: one 9-inch pie.**

TimeSavers

• For easier slicing of the steak, freeze it 30 to 60 minutes. Slicing steak across the grain makes it more tender. Position the knife at a 45° angle for attractive slices.
• Choose asparagus stalks that are uniform in size to ensure even cooking. The tough part of an asparagus spear will snap off when you bend the spear.

Pork with a Flair

SERVES 4

Pork Marsala • Garlic-Tarragon Green Salad • French rolls
◆ Mellowed-Out Melon Compotes

Pork Marsala

1 (1-pound) pork tenderloin
1 tablespoon butter or margarine
1 tablespoon vegetable oil
1 clove garlic, minced
½ cup marsala
½ cup dry red wine
1 tablespoon tomato paste
½ pound fresh mushroom caps
1 tablespoon chopped fresh parsley
Hot cooked noodles or rice

Cut tenderloin into 4 equal pieces. Place each piece between two sheets of heavy-duty plastic wrap, and flatten to ¼-inch thickness, using a meat mallet or rolling pin.

Heat butter and oil in a large, heavy skillet over medium heat. Add pork, and cook 3 to 4 minutes on each side or until browned. Remove pork from skillet, and keep warm.

Cook garlic in pan drippings in skillet; add wines and tomato paste, stirring until blended. Add mushroom caps, and simmer 3 to 5 minutes.

Return pork to skillet, and cook until thoroughly heated. Sprinkle with parsley, and serve over noodles or rice. **Yield: 4 servings.**

Garlic-Tarragon Green Salad

1 clove garlic, minced
¼ teaspoon salt
⅛ teaspoon freshly ground pepper
Pinch of dry mustard
1 tablespoon tarragon vinegar
¼ cup vegetable oil
8 cups mixed salad greens

Combine first 4 ingredients in a large bowl; blend with a fork. Add vinegar and oil, mixing well. Add lettuce; toss gently. **Yield: 4 to 6 servings.**

Mellowed-Out Melon Compotes

1½ cups cubed cantaloupe
1½ cups cubed honeydew melon
¼ cup amaretto
½ cup slivered almonds, toasted

Combine first 3 ingredients; toss gently to coat. Chill 1 hour. Spoon into individual compotes; sprinkle with almonds, and serve immediately. **Yield: 4 servings.**

TimeSavers

- To clean mushrooms, brush with a damp paper towel or place in a plastic salad spinner for quick rinsing and drying.
- Mince garlic for the entrée and salad at the same time.
- Keep a tube of tomato paste in the refrigerator to use when you need a small amount.
- Buy cut-up melon in the produce section.

Pork Marsala

Kielbasa-Vegetable Dinner

Busy Day Dinner

SERVES 6

Kielbasa-Vegetable Dinner • Spoon Rolls • Tart Lemon Pie

Kielbasa-Vegetable Dinner

3 slices bacon
1½ pounds small red potatoes, thinly sliced
1 cup chopped onion
1½ cups thinly sliced carrot
½ teaspoon dried marjoram
1½ pounds kielbasa sausage, cut into ½-inch
    slices
1½ pounds fresh broccoli flowerets
1 cup water

Cook bacon in a large Dutch oven until crisp; remove bacon, reserving drippings in Dutch oven. Crumble bacon, and set aside.

Cook potato, onion, carrot, and marjoram in reserved drippings in Dutch oven over medium heat 7 minutes, stirring often.

Add kielbasa, broccoli, and water to vegetables in Dutch oven; bring mixture to a boil. Cover, reduce heat, and simmer 15 minutes or until vegetables are crisp-tender, stirring occasionally. Spoon into soup bowls; sprinkle with bacon. **Yield: 6 servings.**

TimeSavers

• To save time, use frozen chopped onion, and buy broccoli flowerets and scraped baby carrots from the produce section.
• Wash the potatoes well, but leave the skins on to save time and preserve nutrients.
• Make batter for rolls ahead of time.

Spoon Rolls

1 package active dry yeast
2 tablespoons warm water (105° to 115°)
½ cup vegetable oil
¼ cup sugar
1 large egg, beaten
4 cups self-rising flour
2 cups warm water (105° to 115°)

Dissolve yeast in 2 tablespoons warm water in a large bowl; let stand 5 minutes. Add oil and remaining ingredients to yeast mixture, and stir until mixture is smooth.

Cover; chill at least 4 hours or up to 3 days.

Stir batter, and spoon into greased muffin pans, filling three-fourths full. Bake at 400° for 20 minutes or until golden. **Yield: 1½ dozen.**

Tart Lemon Pie

3 large eggs
1 medium lemon, unpeeled, quartered, and
    seeded
1¼ cups sugar
2 tablespoons lemon juice
¼ cup butter or margarine, melted
1 unbaked 9-inch pastry shell
Frozen whipped topping, thawed

Combine first 4 ingredients in an electric blender; process 3 minutes or until smooth. Add butter; process 30 seconds. Pour into pastry shell. Bake at 350° for 30 to 35 minutes. Serve pie at room temperature or chilled with whipped topping. **Yield: one 9-inch pie.**

Sausage Ratatouille

One-Dish Dinner for Two

SERVES 2

Sausage Ratatouille • ◆ Mixed Greens with Blue Cheese Vinaigrette
Breadsticks • ◆ Grasshopper Tarts

Sausage Ratatouille

½ pound Italian sausage
1 small onion, chopped
¼ cup olive oil
1 small eggplant (¾ pound), cut into ½-inch
   cubes
1 zucchini, sliced
1 clove garlic, minced
1 large tomato, peeled and chopped
½ teaspoon dried oregano
¼ teaspoon salt
¼ teaspoon pepper
Garnish: fresh parsley sprigs

Remove casings from sausage. Cook sausage in a large skillet over medium heat until browned, stirring to crumble. Drain well; set aside.

Cook onion in hot oil in a large skillet over medium heat, stirring constantly, until tender. Add eggplant, and cook 3 minutes, stirring constantly. Add zucchini and garlic; reduce heat, and simmer 10 minutes. Add tomato, sausage, and seasonings; cover and simmer 5 minutes, stirring once. Garnish, if desired. **Yield: 2 servings.**

TimeSavers

• Cut all the vegetables for entrée and arrange on cutting board in order of use.
• Keep a supply of torn salad greens in the refrigerator for salads.
• Substitute 1 cup frozen whipped topping, thawed, for whipped cream.

Mixed Greens with Blue Cheese Vinaigrette

¼ cup vegetable oil
1½ tablespoons white wine vinegar
1 ounce crumbled blue cheese
½ teaspoon dried oregano
⅛ teaspoon salt
⅛ teaspoon freshly ground pepper
1 cup torn radicchio
1 cup torn Bibb lettuce

Combine first 6 ingredients in a jar; cover tightly and shake. Chill at least 1 hour.

Place salad greens in a bowl. Toss with dressing just before serving. **Yield: 2 servings.**

Grasshopper Tarts

⅔ cup chocolate wafer crumbs
1 tablespoon butter or margarine, melted
½ cup marshmallow cream
1 tablespoon green crème de menthe
½ cup whipping cream, whipped

Combine chocolate wafer crumbs and butter; press onto the bottom and sides of 2 (6-ounce) freezerproof ramekins. Chill 1 hour.

Combine marshmallow cream and crème de menthe, stirring well. Set aside 2 tablespoons whipped cream; fold remaining whipped cream into marshmallow mixture.

Spoon into prepared crusts; top with reserved whipped cream. Cover loosely, and freeze at least 8 hours. **Yield: 2 servings.**

Fireside Supper

SERVES 4 TO 6
Easy Red Beans and Rice • ◆ Overnight Slaw
Quick Corn Muffins • Citrus fruit cup

Easy Red Beans and Rice

1 pound smoked link sausage, cut into ½-inch
   slices
1 medium onion, chopped
1 green pepper, chopped
1 clove garlic, minced
2 (15-ounce) cans kidney beans, drained
1 (16-ounce) can whole tomatoes, undrained
   and chopped
½ teaspoon dried oregano
½ teaspoon pepper
Hot cooked rice

Cook sausage over low heat 5 to 8 minutes.
Add onion, green pepper, and garlic; cook until
tender. Drain, if necessary. Add beans, tomatoes,
and seasonings; simmer, uncovered, 20 minutes.
Serve over rice. **Yield: 4 to 6 servings.**

Overnight Slaw

5 cups shredded cabbage
¼ cup chopped purple onion
¾ cup sugar
¾ cup white vinegar
¾ cup water
2 teaspoons salt

Combine cabbage and purple onion in a large
bowl. Combine sugar and remaining ingredients,
stirring until sugar dissolves. Pour over cabbage
mixture; toss gently.

Cover and chill 8 hours. Serve with a slotted
spoon. **Yield: 4 to 6 servings.**

Quick Corn Muffins

1 (8½-ounce) package corn muffin mix
2 tablespoons chopped onion
1 large egg, beaten
⅓ cup milk

Combine muffin mix and onion; add egg and
milk, stirring just until dry ingredients are moistened. Pour batter into well-greased muffin pans,
filling two-thirds full. Bake at 400° for 15 minutes or until lightly browned. **Yield: 6 to 8
muffins.**

TimeSavers

• Use kitchen shears to chop
canned tomatoes in the can.
• Purchase shredded cabbage or
coleslaw mix and make slaw the
night before. Chop and bag onion
and green pepper for the entrée
and muffins for a headstart.
• Buy chilled citrus sections for
dessert.
• Use a corn muffin mix for a
really quick bread. The yield depends
on the size of the muffin pan.

Easy Red Beans and Rice

Simple and Sensational

SERVES 4

Shrimp and Tortellini • Asparagus with Garlic Butter
Crusty Italian bread • Orange-Glazed Bananas Foster

Shrimp and Tortellini

Shrimp and Tortellini

1 (9-ounce) package refrigerated
   cheese-filled tortellini, uncooked
⅓ cup butter or margarine
1 pound peeled, medium-size fresh shrimp
1 shallot, minced
2 tablespoons chopped fresh basil or
   2 teaspoons dried basil
½ cup grated Parmesan cheese
Garnish: fresh basil

Cook pasta according to package directions;
drain and set aside.

Melt butter in a large skillet over medium-high
heat; add shrimp, minced shallot, and chopped
basil. Cook, stirring constantly, about 5 minutes.
Add pasta and Parmesan cheese. Toss gently, and
garnish, if desired. **Yield: 4 servings.**

Asparagus with Garlic Butter

1 pound fresh asparagus or 1 (10-ounce)
   package frozen asparagus
1½ tablespoons butter
1 clove garlic, minced
½ teaspoon soy sauce

Cut asparagus on the diagonal into 2-inch pieces.
Cook asparagus, covered, in a small amount of
boiling water 4 minutes or until crisp-tender; drain.
Melt butter in a large saucepan, and add garlic
and soy sauce. Cook over low heat, stirring constantly, 1 minute. Add asparagus; toss to coat.
Yield: 4 servings.

Orange-Glazed Bananas Foster

2 bananas, split and quartered
⅓ cup orange juice
2 tablespoons Grand Marnier or other
   orange-flavored liqueur
1 tablespoon butter or margarine
2 tablespoons chopped walnuts
2 tablespoons firmly packed brown sugar
Vanilla ice cream

Arrange bananas in an 8-inch square baking
dish. Combine orange juice and liqueur; pour
over bananas, and dot with butter. Bake at 400°
for 10 minutes, basting occasionally.

Combine walnuts and brown sugar; sprinkle
over bananas, and bake 5 additional minutes.
Serve immediately over ice cream. **Yield: 4
servings.**

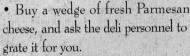

TimeSavers

• Buy a wedge of fresh Parmesan
cheese, and ask the deli personnel to
grate it for you.
• Substitute 2 green onions for 1
shallot, if desired.
• Add a drop of vegetable oil to the
pasta water to prevent it from boiling over.
• Choose asparagus stalks that are
uniform in size to ensure even
cooking.

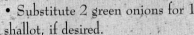

Fast Shrimp Dee-Lish

SERVES 4

Shrimp Dee-Lish • Tomato-Asparagus Salad
Chive-Garlic French Bread • Lemon sherbet

Shrimp Dee-Lish

Vegetable cooking spray
1 cup sliced green onions
½ cup chopped celery
½ cup sliced fresh mushrooms
4 cloves garlic, minced
1 pound peeled, medium-size fresh shrimp
1 (10¾-ounce) can cream of mushroom soup, undiluted
¼ teaspoon Creole seasoning
1 (8-ounce) carton plain yogurt
Hot cooked noodles
Garnish: green onion fan

Coat a large nonstick skillet with cooking spray; place over medium heat until hot. Add green onions and next 3 ingredients; cook until vegetables are tender.

Add shrimp; cook 5 minutes, stirring constantly. Stir in soup and seasoning; bring to a boil.

Remove from heat; stir in yogurt (at room temperature), and serve immediately over noodles. Garnish, if desired. **Yield: 4 servings.**

Tomato-Asparagus Salad

1 pound fresh asparagus
8 romaine lettuce leaves
12 cherry tomatoes, halved
⅓ cup commercial Italian salad dressing
¼ cup grated Parmesan cheese

Snap off tough ends of asparagus. Place asparagus in steaming rack over boiling water;

cover and steam 4 minutes. Drain and plunge into ice water to cool. Drain asparagus well.

Arrange lettuce leaves on individual plates. Arrange asparagus spears and tomato on top; drizzle with salad dressing, and sprinkle with Parmesan cheese. **Yield: 4 servings.**

Note: 1 (16-ounce) can asparagus spears may be substituted for fresh asparagus.

Chive-Garlic French Bread

¼ cup butter or margarine, softened
1 tablespoon minced chives
1 large clove garlic, minced
1 teaspoon lemon juice
10 (1-inch) slices French bread

Combine first 4 ingredients; spread on one side of bread slices. Place buttered side up on a baking sheet. Broil 6 inches from heat (with electric oven door partially opened) 2 to 3 minutes or until lightly browned. **Yield: 10 servings.**

TimeSavers

• Select thin asparagus stalks, as they generally are more tender.
• Spread topping on bread ahead of time; wrap tightly and refrigerate. Unwrap and broil just before serving.
• Dress up the dessert by serving the sherbet in a compote and garnishing with a mint sprig.

Shrimp Dee-Lish

Linguine with Clam Sauce

Linguine with Clam Sauce

1 (16-ounce) package linguine
2 cloves garlic, minced
½ cup butter or margarine, melted
2 (6½-ounce) cans minced clams, drained
½ teaspoon dried basil
½ teaspoon dried oregano
¼ teaspoon salt
¼ teaspoon pepper
½ cup chopped fresh parsley
1 cup grated Parmesan cheese

Cook linguine in a Dutch oven according to package directions. Drain and return to Dutch oven; set aside.

Cook garlic in butter in a medium skillet; add clams and next 4 ingredients. Cook over low heat, stirring constantly, 5 minutes. Pour over hot cooked linguine; add parsley, and toss gently. Place on a warm platter, and top with Parmesan cheese. **Yield: 4 to 6 servings.**

TimeSavers

• To make cleanup easier when grating Parmesan cheese, brush grater lightly with oil before you start.
• Cook linguine in a Dutch oven with plenty of water so pasta has room to move around while cooking.
• Speed up salad preparation by buying pre-washed spinach, sliced mushrooms, and chopped pecans.

Spinach-Pecan Salad

1 cup sliced fresh mushrooms
½ cup commercial Italian salad dressing
1 (10-ounce) package fresh, trimmed spinach, torn into bite-size pieces
⅓ cup golden raisins
⅓ cup coarsely chopped pecans
2 hard-cooked eggs

Toss mushrooms with salad dressing; set aside.

Combine spinach, mushrooms, raisins, and pecans in a bowl; toss gently. Add additional dressing, if necessary. Grate egg over salad before serving. **Yield: 6 servings.**

Crème de Menthe Parfait

1 quart vanilla ice cream, softened
1 pint lime sherbet, softened
½ (8-ounce) carton frozen whipped topping, thawed
¼ cup green crème de menthe

Combine all ingredients in container of an electric blender; blend at medium speed until well mixed.

Spoon into parfait glasses. Place parfaits in freezer 3 to 4 hours. **Yield: 6 servings.**

Dinner on a Platter

SERVES 4

Fish-and-Potato Platter • Fresh fruit with poppy seed dressing
◆ Peanut Butter Pie

Fish-and-Potato Platter

1 (8-ounce) carton plain nonfat yogurt
¼ cup chopped fresh dill
2 tablespoons rice vinegar
2 tablespoons chopped chives
½ teaspoon salt
½ teaspoon pepper
¾ pound small red potatoes, unpeeled and cut
    into ⅛-inch slices
1 pound salmon or amberjack fillets, skinned
    and cut crosswise into 3- x 1½-inch pieces
1 cup broccoli flowerets
2 tablespoons lemon juice

Combine first 6 ingredients in a small bowl; cover and chill.

Overlap potato slices around edge of a microwave-safe, round 12-inch platter. Cover tightly with heavy-duty plastic wrap; fold back a small edge of wrap to allow steam to escape. Microwave at HIGH 3 minutes.

Uncover and place fish in a ring inside potato slices with pieces end to end. Mound broccoli in center of platter. Sprinkle fish and potato with lemon juice; cover.

Microwave at HIGH 8 minutes or until fish is cooked through and potato is tender, giving dish a half-turn at 4-minute intervals. Serve with dill sauce. **Yield: 4 servings.**

Fish-and-Potato Platter

Peanut Butter Pie

1 (8-ounce) package cream cheese, softened
1 cup sifted powdered sugar
1 cup chunky peanut butter
½ cup milk
1 (8-ounce) carton frozen whipped topping,
    thawed
1 (9-inch) graham cracker crust
¼ cup coarsely chopped peanuts

Combine first 4 ingredients in a bowl; beat at medium speed of an electric mixer until blended. Fold in whipped topping. Spoon into crust; sprinkle with peanuts. Chill. **Yield: one 9-inch pie.**

Make It Casual

Casual fare shouldn't take more time to make than to eat. These favorites stand on their own as hassle-free lunches or dinners.

Chili-Chicken Stew, Creamy Onion-and-Potato Soup, Stromboli

Caesar Salad with Tortellini and Asparagus, Crab Bisque, Feta-Tomato Crostini

Mexican Chef Salad, Ham-Pecan-Blue Cheese Pasta Salad, Double-Decker BLT

Honey-Mustard Turkey Salad, Ranch-Style Turkey 'n' Pasta Salad

Tuna-Pasta Salad (page 67)

Chili-Chicken Stew

Winter Warm-Up

SERVES 6
Chili-Chicken Stew • Deli coleslaw
Seasoned Cornbread • Brownie Chip Cookies

Chili-Chicken Stew

6 skinned, boned chicken breast halves
1 medium onion, chopped
1 medium-size green pepper, chopped
2 cloves garlic, minced
1 tablespoon vegetable oil
2 (14½-ounce) cans stewed tomatoes,
    undrained and chopped
1 (15-ounce) can pinto beans, drained
⅔ cup picante sauce
1 teaspoon chili powder
1 teaspoon ground cumin
½ teaspoon salt
Shredded Cheddar cheese, diced avocado,
    sliced green onions, and sour cream

Cut chicken into 1-inch pieces. Cook chicken, onion, green pepper, and garlic in hot oil in a Dutch oven until lightly browned. Add tomatoes and next 5 ingredients; cover, reduce heat, and simmer 20 minutes.

Top individual servings with remaining ingredients. **Yield: 6 servings.**

Seasoned Cornbread

1 (8½-ounce) package corn muffin mix
½ teaspoon poultry seasoning
1 large egg, beaten
⅔ cup milk

Combine muffin mix and poultry seasoning; add egg and milk, stirring just until dry ingredients are moistened. Pour batter into a well-greased 8-inch square baking dish; bake at 400° for 18 to 20 minutes. **Yield: 9 servings.**

Brownie Chip Cookies

1 (23.7-ounce) package brownie mix
2 large eggs
⅓ cup vegetable oil
1 (6-ounce) package semisweet chocolate
    morsels
½ cup chopped pecans

Combine brownie mix, eggs, and oil; beat about 50 strokes with a spoon. Stir in chocolate morsels and pecans. Drop dough by rounded teaspoonfuls onto greased cookie sheets.

Bake at 350° for 10 to 12 minutes. Cool slightly on cookie sheets; then remove to wire racks, and cool completely. **Yield: about 6 dozen.**

TimeSavers

• Use kitchen shears to chop tomatoes in the can and to cut chicken into uniform pieces.
• Buy chopped vegetables, shredded cheese, and deli coleslaw.
• Bake cookies in advance, or serve bakery cookies.

Creamy Onion-and-Potato Soup

2 tablespoons butter or margarine
2 tablespoons all-purpose flour
1 cup chopped onion
1 large clove garlic, minced
2 (14½-ounce) cans ready-to-serve chicken
  broth
4 cups peeled, cubed potato (about 3 large)
½ cup sliced green onions
⅛ teaspoon salt
¼ teaspoon ground white pepper
1 cup milk
Garnish: green onion strips

Melt butter in a Dutch oven over low heat;
add flour, stirring until smooth. Cook, stirring
constantly, 1 minute. Add onion and garlic; cook
1 minute or until onion is tender. Gradually add
broth, stirring constantly. Add potato and next 3
ingredients.

Bring to a boil; cover, reduce heat, and simmer
15 minutes, stirring occasionally, or until potato is
tender. Stir in milk, and heat thoroughly. Garnish,
if desired. **Yield: 7 cups.**

TimeSavers

• Cut potatoes into small cubes to
help them cook faster.
• Buy prewashed spinach, if available.
• Use leftover cooked ham for
biscuits.

Spinach Salad

1 (10-ounce) package fresh, trimmed
  spinach
1 cup strawberries, halved
1 cup pecan halves, toasted
Commercial poppy seed dressing

Tear spinach leaves into bite-size pieces.
Combine spinach, strawberries, and pecans;
drizzle with poppy seed dressing. Serve immediately. **Yield: 6 servings.**

Ham-Cheese Biscuits

2 cups biscuit mix
½ cup minced cooked ham
½ cup (2 ounces) shredded Cheddar cheese
⅔ cup milk

Combine first 3 ingredients in a medium bowl,
stirring well. Sprinkle milk over dry mixture, stirring just until moistened.

Pat dough out onto a floured surface to ½-
inch thickness; cut with a 2-inch biscuit cutter.

Place biscuits on a greased baking sheet. Bake
at 450° for 8 minutes or until lightly browned.
Yield: 14 biscuits.

Creamy Onion-and-Potato Soup

Mexican Chef Salad

A Taste of Tex-Mex

SERVES 4
Mexican Chef Salad • Strawberry Fool
Southern Sangría

Mexican Chef Salad

1 pound ground beef
¾ cup water
1 (1¼-ounce) package taco seasoning mix
8 cups torn iceberg lettuce
1 (16-ounce) can kidney beans, drained and rinsed
2 tomatoes, chopped
1 (2¼-ounce) can sliced ripe olives, drained
½ cup (2 ounces) shredded Cheddar cheese
Commercial guacamole
Tortilla chips

Cook ground beef in a skillet until meat is browned, stirring to crumble; drain. Return meat to skillet; add water and taco seasoning mix. Bring to a boil; reduce heat, and simmer 10 minutes, stirring occasionally.

Layer lettuce, beans, beef mixture, tomato, olives, and cheese. Serve with guacamole and tortilla chips. **Yield: 4 servings.**

Strawberry Fool

2 cups fresh strawberries, hulled
¼ cup sugar
1 cup whipping cream, whipped
Garnish: 4 fresh strawberries

Place 2 cups strawberries and sugar in container of a food processor or electric blender, and process until smooth. Pour mixture into a large bowl.

Fold whipped cream into strawberry mixture. Spoon into individual serving bowls. Garnish, if desired. Serve immediately, or chill 1 hour.
Yield: 4 servings.

Southern Sangría

⅓ cup sugar
⅓ cup lemon juice
⅓ cup orange juice
1 (25.4-ounce) bottle sparkling red grape juice, chilled

Combine first 3 ingredients in a large pitcher, stirring until sugar dissolves. Add grape juice, and gently stir to mix well. Serve over crushed ice. **Yield: 5 cups.**

TimeSavers

• Buy shredded cheese, sliced ripe olives, and guacamole for a head-start on the salad.
• To save time with dessert, substitute frozen strawberries for fresh, and 2 cups frozen whipped topping, thawed, for whipped cream; omit sugar.

Ham-Pecan-Blue Cheese Pasta Salad

Lazy Day Fare

SERVES 6

Ham-Pecan-Blue Cheese Pasta Salad • ◆ Marinated Tomatoes
Crusty rolls • Blueberries and Cointreau

Ham-Pecan-Blue Cheese Pasta Salad

3 cups farfalle (bow tie pasta), uncooked
4 ounces cooked ham, cut into strips
1 cup coarsely chopped pecans
1 (4-ounce) package crumbled blue cheese
2 tablespoons chopped fresh parsley
1 tablespoon minced fresh rosemary or
    1 teaspoon dried rosemary
1 clove garlic, minced
½ teaspoon coarsely ground pepper
¼ cup olive oil
⅓ cup grated Parmesan cheese

Cook pasta according to package directions; drain. Rinse with cold water and drain.

Combine pasta and remaining ingredients except Parmesan cheese, tossing well. Sprinkle with Parmesan cheese. Serve immediately or chill, if desired. **Yield: 6 servings.**

Marinated Tomatoes

3 large tomatoes
⅓ cup olive oil
¼ cup red wine vinegar
1 teaspoon salt
¼ teaspoon pepper
½ clove garlic, crushed
1 tablespoon chopped fresh parsley
1 tablespoon chopped fresh basil or
    1 teaspoon dried basil
2 tablespoons chopped onion

Cut tomatoes into ½-inch-thick slices, and arrange in a large shallow dish; set aside.

Combine remaining ingredients in a jar; cover tightly, and shake vigorously. Pour over tomato slices. Cover and marinate in refrigerator several hours. **Yield: 6 servings.**

TimeSavers

• Rinse cooked pasta in cold water to eliminate chilling salad if you plan to serve it immediately.
• Buy vine-ripened tomatoes and store at room temperature. To speed the ripening process, place tomatoes in a paper bag.
• To chop parsley, place in a glass measuring cup and snip with kitchen shears.

Blueberries and Cointreau

3 cups fresh blueberries, rinsed and drained
¼ cup plus 2 tablespoons Cointreau or other
    orange-flavored liqueur
Sweetened whipped cream

Place ½ cup blueberries in each of 6 stemmed glasses; pour 1 tablespoon Cointreau over each serving.

Top each serving with a dollop of sweetened whipped cream. **Yield: 6 servings.**

Sunday Night Supper

SERVES 4
◆ Honey-Mustard Turkey Salad • Creamy Tomato Soup
Sesame Knots

Honey-Mustard Turkey Salad

2 cups chopped cooked turkey
6 slices bacon, cooked and crumbled
1 (4.5-ounce) jar whole mushrooms, drained
¼ cup sweet red pepper strips
¼ cup sliced green onions
½ cup mayonnaise or salad dressing
2 tablespoons honey
1½ tablespoons Dijon mustard
¾ teaspoon soy sauce
¾ teaspoon lemon juice
1 (2-ounce) package roasted cashews
Lettuce leaves
Sweet red pepper rings
Chow mein noodles

Combine first 5 ingredients in a medium bowl; set aside. Combine mayonnaise and next 4 ingredients; fold into turkey mixture. Cover and chill. Just before serving, stir in cashews. Serve on lettuce leaves and red pepper rings; sprinkle with chow mein noodles. **Yield: 4 servings.**

TimeSavers

• Use leftover cooked turkey or sliced turkey from the deli.
• Get a headstart on the salad by cooking extra breakfast bacon; wrap bacon airtight, and chill up to 5 days or freeze up to 6 weeks.
• Chop canned tomatoes right in the can with kitchen shears.

Creamy Tomato Soup

1 (10¾-ounce) can tomato soup, undiluted
1 (12-ounce) can evaporated milk
1 (14½-ounce) can stewed tomatoes, undrained and chopped
½ cup (2 ounces) shredded Cheddar cheese

Combine soup and milk in a medium saucepan, stirring with a wire whisk. Add tomatoes and cheese.

Cook over low heat until cheese melts and soup is hot. **Yield: 4⅔ cups.**

Sesame Knots

1 (11-ounce) package refrigerated soft breadsticks
2 tablespoons butter or margarine, melted
½ teaspoon sesame seeds or poppy seeds

Separate dough, and loosely tie each piece of dough into a knot. Arrange rolls 1 inch apart on an ungreased baking sheet. Brush with butter; sprinkle with sesame seeds.

Bake at 350° for 15 minutes or until golden brown. **Yield: 10 servings.**

Honey-Mustard Turkey Salad

Cool Summer Lunch

SERVES 6 TO 8

◆ Ranch-Style Turkey 'n' Pasta Salad • Crusty hard rolls • ◆ Green Grapes Surprise

Ranch-Style Turkey 'n' Pasta Salad

Ranch-Style Turkey 'n' Pasta Salad

2 cups penne pasta, uncooked
2 cups chopped cooked turkey
1 small zucchini, sliced
2 small yellow squash, sliced
1 small green pepper, chopped
1 small sweet red pepper, chopped
¼ cup grated Parmesan cheese
¾ cup commercial Ranch-style dressing

Cook pasta according to package directions; drain. Rinse with cold water; drain.

Combine pasta and remaining ingredients in a large bowl. Cover and chill at least 2 hours. Toss before serving. **Yield: 6 to 8 servings.**

Green Grapes Surprise

¼ cup firmly packed light brown sugar
½ cup sour cream
5 cups seedless green grapes, washed and stemmed
Garnish: mint sprigs

Combine brown sugar and sour cream in a large bowl. Stir in grapes. Chill several hours.

Spoon into individual serving dishes. Garnish, if desired. **Yield: 6 to 8 servings.**

An Autumn Favorite

(pictured on page 55)

SERVES 6

◆ Tuna-Pasta Salad • Fresh fruit with Tangy Coconut Dressing • Cheesy Twists

Tuna-Pasta Salad

6 ounces spinach or tricolored corkscrew
   noodles, uncooked
½ cup sliced green onions
½ cup sweet yellow or green pepper strips
½ cup sliced ripe olives
1 cup halved cherry tomatoes
1 carrot, scraped and shredded
2 (6½-ounce) cans chunk light tuna, drained
   and flaked
½ cup vegetable oil
3 tablespoons white wine vinegar
2 tablespoons lemon juice
3 tablespoons minced fresh parsley
½ teaspoon salt
¼ teaspoon pepper
1 green onion, cut into 1-inch pieces
1 large clove garlic, halved
Lettuce leaves

   Cook pasta according to package directions;
drain. Rinse with cold water; drain. Combine
pasta and next 6 ingredients; set aside.
   Combine oil and remaining ingredients except
lettuce leaves in an electric blender, and process
until mixture is smooth.
   Pour dressing over salad, and toss gently.
Cover and chill at least 8 hours, stirring occasionally. Spoon salad over lettuce leaves, using a
slotted spoon. **Yield: 6 to 8 servings.**

Tangy Coconut Dressing

1 (15-ounce) can cream of coconut
1 (6-ounce) can frozen lemonade concentrate,
   thawed and undiluted

   Combine ingredients, stirring until blended.
Serve over fresh fruit. Store remaining dressing
in refrigerator. **Yield: about 2 cups.**

Cheesy Twists

½ cup grated Parmesan cheese
3 tablespoons butter or margarine, softened
½ teaspoon Dijon mustard
1 (10-ounce) can refrigerated buttermilk
   biscuits

   Combine first 3 ingredients; set aside.
   Roll each biscuit into a 5- x 2-inch rectangle;
spread about 2 teaspoons cheese mixture over
rectangle, and cut in half lengthwise. Twist each
strip 2 or 3 times, and place on a lightly greased
baking sheet.
   Bake at 400° for 8 to 10 minutes or until golden.
Yield: 20 twists.

TimeSavers

• Buy precut vegetables to shorten
salad preparation time.
• Remove frozen lemonade from
can, and thaw in the microwave.

Summertime Supper

SERVES 4

Caesar Salad with Tortellini and Asparagus • Mayonnaise Muffins
◆ Summer Fruit Compote

Caesar Salad with Tortellini and Asparagus

Caesar Salad with Tortellini and Asparagus

4 cups hot water
1 (9-ounce) package refrigerated cheese-filled
   tortellini, uncooked
½ pound fresh asparagus, cut into 2-inch
   pieces
¼ cup lemon juice
3 tablespoons olive oil
2 tablespoons water
1 tablespoon Worcestershire sauce
¼ teaspoon freshly ground pepper
1 clove garlic, pressed
1 head romaine lettuce, torn
¼ cup grated Parmesan cheese

Bring water to a boil in a 4-quart Dutch oven.
Add tortellini and asparagus, and cook 4 minutes. Drain; rinse in cold water and drain. Set mixture aside.
Combine lemon juice and next 5 ingredients, stirring with a wire whisk; set aside.
Place lettuce, tortellini, and asparagus in a large bowl; add dressing, tossing gently. Sprinkle with cheese. **Yield: 4 servings.**

TimeSavers

• To boil pasta faster, start with hot water. Cook pasta and asparagus together in the same pot.
• Buy sliced fruit in the produce section for fruit compote.
• Grate the lime for compote before squeezing it. Get more juice by microwaving the lime at HIGH 20 seconds before squeezing.

Mayonnaise Muffins

1 cup self-rising flour
2 tablespoons mayonnaise
½ cup milk

Combine all ingredients; stir until smooth.
Spoon batter into greased muffin pans, filling two-thirds full. Bake at 425° for 10 to 12 minutes. **Yield: 6 muffins.**

Summer Fruit Compote

¼ cup sugar
2 tablespoons rum
1 teaspoon grated lime rind
2 tablespoons fresh lime juice
1 nectarine
1 plum
1 pear
1 peach
4 strawberries

Combine first 4 ingredients. Seed and slice nectarine, plum, and pear; peel, seed, and slice peach. Pour dressing over fruit in a medium bowl; toss lightly. Cover and chill thoroughly.
Spoon into individual compotes; top each serving with a strawberry. **Yield: 4 servings.**

Patio Supper

SERVES 4

Stromboli • ◆ Marinated Artichoke Salad
Potato chips • Dill pickles • Grape Juice-Fruit Refresher

Stromboli

1 (16-ounce) loaf frozen bread dough, thawed
¼ pound thinly sliced ham
¼ pound sliced hard salami
½ teaspoon dried basil, divided
½ teaspoon dried oregano, divided
3 ounces sliced provolone cheese
1 cup (4 ounces) shredded mozzarella cheese
2 tablespoons butter or margarine, melted
1 teaspoon cornmeal

Place bread dough on a lightly greased baking sheet; pat to a 15- x 10-inch rectangle. Arrange ham slices lengthwise down center; place salami on top. Sprinkle with ¼ teaspoon basil and ¼ teaspoon oregano. Arrange provolone cheese over herbs, and top with mozzarella cheese; sprinkle with remaining herbs.

Moisten all edges of dough with water. Bring each long edge of dough to center; press edges together securely to seal. Seal ends.

Brush dough with 1 tablespoon butter. Sprinkle with cornmeal, and carefully invert. Brush top with remaining butter. Bake at 375° for 20 to 22 minutes. **Yield: 4 servings.**

TimeSavers

• Buy sliced meat and cheese at deli.
• Thaw frozen bread dough at room temperature, or follow quick thawing instructions on package.

Marinated Artichoke Salad

1 (6-ounce) jar marinated artichoke hearts, undrained
1 (4-ounce) can sliced mushrooms, drained
1 (4-ounce) can sliced ripe olives, drained
½ cup chopped onion
2 stalks celery, sliced
1 medium tomato, cut into wedges
Lettuce leaves

Combine first 6 ingredients in a large bowl, stirring well. Cover and chill thoroughly.

Transfer salad with a slotted spoon into a lettuce-lined bowl. **Yield: 4 servings.**

Grape Juice-Fruit Refresher

1 quart pineapple or lime sherbet
1⅓ cups sliced fresh strawberries
¼ to ½ cup white grape juice

Spoon sherbet equally into 4 compotes. Top each with ⅓ cup sliced strawberries. Just before serving, pour 1 to 2 tablespoons grape juice over top. **Yield: 4 servings.**

Stromboli

Mexican Egg Salad Tacos

Quick-Fix Lunch

SERVES 6
Mexican Egg Salad Tacos • ◆ Herbed Tomatoes • Peach Crinkle

Mexican Egg Salad Tacos

4 large hard-cooked eggs, chopped
¼ cup (1 ounce) shredded sharp Cheddar cheese
1 tablespoon chopped green onions
2 tablespoons mayonnaise or salad dressing
2 tablespoons salsa
1 tablespoon sour cream
⅛ teaspoon salt
⅛ teaspoon pepper
6 taco shells
Lettuce leaves
¾ cup (3 ounces) shredded sharp Cheddar cheese
Avocado slices
Additional salsa

Combine first 3 ingredients in a medium bowl; set aside.

Combine mayonnaise and next 4 ingredients; fold into egg mixture.

Line taco shells with lettuce. Spoon egg salad evenly into taco shells. Sprinkle 2 tablespoons cheese on each taco. Serve with avocado slices and salsa. Yield: 6 servings.

Herbed Tomatoes

⅓ cup vegetable oil
2 tablespoons white wine vinegar
¼ cup chopped fresh parsley
¼ cup chopped fresh chives
⅛ teaspoon pepper
Pinch of dried thyme
3 tomatoes, unpeeled and quartered
Lettuce

Combine first 6 ingredients in a 2-cup glass measure; mix well. Place tomato in a shallow container; pour dressing over tomato. Cover and chill 8 hours or overnight.

Drain tomato, reserving dressing. Arrange tomato on lettuce leaves; spoon dressing over tomato. Yield: 6 servings.

Peach Crinkle

1 (29-ounce) can sliced peaches, drained
1 teaspoon grated lemon rind
1 (11-ounce) package piecrust mix
1 cup firmly packed brown sugar
¼ cup cold butter or margarine, cut into
   small pieces

Place peaches in a lightly greased 11- x 7- x 1½-inch baking dish. Sprinkle with lemon rind, and set aside.

Combine piecrust mix and sugar; sprinkle over top. Dot with butter.

Bake at 375° for 30 minutes. Serve with vanilla ice cream or frozen yogurt. Yield: 6 servings.

TimeSavers

• Save time and nutrients by not peeling tomatoes.
• To seed avocado, cut lengthwise all the way around and twist halves in opposite directions to separate. Remove seed; brush cut surface with lemon juice to keep from turning brown.

Relax with Soup and Sandwiches

SERVES 4
Double-Decker BLT • Pickles • Broccoli-Cheese Soup
Cookies and fresh fruit • Easy Mint Tea

Double-Decker BLT

1 (13-ounce) loaf unsliced French bread
Olive oil-flavored cooking spray
Garlic-Basil Mayonnaise
Salad greens
4 tomatoes, thinly sliced
16 slices bacon, cooked

Cut bread into 12 slices. Coat one side of each with cooking spray. Grill or toast until golden.

Spread Garlic-Basil Mayonnaise on other side of each bread slice; layer 4 slices with half each of salad greens, tomato slices, and bacon. Top each with a second bread slice and remaining salad greens, tomato, and bacon. Top with remaining bread slices. **Yield: 4 sandwiches.**

Garlic-Basil Mayonnaise

½ cup mayonnaise or salad dressing
1 tablespoon chopped fresh basil or
    1 teaspoon dried basil
¼ teaspoon garlic salt
¼ teaspoon freshly ground pepper

Combine all ingredients; cover and chill.
Yield: ½ cup.

TimeSavers

• Microwave bacon in advance on a microwave-safe rack or paper plate with a double layer of paper towels between each layer of slices. Cook 8 slices at HIGH 6 to 7 minutes.

Broccoli-Cheese Soup

¾ cup water
1 (10-ounce) package frozen chopped broccoli
1 (10¾-ounce) can cream of chicken soup
½ cup milk
⅛ teaspoon ground red pepper
½ cup (2 ounces) shredded Cheddar cheese

Bring water to a boil in a large saucepan; add broccoli. Cover, reduce heat, and simmer 5 minutes or until tender. Stir in soup and milk.

Cook over medium heat, stirring constantly, until thoroughly heated. Stir in pepper. Pour into serving bowls. Top each serving with cheese.
Yield: 1 quart.

Easy Mint Tea

2 cups boiling water
5 regular-size, mint-flavored tea bags
1 cup sugar
¾ cup lemon juice
1½ quarts water
1 cup pineapple juice
2 cups ginger ale

Pour boiling water over tea bags; cover and steep 5 minutes. Remove tea bags, squeezing gently. Add sugar and lemon juice, stirring until sugar dissolves. Stir in 1½ quarts water, pineapple juice, and ginger ale. Serve over ice. **Yield: about 3 quarts.**

Double-Decker BLT

Quick Gourmet Fare

SERVES 6

Feta-Tomato Crostini • Pita chips • Crab Bisque • Fresh fruit

Feta-Tomato Crostini

3 (6-inch) French bread rolls, split
Olive oil
1 (7-ounce) package feta cheese, crumbled
Coarse ground garlic powder with parsley
3 small tomatoes, chopped
1½ tablespoons balsamic vinegar
2 tablespoons chopped fresh mint
Lettuce leaves
Garnish: fresh mint sprigs

Brush cut side of each roll with olive oil; place on a baking sheet. Broil 6 inches from heat (with electric oven door partially opened) 2 minutes or until lightly browned.

Place crumbled cheese evenly on each roll; sprinkle lightly with garlic powder. Place tomato over cheese; drizzle with balsamic vinegar, and sprinkle with mint. Serve on lettuce leaves, and garnish, if desired. Serve immediately. **Yield: 6 servings.**

Feta-Tomato Crostini

Crab Bisque

1 (10¾-ounce) can cream of mushroom soup, undiluted
1 (10¾-ounce) can cream of asparagus soup, undiluted
2 cups milk
1 cup half-and-half
1 (6-ounce) can crabmeat, drained and flaked
¼ to ⅓ cup Chablis or other dry white wine

Combine first 4 ingredients in a saucepan; cook over medium heat until thoroughly heated, stirring occasionally. Add crabmeat and wine; cook until thoroughly heated. **Yield: 6 cups.**

TimeSavers

• Substitute red wine vinegar for balsamic vinegar in crostini, if desired.
• While bisque is heating, prepare crostini.

Kids' Favorites

When time is short and you need fresh ideas for picky eaters, try these no-fuss kid pleasers. They're just right for hectic times.

Strawberry-French Toast Sandwiches, Gulf Coast Fried Shrimp

Big Veggie Sandwich, Corn Chowder, Bacon-Cheese French Bread, Fiesta Dip

Speedy Chili Dogs, Mexican Franks, Sloppy Joes, All-American Pizza Burgers

Easy Cheesy Bobolis, Hearty Stuffed Potatoes, Zesty Broccoli Slaw

Microwave Chili Dogs (page 79)

Easy Breakfast Treat

SERVES 6
Orange Juicy • Strawberry-French Toast Sandwiches • Bacon

Strawberry-French Toast Sandwiches

Orange Juicy

1 (6-ounce) can frozen orange juice
    concentrate, undiluted
1 cup water
1 cup milk
¼ cup sugar
1 teaspoon vanilla extract
2 cups ice cubes

Combine all ingredients in container of an electric blender; process until smooth. Serve immediately. **Yield: 5 cups.**

Strawberry-French Toast Sandwiches

¼ cup plus 2 tablespoons whipped cream cheese
12 slices sandwich bread
3 tablespoons strawberry jam
3 large eggs
3 tablespoons milk
⅛ teaspoon salt
2 to 3 tablespoons butter or margarine,
    divided
Powdered sugar
Garnish: strawberry fans

Spread 1 tablespoon cream cheese on each of six bread slices; spread 1½ teaspoons jam over cream cheese. Top with remaining slices of bread.

Combine eggs, milk, and salt in a shallow dish, beating well. Dip each sandwich into egg mixture, turning to coat both sides.

Melt 2 tablespoons butter in a large skillet; cook 3 sandwiches in butter until browned, turning to brown both sides. Repeat procedure with remaining sandwiches, adding more butter if necessary.

Sprinkle sandwiches with powdered sugar; serve immediately. Garnish, if desired. **Yield: 6 servings.**

TimeSavers

• Microwave bacon on a microwave-safe rack or paper plate. Cover bacon with paper towels; cook 6 slices at HIGH 5 minutes.

Fall Festival

(pictured on page 77)

SERVES 8

Microwave Chili Dogs • ◆ Kraut Relish
Corn chips • Oat 'n' Crunch Brownies

Microwave Chili Dogs

1 pound ground turkey
1 onion, chopped
1 green pepper, chopped (optional)
1 (15-ounce) can tomato sauce
2 tablespoons chili powder
½ teaspoon dried oregano
Dash of garlic powder
8 frankfurters, cooked
8 hot dog buns

Combine turkey, onion, and, if desired, green pepper in a 2-quart casserole. Cover with wax paper, and microwave at HIGH 6 minutes, stirring after 3 minutes; drain. Add tomato sauce and next 3 ingredients, stirring well. Microwave at HIGH 10 minutes, stirring after 5 minutes.

Place frankfurters in hot dog buns. Spoon turkey mixture over frankfurters. **Yield: 8 servings.**

Kraut Relish

1 (16-ounce) jar sauerkraut, drained
½ cup finely chopped celery
½ cup finely chopped green pepper
½ cup finely chopped carrot
½ cup finely chopped onion
¼ cup sugar

Combine all ingredients; cover and chill 8 hours. Serve relish with hot dogs, vegetables, or meats. **Yield: 1 quart.**

Oat 'n' Crunch Brownies

1 (21.5-ounce) package fudge brownie mix
½ cup chopped pecans
⅓ cup quick-cooking oats, uncooked
¼ cup firmly packed brown sugar
¼ teaspoon ground cinnamon (optional)
2 tablespoons butter or margarine, melted
¾ cup candy-coated chocolate pieces

Grease bottom of a 13- x 9- x 2-inch pan. Prepare brownie mix according to package directions; spoon into prepared pan.

Combine pecans, oats, brown sugar, and, if desired, cinnamon; stir in butter. Stir in candy; sprinkle over batter.

Bake at 350° for 35 minutes. Cool and cut into squares. **Yield: 3 dozen.**

TimeSavers

• Substitute plain kraut for Kraut Relish.
• Bake brownies a day ahead.

Speedy Chili Dogs

Backyard Picnic

SERVES 8

Speedy Chili Dogs • ◆ Old-Fashioned Sweet Coleslaw
Potato chips • ◆ Lemon Ice Cream Tarts

Speedy Chili Dogs

1 pound ground beef
1 large onion, chopped
1 clove garlic, crushed
1 (16-ounce) can tomato sauce
¼ teaspoon salt
⅛ teaspoon pepper
1 to 2 tablespoons chili powder
1 cup water
8 frankfurters, cooked
8 hot dog buns, split and toasted
Shredded Cheddar cheese
Chopped green onions

Combine first 3 ingredients in a skillet; cook until beef is browned, stirring until it crumbles. Drain. Add tomato sauce and next 4 ingredients; cover, reduce heat, and simmer 25 minutes, stirring occasionally.

Place frankfurters in hot dog buns. Spoon chili mixture over frankfurters; top with cheese and green onions. **Yield: 8 servings.**

TimeSavers

• Select a packaged slaw mix that has shredded carrot in it.
• Make tarts in advance and freeze.

Old-Fashioned Sweet Coleslaw

5 cups finely chopped cabbage (about 1 small head)
2 carrots, scraped and shredded
1 to 2 tablespoons sugar
½ teaspoon salt
¼ teaspoon pepper
⅓ cup mayonnaise or salad dressing

Combine cabbage and carrot in a large bowl. Sprinkle with sugar, salt, and pepper; toss gently. Stir in mayonnaise. Cover and chill thoroughly. **Yield: 8 servings.**

Lemon Ice Cream Tarts

1 quart vanilla ice cream, slightly softened
1 (6-ounce) can frozen lemonade concentrate, undiluted
12 (3-inch) commercial graham cracker tart shells

Place softened ice cream and lemonade concentrate in container of an electric blender; process until smooth. Pour mixture into tart shells.

Place tart shells on a baking sheet, and freeze until firm. Place frozen tarts in heavy-duty, zip-top plastic bags. Carefully remove filled crusts about 5 minutes before serving. **Yield: 12 (3-inch) tarts.**

Kids' Company Supper

SERVES 10

Mexican Franks • Baked beans

Corn chips with Fiesta Dip • ◆ Frozen Cookie Crunch

Mexican Franks

10 (6-inch) corn tortillas
Vegetable oil
1 (15-ounce) can chili without beans
1 (8-ounce) can tomato sauce, divided
1 tablespoon minced onion
¼ teaspoon hot sauce
10 frankfurters
1 (4.5-ounce) can chopped green chiles, drained
1 cup (4 ounces) shredded Cheddar cheese

Fry tortillas, one at a time, in ¼-inch hot oil 3 to 5 seconds on each side or just until softened. Drain on paper towels. Set aside.

Combine chili, ¼ cup tomato sauce, onion, and hot sauce in a small bowl. Place a frankfurter in center of each tortilla; top each with 2 tablespoons chili mixture. Roll up, and place seam side down in a lightly greased 11- x 7- x 1½-inch baking dish. Combine remaining tomato sauce and remaining chili mixture; pour over tortillas.

Sprinkle with chiles. Cover and bake at 350° for 20 to 25 minutes. Uncover and sprinkle evenly with cheese; bake 5 additional minutes. **Yield: 10 servings.**

Fiesta Dip

1 (8-ounce) package cream cheese, softened
1 (8-ounce) jar mild picante sauce
Garnish: sliced green onions

Combine cream cheese and picante sauce; beat mixture at low speed of an electric mixer until smooth. Spoon into a small bowl, and garnish, if desired. Serve with corn chips or tortillas. **Yield: 2 cups.**

Frozen Cookie Crunch

1 (20-ounce) package cream-filled chocolate sandwich cookies, crushed
½ cup butter or margarine, melted
1 cup chopped pecans
½ gallon vanilla ice cream, softened

Combine first 3 ingredients. Pat one-third of cookie mixture in bottom of a lightly greased 13- x 9- x 2-inch pan; spread half of ice cream on top. Repeat procedure; sprinkle remaining crumbs on top. Freeze 8 hours. **Yield: 15 servings.**

TimeSavers

• Line your baking dishes or pans with aluminum foil for easy cleanup. Grease the foil if the recipe calls for this procedure.
• Soften cream cheese for dip in the microwave. Remove wrapper, place on a microwave-safe plate, and microwave at MEDIUM (50% power) 1 minute.
• Make dessert ahead and freeze.

82   Kids' Favorites

Mexican Franks

Sloppy Joes and Jiffy Beans and Franks

Fourth of July Celebration

SERVES 6

Sloppy Joes • Jiffy Beans and Franks • Potato chips
Dill pickle spears • Root Beer Floats or watermelon slices

Sloppy Joes

1½ pounds ground beef
1 small onion, chopped
1 small green pepper, chopped
1 (10¾-ounce) can tomato soup
1 (8-ounce) can tomato sauce
2 tablespoons brown sugar (optional)
1 tablespoon Worcestershire sauce
1 teaspoon prepared mustard
Pinch of garlic powder
6 hamburger buns, split and toasted

Cook ground beef, onion, and green pepper in a large skillet until beef is browned, stirring to crumble; drain.

Stir in tomato soup and next 5 ingredients; simmer 10 to 15 minutes, stirring mixture often. Serve on toasted buns. **Yield: 6 servings.**

TimeSavers

• Microwave Jiffy Beans and Franks while Sloppy Joe mixture is simmering.
• Allow ice cream time to soften before scooping, or peel away the carton and cut into slices with an electric knife.

Jiffy Beans and Franks

2 (16-ounce) cans pork and beans
½ cup chopped onion
½ cup ketchup
¼ cup firmly packed brown sugar
½ teaspoon dry mustard
4 frankfurters, cut into ⅜-inch slices

Combine first 5 ingredients; spoon into a lightly greased, shallow 2-quart casserole. Cover with heavy-duty plastic wrap; fold back a small edge of wrap to allow steam to escape.

Microwave at HIGH 8 to 9 minutes, stirring once. Add frankfurters. Microwave at HIGH 8 to 9 minutes, stirring once. **Yield: 6 servings.**

Root Beer Floats

1 (1-liter) bottle root beer or other cola, divided
1 quart vanilla ice cream

Pour ½ cup root beer into each of 6 (12-ounce) soda glasses; spoon ice cream equally into glasses. Top each with remaining root beer. **Yield: 6 servings.**

All-American Pizza Burgers

1½ pounds lean ground beef
1½ pounds ground turkey sausage
Vegetable cooking spray
1 (14-ounce) jar pizza sauce, divided
¾ cup grated Parmesan cheese
1 medium onion, chopped (optional)
12 hamburger buns
12 slices mozzarella cheese

Combine ground beef and sausage; shape into 12 patties. Coat grill rack with cooking spray; place on grill over medium-hot coals (350° to 400°).

Place patties on rack, and cook, uncovered, 5 minutes on each side or until done, brushing patties occasionally with ¾ cup pizza sauce. (Discard any remaining pizza sauce used for brushing patties.)

Sprinkle with Parmesan cheese and, if desired, onion. Serve on buns with mozzarella cheese and remaining pizza sauce. **Yield: 12 servings.**

TimeSavers

• Shape ground meat into ½-inch-thick patties (¼ pound each), and stack between sheets of wax paper. If making patties ahead to freeze, place 2 pieces of wax paper between each patty, and place in a freezer bag.
• Preheat gas grill 20 minutes, or light charcoal 30 minutes before grilling burgers.

Ranch-Style Dip

¾ cup low-fat cottage cheese
1 (8-ounce) carton sour cream
1 cup mayonnaise or salad dressing
1 (1-ounce) envelope Ranch-style dressing mix

Place cottage cheese in container of an electric blender or food processor; process until smooth. Add sour cream and remaining ingredients; process until blended, stopping once to scrape down sides. Serve dip with fresh vegetables. **Yield: 2½ cups.**

Easy Chocolate Sauce

1 (14-ounce) can sweetened condensed milk
2 (1-ounce) squares unsweetened chocolate
2 tablespoons butter or margarine
Dash of salt
½ teaspoon vanilla extract

Combine all ingredients in a heavy saucepan; cook over low heat, stirring constantly with a wire whisk, until chocolate melts and mixture is smooth. Serve warm sauce over ice cream. **Yield: 1⅝ cups.**

All-American Pizza Burgers and Ranch-Style Dip with Vegetables

Easy Cheesy Bobolis and Santa's Hats

Saint Nick Party

SERVES 8
Easy Cheesy Bobolis
◆ Carrot and celery sticks with Christmas Confetti Dip • Santa's Hats

Easy Cheesy Bobolis

8 (6-inch) Bobolis
1 (14-ounce) jar pizza sauce
1 (3½-ounce) package pepperoni slices
1 (8-ounce) package shredded mozzarella
    cheese

Place Bobolis on ungreased baking sheets.
Spread pizza sauce evenly over Bobolis. Top
evenly with pepperoni slices, and sprinkle evenly
with cheese.
    Bake at 350º for 15 minutes or until cheese
melts and Bobolis are thoroughly heated. **Yield:
8 servings.**

Christmas Confetti Dip

⅔ cup sour cream
⅓ cup mayonnaise or salad dressing
1 (2-ounce) jar diced pimiento, drained
2 tablespoons finely chopped chives
1 tablespoon finely chopped onion
¼ teaspoon garlic powder

    Combine all ingredients; cover and chill up to
2 days. Serve with carrot and celery sticks.
Yield: about 1¼ cups.

Santa's Hats

½ gallon cherry-vanilla ice cream
1 (1-liter) bottle ginger ale
1 (8.75-ounce) can refrigerated instant
    whipped cream
Red decorator sugar crystals
8 maraschino cherries with stems

    Divide ice cream evenly among 8 mugs or
glasses; pour ½ cup ginger ale over each. Top
each with whipped cream, sugar crystals, and
cherry. **Yield: 8 servings.**

TimeSavers

• Bobolis are baked pizza crusts
available in the deli section of most
supermarkets. Eight (6-inch) pita
bread rounds may be substituted.
• To save time, substitute a commercial dip for the Christmas
Confetti Dip, and purchase pre-cut
celery and carrot sticks.
• Canned instant whipped cream
magically becomes a "furry, white
hat" on Santa's Hats.

Hearty Stuffed Potatoes

School Night Fare

Hearty Stuffed Potatoes • Bacon-Cheese French Bread
Old-Fashioned Strawberry Sodas

Hearty Stuffed Potatoes

4 large potatoes (about 2 pounds)
1 cup chopped fresh or frozen broccoli
1 small onion, chopped
1 cup chopped cooked ham or turkey
1 (2-ounce) jar diced pimiento, drained
Yogurt Sauce

Rinse potatoes, and pat dry. Prick each several times with a fork. Arrange in a circle, 1 inch apart, on a layer of paper towels in microwave oven.

Microwave, uncovered, at HIGH 14 to 17 minutes, turning and rearranging potatoes halfway through cooking time. Let stand 5 minutes.

Place broccoli and onion in a 1-quart glass bowl. Cover with heavy-duty plastic wrap; fold back a small edge of wrap to allow steam to escape. Microwave at HIGH 4 minutes or until tender. Drain.

Add ham and pimiento, and microwave at HIGH 2 to 3 minutes. Stir in Yogurt Sauce, and microwave at MEDIUM (50% power) 2 to 4 minutes or until mixture is thoroughly heated. (Do not boil.) Cut potatoes lengthwise, and top with yogurt mixture. **Yield: 4 servings.**

Yogurt Sauce

1 (8-ounce) carton plain low-fat yogurt
¼ cup mayonnaise or salad dressing
1 tablespoon tarragon vinegar
2 teaspoons cornstarch
1 teaspoon soy sauce
½ teaspoon dried thyme
½ teaspoon dry mustard
¼ teaspoon dried oregano
⅛ teaspoon garlic powder

Combine all ingredients, stirring until blended. **Yield: 1¼ cups.**

Bacon-Cheese French Bread

1 (16-ounce) loaf unsliced French bread, cut into 1-inch-thick slices
5 slices bacon, cooked and crumbled
1 (8-ounce) package shredded mozzarella cheese
¼ cup butter or margarine, melted

Place sliced loaf on aluminum foil. Combine bacon and cheese; place between bread slices. Drizzle with butter, and wrap in foil.

Bake at 350° for 20 minutes or until thoroughly heated. **Yield: 8 servings.**

Old-Fashioned Strawberry Sodas

1 (10-ounce) package frozen strawberries in syrup, thawed
3 cups strawberry ice cream, divided
2 (12-ounce) cans cream soda, divided
Garnish: whipped cream

Mash thawed strawberries with a fork until strawberries are well blended with syrup. Add 1 cup ice cream and ½ cup cream soda; stir well.

Spoon an equal amount of strawberry mixture into 4 (14-ounce) soda glasses; top with remaining ice cream, and fill glasses with remaining soda. Garnish, if desired. **Yield: 4 servings.**

Shrimp Basket Special

SERVES 6
◆ Gulf Coast Fried Shrimp • Corn on the Cob with Herb Butter
◆ Zesty Broccoli Slaw • Applesauce

Gulf Coast Fried Shrimp

4 large eggs, beaten
⅔ cup commercial spicy French dressing
1½ tablespoons lemon juice
¾ teaspoon onion powder
2 pounds peeled, medium-size fresh shrimp
1⅓ cups saltine cracker crumbs
⅓ cup white cornmeal
⅔ cup crushed corn flakes cereal
Vegetable oil
Commercial cocktail sauce

Combine first 4 ingredients; pour over shrimp. Stir gently; cover and chill 3 hours.

Combine cracker crumbs, cornmeal, and crushed corn flakes. Remove shrimp from marinade; discard marinade. Dredge shrimp in crumb mixture.

Pour oil to a depth of 2 to 3 inches in a Dutch oven; heat to 375°. Fry shrimp in hot oil until golden. Serve with cocktail sauce. **Yield: 6 servings.**

TimeSavers

• Commercial corn flake crumbs and cracker meal can be used to dredge shrimp. For easy cleanup, dredge shrimp in a plastic bag.
• Purchase frozen corn on the cob if fresh corn is unavailable.
• Substitute any type of 16-ounce package slaw mix for slaw.

Corn on the Cob with Herb Butter

¼ cup butter or margarine, softened
1 tablespoon chopped fresh parsley
1 tablespoon chopped fresh chives
¼ teaspoon dried salad herbs
About 2 quarts water
6 ears fresh corn

Combine first 4 ingredients; set aside.

Bring water to a boil, and add corn. Return to a boil, and cook 8 to 10 minutes. Drain well. Spread butter mixture over hot corn. **Yield: 6 servings.**

Zesty Broccoli Slaw

½ cup cider vinegar
½ cup vegetable oil
1 clove garlic, pressed
1½ teaspoons dried dillweed
½ teaspoon salt
1 (16-ounce) package fresh broccoli, carrot, and red cabbage slaw mix

Combine first 5 ingredients; pour over slaw mix, stirring gently to coat.

Cover and chill at least 2 hours. Drain slaw mix before serving, or serve with a slotted spoon. **Yield: 6 servings.**

Gulf Coast Fried Shrimp

Spring Holiday Celebration

SERVES 6

Big Veggie Sandwich • Corn Chowder • Cookies • Milk

Big Veggie Sandwich

1 (16-ounce) loaf unsliced whole wheat bread
1 (8-ounce) container chives-and-onion-
   flavored cream cheese
6 lettuce leaves
1 small green pepper, thinly sliced
1 large tomato, thinly sliced
2 avocados, peeled and sliced
1 small cucumber, thinly sliced
¾ cup alfalfa sprouts
¼ to ⅓ cup commercial Italian salad
   dressing

Cut bread into 12 slices, cutting to within ½ inch of bottom crust. Starting at first cut, carefully spread a thin layer of cream cheese on facing sides of both pieces of bread. Repeat procedure with every other cut.

Pull cheese-spread bread slices apart. Place a lettuce leaf between each sandwich and fill equally with vegetables. Drizzle Italian salad dressing into each sandwich. Serve sandwiches immediately, separating at unfilled cuts. **Yield: 6 servings.**

Big Veggie Sandwich

Corn Chowder

1 (10¾-ounce) can cream of potato soup
1 (17-ounce) can reduced-sodium whole
   kernel corn, drained
1⅓ cups milk
1 tablespoon butter or margarine
½ teaspoon pepper
4 slices bacon, cooked and crumbled
2 small green onions, sliced

Combine first 5 ingredients in a saucepan. Cook over medium heat, stirring occasionally, until thoroughly heated. Sprinkle each serving with crumbled bacon and green onions. **Yield: 1 quart.**

TimeSavers

• Save time by making 1 large sandwich and cutting it into 6 servings. The thinner you slice the vegetables, the easier it is to keep the sandwich together.
• Substitute bacon bits for crumbled bacon if you don't have a supply of cooked bacon in the freezer.

Breakfast and Brunch

Serve an omelet for a festive morning treat, or quickly exit the kitchen during the week with other fast-to-fix breakfast menus. Then make a leisurely brunch the highlight of your weekend.

Ambrosia Pancakes with Orange Syrup, Lightnin' Cheese Biscuits

Apple Breakfast Sandwiches, Shrimp-and-Egg Salad Sandwiches, Crabmeat Salad

Easy Mexican Omelet, Shrimp-and-Cheese Omelet, Marmalade Breakfast Pears

Quick Eggs Benedict, Club Soda Waffles, Herbed Cheese Omelet

Easy Pancakes (page 101)

Herbed Cheese Omelet

Lazy Morning Breakfast

SERVES 4
Herbed Cheese Omelet • ◆ Fresh fruit with Sour Cream Sauce • Quick Biscuits

Herbed Cheese Omelet

1 (3-ounce) package cream cheese, softened
1½ teaspoons sour cream
¼ teaspoon lemon juice
¼ teaspoon dried parsley flakes
⅛ teaspoon salt
⅛ teaspoon garlic powder
⅛ teaspoon ground white pepper
⅛ teaspoon dried dillweed
8 large eggs
2 tablespoons water
½ teaspoon ground white pepper
1 tablespoon olive oil
1 tablespoon butter or margarine
2 tablespoons chopped green onions

Combine first 3 ingredients in a large bowl; add parsley flakes and next 4 ingredients, mixing well.

Combine eggs, water, and ½ teaspoon white pepper; stir with a wire whisk or fork until blended.

Heat a heavy 10-inch skillet over medium heat until hot enough to sizzle a drop of water. Add olive oil and butter, and rotate skillet to coat bottom. Pour egg mixture into skillet. As mixture starts to cook, gently lift edges of omelet with a spatula, and tilt skillet so uncooked portion flows underneath.

Spoon cream cheese mixture in center of omelet, and fold sides over filling. Sprinkle with green onions, and serve immediately. **Yield: 4 servings.**

Sour Cream Sauce

¾ cup sour cream
2 tablespoons orange juice concentrate, thawed and undiluted
3 tablespoons honey

Combine all ingredients; cover and chill. Serve over fresh fruit. **Yield: 1 cup.**

Quick Biscuits

2 cups self-rising flour
⅔ cup buttermilk
⅓ cup corn oil

Combine all ingredients in a medium bowl, stirring just until dry ingredients are moistened. Turn dough out onto a floured surface, and knead dough 3 or 4 times.

Roll dough to ½-inch thickness; cut with a 2-inch biscuit cutter. Place biscuits on an ungreased baking sheet.

Bake at 425° for 10 to 12 minutes or until biscuits are golden. **Yield: 1 dozen.**

Note: Mix up a powdered buttermilk blend if you don't have fresh buttermilk on hand.

TimeSaver

• Use as little flour as possible when rolling out biscuits—excess flour toughens the dough.

Easy Mexican Omelet

Zippy Omelet Brunch

SERVES 2

Easy Mexican Omelet • Hash Brown Potatoes
Crusty Broiled Tomatoes • English muffins

Easy Mexican Omelet

3 large eggs
½ teaspoon salt
¼ teaspoon pepper
1 tablespoon water
1 tablespoon butter or margarine
¾ cup (3 ounces) shredded Monterey Jack
   cheese
2 tablespoons sliced jalapeño peppers
2 tablespoons salsa

Combine first 4 ingredients; stir with a wire whisk just until blended.

Heat a heavy 8-inch skillet over medium heat until hot enough to sizzle a drop of water. Add butter, and rotate skillet to coat bottom.

Pour egg mixture into skillet; sprinkle with cheese and jalapeño peppers. As mixture starts to cook, gently lift edges of omelet with a spatula, and tilt skillet so that uncooked portion flows underneath. Fold omelet in half, and transfer to plate. Top with salsa. **Yield: 2 servings.**

TimeSavers

• Begin omelet with a heated non-stick skillet or omelet pan.
• Use leftover cooked potatoes, or cut potatoes into small pieces to cook faster.
• Cut a thin slice off bottom of tomatoes to help them sit flat. Assemble tomatoes ahead and chill, if desired.

Hash Brown Potatoes

1 tablespoon bacon drippings
1 tablespoon butter or margarine
2 cups diced cooked potato
⅓ cup minced onion
1 tablespoon minced fresh parsley
1 clove garlic, minced
Salt and pepper to taste

Melt bacon drippings and butter in a heavy 9-inch skillet. Add remaining ingredients, stirring gently until coated. Cook mixture, uncovered, 15 to 20 minutes or until browned on all sides, turning occasionally. **Yield: 2 servings.**

Crusty Broiled Tomatoes

2 small tomatoes
2 teaspoons Dijon mustard
Dash of salt and black pepper
Dash of ground red pepper
3 tablespoons butter or margarine, melted
¼ cup dry breadcrumbs
¼ cup grated Parmesan cheese

Cut tomatoes in half crosswise. Spread cut side with mustard; sprinkle with salt, pepper, and red pepper.

Combine butter, breadcrumbs, and cheese; spoon evenly over tomato halves. Broil 5½ inches from heat (with electric oven door partially open) 2 to 4 minutes or until lightly browned. Serve immediately. **Yield: 2 servings.**

Sunday Morning Special

SERVES 2

Shrimp-and-Cheese Omelet • Fruit cup
Easy Herb Biscuits • Bloody Marys

Shrimp-and-Cheese Omelet

Shrimp-and-Cheese Omelet

4 large eggs
2 tablespoons water
2 tablespoons butter or margarine, divided
⅓ cup (1.3 ounces) shredded Monterey Jack cheese
½ cup coarsely chopped cooked shrimp
2 tablespoons sliced green onions
1 tablespoon chopped fresh parsley
Garnishes: whole shrimp, green onions

Whisk together eggs and water; set aside.
Heat an 8-inch omelet pan or nonstick skillet over medium heat. Add 1 tablespoon butter, and rotate pan to coat.

Add half of egg mixture. As mixture starts to cook, gently lift edges of omelet with a spatula, and tilt pan so that uncooked portion of omelet flows underneath.

Sprinkle half of omelet with half each of cheese and next 3 ingredients; fold omelet in half. Transfer to a serving plate. Repeat procedure with remaining egg and filling mixtures. Garnish, if desired. Serve immediately. **Yield: 2 servings.**

Easy Herb Biscuits

2 cups biscuit mix
1 tablespoon freeze-dried chives
1 teaspoon dried parsley flakes
¾ cup plain yogurt

Combine all ingredients in a medium bowl, stirring just until dry ingredients are moistened. Turn dough out onto a floured surface, and knead lightly 4 or 5 times.

Roll dough to ½-inch thickness; cut with a 2½-inch biscuit cutter. Place biscuits on a lightly greased baking sheet. Bake at 450° for 8 minutes or until lightly browned. **Yield: 6 biscuits.**

TimeSavers

• Cut time on biscuit preparation by patting dough into a square and cutting into smaller squares with a sharp knife. You'll have no dough scraps.

Favorite Family Breakfast
(pictured on page 95)
SERVES 4
Easy Pancakes • Cranberry-Apple Sauce
Baked Sausage Patties • Orange juice

Easy Pancakes

2½ cups biscuit mix
2 large eggs, beaten
1⅓ cups milk
2 tablespoons vegetable oil

Place biscuit mix in a medium bowl; make a well in center. Combine eggs, milk, and oil; add to biscuit mix, stirring just until dry ingredients are moistened.

Pour about ¼ cup batter for each pancake onto a moderately hot, lightly greased griddle. Turn pancakes when tops are covered with bubbles and edges of pancakes look cooked. **Yield: 16 pancakes.**

Cranberry-Apple Sauce

1 (16-ounce) can whole-berry cranberry sauce
2 small cooking apples, cored and chopped
⅓ cup apple juice

Combine all ingredients in a small saucepan; bring to a boil, stirring constantly. Reduce heat and simmer, stirring occasionally, 6 minutes or until apples are tender.

Serve warm over pancakes. Store sauce in refrigerator. **Yield: 2½ cups.**

Baked Sausage Patties

1 pound ground pork sausage

Shape sausage into 8 patties about ¾-inch thick; place on a rack in a broiler pan. Bake at 375° for 15 to 20 minutes or until done. Drain on paper towels. **Yield: 8 servings.**

To make ahead: Prepare as directed; let cool. Wrap in aluminum foil; chill. Bake at 350° in foil 10 minutes or until thoroughly heated.

TimeSavers

• Stir pancake batter only until dry ingredients are moistened—batter will still be lumpy. Beating batter until smooth produces tough pancakes.
• Save time by using a wide-mouth pitcher to mix and pour pancake batter.
• Make sausage patties and sauce for pancakes ahead of time.

Wake Up to Pancakes

SERVES 4

Ambrosia Pancakes with Orange Syrup • Crisp bacon
Summer Fruit Bowl • Milk

Ambrosia Pancakes with Orange Syrup

Ambrosia Pancakes with Orange Syrup

1 large egg, beaten
1 cup milk
½ cup flaked coconut
1 tablespoon vegetable oil
1 teaspoon grated orange rind
1 cup pancake-and-waffle mix
Orange Syrup

Combine first 5 ingredients, stirring well. Add pancake mix; stir just until dry ingredients are moistened.

Pour about 2 tablespoons batter for each pancake onto a hot, lightly greased griddle. Turn pancakes when tops are covered with bubbles and edges look cooked. Serve with Orange Syrup. **Yield: 12 pancakes.**

Orange Syrup

1 cup orange sections, coarsely chopped
1 cup maple-flavored syrup

Combine ingredients in a small saucepan. Cook until thoroughly heated. **Yield: 1½ cups.**

Summer Fruit Bowl

1½ cups cubed cantaloupe
1 cup sliced fresh strawberries
1 cup cubed fresh pineapple
⅓ cup fresh blueberries

Combine all fruit; toss gently. **Yield: 4 servings.**

TimeSavers

• Use a nonstick griddle or skillet for pancakes. The griddle is hot enough when a drop of water sizzles on it.
• Buy cored, peeled pineapple and cubed cantaloupe from the produce section of your supermarket.

Easy Waffle Breakfast

SERVES 6

Club Soda Waffles • Maple syrup • Bacon or sausage
◆ Colorful Fruit Bowl • Sparkling Apple Juice • Milk

Club Soda Waffles

2¼ cups biscuit mix
3 tablespoons vegetable oil
1 large egg
1 (10-ounce) bottle club soda
Garnish: fresh strawberries

Combine first 3 ingredients in a large mixing bowl; stir until blended. Add club soda; beat at medium speed of an electric mixer until blended.

Bake in a preheated, oiled waffle iron until golden. Garnish, if desired, and serve with maple syrup. **Yield: 14 (4-inch) waffles.**

Club Soda Waffles

Colorful Fruit Bowl

1 (8-ounce) carton plain yogurt
1 tablespoon sugar
1 teaspoon lemon juice
1 cup orange sections, chilled
1 cup grapefruit sections, chilled
1 medium banana, sliced
1 cup sliced strawberries
1 cup cubed honeydew melon

Combine first 3 ingredients; chill. Combine orange sections and remaining fruit, tossing gently.

Drizzle yogurt dressing over each serving; serve immediately. **Yield: 6 servings.**

Sparkling Apple Juice

1 (12-ounce) can frozen apple juice
    concentrate, thawed and undiluted
1 (23-ounce) bottle sparkling mineral water,
    chilled

Combine ingredients; stir gently. Serve immediately over crushed ice. **Yield: about 4½ cups.**

TimeSavers

• Use club soda at room temperature to make waffles extra light. Bake waffles immediately.
• Make a double batch of waffles and freeze leftovers; reheat in a toaster or toaster oven.

Out-of-the-Ordinary Breakfast
SERVES 10
Apple Breakfast Sandwiches • Link sausage
Fruit Cup with Rum • Perky Cranberry Punch • Orange juice

Apple Breakfast Sandwiches

⅓ cup firmly packed brown sugar
2 tablespoons all-purpose flour
½ teaspoon ground cinnamon
1 (10-ounce) can refrigerated buttermilk
    biscuits
1 cup (4 ounces) shredded sharp Cheddar
    cheese
2 large apples, peeled, cored, and cut into
    rings
1 tablespoon butter or margarine, melted

Combine first 3 ingredients in a small bowl;
set aside.

Separate biscuits, and press each into a 3-inch
circle. Place on lightly greased baking sheets;
sprinkle with cheese, and top each with an apple
ring. Sprinkle with reserved sugar mixture, and
drizzle with butter.

Bake at 350° for 15 minutes or until crust is
golden. Serve immediately. **Yield: 10 servings.**

TimeSavers

• Get a head start on your weekend
breakfast by fixing the fruit cup the
night before.
• Cook link sausage while sandwiches bake.

Fruit Cup with Rum

1 (17-ounce) can apricot halves, drained
1 (16-ounce) can sliced peaches, drained
1 (16-ounce) can sliced pears, drained
1 (15¼-ounce) can pineapple chunks, drained
1 (11-ounce) can mandarin oranges, drained
½ cup rum

Combine fruit in a large bowl; add rum, and
toss gently. Cover and chill 8 hours. **Yield: 12
servings.**

Perky Cranberry Punch

2 (32-ounce) bottles cranberry juice
1 (46-ounce) can unsweetened pineapple juice
2 cups water
1 cup firmly packed brown sugar
2 tablespoons whole allspice
2 tablespoons whole cloves
6 (3-inch) sticks cinnamon

Pour first 3 ingredients into a large percolator.
Place brown sugar and remaining ingredients in
percolator basket.

Perk through complete cycle of electric percolator. **Yield: 1 gallon.**

Apple Breakfast Sandwiches

Quick Eggs Benedict

Weekend Eye-Opener

SERVES 6

Quick Eggs Benedict • Cherry tomatoes
Grapefruit in Champagne • Spiced-Up Coffee • Orange juice

Quick Eggs Benedict

6 slices Canadian bacon
1 (11-ounce) can Cheddar cheese soup
2 tablespoons milk
3 tablespoons dry sherry
6 large eggs
3 English muffins, split and toasted
Paprika

Cook bacon over medium heat 3 minutes on each side. Set aside.

Combine soup and milk in a small saucepan; cook over medium heat, stirring until blended. Stir in sherry; reduce heat to low.

Pour water to a depth of 2 inches into a lightly greased deep skillet. Bring water to a boil; reduce heat, and maintain at a light simmer. Break eggs, one at a time, into a saucer. Slip eggs, one at a time, into water, holding saucer as close as possible to surface of water. Simmer 3 to 5 minutes or to desired degree of doneness. Remove eggs with a slotted spoon. Drain eggs on paper towels. Trim edges of eggs, if desired.

Place a slice of Canadian bacon on each toasted muffin half; top with a poached egg, and cover with cheese sauce. Sprinkle with paprika. **Yield: 6 servings.**

Grapefruit in Champagne

4 cups grapefruit sections, chilled
1 cup pink champagne, chilled
Garnish: fresh mint leaves

Combine grapefruit sections and champagne; spoon into 6 stemmed glasses; garnish, if desired. **Yield: 6 servings.**

Spiced-Up Coffee

⅔ cup ground coffee
1 teaspoon vanilla extract
1 teaspoon almond extract
6 cups water

Place coffee in coffee filter or filter basket; spoon flavorings over coffee.

Add water to coffeemaker, and brew. Serve immediately. **Yield: about 6 cups.**

TimeSavers

• A soup-based sauce replaces classic Hollandaise sauce in the entrée.
• Use an egg ring or a clean tuna can (top and bottom removed) to hold the shape of eggs while poaching. Oil the ring before using.
• Purchase refrigerated grapefruit sections.

Anyday Brunch

SERVES 6

Shrimp-and-Egg Salad Sandwiches

Marmalade Breakfast Pears • Mimosas

Shrimp-and-Egg Salad Sandwiches

Shrimp-and-Egg Salad Sandwiches

½ pound peeled, medium-size cooked shrimp,
    coarsely chopped
6 large hard-cooked eggs, chopped
¼ cup finely chopped green onions
2 tablespoons finely chopped celery
1 tablespoon chopped fresh parsley
2 tablespoons capers (optional)
2 teaspoons chopped fresh dill (optional)
3 tablespoons mayonnaise or salad dressing
1 teaspoon lemon juice
1 teaspoon prepared mustard
¼ teaspoon salt
¼ teaspoon hot sauce
Leaf lettuce
3 English muffins, split and toasted
Garnishes: fresh dill, whole shrimp,
    lemon slices

Combine first 5 ingredients; stir in capers and
dill, if desired. Set aside.

Combine mayonnaise and next 4 ingredients,
and gently fold into egg mixture.

Place lettuce on English muffin halves; spoon
egg mixture over lettuce. Garnish, if desired.
Yield: 6 servings.

Marmalade Breakfast Pears

⅓ cup orange marmalade
¼ cup orange juice
2 (16-ounce) cans pear halves, drained
½ cup sour cream
2 teaspoons grated orange rind
½ teaspoon ground cinnamon

Combine marmalade and orange juice in an
8-inch square baking dish. Arrange pears, cut
side down, in dish. Cover and microwave at
HIGH 4 to 5 minutes or until pears are hot. Let
stand 2 minutes, basting pears occasionally with
juice mixture.

Spoon pears and juice into individual bowls.

Combine sour cream, orange rind, and cinnamon, stirring well. Serve over pears. **Yield: 6
servings.**

Mimosas

1 (750-milliliter) bottle champagne, chilled
1 (6-ounce) can frozen orange juice
    concentrate, thawed and diluted

Combine chilled champagne and orange juice
just before serving. **Yield: 1½ quarts.**

TimeSavers

• Cooked pear mixture may be
chilled overnight and served cold.
• Cook eggs in advance. To keep
egg shells from cracking when
hard-cooking eggs, pierce the large
end with an egg piercer. The eggs
will also be easier to peel.
• Thaw orange juice concentrate
in microwave or overnight in
refrigerator.

Summertime Brunch
SERVES 4
◆ Crabmeat Salad • Lightnin' Cheese Biscuits • Sunshine Fizz

Crabmeat Salad

1 dozen fresh asparagus spears
⅓ cup sour cream
⅓ cup mayonnaise or salad dressing
2 teaspoons Dijon mustard
2 teaspoons white wine vinegar
½ teaspoon dried tarragon
¼ teaspoon dried basil
1 tablespoon chopped green onions
½ teaspoon prepared horseradish
4 cups shredded lettuce
1 pound fresh lump crabmeat, drained
4 marinated artichoke hearts, halved
2 hard-cooked eggs, quartered
Garnish: pimiento strips

Snap off tough ends of asparagus. Arrange asparagus in a steaming rack, and place over boiling water. Cover and steam 5 minutes or until crisp-tender. Drain. Chill 1 hour.

Combine sour cream and next 7 ingredients in a small bowl. Line each of 4 individual salad plates with 1 cup lettuce.

Divide crabmeat among plates. Divide artichokes, asparagus, and hard-cooked eggs among plates, and arrange around crabmeat. Serve with dressing. Garnish, if desired. **Yield: 4 servings.**

Lightnin' Cheese Biscuits

2 cups biscuit mix
⅔ cup (2.6 ounces) finely shredded Cheddar
     cheese
½ cup water

Combine all ingredients in a medium bowl, stirring just until moistened. Turn dough out onto a well-floured surface, and knead 15 to 20 times.

Pat dough to ½-inch thickness; cut with a 2½-inch biscuit cutter. Place biscuits on a lightly greased baking sheet. Bake at 450° for 8 to 10 minutes or until lightly browned. **Yield: 1 dozen.**

Sunshine Fizz

1½ cups orange juice, chilled
1½ cups pineapple juice, chilled
1½ cups orange sherbet
¾ cup club soda, chilled
Orange sherbet

Combine first 3 ingredients in container of an electric blender; process until smooth. Stir in club soda, and pour into soda glasses. Add a scoop of orange sherbet to each glass. Serve immediately. **Yield: 4 servings.**

TimeSavers

• Steam asparagus and cook eggs a day ahead. Eggs that are one week old prior to hard-cooking are easier to peel than those that are less than one week old.
• Chill juices and club soda the night before.

Crabmeat Salad

Curried Chicken-Rice Salad

Late-Morning Brunch

SERVES 6

Curried Chicken-Rice Salad • Orange Broccoli
Sour Cream Muffins • Lemon Frappé

Curried Chicken-Rice Salad

3 cups chopped cooked chicken
1½ cups cooked rice
1 cup chopped celery
1 cup seedless green grapes, halved
½ cup chopped pecans, toasted
⅓ cup sweet pickle relish
¾ cup mayonnaise
1 teaspoon curry powder
½ teaspoon salt
¼ teaspoon pepper
Lettuce leaves
1 pint fresh strawberries
1 fresh pineapple, peeled and cut into spears

Combine first 6 ingredients in a medium bowl. Combine mayonnaise and next 3 ingredients; add to chicken mixture, stirring well.

Serve on lettuce leaves with strawberries and pineapple. **Yield: 6 servings.**

Orange Broccoli

1½ pounds broccoli spears
¼ cup butter or margarine, softened
1 tablespoon grated orange rind
2 tablespoons orange juice

Arrange broccoli in a steaming rack, and place over boiling water. Cover and steam 8 to 10 minutes or until tender. Place in a serving bowl.

Combine butter, orange rind, and orange juice in a small bowl. Top broccoli with butter mixture. **Yield: 6 servings.**

Sour Cream Muffins

½ cup butter, softened
1 (8-ounce) carton sour cream
2 cups biscuit mix

Cream butter; stir in sour cream. Gradually add biscuit mix, stirring just until moistened.

Spoon into lightly greased miniature muffin pans, filling two-thirds full. Bake at 350° for 15 minutes or until lightly browned. **Yield: 3 dozen.**

Note: Muffins can be made in regular muffin pans. Bake at 350° for 20 minutes. **Yield: 1 dozen.**

Lemon Frappé

1 (6-ounce) can frozen lemonade concentrate, undiluted
1½ cups water
1 pint lemon ice cream or sherbet
1 (12-ounce) can ginger ale

Combine first 3 ingredients in container of an electric blender; process until smooth. Spoon into pitcher; stir in ginger ale. **Yield: 5 cups.**

TimeSavers

• Purchase chicken from the deli and use quick-cooking rice.
• Buy cored and peeled fresh pineapple.
• Grate orange rind before cutting orange to juice.

Special Occasion Brunch
SERVES 4 TO 6
Ham Roll Casserole • Whipping Cream Biscuits
Fresh fruit with poppy seed dressing • Raspberry Kir

Ham Roll Casserole

2 (10-ounce) packages frozen broccoli spears
8 (1-ounce) slices Swiss cheese
8 (6- x 4-inch) slices cooked ham
1 (10¾-ounce) can cream of mushroom soup,
    undiluted
½ cup sour cream
2 teaspoons Dijon mustard
2 tablespoons sliced almonds

Place broccoli in a 12- x 8- x 2-inch baking dish. Cover tightly with heavy-duty plastic wrap; fold back a small corner of wrap to allow steam to escape. Microwave at HIGH 2 to 3 minutes. Rearrange spears. Cover and microwave at HIGH 3 to 4 minutes. Drain broccoli; set aside.

Place 1 slice of cheese on each ham slice. Divide broccoli into 8 portions; arrange a portion on each ham slice, placing stems in the center and flowerets to the outside. Roll up securely, and place seam side down in greased 12-x 8- x 2-inch baking dish.

Combine soup, sour cream, and mustard; pour over ham rolls. Sprinkle with almonds. Cover with heavy-duty plastic wrap; fold back a small corner of wrap to allow steam to escape. Microwave at HIGH 8 to 10 minutes or until casserole is thoroughly heated, giving dish a half-turn after 5 minutes. **Yield: 4 to 6 servings.**

Conventional directions: Cook broccoli according to package directions. Assemble casserole; cover and bake at 350° for 20 minutes or until bubbly.

Whipping Cream Biscuits

1¾ cups all-purpose flour
2½ teaspoons baking powder
½ teaspoon salt
1 cup whipping cream

Combine flour, baking powder, and salt in a medium bowl; stir until well blended. Add whipping cream; stir with a fork just until moistened.

Turn dough out onto a lightly floured surface, and knead 4 or 5 times. Roll dough to ½-inch thickness; cut with a 2-inch biscuit cutter.

Place biscuits 1-inch apart on an ungreased baking sheet. Bake at 450° for 10 minutes or until lightly browned. Serve hot. **Yield: 1 dozen.**

Variations
Bacon Biscuits: Add ⅓ cup cooked crumbled bacon to dry ingredients.

Cheese Biscuits: Add ½ cup (2 ounces) shredded sharp Cheddar cheese to dry ingredients.

Herb Biscuits: Add 1¼ teaspoons caraway seeds, ½ teaspoon dried whole sage, and ¼ teaspoon dry mustard to dry ingredients.

Raspberry Kir

4 cups Chablis or other dry white wine, chilled
1½ tablespoons Chambord or other
    raspberry liqueur

Pour ⅔ cup wine in each wine glass.

Add ¾ teaspoon Chambord to each one, and stir well. **Yield: 6 servings.**

Ham Roll Casserole

Breakfast Pita Pockets

½ pound ground pork sausage
4 large eggs
¼ cup milk
½ teaspoon dried oregano
⅛ to ¼ teaspoon salt
¼ teaspoon pepper
4 slices Provolone cheese (about 1 ounce each)
4 (6-inch) pita bread rounds

Crumble sausage into a shallow 1-quart casserole. Cover tightly with heavy-duty plastic wrap; fold back a small edge of wrap to allow steam to escape. Microwave at HIGH 3 to 4 minutes or until sausage is browned, stirring once. Drain well on paper towels. Set aside.

Combine eggs and next 4 ingredients in shallow 1-quart casserole, mixing well. Microwave at HIGH 2 to 4 minutes, pushing cooked portion to center at 1-minute intervals.

Cut cheese and pita bread rounds in half. Line each bread half with one piece of cheese. Combine sausage and egg mixture; spoon about ¼ cup sausage-egg mixture into pita pockets.

Wrap each pita pocket in a paper towel. Place 4 pita pockets on a paper plate or glass pizza plate, and microwave at MEDIUM (50% power) 1 to 2 minutes or until warm. Repeat process with remaining sandwiches. **Yield: 4 servings.**

Breakfast Pita Pockets

Yogurt-Granola Fruit Medley

2 bananas, sliced
1 (8-ounce) carton vanilla yogurt
1 cup granola
2 cups seedless grapes

Layer half of banana slices in a 1-quart bowl; lightly spread one-fourth of yogurt on top, and sprinkle with one-fourth of granola.

Arrange half of grapes over granola; spread with one-fourth of yogurt, and sprinkle with one-fourth of granola.

Repeat procedure with remaining ingredients. Cover and chill up to 3 hours. **Yield: 4 servings.**

Company's Coming

Relax and celebrate simplicity with these menus. Whether you wish to host a cookout with panache or an elegant seated dinner, you'll find a quick and easy menu here.

Grilled Salmon Steaks, Pepper Steak Stir-Fry, Mediterranean Chicken

Easy Crab Imperial, Fiery Cajun Shrimp, Lime-Buttered Turkey Tenderloins

Honey-Gingered Pork Tenderloin, Pork Piccata, Lemon-Dill Chicken Sauté

Grouper with Sautéed Vegetables, Tuna Steaks with Tarragon Butter

Baked Chicken with Tarragon Sauce (page 128)

Stir Up a Stir-Fry

SERVES 4

Pepper Steak Stir-Fry • Fresh fruit with Tangy Sauce
Crusty rolls • ◆ Almond Ice Cream Balls

Pepper Steak Stir-Fry

1¼ pounds sirloin steak (1 inch thick)
1 tablespoon cornstarch
¼ cup water
½ cup canned diluted beef broth
¼ cup soy sauce
¼ cup vegetable oil
1 clove garlic, minced
1 teaspoon ground ginger
½ teaspoon salt
½ teaspoon pepper
1 large green pepper, cut into strips
1 large sweet red pepper, cut into strips
1 large onion, thinly sliced
1 (6-ounce) can sliced water chestnuts,
    drained
4 green onions, cut into 1-inch pieces
Hot cooked rice

Partially freeze steak; slice diagonally across the grain into 1½- x ⅛-inch strips. Set aside.

Combine cornstarch and water in a small bowl, stirring until smooth; add beef broth and soy sauce. Set aside.

Heat oil in a skillet over medium-high heat; add garlic, ginger, salt, and pepper, and cook 1 minute, stirring constantly. Add steak, and cook 2 minutes or until browned; remove from skillet. Add pepper strips and onion, and cook 3 minutes or until crisp-tender. Add beef, water chestnuts, green onions, and broth mixture; cook 2 minutes or until thickened. Serve over rice. **Yield: 4 servings.**

Tangy Sauce

⅓ cup frozen lemonade concentrate, thawed
⅓ cup vegetable oil
⅓ cup honey
1 teaspoon celery seeds

Combine all ingredients in container of an electric blender; blend 1 minute. Serve with fresh fruit. **Yield: 1 cup.**

Almond Ice Cream Balls

1 pint vanilla ice cream
1 (2-ounce) package slivered almonds,
    chopped and toasted
½ cup commercial fudge sauce
2 teaspoons amaretto or 1 teaspoon almond
    extract

Scoop ice cream into 4 balls, and place on a baking sheet; freeze at least 1 hour or until firm.

Coat ice cream balls with almonds; freeze.

Combine fudge sauce and amaretto. Place ice cream balls in dessert dishes; top with sauce. Serve immediately. **Yield: 4 servings.**

TimeSavers

• Peppers are easier to slice if you cut from the flesh (not the skin) side.
• Store individually wrapped almond-coated ice cream balls in a freezer bag or container for a quick dessert.

Pepper Steak Stir-Fry

Veal Piccata

A Little Dinner for Two

SERVES 2

Veal Piccata • Green Beans with Buttered Pecans
Sparkling Mushrooms • Whole-grain hard rolls • Lemon sherbet

Veal Piccata

4 veal cutlets (about ¾ pound)
¼ cup all-purpose flour
½ teaspoon salt
¼ teaspoon pepper
1½ tablespoons peanut or vegetable oil
3 tablespoons vermouth or dry white wine
2 tablespoons butter or margarine
2 tablespoons lemon juice
2 teaspoons grated lemon rind
Garnishes: lemon slices, parsley

Place cutlets between two sheets of heavy-duty plastic wrap; flatten to ⅛-inch thickness, using a meat mallet or rolling pin.

Combine flour, salt, and pepper; dredge cutlets in flour mixture. Cook in oil in a skillet over medium heat 1 minute on each side. Remove from skillet; keep warm.

Add vermouth to skillet; cook until thoroughly heated. Add butter and lemon juice; heat just until butter melts. Pour over cutlets, and sprinkle with lemon rind. Garnish, if desired. **Yield: 2 servings.**

TimeSavers

• Store veal in the coldest part of the refrigerator for no more than 2 days.
• Use a plastic bag for dredging veal to make cleanup a snap.
• Grate lemon rind while lemon is whole, and then cut lemon in half to juice.

Green Beans with Buttered Pecans

2 cups water
¼ teaspoon salt
½ pound trimmed green beans
1 tablespoon butter or margarine
2 tablespoons chopped pecans
⅛ teaspoon pepper

Bring water and salt to a boil in a medium saucepan. Add green beans; cook, uncovered, 10 minutes or just until crisp-tender. Drain beans, and set aside.

Melt butter in a nonstick skillet; add pecans, and cook until golden, stirring often. Add beans; toss gently, and cook until thoroughly heated. Sprinkle with pepper. **Yield: 2 servings.**

Sparkling Mushrooms

1 (8-ounce) carton small whole mushrooms
2 tablespoons olive oil
½ teaspoon dried rosemary
⅛ teaspoon salt
⅛ teaspoon pepper
½ cup champagne or sparkling wine

Cook mushrooms in olive oil in a large skillet over medium-high heat, stirring constantly, 1 to 2 minutes.

Add rosemary, salt, and pepper; cook 1 minute. Stir in champagne; reduce heat, and simmer 5 minutes. **Yield: 2 servings.**

Hot Off the Coals

SERVES 6
◆ Honey-Gingered Pork Tenderloin • Vegetable Kabobs
Garlic bread • ◆ Strawberries Jamaica

Honey-Gingered Pork Tenderloin

2 (¾-pound) pork tenderloins
¼ cup honey
¼ cup soy sauce
¼ cup oyster sauce
2 tablespoons brown sugar
1 tablespoon minced fresh gingerroot
1 tablespoon minced garlic
1 tablespoon ketchup
¼ teaspoon ground red pepper
¼ teaspoon ground cinnamon
Garnish: fresh parsley sprigs

Place tenderloins in an 11- x 7- x 1½-inch dish. Combine honey and next 8 ingredients, stirring well; pour over tenderloins. Cover and marinate in refrigerator 8 hours, turning occasionally.

Remove tenderloins from marinade; pour marinade into a saucepan, and bring to a boil.

Grill tenderloins, covered with grill lid, over medium-hot coals (350° to 400°) 15 minutes or until meat thermometer registers 160°, turning often and basting with reserved marinade.

Cut tenderloins into thin slices, and arrange on a serving platter. Garnish, if desired. **Yield: 6 servings.**

TimeSavers

• Look for pork tenderloin packaged in vacuum-sealed plastic bags at the meat counter.
• Purchase oyster sauce, a popular Oriental seasoning, at your local supermarket.

Vegetable Kabobs

3 medium onions, quartered
1 medium zucchini, cut into 1-inch slices
3 medium-size yellow squash, cut into 1-inch slices
12 medium fresh mushrooms
12 cherry tomatoes
¼ cup butter or margarine, melted
¼ teaspoon ground cumin

Arrange vegetables on 6 skewers. Combine butter and cumin; brush vegetables with butter mixture.

Grill kabobs, covered with grill lid, over medium-hot coals (350° to 400°) 10 to 15 minutes or until zucchini and yellow squash are crisp-tender, turning occasionally and brushing with butter mixture. **Yield: 6 servings.**

Strawberries Jamaica

1 (3-ounce) package cream cheese, softened
½ cup firmly packed brown sugar
1½ cups sour cream
1 to 2 tablespoons Grand Marnier or orange juice
Fresh strawberries

Beat cream cheese at medium speed of an electric mixer until smooth. Add brown sugar, sour cream, and Grand Marnier, stirring until blended. Cover and chill 8 hours. Serve with strawberries. **Yield: 2 cups.**

Honey-Gingered Pork Tenderloin

Dinner with Italian Flavors

SERVES 6

Pork Piccata • ◆ Quick Summer Italian Salad
Italian bread • Sorbet

Pork Piccata

2 (¾-pound) pork tenderloins
½ cup all-purpose flour
½ teaspoon salt
¼ teaspoon pepper
3 tablespoons olive oil
½ cup Chablis or other dry white wine
½ cup lemon juice
3 tablespoons butter or margarine
¼ cup chopped fresh parsley
1½ tablespoons capers
Hot cooked fettuccine
Garnishes: lemon slices, fresh parsley sprigs

Cut each tenderloin into 6 (2-ounce) medaillons. Place, cut side down, between 2 sheets of heavy-duty plastic wrap; flatten to ¼-inch thickness, using a meat mallet or rolling pin.

Combine flour, salt, and pepper; dredge pork in flour mixture.

Cook half of pork in 1½ tablespoons olive oil in a large skillet over medium heat about 2 minutes on each side or until lightly browned. Remove from skillet; keep warm. Repeat procedure.

Add wine and lemon juice to skillet; cook until thoroughly heated. Add butter, chopped parsley, and capers, stirring until butter melts.

Arrange pork over pasta; drizzle with wine mixture. Garnish, if desired. Serve immediately. Yield: 6 servings.

Pork Piccata

Quick Summer Italian Salad

15 small fresh mushrooms
1 large cucumber, unpeeled and sliced
1 large green pepper, cut into strips
2 medium tomatoes, cut into wedges
½ cup chopped green onions
1 cup commercial Italian salad dressing
Lettuce leaves

Clean mushrooms with damp paper towels. Remove stems, and reserve for another use. Combine mushroom caps and next 5 ingredients in a large bowl; toss gently. Cover and chill. Serve on lettuce leaves. Yield: 6 servings.

124   Company's Coming

Special Occasion Luncheon
(pictured on page 4)
SERVES 6
Lemon-Dill Chicken Sauté • ◆ Marinated Salad
French bread • Peachy Sherbet Cooler

Lemon-Dill Chicken Sauté

½ cup dry breadcrumbs
1½ teaspoons lemon-pepper seasoning
½ teaspoon dried dillweed
6 skinned and boned chicken breast halves
1 large egg, beaten
2 tablespoons vegetable oil

Combine first 3 ingredients in a dish. Dip chicken in egg; dredge in breadcrumb mixture.

Heat oil in a large skillet over medium heat. Add chicken, and cook 5 minutes on each side or until golden. Cover and cook 5 minutes. **Yield: 6 servings.**

Marinated Salad

1 (15-ounce) can white asparagus spears, drained
1 (14-ounce) can artichoke hearts, drained and cut in half
1 (14-ounce) can hearts of palm, drained and cut into ½-inch slices
1 (4-ounce) can sliced mushrooms, drained
¼ cup sliced ripe olives
¼ cup sliced pimiento-stuffed olives
12 cherry tomatoes, halved
½ purple onion, sliced and separated into rings
1 (8-ounce) bottle Italian salad dressing
Romaine lettuce

Combine all ingredients except romaine lettuce in a bowl, stirring gently. Chill at least 30 minutes. Drain salad, and serve on lettuce. **Yield: 6 servings.**

TimeSavers

• For easy cleanup, use a plastic bag to dredge chicken.
• Layer salad in a glass bowl for a showy presentation; chill 8 hours.
• Get a head start on dessert by peeling and halving peaches. Place in a bowl, and cover with pineapple juice to prevent discoloration. Drain before serving.

Peachy Sherbet Cooler

3 peaches, peeled and halved
1 pint lime sherbet
1½ cups fresh raspberries
2 tablespoons peach schnapps

Place peach halves in individual serving dishes; top with a scoop of sherbet. Sprinkle with raspberries. Spoon 1 teaspoon peach schnapps over sherbet. Serve immediately. **Yield: 6 servings.**

Chicken-and-Rice Dinner
SERVES 4
Mediterranean Chicken • Hot cooked rice • Red Cabbage-Citrus Salad
Baked Ranch Tomatoes • Frozen yogurt • White wine

Mediterranean Chicken

4 skinned and boned chicken breast halves
3 tablespoons all-purpose flour
2 tablespoons olive oil
1 (14½-ounce) can ready-to-serve chicken
    broth
¼ cup sliced ripe olives
2 tablespoons capers
⅛ teaspoon pepper
1 (14-ounce) can whole artichoke hearts,
    rinsed and halved

Dredge chicken in flour; set aside.

Heat oil in a large skillet over medium-high heat. Add chicken, and cook 3 minutes on each side or until lightly browned.

Add chicken broth and next 3 ingredients. Bring to a boil; reduce heat, and simmer 15 minutes or until thickened and bubbly.

Stir in artichoke halves, and cook until mixture is thoroughly heated. **Yield: 4 servings.**

TimeSavers

• Dredge chicken in a plastic bag for easy cleanup.
• Cut salad preparation time by buying shredded cabbage and refrigerated orange sections.
• Cut a thin slice off the bottom of tomatoes to help them sit flat on the plate.

Red Cabbage-Citrus Salad

2 cups shredded red cabbage
4 large oranges, peeled and sectioned
½ cup coarsely chopped pecans, toasted
¼ cup chopped green onions
Commercial poppy seed dressing or sweet-
    and-sour salad dressing

Arrange cabbage evenly on individual salad plates; place orange sections in center. Sprinkle with pecans and green onions. Serve with dressing. **Yield: 4 to 6 servings.**

Baked Ranch Tomatoes

2 tomatoes, cut in half
Vegetable cooking spray
¼ teaspoon dried Italian seasoning
1½ tablespoons commercial Ranch-style
    dressing
Garnish: fresh parsley sprigs

Place tomato halves in an 8-inch square pan. Coat top of halves with cooking spray.

Bake tomato halves at 350° for 15 minutes.

Sprinkle with Italian seasoning, and top evenly with dressing.

Broil 3 inches from heat (with electric oven door partially opened) 2 to 3 minutes or until tomato halves begin to brown. Garnish, if desired. **Yield: 4 servings.**

Mediterranean Chicken

Baked Chicken with Tarragon Sauce

8 skinned and boned chicken breast halves
½ teaspoon salt
¼ teaspoon pepper
3 tablespoons lemon juice
½ cup mayonnaise or salad dressing
1 cup finely chopped celery
1 teaspoon dried tarragon
1 pound trimmed fresh spinach
3 medium tomatoes, cut into wedges
Garnish: celery leaves

Sprinkle chicken with salt and pepper. Arrange chicken in a lightly greased 13- x 9- x 2-inch pan; sprinkle with lemon juice.

Bake at 375° for 20 minutes or until tender. Chill 1 hour.

Combine mayonnaise, celery, and tarragon; set mixture aside.

Wash spinach, and pat dry. Arrange spinach on individual plates. Arrange chicken and tomato wedges over spinach. Spoon mayonnaise mixture over chicken. Garnish, if desired. **Yield: 8 servings.**

Note: For chicken salad, cooked chicken may be coarsely chopped and combined with mayonnaise mixture.

TimeSavers

• Purchase pre-packaged spinach.
• Prepare parfaits ahead. Toast almonds in microwave, soften ice cream, and thaw frozen topping.

Marinated Squash Medley

¾ cup olive oil
⅓ cup tarragon-flavored wine vinegar
2 tablespoons finely chopped shallots
1 clove garlic, minced
½ teaspoon salt
¼ teaspoon pepper
¼ teaspoon dried thyme
3 medium-size yellow squash, sliced
3 medium zucchini, sliced

Combine first 7 ingredients in a jar. Cover tightly, and shake vigorously.

Pour dressing over squash; toss gently. Cover and chill 4 hours. **Yield: 8 servings.**

Coffee Crunch Parfaits

1 quart coffee ice cream, softened
1 (2-ounce) package slivered almonds, chopped and toasted
2 (1⅛-ounce) English toffee-flavored candy bars, crushed
½ cup chocolate syrup
1 cup frozen whipped topping, thawed

Spoon ¼ cup ice cream into each of 8 (4-ounce) parfait glasses; freeze 15 minutes or until firm.

Layer half each of chopped almonds, crushed candy bars, and chocolate syrup evenly into glasses. Repeat layers with remaining ice cream, almonds, candy bars, and chocolate syrup.

Cover and freeze until firm. Top parfaits with whipped topping. **Yield: 8 parfaits.**

Saturday Night Buffet

SERVES 4 TO 6

Lime-Buttered Turkey Tenderloins • Asparagus-Carrot-Squash Toss
Almond Rice • Hot fudge sundaes

Lime-Buttered Turkey Tenderloins

¼ cup butter or margarine, melted
¼ cup lime juice
2 teaspoons dry mustard
2 teaspoons garlic salt
2 (¾-pound) turkey breast tenderloins
Garnishes: lime wedges, fresh parsley

Combine first 4 ingredients; divide in half.

Grill turkey, covered with grill lid, over medium-hot coals (350º to 400º) 4 to 5 minutes on each side or until meat thermometer registers 170º, turning once and basting often with half of marinade.

Cook remaining marinade in a small saucepan until thoroughly heated; serve warm with sliced turkey. Garnish, if desired. **Yield: 4 to 6 servings.**

Lime-Buttered Turkey Tenderloins

Asparagus-Carrot-Squash Toss

½ pound asparagus, cut into 1-inch pieces
½ pound carrots, cut into very thin strips
1 yellow squash, sliced
3 tablespoons butter or margarine, melted
3 tablespoons lemon juice
1 tablespoon chopped fresh dill or 1 teaspoon dried dillweed
¼ teaspoon salt

Combine vegetables, and place in a steamer rack over boiling water in a Dutch oven. Steam 8 to 10 minutes or until vegetables are crisp-tender.

Combine butter and remaining ingredients, and toss gently with vegetables. Serve immediately. **Yield: 4 to 6 servings.**

Almond Rice

1 (10½-ounce) can chicken broth, undiluted
1¼ cups water
1 cup long-grain rice, uncooked
½ cup slivered almonds
2 tablespoons butter or margarine, melted

Combine broth and water in a heavy saucepan; bring to a boil, and add rice. Cover, reduce heat, and simmer 20 minutes or until liquid is absorbed.

Cook almonds in butter in a skillet until lightly browned; stir into rice. **Yield: 4 to 6 servings.**

Company's Coming 129

Grouper with Sautéed Vegetables

Fast Fish Feast

SERVES 4
Grouper with Sautéed Vegetables • Parmesan Noodles
Lettuce Wedges with Pimiento Dressing • Pineapple sherbet

Grouper with Sautéed Vegetables

1 small onion, thinly sliced
1 small green pepper, cut into strips
1 tablespoon olive oil
1 teaspoon garlic salt, divided
¾ teaspoon dried thyme, divided
1 medium tomato, peeled, seeded, and
   chopped
1 (1-pound) grouper fillet
3 tablespoons lemon juice
¼ teaspoon hot sauce
Garnishes: leaf lettuce, lemon wedges

Combine first 3 ingredients in a 9-inch pieplate; sprinkle with ½ teaspoon garlic salt and ¼ teaspoon thyme. Microwave, uncovered, at HIGH 2 to 3 minutes. Stir in chopped tomato; microwave at HIGH 1 minute.

Cut fillet into 4 equal portions, and arrange in an 8-inch square baking dish, with thickest portions of fish toward outside of dish.

Combine lemon juice, hot sauce, remaining ½ teaspoon garlic salt, and ½ teaspoon thyme in a small bowl; pour over fish. Cover with wax paper, and microwave at HIGH 6 to 7 minutes or until fish flakes easily when tested with a fork. Drain.

Spoon vegetable mixture over fish; microwave at MEDIUM-HIGH (70% power) 1 minute. Garnish, if desired. **Yield: 4 servings.**

Parmesan Noodles

1 (8-ounce) package medium egg noodles
3 tablespoons butter or margarine, melted
⅛ teaspoon garlic powder
2 tablespoons chopped fresh parsley
2 tablespoons grated Parmesan cheese

Cook noodles according to package directions; drain well.

Toss noodles with butter, garlic powder, and parsley. Spoon into a serving bowl, and sprinkle with Parmesan cheese. Serve immediately. **Yield: 4 servings.**

Lettuce Wedges with Pimiento Dressing

3 tablespoons olive or vegetable oil
3 tablespoons red wine vinegar
1 tablespoon diced pimiento
1 teaspoon sugar
¼ teaspoon salt
¼ teaspoon pepper
1 medium head Boston lettuce, quartered

Combine first 6 ingredients in a jar. Cover tightly, and shake vigorously. Serve dressing over lettuce quarters. **Yield: 4 servings.**

TimeSavers
- Buy precut vegetables at a salad bar if you don't have a chopped supply in refrigerator.
- Make salad dressing the night before to allow flavors to blend.

Grilled Salmon Steaks

A Summer Delight

SERVES 4

Grilled Salmon Steaks • Sautéed zucchini strips ◆ Tomato-Feta Salad
Crusty rolls • ◆ Double-Delight Ice Cream Pie

Grilled Salmon Steaks

¼ cup mayonnaise
1 teaspoon chopped fresh dill or ¼ teaspoon
     dried dillweed
4 (1-inch-thick) salmon steaks
Garnishes: lemon halves, fresh dill sprigs

Combine mayonnaise and dill; spread on both sides of salmon.

Cook salmon, covered with grill lid, over medium-hot coals (350° to 400°) 5 to 6 minutes on each side or until done. Garnish, if desired. **Yield: 4 servings.**

Tomato-Feta Salad

¾ cup crumbled feta cheese
¼ cup chopped green onions
¾ teaspoon vegetable oil
½ teaspoon dried oregano
3 medium tomatoes, cut into wedges
Boston lettuce leaves

Combine first 5 ingredients; toss gently. Cover and chill at least 2 hours. Spoon onto Boston lettuce leaves to serve. **Yield: 4 servings.**

Double-Delight Ice Cream Pie

1½ cups butter pecan ice cream, softened
1 (9-inch) graham cracker crust
2 (1⅛-ounce) English toffee-flavored candy
     bars, crushed
1½ cups vanilla ice cream, softened

Spread butter pecan ice cream in graham cracker crust. Sprinkle with half of crushed candy bars; freeze. Spread vanilla ice cream over top, and sprinkle with remaining crushed candy bars; freeze until firm. **Yield: one 9-inch pie.**

TimeSavers

• Preheat gas grill 20 minutes or light charcoal fire 30 minutes ahead.
• Save time and nutrients by not peeling the tomatoes.
• Make pie ahead; soften solidly frozen ice cream by microwaving at HIGH 10 seconds or until soft.

Elegant Tuna Dinner

SERVES 4

Tuna Steaks with Tarragon Butter
Buttered orzo and parsley • Vegetable Sauté • Sourdough Wedges
Angel food cake and strawberries

Tuna Steaks with Tarragon Butter

¼ cup butter or margarine, softened
½ teaspoon lemon juice
1 teaspoon minced fresh tarragon or ½
    teaspoon dried tarragon
4 (½-pound) tuna steaks (about ¾ inch thick)
½ teaspoon salt
½ teaspoon freshly ground pepper
2 tablespoons olive oil

Combine first 3 ingredients; shape into a 1-inch-thick log; cover and chill until firm.

Sprinkle tuna with salt and pepper on all sides. Heat olive oil in a nonstick skillet over medium heat; cook tuna 5 minutes on each side or until desired degree of doneness. Slice tarragon butter, and serve with tuna. **Yield: 4 servings.**

Vegetable Sauté

2 tablespoons olive oil
1 large zucchini, sliced
1 large yellow squash, sliced
1 carrot, scraped and sliced
1 clove garlic, crushed
½ teaspoon pepper
¼ teaspoon hot sauce

Heat olive oil in a large skillet until hot; add remaining ingredients, and toss gently. Cover, reduce heat, and cook 10 minutes or until crisp-tender. **Yield: 4 servings.**

Sourdough Wedges

4 (2-ounce) sourdough rolls, cut into quarters
Butter-flavored cooking spray
1 tablespoon grated Parmesan cheese
¼ teaspoon paprika

Coat cut surfaces of rolls with cooking spray. Combine Parmesan cheese and paprika; sprinkle mixture on cut surfaces, and place bread on a baking sheet.

Broil 6 inches from heat (with electric oven door partially opened) 2 to 3 minutes or until rolls are golden. **Yield: 4 servings.**

TimeSavers

• If desired, substitute rice for orzo, a rice-shaped pasta which cooks quickly.
• Shape and chill tarragon butter in advance, or, if short on time, dollop tarragon butter on tuna steaks.
• Purchase angel food cake from the bakery of your local supermarket, or make one from a mix. Serve with fresh strawberries or other fruits in season.

Tuna Steaks with Tarragon Butter

Easy Crab Imperial

Imperial Dinner

SERVES 4

Easy Crab Imperial • Minted Peas and Peppers • Sliced tomatoes
Sesame rolls • Mocha Polka

Easy Crab Imperial

1 pound fresh lump crabmeat, drained
⅔ cup mayonnaise or salad dressing
1 tablespoon chopped fresh parsley
2 teaspoons lemon juice
3 to 4 tablespoons grated Parmesan cheese
Paprika

Combine first 4 ingredients. Spoon about ½ cup mixture into 4 shell-shaped baking dishes; sprinkle with cheese. Bake at 350° for 15 minutes or until thoroughly heated. Sprinkle with paprika. **Yield: 4 servings.**

Minted Peas and Peppers

½ pound fresh snow pea pods
1 tablespoon butter or margarine
1 large sweet red pepper, cut into ¼-inch strips
2 tablespoons chopped onion
1 teaspoon chopped fresh mint
¼ teaspoon salt

Wash snow peas; trim ends, and remove any tough strings. Set aside.

Place butter in a shallow 1½-quart casserole; microwave at HIGH 35 seconds or until melted. Add snow peas, red pepper, and remaining ingredients.

Cover tightly with heavy-duty plastic wrap; fold back a small corner of wrap to allow steam to escape. Microwave at HIGH 4 minutes or until vegetables are crisp-tender, stirring after 2 minutes. Serve immediately. **Yield: 4 servings.**

Mocha Polka

1 pint chocolate ice cream
2 cups cold coffee
1 tablespoon rum
Whipped cream
Ground nutmeg

Combine first 3 ingredients in container of an electric blender; process until smooth. Pour into glasses, and top with whipped cream. Sprinkle with nutmeg, and serve immediately. **Yield: 4 cups.**

TimeSavers

• Easy Crab Imperial may be baked in 4 baked (3-inch) pastry shells.
• Substitute frozen snow peas for fresh ones.
• Halve and seed red pepper; then place, skin side down, on cutting board and slice. It is easier to slice a pepper if cut from the flesh (not the skin) side.

Festive Shrimp Supper

SERVES 6

Shrimp Scampi • ◆ Marinated Asparagus and Hearts of Palm
French bread • ◆ Easy Individual Trifles • White wine

Shrimp Scampi

1 medium onion, finely chopped
4 cloves garlic, minced
½ cup butter or margarine, melted
½ teaspoon dried tarragon
2 tablespoons fresh lemon juice
½ teaspoon steak sauce
½ teaspoon Worcestershire sauce
¼ teaspoon hot sauce
2 pounds peeled, jumbo fresh shrimp
2 tablespoons chopped fresh parsley
Hot cooked fettuccine

Cook onion and garlic in butter in a large skillet over medium heat, stirring constantly, 3 to 4 minutes; add tarragon and next 4 ingredients. Bring to a boil; add shrimp, and cook, stirring constantly, 5 to 6 minutes or until shrimp turn pink. Sprinkle with parsley. Serve over fettuccine. **Yield: 6 servings.**

Marinated Asparagus and Hearts of Palm

1½ pounds fresh asparagus
1 (14-ounce) can hearts of palm, drained and cut into ½-inch slices
½ cup vegetable oil
¼ cup cider vinegar
1 clove garlic, crushed
¾ teaspoon salt
½ teaspoon pepper
Cherry tomatoes

Snap off tough ends of asparagus. Place asparagus in steaming rack over boiling water; cover and steam 4 minutes. Drain and submerge in ice water to cool. Drain asparagus well.

Combine asparagus and hearts of palm in a heavy-duty, zip-top plastic bag. Combine oil and next 4 ingredients in a jar; cover and shake vigorously. Pour over vegetables. Seal bag, and marinate in refrigerator 8 hours; turn bag occasionally. Add tomatoes. **Yield: 6 servings.**

Easy Individual Trifles

1 (3-ounce) package ladyfingers
¼ cup seedless raspberry jam
2 tablespoons dry sherry
2 tablespoons orange juice
2 cups milk
1 (3.4-ounce) package vanilla instant pudding mix
1 (8.5-ounce) can refrigerated instant whipped cream
2 tablespoons slivered almonds, toasted

Halve ladyfingers lengthwise. Spread 1 teaspoon jam on bottom half of each ladyfinger; cover each with top, and cut in half crosswise.

Arrange 4 filled halves in each individual serving dish; drizzle each with 1 teaspoon sherry and 1 teaspoon orange juice.

Combine milk and pudding mix in a 1-quart container; cover tightly, and shake 45 seconds. Pour over ladyfingers.

Chill at least 4 hours. Just before serving, top with whipped cream and almonds. **Yield: 6 servings.**

Fiery Cajun Feast

SERVES 6 TO 8

Fiery Cajun Shrimp • Corn on the Cob
◆ Green salad with Vinaigrette Dressing • French bread
Watermelon slices

Fiery Cajun Shrimp

1 cup butter, melted
1 cup margarine, melted
½ cup Worcestershire sauce
¼ cup lemon juice
¼ cup ground pepper
2 teaspoons hot sauce
2 teaspoons salt
4 cloves garlic, minced
5 pounds unpeeled, medium-size fresh shrimp
2 lemons, thinly sliced
French bread

Combine first 8 ingredients; pour half of mixture into a large ceramic heat-proof dish. Layer shrimp and lemon slices in sauce; pour remaining sauce over shrimp and lemon.

Bake, uncovered, at 400° for 20 minutes or until shrimp turn pink, stirring twice. Drain sauce, and serve with shrimp and French bread. **Yield: 6 to 8 servings.**

Fiery Cajun Shrimp

Vinaigrette Dressing

¼ cup white wine vinegar
1 teaspoon lemon juice
⅛ teaspoon garlic powder or 1 clove garlic, minced
½ teaspoon Dijon mustard
⅛ teaspoon salt
½ cup olive oil

Combine first 5 ingredients; slowly add olive oil, stirring constantly with a wire whisk until blended. Serve over green salad. **Yield: ¾ cup.**

TimeSavers

• Melt butter and margarine in a 4-cup glass measure in microwave.
• Make Vinaigrette Dressing ahead. Mince enough garlic and squeeze lemon juice for dressing and shrimp.

Southern Living®

ALL-TIME FAVORITE
CHICKEN
RECIPES

Contents

Chicken—A Perfect Choice

You can always count on chicken to be a favorite with family and guests. Its popularity is due in part to the endless variety of dishes it creates: dinner entrées, luncheon specialties, or tempting appetizers. Thanks to its delicate flavor, chicken teams well with fruits and vegetables and takes naturally to many seasonings and cooking methods.

Chicken—What's Available

At the supermarket, chicken is available in a variety of cuts and products. You'll find packages of whole chicken, chicken halves or quarters, cut-up parts, breast halves, boned breasts, thighs, drumsticks, and wings, plus a variety of semi-prepared and fully cooked products. Select the cut that best suits your time and budget requirements. Keep in mind that the less processed the chicken, the less expensive it will be per pound.

• **Whole broiler-fryer**: This all-purpose chicken is usually the least expensive per pound and weighs 3 to 4½ pounds. It's suitable not only for broiling and frying, but also for roasting, baking, and grilling, and is packaged with and without neck and giblets.

• **Young roaster**: Also known as a roasting chicken, this large, meaty chicken ranges from 5 to 8 pounds and provides more meat per pound than smaller chickens.

• **Cut-up chicken**: Usually a whole broiler-fryer cut into 8 pieces, this package yields 2 breast halves and 2 each of thighs, drumsticks, and wings.

• **Broiler halves or splits**: A broiler is cut into 2 pieces of approximately equal weight and is ideal for grilling.

• **Broiler quarters**: Leg quarters and breast quarters are usually packaged separately. A leg quarter, which is all dark meat, includes a drumstick, thigh, and back portion. A breast quarter, which is all white meat, includes a wing, breast, and back portion.

• **Leg**: The whole leg is all dark meat with unseparated drumstick and thigh.

• **Drumstick**: This is the lower portion of the leg. Allow 2 drumsticks per adult serving.

• **Thigh**: This meaty portion above the knee joint is a favorite of those who prefer dark meat. Thighs are also available skinned and boned and can usually be substituted for skinned and boned chicken breast halves. Allow 1 or 2 thighs per person, depending on the special dish size. See the recipe for Soy-Lime Grilled Chicken Thighs on page 267.

• **Breast halves or split breast**: Popular because of their tender, meaty character, breasts are all white meat. They can be purchased whole or split, bone-in or boned, and skin-on or skinned.

• **Wing**: The whole wing has 3 sections attached and is all white meat.

• **Drummette**: This first section of the wing makes ideal hors d'oeuvres.

• **Giblets**: The gizzard, liver, and heart are 100 percent edible, and when simmered for a few hours, add flavor to your chicken broth.

• **Ground chicken**: Popular as a low-fat replacement for ground beef or pork, ground chicken is made from skinned and boned thigh meat.

• **Other packaged products**: A wide selection of prepared and semi-prepared products are available frozen and fresh in your local supermarket. Partially prepared products include chicken pieces that have been marinated or seasoned but haven't been cooked. Some of the fully cooked products include roasters and whole broilers that are ready to eat.

Tips on Buying and Storing Chicken

• Check for the USDA Grade A inspection mark on a label to insure the chicken meets highest government standards for safety and wholesomeness.

• Check the "sell by" date on package label indicating the last day the products should be sold. Chicken will retain its freshness for a few days after this date if properly refrigerated.

• A chicken's skin color ranges from white to deep yellow, depending on the chicken's diet. Color doesn't indicate a difference in nutritional value, flavor, fat content, or tenderness. Color of giblets also varies and doesn't indicate a taste difference.

• Refrigerate raw chicken promptly after you purchase it. Never leave chicken on a countertop at room temperature.

• Tray-packed raw chicken can be safely stored in its original wrap for up to 2 days in the coldest part of the refrigerator. Freeze raw chicken if it is not to be used within 2 days.

• Never let cooked chicken stand at room temperature for more than 2 hours. If not eaten immediately, cooked chicken should be kept either hot (between 140° and 165°) or refrigerated at 40° or less. Store cooked chicken for picnics in an ice chest or insulated container.

• Cooked chicken, properly wrapped and refrigerated, should be used within 2 days.

• If cooked chicken is stuffed, remove stuffing and refrigerate chicken and stuffing in separate containers.

Handle Chicken with Care

Chicken, like all fresh meat, is very perishable and must be handled with care to maintain top quality. Use these tips when handling and preparing chicken:

• Wash hands thoroughly with hot soapy water before and after handling raw poultry.

• Cut raw poultry on acrylic or hard plastic cutting boards rather than wooden or porous surfaces that are hard to clean thoroughly.

• Clean countertops, cutting surfaces, and utensils with hot soapy water after handling raw chicken in order to prevent spreading bacteria to other foods.

• Rinse chicken and pat dry with paper towels before cooking.

• Marinate chicken in the refrigerator. When grilling chicken, do not place cooked chicken on the same plate used to transport raw chicken to the grill without washing the plate.

• If leftovers need to be reheated, cover to retain moisture and to insure that chicken heats all the way through.

Freezing and Thawing Guide

Chicken is very perishable and should be cooked within 2 days of purchasing. If it is not cooked within that time, follow these tips for freezing and thawing:

• Remove raw chicken from original package; wash and pat dry. For best results, wrap chicken pieces individually or in portions to suit your family size. Wrap tightly in heavy-duty plastic wrap, aluminum foil, or freezer paper; store in a large plastic freezer bag. To prevent freezer burn, press air out of bag before sealing. Label package with date and contents.

• Prepare cooked chicken for freezing as indicated above. If chicken is cooked in a sauce, gravy, or other liquid, pack it in a sturdy freezer container with a tight-fitting lid.

• Do not freeze a stuffed chicken for later roasting. Always stuff chicken just before cooking.

• Thaw chicken that is well wrapped in the refrigerator—never at room temperature. Allow 24 hours to thaw a 4-pound whole chicken in the refrigerator and 3 to 9 hours for chicken parts, depending on the weight of the chicken.

• To thaw chicken safely in cold water, place chicken in a watertight plastic bag and submerge in cold water; change water frequently. It takes about 2 hours to thaw a whole chicken.

• Use the microwave for quick thawing of chicken (cooked or uncooked). Defrosting time varies according to whether chicken is whole or parts are frozen together. Remove the chicken from the freezer wrapping, place in a microwave-safe dish, and cover. Microwave at DEFROST or MEDIUM-LOW (30% power) 2 minutes. Let stand 2 minutes. Separate chicken parts as they begin to thaw, and rotate chicken to prevent overcooking of certain parts. Repeat if necessary.

• Cooked or uncooked chicken that has been thawed should not be refrozen. Cook the thawed chicken immediately or refrigerate it until cooking time.

Guidelines for Chicken Cookery

Whatever your choice of cooking method, always cook chicken well-done, not medium or rare. Follow these suggestions for cooking chicken safely:

• A meat thermometer provides the most accurate doneness test for cooking chicken. For a whole chicken, a meat thermometer inserted into the thickest part of the thigh (not touching bone or fat) should register 180°. The legs should move freely when twisted, and juices should be clear. Chicken breasts should reach an internal temperature of 170°.

• Without the use of a thermometer, check visually for doneness by piercing chicken with a fork or cutting chicken with a knife. The juices should run clear, and the chicken should no longer look pink.

• When microwaving chicken, it is better to undercook than overcook because it can be returned to the microwave for additional cooking if it isn't done.

• Do not partially cook chicken and store it to be finished later, as this delay can promote the growth of bacteria.

For Quick Chopped Cooked Chicken

Many recipes call for tender chunks of chopped cooked chicken. To cook, follow directions on page 145 for Simmering or Microwaving.

• 1 pound skinned and boned breast or thigh meat yields about 2 cups chopped cooked chicken. A single chicken breast will yield about ½ cup chopped cooked chicken.

• A 3-pound broiler-fryer yields 2½ to 3 cups chopped cooked chicken.

• A 6- to 7-pound roaster yields about 7 cups chopped cooked chicken.

• Leftover chopped cooked chicken can be stored in freezer bags and frozen up to 1 month.

Basic Cooking Techniques

These basic cooking methods can be the beginning of many creative chicken dishes.

The popularity of chicken is quite understandable since it can be the basis for any number of dishes and takes well to a variety of cooking methods.

Frying

Step 1: Dredge chicken pieces in seasoned flour.

Step 2: Pour vegetable oil to depth of 1 inch in a heavy skillet; heat to medium-high temperature. Add chicken and cook, uncovered, for 10 minutes, turning to brown both sides. Reduce heat to medium-low; cover and cook 20 minutes or until chicken is tender. Drain on paper towels.

Simmering

Place broiler-fryer (whole or cut-up) or about 3 pounds of skinned chicken pieces in a Dutch oven. Add 4 cups water, 1 teaspoon salt, ¼ teaspoon pepper, 3 celery tops, and 1 onion, quartered. Cover and simmer 45 minutes or until chicken is tender. Remove chicken from Dutch oven and cool. Skin and bone chicken; cut chicken into bite-size pieces. (For boned chicken breasts, simmer 15 to 20 minutes.)

Roasting

Season whole chicken inside and out with salt and pepper. If stuffing chicken, spoon dressing loosely into cavity. Tie legs together with string, or close cavity with skewers. Hook wing tips under back of chicken. Place, breast side up, on a rack in a shallow roasting pan. Bake at 350° for 1½ hours or until internal temperature reaches 180°, basting as recipe directs. Let stand 10 minutes before carving.

Microwaving

Remove skin from chicken. Arrange chicken pieces in a shallow microwave dish in a single layer with meatier parts toward outside of dish. Brush chicken with melted butter. Cover loosely with wax paper or heavy-duty plastic wrap with corner vented. Microwave parts at HIGH and whole chicken on MEDIUM (50% power). Microwave about 6 minutes per pound, rotating or rearranging to promote even cooking. Sprinkle with salt and let stand, covered, 5 to 10 minutes.

Grilling

Place chicken halves, quarters, or pieces, skin side up, on prepared grill positioned 6 to 8 inches above heat source. Grill chicken over direct or indirect heat, turning frequently with tongs. (See page 275 for instructions.) For extra flavor and juiciness, brush chicken often with a basting sauce. Brush with a sweet sauce in last 15 minutes of grilling only to avoid overbrowning.

Preparation Techniques

These techniques and tips for preparing chicken will help you with the wide assortment of recipes in this book.

Boning a Chicken Breast

If you're in a hurry, skinned and boned chicken breast halves make cooking quick and easy. If you have time, however, you may appreciate the economy of boning the breasts at home.

Step 1: Carefully remove the skin from the chicken breast, and discard. Split the breast in half lengthwise with a sharp knife.

Step 2: Starting at the breast-bone side of the chicken, slice meat away from the bone, using a thin, sharp knife, cutting as close to the bone as possible. Remove the tendon; this prevents shrinkage and makes the meat tender for serving.

Skinning Chicken Pieces

Almost half the fat in chicken comes from the skin and the pockets of fat just under the skin. To lower the fat content even further, remove the skin and cut away any excess fat before or after cooking.

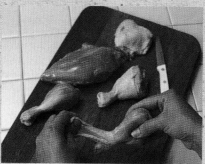

Cutting Chicken into Strips

To prepare chicken for stir-fries and other dishes calling for chicken strips, place skinned and boned chicken on a cutting surface. Cut each breast half into 3 or 4 long, thin strips (about ¾-inch wide), using a sharp knife. Then proceed as recipe directs.

Flattening a Chicken Breast

Place skinned and boned chicken breast between 2 sheets of wax paper or heavy-duty plastic wrap. Press out and down from center with a meat mallet so breast flattens evenly to desired thickness. This yields a thinner breast that rolls or stuffs easily and cooks quickly.

Marinating Chicken

Enhance the flavor of grilled, roasted, or microwaved chicken by refrigerating it in a flavorful marinade. Place chicken in a shallow dish or heavy-duty, zip-top plastic bag; add marinade and refrigerate. Drain chicken; cook as desired.

Appetizers and Snacks

When it comes to versatility in appetizers and snacks, there's no match for chicken. Enjoy drummettes, pizza, nachos, and sandwiches— all perfect for chicken nibbling.

Coconut Curried Chicken Balls, Festive Chicken Spread, Wine Pâté

Peppery Chicken in Pita, Marinated Chicken in a Sandwich, Chicken Crêpes

Chicken-Chile Cheesecake, Curried Chicken Cheesecake, Rumaki, Hot Buffalo Wings

Spicy Chicken Strips, Chicken Almondette Fingers, Chicken Nachos

Southwestern Chicken Drummettes (page 152)

Coconut Curried Chicken Balls

⅔ cup raisins
2 tablespoons dark rum
4 skinned chicken breast halves
1⅓ cups pineapple cream cheese
3 tablespoons mango chutney
3 tablespoons mayonnaise or salad dressing
1 tablespoon teriyaki sauce
2 teaspoons curry powder
½ teaspoon ground ginger
½ teaspoon salt
¼ teaspoon red pepper
1 cup sliced almonds, toasted
1½ cups flaked coconut
Garnishes: apricots, orange slices, kiwifruit

Combine raisins and rum; set aside.

Place chicken in a large saucepan; cover with water. Bring to a boil; cover, reduce heat, and simmer 25 minutes or until tender. Remove chicken; let cool slightly, and bone. Position knife blade in food processor bowl; add half of chicken. Pulse 2 or 3 times until chicken is coarsely chopped. Repeat with remaining chicken.

Combine cream cheese and next 7 ingredients. Drain raisins. Add raisins, chicken, and almonds to cream cheese mixture, stirring until blended. Shape mixture into 1-inch balls; roll in coconut. Chill before serving. Arrange on a platter, and garnish, if desired. **Yield: 44 appetizers.**

Note: These may be frozen up to 1 week.

Chicken Salad Spread

1½ cups coarsely ground cooked chicken
¼ cup sweet pickle relish
3 to 4 tablespoons mayonnaise
2 tablespoons finely chopped onion
¾ teaspoon salt
½ teaspoon celery seeds
¼ teaspoon pepper

Combine all ingredients, stirring well. Store in refrigerator; serve with crackers. **Yield: 1½ cups.**

Festive Chicken Spread

1 (8-ounce) package cream cheese, softened
3 tablespoons mayonnaise
1 tablespoon lemon juice
½ teaspoon salt
¼ teaspoon ground ginger
⅛ teaspoon pepper
4 drops of hot sauce
2 cups diced cooked chicken
2 hard-cooked eggs, diced
¼ cup diced green onions
3 tablespoons chopped green pepper
Green pepper strips
2 tablespoons sesame seeds, toasted
3 tablespoons chopped black olives
3 tablespoons chopped sweet red pepper
5 slices cucumber, halved (optional)
Parsley sprigs (optional)

Combine first 7 ingredients in a large bowl; beat at medium speed of an electric mixer until smooth. Add chicken, eggs, green onions, and chopped green pepper; stir well.

Line a 1-quart bowl or mold with plastic wrap. Spoon mixture into bowl; press firmly with the back of a spoon. Cover and chill at least 4 hours.

Invert bowl onto serving platter. Remove bowl, and peel off plastic wrap. Garnish mound with green pepper strips, sesame seeds, black olives, and sweet red pepper. Arrange cucumber slices and parsley sprigs around bottom of mound, if desired; serve with assorted crackers. **Yield: 3 cups.**

Wine Pâté

¼ cup butter or margarine
1 pound chicken livers
½ cup sliced fresh mushrooms
⅓ cup chopped green onions
1 clove garlic, minced
¾ teaspoon salt
½ cup dry white wine
½ cup butter or margarine, softened
Pinch of dried dillweed
3 or 4 drops of hot sauce

Melt ¼ cup butter in a skillet. Add livers and next 4 ingredients; sauté 5 minutes. Add wine and remaining ingredients; cover and simmer 10 minutes. Cool slightly.

Pour mixture into container of an electric blender; blend until smooth. Pour into a lightly oiled 3-cup mold; cover and chill at least 8 hours. Unmold and serve pâté with assorted crackers. **Yield: 3 cups.**

Chicken Liver Pâté

⅓ cup finely chopped onion
2 tablespoons butter or margarine, melted
½ pound chicken livers
¼ teaspoon salt
2 tablespoons dry sherry
½ cup butter, softened

Cook onion in 2 tablespoons butter in a skillet over medium heat until tender; add chicken livers and cook 10 to 15 minutes, stirring often.

Pour livers into container of an electric blender. Add salt and sherry; process until smooth. Cool mixture.

Combine liver mixture and ½ cup butter; place in a small bowl or crock, and serve with crackers. **Yield: about 1½ cups.**

Chicken-Chile Cheesecake

1⅓ cups finely crushed tortilla chips
¼ cup butter or margarine, melted
3 (8-ounce) packages cream cheese, softened
4 large eggs
1 teaspoon chili powder
1 teaspoon Worcestershire sauce
¼ teaspoon salt
3 tablespoons minced green onions
1½ cups finely shredded cooked chicken
2 (4.5-ounce) cans chopped green chiles, drained
1½ cups (6 ounces) shredded Monterey Jack cheese
1 (16-ounce) carton sour cream
1 teaspoon seasoned salt
Garnish: minced green onions
Picante sauce

Combine tortilla chips and butter; press on bottom and 1 inch up sides of a 9-inch spring-form pan. Set aside.

Beat cream cheese at high speed of an electric mixer until light and fluffy; add eggs, one at a time, beating well after each addition. Stir in chili powder and next 3 ingredients.

Pour half of cream cheese mixture into prepared pan. Sprinkle with chicken, chiles, and cheese; carefully pour remaining cream cheese mixture on top.

Bake at 350° for 10 minutes; reduce heat to 300°, and bake an additional hour or until set. Cool completely on a wire rack.

Combine sour cream and seasoned salt, stirring well; spread evenly on top of cheesecake. Cover and chill at least 8 hours. Garnish, if desired, and serve with picante sauce. **Yield: 8 servings or 24 appetizer servings.**

Curried Chicken Cheesecake

Curried Chicken Cheesecake

1⅓ cups round buttery cracker crumbs
¼ cup butter or margarine, melted
1½ teaspoons chicken-flavored bouillon
    granules
1 tablespoon boiling water
3 (8-ounce) packages cream cheese, softened
3 large eggs
1 (8-ounce) carton sour cream
3 tablespoons grated onion
3 tablespoons minced celery
1 tablespoon all-purpose flour
2 to 3 teaspoons curry powder
¼ teaspoon salt
1½ cups chopped cooked chicken
½ cup chopped almonds, toasted
⅓ cup golden raisins
Lettuce leaves
Garnishes: chopped sweet red pepper, flaked
    coconut, chopped green pepper
Assorted condiments
Curried Sour Cream Sauce

Combine crumbs and butter; press on bottom and 1 inch up sides of a 9-inch springform pan. Set aside.

Combine bouillon granules and boiling water; stir until granules dissolve.

Beat cream cheese at high speed of an electric mixer until light and fluffy; add eggs, one at a time, beating well after each addition. Add bouillon mixture, sour cream, and next 5 ingredients; beat at low speed until blended. Stir in chicken, almonds, and raisins.

Pour mixture into prepared pan. Bake at 300° for 45 minutes or until set. Turn oven off, and partially open oven door; leave cheesecake in oven 1 hour. Remove from oven, and let cool completely on a wire rack. Cover and chill.

Unmold cheesecake onto a lettuce-lined platter; garnish, if desired. Serve cheesecake with several of the following condiments: flaked coconut, toasted slivered almonds, chutney, chopped green or sweet red pepper, raisins, and crumbled cooked bacon. Serve with Curried Sour Cream Sauce. **Yield: 8 servings or 24 appetizer servings.**

Curried Sour Cream Sauce

1 (8-ounce) carton sour cream
1½ teaspoons curry powder
⅛ teaspoon ground ginger

Combine all ingredients, stirring well; cover and chill. **Yield: 1 cup.**

Rumaki

About ½ pound chicken livers
¼ cup soy sauce
1½ tablespoons dry white wine
2 cloves garlic, minced
⅛ teaspoon ground ginger
1 (6-ounce) can water chestnuts, drained
12 slices bacon, cut into thirds

Cut chicken livers in about 1-inch pieces. Combine soy sauce, wine, garlic, and ginger in a shallow dish or heavy-duty zip-top plastic bag; mix well. Add chicken livers. Cover dish or seal bag and marinate in refrigerator 2 to 3 hours.

Cut water chestnuts in half. Place a water chestnut half and a piece of chicken liver on each piece of bacon. Roll up, and secure with a wooden pick.

Arrange appetizers on paper-towel-lined microwave-safe platters, placing no more than a dozen appetizers on each. Cover and refrigerate up to 2 hours.

Cover platters with paper towels when ready to microwave. Microwave each platter at HIGH 4½ to 7 minutes or until bacon is crisp and liver is done, giving dish one half-turn. **Yield: about 3 dozen.**

Note: Rumaki may be microwaved without final chilling. Microwave time will be the same.

Hot Buffalo Wings

2½ pounds chicken wings
1 teaspoon salt
¼ teaspoon pepper
Vegetable oil
¼ cup hot sauce
¼ cup water
¼ cup butter or margarine
1 tablespoon cider vinegar

Cut chicken wings in half at joint; cut off tips of wings, and discard. Sprinkle chicken with salt and pepper.

Pour oil to depth of 2 inches into a large, heavy skillet; heat to 350°. Fry wings, about 1 dozen at a time, for 10 minutes. Drain on paper towels. Arrange wings in a 13- x 9- x 2-inch dish.

Combine hot sauce and remaining ingredients in a small saucepan; cook over low heat until butter melts. Pour over fried wings.

Bake, uncovered, at 350° for 10 to 15 minutes or until hot. **Yield: 3 dozen appetizers.**

Southwestern Chicken Drummettes

(pictured on page 147)

⅔ cup fine, dry breadcrumbs
⅔ cup finely crushed corn chips
1 (1¼-ounce) package taco seasoning mix
2 pounds chicken drummettes, skinned
1 (16-ounce) jar taco sauce, divided
Garnish: fresh cilantro sprigs

Combine first 3 ingredients in a small bowl. Dip drummettes, one at a time, into ½ cup taco sauce, and dredge in crumb mixture; place on a lightly greased baking sheet.

Bake at 375° for 30 to 35 minutes. Serve with remaining taco sauce. Garnish, if desired. **Yield: 8 to 10 appetizer servings.**

Spicy Chicken Strips

8 skinned and boned chicken breast halves
¾ cup all-purpose flour
1 to 1½ teaspoons chili powder
¾ teaspoon salt
½ teaspoon garlic powder
¼ teaspoon ground cumin
¼ teaspoon pepper
1 large egg, beaten
½ cup water
Vegetable oil
Tomato-Garlic Dip

Cut chicken into long, thin strips (about ¾-inch wide). Combine flour and next 5 ingredients; stir well. Stir in egg and water. Dip chicken strips in batter.

Fry strips, a few at a time, in hot oil (375°) for 2 to 3 minutes or until golden. Drain on paper towels. Serve immediately with Tomato-Garlic Dip. **Yield: 16 appetizer servings.**

Tomato-Garlic Dip

1 (6-ounce) can tomato paste
⅓ cup mayonnaise
¼ cup sour cream
¼ cup tomato sauce
2 cloves garlic, crushed
¼ teaspoon ground cumin
¼ teaspoon chili powder
¼ teaspoon hot sauce

Combine all ingredients in a small bowl; stir well. Serve dip in a hollowed-out cabbage bowl, if desired. **Yield: 1½ cups.**

Spicy Chicken Strips

Chicken Almondette Fingers

1 (8-ounce) package tempura batter mix
1 (12-ounce) can beer
1 cup flaked coconut
½ cup sliced almonds
6 skinned and boned chicken breast halves,
    cut into 24 strips
Vegetable oil
Honey-Poppy Seed Sauce

Combine tempura batter mix and beer; pour into a shallow dish, and set aside. Combine coconut and almonds. Dip each chicken strip into batter mixture, and dredge in coconut mixture.

Pour oil to depth of 1½ inches in a Dutch oven; heat to 350°. Fry chicken strips 2 minutes on each side or until golden; drain. Serve with Honey-Poppy Seed Sauce. **Yield: 24 appetizers.**

Honey-Poppy Seed Sauce

½ cup honey
½ cup mayonnaise or salad dressing
1 teaspoon poppy seeds

Combine all ingredients in a small bowl. **Yield: 1 cup.**

Gruyère-Chicken Pizza

1 (8-ounce) carton sour cream
1 tablespoon all-purpose flour
1½ cups chopped cooked chicken
1½ cups (6 ounces) grated Gruyère cheese,
    divided
¼ teaspoon ground cumin
⅛ teaspoon hot sauce
1 clove garlic, minced
1 Crispy Pizza Crust
⅓ cup sliced ripe olives
¼ cup chopped green onions
2 tablespoons grated Parmesan cheese

Combine sour cream and flour in a large bowl, stirring well. Stir in chicken, 1 cup Gruyère cheese, cumin, hot sauce, and garlic. Spread chicken mixture over Crispy Pizza Crust. Top with olives, green onions, remaining ½ cup Gruyère cheese, and Parmesan cheese. Bake at 450° for 15 minutes or until cheese melts. **Yield: one 12-inch pizza.**

Crispy Pizza Crusts

1 package active dry yeast
1 cup warm water (105° to 115°)
3 to 3¼ cups all-purpose flour, divided
1 tablespoon olive or vegetable oil
1 teaspoon salt
1 to 2 teaspoons yellow cornmeal

Combine yeast and warm water in a 2-cup liquid measuring cup; let stand 5 minutes. Combine yeast mixture, 1½ cups flour, oil, and salt in a large mixing bowl; beat at medium speed of an electric mixer until mixture is well blended. Gradually stir in enough of remaining flour to make a firm dough.

Turn dough out onto a lightly floured surface, and knead until smooth and elastic (about 5 minutes). Place in a well-greased bowl, turning to grease top. Cover and let rise in a warm place (85°), free from drafts, 1 hour or until dough is doubled in bulk.

Punch dough down; divide in half. Roll each portion to a 12-inch circle on a lightly floured surface. Transfer dough to 2 ungreased 12-inch pizza pans sprinkled with cornmeal. Fold over edges of dough, and pinch to form a rim; prick with a fork. Bake at 450° for 5 minutes for soft crust or 10 minutes for crisper crust. **Yield: two 12-inch pizza crusts.**

Note: Baked Crispy Pizza Crusts may be wrapped tightly and frozen up to one month. To use, remove from freezer, and let stand 30 minutes. Remove wrapping, and top as directed above with chicken mixture and Gruyère cheese.

Chicken Nachos

4 skinned and boned chicken breast halves
1 teaspoon salt
1½ teaspoons ground cumin
2 tablespoons butter or margarine
½ cup diced onion
¼ cup diced green pepper
1 (4.5-ounce) can chopped green chiles, undrained
⅔ cup chopped tomato
1 teaspoon ground cumin
¼ teaspoon salt
⅛ teaspoon pepper
About 3 dozen round tortilla chips
3 cups (12 ounces) shredded Monterey Jack cheese
¾ cup sour cream
About 3 dozen jalapeño pepper slices
Paprika (optional)

Combine chicken and 1 teaspoon salt in a large saucepan; cover with water. Bring to a boil; cover, reduce heat, and simmer 8 minutes. Drain chicken, reserving ⅔ cup broth.

Place chicken and 1½ teaspoons cumin in container of food processor; process until coarsely ground. Set aside.

Melt butter in a large skillet over medium heat. Add onion and green pepper; cook, stirring constantly, until tender. Add chicken, reserved broth, chiles, and next 4 ingredients; simmer, uncovered, 10 minutes or until liquid evaporates.

Place tortilla chips on baking sheets, and spoon about 1 tablespoon chicken mixture on each. Top each nacho with 1 heaping tablespoon cheese.

Broil nachos 5 inches from heat (with electric oven door partially opened) until cheese melts. Remove from oven, and top each nacho with 1 teaspoon sour cream and a jalapeño pepper slice. Sprinkle with paprika, if desired, and broil 30 seconds. Serve immediately. **Yield: about 3 dozen.**

Cheesy Chicken-Tortilla Stack

½ cup vegetable oil
6 (8-inch) flour tortillas
1 (8-ounce) carton sour cream
½ teaspoon seasoned salt
½ teaspoon hot sauce
2½ cups shredded cooked chicken
2½ cups (10 ounces) shredded Monterey Jack cheese
1¼ cups (5 ounces) shredded Longhorn cheese
½ cup plus 2 tablespoons minced green onions
1½ tablespoons butter or margarine, melted
⅓ cup shredded lettuce
¼ cup chopped tomato

Heat oil to 375° in a 10-inch skillet. Fry tortillas, one at a time, in hot oil 3 to 5 seconds on each side or until tortillas hold their shape and begin to crisp. Drain tortillas well on paper towels; set aside.

Combine sour cream, seasoned salt, and hot sauce. Place 1 tortilla on a lightly greased baking sheet; spread about 1 tablespoon sour cream mixture over tortilla. Sprinkle with ½ cup shredded chicken, ½ cup Monterey Jack cheese, ¼ cup Longhorn cheese, and 2 tablespoons green onions. Repeat all layers 4 times. Top with remaining tortilla. Reserve remaining sour cream mixture. Brush top tortilla and edges of tortillas with melted butter.

Cover with foil; bake at 400° for 25 minutes. Immediately remove foil after baking; place tortilla stack on serving plate. Spread remaining sour cream mixture on top tortilla; sprinkle with shredded lettuce and chopped tomato. Cut into wedges, and serve immediately. **Yield: 4 servings.**

Peppery Chicken in Pita

Peppery Chicken in Pita

6 skinned and boned chicken breast halves
   (about 1½ pounds)
¼ cup teriyaki sauce
1 teaspoon dried thyme
1 teaspoon ground white pepper
1 teaspoon black pepper
½ teaspoon garlic powder
½ teaspoon ground red pepper
2 tablespoons olive oil, divided
⅓ cup mayonnaise or salad dressing
1 tablespoon prepared horseradish
6 (8-inch) pita bread rounds
2 cups shredded lettuce

Cut chicken lengthwise into ½-inch-wide strips, and place in a shallow dish. Pour teriyaki sauce over chicken; cover and marinate in refrigerator 2 hours.

Remove chicken from marinade, discarding marinade. Combine thyme and next 4 ingredients; sprinkle evenly over chicken.

Heat 1 tablespoon olive oil in a large skillet over medium-high heat. Cook half of chicken 5 to 7 minutes, turning once. Drain on paper towels. Repeat procedure with remaining olive oil and chicken.

Combine mayonnaise and horseradish. Spread each pita round with about 1 tablespoon mayonnaise mixture; sprinkle evenly with lettuce, and top with chicken. Fold two sides of pita over chicken, and secure with a wooden pick. **Yield: 6 servings.**

Note: Before spreading pita rounds with mayonnaise mixture, wrap in heavy-duty plastic wrap, and microwave at HIGH 45 seconds or until thoroughly heated. This will prevent bread from cracking when folding.

Marinated Chicken in a Sandwich

8 skinned and boned chicken breast halves
1 cup soy sauce
½ cup pineapple juice
¼ cup dry sherry
¼ cup firmly packed brown sugar
¾ teaspoon minced fresh garlic
8 slices Monterey Jack cheese
8 Kaiser rolls, sliced in half horizontally
Mustard Sauce
Leaf lettuce

Place chicken in a large shallow dish. Combine soy sauce and next 4 ingredients, mixing well. Set aside ½ cup marinade and pour remainder over chicken. Cover and marinate in refrigerator 30 minutes. Remove from marinade; discard marinade.

Cook chicken, covered, over medium coals (300° to 350°) 15 minutes or until done, turning and basting with reserved marinade approximately every 5 minutes. Place slice of cheese on each chicken breast, and grill 2 additional minutes or until cheese melts. Remove chicken from grill.

Spread each side of rolls with Mustard Sauce; place chicken breast on bottom half of each roll; top with lettuce. Cover with roll top, and serve immediately. **Yield: 8 servings.**

Mustard Sauce

½ cup dry mustard
⅔ cup white vinegar
⅔ cup sugar
1 large egg

Combine all ingredients in container of an electric blender and blend until smooth.

Cook mixture in a heavy saucepan over medium heat, stirring constantly, about 7 minutes or until smooth and thickened. Store in an airtight container in refrigerator. **Yield: 1⅓ cups.**

Open-Faced Chicken Sandwiches

2 tablespoons butter or margarine
2 tablespoons all-purpose flour
1 cup milk
½ teaspoon salt
⅛ teaspoon white pepper
½ cup (2 ounces) shredded Cheddar cheese
1 pound sliced cooked chicken
4 slices sandwich bread, toasted
8 slices bacon, cooked, drained, and crumbled
¼ cup grated Parmesan cheese

Melt butter in a heavy saucepan over low heat; add flour, stirring until smooth. Cook, stirring constantly, 1 minute. Gradually add milk; cook over medium heat, stirring constantly, until thickened and bubbly. Add salt, pepper, and Cheddar cheese, stirring until cheese melts.

Place chicken on toast, and cover with sauce. Sprinkle with bacon and Parmesan cheese. Bake at 400° for 10 minutes. Yield: 4 servings.

Chicken Crêpes

3 cups finely chopped cooked chicken
1½ cups freshly grated Parmesan cheese, divided
1 tablespoon butter or margarine
¼ pound finely chopped fresh mushrooms
½ teaspoon salt
¼ teaspoon pepper
¼ teaspoon ground nutmeg
⅓ cup butter or margarine
⅓ cup all-purpose flour
3 cups milk
1 cup whipping cream
Basic Crêpes

Combine chicken and 1 cup cheese in a large bowl; set aside.

Melt 1 tablespoon butter in a medium skillet. Add mushrooms; cook, stirring constantly, until tender.

Stir in salt, pepper, and nutmeg. Set aside.

Melt ⅓ cup butter in a heavy saucepan over low heat; add flour and cook, stirring constantly, 1 minute. Gradually add milk; cook over medium heat, stirring constantly, until thickened and bubbly. Stir in whipping cream.

Add mushroom mixture and ⅔ cup sauce to chicken mixture, stirring well. Spoon ⅓ cup mixture into center of each crêpe, and roll up tightly; place crêpes, seam side down, in a lightly greased 13- x 9- x 2-inch baking dish.

Pour remaining sauce over crêpes, and bake at 350° for 25 minutes. Sprinkle with remaining ½ cup Parmesan cheese, and bake 5 additional minutes. Yield: 8 servings.

Basic Crêpes

1 cup all-purpose flour
¼ teaspoon salt
1¼ cups milk
2 large eggs
2 tablespoons butter or margarine, melted
Vegetable oil

Combine first 3 ingredients, beating at medium speed of an electric mixer until smooth. Add eggs, and beat well; stir in melted butter.

Refrigerate batter 1 hour. (This allows flour particles to swell and soften so crêpes will be light in texture.)

Brush bottom of a 6-inch crêpe pan or heavy skillet lightly with oil; place over medium heat until hot.

Pour 2 tablespoons batter into pan; quickly tilt pan in all directions so batter covers bottom of pan. Cook 1 minute or until crêpe can be shaken loose from pan. Turn crêpe over, and cook about 30 seconds. Place crêpe on a dish towel to cool. Repeat with remaining batter.

Stack crêpes between sheets of wax paper, and place in an airtight container, if desired. Refrigerate up to 2 days or freeze up to 3 months. Yield: 16 to 18 (6-inch) crêpes.

Salad Sampler

Chicken salad is still in style but with some surprisingly
different versions. You'll find new favorites here to serve
for brunch, lunch, or a light supper.

Old-Fashioned Chicken Salad, Chicken-Fruit Salad, Poulet Rémoulade

Chicken Salad in Puff Pastry, Marinated Chicken-Grape Salad, Chicken Salad Oriental

Chutney-Chicken Salad, Aspic-Topped Chicken Salad, Dilled Chicken Salad

Broccoli-Chicken Salad, BLT Chicken Salad, Grilled Chicken Salad

Clockwise from top: Aspic-Topped Chicken Salad, Southwestern
Chicken Salad, and Fruited Chicken Salad (pages 160, 174, and 165)

Old-Fashioned Chicken Salad

4 cups chopped cooked chicken
2 hard-cooked eggs, chopped
1 cup chopped celery
¼ cup chopped onion
¾ teaspoon salt
½ teaspoon celery salt
⅛ to ¼ teaspoon white pepper
Dash of red pepper
2 tablespoons lemon juice
½ to ¾ cup mayonnaise
Paprika
Garnishes: fresh parsley sprigs, cherry tomatoes

Combine first 9 ingredients; toss gently. Fold in mayonnaise; cover and chill 2 hours.

Spoon salad into a serving dish; sprinkle with paprika. Garnish, if desired. Yield: 6 servings.

Chutney-Chicken Salad

4½ cups chopped cooked chicken
¾ cup mayonnaise
½ cup chutney
1½ teaspoons curry powder
¼ teaspoon salt
1 tablespoon lime juice
1½ cups sliced almonds, toasted
Lettuce leaves
Garnish: apple slices

Combine first 6 ingredients in a large bowl; toss to mix. Cover and let chill thoroughly.

Stir in toasted almonds before serving. Serve salad on lettuce leaves. Garnish, if desired. Yield: 6 servings.

Aspic-Topped Chicken Salad

(pictured on page 159)

1 envelope unflavored gelatin
½ cup cold water
3 cups tomato juice
3 cups finely chopped celery, divided
2 tablespoons chopped onion
1 tablespoon Worcestershire sauce
Dash of salt
¼ teaspoon white pepper
1 envelope unflavored gelatin
¼ cup cold water
1 cup mayonnaise
1 cup whipping cream, whipped
3 cups chopped cooked chicken (about 6 breast halves)
Lettuce leaves

Sprinkle 1 envelope gelatin over ½ cup cold water; let stand 1 minute.

Combine tomato juice, 1 cup celery, and onion in a saucepan; bring to a boil, and cook 1 minute. Remove from heat; strain, discarding vegetables.

Combine vegetable liquid and gelatin mixture, stirring until gelatin dissolves. Stir in Worcestershire sauce, salt, and pepper. Pour mixture into a lightly oiled 11-cup mold; chill until the consistency of unbeaten egg white.

Sprinkle 1 envelope gelatin over ¼ cup cold water in a small saucepan; let stand 1 minute. Cook over medium heat until gelatin dissolves. Remove from heat; cool.

Fold mayonnaise and gelatin mixture into whipped cream. Fold in chicken and remaining 2 cups celery; gently spoon over aspic in mold. Chill until firm. Unmold aspic onto a lettuce-lined serving dish. Yield: 8 servings.

Dilled Chicken Salad

8 skinned chicken breast halves
1 teaspoon salt
1 cup chopped celery
3 hard-cooked eggs, chopped
1 (3-ounce) package cream cheese, softened
½ cup mayonnaise or salad dressing
¼ cup sour cream
1½ tablespoons chopped fresh dillweed
1 teaspoon dry mustard
¼ teaspoon salt
⅛ teaspoon pepper
Lettuce leaves
Slices of raw carrot and yellow squash

Combine chicken and 1 teaspoon salt in a Dutch oven; add water to cover. Bring to a boil; cover, reduce heat, and simmer 30 minutes or until tender.

Drain chicken, reserving broth for another use. Bone chicken, and cut into bite-size pieces. Combine chicken, celery, and eggs in a large bowl, and set aside.

Combine cream cheese and next 6 ingredients in a medium bowl. Add to chicken mixture, and toss well. Cover and chill thoroughly.

Serve salad on lettuce leaves with sliced carrot and squash. **Yield: 8 servings.**

Poulet Rémoulade

1½ quarts water
1 teaspoon salt
8 skinned chicken breast halves
1 cup shredded carrot
½ cup chopped celery
1 tablespoon minced fresh parsley
1 tablespoon chopped green onions
1 cup mayonnaise
1 tablespoon dry mustard
1 tablespoon cider vinegar
2 tablespoons olive oil
1 teaspoon paprika
1½ teaspoons prepared horseradish
½ teaspoon Worcestershire sauce
Dash of hot sauce
Garnish: carrot strips

Combine first 3 ingredients in a Dutch oven. Bring to a boil; cover, reduce heat, and simmer 25 to 30 minutes.

Drain chicken, reserving broth for another use. Bone chicken, and cut into bite-size pieces. Combine chicken, shredded carrot, celery, parsley, and green onions in a large bowl; set aside.

Combine mayonnaise and next 7 ingredients. Add to chicken mixture; toss gently. Cover and chill at least 3 hours. Garnish, if desired. **Yield: 6 to 8 servings.**

Quick Chicken for Salad

When time is short and your recipe calls for tender chunks of chicken, remember that chicken and the microwave are ideal partners. For 2 cups chopped cooked chicken:
• Arrange 4 skinned and boned chicken breast halves around sides of an 8-inch square dish. Pour ½ cup water over chicken and sprinkle with pepper.
• Cover with heavy-duty plastic wrap; vent corner. Microwave at HIGH 6 minutes or until juice is no longer pink.
• Let stand, covered, 5 minutes; drain. When cool enough to handle, chop chicken.

Chicken Salad in Puff Pastry

3½ cups chopped cooked chicken
1½ cups chopped celery
½ cup mayonnaise
⅓ cup honey mustard
3 tablespoons finely chopped onion
1 teaspoon salt
¾ teaspoon cracked pepper
½ teaspoon dry mustard
¾ cup slivered almonds, toasted
Puff Pastry Ring
Curly leaf lettuce

Combine chicken and celery in a bowl. Combine mayonnaise and next 5 ingredients; stir well. Add to chicken; toss gently. Stir in almonds.

Split Puff Pastry Ring in half horizontally; remove and discard soft dough inside. Line bottom half of pastry ring with lettuce; top with chicken salad. Replace pastry ring top. **Yield: 12 servings.**

Puff Pastry Ring

1⅓ cups water
⅔ cup butter
1⅓ cups all-purpose flour
¼ teaspoon salt
¼ to ½ teaspoon celery seeds
6 large eggs

Trace a 9-inch circle on parchment paper. Turn paper over, and place on a greased baking sheet.

Combine water and butter in a medium saucepan; bring to a boil. Combine flour, salt, and celery seeds; stir well. Add to butter mixture, all at once, stirring vigorously over medium-high heat until mixture leaves sides of pan and forms a smooth ball. Remove from heat, and let cool 2 minutes.

Add eggs, one at a time, beating thoroughly with a wooden spoon after each addition; beat until dough is smooth.

Spoon dough into a large pastry bag fitted with a large fluted tip. Working quickly, pipe into 12 rosettes on 9-inch circle on baking sheet. Bake at 400° for 40 to 50 minutes or until puffed and golden. Cool on a wire rack. **Yield: 12 servings.**

Chicken Salad in Puff Pastry Techniques

For a fancy pastry ring, pipe dough from a pastry bag, or simply spoon dough onto the parchment paper.

Cool on a wire rack, away from drafts. Carefully slice the cooled ring in half horizontally.

Remove the soft dough from inside of pastry before filling ring with lettuce leaves and chicken salad.

Chicken Salad in Puff Pastry

Chicken-Fruit Salad

Chicken-Fruit Salad

1 small head Bibb lettuce
1 avocado
2 chicken breast halves, cooked and cubed
1 small apple, diced
1 small banana, sliced
1 (8-ounce) can pineapple chunks, drained
½ cup chopped pecans
⅓ to ½ cup mayonnaise or salad dressing

Remove 6 outer leaves of lettuce; tear remaining lettuce. Peel and seed avocado. Slice half of avocado and set aside; chop remaining avocado.

Combine torn lettuce, chopped avocado, chicken, and next 5 ingredients; toss gently. Serve on reserved lettuce leaves, and garnish with avocado slices. **Yield: 2 servings.**

Marinated Chicken-Grape Salad

⅔ cup dry white wine
3 tablespoons lemon juice
4 chicken breast halves, cooked and cut into strips
1 cup mayonnaise
¼ teaspoon salt
⅛ teaspoon white pepper
Red-leaf lettuce
1 cup halved seedless green grapes
1 cup halved seedless red grapes
1½ cups diagonally sliced celery
½ cup cashews

Combine wine and lemon juice; pour over chicken. Cover and chill 2 hours. Drain, reserving marinade. Strain marinade, reserving ⅓ cup. Combine reserved marinade, mayonnaise, salt, and pepper.

Line 4 plates with lettuce. Arrange chicken, grapes, celery, and cashews over lettuce. Serve with mayonnaise mixture. **Yield: 4 servings.**

Fruited Chicken Salad

(pictured on page 159)

4 cups chopped cooked chicken
2 cups diced celery
2 cups halved seedless red or green grapes
1 (15¼-ounce) can pineapple tidbits, drained
1 (11-ounce) can mandarin oranges, drained
1 cup slivered almonds, toasted
½ cup mayonnaise
½ cup sour cream
2 tablespoons lemon juice
¼ teaspoon salt
¼ teaspoon white pepper
Fresh escarole
Cheese Tart Shells

Combine first 6 ingredients, and toss well. Combine mayonnaise and next 4 ingredients; add to chicken mixture, stirring well. Chill.

Arrange escarole around inside edges of 8 Cheese Tart Shells; spoon chicken mixture on top. **Yield: 8 servings.**

Cheese Tart Shells

2 cups all-purpose flour
½ teaspoon salt
¾ cup shortening
1 cup (4 ounces) shredded Cheddar cheese
4 to 5 tablespoons cold water

Combine flour and salt in a bowl; cut in shortening with a pastry blender until mixture is crumbly. Stir in cheese.

Sprinkle cold water, 1 tablespoon at a time, evenly over surface; stir with a fork until dry ingredients are moistened. Shape into 8 balls; cover and chill.

Roll dough into 8 (6½-inch) circles on a lightly floured surface. Line 8 (4½-inch) tart pans with pastry; trim excess pastry.

Bake at 450° for 8 to 10 minutes or until lightly browned. **Yield: 8 tart shells.**

Asparagus-Chicken Salad

1 pound fresh asparagus
1½ cups chopped cooked chicken
3 cups iceberg lettuce, torn into bite-size
    pieces
¼ cup slivered almonds, toasted
¼ cup chopped parsley
1½ tablespoons raisins
1 red apple, unpeeled
Lettuce leaves (optional)
Italian Cream Dressing

Snap off tough ends of asparagus. Remove scales with a knife or vegetable peeler, if desired.

Cook asparagus, covered, in a small amount of boiling water 3 minutes. Plunge in ice water. Drain well.

Cut asparagus into 1½-inch pieces; reserve 8 pieces for garnish. Combine remaining asparagus, chicken, lettuce, almonds, parsley, and raisins in a large bowl. Cut half of apple into ½-inch cubes; stir into chicken mixture. (Reserve remaining apple for garnish.)

Arrange salad in a lettuce-lined bowl, if desired. Garnish with reserved asparagus and apple slices. Pour Italian Cream Dressing over salad. **Yield: 4 servings.**

Italian Cream Dressing

¾ cup sour cream
¼ cup crumbled Gorgonzola cheese or
    blue cheese
1 tablespoon lemon juice
¼ teaspoon garlic powder
Freshly ground pepper

Combine all ingredients in a small bowl; stir well. **Yield: 1 cup.**

Artichoke-Chicken-Rice Salad

2 (6-ounce) jars marinated artichoke hearts,
    undrained
1 (6.9-ounce) package chicken-flavored rice
    and vermicelli mix
2½ cups chopped cooked chicken
1 (6-ounce) can sliced water chestnuts,
    drained and chopped
1 (3-ounce) jar pimiento-stuffed olives,
    drained and sliced
1 cup chopped green onions
1 cup reduced-fat mayonnaise
1½ tablespoons curry powder
1 teaspoon pepper
Lettuce leaves

Drain artichoke hearts, reserving marinade; coarsely chop artichokes.

Cook rice mix according to package directions; stir in reserved marinade. Cool.

Combine artichoke hearts, rice mixture, chopped chicken, and next 3 ingredients.

Combine mayonnaise, curry powder, and pepper; stir into chicken mixture.

Cover and chill 1 to 2 hours. Serve on lettuce leaves. **Yield: 8 servings.**

Broccoli-Chicken Salad

4 cups chopped cooked chicken
¼ cup sliced pimiento-stuffed olives
1 pound fresh broccoli, broken into flowerets
⅔ cup mayonnaise or salad dressing
¼ teaspoon curry powder
Lettuce leaves (optional)

Combine chicken, olives, and broccoli. Combine mayonnaise and curry powder, stirring well; add to chicken mixture, and toss well. Cover and chill. Serve in a lettuce-lined bowl, if desired. **Yield: 6 to 8 servings.**

Chicken Salad Oriental

½ cup uncooked macaroni
2 cups chopped cooked chicken
½ cup sliced green onions
1 (8-ounce) can sliced water chestnuts, drained
½ cup mayonnaise or salad dressing
2 teaspoons soy sauce
¼ teaspoon ground ginger
⅛ teaspoon pepper
2 cups (¾-pound) fresh snow pea pods, blanched
½ cup slivered almonds, toasted

Cook macaroni according to package directions; drain. Combine macaroni and next 3 ingredients; toss well.

Combine mayonnaise and next 3 ingredients, stirring well; fold into chicken mixture. Cover and chill 2 hours.

Divide snow peas among 4 plates. Top with chicken salad, and sprinkle with toasted almonds. **Yield: 4 servings.**

Chicken Salad Oriental

BLT Chicken Salad

BLT Chicken Salad

½ cup mayonnaise
¼ cup commercial barbecue sauce
2 tablespoons grated onion
1 tablespoon lemon juice
½ teaspoon pepper
2 large tomatoes, chopped
8 cups torn leaf lettuce or iceberg lettuce
3 cups chopped cooked chicken
10 slices bacon, cooked and crumbled
2 hard-cooked eggs, sliced

Combine first 5 ingredients in a small bowl; stir well. Cover and chill dressing mixture thoroughly.

Press chopped tomato between several layers of paper towels to remove excess moisture.

Arrange lettuce on individual salad plates; top each serving with tomato and chopped cooked chicken.

Spoon dressing mixture over salads; sprinkle with crumbled bacon, and garnish with egg slices. Serve immediately. **Yield: 4 servings.**

BLT Chicken Salad Technique

This egg slicer makes slicing hard-cooked eggs a simple task; the slices make a pretty garnish.

Layered Chicken Salad

3 cups chopped cooked chicken, divided
2 cups torn lettuce
1 cup cooked long-grain rice
1 (10-ounce) package frozen English peas, thawed
¼ cup chopped fresh parsley
2 large tomatoes, seeded and chopped
1 cup thinly sliced cucumber
1 small sweet red pepper, chopped
1 small green pepper, chopped
Creamy Dressing
Red pepper rings

Layer 1½ cups chicken and lettuce in a 3-quart bowl. Combine rice, peas, and parsley; spoon evenly over lettuce.

Layer tomato, cucumber, chopped red pepper, green pepper, and remaining 1½ cups chicken.

Spoon Creamy Dressing evenly over top of salad, sealing to edge of bowl. Top with red pepper rings; cover and chill 8 hours. Toss before serving. **Yield: 8 servings.**

Creamy Dressing

1 cup mayonnaise
½ cup sour cream
½ cup raisins
½ cup finely chopped onion
¼ cup sweet pickle relish
2 tablespoons milk
½ teaspoon celery seeds
½ teaspoon dillseeds
½ teaspoon dry mustard
½ teaspoon garlic salt

Combine all ingredients; stir well. **Yield: about 2¾ cups.**

Chicken Tortellini Salad

1 pound boneless chicken breasts, cut into strips
2 cloves garlic, minced
2 tablespoons olive oil
1 (8-ounce) package tortellini with Parmesan cheese
2 tablespoons olive oil
3 stalks celery, chopped
1 medium-size red pepper, cut into strips
⅓ cup chopped purple onion
5 ounces smoked Gouda cheese, cut into strips
¾ cup olive oil
¾ cup cider vinegar
2 tablespoons honey
2 tablespoons Dijon mustard
1 teaspoon dry mustard
Bibb lettuce leaves
5 slices Canadian bacon, cut into strips
Garnish: celery leaves

Cook chicken and garlic in 2 tablespoons hot oil, stirring constantly, until chicken is done; drain and set aside.

Cook tortellini according to package directions; drain well. Combine tortellini and 2 tablespoons oil in a large bowl, tossing gently. Add chicken, celery, red pepper, onion, and cheese.

Combine ¾ cup olive oil and next 4 ingredients in a jar; cover tightly, and shake vigorously. Pour mixture over salad, and toss gently.

Serve salad immediately or chill. Arrange on lettuce leaves, and top with Canadian bacon. Garnish, if desired. **Yield: 6 servings.**

Warm Chinese Chicken Salad

¼ cup cider vinegar
2 tablespoons walnut oil
2 tablespoons vegetable oil
2 tablespoons chicken broth
1 teaspoon dried tarragon
½ teaspoon Dijon mustard
½ teaspoon Worcestershire sauce
¼ teaspoon salt
⅛ teaspoon ground nutmeg
2 cups torn Chinese cabbage
2 cups torn romaine lettuce
⅔ cup chopped walnuts, toasted
3 cups coarsely chopped cooked chicken
1½ cups halved seedless red grapes

Combine first 9 ingredients in a small bowl, stirring well. Toss cabbage and lettuce with half of dressing mixture in a large shallow bowl. Sprinkle walnuts over cabbage mixture.

Combine chicken and 3 tablespoons remaining dressing mixture in a skillet over medium heat. Cook, stirring occasionally, until chicken is thoroughly heated.

Toss hot chicken mixture and grape halves with cabbage mixture. Serve salad warm with remaining dressing. **Yield: 4 servings.**

Wow! Chicken Salad

Today's chicken salad goes far beyond being chunks of chicken tossed with mayonnaise, celery, and pickle relish. Pasta and chicken make a splendid partnership in Chicken Tortellini Salad. And for a casual cold weather salad, try Warm Chinese Chicken Salad or one of our hot chicken salads on page 172.

Warm Chinese Chicken Salad

Hot Chicken Salad Casserole

4 cups chopped cooked chicken
1½ cups chopped celery
4 hard-cooked eggs, chopped
1 (2-ounce) jar diced pimiento, drained
1 tablespoon finely chopped onion
¾ cup mayonnaise
2 tablespoons lemon juice
¾ teaspoon salt
1 cup (4 ounces) shredded Cheddar cheese
⅔ cup sliced almonds, toasted

Combine first 8 ingredients in a bowl; mix well. Spoon into a lightly greased 12- x 8- x 2-inch baking dish; cover and bake at 350° for 20 minutes.

Sprinkle with cheese; top with almonds. Bake, uncovered, 3 additional minutes or until cheese melts. **Yield: 6 to 8 servings.**

Hot Mexican Chicken Salads

5 cups chopped cooked chicken
2 cups (8 ounces) shredded sharp Cheddar
      cheese, divided
1 (15-ounce) can red kidney beans, drained
1 large sweet red pepper, chopped
¾ cup finely chopped onion
½ cup sliced ripe olives
½ cup sour cream
½ cup mayonnaise
1 (4.5-ounce) can chopped green chiles
1 (1¼-ounce) package taco seasoning
Vegetable oil
6 (8-inch) flour tortillas
Garnishes: avocado slices, cilantro sprigs

Combine chicken, 1 cup cheese, and next 8 ingredients, stirring well. Cover and chill.

Pour oil to depth of ¼ inch into a large deep skillet; heat to 375°. Fry tortillas, one at a time, until crisp and golden. Drain on paper towels.

Spoon chicken mixture evenly onto fried tortillas. Sprinkle with remaining 1 cup cheese. Place on baking sheets.

Broil 4 inches from heat (with electric oven door partially opened) 30 seconds or just until cheese melts. Garnish, if desired. Serve immediately. **Yield: 6 servings.**

Hot Mexican Chicken Salads Techniques

Slice avocado by peeling top half of skin and holding bottom half intact. Cut and lift out thin wedges from top of avocado.

Broil salads briefly to melt the cheese topping without burning the shells. Garnish salads, and serve immediately.

Hot Mexican Chicken Salads

Southwestern Chicken Salad

(pictured on page 159)

4 skinned chicken breast halves
½ teaspoon salt
¼ cup mayonnaise
¼ cup sour cream
1 (4.5-ounce) can chopped green chiles,
    undrained
1 teaspoon ground cumin
¼ teaspoon salt
⅛ teaspoon pepper
¼ cup chopped onion
4 (8-inch) flour tortillas
1 cup (4 ounces) shredded Longhorn cheese
3 cups shredded lettuce
Garnishes: sour cream, diced tomato
Picante sauce

Place chicken in a large saucepan; add ½ teaspoon salt and water to cover. Bring to a boil; cover, reduce heat, and simmer 30 minutes or until chicken is tender.

Drain chicken, reserving broth for another use. Bone chicken, and shred into small pieces. Set aside.

Combine mayonnaise and ¼ cup sour cream, stirring well. Add chiles and next 3 ingredients; stir well.

Combine chicken and onion; add sour cream mixture, stirring to coat well. Cover and refrigerate 2 hours.

Place tortillas on a baking sheet; sprinkle cheese evenly over each tortilla. Bake at 300° for 10 minutes or until cheese melts; transfer to individual serving plates.

Arrange lettuce on tortillas; top each with one-fourth of chicken mixture. Garnish, if desired. Serve with picante sauce. **Yield: 4 servings.**

Grilled Chicken Salad

4 skinned and boned chicken breast halves
3 tablespoons soy sauce
3 tablespoons butter or margarine, softened
3 (¾-inch-thick) slices French bread
⅓ cup olive oil
2 cloves garlic, crushed
1½ tablespoons lemon juice
2 teaspoons Dijon mustard
2 dashes of hot sauce
1 large head romaine lettuce, torn
¼ cup freshly grated Parmesan cheese
Freshly ground pepper

Place chicken and soy sauce in a heavy-duty, zip-top plastic bag; marinate 30 minutes in refrigerator.

Spread butter over both sides of bread slices; cut slices into ¾-inch cubes. Place on a baking sheet, and bake at 350° for 15 minutes or until croutons are crisp and dry. Set aside.

Remove chicken from soy sauce; discard soy sauce. Grill chicken, covered, over medium coals (300° to 350°) 5 minutes on each side or until done. Cool 5 minutes; slice crosswise into ½-inch-wide strips. Set aside.

Combine olive oil and next 4 ingredients in a large bowl; stir with a wire whisk until blended. Add chicken strips, tossing to coat. Add romaine, cheese, croutons, and pepper, tossing gently to combine. Serve immediately. **Yield: 4 servings.**

Great Grilled Salad

Grilled Chicken Salad, a popular restaurant item, can be prepared quickly at home. For an easier version of this salad, substitute commercial croutons and Caesar salad dressing.

Comfort Food

Down-home chicken classics, such as pot pies and chicken and dumplings, are some of life's greatest comforts. These home-cooked favorites bring us back to basics amidst everyday hustle and bustle.

Chicken Noodle Soup, Biscuit-Topped Chicken Pie, Brunswick Stew

Chicken-and-Sausage Gumbo, Chicken-and-Oyster Gumbo, Kentucky Burgoo

Chili-Chicken Stew, Country Chicken and Dumplings, Chicken-and-Rice Soup

Individual Chicken Pot Pies, Creamy Chicken-and-Broccoli Soup

Chicken Ragoût with Cheddar Dumplings (page 188)

Chicken Noodle Soup

1 (3½- to 4-pound) broiler-fryer
8 to 10 cups water
1 bay leaf
1 tablespoon chopped fresh parsley
1¼ teaspoons salt
¼ teaspoon pepper
¼ teaspoon dried basil
⅛ teaspoon celery seeds
⅛ teaspoon garlic powder
4 medium carrots, chopped
1 small onion, chopped
1 cup uncooked fine egg noodles

Combine first 9 ingredients in a large Dutch oven. Bring to a boil; cover, reduce heat, and simmer 1 hour or until chicken is tender.

Remove chicken from broth; discard bay leaf. Remove skin, bone chicken, and dice meat; set aside.

Add carrot and onion to broth; cover and simmer 30 minutes. Add chicken and noodles; cook 15 additional minutes. **Yield: 2½ quarts.**

Chicken-and-Rice Soup

1 (3½- to 4-pound) broiler-fryer, cut up
   and skinned
2 quarts water
1 medium onion, chopped
2 stalks celery, thinly sliced
1½ teaspoons salt
1 to 1½ teaspoons pepper
1 bay leaf
1 cup uncooked long-grain rice
2 carrots, diced

Combine first 7 ingredients in a Dutch oven. Bring to a boil; cover, reduce heat, and simmer 45 minutes.

Remove chicken, reserving broth. Discard bay leaf. Set chicken aside.

Add rice and carrot to broth; bring to a boil. Cover, reduce heat, and simmer 20 minutes or until rice is tender.

Bone chicken, and cut into bite-size pieces. Add chicken to broth; heat thoroughly. **Yield: 2 quarts.**

Creamy Chicken-and-Broccoli Soup

½ cup sliced fresh mushrooms
½ cup chopped onion
¼ cup butter or margarine, melted
¼ cup all-purpose flour
2 cups half-and-half
1½ cups chicken broth
1 cup chopped cooked chicken
1 cup frozen chopped broccoli, thawed
½ teaspoon dried rosemary
½ teaspoon salt
¼ teaspoon dried thyme
¼ teaspoon pepper

Cook mushrooms and onion in butter in a medium saucepan over low heat until tender; add flour, stirring until smooth. Cook, stirring constantly, 1 minute.

Add half-and-half and chicken broth; cook over medium heat, stirring constantly, until mixture is thickened and bubbly.

Stir in chicken and remaining ingredients. Cover and simmer 10 minutes, stirring occasionally. **Yield: 1 quart.**

Soup's On!

When you have leftover chopped cooked chicken, store it in freezer bags, and freeze up to 1 month. The tender chunks of meat are then ready to use in salads or soups like our Creamy Chicken-and-Broccoli Soup.

Creamy Chicken-and-Broccoli Soup

Brunswick Stew

Brunswick Stew

8 skinned and boned chicken breast halves
1½ cups chopped onion
1 cup chopped green pepper
1 tablespoon vegetable oil
3 (16-ounce) cans tomatoes, undrained and
    chopped
1 (8-ounce) can tomato sauce
¼ cup sugar
3 tablespoons white vinegar
2 tablespoons Worcestershire sauce
2 tablespoons all-purpose flour
1 cup water
1 pound red potatoes, peeled and cubed
1 (16-ounce) can pork and beans
1 tablespoon hot sauce
1½ teaspoons salt
½ teaspoon ground turmeric
½ teaspoon pepper
1 (16-ounce) can whole kernel corn, drained
1 (16-ounce) can lima beans, drained

Place chicken in a large Dutch oven; add water to cover. Bring to a boil; cover, reduce heat, and simmer 20 minutes or until chicken is tender.

Remove chicken from broth, reserving broth for another use. Let chicken cool. Chop chicken, and set aside.

Cook onion and green pepper in hot oil in Dutch oven, stirring constantly. Add chicken, tomatoes, and next 4 ingredients.

Combine flour and 1 cup water, stirring until smooth. Stir flour mixture into chicken mixture.

Add potato and next 5 ingredients; stir well. Cover and cook over medium heat 20 to 30 minutes or until potato is tender, stirring occasionally. Add corn and lima beans, and cook 10 minutes or until thoroughly heated. **Yield: 4 quarts.**

Brunswick Stew Technique

Use a vegetable peeler with a swiveling blade to peel the potatoes. The blade will conform to the shape of each potato.

Chili-Chicken Stew

6 skinned and boned chicken breast halves
1 medium onion, chopped
1 medium-size green pepper, chopped
2 cloves garlic, minced
1 tablespoon vegetable oil
2 (14½-ounce) cans stewed tomatoes,
    undrained and chopped
1 (15-ounce) can pinto beans, drained
⅔ cup picante sauce
1 teaspoon chili powder
1 teaspoon ground cumin
½ teaspoon salt
Condiments: shredded Cheddar cheese, sour
    cream, diced avocado, sliced green onions

Cut chicken into 1-inch pieces. Cook chicken and next 3 ingredients in hot oil in a Dutch oven until lightly browned.

Add tomatoes and next 5 ingredients; cover, reduce heat, and simmer 20 minutes. Top individual servings with desired condiments. **Yield: 6 servings.**

White Lightning Texas Chili

1 pound dried navy beans
4 (14½-ounce) cans ready-to-serve chicken
    broth, divided
1 large onion, chopped
2 cloves garlic, minced
1 tablespoon ground white pepper
1 tablespoon dried oregano
1 tablespoon ground cumin
1 teaspoon salt
½ teaspoon ground cloves
5 cups chopped cooked chicken
1 (4.5-ounce) can chopped green chiles,
    undrained
1 cup water
1 jalapeño pepper, seeded and chopped
    (optional)
Shredded Monterey Jack cheese
Commercial salsa
Sour cream
Sliced green onions

Sort and wash beans; place in a large Dutch
oven. Cover with water 2 inches above beans; let
soak 8 hours. Drain beans, and return to pan.

Add 3 cans chicken broth and next 7 ingredients; bring to a boil. Cover, reduce heat, and simmer 2 hours or until beans are tender, stirring
occasionally.

Add remaining can of chicken broth, chicken,
and next 3 ingredients. Cover and simmer 1 hour,
stirring occasionally.

Serve with cheese, salsa, sour cream, and
green onions. **Yield: 2½ quarts.**

Making a Roux

Roux, the basis of many authentic
Louisiana recipes, should be stirred
constantly until it reaches a rich,
dark brown color.

Chicken-and-Sausage Gumbo

1 pound hot smoked sausage, cut into ¼-inch
    slices
4 skinned chicken breast halves
¼ to ⅓ cup vegetable oil
¾ cup all-purpose flour
1 cup chopped onion
½ cup chopped green pepper
½ cup sliced celery
2 quarts hot water
3 cloves garlic, minced
2 bay leaves
2 teaspoons Creole seasoning
½ teaspoon dried thyme
1 tablespoon Worcestershire sauce
½ to 1 teaspoon hot sauce
½ cup sliced green onions
¼ teaspoon salt (optional)
Hot cooked rice
Gumbo filé (optional)

Brown sausage in a Dutch oven over medium
heat. Remove to paper towels, reserving drippings.

Brown chicken in drippings; remove to paper
towels, reserving drippings. Measure drippings,
adding enough oil to measure ½ cup. Heat in
Dutch oven over medium heat until hot.

Add flour to hot oil; cook, stirring constantly,
until roux is the color of chocolate (about 30
minutes). Add onion, green pepper, and celery;
cook until vegetables are tender, stirring often.

Stir in water; bring to a boil. Return chicken
to pan; add garlic and next 5 ingredients. Reduce
heat; simmer, uncovered, 1 hour.

Remove chicken; return sausage to pan, and
cook, uncovered, 30 minutes. Stir in green
onions; cook, uncovered, 30 minutes. Add salt,
if desired.

Bone chicken, and cut into strips. Add to
gumbo, and thoroughly heat. Remove bay leaves;
serve gumbo over rice. Sprinkle with gumbo filé,
if desired. **Yield: 8 servings.**

Chicken-and-Sausage Gumbo

Chicken-and-Oyster Gumbo

1 (5-pound) hen
2½ quarts water
2 teaspoons salt
¾ cup vegetable oil
1 cup all-purpose flour
2 large onions, chopped
¼ cup chopped fresh parsley
1 teaspoon whole allspice
1 teaspoon dried crushed red pepper
5 bay leaves
½ teaspoon pepper
2 (12-ounce) containers fresh oysters, undrained
Salt to taste
2 teaspoons gumbo filé
Hot cooked rice

Combine first 3 ingredients in a Dutch oven. Bring to a boil; cover, reduce heat, and simmer 1½ hours or until hen is tender.

Remove hen from broth, reserving 8½ cups broth. Remove skin, bone hen, and cut meat into pieces. Set aside.

Combine oil and flour in Dutch oven; cook over medium heat, stirring constantly, until roux is the color of chocolate (about 30 minutes).

Add onion and parsley to roux; cook 10 minutes, stirring frequently. Gradually add reserved broth to roux, stirring constantly.

Combine allspice, red pepper, and bay leaves in a cheesecloth bag; add to broth mixture. Add pepper; simmer 2½ hours, stirring occasionally.

Add chicken and oysters; simmer 10 minutes. Remove from heat, and discard spice bag.

Add additional salt, if desired. Stir in gumbo filé. Serve over rice. **Yield: about 3½ quarts.**

Kentucky Burgoo

1 (4-pound) broiler-fryer
1 pound beef for stewing, cut into 2-inch pieces
1 pound veal for stewing, cut into 2-inch pieces
1 stalk celery with leaves
1 carrot, scraped
1 onion, quartered
6 fresh parsley sprigs
4 quarts water
1 (10¾-ounce) can tomato puree
1½ tablespoons salt
1 tablespoon sugar
3 tablespoons Worcestershire sauce
1½ teaspoons pepper
½ teaspoon ground red pepper
4 large tomatoes, peeled and chopped
2 large onions, chopped
2 large green peppers, chopped
2 cups sliced celery
2 cups chopped cabbage
1 (16-ounce) package frozen lima beans
1 (16-ounce) package frozen sliced okra
2 (8¾-ounce) cans whole kernel corn

Combine first 14 ingredients in a large stockpot. Bring to a boil; cover, reduce heat, and simmer 3 hours. Remove from heat, and let cool.

Strain soup, discarding vegetables; return meat and stock to stockpot. Let chicken cool; remove skin, bone, and chop chicken. Return chopped chicken to soup; cover and refrigerate 8 hours.

Skim and discard fat from surface of soup; add tomato and remaining ingredients. Bring to a boil; cover, reduce heat, and simmer 1 hour.

Uncover; simmer 1 hour and 45 minutes to 2 hours, stirring frequently. **Yield: 5 quarts.**

What's Gumbo Filé?

Gumbo filé, a seasoning used to thicken and flavor gumbo, is made from the ground dried leaves of the sassafras tree. Stir filé into a dish after it's removed from the heat—cooking makes filé stringy and tough.

Kentucky Burgoo

Double-Crust Chicken Pot Pie

6 skinned and boned chicken breast halves
1 medium onion, chopped
2 tablespoons butter or margarine, melted
1 cup sliced fresh mushrooms
¾ cup chopped carrot
1 stalk celery, chopped
¾ cup frozen English peas
¾ cup peeled, chopped potato
1 cup chicken broth
¼ cup Chablis or other dry white wine
½ teaspoon dried parsley flakes
¼ teaspoon ground white pepper
1 bay leaf
2 tablespoons cornstarch
2 tablespoons water
1 (10¾-ounce) can cream of mushroom soup, undiluted
½ cup sour cream
¾ cup (3 ounces) shredded Cheddar cheese
Celery Seed Pastry
1 egg yolk, lightly beaten
1 tablespoon half-and-half or milk

Cut chicken into 1-inch pieces. Cook chicken and onion in melted butter in a Dutch oven 5 minutes.

Stir in mushrooms and next 9 ingredients. Bring to a boil; cover, reduce heat, and simmer 15 minutes or until vegetables are tender.

Combine cornstarch and water, stirring until blended; add to chicken mixture. Cook over medium heat, stirring constantly, until mixture comes to a boil. Remove from heat. Remove bay leaf. Stir in soup, sour cream, and cheese.

Roll half of Celery Seed Pastry to ⅛-inch thickness on a floured surface. Fit pastry into a deep 2-quart casserole. Spoon chicken mixture into pastry.

Roll remaining pastry to ⅛-inch thickness, and place over chicken mixture; trim, seal, and flute edges.

Reroll pastry trimmings; make chicken-shaped cutouts. Dampen cutouts with water, and arrange on top of pastry. Cut slits in pastry.

Combine egg yolk and half-and-half; brush over pastry. Bake at 400° for 30 minutes or until golden. Shield pastry with aluminum foil to prevent excessive browning. **Yield: 6 servings.**

Celery Seed Pastry

3 cups all-purpose flour
2 teaspoons celery seeds
1 teaspoon salt
1 cup shortening
4 to 6 tablespoons cold water

Combine first 3 ingredients; cut in shortening with a pastry blender until mixture is crumbly.

Sprinkle cold water, 1 tablespoon at a time, evenly over surface; stir with a fork until dry ingredients are moistened. Shape dough into a ball; chill. **Yield: pastry for one double-crust pie.**

Double-Crust Chicken Pot Pie Techniques

Roll half of pastry to ⅛-inch thickness; fit pastry into a deep 2-quart casserole.

Brush pastry with an egg yolk and half-and-half wash to give finished crust a rich color and glossy sheen.

Double-Crust Chicken Pot Pie

Individual Chicken Pot Pies

Individual Chicken Pot Pies

1 cup chopped onion
1 cup chopped celery
1 cup chopped carrot
⅓ cup butter or margarine, melted
½ cup all-purpose flour
2 cups chicken broth
1 cup half-and-half
4 cups chopped cooked chicken
1 cup frozen English peas, thawed
1 teaspoon salt
¼ teaspoon pepper
Basic Pastry

Cook first 3 ingredients in butter in a skillet over medium heat until tender. Add flour; stir until smooth. Cook, stirring constantly, 1 minute.

Add chicken broth and half-and-half; cook, stirring constantly, until thickened and bubbly.

Stir in chicken, peas, salt, and pepper.

Divide Basic Pastry into 8 equal portions. Roll 4 portions of pastry into 10-inch circles on a floured surface. Place in 4 (6-inch) pie pans.

Spoon chicken mixture evenly into each of the prepared pie pans.

Roll remaining 4 portions of pastry to 7-inch circles on a floured surface. Place pastry circles over filling; fold edges under and flute. Cut slits in tops to allow steam to escape.

Bake, uncovered, at 400° for 35 minutes or until crust is golden brown. **Yield: 4 servings.**

Basic Pastry

4 cups all-purpose flour
2 teaspoons salt
1½ cups plus 1 tablespoon shortening
⅓ to ½ cup cold water

Combine flour and salt; cut in shortening with a pastry blender until mixture is crumbly. Sprinkle cold water, 1 tablespoon at a time, over surface; stir with a fork until dry ingredients are moistened. Shape into a ball; chill. **Yield: pastry for 4 (6-inch) pies.**

Biscuit-Topped Chicken Pie

1 (3-pound) broiler-fryer, cut up
1½ teaspoons salt, divided
1 cup chopped carrot
1 cup frozen English peas, thawed
2½ cups diced potato
¼ cup chopped celery
½ teaspoon white pepper
1 teaspoon onion powder
¾ teaspoon poultry seasoning
3 tablespoons all-purpose flour
1 (5-ounce) can evaporated milk
1 cup chopped fresh mushrooms
Biscuit Topping
Butter or margarine, melted (optional)

Place chicken in a Dutch oven; add 1 teaspoon salt and water to cover. Bring to a boil; cover, reduce heat, and simmer 45 minutes or until chicken is tender.

Drain chicken, reserving 2¾ cups broth. Set chicken aside. Add remaining ½ teaspoon salt, carrot, and next 6 ingredients to broth; cook 20 minutes or until vegetables are tender.

Combine flour and milk; add to vegetable mixture, stirring constantly until mixture is thickened.

Bone chicken, and cut into bite-size pieces. Stir chicken and mushrooms into vegetable mixture. Spoon into a lightly greased 13- x 9- x 2-inch baking dish. Arrange Biscuit Topping rounds over chicken mixture.

Bake at 400° for 25 minutes or until biscuits are golden. Brush tops of biscuits with butter, if desired. **Yield: 6 to 8 servings.**

Biscuit Topping

½ cup shortening
2 cups self-rising flour
⅔ cup milk

Cut shortening into flour with a pastry blender until mixture is crumbly. Add milk, and mix well.

Turn dough out onto a lightly floured surface. Roll dough to ⅓-inch thickness; cut rounds with a 2¾-inch biscuit cutter. **Yield: 15 biscuit rounds.**

Country Chicken and Dumplings

1 (3- to 3½-pound) broiler-fryer
2 quarts water
2 stalks celery, cut into pieces
1 teaspoon salt
2 cups all-purpose flour
2 teaspoons baking powder
½ teaspoon salt
¼ cup butter or margarine, softened

Place chicken in a Dutch oven; add water, celery, and 1 teaspoon salt. Bring to a boil; cover, reduce heat, and simmer 1 hour or until chicken is tender.

Remove chicken from broth, and cool. Discard celery. Bone chicken, and cut into bite-size pieces; set aside chicken and ¾ cup broth. Leave remaining broth in pan.

Combine flour, baking powder, and ½ teaspoon salt; cut in butter until mixture is crumbly. Add ¾ cup reserved broth, stirring with a fork until dry ingredients are moistened. Turn dough out onto a well-floured surface, and knead.

Pat dough to ½-inch thickness. Cut dough in 4- x ½-inch pieces, and sprinkle with additional flour.

Bring broth to a boil. Drop dough, one piece at a time, into boiling broth, gently stirring after each addition. Reduce heat to low; cover and cook 8 to 10 minutes. Stir in chicken, and serve immediately. **Yield: 4 servings.**

Chicken Ragoût with Cheddar Dumplings

(pictured on page 175)

2 cups diagonally sliced carrot
1 cup sweet red pepper strips
3 tablespoons butter or margarine
¼ cup all-purpose flour
2 cups chicken broth
1 cup milk
1 tablespoon lemon juice
½ teaspoon salt
½ teaspoon pepper
3 cups chopped cooked chicken
1 cup frozen English peas, thawed
2 cups biscuit mix
⅔ cup milk
¾ cup (3 ounces) shredded Cheddar cheese
1 (2-ounce) jar diced pimiento, drained

Arrange carrot and pepper strips in a steamer basket; place over boiling water. Cover and steam 8 minutes or until crisp-tender; set aside.

Melt butter in a large heavy saucepan over low heat; add flour, stirring until smooth. Cook, stirring constantly, 1 minute.

Add chicken broth and 1 cup milk; cook over medium heat, stirring constantly, until mixture is thickened and bubbly. Remove from heat. Stir in lemon juice, salt, and pepper. Add chicken, steamed vegetables, and peas, stirring gently. Spoon into a lightly greased 11- x 7- x 1½-inch baking dish.

Combine biscuit mix and ⅔ cup milk, stirring until dry ingredients are moistened. Stir vigorously 30 seconds. Turn out onto a lightly floured surface, and knead 4 or 5 times.

Roll dough into a 12- x 9-inch rectangle. Sprinkle with cheese and pimiento, leaving a ½-inch border; roll up jellyroll fashion, starting with a long side, and turn seam side down. Cut into 1-inch-thick slices, and place over chicken mixture.

Bake at 400° for 30 minutes or until golden brown. **Yield: 6 servings.**

Chicken à la King

6 skinned chicken breast halves
8 fresh mushroom caps, sliced
1 green pepper, chopped
2 tablespoons butter or margarine, melted
¼ cup plus 1 tablespoon butter or margarine
¼ cup plus 1 tablespoon all-purpose flour
5 cups half-and-half, divided
¼ cup dry sherry
4 egg yolks
2 tablespoons sherry
1 tablespoon diced pimiento
1 teaspoon salt
¼ teaspoon white pepper
Diced pimiento (optional)
Cornbread or toast points

Place chicken in a Dutch oven; cover with water. Bring to a boil; cover, reduce heat, and simmer 25 minutes or until chicken is tender.

Remove chicken from broth; reserve broth for another use. Cool, bone, and chop chicken; set aside.

Cook mushrooms and green pepper in 2 tablespoons butter in a skillet until crisp-tender. Drain and set aside.

Melt ¼ cup plus 1 tablespoon butter in a Dutch oven over low heat; add flour, stirring until smooth. Cook 1 minute, stirring constantly.

Add 4½ cups half-and-half and ¼ cup sherry; cook over medium heat, stirring constantly, until mixture is thickened and bubbly.

Beat egg yolks until thick and lemon colored; add remaining ½ cup half-and-half. Gradually stir about one-fourth of hot mixture into yolk mixture; add to remaining hot mixture, stirring constantly.

Add chicken, sautéed vegetables, 2 tablespoons sherry, and next 3 ingredients.

Cook over medium heat, stirring constantly, until mixture is bubbly. Sprinkle additional diced pimiento over top, if desired. Serve over cornbread or toast points. **Yield: 8 servings.**

Roasted and Baked

You'll find great variety in this collection of roasted and baked chicken. From casual Oven-Barbecued Chicken to elegant Rosemary-Riesling Chicken, our choices range from simple to all dressed up.

Herb-Roasted Chicken, Wild Rice-Stuffed Chicken, Creole Chicken

Spicy Almond Chicken, Orange-Pecan Chicken Drummettes, Golden Fruited Chicken

Rice-Stuffed Roasted Chicken, Roast Chicken with Pineapple-Mustard Glaze

Oven-Barbecued Chicken, Crispy Walnut Chicken, Basil Chicken

Herb Garden Chicken (page 191)

Herb-Roasted Chicken

Herb-Roasted Chicken

2 tablespoons butter or margarine, melted
⅓ cup white vinegar
3 tablespoons lemon juice
3 tablespoons chopped fresh tarragon
2 tablespoons olive oil
1 clove garlic, minced
1 teaspoon salt
1 teaspoon freshly ground pepper
1 pound round red potatoes, unpeeled
1 cup diagonally sliced celery
1 (2-ounce) jar sliced pimiento, drained
¼ cup chopped fresh parsley
1 (5- to 6-pound) stewing chicken
Garnishes: fresh parsley, fresh tarragon

Combine first 8 ingredients in a small bowl, mixing well. Set aside.

Cover potatoes with water in saucepan; cook, covered, over medium heat 15 minutes or until tender. Drain potatoes; cool.

Cut potatoes into bite-size pieces. Add celery, pimiento, and ¼ cup parsley, tossing gently. Add 2 tablespoons tarragon-oil mixture, tossing to coat. Set aside.

Remove giblets from cavity of chicken, and reserve for another use. Rinse chicken with cold water; pat dry with paper towels. Fold neck skin over back; secure with a wooden pick. Lift wingtips up and over back, and tuck under chicken.

Stuff chicken with potato mixture. Close cavity with wooden picks or skewers; tie ends of legs together with string or cord. Place chicken, breast side up, on a roasting rack. Brush entire chicken with remaining tarragon-oil mixture.

Insert meat thermometer in meaty part of thigh, making sure it does not touch bone. Bake at 375° until meat thermometer inserted in meaty part of thigh registers 180° (about 2 hours), basting frequently with tarragon-oil mixture. Let cool 10 to 15 minutes before slicing. Place on a serving platter; garnish, if desired. **Yield: 4 servings.**

Herb Garden Chicken

(pictured on page 189)

⅓ cup chopped onion
⅓ cup diced carrot
⅓ cup diced celery
1 tablespoon chopped fresh parsley
3 tablespoons Chablis or other dry white wine
1 (3- to 3½-pound) broiler-fryer
2 cloves garlic, peeled and halved
⅓ cup butter or margarine, melted
⅓ cup Chablis or other dry white wine
2 teaspoons chopped fresh basil
2 teaspoons chopped fresh oregano
2 teaspoons chopped fresh thyme
½ teaspoon salt
¼ teaspoon ground white pepper
Garnishes: basil, oregano, thyme sprigs

Combine first 5 ingredients in a small bowl; toss gently. Set aside.

Remove giblets and neck from chicken; reserve for another use. Rinse chicken with cold water; pat dry with paper towels. Rub skin of chicken with cut side of each garlic clove half.

Stuff chicken with garlic halves and reserved vegetable mixture. Close cavity with skewers; tie ends of legs together with string or cord. Lift wingtips up and over back of chicken, and tuck under chicken.

Place chicken, breast side up, on a rack in a shallow roasting pan.

Combine butter and next 6 ingredients in a small bowl; stir well. Brush chicken generously with butter mixture.

Bake, uncovered, at 375° for 1½ hours or until meat thermometer inserted in meaty part of thigh registers 180°, basting occasionally with any remaining butter mixture. Place chicken on a serving platter. Garnish, if desired. **Yield: 4 servings.**

Wild Rice-Stuffed Chicken

1 (6-ounce) package long grain and wild rice
   mix
3 tablespoons butter or margarine, melted
½ teaspoon dried thyme, crushed
⅛ teaspoon onion powder
1½ cups seedless green grapes, halved
1 (3- to 3½-pound) broiler-fryer
Salt
2 tablespoons soy sauce
2 tablespoons white wine
Garnish: green grapes

Cook rice mix according to package directions. Add butter and next 3 ingredients; stir well.

Season cavity of chicken with salt; place chicken, breast side up, on a rack in a shallow roasting pan. Stuff lightly with half of rice mixture. Close cavity with skewers or wooden picks.

Bake at 375° for 1 hour. Combine soy sauce and wine; baste chicken with soy mixture, and bake 30 more minutes or until meat thermometer inserted in meaty part of thigh registers 180° and in rice mixture registers 165°.

Spoon remaining rice mixture into a lightly greased 1-quart casserole; bake in oven with chicken the last 15 to 20 minutes of baking time.

Place chicken on a serving platter, and spoon rice around it. Garnish with grapes, if desired.
Yield: 4 to 6 servings.

Microwave Directions:

Cook rice mix according to package directions. Add butter and next 3 ingredients; stir well.

Season cavity of chicken with salt, and stuff lightly with half of rice mixture. Close cavity with skewers or wooden picks.

Place chicken, breast side down, on a microwave roasting rack in a 12- x 8- x 2-inch baking dish. Microwave at HIGH 3 minutes. Microwave at MEDIUM (50% power) 20 minutes. Turn chicken, breast side up.

Combine soy sauce and wine; baste chicken with soy mixture. Microwave at MEDIUM 25 to 30 minutes or until instant-read thermometer inserted in meaty part of thigh registers 180° and in rice mixture registers 165°.

Spoon remaining rice mixture into a lightly greased 1-quart casserole. Microwave at HIGH 6 to 8 minutes or until thoroughly heated.

Place chicken on a serving platter, and spoon rice around it. Garnish, if desired.

Rice-Stuffed Roasted Chicken

2½ cups cooked brown rice
1 cup chopped apple
½ cup chopped dried prunes
½ cup chopped dried apricots
¼ cup chopped celery
¼ teaspoon garlic powder
½ teaspoon grated lemon rind
1 teaspoon ground ginger
¼ teaspoon salt
¼ cup butter or margarine, melted
1 (2½- to 3-pound) broiler-fryer
2 tablespoons butter or margarine, melted
¼ teaspoon paprika

Combine first 10 ingredients in a large bowl; mix well.

Place chicken, breast side up, on a rack in a shallow roasting pan. Stuff cavity lightly with brown rice mixture. Close cavity with wooden picks or skewers.

Combine 2 tablespoons melted butter and paprika; brush over chicken. Bake at 375° for 1½ hours or until meat thermometer inserted in meaty part of thigh registers 180° and in rice mixture registers 165°.

Spoon remaining rice mixture into a lightly greased 1-quart casserole; bake in oven with chicken the last 15 to 20 minutes of baking time.

Place chicken on a serving platter, and spoon rice around it. **Yield: 4 servings.**

Creole Chicken

Creole Chicken

1   medium onion, sliced
8   cloves garlic, minced
¼   cup olive oil
½   cup orange juice
⅓   cup fresh lime juice
3   tablespoons Chablis or chicken broth
1   teaspoon sugar
1   teaspoon salt
¼   teaspoon pepper
1   teaspoon white vinegar
1   (3- to 3½-pound) broiler-fryer
Garnishes: lime slices, orange slices, fresh
      cilantro

Cook onion and garlic in olive oil in a medium saucepan over medium-high heat 2 minutes. Add orange juice and next 6 ingredients.

Bring to a boil. Remove from heat; cool. Reserve ¼ cup marinade, and refrigerate it.

Place chicken in a shallow dish or heavy-duty, zip-top plastic bag. Pour remaining marinade over chicken. Cover or seal, and refrigerate 8 hours, turning chicken occasionally.

Remove chicken from marinade; discard marinade. Dry chicken with a paper towel. Place on a lightly greased rack, and place rack in a broiler pan.

Bake at 400° for 15 minutes; reduce heat to 350°, and bake 1 hour or until meat thermometer in thigh registers 180°, basting with reserved ¼ cup marinade. Cover chicken with aluminum foil after 1 hour to prevent excessive browning. Place on a serving platter, and garnish, if desired. **Yield: 4 servings.**

Roast Chicken with Pineapple-Mustard Glaze

Roast Chicken with Pineapple-Mustard Glaze

2 (2½- to 3-pound) broiler-fryers, quartered
4 large cloves garlic, sliced
¼ cup butter or margarine, melted
¼ cup minced fresh parsley
1 teaspoon dried thyme
1 (20-ounce) can sweetened pineapple chunks
⅓ cup honey
¼ cup Dijon mustard
1 tablespoon cornstarch
Hot cooked rice
Garnish: fresh parsley sprigs

Place chicken, skin side up, on a rack in a roasting pan. Place garlic slices under skin of chicken.

Combine butter, parsley, and thyme; brush over chicken. Bake at 350° for 45 minutes.

Drain pineapple, reserving juice. Combine ¼ cup pineapple juice, honey, and mustard. Brush mixture over chicken, and bake 15 to 20 additional minutes or until juices run clear.

Combine cornstarch, remaining honey mixture, pineapple, and remaining juice in a saucepan; cook over medium heat, stirring constantly, until thickened and bubbly. Boil 1 minute, stirring constantly. Serve chicken and sauce over cooked rice. Garnish, if desired. **Yield: 8 servings.**

Spicy Almond Chicken

3 tablespoons butter or margarine
1 (3- to 3½-pound) broiler-fryer, cut up and skinned
1 (14-ounce) jar red currant jelly
½ cup prepared mustard
½ cup slivered almonds
3 tablespoons brown sugar
2 tablespoons lemon juice
½ teaspoon ground cinnamon

Melt butter in a large skillet over medium heat. Add chicken, and cook about 10 minutes or until lightly browned on all sides.

Place chicken in a lightly greased 13- x 9- x 2-inch baking dish.

Add jelly and remaining ingredients to skillet; cook over medium heat until jelly melts, stirring occasionally. Pour over chicken.

Cover and bake at 350° for 30 minutes. Uncover and bake 10 additional minutes or until juices run clear. **Yield: 4 servings.**

Chicken in Foil

1 (2½-pound) broiler-fryer, skinned and quartered
¼ teaspoon garlic salt
⅛ teaspoon paprika
1 large onion, cut into 4 slices
1 large potato, cut into 8 slices
2 carrots, scraped and cut into ¾-inch pieces
2 stalks celery, cut into ¾-inch pieces
1 (4-ounce) can sliced mushrooms, drained
1 (10¾-ounce) can cream of chicken soup, undiluted

Cut 4 (24- x 18-inch) pieces of heavy-duty aluminum foil.

Place a chicken quarter in center of each; sprinkle with garlic salt and paprika. Top evenly with onion and next 4 ingredients.

Spoon soup evenly over each portion. Seal each packet, and place on a 15- x 10- x 1-inch jellyroll pan.

Bake at 400° for 1 hour and 15 minutes or until juices run clear. **Yield: 4 servings.**

Barbecue in the Oven

Southerners can barbecue chicken outdoors almost all year long, but if the weather keeps you indoors, consider Oven-Barbecued Chicken or Barbecued Chicken Legs and Thighs. Once the chicken goes into the oven, neither recipe needs much more attention.

Oven-Barbecued Chicken

½ cup all-purpose flour
1 teaspoon paprika
½ teaspoon salt
⅛ teaspoon pepper
1 (2½- to 3-pound) broiler-fryer, cut up
¼ cup butter or margarine, melted
½ cup ketchup
½ medium onion, chopped
2 tablespoons water
1 tablespoon white vinegar
1 tablespoon Worcestershire sauce
½ teaspoon salt
½ teaspoon chili powder
¼ teaspoon pepper

Combine first 4 ingredients; stir well. Dredge chicken in flour mixture.

Pour butter into a 13- x 9- x 2-inch pan. Arrange chicken in pan, skin side down. Bake at 350° for 30 minutes.

Combine ketchup and remaining ingredients, stirring well.

Remove chicken from oven, and turn; spoon sauce over chicken. Bake 30 additional minutes. **Yield: 4 servings.**

Barbecued Chicken Legs and Thighs

4 chicken legs, skinned
4 chicken thighs, skinned
¾ cup ketchup
⅓ cup firmly packed brown sugar
3 tablespoons Worcestershire sauce
2 tablespoons orange juice
1 tablespoon dried onion flakes
1 tablespoon prepared mustard
½ teaspoon garlic powder

Place chicken in a greased 13- x 9- x 2-inch baking dish; set aside.

Combine ketchup and remaining ingredients, and pour over chicken.

Bake at 350° for 1 hour, turning chicken once. **Yield: 4 to 6 servings.**

Crispy Walnut Chicken

3 cups crispy rice cereal
½ cup walnuts
½ cup butter or margarine, melted
1 teaspoon garlic powder
½ teaspoon salt
½ teaspoon pepper
3 pounds chicken pieces, skinned

Position knife blade in food processor bowl. Add cereal and walnuts; top with cover, and process until finely ground. Set aside.

Combine butter and next 3 ingredients; stir well. Dredge chicken in butter mixture and then in cereal mixture.

Arrange chicken in a 15- x 10- x 1-inch jelly-roll pan; pour any remaining butter mixture over chicken. Bake at 350° for 1 hour or until chicken is tender. **Yield: 6 servings.**

Crispy Walnut Chicken

Orange-Pecan Chicken Drummettes

1 (6-ounce) can frozen orange juice
　　concentrate, thawed and undiluted
3 large eggs, lightly beaten
2 tablespoons water
1 cup all-purpose flour
⅓ cup finely chopped pecans
3 pounds chicken drummettes, skinned
⅓ cup butter or margarine, melted
Red Hot Sauce
Hot cooked rice

Combine first 3 ingredients, and set aside. Combine flour and pecans, and set aside.

Dip drummettes in orange juice mixture; dredge in flour mixture. Pour butter into a 15- x 10- x 1-inch jellyroll pan; arrange drummettes in a single layer. Bake at 375° for 25 minutes.

Spoon Red Hot Sauce over drummettes, and bake 30 additional minutes. Serve over rice. **Yield: 8 to 10 servings.**

Red Hot Sauce

2 cups ketchup
¾ cup firmly packed brown sugar
1 to 2 teaspoons hot sauce

Combine all ingredients, stirring until smooth. **Yield: 2½ cups.**

Cutting Wings into Drummettes

A drummette, the first section and meatier portion of a chicken wing, is cut to resemble a miniature drumstick. If you're short on time, the supermarket butcher can do the trimming and skinning, if desired.

Rosemary-Riesling Chicken

8 skinned chicken breast halves
Salt and pepper
2 tablespoons vegetable oil
¼ cup minced shallots or onion
2 cloves garlic, crushed
1 cup Riesling wine or other dry white wine
⅓ cup chicken broth
1 tablespoon minced fresh rosemary or 1
　　teaspoon dried rosemary
1 cup whipping cream
Hot cooked rice

Sprinkle chicken with salt and pepper. Brown chicken in oil in a large nonstick skillet over medium-high heat.

Remove chicken from skillet, reserving drippings in skillet. Place chicken in a 13- x 9- x 2-inch baking dish.

Add shallots and garlic to drippings in skillet, and cook until tender. Add wine; cook over high heat, deglazing skillet by scraping particles that cling to bottom. Cook until wine is reduced to about ½ cup.

Add chicken broth; stir well. Bring just to a boil; pour over chicken in baking dish. Sprinkle with rosemary.

Cover and bake at 350° for 20 to 30 minutes or until chicken is tender. Place chicken on a serving platter.

Transfer juices and drippings in baking dish to skillet. Simmer until mixture is reduced to about ½ cup.

Add cream; cook over high heat, stirring constantly, 4 minutes or until mixture is thickened. Remove from heat, and pour sauce over chicken. Serve with rice. **Yield: 8 servings.**

Rosemary-Riesling Chicken

Golden Fruited Chicken

Golden Fruited Chicken

6 skinned chicken breast halves
1 teaspoon ground ginger
¼ teaspoon salt
⅛ teaspoon pepper
⅛ teaspoon dried rosemary, crushed
2 cups orange marmalade
¼ cup apple juice
¼ cup orange juice
8 ounces dried apricots (about 1¼ cups)
8 ounces golden raisins (about 1½ cups)
⅓ cup firmly packed brown sugar
Garnishes: rosemary sprigs, orange rind

Place chicken in a lightly greased shallow roasting pan. Combine ginger, salt, pepper, and rosemary; sprinkle over chicken.

Cook marmalade in a saucepan over low heat until softened. Stir in juices; pour over chicken. Bake, uncovered, at 375° for 20 minutes.

Remove from oven; add apricots and raisins to liquid in pan. Sprinkle entire mixture with brown sugar. Bake 30 to 40 additional minutes or until golden brown, basting frequently with pan juices.

Arrange chicken and fruit on a serving platter. Pour some of pan juices over chicken. Garnish, if desired. Serve immediately. **Yield: 6 servings.**

Golden Fruited Chicken Technique

Pour the marmalade and juice mixture over the chicken, coating well.

Baked Lemon Chicken

4 skinned chicken breast halves
⅓ cup lemon juice
½ cup butter or margarine, melted
1 teaspoon garlic powder
1 teaspoon poultry seasoning
½ teaspoon salt
¼ teaspoon pepper
Hot cooked rice (optional)

Place chicken in a lightly greased 11- x 7- x 1½-inch baking dish. Combine remaining ingredients except rice; pour over chicken.

Bake, uncovered, at 350° for 1 hour or until juices run clear, basting frequently. Serve with rice, if desired. **Yield: 4 servings.**

Basil Chicken

½ cup dry white wine
¼ cup olive oil
¼ cup chopped fresh basil
2 cloves garlic, minced
Dash of hot sauce
4 skinned and boned chicken breast halves

Combine first 5 ingredients in a small bowl; reserve ¼ cup marinade and refrigerate. Place chicken in a shallow dish or heavy-duty, zip-top plastic bag. Pour remaining marinade over chicken. Cover or seal, and refrigerate 8 hours, turning chicken occasionally.

Remove chicken from marinade; discard marinade. Place chicken in a greased 8-inch square dish.

Bake at 350° for 10 minutes; turn chicken. Brush with reserved marinade, and bake 10 more minutes or until juices run clear. **Yield: 4 servings.**

Note: Chicken may be grilled 5 inches from hot coals for 5 minutes. Turn chicken; brush with reserved marinade, and grill 5 additional minutes.

Pecan Chicken

4 skinned and boned chicken breast halves
¼ cup honey
¼ cup Dijon mustard
1 cup finely chopped pecans

Place chicken between 2 sheets of heavy-duty plastic wrap; flatten to ¼-inch thickness, using a meat mallet or rolling pin. Set aside.

Combine honey and mustard; spread on both sides of chicken, and dredge chicken in pecans.

Arrange chicken in a lightly greased shallow baking dish. Bake at 350° for 30 minutes or until juices run clear. **Yield: 4 servings.**

Parmesan Chicken

1 large egg, lightly beaten
1 tablespoon milk
½ cup grated Parmesan cheese
¼ cup all-purpose flour
1 teaspoon paprika
½ teaspoon salt
¼ teaspoon pepper
4 skinned chicken breast halves
3 tablespoons butter or margarine, melted

Combine egg and milk in a small bowl; stir well. Combine cheese and next 4 ingredients; stir well.

Dip chicken in egg mixture; dredge in flour mixture. Arrange chicken in an 11- x 7- x 1½-inch baking dish. Drizzle melted butter over top.

Bake at 350° for 40 to 45 minutes or until juices run clear. **Yield: 4 servings.**

Note: Six large chicken thighs may be substituted for chicken breasts. Bake as directed for 35 to 40 minutes.

Crunchy Seasoned Chicken

½ cup sour cream
2 tablespoons lemon juice
1½ tablespoons Worcestershire sauce
1½ teaspoons celery salt
¼ teaspoon garlic powder
¼ teaspoon onion powder
⅛ teaspoon pepper
6 skinned chicken breast halves
1¾ cups saltine cracker crumbs (about 40 crackers)
1½ teaspoons paprika
2 tablespoons butter or margarine, melted
Garnish: lemon slices

Combine first 7 ingredients in a small bowl; mix well. Brush mixture on chicken, coating well.

Place chicken in a 13- x 9- x 2-inch dish; cover and refrigerate 8 hours.

Combine cracker crumbs and paprika; roll chicken in cracker crumb mixture, coating well.

Place chicken in a lightly greased 3-quart casserole. Drizzle with melted butter.

Bake, uncovered, at 350° for 1 hour or until juices run clear. Garnish, if desired. **Yield: 6 servings.**

Roasting & Baking Tips

• To quickly coat chicken before baking, combine dry coating ingredients in a plastic bag. Add a few chicken pieces and shake until they are evenly coated.

• When stuffing a chicken, count on about ¾ cup dressing per pound.

• For safety, do not stuff a chicken until just before cooking.

Versatile Chicken Breasts

Whether on or off the bone, chicken breasts make any occasion special.
Simply sauced, shaped into rollups, or wrapped in pastry—
all offer great taste and eye appeal.

Creamy Almond Chicken, Champagne Chicken, Chicken Véronique

Chicken Breasts Lombardy, Fontina-Baked Chicken, Hearts of Palm Chicken Rolls

Dijon-Herb Chicken, Pesto-Stuffed Chicken Rolls, Chicken in Mushroom Sauce

Chicken Cordon Bleu, Spinach-Stuffed Chicken in Puff Pastry

Dijon Chicken with Pasta (page 207)

Quick Chicken

Vegetable cooking spray
4 skinned and boned chicken breast halves
½ cup water
¼ teaspoon salt

Coat a nonstick skillet with cooking spray; place over medium heat until hot. Add chicken, and cook 12 minutes, turning once.

Add water and salt; cover, and simmer 5 minutes. Drain chicken, and serve with one of the following sauces or toppings. **Yield: 4 servings.**

Rainbow Pepper Topping

1 small onion, sliced and separated into rings
1 clove garlic, minced
2 tablespoons olive oil
1 small sweet red pepper, cut into strips
1 small green pepper, cut into strips
1 small yellow pepper, cut into strips
½ cup dry sherry
1 tablespoon chopped fresh parsley
¼ teaspoon salt
¼ teaspoon pepper
Hot cooked pasta
Garnish: fresh parsley sprig

Cook onion and garlic in olive oil in a skillet over medium heat 1 minute. Add peppers, and cook, stirring constantly, 2 minutes.

Add sherry, parsley, salt, and pepper; simmer 2 minutes. Spoon pepper mixture over chicken and pasta; garnish, if desired. Serve immediately. **Yield: 4 servings.**

Note: For a more formal presentation, serve the chicken breasts and sauce over a curly pasta.

Basil and Cream Sauce

2 tablespoons chopped shallots
¼ cup chopped green onions
1 tablespoon butter or margarine, melted
1 cup half-and-half
⅛ teaspoon pepper
2 teaspoons dried basil or 2 tablespoons chopped fresh basil
2 slices bacon, cooked and crumbled

Cook shallots and green onions in butter in a skillet until crisp-tender. Add half-and-half; simmer 5 minutes or until cream is reduced and slightly thickened.

Stir in pepper, basil, and bacon. Spoon sauce over chicken, and serve immediately. **Yield: ½ cup.**

Chervil-and-Savory Sauce

¼ cup chopped onion
1½ teaspoons butter or margarine, melted
¼ cup dry white wine
½ teaspoon dried chervil
⅛ teaspoon salt
⅛ teaspoon dried savory
⅛ teaspoon pepper
½ cup plain yogurt

Cook onion in butter until crisp-tender. Add wine, and simmer over low heat until wine almost evaporates (about 5 minutes).

Add seasonings; gently stir in yogurt (at room temperature).

Cook over low heat, stirring constantly, until thoroughly heated (do not boil). Spoon sauce over chicken, and serve immediately. **Yield: ⅔ cup.**

Green Peppercorn Butter Sauce

½ cup butter or margarine, melted
2 tablespoons whole green peppercorns,
    drained
2 teaspoons lemon juice
2 teaspoons Worcestershire sauce
1 teaspoon Dijon mustard

Combine all ingredients in a small saucepan. Cook over low heat, stirring gently; do not boil. Spoon sauce over chicken, and serve immediately. **Yield: about ½ cup.**

Country Ham Sauce

½ cup diced cooked country ham
1 clove garlic, minced
1 teaspoon butter or margarine, melted
1 teaspoon white wine Worcestershire sauce
½ teaspoon lemon juice
¼ teaspoon paprika
⅛ teaspoon white pepper
½ cup sour cream

Cook ham and garlic in butter 2 to 3 minutes. Stir in Worcestershire sauce and next 3 ingredients.

Fold in sour cream, and cook over low heat until thoroughly heated (do not boil). Spoon over chicken; serve immediately. **Yield: about ¾ cup.**

Chicken Curry Sauce

½ cup finely chopped onion
2 tablespoons butter or margarine, melted
1 (10¾-ounce) can cream of chicken soup,
    undiluted
½ cup half-and-half
1 tablespoon lemon juice
1 teaspoon curry powder
½ teaspoon ground ginger
Hot cooked rice
Condiments: chutney, toasted coconut, raisins,
    sliced green onions, and peanuts

Cook onion in butter in a saucepan until tender. Stir in soup and next 4 ingredients; cook over medium heat until thoroughly heated, stirring occasionally.

Spoon cooked rice onto a serving plate. Place chicken on rice, and spoon sauce over chicken.

Serve with several of the condiments. **Yield: about 2 cups.**

Team Chicken and Sauces

These six versatile sauces and toppings prove that good food often comes from the easy combination of just a few ingredients. These recipes honor simplicity and transform Quick Chicken into fast and fancy fare.

The sauces that accompany Quick Chicken call for a few carefully chosen ingredients that intensify taste and eye appeal. Follow our easy method of cooking the chicken breasts, prepare your choice of sauce, cook rice or pasta, and have dinner on the table in a flash.

Creamy Almond Chicken

⅔ cup sliced almonds
¼ cup butter or margarine, divided
6 skinned and boned chicken breast halves
⅛ teaspoon salt
⅛ teaspoon pepper
1½ cups whipping cream
1 tablespoon Dijon mustard
2 tablespoons orange marmalade
⅛ teaspoon red pepper
Hot cooked rice

Cook almonds in 1 tablespoon butter in a skillet, stirring constantly, until lightly browned. Set almonds aside.

Place chicken between 2 sheets of heavy-duty plastic wrap; flatten to ¼-inch thickness, using a meat mallet or rolling pin. Sprinkle chicken with salt and pepper.

Melt remaining 3 tablespoons butter in skillet over medium-high heat. Add chicken, and cook about 1 minute on each side or until golden brown.

Reduce heat to medium; add ½ cup almonds, whipping cream, and next 3 ingredients, stirring well.

Cook about 10 minutes or until sauce thickens. Sprinkle with remaining almonds; serve with rice. **Yield: 6 servings.**

Champagne Chicken

2 tablespoons all-purpose flour
½ teaspoon salt
Dash of pepper
4 skinned and boned chicken breast halves
2 tablespoons butter or margarine, melted
1 tablespoon olive oil
¾ cup champagne or dry white wine
¼ cup sliced fresh mushrooms
½ cup whipping cream

Combine flour, salt, and pepper; lightly dredge chicken in flour mixture.

Heat butter and oil in a large skillet; add chicken, and cook about 4 minutes on each side.

Add champagne; cook over medium heat about 12 minutes or until chicken is tender. Remove chicken, and set aside.

Add mushrooms and whipping cream to skillet; cook over low heat, stirring constantly, just until thickened. Add chicken, and cook until heated. **Yield: 4 servings.**

Chicken Véronique

¼ cup all-purpose flour
1 teaspoon salt
½ teaspoon pepper
8 skinned and boned chicken breast halves
½ cup butter or margarine
1 tablespoon currant jelly
⅔ cup Madeira wine
1½ cups seedless green grapes
Garnish: green grapes

Combine flour, salt, and pepper; dredge chicken in flour mixture.

Cook chicken in butter in a large skillet over medium heat until golden brown on each side. Cover, reduce heat, and cook 10 minutes or until chicken is tender.

Remove chicken to serving platter, reserving pan drippings.

Stir jelly and wine into pan drippings; cook until heated. Stir in 1½ cups grapes; cook just until heated. Spoon wine sauce over chicken. Garnish, if desired. **Yield: 8 servings.**

Dijon-Herb Chicken

8 skinned and boned chicken breast halves
¼ cup butter or margarine, melted
¼ cup lemon juice
2 tablespoons Worcestershire sauce
1 tablespoon Dijon mustard
½ teaspoon salt
2 tablespoons chopped fresh chives
2 tablespoons chopped fresh parsley

Cook chicken in butter in a skillet over medium heat 10 minutes on each side. Remove chicken to a serving platter, reserving pan drippings in skillet; keep chicken warm.

Add lemon juice and next 3 ingredients to pan drippings. Bring to a boil, stirring occasionally.

Stir in chives and parsley. Pour over chicken. **Yield: 8 servings.**

Tarragon Chicken

6 skinned chicken breast halves
½ teaspoon salt
¼ teaspoon pepper
1 tablespoon chopped fresh tarragon or
    1 teaspoon dried tarragon
½ cup diced onion
1 tablespoon butter or margarine, melted
1½ cups Chablis or other dry white wine
¼ cup water
⅓ cup whipping cream
2 tablespoons butter or margarine
2 tablespoons all-purpose flour
⅛ teaspoon pepper
Hot cooked rice

Place chicken in a lightly greased 12- x 8- x 2-inch baking dish; sprinkle with salt, ¼ teaspoon pepper, tarragon, and onion. Add 1 tablespoon butter, wine, and water.

Cover and bake at 350° for 1 hour or until chicken is tender. Remove to serving platter, and keep warm.

Pour drippings into a heavy saucepan. Bring to a boil, and cook until drippings are reduced to 1 cup; pour drippings into a small bowl. Add whipping cream; mix well, and set aside.

Melt 2 tablespoons butter in a saucepan over low heat; add flour, stirring until smooth. Cook 1 minute, stirring constantly. Gradually add whipping cream mixture; cook over medium heat, stirring constantly, until mixture is thickened and bubbly.

Stir in ⅛ teaspoon pepper. Serve chicken and gravy over rice. **Yield: 6 servings.**

Dijon Chicken with Pasta

(pictured on page 203)

6 chicken breast halves
¾ cup butter or margarine, softened
⅓ cup sliced green onions
¼ cup chopped fresh parsley
3½ tablespoons Dijon mustard
12 ounces uncooked fettuccine
Garnish: fresh parsley sprigs

Loosen skin from chicken, forming a pocket without detaching skin. Set aside.

Combine butter and next 3 ingredients, mixing well. Place 1½ tablespoons butter mixture under skin of each piece of chicken; reserve remaining mixture.

Place chicken, skin side up, in a lightly greased 13- x 9- x 2-inch baking dish. Bake at 350° for 1 hour, basting occasionally with pan drippings.

Cook fettuccine in a Dutch oven according to package directions; drain and return to pan. Add remaining butter mixture, tossing well. Serve with chicken. Garnish, if desired. **Yield: 6 servings.**

Chicken in Mushroom Sauce

Chicken in Mushroom Sauce

2 tablespoons sliced almonds
6 skinned chicken breast halves
1 cup plus 2 tablespoons Marsala wine, divided
1 (10¾-ounce) can cream of mushroom soup, undiluted
1 (6-ounce) jar mushrooms, drained
½ teaspoon pepper
1 cup (4 ounces) shredded Swiss cheese
⅓ cup herb-seasoned stuffing mix, crushed
¼ cup chopped fresh parsley
1 tablespoon butter or margarine
Paprika

Place almonds in a 9-inch pieplate. Microwave, uncovered, at HIGH 3 to 4 minutes or until toasted, stirring twice. Set almonds aside.

Place chicken in a shallow dish; pour 1 cup wine over chicken. Cover and marinate in refrigerator 1 hour. Drain chicken, discarding wine.

Arrange chicken on a 12-inch round glass platter or in a 13- x 9- x 2-inch baking dish with thickest portions toward the outside.

Combine remaining 2 tablespoons wine, soup, mushrooms, and pepper; spoon over chicken. Cover with wax paper, and microwave at HIGH 16 to 18 minutes, giving dish a half-turn at 5 minute intervals.

Sprinkle with cheese. Microwave, uncovered, at HIGH 1 to 2 minutes or until cheese melts. Combine stuffing mix and parsley; sprinkle over chicken.

Place butter in a 1-cup glass measure. Microwave, uncovered, at HIGH 20 seconds or until melted; drizzle over chicken. Microwave chicken, uncovered, at HIGH 1 to 2 minutes or until instant-read thermometer registers 170°.

Sprinkle with paprika. Top with reserved toasted almonds. **Yield: 6 servings.**

Chicken in Mushroom Sauce Techniques

Sliced almonds will toast slowly in the microwave. Be sure to stir them occasionally for even browning.

Arrange chicken breasts with the thick, meaty portions to the outside of a large-rimmed platter or a baking dish.

Top the chicken with a mixture of stuffing mix and parsley. Sprinkle with paprika and almonds before serving.

Chicken Breasts Lombardy

Chicken Breasts Lombardy

1 cup sliced fresh mushrooms
2 tablespoons butter or margarine, melted
8 skinned and boned chicken breast halves
⅓ cup all-purpose flour
⅓ cup butter or margarine, melted and divided
½ cup Marsala wine
⅓ cup chicken broth
¼ teaspoon salt
⅛ teaspoon pepper
½ cup (2 ounces) shredded fontina or
   mozzarella cheese
½ cup grated Parmesan cheese
¼ cup chopped green onions

Cook mushrooms in 2 tablespoons butter in a large skillet, stirring constantly, until tender. Remove from heat, and set mushrooms aside.

Cut each chicken breast half in half lengthwise. Place chicken between 2 sheets of heavy-duty plastic wrap; flatten to ⅛-inch thickness, using a meat mallet or rolling pin.

Dredge chicken lightly in flour. Place 5 or 6 pieces of chicken in 1 to 2 tablespoons butter in large skillet; cook over medium heat 3 to 4 minutes on each side or until golden.

Place chicken in a lightly greased 13- x 9- x 2-inch baking dish, overlapping edges. Repeat procedure with remaining chicken and butter. Reserve pan drippings in skillet. Sprinkle reserved mushrooms over chicken.

Add wine and broth to reserved pan drippings in skillet. Bring to a boil; reduce heat, and simmer, uncovered, 8 minutes, stirring occasionally. Stir in salt and pepper. Pour sauce evenly over chicken.

Combine cheeses and green onions; sprinkle over chicken. Bake, uncovered, at 375° for 20 minutes. Broil 6 inches from heat (with electric oven door partially opened) 1 to 2 minutes or until lightly browned. **Yield: 6 to 8 servings.**

Note: ⅓ cup white wine and 2 tablespoons brandy may be substituted for Marsala wine.

Fontina-Baked Chicken

½ cup all-purpose flour
¼ teaspoon dried oregano
¼ teaspoon pepper
¼ teaspoon paprika
¼ teaspoon poultry seasoning
⅛ teaspoon red pepper
2 tablespoons Parmesan cheese
6 skinned and boned chicken breast halves
2 large eggs, beaten
½ cup butter or margarine, divided
½ pound fresh mushrooms, halved
½ pound cooked ham, diced
2 cups (8 ounces) shredded fontina cheese,
   divided

Combine first 7 ingredients, mixing well. Dip chicken in beaten egg; dredge in flour mixture.

Melt ¼ cup butter in a large skillet over medium heat. Add chicken, and cook about 8 minutes on each side or until golden brown.

Remove chicken, and drain on paper towels. Place in a greased 12- x 8- x 2-inch baking dish or individual au gratin dishes.

Melt remaining ¼ cup butter in skillet. Cook mushrooms in butter, stirring constantly, 4 minutes or until tender; drain. Layer mushrooms and ham over chicken. Sprinkle with 1 cup fontina cheese.

Cover and bake at 350° for 35 minutes. Uncover; sprinkle with remaining 1 cup cheese, and bake 5 additional minutes. **Yield: 6 servings.**

Prize-Winning Chicken

Chicken Breasts Lombardy has long been a favorite at our *Southern Living* luncheons, and we've recommended it to many readers requesting an entrée for a special occasion.

Roquefort Chicken

1 cup fresh sourdough breadcrumbs
1 (1½-ounce) can grated Parmesan cheese
¼ teaspoon salt
¼ teaspoon freshly ground pepper
1¼ teaspoons dried thyme
3 tablespoons butter or margarine, melted
3 tablespoons olive oil
¼ cup milk
1 tablespoon white wine Worcestershire sauce
8 skinned and boned chicken breast halves
Roquefort Sauce

Combine first 5 ingredients in a pieplate. Combine butter, oil, milk, and Worcestershire sauce. Dip chicken in milk mixture, and dredge in crumb mixture.

Arrange chicken in a lightly greased 15- x 10- x 1-inch jellyroll pan. Bake at 350° for 30 to 35 minutes or until tender. Serve with Roquefort Sauce drizzled over chicken. **Yield: 8 servings.**

Roquefort Sauce

1 shallot, chopped
1 stalk celery with leaves, chopped
2 tablespoons butter or margarine, melted
½ cup white wine
1 (10¾-ounce) can condensed chicken broth, undiluted
1 cup whipping cream
2 tablespoons crumbled Roquefort cheese
1 tablespoon chopped fresh chives

Cook shallot and celery in butter over medium heat in a medium saucepan, stirring constantly, until tender.

Add wine and chicken broth. Bring to a boil, and cook over medium heat, stirring frequently, until liquid is reduced to about 1 cup (about 15 minutes). Strain.

Return broth mixture to saucepan. Add whipping cream, and return to a boil; reduce heat and simmer about 15 minutes or until mixture is reduced to about 1 cup, stirring frequently.

Remove from heat; add cheese, and stir until cheese melts. Stir in chopped chives. **Yield: 1 cup.**

Chicken Cordon Bleu

4 large chicken breast halves
4 (1-ounce) slices cooked ham
4 (1-ounce) slices Swiss or Gruyère cheese
Salt and pepper
2 tablespoons butter or margarine, melted
1 (10¾-ounce) can mushroom soup, undiluted
1 (4-ounce) can sliced mushrooms, drained
¼ teaspoon garlic powder
⅛ teaspoon curry powder
¼ cup Chablis or other dry white wine
½ cup sour cream
Whole wheat toast points
Garnish: fresh parsley sprigs

Loosen skin from chicken, forming a pocket without detaching skin. Arrange 1 slice each of ham and cheese under skin of each breast half; secure skin with wooden picks.

Sprinkle chicken with salt and pepper; place in an ungreased baking dish.

Bake, uncovered, at 375° for 30 to 40 minutes or until meat thermometer registers 170°, basting with melted butter after 20 minutes.

Remove chicken from drippings; set aside, and keep warm. Pour pan drippings into a skillet, and cook over high heat until liquid is reduced to about ¼ cup.

Add soup, mushrooms, garlic powder, and curry powder; stir well. Cook over medium heat until thoroughly heated. Stir in wine and sour cream. Remove from heat.

Remove wooden picks from chicken. Serve mushroom sauce with chicken over whole wheat toast points. Garnish, if desired. **Yield: 4 servings.**

Chicken Cordon Bleu

Hearts of Palm Chicken Rolls

12 skinned and boned chicken breast halves
½ teaspoon salt
½ teaspoon white pepper
¼ cup butter or margarine, melted
2 (14.4-ounce) cans hearts of palm, drained
Béarnaise Sauce
Garnish: fresh tarragon sprigs

Place chicken between 2 sheets of heavy-duty plastic wrap; flatten to ¼-inch thickness, using a meat mallet or rolling pin. Sprinkle with salt and pepper; brush with butter.

Roll each piece of chicken around a heart of palm. Place seam side down on a lightly greased 15- x 10- x 1-inch jellyroll pan. Brush chicken rolls with remaining butter.

Cover and bake at 350° for 1 hour. Spoon Béarnaise Sauce over chicken rolls. Garnish, if desired. **Yield: 12 servings.**

Béarnaise Sauce

3 tablespoons white wine vinegar
2 teaspoons minced shallots
1½ teaspoons chopped fresh tarragon
        or ½ teaspoon dried tarragon
3 egg yolks
⅛ teaspoon salt
⅛ teaspoon red pepper
2 tablespoons lemon juice
½ cup butter or margarine

Combine vinegar and shallots in a small saucepan; bring to a boil over medium heat. Reduce heat, and simmer until half of liquid evaporates.

Strain vinegar mixture, reserving liquid; discard solids. Cool slightly; stir in tarragon. Set aside.

Beat egg yolks, salt, and pepper in top of a double boiler; add lemon juice, stirring constantly.

Add one-third of butter to egg mixture; cook over hot (not boiling) water, stirring constantly, until butter melts.

Add another one-third of butter, stirring constantly. As sauce thickens, stir in remaining butter; cook until thickened. Immediately remove from heat. Add vinegar mixture to sauce, stirring well. Serve immediately. **Yield: ¾ cup.**

Pesto-Stuffed Chicken Rolls

6 large skinned and boned chicken breast halves
¼ teaspoon salt
¼ teaspoon pepper
1 (3-ounce) package cream cheese, softened
¼ cup commercial pesto
½ cup finely chopped sweet red pepper
¾ cup corn flake crumbs
½ teaspoon paprika
Vegetable cooking spray
Garnish: fresh basil sprigs

Place chicken between 2 sheets of heavy-duty plastic wrap; flatten to ¼-inch thickness, using a meat mallet or rolling pin. Sprinkle with salt and pepper; set aside.

Combine cream cheese, pesto, and sweet red pepper in a small bowl, stirring with a fork until smooth. Spread 2 tablespoons over each chicken breast; roll up lengthwise, securing with wooden picks.

Combine corn flake crumbs and paprika; dredge chicken rolls in crumb mixture. Place in an 11- x 7- x 1½-inch baking dish coated with cooking spray.

Bake, uncovered, at 350° for 35 minutes; let stand 10 minutes. Remove wooden picks, and slice into 1-inch rounds. (An electric knife works best.) Garnish, if desired. **Yield: 6 servings.**

Note: Chicken Rolls may be prepared ahead. Prepare as directed above; do not bake. Cover and refrigerate overnight. Remove from refrigerator; let stand, covered, 30 minutes. Uncover and bake as directed above.

Pesto-Stuffed Chicken Rolls

Chicken Rollups

1 (6-ounce) package wild rice-and-mushroom
    stuffing mix
6 large skinned and boned chicken breast halves
¼ teaspoon pepper
2 tablespoons butter or margarine, melted
2 tablespoons Dijon mustard
1¼ cups ground pecans
3 tablespoons vegetable oil
¾ cup chicken broth
¾ cup sour cream

Prepare wild rice-and-mushroom stuffing mix according to package directions. Set aside.

Place each chicken breast between 2 sheets of heavy-duty plastic wrap. Flatten to ¼-inch thickness, using a meat mallet or rolling pin.

Divide stuffing mixture evenly, and place on top of each chicken breast; fold sides of chicken breast over stuffing, roll up, and secure with wooden picks. Sprinkle with pepper.

Combine butter and mustard in a small bowl; stir well. Brush mustard mixture over chicken, completely coating all sides; roll in pecans.

Brown chicken on all sides in hot oil in skillet; drain and discard pan drippings, retaining chicken in skillet. Add chicken broth to skillet; cover, reduce heat, and simmer 20 minutes.

Place chicken on a serving dish; keep warm. Stir sour cream into broth in skillet; cook over low heat, stirring constantly, until heated. Spoon over chicken. **Yield: 6 servings.**

Chicken Alouette

1 (17½-ounce) package frozen puff pastry
    sheets, thawed
2 teaspoons all-purpose flour
1 (4-ounce) container garlic-and-spice-
    flavored Alouette cheese
6 skinned and boned chicken breast halves
½ teaspoon salt
⅛ teaspoon pepper
1 large egg, beaten
1 tablespoon water
Garnish: kale leaves

Unfold pastry sheets, and sprinkle each with 1 teaspoon flour. Roll each sheet into a 14- x 12-inch rectangle on a lightly floured surface.

Cut one sheet into 4 (7- x 6-inch) rectangles; cut second sheet into 2 (7- x 6-inch) rectangles and 1 (14- x 6-inch) rectangle.

Set large rectangle aside. Shape each small rectangle into an oval by trimming off corners. Spread pastry ovals evenly with cheese.

Sprinkle chicken with salt and pepper, and place one piece in center of each pastry oval. Lightly moisten pastry edges with water. Fold ends over chicken; fold sides over, and press to seal.

Place bundles, seam side down, on a lightly greased baking sheet.

Cut large pastry rectangle into 24 (14- x ¼-inch) strips. Twist 2 strips together, and place crosswise over a chicken bundle, trimming and reserving excess braid. Twist 2 additional strips, and place lengthwise over bundle, trimming and tucking ends under. Repeat procedure with remaining strips and bundles.

Cover and refrigerate up to 2 hours, if desired.

Combine egg and 1 tablespoon water; brush over pastry bundles. Bake at 400° on lower oven rack 25 minutes or until bundles are golden brown. Garnish, if desired. **Yield: 6 servings.**

Note: ½ cup chives-and-onion-flavored cream cheese may be substituted for Alouette cheese.

Chicken Alouette

Spinach-Stuffed Chicken in Puff Pastry

Spinach-Stuffed Chicken in Puff Pastry

4 skinned and boned chicken breast halves
½ teaspoon salt
½ teaspoon pepper
1 (10-ounce) package frozen spinach, thawed and drained
¾ cup (3 ounces) shredded Gruyère or Swiss cheese
½ cup finely chopped prosciutto or cooked ham (about 3 ounces)
¼ teaspoon salt
⅛ teaspoon pepper
Dash of ground nutmeg
1 (17¼-ounce) package frozen puff pastry sheets, thawed
1 large egg, lightly beaten
1 teaspoon water
1 (0.9-ounce) package béarnaise sauce mix

Place chicken between two sheets of heavy-duty plastic wrap; flatten to ⅛-inch thickness, using a meat mallet or rolling pin. Sprinkle chicken with ½ teaspoon each of salt and pepper.

Combine spinach and next 5 ingredients; shape into 4 balls, placing 1 in center of each chicken breast. Fold chicken over spinach.

Roll each sheet of puff pastry into a 12-inch square. Cut a 1-inch strip from side of each sheet, setting aside for garnish. Cut each sheet in half, making 4 (5½- x 6-inch) rectangles.

Place stuffed chicken breasts in center of pastry rectangles; fold sides over chicken. Combine egg and water, and brush on pastry seams, pinching to seal. Place seam side down on a lightly greased 15- x 10- x 1-inch jellyroll pan.

Cut decorative stems and leaves or desired shapes from reserved pastry strips. Brush back of cutouts with egg mixture, and arrange on chicken bundles.

Chill bundles and remaining egg mixture 1 hour. Brush bundles with egg mixture, and bake at 400° for 20 to 25 minutes or until golden.

Prepare béarnaise sauce according to package directions. Spoon 2 tablespoons sauce in each plate; top with bundles. **Yield: 4 servings.**

Spinach-Stuffed Chicken in Puff Pastry Techniques

Flatten chicken with a meat mallet; form spinach mixture into balls, and place in center of each breast.

Fold chicken over spinach; invert onto a cut rectangle of pastry. Fold ends of pastry over chicken.

Brush seams with egg mixture; press edges to seal. Make cutouts from reserved pastry; apply to bundles.

Chicken Breasts in Phyllo Pastry

1 cup mayonnaise or salad dressing
⅔ cup chopped green onions
3½ tablespoons fresh lemon juice
1 small clove garlic, minced
¾ teaspoon dried tarragon
8 skinned and boned chicken breast halves
¼ teaspoon salt
⅛ teaspoon pepper
16 sheets commercial frozen phyllo pastry, thawed
Butter-flavored vegetable cooking spray
3½ tablespoons grated Parmesan cheese

Combine first 5 ingredients in a small bowl; set aside.

Sprinkle chicken with salt and pepper. Place one sheet of phyllo pastry on a sheet of plastic wrap; spray evenly with cooking spray. Place another sheet of phyllo on top; spray with cooking spray.

Spread about 3 tablespoons mayonnaise mixture on both sides of 1 chicken breast; place breast diagonally in one corner of stacked pastry sheets. Fold corner over breast; fold sides over, and carefully roll up in pastry. Place seam side down in an ungreased 15- x 10- x 1-inch jellyroll pan.

Repeat procedure with remaining phyllo, cooking spray, mayonnaise mixture, and chicken breasts. Spray tops of pastry bundles with cooking spray; sprinkle with Parmesan cheese.

Bake at 350° for 40 to 45 minutes or until chicken breasts are done. Serve immediately.
Yield: 8 servings.

Note: Melted butter or margarine may be substituted for butter-flavored cooking spray.

Chicken and Vegetables en Papillote

6 skinned and boned chicken breast halves
¼ cup orange juice
¼ cup teriyaki sauce
1½ tablespoons sesame oil
½ teaspoon grated fresh gingerroot
2 to 3 tablespoons vegetable oil
6 green onions, chopped
2 medium carrots, cut into very thin strips
2 small yellow squash, thinly sliced

Place chicken between 2 sheets of heavy-duty plastic wrap. Flatten chicken to ¼-inch thickness, using a meat mallet or rolling pin. Combine orange juice and next 3 ingredients; reserve 3 tablespoons marinade, and refrigerate.

Place chicken in a shallow dish; pour remaining marinade over chicken. Cover and refrigerate 30 minutes, turning occasionally.

Cut six 15- x 12-inch pieces parchment paper or aluminum foil; fold in half lengthwise, creasing firmly. Trim each into a large heart shape. Place hearts on baking sheets. Brush one side of each heart with vegetable oil, leaving edges ungreased.

Remove chicken from marinade, and discard marinade; place a chicken breast half on one half of each parchment heart near the crease.

Arrange vegetables over chicken. Spoon reserved 3 tablespoons marinade over vegetables.

Fold over remaining halves of parchment hearts. Starting with rounded edge of each heart, pleat and crimp edges together to make a seal. Twist end tightly to seal.

Bake at 350° for 20 minutes or until bags are puffed and lightly browned and chicken is done.
Yield: 6 servings.

Chicken Combos

Ways to combine chicken with other ingredients are limited only by your imagination. To get you started creating your own combinations, we've included some of our tastiest "chicken and …" dishes.

Chicken Divan Casserole, Creole Chicken and Grits, Chicken Pilaf

Tipsy Chicken and Dressing, Chicken Fettuccine Supreme, Country Captain Chicken

Creamy Chicken-and-Ham Medley, Shrimp-and-Chicken Casserole, Chicken Curry

Chicken-Wild Rice Casserole, Ginger-Nut Chicken, Chicken Lasagna

Creamy Chicken-and-Ham Medley (page 223)

Chicken Divan Casserole

Chicken Divan Casserole

4 skinned chicken breast halves
1 fresh rosemary sprig
½ teaspoon salt
¼ teaspoon pepper
2 tablespoons butter or margarine
¼ cup all-purpose flour
1 cup milk
1 egg yolk, beaten
1 cup sour cream
½ cup mayonnaise
½ teaspoon grated lemon rind
2 tablespoons lemon juice
½ teaspoon salt
¼ to ½ teaspoon curry powder
2 (10-ounce) packages frozen broccoli spears,
    thawed and drained
⅓ cup grated Parmesan cheese
Paprika

Place first 4 ingredients in a large saucepan; add water to cover. Bring to a boil. Cover, reduce heat, and simmer 15 to 20 minutes or until chicken is tender. Drain, reserving ½ cup broth. Discard rosemary.

Let chicken cool slightly. Bone and chop chicken; set aside.

Melt butter in a heavy saucepan over low heat; add flour, stirring until smooth. Cook 1 minute, stirring constantly. Gradually add milk and reserved broth; cook over medium heat, stirring constantly, until thickened and bubbly.

Stir one-fourth of hot mixture into egg yolk; add to remaining hot mixture and cook, stirring constantly, 1 minute. Remove from heat; stir in sour cream and next 5 ingredients.

Layer half each of broccoli, chicken, and sauce in a greased 2-quart casserole. Repeat layers. Sprinkle with Parmesan cheese.

Bake, uncovered, at 350° for 30 to 35 minutes. Sprinkle with paprika. **Yield: 4 to 6 servings.**

Creamy Chicken-and-Ham Medley

(pictured on page 221)

1 tablespoon butter or margarine
½ cup sliced fresh mushrooms
⅓ cup butter or margarine
⅓ cup all-purpose flour
2½ to 3 cups milk, divided
1 cup whipping cream
1 cup freshly grated Parmesan cheese
½ teaspoon salt
¼ teaspoon pepper
¼ teaspoon ground nutmeg
Dash of ground red pepper
2 cups chopped cooked chicken
2 cups chopped cooked ham
2 (10-ounce) packages frozen puff pastry
    shells, baked
Paprika

Melt 1 tablespoon butter in a large saucepan over medium heat; add mushrooms, and cook, stirring constantly, until tender. Remove from saucepan; set aside.

Melt ⅓ cup butter in saucepan over low heat; add flour, stirring until smooth. Cook, stirring constantly, 1 minute. Gradually add 2½ cups milk; cook over medium heat, stirring constantly, until thickened and bubbly.

Stir in whipping cream and next 5 ingredients. Cook, stirring constantly, until cheese melts and mixture is smooth; stir in chicken, ham, and reserved mushrooms.

Add enough of remaining ½ cup milk for a thinner consistency, if desired. To serve, spoon into baked shells, and sprinkle with paprika. **Yield: 12 servings.**

Note: Creamy Chicken-and-Ham Medley may be served over hot, cooked angel hair pasta instead of pastry. Sprinkle with freshly grated Parmesan cheese, if desired.

Shrimp-and-Chicken Casserole

1 (2½- to 3-pound) broiler-fryer
1 teaspoon salt
4 cups water
1 pound unpeeled, medium-size fresh shrimp
2 (16-ounce) packages frozen broccoli cuts, thawed and well drained
1 cup mayonnaise or salad dressing
1 (10¾-ounce) can cream of chicken soup, undiluted
1 (10¾-ounce) can cream of celery soup, undiluted
3 tablespoons lemon juice
¼ teaspoon white pepper
1 cup (4 ounces) shredded Cheddar cheese
½ cup soft breadcrumbs
1 tablespoon butter or margarine, melted
Paprika
Garnishes: shrimp and fresh parsley sprigs

Combine chicken and salt in a Dutch oven; add enough water to cover, and bring to a boil. Cover, reduce heat, and simmer 45 minutes or until chicken is tender. Drain; let chicken cool slightly. Bone chicken; cut into bite-size pieces, and set aside.

Bring 4 cups water to a boil; add shrimp, and cook 3 to 5 minutes. Drain; rinse with cold water. Peel and devein shrimp. Set 3 shrimp aside for garnish, if desired.

Spread broccoli evenly in a lightly greased 13- x 9- x 2-inch baking dish; set aside. Combine mayonnaise and next 4 ingredients; spread one-third over broccoli. Set aside remaining sauce.

Combine chicken and shrimp; spread evenly over casserole, and top with remaining sauce. Cover and chill up to 8 hours.

Remove casserole from refrigerator, and let stand at room temperature 30 minutes. Bake, covered, at 350° for 30 minutes. Uncover; sprinkle with cheese.

Combine breadcrumbs and butter; sprinkle over cheese. Bake 15 additional minutes or until casserole is hot and bubbly. Sprinkle with paprika. Garnish, if desired. **Yield: 10 servings.**

Note: Casserole may be assembled and baked immediately. Six chicken breast halves may be substituted for broiler-fryer.

Tipsy Chicken and Dressing

1 (8-ounce) package cornbread stuffing mix
2 large eggs
3 slices bread, crumbled
1 (14½-ounce) can chicken broth, undiluted
1 small onion, finely chopped
1 stalk celery, finely chopped
1 (14-ounce) can artichoke hearts, drained and quartered
8 skinned and boned chicken breast halves
8 (1-ounce) slices Swiss cheese
1 (10¾-ounce) can cream of celery soup, undiluted
1 cup white wine
½ teaspoon dried basil
4 mushrooms, sliced
¼ cup grated Parmesan cheese
2 tablespoons minced parsley
Garnish: fresh parsley sprigs

Combine first 6 ingredients; mix well. Divide mixture among 8 lightly greased individual 2-cup casserole dishes. Place 3 artichoke quarters in middle of dressing mixture in each dish; place chicken over artichokes. Top with Swiss cheese.

Combine soup, wine, and basil; pour over chicken. Top with mushrooms, Parmesan cheese, and minced parsley.

Cover and bake at 350° for 40 minutes. Uncover and bake 10 additional minutes. Garnish, if desired. **Yield: 8 servings.**

Creole Chicken and Grits

½ cup all-purpose flour
½ cup plus 3 tablespoons vegetable oil, divided
1 medium onion, chopped
1 medium-size green pepper, chopped
2 cloves garlic, minced
1 (10¾-ounce) can chicken broth, undiluted
1 (8-ounce) can tomato sauce
3 bay leaves
3 tablespoons all-purpose flour
1 teaspoon garlic salt
1 teaspoon ground red pepper
1 teaspoon dried oregano
1 teaspoon pepper
½ teaspoon dried thyme
2 pounds skinned and boned chicken breast
   halves, cut into bite-size pieces
Garlic-Cheese Grits

Combine ½ cup flour and ½ cup oil in a Dutch oven. Cook over medium-low heat, stirring constantly, 20 to 30 minutes or until roux is caramel-colored.

Add onion, green pepper, and garlic; cook, stirring constantly, 4 minutes. Add chicken broth, tomato sauce, and bay leaves. Cover, reduce heat, and simmer 20 minutes.

Combine 3 tablespoons flour and next 5 ingredients; dredge chicken in flour mixture.

Heat remaining 3 tablespoons oil in a large nonstick skillet over medium heat. Brown chicken on all sides in skillet in batches. Remove chicken from skillet; add to Dutch oven. Cover and simmer over low heat 5 minutes. Remove bay leaves. Serve over Garlic-Cheese Grits. **Yield: 8 servings.**

Garlic-Cheese Grits

7 cups water
1 teaspoon salt
2 cups quick-cooking grits, uncooked
2 (6-ounce) rolls process cheese food with garlic

Bring water to a boil in a Dutch oven; stir in salt and grits. Return mixture to a boil; reduce heat, and simmer 4 minutes, stirring occasionally. Add cheese, stirring until cheese melts.

Remove from heat. Press grits firmly into a greased 8-cup ring mold. Let stand 10 to 15 minutes. Unmold onto a serving plate. **Yield: 8 cups.**

Chicken Pilaf

½ cup all-purpose flour
1 teaspoon paprika
½ teaspoon salt
Dash of pepper
8 skinned and boned chicken breast halves
3 tablespoons butter or margarine
2 cups boiling water
2 chicken-flavored bouillon cubes
4 medium carrots, diced
1 medium onion, chopped
1 cup uncooked regular rice
½ teaspoon dried thyme

Combine first 4 ingredients. Cut each chicken breast half in half lengthwise; dredge in flour mixture.

Melt butter over medium heat in a large, heavy ovenproof skillet; add chicken, and brown on both sides. Remove chicken from skillet, and set aside. Reserve drippings in skillet.

Combine boiling water and bouillon cubes, stirring until bouillon dissolves.

Cook carrot and onion in reserved drippings in skillet until tender. Add rice; cook over low heat until lightly browned. Add bouillon mixture and thyme, stirring well. Arrange chicken over rice mixture.

Cover and bake at 350° for 1 hour. **Yield: 8 servings.**

Country Captain Chicken

Country Captain Chicken

½ cup all-purpose flour
1 teaspoon salt
½ teaspoon pepper
1 (2½- to 3-pound) broiler-fryer, cut up
Vegetable oil
2 medium onions, chopped
2 medium-size green peppers, chopped
¼ cup chopped celery
1 clove garlic, minced
2 (16-ounce) cans whole tomatoes, undrained
    and chopped
¼ cup currants
2 teaspoons curry powder
¾ teaspoon salt
½ teaspoon ground white pepper
½ teaspoon ground thyme
3 cups hot cooked rice
1½ tablespoons minced fresh parsley
3 tablespoons cornstarch
¼ cup cold water
¼ cup sliced natural almonds, toasted

Combine first 3 ingredients; stir well. Dredge chicken in flour mixture.

Pour oil to a depth of ½ inch into a large heavy skillet. Fry chicken in hot oil (350°) until browned.

Arrange chicken in a 13- x 9- x 2-inch baking dish; set aside. Drain pan drippings, reserving 2 tablespoons drippings in skillet.

Cook onion, green pepper, celery, and garlic in pan drippings until vegetables are tender. Add tomatoes and next 5 ingredients; stir well. Spoon sauce over chicken in baking dish.

Cover and bake at 350° for 40 to 50 minutes or until chicken is tender.

Transfer chicken to a large serving platter with a slotted spoon, reserving sauce in baking dish. Combine rice and parsley, tossing gently to combine; spoon around chicken. Set aside, and keep warm.

Transfer sauce to a medium saucepan. Combine cornstarch and water, stirring until smooth; stir into sauce. Bring sauce to a boil; cook, stirring constantly, 1 minute or until slightly thickened. Spoon sauce over chicken. Sprinkle almonds over chicken. Serve immediately. **Yield: 4 servings.**

Chicken-Wild Rice Casserole

1 (6-ounce) package long grain and wild rice
¼ cup butter or margarine
¼ cup all-purpose flour
½ teaspoon salt
¼ teaspoon pepper
1 (13-ounce) can evaporated milk
½ cup chicken broth
2½ cups chopped cooked chicken
1 (3-ounce) can sliced mushrooms, drained
1 (14-ounce) can artichoke hearts, drained
    and chopped
¼ cup chopped pimiento (optional)
¼ cup slivered almonds, lightly toasted

Prepare rice according to package directions; set aside.

Melt butter in a heavy saucepan over low heat; add flour, salt, and pepper, stirring until smooth. Cook, stirring constantly, 1 minute. Gradually add milk and broth; cook over medium heat, stirring constantly, until thickened and bubbly.

Combine sauce, rice, chicken, mushrooms, artichokes, and, if desired, pimiento. Spoon into a lightly greased 2-quart casserole. Sprinkle with almonds.

Bake, uncovered, at 350° for 30 to 35 minutes or until thoroughly heated. **Yield: 6 servings.**

Note: To make ahead, prepare as directed above, but do not bake. Cover and refrigerate up to 8 hours. Let stand, covered, at room temperature 30 minutes. Uncover and bake as directed.

Chicken Curry

6 skinned chicken breast halves
2 cloves garlic
2 bay leaves
4 whole peppercorns
1 teaspoon salt
1 carrot, sliced
1 onion, sliced
½ cup chopped celery
1 apple, peeled, cored, and chopped
3 tablespoons butter or margarine, melted
1½ tablespoons curry powder
½ teaspoon chili powder
3 tablespoons all-purpose flour
¼ teaspoon ground mace
¼ teaspoon ground allspice
¼ teaspoon ground nutmeg
¼ teaspoon ground cinnamon
¼ teaspoon ground cloves
Hot cooked rice
Condiments: flaked coconut, chopped peanuts,
    chopped green onions, chutney, raisins,
    cooked and crumbled bacon
Garnish: celery leaves

Combine first 5 ingredients in a Dutch oven; add water to cover. Bring to a boil over medium heat; cover, reduce heat, and simmer 35 to 40 minutes or until chicken is tender. Drain; discard peppercorns, bay leaves, and garlic. Reserve 2 cups broth. Bone chicken; cut into bite-size pieces.

Cook carrot and next 3 ingredients in butter in a Dutch oven over medium heat, stirring constantly, 10 minutes or until tender. Add curry powder and chili powder, and cook 5 minutes, stirring occasionally.

Stir in ¾ cup reserved broth. Place apple mixture in container of an electric blender, and process until smooth. Add flour, and process until well blended.

Return mixture to Dutch oven, and cook until thickened. Gradually add 1¼ cups reserved chicken broth and cook, stirring constantly, 5 minutes.

Add mace and next 4 ingredients; gently stir in chicken.

Serve over rice with assorted condiments. Garnish, if desired. **Yield: 6 servings.**

Ginger-Nut Chicken

1 tablespoon butter or margarine
2 skinned and boned chicken breast halves
1½ cups broccoli flowerets
½ cup green onions, cut into 1-inch pieces
½ cup celery, cut into 1-inch pieces
3 (⅛-inch) slices fresh gingerroot
2 tablespoons cornstarch
½ cup water, divided
1 tablespoon soy sauce
¼ teaspoon lemon-pepper seasoning
⅛ teaspoon garlic salt
⅓ cup dry-roasted peanuts
Hot cooked rice

Place butter in a 1½-quart casserole. Microwave at HIGH 45 seconds or until melted.

Cut chicken into bite-size pieces. Add to casserole, and coat with butter. Cover and microwave at HIGH 4 minutes, stirring after 2 minutes.

Add broccoli and next 3 ingredients. Microwave at HIGH 2 minutes.

Combine cornstarch and ¼ cup water in a glass measuring cup, stirring well. Add remaining ¼ cup water, soy sauce, lemon-pepper seasoning, and garlic salt; stir well. Pour cornstarch mixture over chicken and vegetables.

Cover and microwave at HIGH 2 to 3 minutes or until sauce is slightly thickened; stir once. Stir in peanuts. Remove ginger, and serve over rice. **Yield: 2 to 3 servings.**

Ginger-Nut Chicken

Chicken Cacciatore

¼ cup all-purpose flour
½ teaspoon salt
½ teaspoon pepper
8 skinned and boned chicken breast halves
¼ cup olive oil
1 large onion, chopped
3 or 4 cloves garlic, minced
½ pound fresh mushrooms, sliced
2 (16-ounce) cans whole tomatoes, undrained and quartered
1 (4-ounce) jar whole pimientos, undrained and sliced
3 bay leaves
½ cup sweet vermouth
1 teaspoon dried thyme
1 teaspoon dried oregano
½ teaspoon salt
¼ teaspoon pepper
2 medium-size green peppers, seeded and cut into strips
Hot cooked spaghetti

Combine first 3 ingredients; dredge chicken in flour mixture. Brown chicken in hot oil in a Dutch oven over medium-high heat. Remove chicken from Dutch oven, reserving drippings; drain chicken on paper towels.

Cook onion and garlic in drippings in Dutch oven over medium heat 5 minutes. Stir in mushrooms and next 8 ingredients. Add chicken to mixture in Dutch oven. Bring to a boil; reduce heat, and simmer, uncovered, 30 minutes, stirring occasionally. Stir in green pepper; cook, uncovered, 30 minutes, stirring occasionally. Remove and discard bay leaves. Serve over spaghetti. **Yield: 8 servings.**

Note: "Cacciatore" means hunter's style in Italian. Served with generous amounts of spaghetti, this classic dish always includes tomatoes, mushrooms, onions, and herbs.

Chicken Fettuccine Supreme

¼ cup butter or margarine
1¼ pounds skinned and boned chicken breast halves, cut into ¾-inch pieces
3 cups sliced fresh mushrooms
1 cup chopped green onions
1 small sweet red pepper, cut into thin strips
1 clove garlic, crushed
½ teaspoon salt
½ teaspoon pepper
10 ounces uncooked fettuccine
¾ cup half-and-half
½ cup butter or margarine, melted
¼ cup chopped fresh parsley
¼ teaspoon salt
¼ teaspoon pepper
½ cup grated Parmesan cheese
1 cup chopped pecans, toasted

Melt ¼ cup butter in a large skillet over medium heat; add chicken, and cook, stirring constantly, until browned. Remove chicken from skillet, reserving pan drippings in skillet; set chicken aside.

Add mushrooms and next 5 ingredients to pan drippings in skillet, and cook, stirring constantly, until vegetables are tender.

Add chicken; reduce heat, and cook 15 minutes or until chicken is tender and mixture is thoroughly heated. Set aside, and keep warm.

Cook fettuccine according to package directions, omitting salt; drain. Place fettuccine in a large bowl.

Combine half-and-half and next 4 ingredients in a small bowl; stir well. Add to fettuccine; toss gently to combine.

Add chicken mixture and Parmesan cheese to fettuccine; toss gently to combine. Sprinkle with pecans, and serve immediately. **Yield: 6 servings.**

Chicken Fettuccine Supreme

Creamy Chicken Tetrazzini

Creamy Chicken Tetrazzini

1 (3- to 4-pound) broiler-fryer
1 teaspoon salt
1 teaspoon pepper
1 (8-ounce) package spaghetti
1 large green pepper, chopped
1 cup sliced fresh mushrooms
1 small onion, chopped
¼ cup butter or margarine, melted
¼ cup all-purpose flour
½ teaspoon salt
½ teaspoon garlic powder
½ teaspoon poultry seasoning
½ teaspoon pepper
1 cup half-and-half
2 cups (8 ounces) shredded sharp Cheddar
    cheese, divided
1 (10¾-ounce) can cream of mushroom soup,
    undiluted
¾ cup grated Parmesan cheese, divided
¼ cup dry sherry
1 (4-ounce) jar sliced pimiento, drained
1 teaspoon paprika
¾ cup sliced almonds, toasted

Combine first 3 ingredients in a Dutch oven; add water to cover. Bring to a boil. Cover, reduce heat, and simmer 45 minutes or until chicken is tender. Remove chicken from broth, reserving broth.

Let chicken cool slightly. Bone and coarsely shred chicken; set aside.

Add enough water to reserved broth to measure 3 quarts; bring to a boil. Cook spaghetti in broth according to package directions. Drain and set aside.

Cook green pepper, mushrooms, and onion in butter in a Dutch oven over medium heat, stirring constantly, until tender. Add flour and next 4 ingredients; stir until smooth. Cook, stirring constantly 1 minute. Gradually stir in half-and-half, and cook until thickened, stirring gently.

Add ¾ cup Cheddar cheese, stirring until cheese melts. Add chicken, mushroom soup, ½ cup Parmesan cheese, sherry, and pimiento; stir well.

Combine chicken mixture and cooked spaghetti, tossing gently until thoroughly combined. Spoon into a greased 13- x 9- x 2-inch baking dish.

Bake, uncovered, at 350° for 20 to 25 minutes or until thoroughly heated.

Combine remaining ¼ cup Parmesan cheese and paprika; stir well. Sprinkle remaining 1¼ cups Cheddar cheese in diagonal rows across top of casserole. Repeat procedure with almonds and Parmesan-paprika mixture. Bake 5 additional minutes or until Cheddar cheese melts. **Yield: 6 to 8 servings.**

Chicken Manicotti

8 manicotti shells
1 (10¾-ounce) can creamy chicken mushroom
    soup, undiluted
½ cup sour cream
2 cups chopped cooked chicken
¼ cup chopped onion
2 tablespoons butter or margarine, melted
1 (4-ounce) can sliced mushrooms, undrained
1 cup (4 ounces) shredded Cheddar or
    Monterey Jack cheese

Cook manicotti shells according to package directions, omitting salt; drain and set aside.

Combine soup and sour cream; stir well. Combine half of soup mixture and chicken; stir well. Set aside remaining soup mixture. Stuff manicotti shells with chicken mixture; place in a greased 11- x 7- x 1½-inch baking dish.

Cook onion in butter over medium heat in a large skillet, stirring constantly, until tender; add mushrooms and reserved soup mixture. Spoon over manicotti.

Bake, uncovered, at 350° for 15 minutes. Sprinkle with cheese, and bake 5 additional minutes. **Yield: 4 servings.**

Cheesy Chicken Spaghetti

1 (6-pound) hen
1 (10-ounce) package spaghetti
1½ cups chopped onion
1 cup chopped green pepper
1 cup chopped celery
1 (4-ounce) jar diced pimiento, drained
1 (6-ounce) jar sliced mushrooms, drained
1 (16-ounce) loaf process American cheese,
    cubed
½ teaspoon salt
½ teaspoon pepper

Place hen in a Dutch oven; add water to cover. Bring to a boil; cover, reduce heat, and simmer 1½ hours or until tender.

Remove hen, reserving 6 cups broth; let hen cool slightly. Bone, and cut into bite-size pieces; set aside.

Bring 1 quart reserved broth to a boil in Dutch oven; gradually add spaghetti. Cook, uncovered, over medium heat 10 to 13 minutes. Do not drain.

Combine onion, green pepper, celery, and remaining 2 cups reserved broth in a medium saucepan. Bring to a boil; reduce heat and simmer 10 minutes or until vegetables are tender. Drain.

Add chicken, cooked vegetables, pimiento, and mushrooms to spaghetti, stirring well. Add cheese cubes, salt, and pepper, stirring until cheese melts. **Yield: 8 servings.**

Extra Chicken Broth?

• Fresh broth can be refrigerated 3 to 4 days.
• Freeze broth in a variety of containers or try ice-cube trays. Transfer the cubes to a plastic bag once frozen. Each cube yields about 2 tablespoons of broth.

Chicken Lasagna

1 (2½- to 3-pound) broiler-fryer
6 cups water
1 teaspoon salt
1 clove garlic, minced
2 tablespoons butter, melted
1 (10¾-ounce) can cream of celery soup,
    undiluted
½ teaspoon dried oregano
¼ teaspoon pepper
8 lasagna noodles, uncooked
1 (8-ounce) loaf process American cheese, cut
    in ¼-inch slices, divided
2 cups (8 ounces) shredded mozzarella
    cheese, divided
2 tablespoons grated Parmesan cheese

Combine first 3 ingredients in a Dutch oven; bring to a boil. Cover, reduce heat, and simmer 45 minutes or until chicken is tender.

Drain, reserving broth, and let cool slightly. Bone chicken and cut into bite-size pieces; set aside.

Cook garlic in butter in a skillet over medium-high heat, stirring constantly, 2 minutes. Add celery soup, ¾ cup reserved chicken broth, oregano, and pepper.

Cook lasagna noodles according to package directions in remaining reserved chicken broth, adding more water, if necessary; drain.

Spoon a small amount of sauce into a lightly greased 11- x 7- x 1½-inch baking dish. Layer with half each of lasagna noodles, sauce, chicken, and American and mozzarella cheeses. Repeat procedure with noodles, sauce, and chicken, reserving remaining cheeses to add later.

Bake at 350° for 25 minutes; top with remaining cheeses, and bake 5 additional minutes. Let stand 10 minutes. **Yield: 6 servings.**

Note: To save time, cook chicken in a pressure cooker; follow manufacturer's instructions.

From the Skillet and Wok

These recipes prove that there's more than one way to fry chicken.
Choose from pan-fried, deep-fried, and stir-fried favorites.

Crispy Fried Chicken, Spicy Fried Chicken, Italian Chicken Cutlets

Fried Cheese-Stuffed Chicken Thighs, Chicken Kiev, Cashew-Chicken Stir-Fry

Italian-Seasoned Fried Chicken, Chicken Piccata, Bourbon Chicken with Gravy

Chicken Scaloppine with Lemon Sauce, Crispy Chicken Croquettes

Chicken-in-a-Garden (page 247)

Crispy Fried Chicken

Crispy Fried Chicken

1 (3- to 3½-pound) broiler-fryer, cut up
½ teaspoon salt
⅛ teaspoon black pepper
1½ cups all-purpose flour
1 teaspoon salt
¾ teaspoon black pepper
½ teaspoon ground red pepper
¼ teaspoon paprika
1 large egg, beaten
½ cup buttermilk
Vegetable oil

Season chicken with ½ teaspoon salt and ⅛ teaspoon black pepper; set aside.

Combine flour and next 4 ingredients; stir well, and set aside. Combine egg and buttermilk; stir well.

Dip chicken in egg mixture; dredge in flour mixture, coating each piece well. Repeat procedure, heavily coating chicken pieces.

Pour oil to depth of 1 inch into a large heavy skillet; heat to 350°. Fry chicken 20 to 25 minutes or until golden, turning to brown both sides. Drain well on paper towels. **Yield: 4 servings.**

Spicy Fried Chicken

6 skinned and boned chicken breast halves
2 cups water
2 tablespoons hot sauce
1 cup self-rising flour
1 teaspoon garlic salt
½ teaspoon pepper
1 teaspoon paprika
1 teaspoon red pepper
Vegetable oil

Place chicken in a shallow dish or heavy-duty, zip-top plastic bag. Combine water and hot sauce; pour over chicken. Cover or seal, and marinate 1 hour in refrigerator, turning once.

Combine flour and next 4 ingredients. Remove chicken from marinade, and dredge in flour mixture, coating well. Discard marinade.

Pour oil to depth of 1 inch into a heavy skillet; heat to 350°. Fry chicken 5 to 6 minutes on each side or until golden brown. Drain well on paper towels. **Yield: 6 servings.**

Italian-Seasoned Fried Chicken

¾ cup Italian-seasoned breadcrumbs
½ cup grated Parmesan cheese
¼ cup minced fresh parsley
¾ teaspoon dried oregano
1 large egg, beaten
½ cup milk
1 tablespoon all-purpose flour
1 (3- to 3½-pound) broiler-fryer, cut up
Vegetable oil

Combine first 4 ingredients; stir well, and set aside. Combine egg, milk, and flour; stir well. Dip chicken in egg mixture; dredge in breadcrumb mixture, coating well.

Pour oil to depth of 1 inch into a large, heavy skillet; heat to 350°. Fry chicken 20 to 25 minutes or until golden, turning to brown both sides. Drain well on paper towels. **Yield: 4 servings.**

Fried Chicken Technique

Fry chicken pieces in 1 inch of hot oil until golden, turning with tongs to brown both sides evenly.

Italian Chicken Cutlets

6 skinned and boned chicken breast halves
1 cup Italian-seasoned breadcrumbs
½ cup freshly grated Romano or Parmesan
     cheese
¼ cup all-purpose flour
1 (0.8-ounce) envelope light Italian salad
     dressing mix
2 teaspoons dried oregano
¼ teaspoon garlic powder
2 large eggs, beaten
⅓ cup vegetable oil
Garnish: green onion strips

Place chicken between 2 sheets of heavy-duty plastic wrap; flatten to ¼-inch thickness, using a meat mallet or rolling pin.

Combine breadcrumbs and next 5 ingredients; dip chicken in eggs, and dredge in breadcrumbs.

Heat oil in a large skillet over medium heat. Add chicken, and cook 3 to 4 minutes on each side or until golden brown, adding extra oil if necessary. Drain on paper towels. Garnish, if desired. **Yield: 6 servings.**

Chicken Piccata

6 skinned and boned chicken breast
     halves
⅓ cup all-purpose flour
1 teaspoon salt
¼ teaspoon pepper
¼ cup butter or margarine
¼ cup lemon juice
1 lemon, thinly sliced
2 tablespoons chopped fresh parsley

Place chicken between 2 sheets of heavy-duty plastic wrap; flatten to ¼-inch thickness, using a meat mallet or rolling pin.

Combine flour, salt, and pepper; dredge chicken in flour mixture.

Melt butter in a large skillet over medium heat. Add chicken, and cook 3 to 4 minutes on each side or until golden brown. Remove chicken, and drain on paper towels; keep warm.

Add lemon juice and lemon slices to pan drippings in skillet; cook until thoroughly heated. Pour lemon mixture over chicken; sprinkle with parsley. **Yield: 6 servings.**

Chicken Scaloppine with Lemon Sauce

6 skinned and boned chicken breast halves,
     halved
1 cup all-purpose flour
¼ teaspoon pepper
2 large eggs, beaten
¼ cup butter or margarine
¼ cup vegetable oil
½ to ¾ pound fresh mushrooms, thinly sliced
¼ cup water
½ cup Chablis or other dry white wine
½ cup lemon juice
½ cup chopped fresh parsley

Place chicken between 2 sheets of heavy-duty plastic wrap; flatten to ¼-inch thickness, using a meat mallet or rolling pin.

Combine flour and pepper; dip chicken in egg, and dredge in flour mixture.

Heat butter and oil in a heavy skillet; cook chicken in skillet over medium heat about 4 minutes on each side or until golden brown. Place chicken on a serving platter; keep warm.

Add mushrooms and water to pan drippings; cook over medium heat, stirring often, about 3 minutes. Spoon mushrooms over chicken.

Add wine and lemon juice to skillet; heat thoroughly. Pour sauce over chicken; sprinkle with parsley. **Yield: 6 servings.**

Bourbon Chicken with Gravy

¼ cup butter or margarine
4 pounds skinned chicken pieces
¾ cup bourbon, divided
1 medium onion, finely chopped
2 tablespoons dried parsley flakes
1 teaspoon dried thyme
½ teaspoon salt
⅛ teaspoon pepper
¼ cup whipping cream

Melt butter in a large, heavy skillet over medium heat; add chicken, and brown on both sides. Add ¼ cup bourbon. Carefully ignite bourbon with a long match, and let burn until flames die.

Add onion and next 4 ingredients. Stir in remaining ½ cup bourbon, stirring until blended. Bring to a boil; cover, reduce heat, and simmer 30 minutes or until chicken is tender. Place on a serving plate, reserving liquid in skillet.

Add whipping cream to skillet; bring to a boil, stirring constantly. Cook over medium heat until thickened. Serve with chicken. **Yield: 6 servings.**

Sautéed Chicken Livers

1 pound chicken livers
⅓ cup Chablis or other dry white wine
2½ tablespoons lemon juice
¼ teaspoon salt
¼ teaspoon pepper
½ to ¾ cup all-purpose flour
3 to 4 tablespoons vegetable oil

Cut chicken livers in half. Combine wine and lemon juice in a shallow dish; add livers and toss. Cover and marinate in refrigerator 30 minutes.

Drain livers. Sprinkle with salt and pepper; dredge in flour. Cook in hot oil about 5 minutes or until done. Drain well, and serve immediately. **Yield: 4 servings.**

Chicken Cutlet Shortcuts

- Save time by buying skinned and boned chicken breasts.
- Save money by pounding these breasts into convenient cutlets. Place chicken breasts between 2 sheets of heavy-duty plastic wrap. Starting at the center and working outward, gently pound chicken to desired thickness with the flat side of a meat mallet.

Fried Cheese-Stuffed Chicken Thighs

8 skinned and boned chicken thighs
½ (8-ounce) package Swiss cheese
8 slices bacon, partially cooked
2 egg whites, slightly beaten
1½ tablespoons lemon juice
¾ cup all-purpose flour
1½ teaspoons lemon-pepper seasoning
Vegetable oil

Place chicken between 2 sheets of heavy-duty plastic wrap; flatten to ¼-inch thickness, using a meat mallet or rolling pin.

Slice cheese lengthwise to make 8 even strips. Place 1 strip of cheese in center of each chicken thigh. Fold long sides of chicken over cheese; fold ends of chicken over, and wrap each with a slice of bacon. Secure with wooden picks.

Combine egg white and lemon juice; combine flour and lemon-pepper seasoning. Dip chicken in egg mixture; dredge in flour mixture.

Pour oil to depth of 1 inch into a heavy skillet; heat to 350°. Fry chicken 15 minutes or until golden, turning once. Drain on paper towels. **Yield: 8 servings.**

Crispy Chicken Croquettes

2 tablespoons chopped onion
1 tablespoon butter or margarine, melted
1 tablespoon all-purpose flour
¾ cup water
1¼ teaspoons chicken-flavored bouillon granules
½ teaspoon dry mustard
½ teaspoon pepper
4 cups finely chopped cooked chicken
1 large egg, beaten
3 tablespoons dry white wine
1 cup round buttery cracker crumbs
Vegetable oil
Peppery Cream Sauce

Cook onion in butter in a large saucepan until tender. Add flour, stirring until smooth. Cook, stirring constantly, 1 minute. Gradually add water; cook over medium heat, stirring constantly, until sauce is thickened and bubbly.

Stir in bouillon granules and next 5 ingredients. Cook over medium heat, stirring constantly, 3 to 5 minutes. Remove from heat; cover and chill.

Shape mixture into croquettes, and roll in cracker crumbs. Pour oil to depth of 2 to 3 inches into a Dutch oven; heat to 350°. Fry croquettes until golden brown. Drain on paper towels. Serve with Peppery Cream Sauce. **Yield: 10 croquettes.**

Peppery Cream Sauce

3 tablespoons butter or margarine
3 tablespoons all-purpose flour
1½ cups milk
½ teaspoon salt
½ teaspoon pepper

Melt butter in a heavy saucepan over low heat; add flour, stirring until smooth. Cook, stirring constantly, 1 minute. Gradually add milk; cook over medium heat, stirring constantly, until sauce is thickened and bubbly. Stir in salt and pepper.
Yield: 1½ cups.

Chicken Kiev

¼ cup plus 2 tablespoons butter, softened
1 tablespoon chopped fresh parsley
1 small clove garlic, minced
¼ teaspoon dried tarragon
¼ teaspoon salt
⅛ teaspoon ground white pepper
6 skinned and boned chicken breast halves
1 large egg, beaten
1 tablespoon water
½ cup all-purpose flour
1½ to 2 cups soft breadcrumbs
Vegetable oil

Combine first 6 ingredients in a small bowl; stir until blended. Shape butter mixture into a 3-inch stick; cover and freeze about 45 minutes or until firm.

Place chicken between 2 sheets of heavy-duty plastic wrap; flatten to ¼-inch thickness, using a meat mallet or rolling pin.

Cut butter into 6 pats; place one pat in center of each chicken breast. Fold long sides of chicken over butter; fold ends over, and secure with wooden picks.

Combine egg and water, beating well. Dredge chicken in flour; dip in egg mixture, and dredge in breadcrumbs.

Pour oil to depth of 2 to 3 inches into a Dutch oven; heat to 350°. Fry chicken 3 to 4 minutes on each side or until browned. Drain well on paper towels. **Yield: 6 servings.**

Chicken Kiev

Considered an elegant entrée, this famous Russian dish is worth the effort. Take care when cutting into Chicken Kiev as the traditional herbed butter may spurt out.

Chicken Kiev

Cashew-Chicken Stir-Fry

1½ pounds skinned and boned chicken breast
    halves
½ cup Chablis or other dry white wine
½ cup teriyaki sauce
1 tablespoon grated fresh gingerroot
1 clove garlic, crushed
2 tablespoons vegetable oil, divided
1 cup diagonally sliced celery
½ cup sliced green onions
2 tablespoons soy sauce
1 tablespoon plus 1 teaspoon cornstarch
2 teaspoons brown sugar
2 teaspoons chicken-flavored bouillon granules
1¼ cups boiling water
½ cup roasted cashews
Chow mein noodles

Cut chicken lengthwise into thin strips; place
in a large shallow dish. Combine wine, teriyaki
sauce, gingerroot, and garlic; stir well. Pour
marinade mixture over chicken; toss gently to
coat. Cover and marinate in refrigerator at least
2 hours. Drain chicken, discarding marinade.

Pour 1 tablespoon oil around top of preheated
wok, coating sides; heat at medium-high (350°) for
2 minutes. Add celery and green onions, and stir-fry
2 to 3 minutes or until vegetables are crisp-tender.
Remove vegetables from wok, and set aside.

Add remaining 1 tablespoon oil to wok. Add
chicken, and stir-fry 3 to 4 minutes or until chicken
is done. Remove chicken from wok, and set aside.

Combine soy sauce, cornstarch, and brown
sugar in a small bowl, stirring well. Dissolve
bouillon granules in boiling water; add cornstarch
mixture, stirring well. Add to wok; cook, stirring
gently, until mixture is thickened.

Add reserved vegetables, chicken, and
cashews to wok; stir-fry 30 seconds or until thoroughly heated. Serve over chow mein noodles.
Yield: 6 servings.

Cashew-Chicken Stir-Fry Techniques

Cut chicken lengthwise into thin strips; marinate
in refrigerator at least 2 hours.

Stir-fry celery and green onions in hot oil in a wok
2 to 3 minutes or until crisp-tender.

Dissolve bouillon granules in boiling water; add
cornstarch mixture and stir well.

Cashew-Chicken Stir-Fry

Szechuan Chicken with Cashews

1 pound skinned and boned chicken breast
    halves
2 tablespoons water
2 tablespoons soy sauce
1 teaspoon sherry
1 tablespoon cornstarch
3 tablespoons vegetable oil
2 dried whole red peppers
2 tablespoons chopped fresh gingerroot
5 tablespoons water
2 tablespoons soy sauce
1 tablespoon dry sherry
1 tablespoon cornstarch
1 tablespoon sugar
1 teaspoon coarsely ground black pepper
2 teaspoons white vinegar
1 teaspoon vegetable oil
½ cup coarsely chopped fresh mushrooms
1 green pepper, cut into thin strips
4 green onions, cut into ½-inch pieces
2 stalks celery, diagonally sliced
1 cup cashews
Hot cooked rice

Place chicken between 2 sheets of heavy-duty plastic wrap; flatten to ¼-inch thickness, using a meat mallet or rolling pin. Cut chicken into bite-size pieces.

Combine 2 tablespoons water and next 3 ingredients in a medium bowl; mix well. Add chicken; cover and refrigerate 20 minutes.

Pour 3 tablespoons oil around top of preheated wok, coating sides; heat at medium-high (350°) for 2 minutes. Add red peppers; stir-fry 1 minute, and discard. Add gingerroot to hot oil; stir-fry 1 minute, and discard.

Combine 5 tablespoons water and next 7 ingredients; mix well, and set aside.

Add chicken, mushrooms, green pepper, green onions, and celery. Stir-fry about 5 minutes or until vegetables are crisp-tender.

Pour reserved soy sauce mixture over chicken mixture; add cashews and cook, stirring constantly, until thickened. Serve over hot cooked rice.
Yield: 4 servings.

Princess Chicken

2 tablespoons cornstarch
2 tablespoons soy sauce
1 pound skinned and boned chicken breast
    halves, cut into 1-inch pieces
2 tablespoons soy sauce
1 tablespoon sugar
1 tablespoon rice wine or white wine
1 teaspoon cornstarch
1 teaspoon sesame oil
¼ cup peanut or vegetable oil
5 or 6 dried whole red peppers
2 teaspoons grated fresh gingerroot
½ cup chopped dry-roasted peanuts

Combine 2 tablespoons cornstarch and 2 tablespoons soy sauce in a medium bowl; stir well. Add chicken, mixing well. Cover and refrigerate 30 minutes.

Combine 2 tablespoons soy sauce, sugar, and next 3 ingredients; mix well, and set aside.

Pour peanut oil around top of preheated wok, coating sides; heat at medium-high (350°) for 1 minute. Add chicken, and stir-fry 2 minutes. Remove and drain on paper towels.

Reserve 2 tablespoons drippings in wok. Heat at medium-high (350°) for 30 seconds. Add red peppers, and stir-fry until dark brown. Add ginger- root and chicken; stir-fry 1 minute. Add wine mixture. Cook until slightly thickened. Stir in peanuts. **Yield: 4 servings.**

Lemon Chicken and Vegetables

3 tablespoons vegetable oil, divided
4 skinned and boned chicken breast halves,
    cut into ½-inch strips
1 lemon, sliced
½ cup sliced celery
½ medium onion, sliced
1 cup sliced yellow squash or zucchini
½ cup sliced fresh mushrooms
½ cup sweet red pepper strips
½ cup frozen English peas, thawed
½ cup fresh snow pea pods
1 teaspoon pepper
1 tablespoon lemon juice

Heat 1½ tablespoons oil to medium-high (350°) in a large skillet. Add chicken and lemon slices, and stir-fry 2 minutes or until lightly browned. Remove from skillet. Set aside.

Heat remaining 1½ tablespoons oil to medium-high in skillet. Add celery and next 4 ingredients; stir-fry 2 minutes or until vegetables are crisp-tender.

Add chicken, peas, and remaining ingredients to skillet. Stir-fry on medium-high until thoroughly heated. Serve immediately. **Yield: 4 servings.**

Orange Chicken Stir-Fry

3 tablespoons vegetable oil
6 skinned and boned chicken breast halves,
    cut into 1-inch pieces
2 tablespoons grated orange rind
1 teaspoon freshly grated gingerroot
¼ teaspoon hot sauce
4 green onions, cut into ¼-inch slices
1 cup orange juice
⅓ cup soy sauce
¼ cup sugar
1½ tablespoons cornstarch
2 oranges, peeled, seeded, and sectioned
Hot cooked rice

Pour oil around top of preheated wok, coating sides; heat at medium-high (350°) for 2 minutes. Add chicken and stir-fry 2 minutes or until lightly browned. Remove from wok, and drain well on paper towels.

Add orange rind, gingerroot, and hot sauce to wok; stir-fry 1½ minutes.

Return chicken to wok; stir-fry 3 minutes.

Combine green onions and next 4 ingredients; mix well. Add orange juice mixture and orange sections to wok; stir-fry 3 minutes or until thickened. Serve over rice. **Yield: 6 servings.**

Chicken-Vegetable Stir-Fry

½ cup soy sauce
¼ cup vegetable oil or sesame seed oil
2 teaspoons sesame seeds
6 skinned and boned chicken breast halves
2 cups broccoli flowerets
1 onion, thinly sliced and separated into rings
½ pound fresh snow pea pods
½ cup thinly sliced celery
½ cup sliced fresh mushrooms
1 tablespoon cornstarch
½ cup water
Hot cooked brown rice

Combine first 3 ingredients in a medium bowl, stirring well; set aside. Cut chicken into 2-inch strips, and add to marinade, mixing well. Cover and refrigerate at least 30 minutes.

Preheat wok to medium-high (350°). Add chicken mixture, and stir-fry 2 to 3 minutes. Remove chicken from wok, and set aside.

Add broccoli and onion to wok; stir-fry 2 minutes. Add snow peas, celery, and mushrooms; stir-fry 2 minutes or until vegetables are crisp-tender. Add chicken to wok.

Combine cornstarch and water; add to wok. Cook, stirring constantly, until thickened. Serve over brown rice. **Yield: 6 servings.**

Chicken Chinese

Chicken Chinese

2 skinned and boned chicken breast halves,
    cut into thin strips
2 cloves garlic, minced
½ teaspoon peeled, grated gingerroot
2 tablespoons peanut oil, divided
1 sweet red pepper, cut into thin strips
1 medium onion, cut into thin strips
1 cup broccoli flowerets
1 (13¾-ounce) can ready-to-serve, fat-free,
    reduced-sodium chicken broth
1½ tablespoons cornstarch
2 tablespoons commercial plum sauce
1 tablespoon Worcestershire sauce
1 tablespoon soy sauce
Chow mein noodles

Combine chicken strips, garlic, and ginger-root; toss gently. Cover and chill in refrigerator 30 minutes.

Pour 1 tablespoon peanut oil around top of a preheated wok, coating sides; heat at medium-high (350°) for 1 minute. Add chicken; stir-fry 3 minutes. Remove chicken from wok; set aside.

Pour remaining 1 tablespoon peanut oil into wok. Add red pepper, onion, and broccoli; stir-fry 2 minutes. Remove from wok; set aside.

Combine chicken broth and next 4 ingredients, stirring until smooth; add to wok. Bring to a boil, stirring constantly, for 1 minute. Add chicken and vegetables; cook until thoroughly heated. Serve with noodles. **Yield: 2 servings.**

Chicken-in-a-Garden

(pictured on page 235)

3 tablespoons peanut or vegetable oil, divided
2 tablespoons soy sauce, divided
1½ teaspoons cornstarch
½ teaspoon garlic powder
¼ teaspoon pepper
6 skinned and boned chicken breast halves,
   cut into 1-inch pieces
3 green peppers, cut into 1-inch pieces
1 cup diagonally sliced celery (1-inch pieces)
8 scallions, cut into ½-inch slices
1 (6-ounce) package frozen snow pea pods,
   thawed and drained
2½ tablespoons cornstarch
¾ cup water
¾ teaspoon chicken-flavored bouillon granules
⅛ teaspoon ground ginger
3 medium tomatoes, peeled and cut into eighths
Hot cooked rice

Combine 1 tablespoon oil, 1 tablespoon soy sauce, 1½ teaspoons cornstarch, garlic powder, and pepper in a medium bowl; stir well. Add chicken; cover and refrigerate 20 minutes.

Pour remaining 2 tablespoons oil around top of preheated wok, coating sides; heat at medium-high (350°) for 2 minutes. Add green pepper, and stir-fry 4 minutes. Add celery, scallions, and snow peas; stir-fry 2 minutes. Remove vegetables from wok, and set aside.

Combine remaining 1 tablespoon soy sauce and 2½ tablespoons cornstarch; stir in water, bouillon granules, and ginger. Set mixture aside.

Add chicken to wok, and stir-fry 3 minutes; add stir-fried vegetables, tomato, and bouillon mixture. Stir-fry over low heat (225°) for 3 minutes or until thickened and bubbly. Serve over rice.
Yield: 6 servings.

Sweet-and-Sour Chicken

1 (20-ounce) can pineapple chunks, undrained
¼ cup cider vinegar
3 tablespoons soy sauce
3 tablespoons dry sherry
1 tablespoon sugar
1 tablespoon cornstarch
½ teaspoon salt
1 large egg, beaten
⅓ cup water
½ cup all-purpose flour
1 pound skinned and boned chicken breast
   halves, cut into 1-inch pieces
¾ cup peanut oil
1 sweet red pepper, cut into strips
1 green pepper, cut into strips
1 small onion, sliced and separated into rings
Hot cooked rice

Drain pineapple, reserving juice; set pineapple aside. Combine juice, vinegar, and next 5 ingredients, stirring until smooth; set aside.

Combine egg, water, and flour in a small bowl; stir until blended. Add chicken to batter, stirring until well coated.

Pour oil around top of preheated wok, coating sides; heat at medium-high (350°) for 2 minutes.

Add half of chicken, and stir-fry until lightly browned. Drain on paper towels; set aside. Repeat with remaining chicken. Set aside.

Drain oil from wok, reserving 2 tablespoons in wok; heat to 350°. Add red pepper, green pepper, and onion; stir-fry 1 to 2 minutes or until crisp-tender. Remove from wok; set aside.

Stir cornstarch mixture, and add to wok. Cook, stirring constantly, until smooth and thickened. Add reserved chicken, vegetables, and pineapple; stir gently, and cook until thoroughly heated. Serve over rice. **Yield: 4 servings.**

Sizzling Walnut Chicken

4 skinned and boned chicken breast halves
1 tablespoon sherry
1 teaspoon salt
⅛ teaspoon pepper
2 egg whites
¼ cup cornstarch
2 to 2½ cups finely chopped walnuts
Vegetable oil
Gingered Plum Sauce

Cut chicken into bite-size pieces; sprinkle with sherry, salt, and pepper. Set aside.

Beat egg whites at high speed of an electric mixer until foamy. Gradually add cornstarch, beating until stiff peaks form. Gently fold in chicken. Roll each chicken piece in chopped walnuts.

Pour oil to depth of 2 inches into a large heavy skillet; heat to 350°. Fry chicken 5 to 6 minutes on each side or until golden brown. Drain on paper towels. Serve chicken with Gingered Plum Sauce. **Yield: 4 servings.**

Gingered Plum Sauce

1 cup plum jam
1 tablespoon ketchup
2 teaspoons grated lemon rind
1 tablespoon lemon juice
2 teaspoons cider vinegar
½ teaspoon ground ginger
½ teaspoon anise seeds, crushed
¼ teaspoon dry mustard
¼ teaspoon ground cinnamon
⅛ teaspoon ground cloves
⅛ teaspoon hot sauce

Heat plum jam in a small saucepan over medium heat until melted. Stir in remaining ingredients. Bring mixture to a boil; cook, stirring constantly, 1 minute. **Yield: 1¼ cups.**

Chicken Tempura Delight

1 large egg, beaten
2 tablespoons all-purpose flour
1 tablespoon water
½ teaspoon salt
2 pounds skinned and boned chicken breast halves, cut into 1-inch pieces
All-purpose flour
¾ cup peanut oil
Sweet-and-Sour Pineapple Sauce

Combine first 4 ingredients; mix well, and chill 1 hour. Dip chicken into batter; dredge in flour.

Pour oil around top of preheated wok, coating sides; heat at medium-high (350°) for 2 minutes. Add chicken, and stir-fry until lightly browned. Drain on paper towels. Serve with Sweet-and-Sour Pineapple Sauce. **Yield: 8 servings.**

Sweet-and-Sour Pineapple Sauce

1 (8-ounce) can crushed pineapple
1 (6-ounce) can unsweetened pineapple juice
2 tablespoons sugar
1 tablespoon cornstarch
2 teaspoons prepared mustard
2 tablespoons cider vinegar

Drain pineapple, reserving liquid. Combine reserved liquid and pineapple juice, adding enough water if necessary to equal 1 cup liquid. Combine ¾ cup juice and sugar in a small saucepan; cook over medium heat, stirring constantly, until sugar dissolves.

Combine cornstarch and remaining ¼ cup pineapple juice; stir into pineapple juice mixture in saucepan. Bring to a boil over medium heat, and boil 1 minute, stirring constantly.

Add mustard, vinegar, and pineapple; mix well. Chill. **Yield: 1½ cups.**

South by Southwest

From fajitas and flautas to tamales and chalupas, Southwestern chicken dishes offer a fiesta of tastes and colors. Now you can enjoy Mexico's unique flavors without leaving home.

Lime Soup, Spicy Tortilla Soup, No-Fuss Fajitas, Chicken Tamales

Spicy Tex-Mex Chicken, Chicken-Tomatillo Enchiladas, Pollo en Mole de Cacahuate

Chicken Flautas with Guacamole, Chicken-Olive Chalupas, Easy Chicken Enchiladas

Chicken Tostadas, Chilaquiles con Pollo, Mexican Chicken Rolls

Mexican Stir-Fry (page 260)

Lime Soup

1 (3- to 3½-pound) broiler-fryer, cut up
6 cups water
1 medium onion, quartered
1 stalk celery
3 fresh cilantro or parsley sprigs
6 whole peppercorns
2 teaspoons salt
½ teaspoon dried thyme
1 medium-size green pepper, chopped
1 medium onion, chopped
2 tablespoons vegetable oil
2 large tomatoes, peeled and chopped
1½ teaspoons grated lime rind
Juice of 2 limes
3 tablespoons chopped fresh cilantro or parsley
¼ teaspoon salt
¼ teaspoon pepper
8 corn tortillas
Vegetable oil
Garnishes: lime slices, fresh cilantro

Place first 8 ingredients in a large Dutch oven; bring to a boil. Cover, reduce heat, and simmer 1 hour. Remove chicken, reserving broth; let chicken cool. Bone and chop chicken; set aside. Strain broth to remove vegetables; set broth aside, and discard vegetables.

Cook green pepper and chopped onion in 2 tablespoons oil in Dutch oven, stirring constantly, until crisp-tender. Stir in tomato, and cook 5 minutes. Add reserved broth, lime rind, lime juice, and 3 tablespoons cilantro. Bring to a boil; reduce heat, and simmer, uncovered, 20 minutes.

Stir in chicken, ¼ teaspoon salt, and pepper; simmer, uncovered, 10 minutes.

Cut each tortilla into 8 wedges; fry in hot oil until crisp. Drain. To serve, place 8 tortilla wedges in each soup bowl; add soup, and garnish, if desired. **Yield: 2 quarts.**

Spicy Tortilla Soup

1 large onion, coarsely chopped
Vegetable oil
4 corn tortillas, coarsely chopped
6 cloves garlic, minced
1 tablespoon chopped fresh cilantro or parsley
2 (10¾-ounce) cans tomato puree
2 quarts chicken broth
1 tablespoon ground cumin
2 teaspoons chili powder
2 bay leaves
⅛ teaspoon ground red pepper
3 corn tortillas
2 skinned and boned chicken breast halves, cut into strips
1 avocado, peeled, seeded, and cubed
1 cup (4 ounces) shredded Cheddar cheese

Position knife blade in food processor bowl; add chopped onion, and process until smooth. Measure 1 cup onion puree, and set aside; reserve any remaining puree for another use.

Heat 3 tablespoons vegetable oil in a Dutch oven over medium heat; cook 4 chopped tortillas, garlic, and cilantro in hot oil until tortillas are soft.

Add 1 cup onion puree, tomato puree, and next 5 ingredients. Bring to a boil; cover, reduce heat, and simmer 30 minutes. Remove and discard bay leaves.

Cut 3 tortillas into thin strips. Pour oil to depth of ½ inch into a large, heavy skillet. Fry strips in hot oil over medium heat until browned. Remove tortillas, reserving ½ tablespoon oil in skillet; drain tortillas on paper towels, and set aside.

Add chicken strips to skillet; cook over medium heat, stirring constantly, about 8 minutes or until chicken is done.

Spoon soup into bowls; add chicken strips, avocado, and cheese. Top with tortilla strips. Serve immediately. **Yield: 2½ quarts.**

Spicy Tortilla Soup

No-Fuss Fajitas

No-Fuss Fajitas

3 tablespoons lemon juice
¾ teaspoon salt
¼ teaspoon coarsely ground pepper
¼ teaspoon garlic powder
½ teaspoon liquid smoke
3 skinned and boned chicken breast halves,
    cut into strips
6 (6-inch) flour tortillas
2 tablespoons vegetable oil
1 green or sweet red pepper, cut into strips
1 medium onion, sliced and separated into rings
Condiments: chopped tomato, green onions,
    lettuce, guacamole, sour cream, shredded
    cheese, and picante sauce

Combine first 5 ingredients in a medium
bowl; reserve 1½ tablespoons marinade. Add
chicken to remaining marinade in bowl; stir to
coat. Cover and refrigerate at least 30 minutes.
Drain chicken, discarding marinade.

Wrap tortillas in aluminum foil; bake at 350°
for 15 minutes.

Heat oil in a heavy skillet. Add chicken; cook,
stirring constantly, 2 to 3 minutes. Add 1½ tablespoons reserved marinade, pepper, and onion;
cook, stirring constantly, until vegetables are
crisp-tender. Remove from heat.

Divide mixture evenly, and spoon a portion
onto each tortilla. If desired, top with several
condiments; then wrap. **Yield: 6 fajitas.**

Flavors of Mexico

Cilantro or coriander: pungent herb
that closely resembles flat leaf parsley
Jalapeño: hot green pepper (about 2
inches long); available fresh and canned
Tomatillo: small, firm green tomato-
like fruit covered with a papery husk;
tastes similar to a slightly green plum

Chicken Flautas with Guacamole

¼ cup chopped onion
1 clove garlic, minced
Vegetable oil
1½ teaspoons cornstarch
¼ cup chicken broth
1 cup cooked shredded chicken
½ teaspoon salt
¼ teaspoon pepper
2 tablespoons chopped green chiles
6 (6-inch) corn tortillas
Guacamole

Cook onion and garlic in 1 tablespoon oil in a
skillet, stirring constantly, until tender; set aside.

Combine cornstarch and chicken broth; add
cornstarch mixture, chicken, and next 3 ingredients to onion mixture. Cook over medium heat,
stirring constantly, until mixture thickens; set
aside.

Pour oil to depth of ¼ inch into a medium
skillet; heat to 375°. Fry tortillas, one at a time,
about 5 seconds on each side or just until softened.
Drain on paper towels.

Spread about 2 tablespoons chicken mixture
in center of each tortilla. Roll up each tortilla
tightly, and secure with a wooden pick. Heat oil
in skillet to 375°. Add flautas, and brown on all
sides; drain on paper towels. Serve with
Guacamole. **Yield: 2 servings.**

Guacamole

1 ripe avocado, peeled, seeded, and mashed
2 tablespoons chopped onion
1 medium tomato, peeled and chopped
1 clove garlic, minced
2 tablespoons lemon juice
¼ teaspoon salt
¼ teaspoon pepper

Combine all ingredients in a small bowl, stirring until blended. **Yield: 1¾ cups.**

Chicken Tamales

2 dozen dried cornhusks
2 (2½- to 3-pound) broiler-fryers, cut up
1 medium onion, chopped
1 tablespoon vegetable oil
1 (4-ounce) can taco sauce
1 teaspoon salt
1 teaspoon ground cumin
1 cup shortening
2 teaspoons chili powder
½ teaspoon salt
2½ cups instant corn masa
Commercial salsa

Cover dried cornhusks with hot water; let stand 1 hour or until softened. Drain well, and pat with paper towels to remove excess water.

Place chicken in a large Dutch oven; add water to cover. Bring to a boil over medium heat; cover, reduce heat, and simmer 45 minutes or until tender; drain, reserving 1 cup broth. Bone and finely chop chicken to make 4 cups. Set chopped chicken aside.

Cook onion in hot oil in a large skillet over medium heat until tender. Stir in chicken, taco sauce, 1 teaspoon salt, and cumin. Set aside.

Cream shortening; add reserved 1 cup broth, chili powder, and ½ teaspoon salt, mixing well. Gradually add corn masa, mixing well; beat 10 minutes at medium speed of a heavy-duty electric mixer until light and fluffy.

Cut each cornhusk to make a 4-inch square. Place about 2 tablespoons masa dough in center of each husk, spreading to within ½ inch of edges. Place about 2 tablespoons chicken mixture on each dough square, spreading evenly. Fold in one edge; roll up tamales, starting with an adjoining side, leaving opposite end open. Tie with string or narrow strip of softened cornhusk.

Place a steaming rack or metal colander in a large pot, and place a cup in center of rack. Add just enough water to fill pot below rack level to keep tamales above water. Stand tamales on folded ends around the cup. Bring water to a boil. Cover and steam 1 hour or until tamale dough pulls away from husks; add more water as necessary. Serve with salsa. **Yield: 2 dozen.**

Chicken-Olive Chalupas

Vegetable oil
6 (10-inch) flour tortillas
2 (16-ounce) cans refried beans
Chicken-Olive Filling
½ medium head iceberg lettuce, shredded
2 medium tomatoes, chopped
6 green onions, chopped
2 avocados, peeled and chopped
Taco sauce
Sour cream

Pour oil to depth of ¼ inch into a large skillet; heat to 375°.

Fry tortillas, one at a time, about 20 seconds on each side or until crisp and golden. Drain on paper towels.

Spread an equal amount of beans on each tortilla. Top with equal amounts of Chicken-Olive Filling and next 4 ingredients. Serve with taco sauce and sour cream. **Yield: 6 servings.**

Chicken-Olive Filling

2 (1.25-ounce) packages taco seasoning mix
2 cups water
3 cups chopped cooked chicken
1 (6-ounce) can pitted ripe olives, drained and sliced

Combine taco seasoning mix and water in a medium skillet, stirring well; bring to a boil. Reduce heat, and simmer 5 minutes, stirring occasionally.

Stir in chicken and olives; simmer 3 additional minutes. **Yield: about 4 cups.**

Chicken Tostadas

Chicken Tostadas

4 skinned and boned chicken breast halves,
   cut into ¼-inch-wide strips
¼ cup chopped onion
2 tablespoons butter or margarine, melted
1 (16-ounce) jar salsa
1 (1¼-ounce) package taco seasoning mix
1 (16-ounce) can refried beans
1 (4½-ounce) package tostada shells
2 small tomatoes, chopped
2 cups shredded lettuce
1 cup (4 ounces) shredded Cheddar cheese

Cook half each of chicken strips and onion in 1 tablespoon butter in a large skillet over medium-high heat 2 to 3 minutes, stirring often. Remove mixture, and set aside. Repeat procedure with remaining chicken, onion, and butter.

Return chicken mixture to skillet; add salsa and taco seasoning mix. Cook over low heat 10 minutes, stirring occasionally.

Heat refried beans in a small saucepan; set aside.

Place tostada shells on a baking sheet, slightly overlapping. Bake at 350° for 5 minutes. Spread about 2 tablespoons refried beans on each tostada; top evenly with chicken mixture, tomato, lettuce, and cheese. **Yield: 6 servings.**

Mexican Tostadas

Our recipe is a slight variation of the crisp-fried corn or flour tortilla native to Mexico. Both are piled with beef or chicken, lettuce, tomato, and cheese.

Easy Chicken Enchiladas

2 cups chopped cooked chicken
2 cups sour cream
1 (10¾-ounce) can cream of chicken soup
1½ cups (6 ounces) shredded Monterey Jack cheese
1½ cups (6 ounces) shredded longhorn cheese
1 (4.5-ounce) can chopped green chiles, drained
2 tablespoons chopped onion
⅛ teaspoon salt
¼ teaspoon pepper
10 (10-inch) flour tortillas
Vegetable oil
1 cup (4 ounces) shredded longhorn cheese

Combine first 9 ingredients; mix well. Fry tortillas, one at a time, in 2 tablespoons oil in a skillet 5 seconds on each side or until softened; add additional oil, if necessary. Drain.

Place a heaping ½ cup chicken mixture on each tortilla; roll up each tortilla, and place seam side down in a 13- x 9- x 2-inch baking dish.

Cover and bake at 350° for 20 minutes. Sprinkle with 1 cup longhorn cheese, and bake, uncovered, 5 additional minutes. **Yield: 5 servings.**

Chicken-Tomatillo Enchiladas

5 skinned chicken breast halves
2 (3-ounce) packages cream cheese, softened
⅓ cup half-and-half
¾ cup finely chopped onion
½ teaspoon salt
Tomatillo Sauce
12 (6-inch) corn tortillas
¾ cup (3 ounces) shredded Cheddar cheese
¾ cup (3 ounces) shredded Monterey Jack cheese
Condiments: shredded lettuce, chopped tomatoes, sliced ripe olives, sour cream

Place chicken in a Dutch oven; add water to cover. Bring to a boil; cover, reduce heat, and simmer 35 minutes or until tender.

Remove chicken, reserving 2½ cups broth for Tomatillo Sauce. Bone and chop chicken; set aside.

Beat cream cheese and half-and-half at medium speed of an electric mixer until smooth. Stir in chicken, onion, and salt; set aside.

Spread ¾ cup Tomatillo Sauce in a lightly greased 13-x 9- x 2-inch baking dish; set aside.

Soften tortillas according to package directions.

Spread about 1½ tablespoons Tomatillo Sauce over each tortilla; spoon ¼ cup chicken mixture down center of each. Roll up tortillas, and place, seam side down, in baking dish.

Cover and bake enchiladas at 350° for 25 minutes.

Sprinkle with cheeses. Serve with remaining Tomatillo Sauce and condiments. **Yield: 6 servings.**

Tomatillo Sauce

½ pound fresh tomatillos
4 to 6 jalapeño peppers, seeded and chopped
2½ cups reserved chicken broth
2 tablespoons cornstarch
2 tablespoons water
2 tablespoons chopped fresh cilantro or parsley
1 teaspoon salt

Remove husks from tomatillos; rinse tomatillos.

Combine tomatillos, peppers, and broth in a saucepan. Bring to a boil; reduce heat, and simmer 6 minutes.

Combine cornstarch and water; stir into tomatillo mixture. Add cilantro and salt. Bring to a boil; boil, stirring constantly, 1 minute. Cool slightly.

Pour into container of an electric blender or food processor; process until smooth, stopping once to scrape down sides. **Yield: 3 cups.**

Note: Two (11-ounce) cans tomatillos, drained and chopped, may be substituted for fresh tomatillos.

Chicken-Tomatillo Enchiladas

Chilaquiles con Pollo

1 (3- to 3½-pound) broiler-fryer
6 cups water
1 teaspoon salt
Vegetable oil
4 (8-ounce) packages frozen corn tortillas, thawed
2 (10¾-ounce) cans cream of mushroom soup
2 (10¾-ounce) cans cream of chicken soup
2 (10-ounce) cans tomatoes and green chiles, undrained
2 (16-ounce) cans stewed tomatoes, undrained
1 fresh serrano chile or jalapeño pepper, broiled, peeled, seeded, and chopped
4 medium onions, chopped
1 bunch green onions, chopped
1½ teaspoons garlic powder
1 teaspoon ground cumin
5 cups (20 ounces) shredded Cheddar cheese
3 cups (12 ounces) shredded Monterey Jack cheese

Combine first 3 ingredients in a Dutch oven; bring to a boil. Cover, reduce heat, and simmer 1 hour or until chicken is tender.

Remove chicken from broth; cool and cut into bite-size pieces. Strain broth, and set aside 1⅓ cups (reserve remaining broth for another use).

Pour oil to depth of ⅛ inch in a large skillet; heat to 375°. Using tongs, carefully arrange 3 tortillas in oil; cook 3 to 5 seconds on each side. Drain on paper towels. Repeat cooking procedure with remaining tortillas; add oil to skillet if necessary. Tear each tortilla into 8 pieces; set aside. Reserve oil in skillet.

Combine reserved 1⅓ cups broth, mushroom soup, and next 4 ingredients in Dutch oven; simmer 30 minutes, stirring frequently.

Cook onions, garlic powder, and cumin in reserved oil in skillet until onions are tender but not brown. Stir onions and chicken into soup mixture.

Spread one-fourth of tortillas in a 13- x 9- x 2-inch baking dish. Sprinkle half of Cheddar

cheese over tortillas; pour one-fourth of sauce over cheese. Spread one-fourth of tortillas over sauce. Pour one-fourth of sauce over tortillas; sprinkle top with half of Monterey Jack cheese.

Repeat layering sequence in another 13- x 9- x 2-inch baking dish. Bake casseroles at 350° for 20 to 30 minutes or until bubbly. **Yield: 24 servings.**

Note: Casseroles may be frozen before baking; thaw completely in refrigerator, and bake as directed.

Montezuma Tortilla Pie

2 cups peeled chopped tomato
2 small cloves garlic
¼ teaspoon sugar
½ teaspoon salt
½ cup water
3 tablespoons peanut or safflower oil
⅓ cup chopped onion
2 (4.5-ounce) cans chopped green chiles, drained
24 corn tortillas
Vegetable oil
2 cups chopped cooked chicken
1½ cups sour cream
1¾ cups (7 ounces) shredded Cheddar cheese

Combine first 5 ingredients in container of an electric blender; process 1 minute or until smooth. Pour into a skillet; cook 8 minutes over medium heat, stirring often. Set sauce aside.

Heat peanut oil in a skillet; add onion, and cook until tender. Add chiles; cover, reduce heat, and simmer 4 minutes. Set aside.

Fry tortillas, one at a time, in 2 tablespoons hot oil (375°) about 5 seconds on each side or just until tortillas are softened. Add additional oil, if necessary. Drain on paper towels.

Place 8 tortillas in a lightly greased 13- x 9- x 2-inch baking dish. Layer half each of chicken and chile mixture; top with one-third each of sauce, sour cream, and cheese.

Repeat all layers, starting with tortillas; top with

remaining tortillas, sauce, sour cream, and cheese.

Bake at 350° for 25 minutes; serve immediately.
Yield: 6 to 8 servings.

Breast-of-Chicken Fiesta

1 cup Cheddar cheese cracker crumbs
2 tablespoons taco seasoning mix
8 skinned and boned chicken breast halves
4 green onions, chopped
2 tablespoons butter or margarine, melted
2 cups whipping cream
1 cup (4 ounces) shredded Monterey Jack cheese
1 cup (4 ounces) shredded Cheddar cheese
1 (4.5-ounce) can chopped green chiles, drained
½ teaspoon chicken-flavored bouillon granules

Combine cracker crumbs and seasoning mix
in a small bowl, stirring well. Dredge chicken in
crumb mixture; place in a greased 13- x 9- x 2-
inch baking dish.

Cook green onions in butter in a large skillet
over medium heat until tender. Stir in whipping
cream and remaining ingredients; pour over
chicken. Bake, uncovered, at 350° for 45 minutes.
Yield: 8 servings.

Start with Tortillas

Chalupa: fried tortilla spread with
an assortment of toppings
Enchilada: softened tortilla filled
with meat or cheese and rolled or
folded before being topped with a
sauce and baked
Fajita: originally made with marinated, grilled skirt steak; also popular with chicken cut into strips
and wrapped in warm flour tortillas
Flauta: corn tortilla rolled around
chicken or meat and fried until crisp

Mexican Pollo en Pipián

6 dried ancho chiles
½ cup hot water
1 (4-pound) broiler-fryer, cut up
2 medium onions, quartered
½ green pepper, cut into strips
2 carrots, cut into 4 pieces
1 (10½-ounce) can chicken broth
3½ cups water
1 teaspoon dried coriander seeds
¼ cup creamy peanut butter
½ teaspoon salt
¼ teaspoon ground cinnamon
¼ teaspoon dried thyme
⅛ teaspoon ground cloves
Hot cooked rice
Flour tortillas

Remove stems and seeds from chiles. Chop
chiles. Combine chiles and ½ cup hot water in a
small bowl; cover and set aside 1 hour. Drain
well, and set chiles aside.

Combine chicken and next 5 ingredients in a
large Dutch oven. Place coriander seeds on a 6-
inch square of cheesecloth; tie with string. Add
cheesecloth bag to chicken mixture. Bring to a
boil; cover, reduce heat, and simmer 1 hour.

Remove chicken and vegetables from broth;
set aside. Remove and discard cheesecloth bag.
Strain broth; reserve 1 cup broth, and return 2
cups remaining broth to Dutch oven. Let chicken
cool. Skin, bone, and chop chicken; return chick-
en and vegetables to Dutch oven.

Combine chiles and reserved 1 cup chicken
broth in container of an electric blender; process
until smooth. Add peanut butter; process until
smooth. Add peanut butter mixture, salt, and next
3 ingredients to chicken mixture; stir well. Bring
to a boil; cover, reduce heat, and simmer 30 minutes.
Serve over rice with tortillas. **Yield: 4 servings.**

Mexican Chicken Rolls

½ cup fine, dry breadcrumbs
¼ cup grated Parmesan cheese
1 teaspoon chili powder
¼ teaspoon ground cumin
¼ teaspoon pepper
8 skinned and boned chicken breast halves
1 (8-ounce) package Monterey Jack cheese
   with peppers
⅓ cup butter or margarine, melted

Combine first 5 ingredients in a shallow dish; set aside.

Place chicken between 2 sheets of heavy-duty plastic wrap; flatten to ¼-inch thickness, using a meat mallet or rolling pin. Cut cheese crosswise into 8 equal slices; place a slice of cheese on each chicken breast. Roll up from short side, and secure with wooden picks.

Dip chicken rolls in butter, and dredge in breadcrumb mixture. Place rolls, seam side down, in a lightly greased 11- x 7- x 1½-inch baking dish; bake at 350° for 25 to 30 minutes. **Yield: 8 servings.**

Mexican Stir-Fry

(pictured on page 249)

4 skinned and boned chicken breast halves
2 tablespoons Mexican-seasoned chili powder
2 teaspoons cornstarch
½ cup chicken broth
2 tablespoons olive oil, divided
1 cup frozen whole kernel corn, thawed
2 medium tomatoes, seeded and diced
1 cup canned black beans, drained
¼ teaspoon salt

Cut chicken into thin strips; toss with chili powder, coating well. Let stand 10 minutes. Combine cornstarch and chicken broth; set aside.

Pour 1 tablespoon oil around top of preheated wok or skillet, coating sides; heat at medium-high (350°) for 2 minutes. Add chicken; stir-fry 3 to 4 minutes. Remove from wok, and set aside.

Pour remaining 1 tablespoon olive oil into wok; add corn and tomato, and stir-fry 2 minutes. Return reserved chicken to wok. Add broth mixture, beans, and salt; cook, stirring constantly, until thickened. **Yield: 4 servings.**

Spicy Tex-Mex Chicken

4 large eggs, beaten
¼ cup green chile salsa
¼ teaspoon salt
2 cups fine, dry breadcrumbs
2 teaspoons chili powder
2 teaspoons ground cumin
1½ teaspoons garlic salt
½ teaspoon ground oregano
6 skinned and boned chicken breast halves
¼ cup butter or margarine
Shredded lettuce
1 (8-ounce) carton sour cream
⅓ cup chopped green onions
12 cherry tomatoes
Garnishes: avocado slices, lime wedges
Additional salsa

Combine first 3 ingredients in a shallow bowl; set aside.

Combine breadcrumbs and next 4 ingredients in a shallow pan, and mix well.

Dip chicken in egg mixture, and dredge in breadcrumb mixture; repeat, and set aside.

Melt butter in a 13- x 9- x 2-inch pan. Place chicken in pan, turning once to coat with butter. Bake, uncovered, at 375° for 30 to 35 minutes.

Arrange chicken on a bed of shredded lettuce on a large platter. Top each serving with a dollop of sour cream, and sprinkle with green onions; arrange cherry tomatoes on platter. Garnish, if desired; serve with additional salsa. **Yield: 6 servings.**

Grilled Lime-Jalapeño Chicken

4 skinned and boned chicken breast halves
¼ cup vegetable oil
½ cup lime or lemon juice
1½ teaspoons garlic powder
1 tablespoon minced jalapeño pepper
¼ teaspoon salt
⅛ teaspoon pepper
Garnishes: lime wedges, jalapeño peppers,
    cherry tomatoes, fresh parsley sprigs

Place chicken between 2 sheets of heavy-duty plastic wrap; flatten to ¼-inch thickness, using a meat mallet or rolling pin. Set aside.

Combine oil and next 3 ingredients; reserve ¼ cup marinade, and refrigerate. Place remaining marinade in a heavy-duty, zip-top plastic bag. Add chicken; seal and marinate in refrigerator 1 hour. Remove chicken from marinade, discarding marinade.

Sprinkle chicken with salt and pepper. Grill chicken, covered with grill lid, over medium-hot coals (350° to 400°) 7 minutes on each side, basting twice with reserved ¼ cup marinade. Garnish, if desired. **Yield: 4 servings.**

Grilled Lime-Jalapeño Chicken

Poached Chicken with Black Beans and Salsa

1 cup chicken broth
6 skinned and boned chicken breast halves
¼ cup dry white wine
¼ teaspoon salt
¼ teaspoon pepper
1 (15-ounce) can black beans, undrained
2 teaspoons balsamic or red wine vinegar
Dash of red pepper
Salsa

Bring chicken broth to a boil in a large skillet. Add chicken and next 3 ingredients; cover, reduce heat, and simmer 15 to 20 minutes. Remove from heat.

Pour beans into a container of an electric blender; process until smooth. Combine beans, vinegar, and red pepper in a saucepan; heat thoroughly, stirring occasionally. Add 1 to 2 tablespoons broth from chicken if mixture is too thick.

Divide bean mixture on individual serving plates; drain chicken, and arrange over bean puree. Top with salsa. Serve immediately. **Yield: 6 servings.**

Salsa

1 large tomato, diced
1 serrano or other hot green chile pepper, minced
1 small onion, diced
1 clove garlic, minced
½ cup cilantro or parsley, finely chopped
¼ teaspoon salt
⅛ teaspoon pepper

Combine all ingredients; refrigerate 2 to 3 hours. **Yield: 1½ cups.**

Pollo en Mole de Cacahuate (Chicken with Peanut Mole Sauce)

1 (3-pound) broiler-fryer, cut up and skinned
Salt
1 teaspoon paprika
All-purpose flour
1 cup vegetable oil
¼ cup all-purpose flour
3 tablespoons creamy peanut butter
2 cloves garlic, pressed
2 tablespoons chili powder
1 teaspoon ground cumin
2½ cups water
1 teaspoon Worcestershire sauce
¼ teaspoon salt
Garnish: fresh parsley sprigs

Season chicken with salt and paprika; dredge in flour. Brown chicken in hot oil over medium heat in a large skillet. Remove chicken from skillet, and drain on paper towels; reserve ⅓ cup pan drippings. Place chicken in a 13- x 9- x 2-inch baking dish.

Return reserved pan drippings to skillet; stir in ¼ cup flour, and cook, stirring constantly, 1 minute. Add peanut butter and next 3 ingredients; cook, stirring constantly, until bubbly. Gradually add water; cook over medium heat, stirring until thickened. Stir in Worcestershire sauce and ¼ teaspoon salt.

Pour sauce over chicken; bake, uncovered, at 350° for 30 minutes. Garnish, if desired. **Yield: 4 servings.**

Sauce It

<u>Mole:</u> highly seasoned sauce often served with chicken; may contain Mexican chocolate but not essential
<u>Salsa:</u> cooked or uncooked sauce made with tomatoes, chiles, and seasonings

Outdoor Specialties

Nothing from the grill tastes better than chicken. So fire up
the coals, sniff the enticing aroma, and savor
the tantalizing flavors of these winners.

Grilled Cumin Chicken, Grilled Teriyaki Chicken, Grilled Chicken

Garlic-Grilled Chicken, Basil-Grilled Chicken, Pesto Chicken with Basil Cream

Chicken with White Barbecue Sauce, Marinated Chicken Breasts, Chicken Kabobs

Soy-Lime Grilled Chicken Thighs, Grilled Ginger-Orange Chicken

Chicken grilled with
Spicy Southwest Barbecue Sauce (page 276)

Grilled Cumin Chicken

2 (2½- to 3-pound) broiler-fryers, quartered
Juice of 3 lemons
2 tablespoons vegetable oil
2 tablespoons ground cumin
1 teaspoon salt
1 tablespoon coarsely ground pepper
2½ teaspoons celery salt
¼ teaspoon red pepper

Place chicken in a large shallow dish; pour lemon juice over chicken. Cover and marinate in refrigerator 2 to 3 hours, turning once. Remove chicken from lemon juice; rub with oil.

Combine cumin and remaining ingredients; stir well. Sprinkle seasoning over chicken.

Grill chicken, skin side up, over medium-hot coals (350° to 400°) 30 to 35 minutes or until juices run clear, turning once. **Yield: 8 servings.**

Chicken with White Barbecue Sauce

1½ cups mayonnaise
⅓ cup apple cider vinegar
¼ cup lemon juice
2 tablespoons sugar
2 tablespoons freshly ground pepper
2 tablespoons white wine Worcestershire sauce
1 (2½- to 3-pound) broiler-fryer, quartered

Combine first 6 ingredients in a small bowl; stir well. Arrange chicken in a shallow dish; pour ¾ cup sauce over chicken, turning to coat. Cover and refrigerate remaining sauce. Cover chicken and marinate in refrigerator 6 to 8 hours, turning occasionally.

Remove chicken, discarding marinade; arrange in a 12- x 8- x 2-inch baking dish with skin side down and thicker portion of chicken toward outside of dish. Cover with wax paper, and microwave at HIGH 10 to 12 minutes; turn and rearrange chicken after 5 minutes.

Grill chicken, skin side up, over medium-hot coals (350° to 400°) 15 to 20 minutes or until juices run clear, turning once and basting with half of reserved marinade. Serve with remaining reserved sauce. **Yield: 4 servings.**

Grilled Teriyaki Chicken

4 cups dry white wine
½ cup lemon juice
¼ cup teriyaki sauce
1 tablespoon minced onion
1 clove garlic, minced
2 bay leaves
1 tablespoon bouquet garni
½ teaspoon seasoned salt
½ teaspoon seasoned pepper
½ teaspoon lemon-pepper seasoning
2 black peppercorns
2 (2½- to 3-pound) broiler-fryers, halved
Garnishes: lemon slices, curly endive

Combine first 11 ingredients in a large shallow container; mix well. Reserve 2 cups marinade, and refrigerate. Place chicken in container; cover and marinate in refrigerator 8 hours, turning chicken often. Remove chicken and discard marinade.

Grill chicken, covered with grill lid, over medium-hot coals (350° to 400°) 50 to 60 minutes or until juices run clear, turning and basting often with reserved marinade. Garnish, if desired. **Yield: 4 to 8 servings.**

Microwave Speeds Grilling

Give chicken a jump start by partially cooking it in the microwave and immediately finishing it on the grill. While coals are heating, microwave chicken at HIGH 3 to 5 minutes per pound; then grill 15 to 20 minutes.

Grilled Teriyaki Chicken

Soy-Lime Grilled Chicken Thighs

Soy-Lime Grilled Chicken Thighs

8 large chicken thighs, skinned (about 2 pounds)
½ cup soy sauce
¼ cup chopped green onions
¼ cup lime juice
2 tablespoons dark brown sugar
1 tablespoon honey
1 teaspoon dried crushed red pepper
1 large clove garlic, crushed
Garnishes: lime wedges, fresh parsley sprigs

Place chicken in an 11- x 7- x 1½-inch baking dish. Combine soy sauce and next 6 ingredients; stir well. Reserve ¼ cup marinade, and refrigerate. Pour remaining marinade over chicken. Cover and marinate in refrigerator 8 hours, turning occasionally.

Drain chicken, discarding marinade. Grill chicken, covered with grill lid, over medium-hot coals (350° to 400°) 8 minutes on each side or until done, basting frequently with reserved marinade. Garnish, if desired. **Yield: 4 servings.**

Soy-Lime Grilled Chicken Thighs Technique

Marinate these meaty chicken thighs in a mixture of soy sauce, lime juice, brown sugar, and seasonings.

Marinated Chicken Breasts

6 skinned and boned chicken breast halves
½ cup firmly packed brown sugar
⅓ cup olive oil
¼ cup cider vinegar
3 cloves garlic, crushed
3 tablespoons coarse-grain mustard
1½ tablespoons lemon juice
1½ tablespoons lime juice
1½ teaspoons salt
¼ teaspoon pepper

Place chicken in a large shallow dish. Combine remaining ingredients; stir well, and pour over chicken. Cover and marinate in refrigerator 2 hours.

Remove chicken from marinade, discarding marinade. Grill chicken, covered with grill lid, over medium-hot coals (350° to 400°) 8 to 10 minutes on each side or until done. **Yield: 6 servings.**

Grilled Chicken

½ cup white vinegar
½ cup balsamic vinegar
½ cup water
1 teaspoon chili powder
½ teaspoon dried oregano
½ teaspoon freshly ground black pepper
1 bay leaf, crushed
4 skinned and boned chicken breast halves

Combine first 7 ingredients; reserve ¼ cup marinade, and refrigerate. Place remaining marinade and chicken in a heavy-duty, zip-top plastic bag. Seal and marinate in refrigerator 20 minutes; remove chicken from marinade, discarding marinade.

Grill chicken, covered with grill lid, over medium-hot coals (350° to 400°) 8 to 10 minutes on each side, basting twice with reserved marinade. **Yield: 4 servings.**

From top: Grilled Ginger-Orange Chicken and Grilled Chicken with Vegetables Vinaigrette

Grilled Ginger-Orange Chicken

¼ cup orange marmalade
¼ cup Dijon mustard
2 tablespoons orange juice
2 green onions, finely chopped
6 skinned chicken breast halves
Ginger Butter
Garnishes: orange wedges, kale, green onion,
    orange rind strips

Combine first 4 ingredients; brush on both sides of chicken. Grill chicken, uncovered, over medium coals (300° to 350°) 9 to 10 minutes on each side or until meat thermometer registers 170°. Serve with Ginger Butter; garnish, if desired. **Yield: 6 servings.**

Ginger Butter

½ cup butter or margarine, softened
½ teaspoon grated orange rind
¼ teaspoon ground ginger

Combine all ingredients; chill. Shape butter into curls, if desired. **Yield: ½ cup.**

Grilled Chicken with Vegetables Vinaigrette

4 skinned and boned chicken breast halves
1 (16-ounce) bottle olive oil vinaigrette salad
    dressing, divided
2 sweet red peppers, seeded
2 small zucchini
2 carrots, scraped
2 small yellow squash

Combine chicken and ¾ cup salad dressing in a shallow dish; cover and marinate in refrigerator 4 hours. Cut vegetables into ¼-inch strips; place in a shallow dish. Add ¾ cup salad dressing, tossing to coat. Cover and marinate in refrigerator 4 hours.

Remove chicken from marinade, discarding marinade. Grill chicken, covered with grill lid, over medium coals (300° to 350°) 5 to 6 minutes on each side, basting twice with remaining salad dressing.

Remove vegetables from marinade; drain and discard marinade. Arrange vegetables in steaming rack, and place over boiling water. Cover and steam 3 to 4 minutes or until crisp-tender. Serve chicken on steamed vegetables. **Yield: 4 servings.**

Garlic-Grilled Chicken

4 skinned and boned chicken breast halves
1 cup picante sauce
2 tablespoons vegetable oil
1 tablespoon lime juice
2 cloves garlic, minced
½ teaspoon ground cumin
½ teaspoon dried oregano, crushed
¼ teaspoon salt
Additional picante sauce

Place chicken between 2 pieces of heavy-duty plastic wrap; flatten to ¼-inch thickness, using a meat mallet or rolling pin. Cut chicken into 1-inch-wide strips; place in a shallow container.

Combine 1 cup picante sauce and next 6 ingredients, mixing well. Reserve ⅓ cup marinade, and refrigerate. Pour remaining marinade over chicken; cover and marinate in refrigerator 1 to 2 hours.

Thread chicken onto skewers; grill over medium-hot coals (350° to 400°) 6 to 8 minutes or until done, turning occasionally and basting with reserved marinade. Serve with picante sauce. **Yield: 4 servings.**

Pesto Chicken with Basil Cream

8 skinned and boned chicken breast halves
8 (1-ounce) slices prosciutto or ham
½ cup Pesto
¼ cup olive oil
2 cloves garlic, minced
¼ teaspoon pepper
Basil Cream
Garnish: fresh basil

Place chicken between two sheets of heavy-duty plastic wrap; flatten to ¼-inch thickness, using a meat mallet or rolling pin.

Place 1 slice of prosciutto and 1 tablespoon Pesto in center of each piece of chicken. Roll up crosswise, and secure with a wooden pick. Place in a pan; cover and refrigerate 8 hours, if desired. Let stand at room temperature 30 minutes before grilling.

Combine olive oil, garlic, and pepper. Grill chicken, covered with grill lid, over medium coals (300° to 350°) 15 to 20 minutes or until done, turning and brushing occasionally with olive oil mixture. Serve with Basil Cream. Garnish, if desired. **Yield: 8 servings.**

Pesto

2 cups packed fresh basil
2 cloves garlic
¼ teaspoon salt
¼ teaspoon freshly ground pepper
½ cup freshly grated Parmesan cheese
½ cup freshly grated Romano cheese
½ cup olive oil

Remove stems from basil. Wash basil leaves thoroughly in lukewarm water, and drain well.

Position knife blade in food processor bowl. Add basil and next 5 ingredients, and top with cover; process until smooth. With food processor running, pour oil through food chute in a slow, steady stream until combined. **Yield: 1 cup.**

Basil Cream

⅓ cup dry white wine
3 shallots, chopped (about ¼ cup)
1½ cups whipping cream
¼ cup minced fresh basil
1 cup chopped tomato

Combine wine and shallots in a medium saucepan; bring to a boil, and cook about 2 minutes or until liquid is reduced to about ¼ cup.

Add whipping cream; return to a boil, and cook, stirring constantly, 8 to 10 minutes or until reduced to about 1 cup. Stir in basil and tomato; cook just until heated. **Yield: about 2 cups.**

Note: Chicken may be grilled in advance and reheated. To reheat, reserve ¼ cup basting mixture, and chill. Place chicken rolls on jellyroll pan; cover with foil, and chill. Remove from refrigerator; let stand at room temperature 30 minutes. Reheat chicken rolls, covered, at 350° for 15 to 20 minutes. Uncover and brush chicken with reserved basting mixture. Bake, uncovered, 5 to 10 additional minutes or until thoroughly heated.

Double-Up Grilling

• Grill extra chicken and enjoy it later served cold or reheated in the microwave.
• Leftover grilled chicken is delicious in salads and pasta dishes.
• Grilled chicken may be frozen up to 3 months. Defrost in refrigerator or at LOW (10% power) in the microwave.

Basil-Grilled Chicken

¾ teaspoon coarsely ground pepper
4 skinned chicken breast halves
⅓ cup butter or margarine, melted
¼ cup chopped fresh basil
½ cup butter or margarine, softened
2 tablespoons minced fresh basil
1 tablespoon grated Parmesan cheese
¼ teaspoon garlic powder
⅛ teaspoon salt
⅛ teaspoon pepper
Garnish: fresh basil sprigs

Press ¾ teaspoon pepper into meaty sides of chicken. Combine ⅓ cup melted butter and ¼ cup chopped basil; stir well. Set aside half of butter mixture. Brush chicken lightly with remaining butter mixture.

Combine ½ cup softened butter and next 5 ingredients in a small bowl; beat at low speed of an electric mixer until blended and smooth. Transfer to a small serving bowl; set aside.

Grill chicken over medium coals (300° to 350°) 8 to 10 minutes on each side or until meat thermometer registers 170°, basting frequently with reserved melted butter mixture. Serve with basil-butter mixture. Garnish, if desired. **Yield: 4 servings.**

Basil-Grilled Chicken

Sesame Chicken Kabobs

6 skinned and boned chicken breast halves
¼ cup plus 2 tablespoons teriyaki sauce
¼ cup soy sauce
2 tablespoons sesame seeds
3 tablespoons vegetable oil
2 tablespoons dark sesame oil
2 medium-size sweet red peppers, cut into
    1-inch pieces
2 medium-size yellow peppers, cut into 1-inch
    pieces
4 small purple onions, cut into wedges
Garnish: fresh basil sprigs

Cut chicken into 1-inch pieces; arrange in a shallow container.

Combine teriyaki sauce and next 4 ingredients, stirring well. Reserve ⅓ cup marinade, and refrigerate. Pour remaining marinade over chicken; cover and marinate in refrigerator 3 hours.

Soak 6 (12-inch) wooden skewers in water at least 30 minutes. Remove chicken from marinade, discarding marinade. Thread chicken alternately with peppers and onion onto skewers.

Grill kabobs, covered with grill lid, over medium-hot coals (350° to 400°) 3 to 5 minutes on each side or until chicken is done, basting frequently with reserved marinade. Garnish, if desired. **Yield: 6 servings.**

Mastering Marinades

- Because chicken absorbs flavors quickly, it doesn't necessarily require lengthy marinating time.
- Marinate chicken in the refrigerator in a glass or nonmetallic bowl or a heavy-duty, zip-top plastic bag.
- Drain chicken and discard marinade. To baste chicken during grilling, use a portion of marinade previously set aside.

Sesame Chicken Kabobs Techniques

Seed peppers by cutting them in half and removing seeds and membranes with hands.

Chicken pieces quickly absorb the strong flavor combination of dark sesame oil, teriyaki sauce, and soy sauce.

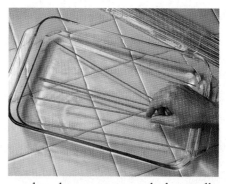

Soak wooden skewers in water before grilling. This prevents them from burning on the grill.

Sesame Chicken Kabobs

Chicken Kabobs

8 slices bacon, cut in half
4 skinned and boned chicken breast halves
1 (15¼-ounce) can unsweetened pineapple
    chunks
1 large onion, cut into 16 pieces
2 large green peppers, cut into 16 pieces
16 cherry tomatoes
½ cup white wine
3 tablespoons Worcestershire sauce
⅛ teaspoon pepper

Cook bacon in a skillet 1 to 3 minutes or until transparent; drain and set aside.

Cut each chicken breast into 4 strips. Drain pineapple, reserving juice. Combine chicken, pineapple chunks, bacon, onion, green pepper, and cherry tomatoes in a shallow dish.

Combine ½ cup reserved pineapple juice, wine, and remaining ingredients; stir well. Reserve ⅓ cup marinade, and refrigerate. Pour remaining marinade over chicken mixture; cover and marinate in refrigerator 8 hours, stirring occasionally.

Drain and discard marinade. Wrap a piece of bacon around each piece of chicken; alternate with vegetables on skewers.

Grill kabobs about 6 inches from medium-hot coals (350° to 400°) 20 minutes or until done, turning and basting often with reserved marinade. **Yield: 4 servings.**

Chicken Kabobs Supreme

4 skinned and boned chicken breast halves
½ cup vegetable oil
¼ cup soy sauce
¼ cup Chablis or other dry white wine
¼ cup light corn syrup
1 tablespoon sesame seeds
2 tablespoons lemon juice
¼ teaspoon garlic powder
¼ teaspoon ground ginger
1 small pineapple, cut into 1-inch pieces
1 large green pepper, cut into 1-inch pieces
2 medium onions, quartered
3 small zucchini, cut into 1-inch pieces
½ pound fresh mushroom caps
1 pint cherry tomatoes (optional)

Cut chicken into 1-inch pieces; arrange in a shallow dish, and set aside.

Combine oil and next 7 ingredients; mix well. Reserve ½ cup marinade, and refrigerate. Pour remaining marinade over chicken; cover and marinate in refrigerator at least 2 hours.

Remove chicken from marinade, discarding marinade. Alternate chicken, pineapple, and vegetables on skewers.

Grill kabobs about 6 inches from medium-hot coals (350° to 400°) 15 to 20 minutes or until done, turning and basting often with reserved marinade. **Yield: 6 servings.**

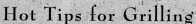

Hot Tips for Grilling

- **Leave** the skin on when grilling and remove it before eating, if desired, to prevent dryness.
- **Flatten** chicken halves with heel of hand before placing on grill for even cooking.
- **Handle** chicken with tongs instead of a fork to prevent piercing and loss of juices.
- **Cook** chicken until well done, not medium or rare. An instant-read thermometer should reach a temperature of 180° or, for chicken breasts, an internal temperature of 170°.

Chicken Bundles with Bacon Ribbons

12 whole skinned and boned chicken breasts
1 cup molasses
½ teaspoon ground ginger
¼ teaspoon garlic powder
2 tablespoons Worcestershire sauce
¼ cup soy sauce
¼ cup olive oil
¼ cup lemon juice
2 pounds mushrooms, sliced and divided
20 green onions, sliced and divided
½ cup butter, melted and divided
½ to 1 teaspoon spike seasoning, divided
24 slices bacon

Place chicken between two sheets of heavy-duty plastic wrap; flatten to ¼-inch thickness, using a meat mallet or rolling pin. Place chicken in a large shallow container, and set aside.

Combine molasses and next 6 ingredients; stir well. Reserve ½ cup marinade, and refrigerate. Pour remaining marinade over chicken, and marinate in refrigerator 8 hours.

Cook half each of mushrooms and green onions in ¼ cup butter, stirring constantly until liquid evaporates; add half of spike seasoning and stir well. Repeat process with remaining mushrooms, green onions, butter, and spike seasoning.

Make each chicken bundle by laying 2 slices bacon in a crosswise pattern on a flat surface. Place a whole chicken breast in center of bacon. Top each with 3 tablespoons mushroom mixture. Fold over sides and ends of chicken to make a square-shaped pouch. Pull bacon around, and tie ends under securely.

Grill chicken over low coals (under 300°) 45 to 55 minutes or until done, turning and basting with reserved marinade every 15 minutes. **Yield: 12 servings.**

Note: Spike seasoning can be found in most supermarkets.

Great Grilling

The key to perfectly grilled chicken is low temperature and nonrushed cooking time. When preparing the grill, consider whether you'll cook using direct or indirect heat.

Grilling with direct heat:
• **Arrange** the coals in a single layer; allow 1 pound charcoal to 2 pounds chicken. Light charcoal 30 minutes before grilling. If using a gas grill, preheat grill for 20 minutes. Coals are ready when covered with light gray ash.
• **Coat** food rack with cooking spray or vegetable oil; place rack 6 to 8 inches above coals.
• **Place** chicken on rack, skin side up, with smaller pieces near the edges.
• **Turn** chicken often during cooking for even doneness.

Grilling with indirect heat:
• **Place** 2 cups hickory or mesquite chips in center of a large square of aluminum foil; fold into a rectangle, and seal. Punch several holes in top of packet.
• **Arrange** charcoal or lava rocks on each side of grill, leaving center empty. Place packet on one side of coals or rocks, and ignite. Let charcoal burn 30 minutes until coals turn white. If using a gas grill, preheat grill for 20 minutes. Place a drip pan in center.
• **Coat** food rack with cooking spray or vegetable oil; place rack 6 to 8 inches above coals.
• **Place** chicken, skin side up, on rack directly over medium-hot coals (350° to 400°); cook, covered with grill lid, about 15 minutes.
• **Turn** chicken, and cook, covered with grill lid, 10 to 15 minutes or until golden. Move chicken over drip pan; cook, covered with grill lid, indirectly 25 to 35 minutes, brushing often with sauce and turning skin side up after 5 minutes.

Maple Syrup Barbecue Sauce

1 cup maple syrup
1 cup ketchup
1 cup finely chopped onion
¼ cup firmly packed brown sugar
¼ cup cider vinegar
¼ cup lemon juice
¼ cup water
2 tablespoons olive oil
2 tablespoons Worcestershire sauce
2 teaspoons finely chopped garlic
2 teaspoons grated lemon rind
1 teaspoon salt
¼ teaspoon hot sauce

Combine all ingredients in a saucepan.
Bring to a boil; reduce heat, and simmer 20 minutes. Cool.
Pour mixture into container of an electric blender; process until smooth.
Remove 1 cup sauce, and brush over chicken the last 30 minutes of cooking time. Serve chicken with remaining sauce. Refrigerate sauce up to 1 month. **Yield: 3½ cups.**

Herbed Lemon Barbecue Sauce

¾ cup lemon juice
2 cloves garlic, peeled
1 tablespoon onion powder
1½ teaspoons salt
1½ teaspoons paprika
1½ cups vegetable oil
1 tablespoon dried basil
1 teaspoon dried thyme

Combine first 5 ingredients in container of an electric blender; process on high 1 minute. With blender on high, add oil in a slow, steady stream; process 1 minute. Add basil and thyme; process on low 30 seconds.

Remove 1 cup sauce, and refrigerate.
Pour remaining sauce over chicken; cover and marinate in refrigerator 8 hours. Drain and blot off excess sauce.
Brush reserved 1 cup sauce over chicken the last 30 minutes of cooking time. **Yield: 2 cups.**

Spicy Southwest Barbecue Sauce

(pictured on page 263)

6 cloves garlic, unpeeled
2 cups ketchup
2 stalks celery, chopped
1 cup water
½ cup chopped onion
½ cup firmly packed brown sugar
½ cup butter or margarine
½ cup Worcestershire sauce
½ cup cider vinegar
3 tablespoons chili powder
2 teaspoons instant coffee granules
1½ to 2 teaspoons dried crushed red pepper
½ teaspoon salt
½ teaspoon ground cloves
Garnish: whole red peppers

Bake garlic in a small pan at 350° for 20 to 30 minutes or until lightly browned. Cool and peel.
Combine garlic and remaining ingredients except garnish in a medium saucepan.
Bring to a boil; reduce heat, and simmer 20 minutes. Cool.
Pour mixture into container of an electric blender; process until smooth, stopping once to scrape down sides.
Remove 1 cup sauce, and brush over chicken the last 30 minutes of cooking time. Serve chicken with remaining sauce. Refrigerate sauce up to 1 month. **Yield: 4½ cups.**

Easy Barbecue Sauce

Easy Barbecue Sauce

1 (16-ounce) can tomato sauce
1 cup chopped onion
½ cup Worcestershire sauce
¼ cup butter or margarine
¼ cup vegetable oil
2 tablespoons sugar
2 tablespoons dark brown sugar
2 teaspoons instant coffee granules
1 teaspoon salt
1 teaspoon garlic powder
1 teaspoon pepper
½ teaspoon ground ginger
½ teaspoon ground allspice

Combine all ingredients in a medium saucepan. Bring to a boil; reduce heat, and simmer 10 minutes, stirring occasionally.

Brush on chicken during grilling, broiling, or baking. Refrigerate sauce in a tightly covered container up to 1 month. **Yield: 3½ cups.**

Baste on a Sauce

Brush barbecue sauces onto chicken during the last 10 to 20 minutes of grilling, especially sauces that are tomato-based or contain sugar. These can cause flare-ups when basted on chicken directly over heat source.

Southern Living®

ALL-TIME FAVORITE

PASTA
RECIPES

Contents

Pasta Primer

Bring on the pasta! For versatility and ease of preparation, pasta is hard to beat.
It is healthy and fits any budget. It can serve one or two or a crowd.
A meal built on a base of pasta can be casual or elegant, leisurely or quick.
From alphabets to ziti, there is a pasta to please almost every palate.

Pasta—What's Available

Pasta, available in a variety of shapes, sizes, and flavors, may be dried or fresh. However, the nutritional value of all the types is about the same.

Dried pasta is a favorite because it is inexpensive and has a long shelf life. Fresh pasta is made with eggs and flour and cooks a bit more quickly than the dried pasta. Look for fresh pasta in the refrigerated section at the supermarket, or follow our step-by-step instructions beginning on page 284 to make your own.

In Shape with Pasta

Choose a pasta shape and sauce that complement each other. To help identify the many shapes of pasta, use the Guide to Pasta on pages 282 and 283.

Long Shapes. Spaghetti, fettuccine, linguine, and angel hair are the most popular and versatile. Team thick strands with heavy, hearty sauces and thin strands with light, delicate sauces.

Medium Shapes. Penne, ziti, rigatoni, and mostaccioli (all tubular shapes) have holes and ridges and pair well with chunky, hearty sauces. Bow ties, elbow macaroni, radiatore (fat, rippled pasta), wagon wheels, and medium shells are popular in salads, casseroles, and stews.

Small Shapes. Ditalini (small tubular pasta), orzo (rice-shaped pasta), and alphabets are suited for soups, salads, and sauces with small chopped vegetables.

Egg Noodles. Available in fine, medium, wide, and extra wide, these are commonly used in casseroles and soups. As the name implies, egg noodles contain egg; most other dry pastas do not.

Specialty Shapes. Lasagna, manicotti, and jumbo shells are almost always used in baked dishes. Ravioli and tortellini are filled with meat, cheese, or other ingredients.

Perfect Pasta Every Time

• Cook pasta in a pasta pot with a removable perforated inner basket, or create one using a large Dutch oven or stockpot with a colander or large wire basket placed inside. The pasta needs plenty of room to bubble in boiling water. To drain, lift the basket, and shake off excess water.

• Use 4 to 6 quarts of water to cook 1 pound of dried pasta. Add pasta gradually to rapidly boiling water so that the water never stops boiling. (A rapid boil means the water is bubbling and moving around swiftly.) After all pasta has been added, stir once, and begin timing.

• Add salt and 1 teaspoon oil to boiling water, if desired. The oil helps keep the pasta from sticking; however, too much oil will cause the sauce to slide off the pasta. If you do not add oil, stir pasta frequently to prevent sticking.

• Cooking times vary with the size, shape, and moisture content of the pasta. Dried pasta cooks in 4 to 15 minutes, while refrigerated pasta requires only 2 to 3 minutes. Follow package directions. Begin checking pasta for doneness 1 minute before its minimum cooking time. Remove a piece of pasta from the water, and cut a bite from it. It is ready when it is al dente ("to the tooth" in Italian)—firm but tender, chewy not soggy.

• If the pasta is to be used in a dish that requires further cooking, slightly undercook the pasta.

• Drain pasta immediately. If pasta is to be reheated or chilled, rinse under cold water to stop the cooking process and to remove excess starch.

• Rinse pasta under running water if it sticks together. For warm pasta dishes, use hot water, and for cold pasta dishes use cold water.

• Save a small amount of the hot cooking liquid to toss with the pasta if it seems too dry.

• Get a head start on a future meal by cooking a little extra. To store cooked pasta, toss lightly with 1 to 2 teaspoons vegetable oil to prevent sticking. Cover and chill up to 4 days, or freeze up to 6 months.

• To reheat cooked pasta, place it in a colander, and run hot water over it. Or drop the pasta in boiling water, let stand for 1 to 2 minutes, and then drain.

Interchanging Pasta Shapes

Give pasta dishes a new twist by using a different shape pasta. It is best to substitute a pasta that is similar in size and thickness to the one called for in the recipe. Here are some pastas that may be interchanged:

• Spaghetti, Thin Spaghetti, or Linguine
• Vermicelli, Thin Spaghetti, or Angel Hair
• Radiatore or Elbow Macaroni
• Wagon Wheels or Elbow Macaroni
• Elbow Macaroni or Medium Shells
• Mostaccioli, Penne, or Ziti
• Rotini or Ziti
• Bow Ties or Rigatoni
• Bow Ties or Ziti
• Orzo, Alphabets, or Ditalini

Pasta Measures Up

Uncooked pasta of similar sizes and shapes may be interchanged in recipes if it is measured by weight, not volume. Cooked pasta, however, should be substituted cup for cup. In general, allow 1 to 2 ounces of uncooked pasta or ½ to 1 cup cooked pasta per person.

Linguine, Spaghetti, or Vermicelli:
    4 ounces dry = 2 to 3 cups cooked
    8 ounces dry = 4 to 5 cups cooked
    16 ounces dry = 8 to 9 cups cooked

Macaroni, Penne, Rotini, or Shells:
    4 ounces dry = 2½ cups cooked
    8 ounces dry = 4½ cups cooked

Fine or Medium Egg Noodles:
    4 ounces dry = 2 to 3 cups cooked
    8 ounces dry = 4 to 5 cups cooked

Guide to Pasta . . .

. . . from A to Z

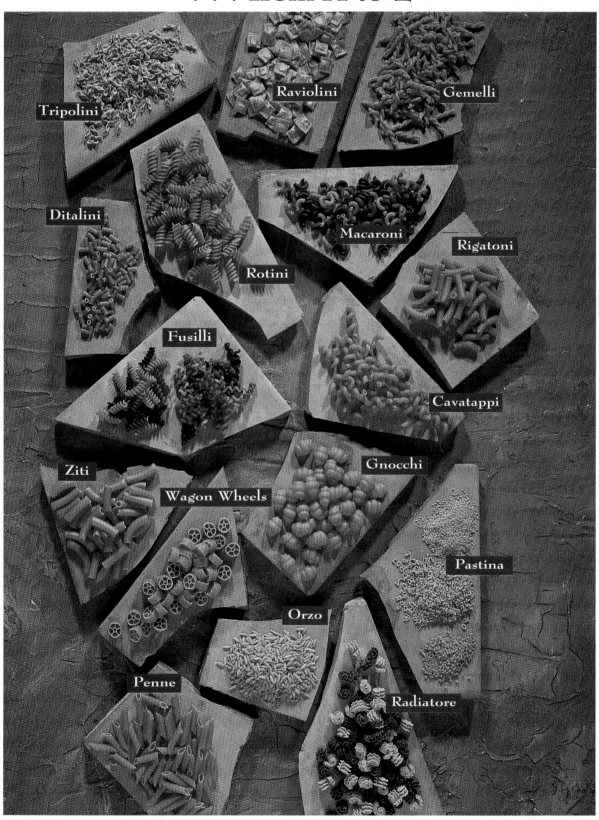

Tripolini

Raviolini

Gemelli

Ditalini

Rotini

Macaroni

Rigatoni

Fusilli

Cavatappi

Ziti

Wagon Wheels

Gnocchi

Pastina

Orzo

Penne

Radiatore

Make Your Own Pasta

If you enjoy pasta, you can double the enjoyment by making your own. The procedure takes some practice, but once you get the knack, it is simple and fun. And pasta purists maintain that there is a world of difference in terms of flavor and texture between the homemade and purchased varieties.

The differences between brands of flour account for the wide range in flour and water amounts called for in our recipe. Start with the minimum amount of flour and water; if the dough seems too dry, add a few more drops of water. If too sticky, knead in a little extra flour. The dough should be firm at the beginning. It will soften as it is kneaded and worked through the pasta machine or rolled out by hand.

Work with the dough, and give it a chance to soften before you add extra water. Otherwise, you might have to add more flour later. Experience is the best guide to knowing when the dough is the right consistency.

Roll the dough in a pasta rolling machine, or roll it out by hand. Most pasta machines have attachments for quickly cutting strips of rolled dough into different widths. You may also use a fluted-edged pastry wheel, a plain-edged roller, a pizza cutter, or a sharp knife with a thin blade to cut the dough into strips.

If you make your own ravioli (see page 286 for recipe), you may want to use a special ravioli rolling pin.

Allow cut pasta to dry 15 to 30 minutes before cooking. Hang it over a wooden drying rack, or spread it out on a kitchen towel to dry. Handle with care; freshly made pasta dough is delicate.

Homemade pasta cooks faster than commercial pasta (in just 1 to 2 minutes). To cook, add fresh pasta to boiling water with salt and a small amount of oil to keep it from sticking.

Homemade Pasta

3 large eggs
3 to 4 cups all-purpose flour
1 teaspoon salt
2 to 4 tablespoons water
3 quarts boiling water
1 teaspoon salt
1 tablespoon olive oil

Beat eggs in a large mixing bowl, using a wire whisk. Add one-fourth of flour and 1 teaspoon salt; beat with a wire whisk until blended. Work in remaining flour and 2 to 4 tablespoons water (add 1 tablespoon at a time) to form dough.

Knead dough gently, and divide dough in half. Working with one portion at a time, pass dough through smooth rollers of pasta machine on widest setting. Generously dust dough with flour, and fold in half.

Repeat rolling, dusting, and folding procedure about 10 times or until dough is smooth and pliable.

Cut dough into 2 pieces. Pass each piece through rollers. Continue moving width gauge to narrower settings; pass dough through rollers once at each setting, dusting with flour, if needed.

Roll dough to thinness desired, about $^1/_{16}$ inch. Pass each dough sheet through the cutting rollers of machine.

Hang noodles over a wooden drying rack, or spread on a dry towel. Dry pasta no longer than 30 minutes. Repeat rolling and drying procedures with remaining portion of dough.

Combine boiling water, 1 teaspoon salt, and olive oil in a large Dutch oven. Add noodles; cook 2 to 3 minutes or until tender. Drain. Use in recipes that call for cooked noodles. **Yield: 10 cups.**

Homemade Pasta Techniques

To make Homemade Pasta, beat eggs in a large mixing bowl with a wire whisk.

Gradually add enough flour and water to form a soft dough.

Knead dough gently, and divide in half. Work with only one portion of dough at a time.

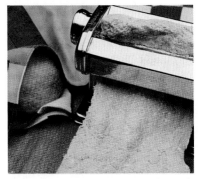

Pass one portion of dough through smooth rollers of pasta machine on widest setting. Repeat rolling, dusting, and folding procedure until dough is smooth and pliable.

Once smooth, cut dough in half, and pass dough through narrower settings until desired thinness is reached, dusting with flour, if needed.

Pass dough through desired cutting rollers of pasta machine.

Cook Homemade Pasta 2 to 3 minutes or until tender. Serve the noodles plain or with a sauce.

Dry pasta over a wooden rack no longer than 30 minutes.

Homemade Ravioli

1 cup ricotta cheese
1 (10-ounce) package frozen chopped spinach,
  thawed and squeezed almost dry
½ cup grated Parmesan cheese
2 egg yolks
2 tablespoons butter or margarine, softened
½ teaspoon ground nutmeg
½ teaspoon salt
¼ teaspoon pepper
1 recipe Homemade Pasta (recipe on page
  284)
4 quarts boiling water
½ teaspoon salt
½ cup butter or margarine, melted
Grated Parmesan cheese
Chopped fresh parsley

Combine first 8 ingredients, stirring well; set aside.

Prepare dough for Homemade Pasta; divide dough into 4 equal portions. Set 2 portions aside. Pass each of 2 pieces of dough, one at a time, through rollers of pasta machine, starting at widest setting.

Continue moving width gauge to narrower settings, passing dough through rollers once at each setting and dusting with flour, if needed. Roll dough to desired thinness, about ¹⁄₁₆ inch thick, 6 inches wide, and 36 inches long.

Place 2 strips of dough on a lightly floured work surface. Roll each rectangle of dough with a ravioli rolling pin, using heavy pressure to make indentations. Spoon 1 teaspoon spinach mixture in center of each square of pattern on one rectangle of dough. Brush water along lines of pattern and edge of dough.

Align remaining rectangle over filled rectangle so rolled ravioli indentations are aligned. Use a fluted pastry wheel to cut through both layers of dough along pattern lines. Dry about 1 hour.

Repeat above rolling and filling procedures with remaining dough and filling ingredients.

Combine boiling water and ½ teaspoon salt in a large Dutch oven. Add half of ravioli; cook 10 to 12 minutes. Drain. Cook remaining ravioli.

Dip ravioli in melted butter; place on baking sheets in a single layer, and sprinkle with Parmesan cheese. Broil 6 inches from heat (with electric oven door partially opened) 3 to 4 minutes or until lightly browned. Place in serving container, and sprinkle with parsley. **Yield: 6 to 8 servings.**

Note: Homemade ravioli in no way resembles (nor should it) the canned versions. Although ravioli is often served with a mushroom or tomato sauce, a simple topping of melted butter and Parmesan cheese on this homemade version will win compliments every time.

Clockwise from top: Whole Wheat Linguine (page 287), Orange Noodles (page 287), Pimiento Pasta (page 288), and Broccoli Pasta (page 288)

Whole Wheat Linguine

1½ cups whole wheat flour
½ teaspoon salt
2 large eggs
2 tablespoons water
2 tablespoons olive oil
2 quarts water
¾ teaspoon salt
2 teaspoons vegetable oil

Position stainless steel chopping blade in food processor bowl. Combine first 5 ingredients in processor, and process until well blended.

Turn dough out onto a lightly floured surface, and knead 1 to 2 minutes. Shape dough into a ball, and place in a zip-top plastic bag. Chill dough 30 minutes.

Cut dough into 4 portions, and return 3 portions to bag. Pat remaining portion into a 4-inch square. Pass square through smooth rollers of pasta machine on widest setting. Fold dough crosswise into thirds. Repeat entire procedure with remaining 3 portions of dough.

Repeat rolling and folding about 10 times or until dough becomes smooth and pliable. Move rollers to next widest setting; pass dough through rollers.

Continue moving width gauge to narrower settings; pass dough through rollers once at each setting until ⅟₁₆-inch thickness, dusting lightly with flour, if needed.

Pass dough through linguine cutting rollers of machine. Hang pasta over a wooden rack, or spread on a dry towel for 30 minutes.

Combine water, ¾ teaspoon salt, and vegetable oil in a large Dutch oven; bring to a boil. Add pasta, and cook 1 to 2 minutes or until tender; drain. Serve with fresh tomato sauce or clam sauce. **Yield: about 4 servings.**

Orange Noodles

3 cups all-purpose flour
½ teaspoon salt
3 large eggs
¼ cup plus 1 tablespoon frozen orange juice
    concentrate, thawed and undiluted
2 tablespoons grated orange rind
3 quarts water
1 teaspoon salt
1 tablespoon vegetable oil

Position stainless steel chopping blade in food processor bowl. Combine first 5 ingredients in processor, and process until well blended.

Turn dough out onto a lightly floured surface, and knead 8 to 10 minutes. Shape dough into a ball, and place in a zip-top plastic bag. Chill dough 1 hour.

Cut dough into 8 portions, and return 7 portions to bag. Pat remaining portion into a 4-inch square. Pass square through smooth rollers of pasta machine on widest setting. Fold dough crosswise into thirds. Repeat entire procedure with remaining 7 portions of dough.

Repeat rolling and folding about 10 times or until dough becomes smooth and pliable. Move rollers to next widest setting; pass dough through rollers.

Continue moving width gauge to narrower settings; pass dough through rollers once at each setting until ⅟₁₆-inch thickness, dusting lightly with flour, if needed.

Pass dough through linguine cutting rollers of machine, or cut with fluted pastry cutter, if desired. Hang pasta over a wooden rack, or spread on a dry towel for 30 minutes.

Combine water, 1 teaspoon salt, and oil in a large Dutch oven; bring to a boil. Add pasta, and cook 1 to 2 minutes or until tender; drain. Serve immediately, plain or buttered. **Yield: 6 servings.**

Pimiento Pasta

2 (4-ounce) jars sliced pimiento, drained
1 large egg
1 tablespoon dry white wine
3 to 3½ cups all-purpose flour
½ teaspoon salt
3 quarts water
1½ teaspoons salt
1 tablespoon olive oil or vegetable oil

Position stainless steel chopping blade in food processor bowl. Combine first 5 ingredients in processor, and process until well blended.

Turn dough out onto a lightly floured surface; knead until smooth. Shape dough into a ball, and place in a zip-top plastic bag. Chill dough 1 hour.

Cut dough into 8 portions, and return 7 portions to bag. Pat remaining portion into a 4-inch square. Pass square through smooth rollers of pasta machine on widest setting. Fold dough crosswise into thirds. Repeat entire procedure with remaining 7 portions of dough.

Repeat rolling and folding about 10 times or until dough becomes smooth and pliable. Move rollers to next widest setting; pass dough through rollers.

Continue moving width gauge to narrower settings; pass dough through rollers once at each setting until ¹⁄₁₆-inch thickness, dusting lightly with flour, if needed.

Pass dough through desired cutting rollers of machine. Hang pasta over a wooden rack, shape into nests, or spread on a dry towel for 30 minutes.

Combine water, 1½ teaspoons salt, and oil in a large Dutch oven; bring to a boil. Add pasta, and cook 1 to 2 minutes or until tender; drain. Serve immediately, plain, buttered, or with a chicken or meat sauce. **Yield: 6 servings.**

Broccoli Pasta

1 (10-ounce) package frozen chopped broccoli
4 cups all-purpose flour
3 large eggs
1 tablespoon lemon juice
1 teaspoon salt
3 quarts water
1½ teaspoons salt
1 tablespoon olive oil or vegetable oil

Cook broccoli according to package directions; drain. Place on paper towels; pat dry.

Position stainless steel chopping blade in food processor bowl. Add broccoli and next 4 ingredients. Process until well blended.

Turn dough out onto a lightly floured surface, and knead about 5 minutes. Shape dough into a ball, and place in a zip-top plastic bag. Chill dough at least 1 hour.

Cut dough into 8 portions, and return 7 portions to bag. Pat remaining portion into a 4-inch square. Pass square through smooth rollers of pasta machine on widest setting. Fold dough crosswise into thirds. Repeat entire procedure with remaining 7 portions of dough.

Repeat rolling and folding 10 times or until dough becomes smooth and pliable. Move rollers to next widest setting; pass dough through rollers.

Continue moving width gauge to narrower settings; pass dough through rollers once at each setting until ¹⁄₁₆-inch thickness, dusting lightly with flour, if needed.

Pass dough through desired cutting rollers of machine. Hang pasta over a wooden rack, or spread on a dry towel for 30 minutes.

Combine 3 quarts water, 1½ teaspoons salt, and oil in a large Dutch oven; bring to a boil. Add pasta, and cook 3 to 4 minutes or until tender. Drain; serve immediately, plain or topped with Parmesan cheese or a sauce. **Yield: 6 servings.**

Note: Substitute 1 (10-ounce) package frozen spinach for broccoli, if desired.

Mainstay Meats

Move over spaghetti and lasagna—manicotti, fettuccine, and tortellini now have equal space in the pantry. Turn these shapes into main dishes to add spark to weeknight or weekend dining.

Pot Roast in Sour Cream, Roquefort Beef Roulades, Veal Marsala

Party Pasta with Prosciutto, Fettuccine with Ham and Peas, Tortellini au Gratin

Red Pepper Round Steak, Classic Beef Stroganoff, One-Step Lasagna, Cavatini

Italian Zucchini Spaghetti, Beefy Tomato-Stuffed Shells, Pasticcio

Meaty Spaghetti with Mushrooms (page 298)

Pot Roast in Sour Cream

1 (3½- to 4-pound) boneless rump roast
2 tablespoons vegetable oil
½ cup water
½ teaspoon beef-flavored bouillon granules
1 bay leaf
½ teaspoon salt
½ teaspoon coarsely ground pepper
2 onions, quartered
2 carrots, scraped and cut into pieces
2 tablespoons all-purpose flour
3 tablespoons water
1 (8-ounce) carton sour cream
Hot cooked noodles

Brown roast on all sides in hot oil in a large Dutch oven. Combine ½ cup water and bouillon granules; add to Dutch oven. Add bay leaf, salt, and pepper.

Cover, reduce heat, and simmer 2½ hours. Add onion and carrot; cover and cook 30 minutes or until vegetables and meat are tender.

Remove roast and vegetables from Dutch oven; keep warm. Remove and discard bay leaf. Combine flour and 3 tablespoons water; stir into pan drippings. Cook, stirring constantly, until gravy is smooth and thickened.

Add sour cream and vegetables to gravy, and cook, stirring constantly, until vegetables are thoroughly heated. Place cooked noodles on a serving platter. Slice roast, and arrange over noodles. Serve with gravy. **Yield: 6 to 8 servings.**

Roquefort Beef Roulades

1 (3-ounce) can sliced mushrooms, undrained
2 (1-pound) round steaks
¼ teaspoon pepper
½ cup chopped onion, divided
1 (4-ounce) package Roquefort cheese, divided
2 tablespoons all-purpose flour
2 tablespoons vegetable oil
1 (12-ounce) can vegetable juice
2 tablespoons Worcestershire sauce
Hot cooked noodles

Drain mushrooms, reserving liquid; set aside.

Trim excess fat from steak. Cut each steak into 3 pieces, and pound to ¼-inch thickness, using a smooth-surfaced meat mallet.

Sprinkle pepper, mushrooms, half of onion, and half of cheese on steaks; roll up, and secure with wooden picks. Dredge steaks in flour, coating evenly. Brown steaks in hot oil in a large skillet; drain.

Return steaks to skillet, and add vegetable juice, reserved mushroom liquid, Worcestershire sauce, and remaining onion. Bring to a boil; cover, reduce heat, and simmer 45 minutes.

Arrange steaks on a platter over hot cooked noodles. Add remaining cheese to sauce, stirring until blended. Spoon sauce over steaks. **Yield: 6 servings.**

Keep the Pasta Platter Hot

Pasta is best served piping hot, but it cools quickly when placed on serving dishes that are at room temperature. To avoid the cool down, preheat the serving platter or bowls. Warm heat-proof dishes in a 250° oven about 10 minutes, or drain some of the hot pasta cooking liquid into the serving bowl and let stand about 2 minutes. Pour off the water, and transfer the pasta to the dish.

Red Pepper Round Steak

Red Pepper Round Steak

1 (1-pound) round steak
½ teaspoon salt
⅛ teaspoon pepper
2 tablespoons chopped onion
2 tablespoons vegetable oil
1 large sweet red pepper, chopped
1 beef-flavored bouillon cube
1 cup hot water
1 (14½-ounce) can tomato wedges, drained
1 tablespoon cornstarch
¼ cup water
2 teaspoons soy sauce
Hot cooked noodles

Partially freeze steak; slice diagonally across grain into ¼-inch-wide strips. Cut strips into 2-inch pieces. Sprinkle steak with salt and pepper.

Cook steak and onion in hot oil in a heavy skillet, stirring constantly, until steak is browned. Add chopped red pepper.

Dissolve bouillon cube in 1 cup hot water; add to steak, and bring to a boil. Cover, reduce heat, and simmer 40 minutes. Add tomatoes.

Combine cornstarch, ¼ cup water, and soy sauce, stirring well; stir into steak mixture. Bring to a boil, and cook, stirring constantly, 1 minute. Serve over noodles. **Yield: 4 servings.**

Classic Beef Stroganoff

1 pound (½-inch-thick) boneless sirloin steak
½ pound sliced fresh mushrooms
¼ cup chopped onion
1 clove garlic, crushed
3 tablespoons butter or margarine, melted
2 tablespoons all-purpose flour
1 (10½-ounce) can beef consommé
3 tablespoons dry sherry
1 tablespoon lemon juice
¼ teaspoon pepper
1 (8-ounce) carton sour cream
Parslied Noodles
Garnish: fresh parsley sprigs

Partially freeze steak. Slice steak diagonally across grain into 3- x ¼-inch strips; set aside.

Cook mushrooms, onion, and garlic in butter in a large skillet, stirring constantly, until vegetables are tender.

Add steak strips, and cook over medium-high heat until browned, stirring frequently. Add flour and next 4 ingredients, stirring well. Bring to a boil; reduce heat, and simmer 15 minutes, stirring occasionally.

Stir in sour cream; cook until thoroughly heated (do not boil). Serve over Parslied Noodles. Garnish, if desired. **Yield: 4 servings.**

Parslied Noodles

4 ounces medium egg noodles, uncooked
2 tablespoons butter or margarine, melted
2 teaspoons chopped fresh parsley

Cook noodles according to package directions; drain well. Combine noodles, butter, and parsley in a large bowl; toss gently. Serve immediately. **Yield: 3 cups.**

Classic Beef Stroganoff Techniques

Stir consommé into meat mixture. Beef consommé is a clarified beef broth used frequently as a flavorful sauce base.

Do not boil mixture after adding sour cream; intense heat causes sour cream to curdle.

Gently toss hot cooked noodles with melted butter and chopped fresh parsley. Top with stroganoff, and serve immediately.

Classic Beef Stroganoff

Cream Cheese Lasagna

Cream Cheese Lasagna

1 pound ground beef
½ cup chopped onion
1 (8-ounce) can tomato sauce
1 (6-ounce) can tomato paste
¼ cup water
1 tablespoon dried parsley flakes
2 teaspoons dried Italian seasoning
1 teaspoon beef-flavored bouillon granules
¼ teaspoon garlic powder
1 (8-ounce) package cream cheese, softened
1 cup cottage cheese
¼ cup sour cream
2 large eggs, beaten
1 (8-ounce) package lasagna noodles, cooked
    and drained
1 (3½-ounce) package sliced pepperoni
2 cups (8 ounces) shredded mozzarella cheese
½ cup grated Parmesan cheese
Garnish: green pepper rings

Cook beef and onion in a heavy skillet, stirring until meat browns and crumbles; drain. Return to skillet, and stir in tomato sauce and next 6 ingredients; cook over low heat 10 minutes.

Combine cream cheese, cottage cheese, sour cream, and eggs; stir well.

Spoon a small amount of meat sauce into a lightly greased 13- x 9- x 2-inch baking dish. Layer with half each of lasagna noodles, cheese mixture, pepperoni, meat sauce, and mozzarella cheese.

Repeat layers; sprinkle with Parmesan cheese.

Cover and bake at 350° for 30 minutes. Let stand 10 minutes before serving. Garnish, if desired. **Yield: 6 servings.**

Microwave Directions:

Crumble ground beef into a 2-quart baking dish; add onion. Cover with wax paper, and microwave at HIGH 4 to 6 minutes or until meat is no longer pink, stirring twice. Drain.

Stir in tomato sauce and next 6 ingredients.

Cover and microwave at HIGH 2 to 3 minutes or until thoroughly heated, stirring once.

Combine cream cheese, cottage cheese, sour cream, and eggs; stir well.

Layer ingredients in a lightly greased 13- x 9- x 2-inch baking dish as directed.

Cover and microwave at MEDIUM HIGH (70% power) 6 to 8 minutes, giving dish a half-turn after 5 minutes. Let stand 10 minutes before serving. Garnish, if desired.

One-Step Lasagna

1 pound lean ground beef
1 (15¼-ounce) jar spaghetti sauce
½ cup water
¼ cup dry red wine
8 lasagna noodles, uncooked
2 cups cottage cheese
3 cups (12 ounces) shredded mozzarella cheese
½ cup grated Parmesan cheese

Crumble beef into a microwave-safe colander; place colander in a 9-inch pieplate. Cover and microwave at HIGH 5 to 6 minutes or until meat is no longer pink, stirring after 3 minutes.

Combine beef, spaghetti sauce, water, and wine. Spread one-third of meat sauce in a lightly greased 13- x 9- x 2-inch baking dish.

Arrange 4 uncooked lasagna noodles on sauce. Layer 1 cup cottage cheese and 1 cup mozzarella cheese over noodles. Spoon half of remaining sauce over cheese.

Repeat layers; sprinkle with Parmesan cheese. Cover tightly with heavy-duty plastic wrap; fold back a small corner of wrap.

Microwave at MEDIUM (50% power) 32 to 35 minutes, giving dish a half-turn after 15 minutes. Sprinkle with remaining 1 cup mozzarella cheese, and microwave, uncovered, at MEDIUM 2 minutes. Let stand 10 minutes. **Yield: 6 servings.**

Specialty Lasagna

Specialty Lasagna

1½ pounds ground beef
¾ cup chopped onion
3 cloves garlic, minced
2 (8-ounce) cans tomato sauce
1 (6-ounce) can tomato paste
1 (4-ounce) can sliced mushrooms, drained
¼ cup red wine vinegar
2 teaspoons dried Italian seasoning
½ teaspoon dried oregano
¼ teaspoon garlic powder
¼ teaspoon salt
¼ teaspoon pepper
1 (8-ounce) package cream cheese, softened
¾ cup ricotta cheese
½ cup sour cream
1 large egg
6 lasagna noodles, uncooked
1¼ cups (5 ounces) shredded mozzarella cheese
½ cup grated Parmesan cheese
1 (6-ounce) package mozzarella cheese slices, cut into ½-inch-wide strips

Crumble ground beef into a 2-quart baking dish; add onion and minced garlic. Cover with wax paper; microwave at HIGH 5 to 6 minutes or until meat is no longer pink, stirring twice. Drain well.

Stir in tomato sauce and next 8 ingredients. Cover and microwave at HIGH 3 to 4 minutes or until thoroughly heated, stirring once.

Beat cream cheese until smooth. Stir in ricotta cheese, sour cream, and egg.

Place noodles in a 13- x 9- x 2-inch baking dish; add water to cover. Cover tightly with heavy-duty plastic wrap; fold back a small corner of wrap to allow steam to escape. Microwave at HIGH 12 to 13 minutes, rearranging noodles after 7 minutes. Drain; pat dry.

Layer half each of cooked noodles, cream cheese mixture, and meat mixture in a greased 13- x 9- x 2-inch baking dish. Sprinkle meat mixture with shredded mozzarella cheese. Repeat layers. Sprinkle with Parmesan cheese.

Cover and microwave at MEDIUM HIGH (70% power) 10 to 12 minutes or until thoroughly heated, giving dish a half-turn after 7 minutes.

Arrange mozzarella strips in a lattice design over lasagna. Cover lasagna, and microwave at MEDIUM HIGH 2 to 3 minutes or until cheese melts. Let stand 5 minutes. **Yield: 6 servings.**

Specialty Lasagna Techniques

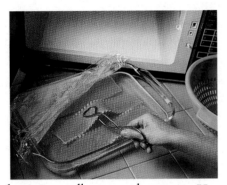

Cook lasagna noodles covered in water. Use tongs to carefully rearrange noodles halfway through cooking time.

For a decorative topping, add strips of mozzarella cheese in a lattice design during last 3 minutes of cooking.

Meaty Spaghetti with Mushrooms

(pictured on page 289)

½ pound ground beef
½ pound hot Italian sausage
1 medium onion, chopped
¾ pound fresh mushrooms, sliced
1 cup diced green pepper
4 cloves garlic, minced
3 tablespoons olive oil
2 (16-ounce) cans whole tomatoes, undrained and coarsely chopped
2 (8-ounce) cans tomato sauce
2 (6-ounce) cans tomato paste
¾ cup water
½ cup dry white wine
1 to 2 tablespoons sugar
1½ teaspoons dried basil
1½ teaspoons dried oregano
1 bay leaf
½ teaspoon salt
½ teaspoon garlic powder
¼ teaspoon ground thyme
¼ teaspoon freshly ground pepper
1 (12-ounce) package thin spaghetti, uncooked
Freshly grated Parmesan cheese

Cook first 3 ingredients in a large Dutch oven, stirring until meat browns and crumbles. Drain well, and set aside.

Cook mushrooms, green pepper, and garlic in olive oil in Dutch oven until tender; add meat mixture. Add tomatoes and next 12 ingredients. Bring to a boil.

Cover, reduce heat, and simmer 25 minutes, stirring occasionally. Uncover and cook 20 minutes, stirring occasionally.

Cook spaghetti according to package directions; drain.

Remove bay leaf from spaghetti sauce. Serve sauce over hot cooked spaghetti; sprinkle with Parmesan cheese. **Yield: 8 servings.**

Quick Spaghetti

1 large onion, chopped
1 green pepper, chopped
1 pound ground beef
1 (3½-ounce) package sliced pepperoni, chopped
1 (32-ounce) jar spaghetti sauce with mushrooms
1 (12-ounce) package spaghetti, uncooked
1 cup (4 ounces) shredded mozzarella cheese
1 tablespoon grated Parmesan cheese

Cook first 4 ingredients in a large skillet over medium heat, stirring until beef browns and crumbles. Remove from heat; drain. Return mixture to skillet.

Add spaghetti sauce to beef mixture, and bring to a boil. Cover, reduce heat, and simmer 20 minutes, stirring occasionally.

Cook spaghetti according to package directions, omitting salt. Drain. Arrange on an oven-proof platter; spoon meat sauce on top. Sprinkle mozzarella cheese over sauce.

Bake at 400° for 3 to 5 minutes. Remove from oven; top with Parmesan cheese. Serve immediately. **Yield: 6 servings.**

Quick Spaghetti

Casserole Spaghetti

1½ pounds ground chuck
1 green pepper, chopped
1 large onion, chopped
½ cup chopped celery
2 cloves garlic, crushed
1 (10¾-ounce) can cream of mushroom soup, undiluted
¾ cup water
1 (16-ounce) can tomatoes, undrained and chopped
2 tablespoons chili powder
½ teaspoon salt
¼ teaspoon pepper
1 (8-ounce) package spaghetti, uncooked
2 ounces sharp Cheddar cheese, cut into ½-inch cubes
1 (5-ounce) jar pimiento-stuffed olives, drained
¾ cup (3 ounces) shredded sharp Cheddar cheese

Cook first 5 ingredients in a Dutch oven, stirring until meat browns and crumbles; drain and return to Dutch oven.

Stir in soup and next 5 ingredients.

Bring soup mixture to a boil over medium heat. Cover, reduce heat, and simmer 1 hour, stirring occasionally.

Cook spaghetti according to package directions; drain.

Stir spaghetti, cheese cubes, and olives into meat sauce. Spoon into a lightly greased 11- x 7- x 1½-inch baking dish.

Cover and bake at 325° for 20 minutes or until thoroughly heated. Sprinkle with ¾ cup shredded cheese, and bake, uncovered, 10 additional minutes. **Yield: 6 to 8 servings.**

Cavatini

1 (16-ounce) package shell macaroni, uncooked
1 pound ground beef
1 pound mild ground pork sausage
1 medium onion, chopped
1 green pepper, chopped
1 (3½-ounce) package sliced pepperoni, chopped
1 (28-ounce) can crushed tomatoes, undrained
1 (26½-ounce) can spaghetti sauce
1 (16-ounce) jar mild salsa
1 (4-ounce) can sliced mushrooms, drained
1 (10-ounce) jar pepperoncini salad peppers, drained and sliced
1 cup grated Parmesan cheese
4 cups (16 ounces) shredded mozzarella cheese

Cook macaroni according to package directions; drain and set aside.

Cook ground beef and next 3 ingredients in a large skillet over medium heat, stirring until meat browns and crumbles. Drain well; set aside.

Combine chopped pepperoni and next 5 ingredients in a large bowl; stir in meat mixture and pasta shells.

Spoon half of pasta mixture into 2 lightly greased 11- x 7- x 1½-inch baking dishes; sprinkle each casserole with ¼ cup Parmesan and 1 cup mozzarella cheeses. Top with remaining pasta mixture.

Bake at 350° for 30 minutes or until heated; top with remaining cheeses. Bake 5 additional minutes. **Yield: 6 servings per casserole.**

Note: Unbaked casseroles may be frozen up to 3 months (freeze cheeses for topping separately). Thaw casseroles in refrigerator 24 hours; let stand at room temperature 30 minutes. Bake at 350° for 40 minutes; sprinkle with cheeses. Bake 5 additional minutes.

Pasticcio

1½ pounds ground beef
1 cup chopped onion
1 (16-ounce) can tomatoes, undrained and
   chopped
1 (6-ounce) can tomato paste
¼ teaspoon dried thyme
1¾ teaspoons salt, divided
1 (8-ounce) package elbow macaroni,
   uncooked
½ cup crumbled feta cheese
4 egg whites, lightly beaten
½ cup butter or margarine
½ cup all-purpose flour
¼ teaspoon ground cinnamon
1 quart milk
4 egg yolks, lightly beaten

Cook ground beef and onion in a large skillet over medium heat, stirring until beef browns and crumbles; drain.

Stir in tomatoes, tomato paste, thyme, and ¾ teaspoon salt; bring to a boil. Cover, reduce heat, and simmer 30 minutes, stirring often.

Cook macaroni according to package directions, adding ¼ teaspoon salt; drain. Stir in feta cheese and egg whites. Add to beef mixture; stir well. Spoon mixture into a lightly greased 13- x 9- x 2-inch baking dish.

Melt butter in a heavy saucepan over low heat; add flour and cinnamon, stirring until smooth. Cook, stirring constantly, 1 minute. Gradually add milk; cook over medium heat, stirring constantly, until mixture is thickened and bubbly. Stir in remaining ¾ teaspoon salt. Gradually stir about one-fourth of hot mixture into yolks; add to remaining hot mixture, stirring constantly. Cook, stirring constantly, 1 minute.

Pour sauce over beef mixture; bake at 350° for 35 to 40 minutes. Remove from oven; let stand 10 minutes. **Yield: 8 servings.**

Pizza Casserole

1 pound lean ground beef
1 large onion, chopped
1 green pepper, chopped
½ teaspoon garlic salt
¼ teaspoon pepper
¼ teaspoon dried oregano
¼ teaspoon dried basil
1 (14-ounce) jar pizza sauce
1 (8-ounce) package macaroni, uncooked
1 (3½-ounce) package sliced pepperoni
1 (4-ounce) package shredded mozzarella
   cheese

Cook ground beef, onion, and green pepper in a large Dutch oven, stirring until meat browns and crumbles. Drain well.

Add garlic salt and next 4 ingredients. Stir well; cover, reduce heat, and simmer 15 minutes.

Cook macaroni according to package directions, omitting salt; drain. Add to meat mixture; stir well. Spoon into a lightly greased 13- x 9- x 2-inch baking dish; top evenly with pepperoni.

Cover and bake at 350° for 20 minutes; top with cheese, and bake, uncovered, 5 additional minutes. **Yield: 6 to 8 servings.**

Did You Know?

Pasticcio, a term derived from the French "pastiche," literally means hodgepodge or potpourri. That's the perfect description for this casserole featuring elbow macaroni layered with a tomato-meat sauce. Feta cheese and cinnamon add authenticity to this Greek dish.

Beefy Tomato-Stuffed Shells

24 jumbo pasta shells, uncooked
1 pound ground beef
½ cup minced onion
½ teaspoon pepper
¼ teaspoon garlic powder
¼ teaspoon dried crushed red pepper
1¼ cups beef broth
1 (7-ounce) jar dried tomatoes in oil, drained
¼ cup pine nuts, toasted
¼ cup fresh basil leaves
2 tablespoons chopped fresh parsley
2 cloves garlic, sliced
¼ cup olive oil
⅓ cup grated Parmesan cheese
1 (32-ounce) jar spaghetti sauce
1½ cups (6 ounces) shredded mozzarella
    cheese
1 to 2 tablespoons chopped fresh parsley

   Cook shells according to package directions;
drain and set aside.
   Cook ground beef and onion in a large skillet,
stirring until meat browns and crumbles; drain.
Add pepper, garlic powder, and red pepper. Cover
and set aside.
   Combine beef broth and next 5 ingredients in
container of an electric blender; cover and process
until well blended. Add olive oil in a slow, steady
stream, and process until combined.
   Stir tomato mixture into ground beef mixture.
Stir in Parmesan cheese.
   Spoon 1 heaping tablespoonful of ground beef
mixture into each shell. Arrange shells in a lightly
greased 13- x 9- x 2-inch baking dish or ovenproof serving dish. Pour spaghetti sauce over top.
   Cover and bake at 375° for 20 to 30 minutes
or until thoroughly heated. Uncover; sprinkle
with mozzarella cheese, and bake 5 additional
minutes or until cheese melts. Sprinkle with
chopped parsley. **Yield: 6 servings.**

Beefy Tomato-Stuffed Shells Techniques

Pine nuts, or pignoli, resemble almonds in shape
but are much smaller and have no skins. Process
with beef broth and other ingredients in a blender
or food processor.

Cook pasta shells in advance so that they will be
cool before being filled with ground beef mixture.

Beefy Tomato-Stuffed Shells

Saucy Manicotti

Saucy Manicotti

¾ pound ground chuck
¾ pound ground hot pork sausage
1 large onion, chopped
5 cloves garlic, minced
2 (15-ounce) cans tomato sauce
1 (14½-ounce) can tomatoes, undrained and
    chopped
1 (6-ounce) can tomato paste
1½ teaspoons dried oregano
1½ teaspoons dried basil
1 teaspoon sugar
¼ teaspoon salt
¼ teaspoon pepper
1 (8-ounce) package manicotti shells,
    uncooked
1 (8-ounce) package cream cheese, softened
½ (8-ounce) carton cream cheese with chives
    and onions
4 cups (16 ounces) shredded mozzarella cheese
1 (16-ounce) carton ricotta cheese
¾ cup grated Parmesan cheese
4 cloves garlic, crushed
¾ teaspoon pepper
½ teaspoon dried oregano

Cook first 4 ingredients in a large Dutch oven over medium heat, stirring until meat browns and crumbles; drain well. Add tomato sauce and next 7 ingredients; bring to a boil. Cover, reduce heat, and simmer 2½ hours, stirring occasionally.

Cook manicotti shells according to package directions; drain and let cool to touch.

Beat cream cheeses in a large bowl at medium speed of an electric mixer until smooth. Add mozzarella cheese and remaining 5 ingredients; stir well. Stuff mixture evenly into cooked shells.

Spoon half of sauce evenly into 2 greased 2½-quart shallow baking dishes. Arrange stuffed shells over sauce. Spoon remaining sauce over shells.

Bake at 350° for 30 to 40 minutes. Let stand 5 minutes before serving. **Yield: 8 servings.**

Cannelloni

3 cups tomato sauce
2 tablespoons grated Parmesan cheese
¼ cup diced onion
1 teaspoon minced garlic
2 tablespoons olive oil
1 (10-ounce) package frozen chopped spinach,
    thawed and drained
1 pound ground beef
2 large eggs, lightly beaten
⅓ cup grated Parmesan cheese
2 tablespoons whipping cream
½ teaspoon dried oregano
12 cannelloni shells, cooked
⅓ cup butter or margarine
⅓ cup all-purpose flour
1 cup milk
1 cup whipping cream
⅛ teaspoon ground white pepper
2 tablespoons butter or margarine

Combine tomato sauce and 2 tablespoons Parmesan cheese in a saucepan; cook over medium heat, stirring constantly, until heated. Spread 1 cup tomato mixture in a lightly greased 13- x 9- x 2-inch baking dish; set aside remaining sauce.

Cook onion and garlic in olive oil in a large skillet until tender. Add spinach, and cook until just tender. Remove from skillet, and set aside.

Brown beef in skillet over medium heat, stirring until it crumbles; drain. Stir in spinach mixture, eggs, and next 3 ingredients.

Stuff cannelloni shells with meat mixture and place on tomato mixture in baking dish; set aside.

Melt ⅓ cup butter in a heavy saucepan over low heat; add flour, stirring until smooth. Cook, stirring constantly, 1 minute. Add milk and 1 cup whipping cream; cook over medium heat, stirring constantly, until thickened. Stir in pepper. Pour sauce over cannelloni; top with reserved tomato mixture. Dot with 2 tablespoons butter. Bake, uncovered, at 375° for 20 minutes. **Yield: 6 servings.**

Stuffed Veal Cutlets

6 (4-ounce) veal cutlets
6 slices prosciutto (about 5 ounces)
4 ounces fontina cheese, cut into 6 strips
¼ teaspoon salt
¼ teaspoon pepper
½ cup all-purpose flour
1 tablespoon butter or margarine, melted
1 tablespoon vegetable oil
1 cup dry white wine
Hot cooked spaghetti

Place cutlets between sheets of heavy-duty plastic wrap; flatten to ⅛-inch thickness, using a meat mallet or rolling pin. Wrap a prosciutto slice around each cheese strip, and place in center of a cutlet. Fold ends of veal cutlets over prosciutto and cheese; fold sides over, and secure with wooden picks.

Sprinkle cutlets with salt and pepper; dredge in flour. Brown on all sides in butter and oil in a heavy skillet. Remove and keep warm.

Add wine to skillet; boil until wine is reduced by half. Add veal; cover and simmer 5 minutes. Serve over spaghetti. **Yield: 6 servings.**

Veal Marsala

¾ cup all-purpose flour
½ teaspoon salt
⅛ teaspoon freshly ground pepper
1¼ pounds thin veal cutlets
½ cup butter or margarine, melted
1¼ cups Marsala wine
Hot cooked vermicelli

Combine flour, salt, and pepper. Dredge veal in flour mixture, and cook in butter 1 to 2 minutes on each side. Place veal on a serving platter; keep warm.

Add wine to skillet, scraping bottom of skillet to loosen browned particles. Cook until bubbly; pour over veal. Serve over vermicelli. **Yield: 4 to 6 servings.**

Note: You may substitute 1 cup dry white wine plus ¼ cup brandy for Marsala wine.

Pork Piccata

2 (¾-pound) pork tenderloins
½ cup all-purpose flour
½ teaspoon salt
¼ teaspoon pepper
3 tablespoons olive oil
½ cup dry white wine
½ cup lemon juice
3 tablespoons butter or margarine
¼ cup chopped fresh parsley
1½ tablespoons capers
Hot cooked fettuccine
Garnishes: lemon slices, fresh parsley sprigs

Cut each tenderloin into 6 (2-ounce) medaillons. Place medaillons, cut side down, between 2 sheets of heavy-duty plastic wrap; flatten to ¼-inch thickness, using a meat mallet or rolling pin.

Combine flour, salt, and pepper; dredge pork in flour mixture.

Cook half of pork in 1½ tablespoons olive oil in a large skillet over medium heat about 2 minutes on each side or until lightly browned. Remove from skillet; keep warm. Repeat procedure.

Add wine and lemon juice to skillet; cook until thoroughly heated. Add butter, chopped parsley, and capers, stirring until butter melts.

Arrange pork over pasta; drizzle with wine mixture. Garnish, if desired. Serve immediately. **Yield: 6 servings.**

Pork Marsala

1 (1-pound) pork tenderloin
1 tablespoon butter or margarine
1 tablespoon vegetable oil
1 clove garlic, minced
½ cup Marsala wine
½ cup dry red wine
1 tablespoon tomato paste
½ pound fresh mushroom caps
1 tablespoon chopped fresh parsley
Hot cooked noodles

Cut tenderloin into 4 equal pieces. Place each piece between two sheets of heavy-duty plastic wrap; flatten to ¼-inch thickness, using a meat mallet or rolling pin.

Heat butter and oil in a large, heavy skillet over medium heat. Add pork, and cook 3 to 4 minutes on each side or until browned. Remove pork from skillet, and keep warm.

Cook garlic in pan drippings in skillet; add wines and tomato paste, stirring until blended. Add mushroom caps, and simmer 3 to 5 minutes. Return pork to skillet, and cook until thoroughly heated. Sprinkle with parsley; serve over noodles. **Yield: 4 servings.**

Pasta Cooking Technique

Add pasta to boiling water in small batches. A few drops of oil added to the water prevents pasta from sticking together.

Ham and Swiss on Noodles

16 ounces egg noodles, uncooked
¼ cup sliced green onions
½ cup butter or margarine, divided
1 (4-ounce) can sliced mushrooms, drained
1 (10-ounce) package frozen English peas,
    thawed and drained
¼ cup all-purpose flour
3 cups milk
½ teaspoon salt
½ teaspoon ground white pepper
2 cups (8 ounces) shredded Swiss cheese
2 cups cubed cooked ham
1 cup chopped canned tomatoes, drained

Cook noodles according to package directions. Drain and keep noodles warm.

Cook green onions in 2 tablespoons melted butter in a large heavy saucepan 3 minutes; add mushrooms and peas, and cook until heated. Remove from saucepan, and set aside.

Melt remaining 6 tablespoons butter in saucepan; add flour, stirring until smooth. Cook, stirring constantly, 1 minute. Gradually add milk, and cook over medium heat, stirring constantly, until mixture is thickened and bubbly. Add salt and pepper, stirring well. Add cheese, and stir until mixture is smooth.

Add vegetables, ham, and tomatoes; mix well. Cook until thoroughly heated. Serve over noodles. **Yield: 8 servings.**

Spaghetti-Ham Pie

6 ounces spaghetti, uncooked
4 cloves garlic, minced
2½ tablespoons olive oil
¼ cup all-purpose flour
¼ teaspoon salt
⅛ teaspoon freshly ground pepper
¾ cup half-and-half
1½ cups milk
¼ to ½ cup chopped cooked ham
¼ cup grated Parmesan cheese, divided

Cook spaghetti according to package directions; drain and set aside.

Cook garlic in olive oil in a Dutch oven over medium heat, stirring constantly, 5 minutes. Stir in flour, salt, and pepper. Cook, stirring constantly, 1 minute.

Add half-and-half and milk; cook over medium heat, stirring constantly, until thickened and bubbly. Stir in spaghetti.

Spoon half of spaghetti mixture into a lightly greased 9-inch pieplate; sprinkle with ham and 2 tablespoons Parmesan cheese. Top with remaining spaghetti mixture; sprinkle with remaining 2 tablespoons Parmesan cheese.

Bake at 425° for 15 to 20 minutes or until lightly browned. **Yield: 6 servings.**

Fettuccine with Ham and Peas

2 cloves garlic, crushed
1 tablespoon butter or margarine, melted
½ pound thinly sliced cooked ham
1 cup frozen English peas, thawed
12 ounces fettuccine, uncooked
½ cup butter or margarine, softened
1 cup grated Parmesan cheese
1 (8-ounce) carton sour cream
½ teaspoon pepper

Cook garlic in 1 tablespoon melted butter in a large skillet over medium heat. Stir in ham and peas; cook, stirring constantly, 3 to 5 minutes. Remove from heat; cover and keep warm.

Cook fettuccine according to package directions, omitting salt. Drain well; place in a large serving bowl. Add ½ cup softened butter, stirring until completely melted; add Parmesan cheese and sour cream, stirring gently to coat well.

Fold ham mixture into fettuccine mixture. Add pepper; toss gently. Serve immediately. **Yield: 6 servings.**

Fettuccine with Ham and Peas Techniques

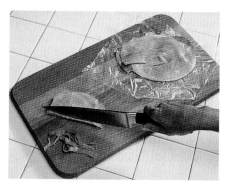

Stack several slices of ham on cutting board; cut ham into ¼-inch slices. Repeat procedure with remaining ham slices.

Thaw peas in microwave oven at HIGH 1 to 2 minutes, stirring to melt ice crystals.

Fettuccine with Ham and Peas

Deluxe Macaroni and Cheese

Deluxe Macaroni and Cheese

1 (8-ounce) package elbow macaroni,
    uncooked
2 cups (8 ounces) shredded Cheddar cheese
2 cups cottage cheese
1 (8-ounce) carton sour cream
1 cup diced cooked ham
3 tablespoons finely chopped onion
1 large egg, lightly beaten
¼ teaspoon salt
¼ teaspoon pepper
1 cup soft breadcrumbs
2 tablespoons butter or margarine, melted
¼ teaspoon paprika
Garnishes: sliced cherry tomatoes, fresh
    parsley sprigs

Cook macaroni according to package directions; drain well.

Place macaroni and next 8 ingredients in a large bowl; stir gently to combine. Spoon mixture into a lightly greased 2-quart baking dish.

Combine breadcrumbs, melted butter, and paprika in a small bowl, stirring well. Sprinkle breadcrumb mixture diagonally across top of casserole, forming stripes.

Bake at 350° for 30 to 40 minutes or until golden. Garnish, if desired. **Yield: 6 servings.**

Chorizo Carbonara

1 (16-ounce) package spaghetti, uncooked
½ pound chorizo sausage, crumbled
1 cup half-and-half
2 cups (8 ounces) shredded Monterey Jack
    cheese with peppers
1 (4½-ounce) can chopped green chiles,
    drained
½ teaspoon ground cumin

Cook spaghetti according to package directions; drain and set aside.

Brown sausage in a nonstick skillet over medium heat. Drain sausage well on paper towels, and set aside.

Heat half-and-half in a small saucepan.

Combine half-and-half, sausage, spaghetti, cheese, and remaining ingredients in a large bowl, tossing until cheese melts. Serve immediately. **Yield: 8 servings.**

Italian Zucchini Spaghetti

1½ pounds hot Italian sausage links, cut into
    bite-size pieces
2 medium-size green peppers, seeded and
    chopped
1 cup chopped onion
2 cloves garlic, minced
3 medium zucchini, coarsely shredded
2 cups chopped peeled tomato
1 (7½-ounce) can tomatoes and jalapeño
    peppers, undrained
1 teaspoon dried Italian seasoning
1 teaspoon chili powder
½ teaspoon salt
1 teaspoon lemon juice
½ teaspoon hot sauce
½ cup grated Parmesan cheese
Hot cooked spaghetti

Cook first 4 ingredients in a Dutch oven, stirring until meat browns; drain well.

Add zucchini and next 7 ingredients; cook over medium heat 10 to 15 minutes or until zucchini is tender, stirring occasionally. Remove from heat; stir in cheese. Serve sauce over spaghetti. **Yield: 8 servings.**

Lasagna Pizza

16 lasagna noodles, uncooked
4 cups (16 ounces) shredded mozzarella cheese
Pizza Sauce
1 (3½-ounce) package sliced pepperoni
1 (8-ounce) can sliced mushrooms, drained
1 small green pepper, cut into strips
1 small onion, sliced and separated into rings
½ cup grated Parmesan cheese

Cook noodles according to package directions; drain. Rinse with cold water, and drain again.

Cover a greased 15- x 10- x 1-inch jellyroll pan with half of noodles, arranging noodles lengthwise in pan, and overlapping sides slightly. (It may be necessary to cut one noodle into smaller pieces to cover pan.)

Sprinkle noodles with half of mozzarella; top with remaining noodles. Spread Pizza Sauce evenly over noodles.

Bake, uncovered, at 375° for 12 minutes. Arrange pepperoni, mushrooms, green pepper, and onion over pizza. Sprinkle with remaining mozzarella and Parmesan cheese. Bake 15 additional minutes. **Yield: 4 to 6 servings.**

Pizza Sauce

1 (8-ounce) can tomato sauce
1 (10¾-ounce) can tomato puree
1 clove garlic, minced
2 teaspoons dried oregano
1 teaspoon dried basil
1 teaspoon dried fennel seeds
¼ teaspoon pepper
⅛ teaspoon salt

Combine all ingredients, mixing well. **Yield: about 2 cups.**

Sausage-Pepperoni Lasagna

1 (8-ounce) package lasagna noodles, uncooked
1 pound ground pork sausage
1 (30-ounce) jar spaghetti sauce
1 large egg, lightly beaten
1 (15-ounce) carton ricotta cheese
1 tablespoon dried parsley flakes
½ teaspoon dried oregano
¼ teaspoon pepper
¼ cup grated Parmesan cheese
2 cups (8 ounces) shredded mozzarella cheese
1 (4.5-ounce) jar sliced mushrooms, drained
1 (3½-ounce) package sliced pepperoni
Garnishes: pepperoni slices, fresh parsley sprigs

Cook lasagna noodles according to package directions, omitting salt; drain.

Brown sausage in a large skillet, stirring until it crumbles; drain. Combine cooked sausage and spaghetti sauce; set aside. Combine egg, ricotta cheese, and next 4 ingredients; set aside.

Spread about ½ cup meat sauce in a lightly greased 13- x 9- x 2-inch baking dish. Layer half of noodles, half of ricotta cheese mixture, one-third of mozzarella cheese, and one-third of remaining meat sauce; repeat layers. Arrange mushrooms and pepperoni slices on top; spoon on remaining sauce.

Bake at 375° for 20 minutes. Sprinkle with remaining mozzarella cheese; bake 5 additional minutes. Let stand 10 minutes before serving. Garnish, if desired. **Yield: 6 to 8 servings.**

Note: To make lasagna ahead, assemble, cover, and refrigerate unbaked casserole 8 hours or overnight. Remove from refrigerator; let stand, covered, 30 minutes. Bake at 375°, uncovered, for 30 minutes; sprinkle with remaining mozzarella cheese. Bake 5 additional minutes; let stand 10 minutes before serving. Garnish, if desired.

Sausage-Pepperoni Lasagna

Tortellini au Gratin

Tortellini au Gratin

¼ pound mild Italian sausage
2 tablespoons finely chopped onion
1 (9-ounce) package refrigerated cheese-filled
    tortellini, uncooked
3 cloves garlic, unpeeled
½ cup whipping cream
½ cup canned diluted chicken broth
½ cup freshly grated Parmesan cheese,
    divided
¼ cup plus 2 tablespoons minced fresh
    parsley, divided
1½ tablespoons minced fresh basil
1 (2-ounce) jar diced pimiento, drained
⅛ teaspoon pepper
2 tablespoons fine, dry breadcrumbs
1½ tablespoons butter or margarine
Garnishes: sliced cherry tomatoes, fresh basil
    sprigs

Remove and discard casing from sausage. Cook sausage and onion in a skillet over medium heat, stirring until sausage browns and crumbles. Drain well; set aside.

Cook tortellini according to package directions, adding unpeeled cloves of garlic to water. Drain well, reserving garlic. Set tortellini aside; peel and crush garlic.

Combine garlic and whipping cream in a medium bowl; beat with a wire whisk until blended. Add reserved sausage mixture, tortellini, chicken broth, ¼ cup plus 2 tablespoons Parmesan cheese, ¼ cup minced parsley, basil, pimiento, and pepper; stir gently to combine.

Place tortellini mixture in a greased 1-quart baking dish. Combine breadcrumbs and remaining 2 tablespoons minced parsley. Sprinkle over tortellini; dot with butter.

Bake at 325° for 40 minutes. Sprinkle remaining 2 tablespoons Parmesan cheese over breadcrumbs; bake 5 additional minutes or until lightly browned. Garnish, if desired. **Yield: 4 servings.**

Spaghetti alla Carbonara

1 (12-ounce) package spaghetti, uncooked
½ cup whipping cream
3 large eggs, beaten
1 cup grated Parmesan cheese, divided
8 slices bacon, cooked and crumbled
¼ cup butter or margarine
¼ cup chopped fresh parsley
1 clove garlic, crushed
½ teaspoon pepper
⅛ teaspoon dried onion powder
⅛ teaspoon dried basil
⅛ teaspoon dried oregano
1 cup cooked English peas

Cook spaghetti according to package directions, omitting salt. Drain; place in a bowl, and keep warm.

Heat whipping cream in a heavy saucepan over medium heat until hot. Gradually stir about one-fourth of hot cream into eggs; add to remaining cream, stirring constantly. Cook, stirring constantly, 1 minute or until mixture reaches 160°.

Add ½ cup cheese and next 8 ingredients, stirring until butter melts. Pour over spaghetti; add peas, and toss. Sprinkle with remaining ½ cup cheese. **Yield: 4 servings.**

Did You Know?

Carbonara is an Italian term referring to pasta dishes with a white cheese sauce of cream, Parmesan cheese, crumbled bacon, and sometimes eggs. Occasionally, English peas are added for extra color and flavor.

Broccoli-Parmesan Fettuccine

2 cups broccoli flowerets
8 ounces fettuccine, uncooked
2 tablespoons butter or margarine
1 (6-ounce) package Canadian bacon, cut into
   thin strips
⅓ cup whipping cream
1½ cups freshly grated Parmesan cheese
½ teaspoon salt
½ teaspoon freshly ground pepper

Cook broccoli in boiling water to cover 3 minutes; drain and plunge into ice water. Drain and set aside.

Cook fettuccine according to package directions; drain and place in a large bowl. Set aside.

Melt butter in a large skillet over medium-high heat. Add Canadian bacon, and cook, stirring constantly, 2 minutes. Stir in broccoli, and cook 1 minute or until thoroughly heated.

Add broccoli mixture, whipping cream, and remaining ingredients to fettuccine; toss gently. Serve immediately. **Yield: 4 servings.**

Party Pasta with Prosciutto

½ cup butter or margarine, divided
2 cups thin prosciutto strips (about ⅓ pound)
1 (12-ounce) package spinach fettuccine,
   uncooked
1½ cups whipping cream
½ cup freshly grated Parmesan cheese
1 (14-ounce) can artichoke hearts, drained
   and halved
½ cup chopped fresh or frozen chives, divided

Melt ¼ cup butter in a skillet. Add prosciutto, and cook over medium heat until browned, stirring often; drain. Set aside.

Cook pasta according to package directions; drain well.

Melt remaining ¼ cup butter in a Dutch oven over medium heat. Add pasta, whipping cream, cheese, artichoke hearts, and ¼ cup chives; toss gently. Arrange on a serving platter.

Sprinkle with prosciutto and remaining chives. Serve immediately. **Yield: 6 servings.**

Note: If prosciutto is not available, you may substitute cooked, crumbled bacon for the cooked prosciutto.

Pasta with Collards and Sausage

1 pound penne or rigatoni (short tubular
   pasta), uncooked
1 pound spicy smoked sausage, sliced
1 (8-ounce) package sliced fresh mushrooms
2 cloves garlic, minced
3 tablespoons olive oil
2 (10-ounce) packages frozen chopped collard
   greens, thawed and well drained
1 tablespoon dried Italian seasoning
2 (14½-ounce) cans chunky Italian-seasoned
   tomatoes, undrained
Freshly grated Parmesan cheese

Cook pasta according to package directions; drain and set aside.

Brown sausage in a Dutch oven; remove from pan, drain on paper towels, and discard drippings. Set sausage aside.

Cook mushrooms and garlic in olive oil in Dutch oven over medium heat, stirring constantly, until mushrooms are tender. Add sausage, collard greens, Italian seasoning, and tomatoes. Cook 10 minutes.

Add pasta, and toss well. Serve with grated Parmesan cheese. **Yield: 8 servings.**

Poultry Pleasers

Pastas of every twirl, curl, and strand team with poultry for enticing fare. The mild flavors of these two basics are complemented by a variety of seasonings.

Italian Chicken, Taste-of-Texas Pasta and Chicken, Cajun Pasta

Turkey with Tarragon Cream, Pasta and Garden Vegetables, Turkey Noodle Bake

Chicken with Artichokes and Mushrooms, Paprika Chicken, Bird's-Nest Chicken

Chicken and Tomatoes over Fettuccine, Pesto Chicken and Pasta

Turkey-Noodle-Poppy Seed Casserole (page 330)

Italian Chicken

2 pounds chicken breasts, thighs, and legs, skinned
1 (14½-ounce) can tomato wedges, drained
1 (6-ounce) can whole mushrooms, drained
1 (6-ounce) can pitted ripe olives, drained
1 (14-ounce) can artichoke hearts, drained
1 (8-ounce) bottle Italian salad dressing
½ cup dry white wine
1 (1-ounce) envelope onion soup mix
1 (8-ounce) package linguine, uncooked

Place chicken pieces in a lightly greased 13- x 9- x 2-inch baking dish. Arrange tomato wedges, mushrooms, olives, and artichoke hearts on top.

Combine salad dressing and wine; pour over vegetables and chicken. Sprinkle with onion soup mix. Cover and bake at 350° for 1 hour or until chicken is tender.

Cook linguine according to package directions; drain. Remove chicken from baking dish, and set aside.

Stir vegetable mixture, and spoon over linguine on a serving platter. Arrange chicken pieces on top, and serve immediately. **Yield: 4 servings.**

Chicken Paprikash

1 (3-pound) broiler-fryer, cut up
¼ cup butter or margarine, melted
½ cup chopped onion
¼ cup all-purpose flour
2 tablespoons Hungarian paprika
2 cups chicken broth
½ teaspoon salt
¼ teaspoon pepper
1 (8-ounce) carton sour cream
Hot cooked noodles

Brown chicken in butter in a Dutch oven over medium heat. Remove chicken, reserving drippings in Dutch oven; drain on paper towels.

Add onion to drippings; cook over medium heat, stirring constantly, until tender. Add flour and paprika; cook, stirring constantly, 1 minute. Gradually add chicken broth; cook, stirring constantly, until thickened and bubbly. Stir in salt and pepper. Add chicken; cover, reduce heat, and simmer 1 hour or until chicken is tender.

Stir in sour cream; cook, stirring constantly, just until thoroughly heated (do not boil). Serve over noodles. **Yield: 4 servings.**

Chicken with Artichokes and Mushrooms

4 skinned and boned chicken breast halves
¼ cup all-purpose flour
2 tablespoons butter or margarine
1 (14-ounce) can artichoke hearts, drained and quartered
1 (4-ounce) can sliced mushrooms, drained
1 cup whipping cream
½ teaspoon cracked pepper
Hot cooked noodles

Place chicken between 2 sheets of heavy-duty plastic wrap; flatten to ¼-inch thickness, using a meat mallet or rolling pin. Dredge chicken lightly in flour.

Melt butter in a large skillet over medium heat. Add chicken, and cook 5 minutes on each side or until golden; cover and cook 5 minutes. Drain drippings from pan.

Add artichokes and next 3 ingredients to skillet; cook, stirring constantly, over low heat until sauce is thickened. Serve over hot cooked noodles. **Yield: 4 servings.**

From top: Taste-of-Texas Pasta and Chicken and Ravioli with Creamy Pesto Sauce (page 382)

Taste-of-Texas Pasta and Chicken

¼ cup olive oil
1 tablespoon lime juice
⅛ teaspoon ground red pepper
4 skinned and boned chicken breast halves
1 (9-ounce) package refrigerated linguine, uncooked
2 tablespoons butter, melted
1 to 1½ teaspoons grated lime rind
1 tablespoon olive oil
1 clove garlic, crushed
1 (16-ounce) jar mild thick-and-chunky salsa
Garnish: lime slices

Combine ¼ cup olive oil, lime juice, and red pepper in a heavy-duty, zip-top plastic bag; seal and shake well. Add chicken; seal and chill 15 minutes.

Cook pasta according to package directions; drain. Add butter and lime rind; toss well, and keep warm.

Remove chicken from marinade; discard marinade. Heat 1 tablespoon oil in a large skillet over medium heat. Add chicken, and cook 10 to 15 minutes or until tender, turning once. Remove chicken, and set aside.

Add garlic to skillet, and cook, stirring constantly, until lightly browned. Add salsa, and bring to a boil. Arrange pasta and chicken on individual serving plates; top with salsa mixture. Garnish, if desired. **Yield: 4 servings.**

Paprika Chicken

1 tablespoon margarine
4 skinned and boned chicken breast halves
1 (10¾-ounce) can reduced-sodium cream of
    mushroom soup, undiluted
1 tablespoon paprika
½ teaspoon dried tarragon
½ teaspoon salt
½ teaspoon ground red pepper
⅓ cup sour cream
Hot cooked egg noodles
Chopped fresh parsley

Melt margarine in a large nonstick skillet over medium-high heat; add chicken, and cook until browned on both sides.

Combine soup and next 4 ingredients; add to skillet, turning chicken to coat. Cover and cook over medium heat 8 minutes or until chicken is tender.

Remove chicken; keep warm. Stir sour cream into pan drippings, and cook 1 minute.

Place chicken on hot cooked noodles; top with sour cream mixture. Sprinkle with chopped fresh parsley. **Yield: 4 servings.**

Chicken Parmesan

6 skinned and boned chicken breast halves
1 large egg, lightly beaten
¼ cup water
½ cup Italian-seasoned breadcrumbs
½ cup grated Parmesan cheese
3 tablespoons butter or margarine
1 (30-ounce) jar spaghetti sauce
Hot cooked egg noodles
1 cup (4 ounces) shredded mozzarella cheese
2 teaspoons grated Parmesan cheese

Place chicken between 2 sheets of heavy-duty plastic wrap. Flatten chicken to ¼-inch thickness, using a meat mallet or rolling pin.

Combine egg and water in a bowl. Combine breadcrumbs and ½ cup Parmesan cheese in a separate bowl. Dip chicken in egg mixture; dredge in breadcrumb mixture.

Melt butter in a skillet over medium heat; add half of chicken, and cook, turning once, until browned. Repeat procedure.

Return chicken to skillet; add spaghetti sauce. Cover and simmer 10 minutes. Place noodles on platter. Spoon chicken and sauce over noodles; sprinkle with mozzarella and 2 teaspoons Parmesan cheese. Cover and let stand until cheeses melt. **Yield: 6 servings.**

Bird's-Nest Chicken

8 nested-style angel hair pasta bundles,
    uncooked
8 skinned and boned chicken breast halves
1 teaspoon salt
½ teaspoon pepper
1 (6-ounce) can sliced mushrooms, drained
1 (10-ounce) package frozen chopped spinach,
    thawed and well drained
1 (10¾-ounce) can cream of chicken soup,
    undiluted
⅔ cup water
3 ounces Monterey Jack cheese, diced
3 ounces Cheddar cheese, diced

Cook angel hair pasta nests according to package directions; drain well, keeping nests intact.

Sprinkle chicken with salt and pepper; arrange in a lightly greased 13- x 9- x 2-inch baking dish. Spoon mushrooms and chopped spinach over chicken. Arrange cooked pasta nests over spinach.

Combine soup and water in a small saucepan; bring to a boil, stirring constantly. Pour sauce evenly over pasta nests. Bake at 375° for 1 hour.

Combine Monterey Jack and Cheddar cheeses; sprinkle over pasta. Bake 5 additional minutes. **Yield: 8 servings.**

Pasta and Garden Vegetables

2 tablespoons butter or margarine
1 tablespoon olive oil
1 pound skinned and boned chicken breasts (about 4 breast halves), cut into strips
1½ cups chopped leeks
3 carrots, scraped and sliced
1 sweet red pepper, cut into 1-inch pieces
½ cup chopped onion
¼ cup chopped fresh parsley
2 teaspoons chopped fresh basil
3 small zucchini, diagonally sliced
2 large tomatoes, diced
½ cup chicken broth
½ teaspoon garlic salt
¼ teaspoon pepper
3 cups rotini (corkscrew pasta), uncooked
2 tablespoons freshly grated Parmesan cheese
2 tablespoons freshly grated Romano cheese

Heat butter and olive oil in a large skillet. Add chicken and next 6 ingredients; cover and simmer 10 minutes.

Add zucchini and next 4 ingredients. Cover and cook 10 minutes or until zucchini is crisp-tender.

Cook rotini according to package directions; drain well. Combine pasta and cheeses in a large bowl; stir well to coat. Add vegetables and chicken, stirring to blend. Serve immediately. **Yield: 6 servings.**

Pesto Chicken and Pasta

1 pound skinned and boned chicken breasts
1 tablespoon vegetable oil
1 cup sliced mushrooms
1 (14½-ounce) can tomato wedges, drained
1 cup chicken broth
1 tablespoon cornstarch
3 tablespoons commercial pesto sauce, divided
8 ounces fettuccine, uncooked

Cut chicken into 1-inch pieces, and set aside.

Place a 10-inch browning skillet in microwave oven; preheat, uncovered, at HIGH 6 minutes or according to manufacturer's instructions. Add oil to hot skillet, tilting to coat surface. Add chicken, stirring well. Microwave, uncovered, at HIGH 3 to 4 minutes or until chicken is no longer pink, stirring every 2 minutes.

Stir in mushrooms and tomato wedges; microwave at HIGH 4 to 5 minutes or until mushrooms are tender.

Combine chicken broth and cornstarch; stir until smooth. Add to chicken mixture; microwave at HIGH 5 to 6 minutes or until slightly thickened. Add 1 tablespoon pesto sauce, stirring well.

Cook fettuccine according to package directions; drain. Combine hot fettuccine and remaining pesto sauce, tossing gently. Serve chicken mixture over pasta. **Yield: 4 servings.**

Cooking Tip

When cooking long pasta shapes (spaghetti, fettuccine, linguine, and angel hair), it's not necessary to break the pasta into shorter pieces. Hold one end of the pasta by the handful, and set the other end in boiling water, pushing pasta gently until it softens enough to submerge.

Cajun Pasta

Cajun Pasta

1½ cups water
½ pound unpeeled medium-size fresh shrimp
2 skinned and boned chicken breast halves,
    cut into ¼-inch strips
½ pound andouille or Cajun smoked sausage,
    sliced
½ cup chopped onion
1 clove garlic, minced
1 tablespoon olive oil
½ cup dry white wine
½ cup chicken broth
1 teaspoon all-purpose flour
1 cup whipping cream
1 tablespoon Cajun or Creole seasoning
2 tablespoons tomato paste
1 teaspoon cracked pepper (optional)
1 green pepper, cut into thin strips
1 sweet red pepper, cut into thin strips
1 (16-ounce) package fettuccine, uncooked

Bring water to a boil; add shrimp, and cook 3 to 5 minutes or until shrimp turn pink. Drain; rinse with cold water. Peel shrimp, and devein, if desired. Set aside.

Cook chicken and next 3 ingredients in olive oil in a large skillet over medium-high heat, stirring often, until meat is lightly browned; remove chicken mixture from skillet, and set aside.

Add wine to skillet. Bring to a boil; reduce heat, and simmer 3 to 5 minutes or until wine is reduced to ¼ cup.

Combine chicken broth and flour, stirring until smooth. Add chicken broth mixture, whipping cream, Cajun seasoning, tomato paste, and if desired, cracked pepper to skillet. Bring to a boil. Reduce heat, and simmer 20 minutes.

Add chicken mixture and pepper strips; cook until thoroughly heated. Keep warm.

Cook fettuccine according to package directions; drain. Combine fettuccine and chicken mixture; toss gently. **Yield: 6 to 8 servings.**

Chicken-Vegetable Spaghetti

4 skinned and boned chicken breast halves,
    cut into 2-inch strips
2 tablespoons olive oil
3 medium zucchini, cut in half lengthwise and
    sliced (about 1 pound)
1 large green pepper, coarsely chopped
½ pound fresh mushrooms, sliced
¼ cup chopped onion
1 clove garlic, minced
1 (30-ounce) jar spaghetti sauce
2 cups (8 ounces) shredded mozzarella cheese,
    divided
8 to 12 ounces spaghetti, uncooked
2 tablespoons chopped fresh parsley

Cook chicken in hot oil in a large skillet, stirring constantly, until no longer pink. Drain and set aside, reserving 1 tablespoon drippings in skillet.

Add zucchini and next 4 ingredients to skillet; cook over medium heat, stirring constantly, until crisp-tender. Stir in chicken and spaghetti sauce; cook until thoroughly heated, stirring occasionally. Stir in 1 cup mozzarella cheese; cook until cheese melts, stirring often.

Cook spaghetti according to package directions; drain. Arrange spaghetti on a large platter, and top with sauce mixture. Sprinkle with remaining 1 cup cheese and parsley. Serve immediately. **Yield: 4 to 6 servings.**

Chicken and Tomatoes over Fettuccine

1 (7-ounce) jar oil-packed dried tomatoes, undrained
6 ounces fettuccine, uncooked
½ cup chopped onion
2 cloves garlic, minced
4 skinned and boned chicken breast halves, cut into strips
3 tablespoons chopped fresh basil or 1 tablespoon dried basil
¼ teaspoon salt
¼ teaspoon pepper

Drain tomatoes, reserving oil. Coarsely chop tomatoes; set aside.

Cook fettuccine according to package directions, omitting salt. Drain and keep warm.

Heat 1 tablespoon reserved oil from tomatoes in a large skillet. Cook onion and garlic in hot oil until tender. Add chicken, and cook, stirring constantly, 8 minutes or until tender.

Add basil and reserved tomatoes to skillet; cook 2 minutes. Stir in salt, pepper, and 2 tablespoons reserved oil from tomatoes.

Place fettuccine on a large platter. Spoon chicken mixture over fettuccine, and toss well. **Yield: 4 servings.**

Try Fresh Basil

Fresh basil, an herb often used in tomato-based pasta dishes, is usually available at supermarkets. To preserve its delicate flavor in long-cooking dishes, add basil near the end of cooking time. Basil bruises easily, so handle it carefully. Cut it with a sharp, thin-bladed stainless-steel knife, or chop it in a food processor using a few 3- to 5-second pulses.

Pasta-Chicken Potpourri

4 ounces penne (short tubular pasta), uncooked
1 teaspoon sesame oil
1½ tablespoons olive oil
1½ tablespoons sesame oil
2 medium carrots, scraped and diagonally sliced
1 small purple onion, chopped
2 medium zucchini, halved lengthwise and sliced
2 cloves garlic, crushed
1½ teaspoons grated fresh ginger
½ teaspoon dried crushed red pepper
2 cups chopped cooked chicken
2 tablespoons soy sauce
2 teaspoons rice wine vinegar
Freshly grated Parmesan cheese

Cook penne pasta according to package directions; drain and toss with 1 teaspoon sesame oil. Set pasta aside.

Pour olive oil and 1½ tablespoons sesame oil around top of preheated wok or large skillet, coating sides; heat at medium-high (375°) for 2 minutes.

Add carrot and onion to wok; stir-fry 3 minutes. Add zucchini and next 3 ingredients; stir-fry 1 minute.

Stir in pasta, chicken, soy sauce, and vinegar; stir-fry 1 minute or until thoroughly heated. Transfer to a serving dish; sprinkle with Parmesan cheese. **Yield: 4 servings.**

Pasta-Chicken Potpourri

Chicken Fettuccine

Chicken Fettuccine

½ pound fresh mushrooms, sliced
1 small sweet red pepper, cut into thin strips
1 small onion, chopped
1 clove garlic, crushed
2 tablespoons butter or margarine, melted
3 cups chopped cooked chicken
1 (8-ounce) package fettuccine, uncooked
½ cup whipping cream
½ cup butter or margarine
½ cup grated Parmesan cheese
2 tablespoons chopped fresh parsley
¼ teaspoon ground white pepper

Cook first 4 ingredients in 2 tablespoons butter in a large skillet over medium heat, stirring constantly, until vegetables are tender. Add chicken, and cook until thoroughly heated. Set aside, and keep warm.

Cook fettuccine according to package directions; drain and place in a large bowl.

Combine whipping cream and ½ cup butter in a small saucepan; cook over low heat until butter melts. Stir in Parmesan cheese, parsley, and white pepper.

Pour whipping cream mixture over hot fettuccine; add chicken mixture. Toss until fettuccine is thoroughly coated. **Yield: 6 to 8 servings.**

Chicken Lasagna Florentine

6 lasagna noodles, uncooked
1 (10-ounce) package frozen chopped spinach, thawed
2 cups chopped cooked chicken
2 cups (8 ounces) shredded Cheddar cheese
⅓ cup finely chopped onion
¼ to ½ teaspoon freshly ground nutmeg
1 tablespoon cornstarch
½ teaspoon salt
¼ teaspoon pepper
1 tablespoon soy sauce
1 (10¾-ounce) can cream of mushroom soup, undiluted
1 (8-ounce) carton sour cream
1 (4.5-ounce) jar sliced mushrooms, drained
⅓ cup mayonnaise or salad dressing
1 cup freshly grated Parmesan cheese
Butter-Pecan Topping

Cook noodles according to package directions; drain and set aside.

Drain spinach well, pressing between layers of paper towels.

Combine spinach, chicken, and next 11 ingredients in a large bowl; stir well to blend.

Arrange 2 noodles in a lightly greased 11- x 7- x 1½-inch baking dish. Spread half of chicken mixture over noodles. Repeat procedure, and top with remaining 2 lasagna noodles. Sprinkle with Parmesan cheese and Butter-Pecan Topping.

Cover and bake at 350° for 55 to 60 minutes or until hot and bubbly. Let stand 15 minutes before cutting. **Yield: 8 servings.**

Butter-Pecan Topping

2 tablespoons butter or margarine
1 cup chopped pecans

Melt butter in a skillet over medium heat; add pecans, and cook 3 minutes. Cool completely. **Yield: 1 cup.**

Ravioli with Parmesan Sauce

3 tablespoons minced shallots or onion
3 tablespoons butter, melted
¾ pound fresh mushrooms, finely chopped
2 teaspoons minced garlic
¾ cup plus 2 tablespoons whipping cream,
    divided
½ cup diced cooked chicken
¼ cup finely chopped prosciutto
¾ teaspoon chopped fresh thyme
⅔ cup ricotta cheese
1¾ cups plus 3 tablespoons grated Parmesan
    cheese, divided
2 egg yolks, beaten
3 cups all-purpose flour
1½ teaspoons salt, divided
3 large eggs
1 tablespoon vegetable oil
1 to 2 tablespoons water
⅓ cup butter
⅓ cup all-purpose flour
2½ cups milk
4 quarts water
½ cup butter, melted
Chopped fresh parsley
Additional chopped fresh thyme

Cook shallots in 3 tablespoons butter 1 minute. Add mushrooms and garlic; cook until liquid evaporates, stirring constantly. Add ¼ cup plus 2 tablespoons whipping cream; cook over medium heat, stirring until liquid is absorbed.

Stir in chicken, prosciutto, and ¾ teaspoon thyme; cool. Stir in ricotta cheese, 3 tablespoons Parmesan cheese, and egg yolks; chill.

Combine 3 cups flour and 1 teaspoon salt; make a well in center. Combine 3 eggs, oil, and 1 tablespoon water; beat well. Add to flour mixture, stirring until blended. Add remaining 1 tablespoon water, if necessary.

Turn dough out onto a floured surface, and knead until smooth and elastic. Cover; let rest 10 minutes.

Divide dough into fourths. Working with one portion at a time (keep unused portions covered), pass dough through pasta machine, starting at widest setting. Continue moving width gauge to narrower settings, passing dough through twice at each setting until about 1/16-inch thick, 6 inches wide, and 48 inches long.

Place one strip of dough on a floured surface. Cut lengthwise into 2-inch-wide strips. Top with about 1½ teaspoons filling at 2-inch intervals. Moisten with water around filling; top with second strip. Press with fingertips to seal. Cut between filling into 2-inch squares. Let dry on a towel 1 hour, turning once. Repeat procedure.

Melt ⅓ cup butter over low heat. Add ⅓ cup flour; stir until smooth. Cook, stirring constantly, 1 minute.

Add milk and remaining ½ cup whipping cream; cook over medium heat, stirring constantly, until thickened and bubbly. Stir in 1½ cups Parmesan cheese; keep sauce warm.

Bring 4 quarts water and remaining ½ teaspoon salt to a boil in a Dutch oven; add half of ravioli at a time, and cook 10 to 12 minutes. Drain. Dip in ½ cup melted butter. Place in a single layer on baking sheets; sprinkle with remaining ¼ cup Parmesan cheese. Broil 6 inches from heat 3 minutes or until golden. Serve with sauce; sprinkle with herbs. **Yield: 6 to 8 servings.**

Ravioli Technique

Working with one portion at a time, pass ravioli dough through rollers of pasta machine.

Ravioli with Parmesan Sauce

Quick Chicken and Pasta

2 quarts water
½ teaspoon salt
4 ounces vermicelli, uncooked
¾ cup frozen English peas
⅓ cup Italian salad dressing
1 cup chopped cooked chicken
¼ teaspoon sweet red pepper flakes
2 tablespoons grated Parmesan cheese

Combine water and salt in a large saucepan; bring to a boil. Add vermicelli and peas. Return water to a boil; reduce heat, and cook 10 minutes. Drain and set aside.

Heat salad dressing in saucepan. Add chicken and red pepper flakes; cook, stirring constantly, 2 minutes.

Add pasta mixture, and cook until thoroughly heated. Sprinkle with Parmesan cheese, tossing mixture well. **Yield: 2 servings.**

Chicken Lasagna

1 (2½- to 3-pound) broiler-fryer
6 cups water
1 teaspoon salt
1 clove garlic, minced
2 tablespoons butter, melted
1 (10¾-ounce) can cream of celery soup, undiluted
½ teaspoon dried oregano
¼ teaspoon pepper
8 lasagna noodles, uncooked
1 (8-ounce) loaf process American cheese, cut in ¼-inch slices, divided
2 cups (8 ounces) shredded mozzarella cheese, divided
2 tablespoons grated Parmesan cheese

Place chicken in a Dutch oven; add water and salt, and bring to a boil. Cover, reduce heat, and

simmer 45 minutes or until tender. Drain, reserving broth, and let cool slightly.

Remove chicken from bone, cutting meat into bite-size pieces; set aside.

Cook garlic in butter in a skillet over medium-high heat, stirring constantly, 2 minutes. Add soup, ¾ cup reserved chicken broth, oregano, and pepper.

Cook lasagna noodles according to package directions in remaining reserved chicken broth, adding more water, if necessary; drain.

Spoon a small amount of sauce into a lightly greased 11- x 7- x 1½-inch baking dish. Layer with half each of noodles, sauce, chicken, and American and mozzarella cheeses. Repeat procedure with noodles, sauce, and chicken, reserving remaining cheeses.

Bake at 350° for 25 minutes; top with remaining cheeses, and bake 5 additional minutes. Let stand 10 minutes. **Yield: 6 servings.**

Turkey-Noodle-Poppy Seed Casserole

(pictured on page 317)

1 (8-ounce) package medium-size egg noodles, uncooked
½ cup chopped onion
¼ cup chopped green pepper
¼ cup butter or margarine, melted
3 tablespoons all-purpose flour
3 cups milk
¼ cup grated Parmesan cheese
1 tablespoon poppy seeds
1 teaspoon salt
⅛ teaspoon ground red pepper
3 cups diced cooked turkey
1 (4-ounce) jar diced pimiento, drained
2 tablespoons grated Parmesan cheese

Cook noodles according to package directions. Drain and set aside.

Cook onion and green pepper in butter in a Dutch oven until tender; add flour, stirring until smooth. Cook, stirring constantly, 1 minute.

Add milk; cook over medium heat, stirring constantly, until thickened and bubbly. Stir in noodles, ¼ cup Parmesan cheese, and next 5 ingredients.

Spoon mixture into a lightly greased 13- x 9- x 2-inch baking dish. Cover and chill 8 hours. To bake, remove from refrigerator, and let stand 30 minutes. Bake, covered, at 350° for 45 minutes. Uncover and sprinkle with 2 tablespoons Parmesan cheese. Bake, uncovered, 10 additional minutes or until thoroughly heated. **Yield: 6 to 8 servings.**

Note: Unbaked casserole may be frozen. To bake, thaw in refrigerator 24 hours. Remove from refrigerator, and let stand 30 minutes. Bake, covered, at 350° for 45 minutes. Uncover and sprinkle with 2 tablespoons cheese. Bake, uncovered, 10 additional minutes or until thoroughly heated.

Microwave Directions:

Prepare casserole as directed in a microwave-safe baking dish; cover and chill 8 hours. Remove from refrigerator, and let stand 30 minutes.

Shield corners of casserole with microwave-safe aluminum foil. Cover baking dish tightly with heavy-duty plastic wrap; fold back a small corner of wrap to allow steam to escape.

Microwave at MEDIUM (50% power) 10 minutes, stirring after 5 minutes. Microwave at HIGH 20 minutes, stirring after 10 minutes.

Uncover and remove shield; sprinkle with 2 tablespoons cheese, and microwave at HIGH 3 minutes.

Note: To microwave frozen casserole, remove from freezer, and shield corners with microwave-safe aluminum foil.

Cover tightly with heavy-duty plastic wrap; fold back a small corner of wrap to allow steam to escape.

Microwave at MEDIUM 30 minutes, stirring after 15 minutes. Microwave at HIGH 10 to 12 minutes, stirring after 5 minutes.

Uncover and remove shield; sprinkle with 2 tablespoons cheese, and microwave at HIGH 3 minutes.

Herbed Turkey Tetrazzini

¼ cup chopped onion
¼ cup chopped fresh mushrooms
¼ cup butter or margarine, melted
¼ cup all-purpose flour
1 cup milk
1 cup chicken broth
½ cup (2 ounces) shredded Swiss or Gruyère cheese, divided
1 tablespoon chopped fresh parsley
1 teaspoon dried tarragon
⅛ teaspoon pepper
Dash of ground nutmeg
2½ cups cooked spaghetti or fettuccine
1½ cups chopped cooked turkey
Garnishes: chopped parsley, red pepper strips

Cook onion and mushrooms in butter in a large, heavy saucepan, stirring constantly, until just tender. Add flour; cook, stirring constantly, 1 minute.

Add milk and chicken broth; cook over medium heat, stirring constantly, until mixture is thickened and bubbly.

Stir in ¼ cup cheese, parsley, and next 5 ingredients, mixing well.

Spoon into a greased 1½-quart baking dish. Bake at 350° for 20 minutes. Sprinkle remaining ¼ cup cheese over top, and bake 5 additional minutes. Garnish, if desired. **Yield: 4 servings.**

Turkey Noodle Bake

Turkey with Tarragon Cream

1 pound cooked turkey breast
2 tablespoons butter or margarine, divided
1 tablespoon all-purpose flour
¾ cup milk
2 tablespoons chopped fresh parsley
½ teaspoon dried tarragon
½ cup sour cream
1 tablespoon Dijon mustard
Hot cooked noodles

Cut turkey into ¼-inch slices. Melt 1 tablespoon butter in a large skillet; add turkey slices, and cook 2 minutes on each side. Arrange turkey on a platter; keep warm.

Melt remaining tablespoon butter in skillet over low heat; add flour, stirring constantly. Gradually add milk; cook over medium heat, stirring constantly, until thickened and bubbly. Remove from heat.

Stir in parsley and next 3 ingredients. Pour sauce over turkey slices. Serve over noodles. **Yield: 4 servings.**

Turkey Noodle Bake

2 pounds ground turkey or beef
2 cups chopped celery
¼ cup chopped green pepper
¼ cup chopped onion
2 tablespoons olive oil
1 (10¾-ounce) can cream of mushroom soup, undiluted
¼ cup soy sauce
1 (8-ounce) can sliced water chestnuts, drained
1 (4.5-ounce) jar sliced mushrooms, drained
1 (4-ounce) jar diced pimiento, drained
1 teaspoon salt
½ teaspoon lemon-pepper seasoning
1 (5-ounce) package egg noodles, uncooked
1 (8-ounce) carton sour cream
¼ cup sliced almonds, toasted
Garnish: celery leaves

Cook first 4 ingredients in olive oil in a Dutch oven over medium heat until meat crumbles, stirring often. Drain. Stir in mushroom soup and next 6 ingredients. Bring to a boil; cover, reduce heat, and simmer 20 minutes, stirring often.

Cook noodles according to package directions; drain. Stir noodles and sour cream into turkey mixture; divide in half.

Spoon mixture into 2 lightly greased 2-quart shallow baking dishes; bake at 350° for 20 minutes or until heated. Top with almonds, and garnish, if desired. **Yield: 4 servings per casserole.**

Note: To freeze Turkey Noodle Bake, line two 2-quart shallow baking dishes with aluminum foil; set aside. Assemble casseroles as directed, and spoon into prepared dishes; freeze. Frozen casseroles may be removed from baking dishes. Wrap in foil, or place in large heavy-duty plastic freezer bags; freeze up to 6 months.

Remove foil, and place frozen casserole in a lightly greased 2-quart shallow baking dish. Cover and bake at 350° for 1 hour and 30 minutes. Top with almonds, and garnish, if desired.

Seafood Sensations

Catch the pasta wave with these delicious pasta and seafood combinations. The pairings are appropriate for family fare or entertaining.

Linguine with Red Clam Sauce, Crawfish Lasagna, Dilled Shrimp

Angel Hair Pasta with Shrimp and Asparagus, Shrimp-and-Vegetable Spaghetti

Scallop Kabobs with Saffron Orzo, Herbed Shrimp and Pasta, Scallops in Wine

Creamy Shrimp and Noodles, Shrimp Scampi, Salmon Fettuccine

Garlic-Buttered Shrimp (page 346)

Linguine with Red Clam Sauce

8 cloves garlic, sliced in half
3 bay leaves, divided
2 tablespoons olive oil
1 cup chopped onion
3 (6½-ounce) cans minced clams, undrained
2 (15-ounce) cans tomato sauce
1 (6-ounce) can tomato paste
½ cup chicken broth
½ cup dry white wine
1½ teaspoons dried basil
1 teaspoon salt
1 teaspoon dried thyme
½ teaspoon ground red pepper
½ teaspoon black pepper
¼ teaspoon ground white pepper
1 (16-ounce) package linguine, uncooked
⅓ cup chopped fresh parsley (optional)

Cook garlic and 2 bay leaves in olive oil in a large saucepan over medium heat 2 minutes, stirring often. Remove and mince 1 tablespoon garlic, discarding any remaining garlic; return minced garlic to saucepan.

Add onion, and cook 6 minutes or until tender and browned, stirring frequently.

Drain clams, reserving 1 cup clam juice; discard remaining juice. Set clams aside. Add reserved clam juice, remaining bay leaf, tomato sauce, and next 9 ingredients to onion mixture. Bring to a boil.

Cover, reduce heat, and simmer 20 minutes, stirring occasionally.

Cook linguine according to package directions; drain and set aside.

Add clams to sauce; simmer 5 minutes. Discard bay leaves. Place linguine on a warm platter; top with sauce. Sprinkle with chopped parsley, if desired. **Yield: 6 to 8 servings.**

Red Clam Sauce Techniques

Cook garlic and bay leaves in olive oil until garlic is golden. The oil takes on a subtle garlic flavor.

Drain canned clams, reserving 1 cup juice. Use clam juice to flavor tomato sauce.

Simmer red clam sauce until thickened. Discard bay leaves before spooning sauce over hot cooked linguine.

Linguine with Red Clam Sauce

Clam Linguine

Clam Linguine

8 ounces linguine, uncooked
2 tablespoons butter
1 clove garlic, minced
2 tablespoons all-purpose flour
1 tablespoon chopped fresh oregano or
    1 teaspoon dried oregano
2 (10-ounce) cans whole clams, undrained
½ cup dry white wine
¼ cup whipping cream
¼ cup grated Parmesan cheese

Cook linguine according to package directions; drain and keep warm.

Melt butter in a large skillet over medium heat; add garlic, and cook, stirring constantly, 1 minute. Add flour and oregano; cook, stirring constantly, 1 minute.

Stir in clams and wine; cook, stirring constantly, 8 minutes or until mixture reduces slightly. Remove from heat.

Stir in whipping cream, and cook over low heat until thoroughly heated. Spoon over linguine; sprinkle with cheese. **Yield: 4 servings.**

Linguine with Clam Sauce

8 ounces linguine, uncooked
2 (6½-ounce) cans minced clams, undrained
½ medium onion, chopped
¼ cup olive oil
1 tablespoon chopped fresh parsley
½ teaspoon garlic powder

Cook linguine in a Dutch oven according to package directions. Drain; return to Dutch oven. Set aside. Drain clams, reserving liquid; set aside.

Cook onion in olive oil in a medium saucepan until tender. Add reserved clam liquid, and simmer 15 minutes. Stir in clams, parsley, and garlic powder. Heat thoroughly.

Add clam mixture to linguine, tossing well. Cook until mixture is thoroughly heated. Serve immediately. **Yield: 4 servings.**

Seafood and Pasta

2 cups sliced fresh mushrooms
¾ cup chopped onion
¼ cup butter or margarine, melted
1 (10¾-ounce) can cream of mushroom soup,
    undiluted
1 cup half-and-half
2 tablespoons grated Parmesan cheese
¼ teaspoon garlic salt
½ teaspoon dried parsley flakes
1 (16-ounce) package refrigerated crab-
    flavored seafood product, chopped
Hot cooked shell macaroni

Cook mushrooms and onion in butter in a large skillet over medium heat, stirring constantly, until tender.

Add mushroom soup and next 5 ingredients. Cook over medium heat, stirring constantly, until thoroughly heated. Serve over shell macaroni. **Yield: 4 servings.**

Seafood Manicotti

2 pounds unpeeled large fresh shrimp
1 quart whipping cream
½ teaspoon salt
¼ teaspoon ground black pepper
¼ teaspoon ground red pepper
14 manicotti shells, uncooked
1 cup chopped onion
1 cup chopped green pepper
¼ cup chopped celery
1 clove garlic, minced
3 tablespoons butter or margarine, melted
1 pound fresh crabmeat, drained and flaked
½ cup (2 ounces) shredded Cheddar cheese
½ cup (2 ounces) shredded Monterey Jack
   cheese with peppers

Peel shrimp, and devein, if desired. Chop and set aside.

Combine whipping cream and next 3 ingredients in a heavy saucepan; cook over medium-high heat 30 minutes or until thickened and reduced to 2 cups. Set aside.

Cook manicotti according to package directions; drain and set aside.

Cook onion and next 3 ingredients in butter in a large Dutch oven over medium-high heat, stirring constantly, 5 minutes or until tender.

Add shrimp and crabmeat, and cook, stirring constantly, 5 minutes or until shrimp turn pink. Cool 10 minutes, and drain well.

Combine seafood mixture and whipping cream mixture.

Fill manicotti shells, and place in 2 lightly greased 11- x 7- x 1½-inch baking dishes. Sprinkle filled shells with cheeses, and cover with aluminum foil.

Bake at 350° for 15 minutes. Uncover and bake 10 additional minutes. Serve immediately.
Yield: 6 to 8 servings.

Crawfish Stroganoff

1 medium onion, chopped
1 medium-size green pepper, seeded and
   chopped
1 tablespoon vegetable oil
¼ cup butter or margarine
⅓ cup all-purpose flour
⅔ cup water
1 pound fresh or frozen peeled crawfish tails
½ teaspoon salt
½ teaspoon pepper
1 (8-ounce) carton sour cream
Hot cooked noodles

Cook onion and green pepper in hot oil in a large skillet, stirring constantly, until tender. Remove from skillet, and set aside.

Melt butter in skillet over low heat; add flour, stirring until smooth. Cook, stirring constantly, 1 minute. Gradually add water; cook over medium heat, stirring constantly, until mixture is thickened and bubbly. Add vegetables, crawfish, salt, and pepper; cover and simmer 30 minutes.

Remove from heat, and stir in sour cream. Cook over medium heat until thoroughly heated. (Do not boil.) Serve over hot cooked noodles.
Yield: 4 servings.

Did You Know?

Many cooks use a flavored seafood product called surimi instead of "real" crabmeat or lobster. Inexpensive whitefish is transformed to imitate the texture, shape, and flavor of crabmeat, shrimp, lobster, or scallops. This seafood product is rich in protein, low in fat and cholesterol, fully cooked, and ready to eat when purchased.

Crawfish Lasagna

1 cup chopped onion
¾ cup chopped celery
¾ cup chopped green pepper
⅓ cup butter or margarine, melted
3 cloves garlic, minced
1 teaspoon dried basil
1 teaspoon dried oregano
¼ teaspoon salt
¼ teaspoon pepper
Dash of hot sauce
½ teaspoon liquid crab boil
⅓ cup all-purpose flour
3 cups milk
1 (8-ounce) carton sour cream
4 cups (16 ounces) shredded Monterey Jack
    cheese, divided
2 pounds fresh or frozen peeled crawfish tails
⅔ cup chopped green onions
⅓ cup chopped fresh parsley
1 teaspoon dried oregano
1 teaspoon dried basil
½ teaspoon salt
½ teaspoon pepper
Dash of hot sauce
9 lasagna noodles, uncooked
½ teaspoon liquid crab boil
1 tablespoon vegetable oil

Crawfish filling for Crawfish Lasagna

Cook first 3 ingredients in butter in a Dutch oven over medium heat, stirring constantly, until tender. Add garlic and next 6 ingredients.

Add flour, stirring until smooth. Cook, stirring constantly, 1 minute. Gradually add milk; cook over medium heat, stirring constantly, until mixture is thickened and bubbly.

Whisk in sour cream and 3 cups cheese, stirring until smooth.

Cook crawfish tails and green onions in a skillet over medium heat until thoroughly heated; drain. Stir into white sauce; add parsley and next 5 ingredients. Simmer over low heat 5 to 6 minutes.

Cook lasagna noodles according to package directions, adding ½ teaspoon crab boil and oil to water; drain.

Place half of noodles in a lightly greased 13- x 9- x 2-inch baking dish. Layer half of sauce over noodles; repeat layers.

Bake at 350° for 40 minutes. Sprinkle with remaining 1 cup cheese, and bake 5 additional minutes. Let lasagna stand 10 minutes before serving. **Yield: 10 to 12 servings.**

Mussels Linguine

2 pounds raw mussels in shells
3 tablespoons olive oil
½ cup chopped fresh parsley
5 cloves garlic, minced
2 tablespoons dry white wine
1 (15½-ounce) jar spaghetti sauce
½ teaspoon dried oregano
⅛ teaspoon freshly ground pepper
8 ounces linguine, uncooked

Remove beards on mussels, and scrub mussel shells well with a brush. Discard opened, cracked, or heavy mussels.

Combine oil, parsley, and garlic in an 11- x 7- x 1½-inch baking dish; microwave at HIGH, uncovered, 3 to 5 minutes. Stir in wine, spaghetti sauce, oregano, and pepper.

Arrange mussels over sauce in a single layer. Cover tightly with heavy-duty plastic wrap; fold back a corner of wrap to allow steam to escape. Microwave at HIGH 6 to 7 minutes or until mussels open. Discard any unopened mussels.

Cook linguine according to package directions; drain. Place cooked linguine on a platter; top with mussels and sauce. **Yield: 4 servings.**

Salmon-Pesto Vermicelli

1 cup firmly packed fresh basil leaves
¼ cup commercial Italian dressing
2 tablespoons water
3 cloves garlic, crushed
1 (1-pound) salmon fillet
¼ teaspoon cracked pepper
Vegetable cooking spray
1 (8-ounce) package vermicelli, cooked
6 lemon wedges (optional)

Combine first 4 ingredients in a food processor bowl fitted with knife blade. Process 2 minutes,

scraping sides of bowl occasionally. Set aside.

Sprinkle fish with pepper, and place, skin side down, on a broiler pan coated with cooking spray.

Broil 6 inches from heat (with electric oven door partially opened) 5 minutes. Carefully turn over, and broil 4 additional minutes or until fish flakes easily when tested with a fork.

Remove fish from pan; cool. Remove and discard skin; break fish into bite-size pieces.

Combine fish, basil mixture, and vermicelli in a large bowl; toss gently. Serve with lemon wedges, if desired. **Yield: 4 to 6 servings.**

Salmon Fettuccine

8 ounces fettuccine, uncooked
1½ tablespoons butter or margarine
1½ tablespoons all-purpose flour
2 cups half-and-half
1 cup freshly grated Parmesan cheese
1½ teaspoons dry sherry
¼ teaspoon salt
¼ teaspoon ground white pepper
1 clove garlic, minced
2 tablespoons butter or margarine, melted
½ pound salmon fillet, cut into 2-inch pieces

Cook fettuccine according to package directions; drain and set aside.

Melt 1½ tablespoons butter in a heavy saucepan over low heat; add flour, stirring until smooth. Cook, stirring constantly, 1 minute.

Add half-and-half; cook over medium heat, stirring constantly, until mixture is thickened and bubbly. Stir in cheese, sherry, salt, and pepper. Keep warm.

Cook garlic in 2 tablespoons butter in a large skillet. Add salmon; cook until fish begins to flake. Add sauce and fettuccine, tossing gently. Cook over low heat just until thoroughly heated. Serve immediately. **Yield: 4 servings.**

Scallop Kabobs with Saffron Orzo

1 (15¼-ounce) can pineapple chunks,
    undrained
½ cup dry white wine
½ cup soy sauce
¼ cup lemon juice
2 tablespoons olive oil
2 tablespoons chopped fresh parsley
1 teaspoon pepper
½ teaspoon garlic powder
1 pound fresh sea scallops
2 medium-size green peppers, seeded and cut
    into 1-inch squares
12 medium-size fresh mushrooms
12 cherry tomatoes
1 cup dry white wine
1 cup water
2 teaspoons chicken-flavored bouillon
    granules
¼ teaspoon ground saffron
1 cup orzo (rice-shaped pasta), uncooked

Drain pineapple, reserving juice. Set pine-apple aside. Combine pineapple juice, ½ cup wine, and next 6 ingredients in a bowl; stir well. Remove half of marinade mixture, and chill.

Place remaining marinade in a large shallow dish. Add pineapple, scallops, green pepper, mushrooms, and tomatoes; toss gently to coat evenly. Cover and chill 1 hour.

Combine 1 cup wine, water, bouillon gran-ules, and saffron in a medium saucepan; stir well. Bring to a boil over medium heat. Add orzo; return to a boil.

Cover, reduce heat to medium-low, and sim-mer 10 to 12 minutes or until orzo is tender. Drain, if necessary. Set aside, and keep warm.

Drain scallop mixture; discard marinade. Alter-nate pineapple, scallops, green pepper, mush-rooms, and tomatoes on 6 (12-inch) metal skewers.

Cook kabobs 4 to 5 inches from medium-hot coals (350° to 400°) 10 to 12 minutes or until

scallops are done, turning and basting frequently with reserved marinade. Arrange orzo on a serv-ing platter. Serve kabobs over warm orzo. **Yield: 6 servings.**

Scallop Kabobs Techniques

Add pineapple, scallops, and vegetables to mari-nade; cover and chill 1 hour.

Alternate pineapple chunks, scallops, green pepper, mushrooms, and tomatoes on 12-inch skewers.

Place saffron-flavored orzo on a serving platter, and arrange kabobs over orzo.

Scallop Kabobs with Saffron Orzo

Scallops in Wine

1 pound fresh bay scallops
¼ cup butter or margarine, melted
½ cup sliced fresh mushrooms
¼ cup chopped onion
1 clove garlic, minced
½ cup dry white wine
3 tablespoons lemon juice
3 tablespoons lime juice
½ teaspoon dried oregano
½ teaspoon celery salt
¼ teaspoon pepper
Hot cooked vermicelli
Garnish: chopped fresh parsley

Cook scallops in butter in a large skillet over medium heat, stirring constantly, 3 minutes or until tender. Remove scallops from skillet, reserving drippings.

Cook mushrooms, onion, and garlic, stirring constantly, 3 to 5 minutes in skillet; remove vegetables, reserving drippings.

Add wine and next 5 ingredients to skillet. Bring to a boil, and cook 8 minutes.

Stir in scallops and vegetables; cook until thoroughly heated. Serve over hot vermicelli, and garnish, if desired. **Yield: 3 to 4 servings.**

Shrimp Scampi

1 pound unpeeled medium-size fresh shrimp
8 ounces angel hair pasta, uncooked
4 cloves garlic, minced
½ cup butter or margarine, melted
⅓ cup dry white wine
¼ teaspoon freshly ground pepper
¾ cup grated Romano cheese
1 tablespoon chopped fresh parsley

Peel shrimp, and devein, if desired; set aside.
Cook pasta according to package directions;

drain and place on a large serving platter, and keep warm.

Cook shrimp and garlic in butter in a large skillet over medium heat, stirring constantly, 3 to 5 minutes or until shrimp turn pink; add wine and pepper. Bring to a boil; cook, stirring constantly, 30 seconds.

Pour shrimp mixture over pasta; sprinkle with cheese and parsley, and toss gently. Serve immediately. **Yield: 4 servings.**

Creamy Shrimp and Noodles

1 pound unpeeled medium-size fresh shrimp
6 ounces fettuccine, uncooked
1 small sweet red pepper, cut into strips
2 tablespoons butter or margarine, melted
1¼ cups milk
2 (0.6-ounce) envelopes cream of chicken-
   flavored instant soup mix
½ cup frozen English peas
3 tablespoons grated Parmesan cheese
¼ teaspoon garlic powder

Peel shrimp, and devein, if desired; set aside.
Cook fettuccine according to package directions; drain and set aside.

Cook shrimp and red pepper in butter in a large skillet over medium-high heat, stirring constantly, 3 minutes or until shrimp turn pink.

Combine milk and soup mix; add to shrimp mixture. Stir in peas, cheese, and garlic powder.

Bring to a boil; reduce heat and simmer, stirring often, 5 minutes or until thickened. Toss shrimp mixture with fettuccine. Serve immediately. **Yield: 3 to 4 servings.**

Herbed Shrimp and Pasta

Herbed Shrimp and Pasta

1 **pound unpeeled medium-size fresh shrimp**
4 **ounces angel hair pasta, uncooked**
2 **cloves garlic, minced**
½ **cup butter, melted**
1 **cup half-and-half**
¼ **cup chopped fresh parsley**
1 **teaspoon chopped fresh dill or ½ teaspoon**
 dried dillweed
¼ **teaspoon salt**
⅛ **teaspoon pepper**
Steamed pepper strips

 Peel shrimp, and devein, if desired; set aside.
Cook pasta according to package directions.

Drain and set aside; keep warm.

 Cook shrimp and garlic in butter in a heavy skillet over medium-high heat, stirring constantly, 3 to 5 minutes or until shrimp turn pink. Remove shrimp, and set aside, reserving garlic and butter in skillet.

 Add half-and-half to skillet; bring to a boil, stirring constantly. Reduce heat to low, and simmer about 15 minutes or until thickened, stirring occasionally. Add shrimp, parsley, and seasonings; stir until blended.

 Serve shrimp over steamed or sautéed red, green, and yellow pepper strips and angel hair pasta. **Yield: 2 to 3 servings.**

Dilled Shrimp

Dilled Shrimp

2 pounds unpeeled large fresh shrimp
½ cup butter or margarine
⅓ cup chopped green onions
2 large cloves garlic, crushed
1 tablespoon lemon juice
1 tablespoon chopped fresh dill or 1 teaspoon
    dried dillweed
1 (2-ounce) jar diced pimiento, drained
3 cups hot cooked medium egg noodles
2 tablespoons butter or margarine
Salt and pepper to taste
Garnish: fresh dill sprigs

Peel shrimp, and devein, if desired; set aside.

Combine ½ cup butter, green onions, and garlic in a 13- x 9- x 2-inch baking dish. Cover tightly with heavy-duty plastic wrap; fold back a small corner of wrap to allow steam to escape.

Microwave at HIGH 1 to 2 minutes or until butter melts and green onions are tender. Add shrimp and lemon juice, stirring to coat.

Cover and microwave at HIGH 4 minutes, stirring after 2 minutes. Stir in chopped dill.

Cover and microwave at HIGH 1 to 3 minutes or until shrimp turn pink. Let stand, covered, 1 minute. Stir in pimiento.

Combine hot cooked noodles, 2 tablespoons butter, salt, and pepper; stir until butter melts. Arrange noodles on a serving platter. Top with shrimp mixture. Garnish, if desired. **Yield: 6 servings.**

Angel Hair Pasta with Shr and Asparagus

8 unpeeled jumbo fresh shrimp
4 ounces angel hair pasta, uncooked
¼ cup olive oil
2 tablespoons minced garlic
1 teaspoon chopped shallots
6 stalks asparagus, cut into 2-inch pieces
¼ cup diced, seeded, and peeled tomato
½ cup sliced shiitake mushroom caps
¼ teaspoon salt
⅛ teaspoon dried crushed red pepper
½ cup dry white wine
1 tablespoon chopped fresh basil
1 tablespoon chopped fresh oregano
1 tablespoon chopped fresh thyme
1 tablespoon chopped fresh parsley
¼ cup freshly grated Parmesan cheese

Peel shrimp, and devein, if desired; set aside.

Cook pasta according to package directions; drain and set aside.

Heat a 9-inch skillet over high heat 1 minute; add oil, and heat 10 seconds. Add shrimp, garlic, and shallots; cook, stirring constantly, 2 to 3 minutes or until shrimp turn pink.

Add asparagus and next 4 ingredients; stir in wine, scraping bottom of skillet to loosen any particles, if necessary. Add pasta, basil, and remaining ingredients; toss gently. Serve immediately. **Yield: 2 servings.**

Note: You may substitute ½ cup sliced fresh mushrooms for shiitake mushrooms.

Shrimp and Pasta

1½ pounds unpeeled medium-size fresh
    shrimp
1 (12-ounce) package spaghetti, uncooked
1 tablespoon Old Bay seasoning
1 cup broccoli flowerets
1 clove garlic, minced
3 tablespoons olive oil
1 bunch green onions, chopped
1 (4-ounce) can sliced mushrooms, drained
1 (4-ounce) can sliced water chestnuts,
    drained
½ cup sour cream
Grated Parmesan cheese

Peel shrimp, and devein, if desired; set aside.

Cook spaghetti according to package directions, omitting salt and adding Old Bay seasoning. Drain and return to Dutch oven; keep warm.

Cook broccoli and garlic in olive oil in a large skillet, stirring constantly, 3 to 4 minutes. Add

green onions; cook 1 minute. Add shrimp, and cook, stirring constantly, 4 minutes.

Stir in mushrooms and water chestnuts; cook until thoroughly heated. Stir in sour cream; heat thoroughly, but do not boil.

Serve over spaghetti; sprinkle with Parmesan cheese. **Yield: 6 servings.**

Garlic-Buttered Shrimp

(pictured on page 333)

2 pounds unpeeled large fresh shrimp
½ cup butter or margarine
½ cup olive oil
¼ cup minced fresh parsley
1 tablespoon plus 1½ teaspoons lemon juice
1 green onion, minced
3 cloves garlic, minced
¼ teaspoon coarsely ground black pepper
8 ounces linguine, uncooked

Peel and devein shrimp, leaving tails intact (tails may be removed, if desired). Set aside.

Place butter in a 13- x 9- x 2-inch baking dish. Microwave, uncovered, at HIGH 1 minute or until melted. Stir in olive oil and next 5 ingredients; arrange shrimp around outer edges of baking dish.

Cover tightly with heavy-duty plastic wrap, and marinate in refrigerator at least 1 hour.

Remove from refrigerator. Fold back a small corner of wrap to allow steam to escape, and microwave at HIGH 7 to 7½ minutes or until shrimp turn pink, rearranging shrimp every 2 minutes.

Cook linguine according to package directions; drain and place on a serving platter. Top pasta with shrimp mixture. Serve immediately. **Yield: 6 servings.**

Shrimp with Pasta Primavera

3 pounds unpeeled medium-size fresh shrimp
1½ cups chopped green onions
3 to 4 cloves garlic, minced
¾ teaspoon salt
¾ teaspoon ground red pepper
¾ teaspoon black pepper
¾ teaspoon dried basil
¾ teaspoon dried oregano
¾ teaspoon dried thyme
1½ cups butter or margarine, melted
1½ pounds fresh mushrooms, sliced
1 cup dry white wine
Pasta Primavera
Garnishes: cherry tomatoes, fresh parsley
     sprigs

Peel shrimp, and devein, if desired; set aside.

Cook green onions and next 7 ingredients in butter in a large skillet over medium heat, stirring often.

Add shrimp, mushrooms, and wine; cook 3 to 4 minutes or until shrimp turn pink, stirring occasionally. Remove from skillet with a slotted spoon, and serve over Pasta Primavera. Garnish, if desired. **Yield: 12 servings.**

Pasta Primavera

2 (12-ounce) packages thin spaghetti or
     vermicelli, uncooked
1 (8-ounce) bottle red wine-and-vinegar salad
     dressing
3 medium-size green peppers, seeded and
     chopped
3 medium-size sweet red peppers, seeded and
     chopped
3 medium-size yellow squash, cut into thin
     strips
1½ cups chopped green onions
¾ cup sliced pitted ripe olives
½ teaspoon salt

Cook spaghetti according to package directions; drain and keep warm.

Combine salad dressing and remaining 6 ingredients in a large skillet; cook over medium heat about 5 minutes or until vegetables are crisp-tender, stirring often. Pour over spaghetti, tossing gently. **Yield: 12 servings.**

Artichoke-and-Shrimp Linguine

1 pound unpeeled medium-size fresh shrimp
8 ounces linguine, uncooked
3 cloves garlic, minced
½ teaspoon dried crushed red pepper
¼ cup olive oil
1 (14-ounce) can artichoke hearts, drained
     and quartered
½ cup ripe olives, sliced
¼ cup fresh lemon juice
⅛ teaspoon salt
⅛ teaspoon pepper
½ cup grated Parmesan cheese

Peel shrimp, and devein, if desired; set aside.

Cook linguine according to package directions; drain and keep warm.

Cook shrimp, garlic, and red pepper in hot oil in a skillet over medium-high heat, stirring constantly, 5 minutes or until shrimp turn pink.

Stir in artichoke hearts and next 4 ingredients. Add to pasta, and sprinkle with cheese. **Yield: 3 to 4 servings.**

Shrimp-and-Fish Lasagna

6 lasagna noodles, uncooked
3 tablespoons vegetable oil, divided
6 cups water
1 pound unpeeled medium-size fresh shrimp
1 large onion, chopped
1 (3-ounce) package cream cheese, softened
1 cup cottage cheese
1 teaspoon Italian seasoning
½ teaspoon salt
¼ teaspoon coarsely ground pepper
⅛ teaspoon salt-free herb-and-spice blend
Dash of ground nutmeg
1 large egg, beaten
1 (10-ounce) package frozen chopped spinach, thawed and drained
1 (10¾-ounce) can cream of celery soup, undiluted
⅓ cup evaporated skim milk
4 flounder fillets (about 1 pound), cut into 1-inch pieces
1 pound crabmeat or crab-flavored seafood product
2 tablespoons lemon juice
3 tablespoons grated Parmesan cheese
3 tablespoons seasoned, dry breadcrumbs
2 tablespoons butter or margarine, melted
⅓ cup (1.33 ounces) shredded Cheddar cheese

Cook noodles according to package directions, adding 1 tablespoon vegetable oil to boiling water; drain. Arrange noodles in a lightly greased 13- x 9- x 2-inch baking dish. Set aside.

Bring 6 cups water to a boil; add shrimp, and cook 1 minute. Drain well; rinse with cold water. Peel shrimp, and devein, if desired; set aside.

Cook onion in remaining 2 tablespoons oil in a large skillet over medium heat, stirring constantly, until translucent.

Add cream cheese and next 7 ingredients to skillet; cook over medium-low heat until cheese is blended, stirring occasionally. Stir in spinach; spoon over lasagna noodles.

Combine shrimp, soup, and next 4 ingredients; stir well. Spoon over spinach mixture.

Combine Parmesan cheese, breadcrumbs, and butter; sprinkle over lasagna.

Bake at 350° for 45 minutes. Sprinkle with Cheddar cheese, and bake 5 additional minutes or until cheese melts. Remove from oven, and let stand 15 minutes before cutting. Yield: 8 servings.

Shrimp-and-Vegetable Spaghetti

1 pound unpeeled medium-size fresh shrimp
4 slices bacon
1 cup chopped onion
1 medium-size green pepper, seeded and chopped
4 carrots, scraped and sliced diagonally
¼ teaspoon garlic powder
2 (14.5-ounce) cans whole tomatoes, undrained and chopped
1 (2.25-ounce) can sliced ripe olives, drained
1 teaspoon dried basil
1 teaspoon dried oregano
¼ teaspoon pepper
¼ teaspoon garlic salt
8 ounces fresh mushrooms, sliced
Hot cooked vermicelli
Grated Parmesan cheese

Peel shrimp, and devein, if desired; set aside.

Cook bacon in a large skillet until crisp; remove bacon, reserving 1 tablespoon drippings in skillet. Crumble bacon, and set aside.

Cook onion and next 3 ingredients in bacon drippings until carrot is crisp-tender. Add tomatoes and next 5 ingredients; bring to a boil. Cover, reduce heat, and simmer 3 to 5 minutes.

Add shrimp and mushrooms; cook 10 minutes. Serve over vermicelli; sprinkle with bacon and cheese. Yield: 6 servings.

Vegetable Variations

For a special luncheon dish or a spur-of-the-moment gathering, team pasta with garden-fresh vegetables. This collection combines pasta with everything from artichokes to zucchini.

Black Bean Spaghetti, Bow Tie Pesto, Caribbean Tomato Pasta

Pasta with Greens, Peppery Pasta, Spinach-Stuffed Manicotti, Vegetable Lasagna

Super-Quick Pasta, Pasta with Peppers and Broccoli, Spaghetti with Vegetables

Orzo Primavera, Pasta Primavera, Linguine with Grilled Vegetables

Roasted Vegetables and Pasta (page 360)

Super-Quick Pasta

Super-Quick Pasta

2½ cups ziti (short tubular pasta), uncooked
2 cups commercial spaghetti sauce
1 cup ricotta cheese
⅛ teaspoon salt
¼ teaspoon pepper
¼ cup chopped fresh parsley
½ cup (2 ounces) shredded mozzarella cheese
Garnish: fresh parsley sprigs

Cook pasta according to package directions; drain and set aside.

Cook spaghetti sauce in a saucepan over medium heat 10 to 12 minutes, stirring occasionally. Remove from heat, and set aside.

Combine pasta, ricotta cheese, salt, and pepper; spoon onto individual serving plates. Stir chopped parsley into spaghetti sauce, and spoon over pasta mixture. Sprinkle with mozzarella cheese, and serve immediately. Garnish, if desired. **Yield: 4 servings.**

Note: For variation, add 1 (14-ounce) can artichoke hearts, drained and quartered, or 1 cup steamed zucchini slices to the spaghetti sauce.

Bow Tie Pesto

1 (16-ounce) package bow tie pasta, uncooked
2 cups tightly packed fresh basil
1½ cups freshly grated Parmesan cheese
1 (1¾-ounce) jar pine nuts
3 cloves garlic, halved
⅔ cup olive oil
1 (14-ounce) can artichoke hearts, drained and quartered
½ cup oil-packed dried tomatoes, drained and cut into thin strips

Cook pasta according to package directions; drain and set aside.

Position knife blade in food processor bowl; add basil and next 3 ingredients. Process until smooth, stopping once to scrape down sides.

Pour olive oil through food chute with processor running; process until smooth. Set pesto mixture aside.

Place pasta in a large bowl. Add 1½ cups pesto mixture and artichoke hearts. (Reserve remaining pesto mixture for another use.)

Sprinkle pasta with tomatoes, and serve hot or cold. **Yield: 8 servings.**

Caribbean Tomato Pasta

3 large vine-ripened tomatoes
¾ cup canned black beans, drained and rinsed
2 tablespoons extra-virgin olive oil
3 cloves garlic, minced
2 tablespoons chopped fresh cilantro
1 tablespoon chopped fresh chives
1 tablespoon fresh lime juice
½ teaspoon ground cumin
¼ teaspoon ground red pepper
¼ teaspoon salt
¼ teaspoon black pepper
4 ounces vermicelli, uncooked
½ cup (2 ounces) shredded Monterey Jack cheese

Peel tomatoes, and coarsely chop over a medium bowl, reserving juice. Combine chopped tomato, reserved juice, beans, and next 9 ingredients; cover and let stand at room temperature at least 1 hour.

Cook pasta according to package directions; drain. Serve tomato mixture over pasta, and sprinkle with cheese. **Yield: 2 servings.**

Black Bean Spaghetti

Black Bean Spaghetti

1 large onion, sliced
1 small sweet red pepper, cut into strips
1 small sweet yellow pepper, cut into strips
1 (8-ounce) package fresh mushrooms, sliced
2 tablespoons olive oil
1 (16-ounce) can whole tomatoes, undrained and chopped
1 (15-ounce) can black beans, drained and rinsed
1 (15½-ounce) can kidney beans, undrained
1 (3½-ounce) jar capers, undrained
¼ cup sliced ripe olives
¼ teaspoon dried rosemary
¾ teaspoon chopped fresh basil or ¼ teaspoon dried basil
¼ teaspoon pepper
Hot cooked angel hair pasta
Freshly grated Parmesan cheese
Garnish: fresh basil leaves

Cook first 4 ingredients in olive oil in a large skillet over medium-high heat, stirring constantly, until tender.

Add tomatoes and next 7 ingredients; bring to a boil. Reduce heat, and simmer 30 minutes, stirring occasionally.

Serve over pasta, and sprinkle with Parmesan cheese. Garnish, if desired. Yield: 6 servings.

Spaghetti with Vegetables

1 cup sliced fresh mushrooms
¾ cup chopped onion
3 cloves garlic, minced
6 large fresh basil leaves, chopped
¼ teaspoon finely ground fennel seeds
¼ cup plus 3 tablespoons olive oil, divided
1½ cups broccoli flowerets
1½ cups cauliflower flowerets
1 (15½-ounce) can red kidney beans, rinsed and drained
¼ to ½ teaspoon salt
2 quarts water
1 teaspoon salt
1 (7-ounce) package spaghetti, uncooked
½ cup freshly grated Parmesan cheese
Freshly ground pepper

Cook first 5 ingredients in 2 tablespoons olive oil, stirring constantly, 3 to 4 minutes or until onion is tender; remove from skillet.

Add 3 tablespoons olive oil to skillet, and cook broccoli and cauliflower, stirring constantly, 5 minutes or until crisp-tender. Add onion mixture, beans, and ¼ to ½ teaspoon salt to vegetables; heat thoroughly. Set aside, and keep warm.

Combine water, 1 tablespoon olive oil, and 1 teaspoon salt; bring to a boil, and add spaghetti. Cook spaghetti 10 to 13 minutes, stirring occasionally. Drain. Add remaining 1 tablespoon olive oil to spaghetti, tossing to coat.

Combine cooked spaghetti, vegetable mixture, and cheese in a large serving bowl, tossing well. Top with freshly ground pepper. Yield: 6 to 8 servings.

Pasta with Greens

1 (8-ounce) package fettuccine, uncooked
1 (16-ounce) package frozen collards or other
    greens
2 to 3 cloves garlic, minced
3 tablespoons olive oil
½ teaspoon salt
¼ teaspoon freshly ground pepper
½ cup freshly grated Parmesan cheese
1 (1¾-ounce) jar pine nuts, toasted
Garnishes: grated Parmesan cheese, toasted
    pine nuts

Cook pasta according to package directions;
drain and set aside.

Cook greens according to package directions;
drain and set aside.

Cook garlic in olive oil in a large skillet over
medium-high heat until tender but not brown.
Add greens, salt, and pepper; cook until heated.

Combine pasta, greens, Parmesan cheese, and
pine nuts in a large serving bowl. Garnish, if desired. **Yield: 2 servings.**

Pasta with Greens

Pasta Potpourri

4 ounces penne or rigatoni (short tubular
    pasta), uncooked
1 teaspoon sesame oil
1½ tablespoons olive oil
1½ tablespoons sesame oil
1 small purple onion, chopped
2 medium carrots, scraped and diagonally
    sliced
2 medium zucchini, halved lengthwise and
    sliced
2 cloves garlic, crushed
1½ teaspoons peeled, grated gingerroot
½ teaspoon dried crushed red pepper
2 tablespoons soy sauce
2 teaspoons rice wine vinegar
1 tablespoon freshly grated Parmesan cheese
2 teaspoons chopped fresh cilantro

Cook pasta according to package directions;
drain and toss with 1 teaspoon sesame oil. Set
pasta aside.

Pour olive oil and 1½ tablespoons sesame oil
around top of a preheated wok, coating sides;
heat at high 1 minute. Add onion and carrot;
cook, stirring constantly, 2 minutes or until onion
is tender.

Add zucchini and next 3 ingredients; cook,
stirring constantly, 1 minute.

Stir in cooked pasta, soy sauce, and vinegar;
cook 1 minute or until thoroughly heated.

Transfer to a serving dish; sprinkle with
cheese and cilantro. **Yield: 4 to 6 servings.**

Note: For a quick main dish, add leftover
chopped cooked chicken or beef.

Peppery Pasta

3 pounds ripe plum tomatoes, peeled and
    quartered
8 green onions, thinly sliced
8 cloves garlic, minced
1 tablespoon olive oil
2 small sweet banana peppers, thinly sliced
⅓ cup chopped fresh oregano or
    2 tablespoons dried oregano
¼ cup chopped fresh basil or 1½ teaspoons
    dried basil
½ teaspoon salt
8 green onions, thinly sliced
3 sweet yellow peppers, cut into thin strips
3 sweet red or orange peppers, cut into thin
    strips
3 tablespoons chopped fresh oregano or
    1 tablespoon dried oregano
1 tablespoon olive oil
10 to 12 crimini or button mushrooms,
    coarsely chopped
1 teaspoon salt
1 teaspoon dried crushed red pepper
1 pound hot cooked mostaccioli (tubular
    pasta)
8 ounces fontina or mozzarella cheese,
    shredded

Position knife blade in food processor bowl;
add one-third of tomato. Pulse 5 or 6 times or
until finely chopped. Remove tomato from bowl,
and set aside. Repeat procedure twice.

Cook 8 green onions and garlic in 1 tablespoon olive oil in a large, heavy saucepan, stirring constantly, 10 minutes or until tender.

Stir in tomato, banana pepper, and next 3
ingredients.

Bring mixture to a boil over medium heat,
stirring constantly; reduce heat, and simmer,
uncovered, 1 hour, stirring occasionally. Remove
from heat; keep tomato mixture warm.

Cook 8 green onions, sweet pepper strips, and
3 tablespoons fresh oregano in 1 tablespoon olive
oil in a large skillet over medium heat, stirring
constantly, 12 to 15 minutes or until vegetables
are crisp-tender. Add mushrooms, 1 teaspoon
salt, and crushed red pepper; cook about 7 minutes or until mushrooms are tender, stirring often.

Place hot cooked pasta on a large serving platter.

Pour tomato mixture over pasta; spoon mushroom mixture over sauce, and sprinkle with
shredded cheese. **Yield: 8 servings.**

Pasta with Peppers and Broccoli

1 pound fresh broccoli
1 (7.5-ounce) jar roasted peppers, drained
    and cut into strips
⅔ cup pine nuts
½ cup olive oil
½ cup chopped fresh parsley
1 (12-ounce) package small shell pasta,
    uncooked
1 cup freshly grated Parmesan cheese
⅛ teaspoon black pepper
⅛ teaspoon ground red pepper

Trim off large leaves of broccoli, and remove
tough ends of lower stalks. Wash broccoli thoroughly, and cut into flowerets. Set aside.

Cook roasted peppers and next 3 ingredients
in a skillet over medium heat until nuts are gold-
en, stirring often.

Cook pasta according to package directions,
adding broccoli the last 2 minutes; drain.

Add roasted pepper mixture, cheese, and
remaining ingredients to pasta. Toss and serve
immediately. **Yield: 6 servings.**

Pasta Primavera

Pasta Primavera

1 pound fresh asparagus
2 cups fresh broccoli flowerets
1 medium onion, chopped
1 large clove garlic, chopped
1 tablespoon olive oil
1 large carrot, scraped and diagonally sliced
1 sweet red pepper, coarsely chopped
1 sweet yellow pepper, coarsely chopped
1 cup whipping cream
½ cup chicken broth
3 green onions, chopped
2 tablespoons chopped fresh basil or
　　2 teaspoons dried basil
½ teaspoon salt
8 ounces linguine, uncooked
½ pound fresh mushrooms, sliced
1 cup freshly grated Parmesan cheese
¼ teaspoon freshly ground pepper

Snap off tough ends of asparagus. Remove scales with a vegetable peeler or knife, if desired. Cut asparagus diagonally into 1½-inch pieces.

Place asparagus pieces and broccoli flowerets in a vegetable steamer over boiling water. Cover; steam 6 to 8 minutes. Set aside.

Cook onion and garlic in oil in a large skillet, stirring constantly, until tender. Add carrot and chopped peppers; cook, stirring constantly, until crisp-tender. Remove from heat; drain.

Combine whipping cream and next 4 ingredients in a medium skillet; cook over medium-high heat 5 minutes, stirring occasionally.

Break linguine noodles in half; cook according to package directions. Drain well; place in a large serving bowl.

Add reserved vegetables, whipping cream mixture, and mushrooms; toss gently. Sprinkle with Parmesan cheese and pepper; toss gently. Serve immediately. **Yield: 8 servings.**

Orzo Primavera

3 quarts water
1 teaspoon salt
2 cups orzo (rice-shaped pasta), uncooked
1 pound fresh asparagus, cut into 1-inch
　　pieces
3 cloves garlic, minced
½ cup chopped sweet red pepper
1 teaspoon butter or margarine, melted
1 tablespoon olive oil
1 cup frozen English peas, thawed
½ cup chicken broth
1 teaspoon grated lemon rind
¼ teaspoon ground white pepper
½ cup freshly grated Parmesan cheese

Combine water and salt in a large Dutch oven; bring to a boil. Add orzo, and cook 5 minutes. Add asparagus, and cook 4 minutes. Drain and set aside in a large serving bowl.

Cook garlic and red pepper in butter and oil in Dutch oven over medium heat, stirring constantly, 1 minute or until crisp-tender. Add peas; cook, stirring constantly, 1 minute. Add broth, lemon rind, and white pepper; bring to a boil, and cook 1 minute.

Add vegetable mixture to orzo mixture, tossing well. Sprinkle with Parmesan cheese. Serve immediately. **Yield: 6 to 8 servings.**

Note: Orzo can be served as a substitute for rice, cooked in soups and stews, or used as the main ingredient in pasta salads.

Garden Spiral Primavera

8 ounces vegetable-flavored rotini (corkscrew pasta), uncooked
2 tablespoons olive oil
¼ cup butter or margarine
1 small onion, thinly sliced
1 clove garlic, minced
1½ cups broccoli flowerets
1 carrot, scraped and sliced
4 ounces fresh mushrooms, sliced
3 tablespoons white wine
1½ teaspoons chopped fresh basil or
   ½ teaspoon dried basil
1½ teaspoons chopped fresh parsley or
   ½ teaspoon dried parsley flakes
¼ teaspoon ground white pepper
½ cup grated Parmesan cheese

Cook pasta according to package directions; drain and set aside.

Heat olive oil and butter in a large skillet; add onion and garlic. Cook over medium heat 2 minutes, stirring frequently. Add broccoli and carrot; cook 2 minutes. Add mushrooms, and cook 1 minute, stirring occasionally.

Add wine, basil, parsley, and pepper; bring to a boil. Cover, reduce heat, and simmer 3 minutes or until vegetables are tender.

Add vegetables and Parmesan cheese to cooked pasta, stirring well. Serve immediately. **Yield: 4 servings.**

Linguine with Grilled Vegetables

2 yellow squash, cut into chunks
2 zucchini, cut into chunks
1 purple onion, quartered
1 small eggplant, unpeeled and cut into chunks
1 sweet red pepper, cut into 1-inch pieces
⅓ cup butter or margarine
2 to 3 teaspoons dried Italian seasoning
½ teaspoon black pepper
2 teaspoons chicken-flavored bouillon granules
2 quarts water
8 ounces linguine, uncooked
¼ cup grated Parmesan cheese

Place first 5 ingredients on a lightly greased 24- x 18-inch piece of heavy-duty aluminum foil; dot with butter, and sprinkle with Italian seasoning and pepper. Seal securely.

Cook on a grill rack over hot coals (400° to 500°) 20 to 30 minutes or until vegetables are tender. Remove from heat, and keep sealed.

Combine bouillon granules and about 2 quarts water in a stockpot; cover and place in hot coals. Bring to a boil; add linguine, and cook until tender. Drain. Top with vegetables; sprinkle with cheese. **Yield: 2 to 3 servings.**

Note: Linguine may be prepared on a conventional cooktop. Cook in bouillon-flavored water according to package directions.

Serving Tip

Serving long, thin pastas such as linguine or fettuccine can be tricky. You may use kitchen tongs or a special wooden pasta fork to transfer the pasta (see page 356). This long-handled fork has 1-inch dowels protruding from the flat surface. These allow you to grab the pasta easily and lift it to plates.

Linguine with Grilled Vegetables

Roasted Vegetables and Pasta

(pictured on page 349)

6 ounces rigatoni (short tubular pasta),
   uncooked
1 (1-ounce) package onion soup mix
2 teaspoons dried thyme
½ cup olive oil, divided
2 carrots, cut into 1-inch slices
1 medium zucchini, cut into 1-inch slices
1 eggplant, cut into 1-inch pieces
½ pound fresh mushrooms, halved
¼ cup white wine vinegar
⅓ cup pine nuts, toasted
Freshly ground pepper

Cook pasta according to package directions, omitting salt and fat. Drain. Rinse and drain again; place in a large bowl, and set aside.

Combine onion soup mix and thyme; stir in ¼ cup olive oil. Add carrot and next 3 ingredients, tossing to coat.

Spread vegetables evenly into a 15- x 10- x 1-inch jellyroll pan. Bake at 450° for 25 minutes, stirring after 15 minutes. Stir into pasta.

Combine remaining ¼ cup olive oil, white wine vinegar, and pine nuts; pour over pasta mixture, tossing to coat. Sprinkle with pepper. Serve immediately. **Yield: 4 to 6 servings.**

To Serve a Frozen Casserole

Most lasagna and manicotti dishes may be covered and frozen up to 4 months. For best results, prepare the recipe, and freeze it before baking. To serve, thaw in refrigerator 24 hours, and bake as recipe directs.

Thaw Vegetable Lasagna, and bake at 375° for 45 minutes; add remaining mozzarella cheese, and bake 5 minutes.

Vegetable Lasagna

12 lasagna noodles, uncooked
2 cups sliced mushrooms
1 cup shredded carrot (about 5 medium
   carrots)
½ cup chopped onion
1 tablespoon vegetable oil
1 (18-ounce) can tomato paste
1 (15-ounce) can tomato sauce
1 (4-ounce) can sliced ripe olives, drained
1½ teaspoons dried oregano
1 teaspoon dried fennel
2 cups cottage cheese, divided
1 (10-ounce) package frozen chopped spinach,
   thawed and well drained
2 (8-ounce) packages sliced mozzarella cheese,
   divided
Grated Parmesan cheese

Cook noodles according to package directions; drain and set aside.

Cook mushrooms, carrot, and onion in oil in a large skillet over medium heat until tender. Stir in tomato paste and next 4 ingredients; bring to a boil. Remove from heat.

Lightly grease two 8-inch square baking dishes; arrange 3 noodles in each dish. Layer one-fourth each of cottage cheese, spinach, vegetable mixture, and mozzarella in each dish. Repeat layers with remaining noodles, cottage cheese, spinach, and vegetable mixture.

Cover and freeze one casserole up to four months. (To serve frozen casserole, see box at left.) Bake remaining casserole at 375° for 30 minutes. Add half of remaining mozzarella slices, and bake 5 additional minutes. Let casserole stand 10 minutes; serve with Parmesan cheese. **Yield: 4 servings per casserole.**

Note: Vegetable Lasagna may be prepared in a 13- x 9- x 2-inch baking dish. Bake at 375° for 40 minutes; top with remaining mozzarella cheese slices, and bake 5 additional minutes.

Vegetable Lasagna

Lasagna Florentine

2 chicken-flavored bouillon cubes
¼ cup water
½ cup butter or margarine
⅓ cup all-purpose flour
⅛ teaspoon salt
⅛ teaspoon dried Italian seasoning
Dash of garlic powder
Dash of ground nutmeg
¼ teaspoon ground white pepper
¼ teaspoon lemon-pepper seasoning
1 cup whipping cream
1 cup half-and-half
¾ cup chopped onion
1 tablespoon butter or margarine, melted
2 (10-ounce) packages frozen chopped
    spinach, thawed
1 large egg, lightly beaten
1½ cups (6 ounces) shredded mozzarella
    cheese
1 (8-ounce) carton sour cream
9 lasagna noodles, uncooked
½ teaspoon salt
½ cup grated Parmesan cheese

Dissolve bouillon cubes in water; set aside. Melt ½ cup butter in a heavy saucepan over low heat. Add flour and next 6 ingredients, stirring until smooth. Cook, stirring constantly, 1 minute.

Add bouillon mixture, whipping cream, and half-and-half to flour mixture; cook over medium heat, stirring until thickened and bubbly. Remove from heat; set aside.

Cook onion in 1 tablespoon butter until tender. Drain spinach well by pressing between layers of paper towels.

Combine spinach, onion, egg, mozzarella cheese, and sour cream in a large bowl; stir well, and set mixture aside.

Cook lasagna noodles according to package directions, adding ½ teaspoon salt; drain.

Layer 3 noodles in a lightly greased 13- x 9- x 2-inch baking dish. Spread with spinach mixture; repeat with 3 noodles. Spread with half of cream sauce; repeat with remaining noodles. Spread with remaining cream sauce; sprinkle with Parmesan cheese.

Bake, uncovered, at 350° for 30 minutes. **Yield: 6 servings.**

Jumbo Shells Florentine

12 jumbo pasta shells, uncooked
1 (10-ounce) package chopped spinach,
    thawed and uncooked
1 small onion, minced
1 large egg, beaten
½ teaspoon salt
⅛ teaspoon pepper
1 cup well-drained cottage cheese
1 (10¾-ounce) can cream of mushroom soup,
    undiluted
⅓ cup water

Cook pasta shells according to package directions; drain and set aside.

Combine spinach, onion, egg, salt, pepper, and cottage cheese; stir gently.

Spoon spinach mixture into pasta shells, and place shells in a lightly greased shallow baking dish. Combine soup and water; pour over shells.

Cover and bake at 350° for 25 minutes. Spoon sauce from bottom of pan over shells, and bake 20 additional minutes. **Yield: 3 main-dish or 6 side-dish servings.**

Pasta Stuffed with Five Cheeses

20 jumbo pasta shells, uncooked
1 (8-ounce) package cream cheese,
    softened
1 cup low-fat cottage cheese
1 cup (4 ounces) shredded mozzarella cheese
1 large egg, lightly beaten
¼ cup grated Parmesan and Romano cheese
    blend
2 tablespoons chopped fresh parsley
2 teaspoons dried basil
½ teaspoon dried oregano
½ teaspoon dried thyme
⅛ teaspoon grated lemon rind
Pinch of ground nutmeg
1 (14½-ounce) can stewed tomatoes,
    undrained
1 (6-ounce) can tomato paste
1 (8-ounce) can tomato sauce
½ cup dry white wine
1 (8-ounce) can mushroom stems and pieces,
    drained
1 teaspoon dried oregano
1 teaspoon dried thyme
1 clove garlic, minced
Garnish: fresh herb sprigs

Cook pasta shells according to package directions; drain and set aside.

Combine cream cheese and next 10 ingredients, mixing well. Stuff jumbo shells with cheese mixture.

Arrange stuffed shells in a lightly greased 13- x 9- x 2-inch baking dish. Cover and bake at 350° for 25 minutes or until thoroughly heated.

Place tomatoes in container of an electric blender or food processor; cover and process until smooth. Pour puree into a Dutch oven; stir in tomato paste and next 6 ingredients.

Bring mixture to a boil; reduce heat, and simmer, uncovered, 20 minutes or until thickened.

Spoon sauce onto serving plates; arrange pasta shells on sauce. Garnish, if desired. **Yield: 4 servings.**

Spinach-Stuffed Manicotti

12 manicotti shells, uncooked
2 (10-ounce) packages frozen chopped
    spinach, thawed and well drained
2 cups (8 ounces) shredded mozzarella cheese
2 cups cottage cheese
½ cup grated Parmesan cheese
1 small onion, diced
2 tablespoons dried parsley flakes
1 teaspoon dried oregano
Dash of hot sauce
Dash of ground nutmeg
1 (32-ounce) jar spaghetti sauce with
    mushrooms, divided
¼ cup grated Parmesan cheese

Cook manicotti shells according to package directions; drain and set aside.

Combine spinach and next 8 ingredients, stirring well. Stuff manicotti shells with spinach mixture.

Spoon 1 cup spaghetti sauce into a lightly greased 13- x 9- x 2-inch baking dish. Arrange stuffed shells over sauce. Spoon remaining sauce over shells; sprinkle with ¼ cup Parmesan cheese.

Cover tightly with aluminum foil, and bake at 350° for 45 minutes or until thoroughly heated. **Yield: 6 servings.**

Spinach-Stuffed Lasagna Ruffles

1 (8-ounce) package lasagna noodles,
    uncooked
1 (8-ounce) package cream cheese, softened
2 (10-ounce) packages frozen chopped
    spinach, thawed and drained
1½ cups freshly grated Parmesan cheese,
    divided
1 (15-ounce) carton ricotta cheese
2 cups (8 ounces) shredded mozzarella cheese
1½ teaspoons dried Italian seasoning
¼ teaspoon salt
1 (32-ounce) jar spaghetti sauce
Garnishes: fresh basil sprigs, grated Parmesan
    cheese

Cook noodles according to package directions; drain and set aside.

Beat cream cheese until smooth. Stir in spinach, 1 cup Parmesan cheese, and next 4 ingredients.

Spread ½ cup cheese mixture evenly over each cooked noodle. Roll noodles up jellyroll fashion, starting at narrow end.

Pour spaghetti sauce into a lightly greased 13- x 9- x 2-inch baking dish. Cut lasagna rolls in half crosswise. Place rolls, cut side down, over sauce in dish. Sprinkle with remaining ½ cup Parmesan cheese.

Cover and bake at 350° for 25 minutes or until lasagna ruffles are thoroughly heated. Garnish, if desired. **Yield: 6 servings.**

Spinach-Stuffed Lasagna Ruffles Techniques

Place cooked lasagna noodles on layers of wax paper. Spread ½ cup spinach-cheese filling evenly over each noodle.

Carefully roll up each lasagna noodle lengthwise, keeping spinach-cheese mixture intact.

Cut each lasagna rollup in half crosswise. Place each half, cut side down, over sauce in dish.

Spinach-Stuffed Lasagna Ruffles

Southwestern Stuffed Shells

Southwestern Stuffed Shells

18 jumbo pasta shells, uncooked
1 (16-ounce) can pumpkin
1 large egg, lightly beaten
½ cup Italian-seasoned breadcrumbs
½ cup grated Parmesan cheese
½ teaspoon ground nutmeg
1 (16-ounce) jar picante sauce or salsa, divided
1 cup (4 ounces) shredded Monterey Jack cheese with peppers
2 tablespoons chopped fresh parsley
Garnish: fresh parsley sprigs

Cook pasta shells according to package directions; drain and set aside.

Combine pumpkin, egg, breadcrumbs, Parmesan cheese, and nutmeg; stuff each shell with mixture.

Spread 1 cup picante sauce in a lightly greased 13- x 9- x 2-inch baking dish. Place filled shells on sauce; top with remaining sauce.

Cover and bake at 350° for 35 minutes or until thoroughly heated. Arrange on individual plates, and sprinkle with Monterey Jack cheese and parsley. Garnish, if desired. **Yield: 3 to 4 servings.**

Satisfying Side Dishes

Mostaccioli Alfredo, Pesto Pasta, and Tortellini Carbonara
are just a sampling of the pasta side dishes that make
great family or entertaining fare.

Garlic Pasta with Marinara Sauce, Fettuccine with Poppy Seeds

Tortellini with Parsley-Caper Sauce, Tortellini Carbonara, St. Louis Toasted Ravioli

Toasted Rice and Pasta, Mostaccioli Alfredo, Lemon-Garlic Pasta, Pesto Pasta

Spinach Pesto-Pasta, Spinach Fettuccine with Mustard Greens

Macaroni and Cheese (page 377)

Garlic Pasta with Marinara Sauce

1 (9-ounce) package refrigerated angel hair
   pasta, uncooked
½ teaspoon salt
4 cloves garlic, minced
2 tablespoons olive oil
½ teaspoon freshly ground pepper
1 (15-ounce) carton refrigerated marinara
   sauce
Grated Parmesan cheese

Cook pasta according to package directions,
adding ½ teaspoon salt; drain.

Cook minced garlic in oil in a small skillet over
medium-high heat, stirring constantly; pour over
pasta, and sprinkle with pepper, tossing gently.

Top pasta with marinara sauce, and sprinkle
with cheese. **Yield: 3 servings.**

Toasted Rice and Pasta

1½ cups long-grain rice, uncooked
4 ounces angel hair pasta or vermicelli,
   uncooked and broken into 1½-inch pieces
2 tablespoons vegetable oil
1 large onion, chopped
2 (14½-ounce) cans ready-to-serve chicken
   broth
¼ cup chopped fresh parsley

Cook rice and pasta in oil in a Dutch oven over
medium heat, stirring constantly, 3 to 5 minutes
or until golden. Add onion, and cook mixture 3
minutes.

Stir in broth; bring to a boil. Cover, reduce
heat to low, and simmer 15 to 17 minutes.

Stir in parsley, and serve immediately. **Yield:
4 to 6 servings.**

Fettuccine with Poppy Seeds

6 ounces fettuccine, uncooked
⅓ cup butter or margarine, melted
¾ teaspoon garlic salt
¾ teaspoon dried parsley flakes
½ teaspoon poppy seeds
⅛ teaspoon pepper
½ cup sour cream
½ cup grated Parmesan cheese

Cook fettuccine according to package directions; drain.

Combine butter and next 4 ingredients; stir in
sour cream.

Combine fettuccine and sour cream mixture;
add cheese, and toss until fettuccine is coated.
Serve immediately. **Yield: 6 servings.**

Fresh Tomato Sauce over Basil Pasta

6 pounds tomatoes, peeled, seeded, and
   chopped (about 7 large)
16 cloves garlic, minced
1 teaspoon salt
½ teaspoon pepper
1 (16-ounce) package linguine, uncooked
¾ cup freshly grated Parmesan cheese
½ cup butter or margarine, softened
¼ cup chopped fresh basil or 1 tablespoon
   dried basil

Combine tomato and garlic in a heavy saucepan; bring to a boil. Reduce heat, and cook 15 to
20 minutes, stirring occasionally. Stir in salt and
pepper; keep warm.

Cook linguine according to package directions; drain. Add Parmesan cheese, butter, and
basil, tossing well. To serve, top pasta with tomato mixture. **Yield: 8 servings.**

Tri-Colored Fettuccine Alfredo

(pictured on page 278)

6 ounces fresh fettuccine, uncooked
5 ounces fresh spinach fettuccine, uncooked
5 ounces fresh tomato or sweet red pepper fettuccine, uncooked
¾ cup butter or margarine, melted
¼ teaspoon garlic powder
2 cups whipping cream
¼ cup grated Asiago cheese
¼ cup grated Romano cheese
¼ cup sour cream
¼ teaspoon salt
¼ cup grated Parmesan cheese
Freshly ground pepper to taste

Cook fettuccine according to package directions; drain well. Place fettuccine in a large Dutch oven.

Combine butter and garlic powder; pour over fettuccine. Gradually add whipping cream and next 4 ingredients; cook over low heat, stirring constantly, until mixture is thoroughly heated (do not boil).

Transfer pasta mixture to a serving platter; sprinkle with Parmesan cheese and pepper to taste. Serve immediately. **Yield: 6 servings.**

Mostaccioli Alfredo

1 (16-ounce) package mostaccioli (tubular pasta), uncooked
1 cup whipping cream
½ cup butter or margarine
½ cup grated Parmesan cheese
¼ cup chopped fresh parsley
1 teaspoon salt
¼ teaspoon freshly ground pepper
⅛ teaspoon garlic powder

Cook mostaccioli according to package directions; drain and set aside.

Combine whipping cream and butter in a Dutch oven; heat until butter melts, stirring occasionally (do not boil).

Add cheese and remaining 4 ingredients; stir well. Add mostaccioli, and toss well. Serve immediately. **Yield: 8 servings.**

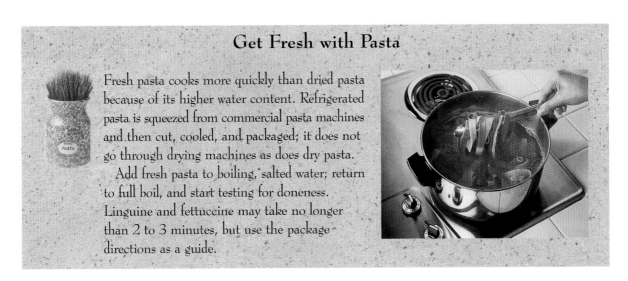

Get Fresh with Pasta

Fresh pasta cooks more quickly than dried pasta because of its higher water content. Refrigerated pasta is squeezed from commercial pasta machines and then cut, cooled, and packaged; it does not go through drying machines as does dry pasta.

Add fresh pasta to boiling, salted water; return to full boil, and start testing for doneness. Linguine and fettuccine may take no longer than 2 to 3 minutes, but use the package directions as a guide.

Fettuccine Alfredo

Fettuccine Alfredo

8 ounces fettuccine, uncooked
½ cup butter
½ cup whipping cream
¾ cup grated Parmesan cheese
¼ teaspoon ground white pepper
2 tablespoons chopped fresh parsley
Garnish: fresh parsley

Cook fettuccine according to package directions, omitting salt. Drain well, and place in a large bowl.

Combine butter and whipping cream in a small saucepan; cook over low heat until butter melts. Stir in cheese, pepper, and parsley.

Pour mixture over hot fettuccine; toss until fettuccine is coated. Garnish, if desired. **Yield: 4 servings.**

Lemon-Garlic Pasta

8 ounces thin spaghetti, uncooked
2 tablespoons butter or margarine
2 tablespoons olive oil
4 to 5 cloves garlic, minced
¼ cup lemon juice
¼ teaspoon salt
½ to 1 teaspoon pepper
⅓ cup chopped fresh parsley

Cook pasta according to package directions; drain and set aside.

Melt butter in a large skillet over medium-high heat; add olive oil and minced garlic. Cook, stirring constantly, 1 minute. Add lemon juice, salt, and pepper.

Bring mixture to a boil; pour over pasta. Add parsley; toss gently. Serve immediately. **Yield: 4 servings.**

Lemon Vermicelli

⅓ cup milk
3 tablespoons butter or margarine
1 (7-ounce) package vermicelli, uncooked
¼ cup lemon juice
⅓ cup grated Parmesan cheese
Garnishes: fresh parsley, lemon twists

Combine milk and butter in a saucepan; cook over low heat until butter melts. Set aside, and keep warm.

Cook vermicelli according to package directions; drain. Rinse with warm water; drain. Place in a bowl, and toss with lemon juice; let stand 1 minute.

Add cheese and warm milk mixture to pasta; toss well. Garnish, if desired. **Yield: 6 servings.**

Green Peas and Pasta

4 ounces spinach linguine, uncooked
1 cup whipping cream
1 cup chicken broth
½ cup freshly grated Parmesan cheese
½ cup frozen English peas
3 slices bacon, cooked and crumbled

Cook linguine according to package directions; drain and keep warm.

Combine whipping cream and chicken broth in a saucepan; bring to a boil. Reduce heat, and simmer 25 minutes or until thickened and reduced to 1 cup. Remove mixture from heat.

Add cheese, peas, and bacon, stirring until cheese melts. Toss with linguine, and serve immediately. **Yield: 2 servings.**

Note: Whipping cream and chicken broth may be simmered longer for a thicker sauce. Peeled, cooked shrimp or chopped, cooked chicken may be added with the cheese, peas, and bacon for a heartier dish.

Noodles Romanoff

Noodles Romanoff

1 (8-ounce) package medium-size curly egg
    noodles, uncooked
1 cup small-curd cottage cheese
1 (8-ounce) carton sour cream
½ cup sliced ripe olives
½ cup sliced green onions
1 teaspoon Worcestershire sauce
½ teaspoon salt
⅛ teaspoon ground red pepper
½ cup (2 ounces) shredded Cheddar cheese

Cook noodles according to package directions, omitting salt. Drain well.

Combine noodles, cottage cheese, and next 6 ingredients, stirring well. Spoon mixture into a lightly greased 11- x 7- x 1½-inch baking dish.

Bake, uncovered, at 350° for 30 minutes. Sprinkle with shredded Cheddar cheese, and bake 5 additional minutes or until cheese melts. **Yield: 6 to 8 servings.**

Traditional Pesto and Linguine

½ cup packed chopped fresh basil
¼ cup chopped fresh parsley
¼ cup grated Parmesan cheese
2 tablespoons pine nuts or walnuts
1 clove garlic, halved
2 tablespoons olive oil
2 tablespoons butter or margarine, softened
¼ teaspoon salt
¼ teaspoon pepper
6 ounces linguine, uncooked

Combine first 9 ingredients in container of an electric blender. Cover and process at high until smooth.

Cook linguine according to package directions; drain. Spoon pesto mixture over linguine. Toss gently; serve immediately. **Yield: 3 to 4 servings.**

Spinach Pesto-Pasta

1 (10-ounce) package frozen chopped spinach,
    thawed
½ cup grated Parmesan cheese
⅓ cup fresh basil leaves
¼ cup pine nuts, toasted
1 teaspoon crushed garlic
½ teaspoon coarsely ground pepper
¼ teaspoon anise seed, ground
¼ teaspoon salt
2 tablespoons butter or margarine, softened
½ cup olive oil
1 (12-ounce) package egg noodles, uncooked

Drain spinach on paper towels.

Combine spinach and next 9 ingredients in a food processor bowl fitted with knife blade. Process 30 seconds, stopping once to scrape down sides.

Cook noodles according to package directions; drain well. Add pesto to hot noodles, tossing gently. Serve immediately. **Yield: 8 to 10 servings.**

Make Fresh Pesto

Pesto, a fresh-tasting sauce that adds flavor and color to pasta, originated in Italy. The first pesto was made with a mortar and pestle, but today you can whip up the uncooked sauce in an electric blender or food processor.

Pesto is usually made with fresh basil, garlic, pine nuts, Parmesan cheese, and olive oil. Make pesto in large batches, and freeze in ice cube trays. When frozen, put pesto cubes in a freezer bag, and freeze up to 6 months.

Pesto Pasta

5 ounces fresh spinach
1 cup fresh parsley sprigs
⅔ cup grated Parmesan cheese
½ cup chopped walnuts, toasted
6 cloves garlic, split
4 anchovy fillets
3 tablespoons minced fresh tarragon or
　 1 tablespoon dried tarragon
1 tablespoon minced fresh basil or 1 teaspoon
　 dried basil
½ teaspoon salt
½ teaspoon pepper
¾ cup olive oil
1 (16-ounce) package thin spaghetti, uncooked
Garnish: fresh basil leaves

Remove stems from spinach. Wash leaves thoroughly in lukewarm water; drain and pat dry.

Position knife blade in food processor bowl; add spinach. Process until spinach is finely chopped.

Add parsley and next 8 ingredients; process until smooth. With processor running, pour oil through food chute in a slow, steady stream until combined.

Cook pasta according to package directions; drain well. Place in a large serving bowl. Toss pasta with pesto. Garnish, if desired. **Yield: 8 to 10 servings.**

Pesto Pasta Techniques

Always wash fresh spinach leaves, and remove tough stems. Drain spinach, and pat dry with paper towels.

Anchovies, a saltwater fish with oily flesh, contribute a pleasing flavor to pesto.

Add olive oil to spinach mixture in a slow, steady stream. It will blend quickly to make a thick pesto.

Pesto Pasta

Spinach Fettuccine with Mustard Greens

1½ pounds fresh mustard greens
10 ounces spinach fettuccine, uncooked
1 cup whipping cream
4 ounces goat cheese
¼ teaspoon salt
½ teaspoon freshly ground pepper
2 tablespoons butter or margarine
2 cloves garlic, minced
¼ cup water
½ cup coarsely chopped walnuts, toasted

Remove and discard stems and any discolored spots from greens. Wash greens thoroughly; drain. Cut into 1-inch strips; set aside.

Cook fettuccine according to package directions; drain and set aside.

Bring whipping cream to a boil in a heavy saucepan; boil until cream is reduced to ¾ cup. Remove from heat; add goat cheese, salt, and pepper, stirring with a spoon or wire whisk until smooth. Set aside.

Melt butter in a large heavy skillet over medium heat; add garlic, and cook 1 minute. Gradually add greens, stirring after each addition until leaves wilt. Add water; cover and cook 10 minutes or until tender, stirring occasionally. Drain.

Return greens to skillet; add cream mixture. Cook over medium heat, stirring constantly, 1 minute or until thoroughly heated.

Combine greens mixture, fettuccine, and walnuts; toss gently. Serve pasta immediately. **Yield: 6 to 8 side-dish servings or 3 to 4 main-dish servings.**

Note: Regular spaghetti noodles may be substituted for spinach fettuccine.

Vermicelli with Fresh Spinach Sauce

1 (8-ounce) package vermicelli, uncooked
2 tablespoons butter or margarine
½ pound fresh chopped spinach
½ teaspoon salt
½ teaspoon pepper
1 cup part-skim ricotta cheese
¼ cup milk
½ cup grated fresh Parmesan cheese

Cook vermicelli according to package directions; drain and set aside.

Melt butter in a large skillet. Add spinach; cook over medium heat, stirring constantly, 10 minutes.

Add salt and next 3 ingredients to spinach; cook over low heat, stirring constantly, until mixture is heated (do not boil).

Add grated Parmesan cheese, tossing well. Serve over hot vermicelli. **Yield: 4 servings.**

Glorious Macaroni

1 (8-ounce) package shell macaroni, uncooked
¼ cup chopped onion
1 (2-ounce) jar diced pimiento, drained
1 tablespoon butter or margarine, melted
2 cups (8 ounces) shredded Cheddar cheese
1 (10¾-ounce) can cream of mushroom soup, undiluted
½ cup mayonnaise
1 (2½-ounce) jar sliced mushrooms, drained

Cook macaroni in a Dutch oven according to package directions; drain.

Cook onion and pimiento in butter until onion is crisp-tender.

Combine macaroni, onion mixture, cheese, and remaining ingredients; mix well. Spoon into a lightly greased 2-quart shallow baking dish.

Bake at 350° for 30 minutes. **Yield: 6 servings.**

Old-Fashioned Macaroni and Cheese

1 (8-ounce) package elbow macaroni, uncooked
2½ cups (10 ounces) shredded Cheddar cheese, divided
2 large eggs, lightly beaten
1½ cups milk
1 teaspoon salt
⅛ teaspoon ground white pepper
Paprika

Cook macaroni according to package directions; drain.

Layer one-third each of macaroni and cheese in a lightly greased 2-quart baking dish. Repeat procedure, and top with remaining macaroni. (Reserve remaining cheese.)

Combine eggs, milk, salt, and pepper; pour over macaroni and cheese.

Cover and bake at 350° for 45 minutes. Uncover and sprinkle with remaining cheese and paprika.

Cover and let stand 10 minutes before serving. **Yield: 6 to 8 servings.**

Macaroni and Cheese
(pictured on page 367)

1 (8-ounce) package elbow macaroni, uncooked
¼ cup butter or margarine
¼ cup plus 2 tablespoons all-purpose flour
¼ teaspoon salt
2 cups milk
2 cups (8 ounces) shredded Cheddar cheese
1 (2-ounce) jar diced pimiento, drained
1 tablespoon butter or margarine
⅓ cup fine, dry breadcrumbs
½ teaspoon dried parsley flakes

Cook macaroni according to package directions; drain and set aside.

Place ¼ cup butter in a 4-cup glass measure; microwave, uncovered, at HIGH 55 seconds or until melted.

Blend in flour and salt, stirring until smooth. Gradually stir in milk; microwave, uncovered, at HIGH 5 to 6 minutes or until thickened, stirring after every minute. Add cheese, stirring until melted; stir in pimiento.

Add cheese sauce to macaroni, stirring well. Place macaroni mixture in a 1½-quart baking dish. Cover with heavy-duty plastic wrap; fold back a small edge of wrap to allow steam to escape.

Microwave at MEDIUM HIGH (70% power) 7 to 8 minutes or until thoroughly heated, stirring after 4 minutes.

Place 1 tablespoon butter in a 1-cup glass measure; microwave, uncovered, at HIGH 35 seconds or until melted. Stir in breadcrumbs and parsley flakes; sprinkle over macaroni mixture. Let stand, uncovered, 1 minute. Serve immediately. **Yield: 6 servings.**

From top: Macaroni and Blue Cheese, Jack-in-the-Macaroni Bake, Creamy Macaroni and Cheese

Creamy Macaroni and Cheese

1 (8-ounce) package elbow macaroni,
   uncooked
4 cups (16 ounces) shredded Cheddar or
   Jarlsberg cheese
1 (8-ounce) carton sour cream
1 cup mayonnaise
2 tablespoons chopped onion
1 cup cheese crackers, crushed
Garnish: green onion fan

Cook macaroni according to package directions; drain. Rinse with cold water; drain.

Combine macaroni and next 4 ingredients. Spoon into a lightly greased 11- x 7- x 1½-inch baking dish; sprinkle with crushed crackers.

Bake at 325° for 30 to 35 minutes. Garnish, if desired. **Yield: 6 to 8 servings.**

Jack-in-the-Macaroni Bake

1 (8-ounce) package elbow macaroni,
   uncooked
2 tablespoons butter or margarine
¼ cup chopped onion
¼ cup chopped sweet red pepper
2 cups (8 ounces) shredded Monterey Jack
   cheese with peppers
1 (10¾-ounce) can cream of celery soup,
   undiluted
½ cup sour cream
Chili powder
Garnish: celery leaves

Cook macaroni according to package directions; drain. Rinse with cold water; drain.

Melt butter in a Dutch oven; add onion and sweet red pepper. Cook over medium heat, stirring constantly, until vegetables are crisp-tender. Remove from heat.

Stir cheese, soup, and sour cream into Dutch oven. Stir in macaroni; spoon into a lightly greased 2-quart shallow baking dish. Sprinkle with chili powder.

Bake at 350° for 30 minutes. Garnish, if desired. **Yield: 6 servings.**

Macaroni and Blue Cheese

1 (8-ounce) package elbow macaroni,
   uncooked
¼ cup butter or margarine
¼ cup all-purpose flour
2 cups milk
1 (4-ounce) package crumbled blue cheese
1 large egg, lightly beaten
1 (2-ounce) jar diced pimiento, drained
½ cup soft breadcrumbs
½ cup walnuts, finely chopped
Garnish: fresh parsley sprig

Cook macaroni according to package directions; drain. Rinse with cold water; drain.

Melt butter in a Dutch oven over low heat; add flour, stirring until mixture is smooth. Cook, stirring constantly, 1 minute. Gradually add milk; cook over medium heat, stirring constantly, until mixture is thickened.

Add blue cheese, stirring until melted. Stir about one-fourth of hot cheese mixture into egg; add to remaining hot mixture, stirring constantly.

Stir in macaroni and pimiento; spoon into a lightly greased 2-quart shallow baking dish. Sprinkle with breadcrumbs and walnuts.

Bake at 350° for 35 minutes. Garnish, if desired. **Yield: 6 servings.**

Mushroom-Macaroni Casserole

1 (8-ounce) package elbow macaroni,
    uncooked
1 (10¾-ounce) can cream of mushroom soup,
    undiluted
1 cup mayonnaise
2 cups (8 ounces) shredded sharp Cheddar
    cheese
1 (4-ounce) can sliced mushrooms, drained
1 (2-ounce) jar diced pimiento, drained
    (optional)
¾ cup crushed round buttery crackers (about
    15 crackers)
1 tablespoon butter or margarine, melted

Cook macaroni according to package directions; drain. Rinse with cold water; drain.

Combine macaroni, soup, and next 3 ingredients; add pimiento, if desired. Spoon into a lightly greased 2-quart baking dish.

Combine cracker crumbs and melted butter; sprinkle evenly over macaroni mixture.

Bake at 300° for 30 minutes or until thoroughly heated. **Yield: 6 to 8 servings.**

Orzo and Olive Bake

½ (16-ounce) package orzo (rice-shaped
    pasta), uncooked
1 large onion, chopped
1 cup chopped celery
2 tablespoons olive oil
1 tablespoon all-purpose flour
1 (16-ounce) can Italian-style tomatoes,
    drained
½ cup canned diluted chicken broth
1 teaspoon dried oregano
1 (4-ounce) can sliced ripe olives, drained
2 cups (8 ounces) shredded mozzarella cheese,
    divided
¾ teaspoon salt
¼ teaspoon ground red pepper

Cook orzo according to package directions; drain and set aside.

Cook onion and celery in oil in a large skillet over medium heat, stirring constantly, until tender. Add flour, stirring constantly until blended.

Add tomatoes, broth, and oregano; simmer 5 minutes. Stir in orzo, olives, 1 cup cheese, and salt. Spoon mixture into a greased 1½-quart baking dish. Sprinkle with remaining cheese and pepper.

Bake, uncovered, at 400° for 20 minutes. **Yield: 6 servings.**

Orzo and Olive Bake Technique

Stir orzo into simmering tomato mixture.

Orzo and Olive Bake

St. Louis Toasted Ravioli

1 large egg, lightly beaten
2 tablespoons milk
¾ cup dry Italian-seasoned breadcrumbs
½ teaspoon salt (optional)
½ (27.5-ounce) package frozen cheese-filled ravioli, thawed
Vegetable oil
Grated Parmesan cheese
Commercial spaghetti sauce or pizza sauce

Combine egg and milk in a small bowl. Place breadcrumbs and, if desired, salt, in a shallow bowl. Dip ravioli in milk mixture, and coat with breadcrumbs.

Pour oil to a depth of 2 inches into a Dutch oven; heat to 350°.

Fry ravioli, a few at a time, 1 minute on each side or until golden. Drain on paper towels.

Sprinkle with Parmesan cheese, and serve immediately with warm spaghetti sauce or pizza sauce. **Yield: about 2 dozen appetizers or 4 to 6 side-dish servings.**

Note: Refrigerated fresh ravioli may be substituted for the frozen. Vary the flavor by using sausage, chicken, Italian, or other meat-filled varieties.

Ravioli with Creamy Pesto Sauce

(pictured on page 319)

2 (9-ounce) packages refrigerated cheese-filled ravioli, uncooked
1 cup whipping cream
1 (2.82-ounce) jar pesto sauce
1 (3-ounce) jar capers, drained (optional)
2 tablespoons pine nuts, toasted

Cook pasta according to package directions; drain well.

Combine whipping cream and pesto sauce in a saucepan; add capers, if desired. Cook over low heat until thoroughly heated, stirring frequently.

Toss ravioli with sauce, and sprinkle with toasted pine nuts. Serve immediately. **Yield: 6 servings.**

Spinach Tortellini with Tomato Sauce

1 (9-ounce) package refrigerated spinach tortellini, uncooked
2 cloves garlic, minced
2 tablespoons chopped onion
2 tablespoons olive oil
½ green pepper, chopped
1 hot pepper, seeded and chopped
2 large tomatoes, peeled and chopped
½ teaspoon dried oregano
½ teaspoon dried basil
½ cup freshly grated Parmesan cheese

Cook tortellini according to package directions; drain. Spoon onto platter.

Cook garlic and onion in olive oil, stirring constantly, 3 minutes or until crisp-tender. Add peppers, and cook 1 minute.

Add tomato, oregano, and basil; cook, stirring constantly, 3 minutes.

Spoon mixture over tortellini, and sprinkle with cheese. Serve immediately. **Yield: 3 to 4 servings.**

Spinach Tortellini with Tomato Sauce

Tortellini Carbonara

Tortellini Carbonara

1 (9-ounce) package refrigerated cheese-filled
   tortellini, uncooked
1 small clove garlic, minced
1½ teaspoons olive oil
½ teaspoon white vinegar
3 slices bacon, cooked and crumbled
⅓ cup grated Parmesan cheese
¼ cup whipping cream
1 tablespoon minced fresh parsley
¼ teaspoon pepper

Cook tortellini according to package directions; drain. Cook garlic in hot oil in a small
saucepan over medium-high heat; stir in vinegar.
   Add garlic mixture, bacon, and remaining
ingredients to tortellini; toss gently to combine.
Serve immediately. **Yield: 3 to 4 servings.**

Tortellini with Parsley-Caper Sauce

1 to 2 cloves garlic
¾ cup finely chopped fresh parsley
¼ cup grated Parmesan cheese
2 tablespoons sunflower kernels
2 tablespoons capers
⅛ teaspoon salt
⅛ teaspoon pepper
½ cup olive oil
1 (9-ounce) package refrigerated cheese-filled
   tortellini, uncooked
1½ teaspoons olive oil

Position knife blade in food processor bowl.
Drop garlic through food chute with processor
running; process 5 seconds or until minced.
   Add parsley and next 5 ingredients; process
until smooth, stopping occasionally to scrape
down sides. Gradually pour ½ cup olive oil
through food chute with processor running,
blending just until mixture is smooth. Set aside.
   Cook tortellini according to package directions; drain. Add 1½ teaspoons olive oil; toss
gently.
   Pour sauce over tortellini, and toss. **Yield: 25
appetizer servings or 3 to 4 side-dish servings.**

Keep Parsley Fresh

Extend the life of fresh parsley by
placing it in a glass jar with a small
amount of water. Cover the jar
tightly, and refrigerate, changing the
water at least every 5 days.

Salad Sampler

Let pasta salad star at your next picnic or casual supper. You'll find the marriage of cold pasta and poultry, meats, or vegetables to be a satisfying match.

Cold Pasta Platter, Chicken-and-Broccoli Pasta, Primavera Salad

Artichokes with Orzo Salad, Bow Tie Pasta Primavera, Garden Tortellini Salad

Smoked Turkey Pasta Primavera, Ham and Cheese Salad, Black-Eyed Pea Salad

Pasta Antipasto, Crabmeat-Shrimp Pasta Salad, Antipasto Kabobs

Cheddar-Pasta Toss (page 389)

Cold Pasta Platter

1 (3-pound) broiler-fryer
¼ cup white wine vinegar
2 teaspoons Dijon mustard
2 teaspoons chopped garlic
½ teaspoon salt
½ teaspoon freshly ground pepper
2 tablespoons olive oil
2 tablespoons vegetable oil
8 ounces vermicelli, uncooked
½ cup mayonnaise
Leaf lettuce
2 tablespoons chopped fresh parsley
    (optional)
Pickled beets
Marinated mushrooms
Marinated artichoke hearts
Cherry tomatoes
Garnish: parsley sprigs

Cold Pasta Platter

Place chicken in a Dutch oven; add water to cover. Bring to a boil; cover, reduce heat, and simmer 45 minutes or until chicken is tender.

Remove chicken from broth, and cool. Bone chicken, and cut into ½-inch pieces; set aside. Reserve broth for other uses, if desired.

Combine vinegar and next 4 ingredients, mixing well. Gradually add olive oil and vegetable oil; whisk until blended. Set dressing aside.

Cook vermicelli according to package directions, omitting salt; drain. Rinse with cold water; drain well.

Combine pasta and dressing, tossing well. Add chicken and mayonnaise, mixing well; cover and chill at least 1 hour.

Spoon mixture into center of a lettuce-lined platter. Sprinkle with chopped parsley, if desired. Arrange beets, mushrooms, artichoke hearts, and tomatoes around pasta. Garnish, if desired.
Yield: about 6 servings.

Chicken-and-Broccoli Pasta

4 skinned chicken breast halves
3 cups broccoli flowerets
8 ounces rotini (corkscrew pasta), uncooked
½ cup chopped walnuts, toasted
½ cup grated fresh Parmesan cheese
1 tablespoon lemon juice
1 teaspoon dried basil
¾ cup mayonnaise

Place chicken in a Dutch oven; add water to cover. Bring to a boil; cover, reduce heat, and simmer 20 to 25 minutes or until chicken is tender.

Remove chicken from broth, and cool. Bone chicken, and chop. Cover and chill.

Place broccoli in a steaming rack; place over boiling water. Cover and steam 7 minutes or until crisp-tender. Let cool.

Cook pasta according to package directions, omitting salt; drain. Rinse with cold water; drain.

Place chicken, broccoli, and pasta in a large bowl; add walnuts and remaining ingredients, and toss gently. Cover and chill. **Yield: 4 to 6 servings.**

Tarragon Pasta-Chicken Salad

1 (8-ounce) bottle Italian salad dressing
¼ cup white wine vinegar
2 tablespoons chopped fresh tarragon
1 clove garlic, minced
4 skinned and boned chicken breast halves
4 ounces shell macaroni, uncooked
2 cups sliced celery
½ cup chopped sweet red pepper or green pepper
¼ cup chopped green onions
1 tablespoon chopped fresh parsley
½ cup mayonnaise

Combine first 4 ingredients in a jar, and cover tightly. Shake vigorously until well mixed.

Place chicken in a heavy-duty, zip-top plastic bag; pour ¾ cup dressing mixture over chicken, reserving remaining mixture. Seal bag, and chill at least 8 hours.

Transfer chicken and marinade from bag to an 11- x 7- x 1½-inch baking dish. Bake at 350° for 25 to 30 minutes or until done. Drain chicken, and cool slightly; coarsely chop.

Cook pasta according to package directions; drain and cool slightly.

Combine chicken, reserved dressing mixture, pasta, celery, and remaining ingredients in a large bowl; toss gently. Cover and chill thoroughly. **Yield: 4 to 6 servings.**

Fruited Pasta Salad

1⅓ cups rotini (corkscrew pasta), uncooked
2 cups chopped cooked chicken
1½ cups sliced celery
1 cup seedless green grapes, halved
¼ cup chopped green pepper
¼ cup chopped purple onion
1 (11-ounce) can mandarin oranges, drained
1 (8-ounce) can sliced water chestnuts, drained
¼ cup commercial buttermilk dressing
¼ cup mayonnaise
1 teaspoon Beau Monde seasoning
¼ teaspoon salt
⅛ teaspoon pepper

Cook pasta according to package directions; drain. Rinse with cold water; drain.

Combine pasta and next 7 ingredients in a large bowl, tossing gently.

Combine buttermilk dressing and next 4 ingredients. Pour over pasta mixture, tossing gently. Cover and chill. **Yield: 4 to 6 servings.**

Pasta Technique

Draining and rinsing hot cooked pasta in cold water helps to cool it quickly before tossing it with other ingredients.

Smoked Turkey Pasta Primavera

1 (12-ounce) package fettuccine, uncooked
1½ pounds fresh broccoli, cut into flowerets
2 medium zucchini, thinly sliced
6 green onions, thinly sliced
1 sweet red pepper, sliced into thin strips
1 (6-ounce) can pitted ripe olives, drained and
    sliced
4 cups chopped cooked smoked turkey
⅔ cup grated Parmesan cheese
½ teaspoon salt
½ teaspoon freshly ground pepper
Basil Sauce
2 cups cherry tomatoes, halved
Lettuce leaves

Primavera Salad

Cook fettuccine according to package directions; drain. Rinse with cold water; drain.

Combine fettuccine and next 9 ingredients. Add Basil Sauce and cherry tomatoes; toss gently.

Cover and chill. Serve on lettuce leaves.
Yield: 12 servings.

Basil Sauce

⅓ cup chopped fresh basil
1 clove garlic
¼ teaspoon dry mustard
¼ teaspoon salt
¼ teaspoon lemon juice
2 teaspoons white wine vinegar
⅓ cup mayonnaise
⅓ cup sour cream

Combine basil and garlic in container of an electric blender or food processor; process 30 seconds or until basil is finely chopped.

Add mustard and next 3 ingredients; process 20 seconds, stopping once to scrape down sides.

Add mayonnaise and sour cream. Stir well.
Yield: ⅔ cup.

Primavera Salad

1 pound broccoli
1 (12-ounce) package bow tie pasta, uncooked
Versatile Vinaigrette
1 (10-ounce) package fresh spinach
1 pound smoked turkey breast, cut into thin
    strips
1 pint cherry tomatoes, halved
½ cup chopped fresh basil
¼ cup chopped fresh parsley
⅓ cup pine nuts, toasted

Remove broccoli leaves, and cut off tough ends of stalks; discard. Wash broccoli thoroughly, and cut into 1-inch pieces.

Cook broccoli in boiling water to cover 1 minute; drain immediately, and plunge into ice water. Drain and pat dry with paper towels; chill.

Cook pasta according to package directions; drain. Rinse with cold water; drain.

Combine pasta and Versatile Vinaigrette, tossing to coat. Place in a large heavy-duty, zip-top plastic bag. Chill at least 2 hours or overnight.

Remove stems from spinach; wash leaves thoroughly, and pat dry.

Combine spinach, broccoli, pasta, turkey, and remaining ingredients, tossing gently. **Yield: 8 to 10 servings.**

Versatile Vinaigrette

⅔ cup vegetable oil
¼ cup white wine vinegar
¼ cup water
1½ teaspoons salt
1 tablespoon freshly ground pepper
1 clove garlic, crushed

Combine all ingredients in a jar. Cover tightly, and shake vigorously. **Yield: 1 cup.**

Ranch-Style Turkey 'n' Pasta Salad

2 cups penne (short tubular pasta), uncooked
2 cups chopped cooked turkey
1 small zucchini, sliced
2 small yellow squash, sliced
1 small green pepper, seeded and chopped
1 small sweet red pepper, seeded and chopped
¼ cup grated Parmesan cheese
¾ cup commercial Ranch-style dressing

Cook pasta according to package directions; drain. Rinse with cold water; drain.

Combine pasta and remaining ingredients in a large bowl. Cover and chill at least 2 hours. Toss before serving. **Yield: 6 to 8 servings.**

Cheddar-Pasta Toss

(pictured on page 385)

1½ cups tri-colored rotini (corkscrew pasta), uncooked
½ (10-ounce) package frozen English peas
1 cup julienne-sliced cooked ham
1 (8-ounce) package Cheddar cheese, cut into ¾-inch cubes
½ cup chopped celery
½ cup sliced ripe olives
3 green onions, chopped
⅓ cup mayonnaise
2 tablespoons red wine vinegar
1 tablespoon olive oil
¼ teaspoon garlic powder
¼ teaspoon pepper
⅛ teaspoon dried oregano
1 (4-ounce) jar diced pimiento, drained
Lettuce leaves

Cook rotini according to package directions; drain. Rinse with cold water; drain.

Cook peas according to package directions; drain well. Combine pasta, peas, ham, and next 4 ingredients in a large bowl; toss gently.

Combine mayonnaise and next 5 ingredients in a small bowl; stir well. Add to pasta mixture; toss gently to coat.

Cover and chill thoroughly. Stir in pimiento just before serving. Serve salad on lettuce leaves. **Yield: 6 servings.**

Ham and Cheese Salad

Ham and Cheese Salad

8 ounces rotini (corkscrew pasta), uncooked
½ pound cooked ham, cut into 2-inch strips
1 cup broccoli flowerets
1 cup frozen English peas, thawed
1 small yellow squash, thinly sliced
1 small sweet red pepper, cut into thin strips
4 ounces Swiss cheese, cubed
½ cup mayonnaise
¼ cup Dijon mustard
¼ cup milk
¼ cup grated Parmesan cheese

Cook pasta according to package directions; drain. Rinse with cold water; drain.

Combine pasta and next 6 ingredients in a large bowl.

Combine mayonnaise, mustard, and milk; stir well. Add to vegetable mixture, tossing gently. Sprinkle with Parmesan cheese. Cover and chill at least 2 hours. **Yield: 6 servings.**

Italian Salad

1 (12-ounce) package rotini (corkscrew pasta), uncooked
2 (6-ounce) jars marinated artichoke hearts, undrained
1¼ cups pitted ripe olives, sliced
1 cup chopped green pepper
¼ pound hard salami, cut into ¼-inch strips
½ cup grated Parmesan cheese
¼ cup chopped onion
¼ cup chopped fresh parsley
1 (0.7-ounce) package Italian salad dressing mix

Cook pasta according to package directions; drain. Rinse with cold water; drain.

Drain artichokes, reserving ¼ cup liquid; set aside. Cut artichoke hearts into quarters; set aside.

Combine pasta, artichokes, reserved artichoke liquid, olives, and remaining ingredients in a large bowl; toss gently. Cover and chill. **Yield: 6 servings.**

Pasta Antipasto

1 cup rotini (corkscrew pasta), uncooked
2 (6-ounce) jars marinated artichoke hearts, undrained
¾ cup commercial Italian salad dressing
¼ teaspoon freshly ground pepper
1 pint cherry tomatoes
½ cup pimiento-stuffed olives
½ cup ripe olives
2 medium carrots, scraped and cut into very thin strips
½ pound fresh mushrooms
1 medium-size green pepper, cut into strips
3 to 4 ounces sliced pepperoni
3 to 4 ounces sliced salami

Cook pasta according to package directions, omitting salt; drain. Rinse with cold water; drain. Set aside.

Drain artichoke hearts, reserving ½ cup artichoke liquid. Add Italian salad dressing and ground pepper to reserved artichoke liquid to make marinade, stirring well.

Combine artichoke hearts, tomatoes, and next 5 ingredients. Add about three-fourths of marinade to vegetable mixture, tossing gently. Cover and chill 8 hours. Add remaining marinade to pasta, tossing gently. Cover and chill 8 hours.

Arrange pepperoni and salami around outer edges of a serving platter. Spoon pasta in a ring within meat, using a slotted spoon. Spoon vegetable mixture in center of platter, using a slotted spoon. **Yield: 8 to 10 servings.**

Pasta Salad

4 ounces spaghetti, uncooked
1 (6-ounce) jar marinated artichoke hearts, undrained
¾ cup sliced fresh zucchini
⅔ cup shredded carrot
2 ounces sliced salami, cut into strips
1 cup (4 ounces) shredded mozzarella cheese
2 tablespoons grated Parmesan cheese
2 tablespoons vegetable oil
2 tablespoons white wine vinegar
¾ teaspoon dry mustard
½ teaspoon dried oregano
½ teaspoon dried basil
1 clove garlic, crushed

Break spaghetti in half, and cook according to package directions, omitting salt; drain. Rinse with cold water; drain.

Drain artichoke hearts, reserving liquid; chop artichokes.

Combine spaghetti, artichokes, and next 5 ingredients; set aside.

Combine reserved artichoke liquid, oil, and next 5 ingredients in a jar. Cover tightly; shake.

Pour dressing over spaghetti mixture; toss gently to coat. Cover and chill 2 to 3 hours.
Yield: 6 to 8 servings.

Salad Dressing Technique

Remove artichokes from liquid, and chop; use reserved liquid in the salad dressing.

Black-Eyed Pea Salad

1 (16-ounce) package dried black-eyed peas
6 cups water
1 (6-ounce) jar marinated artichoke hearts, undrained
2 cups cooked wagon wheel pasta
1 medium-size sweet red pepper, seeded and chopped
1 medium-size green pepper, seeded and chopped
¾ cup canned garbanzo beans
½ cup chopped purple onion
1 (6-ounce) package sliced provolone cheese, cut into strips
1 (3½-ounce) package sliced pepperoni, cut into strips
3 tablespoons chopped fresh parsley
1 (0.7-ounce) envelope Italian salad dressing mix
¼ cup sugar
½ teaspoon pepper
½ cup white wine vinegar
¼ cup vegetable oil

Sort and wash peas; place in a large Dutch oven. Cover with water 2 inches above peas; let soak 8 hours. Drain. Add 6 cups water, and bring to a boil. Cover, reduce heat, and simmer 45 minutes or until peas are tender. Drain and let cool.

Drain artichoke hearts, reserving liquid. Chop artichokes, and set aside.

Combine peas, chopped artichoke, pasta, and next 7 ingredients in a large bowl. Toss gently.

Combine reserved artichoke liquid, salad dressing mix, and next 4 ingredients in a jar; cover tightly, and shake vigorously.

Pour dressing over pea mixture, stirring gently. Cover and chill salad at least 2 hours before serving. **Yield: 12 servings.**

Black-Eyed Pea Salad

Crabmeat-Shrimp Pasta Salad

3 cups water
1 pound unpeeled medium-size fresh shrimp
6 ounces shell macaroni, uncooked
1 cup thinly sliced celery
½ medium-size green pepper, finely chopped
½ medium-size sweet red pepper, finely chopped
½ small purple onion, chopped
2 green onions, chopped
1 tablespoon chopped fresh parsley
¼ cup mayonnaise
¼ cup commercial Italian salad dressing
1 tablespoon lemon juice
½ teaspoon dried oregano, crushed
¼ teaspoon salt
Dash of pepper
8 ounces lump crabmeat, drained

Bring water to a boil; add shrimp, and cook 3 to 5 minutes or just until shrimp turn pink. Drain well; rinse shrimp with cold water. Chill. Peel shrimp, and devein, if desired; set aside.

Cook pasta according to package directions, omitting salt; drain. Rinse with cold water; drain. Stir in celery and next 5 ingredients.

Combine mayonnaise and next 5 ingredients; add to pasta mixture. Stir in crabmeat and shrimp. Cover and chill. **Yield: 7 servings.**

Salad Tip

Cold pasta has a tendency to stick together if it's not rinsed after cooking. For this reason, most of the salad recipes suggest rinsing cooked pasta with cold water before proceeding with the recipe.

Shrimp Vermicelli Salad

5 cups water
1½ pounds unpeeled medium-size fresh shrimp
1 (12-ounce) package vermicelli, uncooked
3 hard-cooked eggs, chopped
1½ cups chopped green onions
1 cup chopped dill pickle
¼ cup minced fresh parsley
1 small green pepper, seeded and chopped
1 (2-ounce) jar diced pimiento, drained
1 (10-ounce) package frozen tiny English peas, thawed and drained
1 cup mayonnaise
1 (8-ounce) carton sour cream
¼ cup lemon juice
2 tablespoons prepared mustard
1 teaspoon celery seeds
1 teaspoon salt
¼ teaspoon pepper
Leaf lettuce
¼ to ½ teaspoon paprika

Bring water to a boil; add shrimp, and cook 3 to 5 minutes or just until shrimp turn pink. Drain well; rinse with cold water. Chill. Peel shrimp, and devein, if desired.

Break vermicelli into 3-inch pieces. Cook according to package directions; drain. Rinse with cold water; drain.

Add shrimp, eggs, and next 6 ingredients to pasta; set aside.

Combine mayonnaise and next 6 ingredients; stir well. Pour over shrimp mixture; toss gently. Cover and chill 2 hours.

Serve on a lettuce-lined platter; sprinkle with paprika. **Yield: 8 servings.**

Shrimp-Pasta Medley

Shrimp-Pasta Medley

5 cups water
1½ pounds unpeeled medium-size fresh shrimp
1 cup rotini (corkscrew pasta), uncooked
1 (6-ounce) package frozen snow pea pods, thawed
1 (4-ounce) can button mushrooms, drained
⅓ to ½ cup grated Parmesan cheese
¼ cup sliced celery
¼ cup sliced pimiento-stuffed olives
¼ cup sliced ripe olives
1 teaspoon chopped parsley
1 teaspoon white wine
¼ teaspoon anise flavoring
1 (8-ounce) bottle Italian salad dressing
Lettuce leaves
Parmesan cheese
Garnish: cherry tomato halves

Bring water to a boil; add shrimp, and cook 3 to 5 minutes or just until shrimp turn pink. Drain well, and rinse with cold water. Chill. Peel shrimp, and devein, if desired.

Cook pasta according to package directions, omitting salt; drain. Rinse with cold water; drain.

Combine pasta, shrimp, snow peas, and next 9 ingredients, tossing well; chill at least 1 hour.

Spoon mixture onto a lettuce-lined platter. Sprinkle with Parmesan cheese. Garnish, if desired. **Yield: 6 servings.**

Bow Tie Shrimp Salad

Bow Tie Shrimp Salad

10 ounces bow tie pasta, uncooked
2 cups water
¾ pound unpeeled medium-size fresh shrimp
1½ cups frozen tiny English peas, thawed
1 (7-ounce) jar dried tomatoes in oil, drained
    and coarsely chopped
1 small purple onion, finely chopped
½ cup finely chopped green pepper
½ cup finely chopped sweet yellow pepper
5 radishes, chopped
2 tablespoons minced fresh parsley
1 tablespoon minced fresh basil
3 tablespoons olive oil
2 tablespoons lemon juice
2 tablespoons white wine vinegar
1 teaspoon Dijon mustard
¼ teaspoon salt
Freshly ground pepper to taste

Cook pasta according to package directions;
drain. Rinse with cold water; drain. Set aside.

Bring 2 cups water to a boil; add shrimp, and
cook 3 to 5 minutes or just until shrimp turn pink.
Drain; rinse with cold water. Chill. Peel shrimp,
and devein, if desired.

Combine pasta, shrimp, peas, and next 7
ingredients in a large salad bowl. Toss gently, and
set aside.

Combine olive oil and next 5 ingredients in a
jar. Cover tightly; shake vigorously. Pour dressing
over pasta mixture; toss gently. **Yield: 8 to 10
servings.**

Bow Tie Shrimp Salad Techniques

Coarsely chopped dried tomatoes add intense
tomato flavor and chewy texture to salad.

Combine salad dressing ingredients in a jar; cover
tightly, and shake vigorously.

Freshly ground pepper from a handheld pepper
mill adds a sharp, lively flavor to salad dressing.

Artichokes with Orzo Salad

Artichokes with Orzo Salad

½ cup orzo (rice-shaped pasta), uncooked
1 carrot, diced
2 green onions, sliced
8 pitted ripe olives
1 tablespoon chopped fresh basil
⅛ teaspoon salt
⅛ teaspoon pepper
Creamy Lemon Dressing, divided
4 artichokes
Lemon wedge
½ cup water
2 teaspoons lemon juice
2 teaspoons vegetable oil
Garnish: ripe olive slices
Chopped fresh parsley

Cook orzo according to package directions; drain. Rinse with cold water; drain.

Combine orzo and next 6 ingredients, mixing well. Stir in 2 tablespoons Creamy Lemon Dressing. Cover and chill.

Wash artichokes by plunging them up and down in cold water. Cut off stem ends, and trim about ½ inch from top of each artichoke. Remove any loose bottom leaves. With scissors, trim away about one-fourth of each outer leaf. Rub top and edge of leaves with a lemon wedge to prevent discoloration.

Place artichokes upside down in a 2½-quart baking dish. Add ½ cup water, lemon juice, and oil. Cover and microwave at HIGH 14 minutes, giving dish a quarter-turn halfway through cooking time. Let stand, covered, 5 minutes. Plunge into cold water. Drain.

Spread artichoke leaves apart; scrape out fuzzy thistle center (choke) with a spoon. Spoon orzo mixture into cavities. Garnish, if desired.

Serve artichokes with remaining Creamy Lemon Dressing. Sprinkle dressing with parsley. **Yield: 4 servings.**

Creamy Lemon Dressing

2 tablespoons lemon juice
2 tablespoons red wine vinegar
1 tablespoon brown mustard
¼ teaspoon garlic powder
2 tablespoons egg substitute
½ cup vegetable oil

Combine first 4 ingredients in container of an electric blender or food processor; process 15 seconds. Add egg substitute, and process 15 seconds. With blender or processor running, gradually add oil, mixing just until well blended. **Yield: ⅔ cup.**

Artichoke-Pasta Salad

2 tablespoons white wine vinegar
2 tablespoons lemon juice
1 teaspoon Dijon mustard
⅓ cup olive oil
¼ cup chopped fresh parsley
2 tablespoons chopped fresh basil
1½ cups orzo (rice-shaped pasta), uncooked
1 (14-ounce) can artichoke hearts, drained
    and quartered
⅔ cup grated Parmesan cheese
Lettuce leaves
4 ounces prosciutto, cut into ½-inch strips
4 green onions, thinly sliced

Combine first 3 ingredients in container of an electric blender or food processor; process until blended. With blender or processor still running, add oil in a slow, steady stream; process until blended. Stir in parsley and basil. Set dressing aside.

Cook orzo according to package directions; drain. Rinse with cold water; drain.

Combine orzo, artichoke hearts, Parmesan cheese, and dressing; toss gently. Cover and chill.

Arrange orzo mixture on a lettuce-lined platter; sprinkle with prosciutto and green onions. **Yield: 6 servings.**

Bow Tie Pasta Primavera

Bow Tie Pasta Primavera

8 ounces bow tie pasta, uncooked
2 tablespoons olive oil, divided
3 green onions, cut into 1-inch pieces
2 cloves garlic, minced
½ pound fresh asparagus
2 cups broccoli flowerets
1 (10-ounce) package frozen English peas,
   thawed and drained
½ pound fresh mushrooms, sliced
1 small tomato, finely chopped
1 small sweet red pepper, seeded and chopped
1 cup freshly grated Parmesan cheese
¼ cup minced fresh parsley
¼ cup white wine vinegar
¼ cup olive oil
½ teaspoon salt
½ teaspoon dried oregano
½ teaspoon dried basil
½ teaspoon dried thyme
¼ teaspoon black pepper
⅛ teaspoon ground red pepper

Cook pasta according to package directions; drain. Rinse with cold water; drain. Place pasta in a large serving bowl; toss with 1 tablespoon olive oil.

Cook green onions and garlic in 1 tablespoon hot olive oil in a large skillet over medium-high heat, stirring constantly, until crisp-tender; add to pasta, tossing gently.

Snap off tough ends of asparagus. Remove scales with a vegetable peeler or knife, if desired. Cut asparagus into 1-inch pieces.

Arrange asparagus and broccoli in a vegetable steamer over boiling water; cover and steam 4 minutes or until crisp-tender.

Add asparagus mixture, peas, and remaining ingredients to pasta mixture; toss gently. Cover and chill 3 to 4 hours, tossing occasionally. **Yield: 8 servings.**

Confetti Orzo Salad

1½ cups orzo (rice-shaped pasta), uncooked
1 carrot, scraped and chopped
1¼ cups chopped sweet red, green, or yellow
   pepper
½ cup peeled, seeded, and chopped cucumber
¼ cup thinly sliced green onions
¼ cup chopped purple onion
¼ cup chopped fresh parsley
2 tablespoons white wine vinegar
½ teaspoon grated lemon rind
3 tablespoons lemon juice
¾ teaspoon salt
⅛ teaspoon coarsely ground pepper
2 cloves garlic, minced
⅓ cup olive oil

Cook orzo according to package directions; drain. Rinse with cold water; drain.

Combine orzo, carrot, and next 5 ingredients; set aside.

Combine vinegar and next 5 ingredients. Gradually add oil, beating with a wire whisk until blended. Pour over orzo mixture, tossing gently. Cover and chill. **Yield: 8 to 10 servings.**

Ramen Noodle Salad

2 cups water
1 (3-ounce) package chicken-flavored Ramen
    noodles
1 teaspoon butter
¼ cup finely chopped celery
¼ cup shredded carrot
¼ cup thinly sliced green onions
1 tablespoon finely chopped green pepper
1 teaspoon lemon juice
1 teaspoon soy sauce
2 tablespoons mayonnaise

Bring water to a boil. Crumble noodles, and add to water; stir in seasoning packet. Return to a boil, and cook 2 minutes, stirring often. Drain.

Combine noodles and butter, stirring until butter melts. Add celery and remaining ingredients, stirring gently to coat. Cover and chill 3 to 4 hours. **Yield: 2 servings.**

Vegetable Pasta Salad

8 ounces rotini (corkscrew pasta), uncooked
1 teaspoon salt
1 medium onion, chopped
1 cup sliced fresh mushrooms
1 clove garlic, minced
2 tablespoons olive oil
1 medium carrot, thinly sliced
1 cup broccoli flowerets
1 medium zucchini, thinly sliced
1 cup frozen English peas
2 tablespoons chopped fresh basil or
    2 teaspoons dried basil
2 tablespoons chopped fresh parsley
1 pint cherry tomatoes, cut in half
Vinaigrette Dressing
Lettuce leaves
Garnish: grated Parmesan cheese

Cook pasta according to package directions, using 1 teaspoon salt; drain. Rinse with cold water; drain. Set aside.

Cook onion, mushrooms, and garlic in 2 tablespoons olive oil in a Dutch oven, stirring constantly, until onion is tender. Add carrot, broccoli, zucchini, and peas; cook 2 minutes.

Add pasta, basil, and parsley to Dutch oven, mixing well. Stir in tomatoes.

Toss pasta mixture with Vinaigrette Dressing, and serve on lettuce leaves. Garnish, if desired. **Yield: 10 to 12 servings.**

Vinaigrette Dressing

⅓ cup olive oil
¼ cup red wine vinegar
1 tablespoon water
1 teaspoon minced onion
1 clove garlic, minced
¼ teaspoon salt
¼ teaspoon sugar
¼ teaspoon paprika
¼ teaspoon pepper
⅛ teaspoon dry mustard

Combine all ingredients in a jar. Cover tightly, and shake vigorously. **Yield: ⅔ cup.**

Toss a Pasta Salad

Turn leftover plain pasta into an impromptu pasta salad—simply add chopped raw or cooked vegetables, and toss with your favorite salad dressing. Add diced or shredded cheese and cooked ham, poultry, or seafood for other variations.

Versatile Pasta Salad

4 ounces rotini (corkscrew pasta), uncooked
1 cup sliced fresh mushrooms
1 cup broccoli flowerets
1 cup diced Cheddar cheese
½ cup shredded carrot
½ cup chopped sweet red pepper
¼ teaspoon seasoned salt
¼ teaspoon pepper
⅓ cup vegetable oil
¼ cup white wine vinegar
1 tablespoon Dijon mustard
¼ cup finely chopped green onions
1 tablespoon minced fresh parsley
2 cloves garlic, crushed
½ teaspoon sugar
½ teaspoon dried basil
¼ teaspoon salt
¼ teaspoon dried oregano
¼ teaspoon dried crushed red pepper flakes

Cook rotini according to package directions; drain. Rinse with cold water; drain.

Combine pasta and next 7 ingredients in a large bowl. Set aside.

Combine vegetable oil and next 10 ingredients in a jar. Cover tightly, and shake vigorously. Pour dressing over pasta mixture; toss well.

Chill in a tightly covered container at least 2 hours and up to 3 days. **Yield: 4½ cups.**

Variations:

Summer Pasta Salad: Substitute 1 small zucchini, thinly sliced, 1 small yellow squash, thinly sliced, and 6 to 8 cherry tomatoes, halved, for mushrooms and broccoli. **Yield: about 4½ cups.**

Pasta Salad Roma: Substitute 1 (14-ounce) can artichoke hearts, drained and quartered, 1 cup cubed salami, 1 cup diced mozzarella cheese, and ½ cup sliced ripe olives for broccoli, carrot, and Cheddar cheese. **Yield: 4 cups.**

Colorful Pasta Salad

1 pound tri-colored rotini (corkscrew pasta), uncooked
1 green pepper, seeded and chopped
1 sweet red pepper, seeded and chopped
1 (8-ounce) can sliced water chestnuts, drained
1 bunch green onions, chopped
Cherry tomatoes (optional)
¾ cup vegetable oil
¼ cup cider vinegar
1½ teaspoons salt
1½ teaspoons pepper
1 clove garlic, crushed

Cook pasta according to package directions, omitting salt; drain. Rinse with cold water; drain.

Combine pasta, peppers, water chestnuts, green onions and, if desired, cherry tomatoes in a bowl.

Combine oil and next 4 ingredients; mix well. Pour over pasta; toss well. Cover and chill 8 hours, stirring occasionally. **Yield: 12 servings.**

Antipasto Kabobs

1 (9-ounce) package refrigerated cheese-filled tortellini, uncooked
1 (14-ounce) can quartered artichoke hearts, drained
1 (6-ounce) jar pitted ripe olives, drained
½ pound (2-inch-round) thin pepperoni slices
1 (8-ounce) bottle reduced-fat Parmesan Italian salad dressing

Cook tortellini according to package directions, omitting salt. Drain and cool.

Thread tortellini and next 3 ingredients onto 25 (6-inch) wooden skewers. Place in a 13- x 9- x 2-inch dish; drizzle with salad dressing, turning to coat.

Cover and chill at least 4 hours. Drain before serving. **Yield: 10 to 12 appetizer servings.**

Tortellini-Pesto Salad

Garden Tortellini Salad

1 (9-ounce) package refrigerated cheese-filled
   tortellini, uncooked
1 (7-ounce) package refrigerated cheese-filled
   spinach tortellini, uncooked
3 cups broccoli flowerets
½ pound carrots, scraped and sliced
2 small green onions, sliced
1 small sweet red pepper, cut into strips
¼ cup finely chopped fresh basil
2 tablespoons egg substitute
1 tablespoon lemon juice
1½ teaspoons Dijon mustard
1½ teaspoons balsamic vinegar
½ cup vegetable oil
¼ cup olive oil
1½ teaspoons grated orange rind
½ teaspoon dried thyme
½ teaspoon salt
⅛ teaspoon ground white pepper

Cook tortellini according to package directions; drain. Rinse with cold water; drain.

Cook broccoli and carrot in a small amount of boiling water 5 minutes or just until crisp-tender; drain well.

Combine tortellini, broccoli, carrot, and next 3 ingredients in a large bowl.

Position knife blade in food processor bowl; add egg substitute and next 3 ingredients. Process 30 seconds. Remove food pusher.

Pour oils slowly through food chute with processor running, blending just until smooth. Add orange rind and next 3 ingredients to dressing; process 30 seconds.

Pour dressing over pasta mixture; toss well. Cover and chill salad at least 2 hours before serving. **Yield: 10 to 12 servings.**

Tortellini-Pesto Salad

1 (9-ounce) package refrigerated cheese-filled
   tortellini, uncooked
1 small sweet red pepper, cut into thin strips
¾ cup broccoli flowerets
⅓ cup carrot slices
⅓ cup sliced pimiento-stuffed olives
½ cup mayonnaise
¼ cup commercial pesto sauce
¼ cup milk
2 tablespoons grated Parmesan cheese
1 tablespoon olive oil
1 teaspoon white wine vinegar
1 clove garlic, minced
Fresh spinach leaves (optional)

Cook tortellini according to package directions; drain. Rinse with cold water; drain.

Combine tortellini and next 4 ingredients in a medium bowl; set aside.

Combine mayonnaise and next 6 ingredients; spoon over tortellini mixture, and toss gently.

Cover and chill until ready to serve. Serve on fresh spinach leaves, if desired. **Yield: 4 to 6 servings.**

Simmering Sauces

Whether you have 10 minutes or an hour to cook, in this chapter you'll find a thick rich sauce perfect for ladling over pasta.

Marinara Sauce, Quick Spaghetti and Meat Sauce, Italian Sauce

Quick Spaghetti Sauce, Southwestern Tomato Sauce, Creamy Tomato Sauce

Bow Tie with Marinara, Spinach Pasta Sauce, Baked Ziti, Italian Tomato Sauce

Dried Tomato Spaghetti Sauce, Grilled Chicken-Pasta Salad

Easy Spaghetti Meat Sauce (page 411)

Marinara Sauce

½ cup chopped onion
2 cloves garlic, crushed
1 tablespoon olive oil
4 (14½-ounce) cans tomatoes, drained and
    chopped
2 tablespoons lemon juice
1 tablespoon dried Italian seasoning
2 bay leaves

Cook onion and garlic in olive oil in a Dutch oven over medium-high heat, stirring constantly, until tender. Stir in tomatoes and remaining ingredients.

Bring mixture to a boil; reduce heat to medium, and cook 20 minutes or until most of liquid evaporates, stirring occasionally.

Remove and discard bay leaves. **Yield: 5 cups.**

Quick Spaghetti and Meat Sauce

½ pound ground beef
1½ cups Marinara Sauce (recipe above)
Hot cooked spaghetti or linguine
2 tablespoons grated Parmesan cheese

Brown beef in a skillet, stirring until it crumbles. Drain; return to skillet.

Stir in Marinara Sauce; cook over medium heat 5 minutes. Serve over pasta, and sprinkle with cheese. **Yield: 2 servings.**

Marinara Magic

Make the Marinara Sauce in 30 minutes, and have a head start on other quick meals. You can also use this sauce in any recipe calling for a marinara sauce.

Bow Tie with Marinara

4 to 8 ounces bow tie pasta, uncooked
1 to 2 cups Marinara Sauce (recipe at left)
Freshly grated Parmesan cheese

Cook pasta according to package directions; drain well.

Combine pasta and Marinara Sauce; sprinkle with cheese. **Yield: 2 to 4 servings.**

Baked Ziti

1 (16-ounce) package ziti (short tubular
    pasta), uncooked
1 pound mild Italian sausage
½ pound ground beef
½ cup chopped onion
3 cups Marinara Sauce (recipe at left)
1 (16-ounce) package sliced mozzarella cheese
¼ cup grated Parmesan cheese

Cook pasta according to package directions; drain and set aside.

Remove sausage from casing. Cook sausage, beef, and onion in a large skillet over medium heat, stirring until meat crumbles. Drain and return to skillet.

Stir Marinara Sauce and cooked ziti into meat mixture. Layer half each of ziti mixture and mozzarella cheese in a lightly greased 13- x 9- x 2-inch baking dish. Spoon remaining ziti mixture over mozzarella cheese; cover with foil.

Bake at 350° for 15 minutes. Remove foil; add remaining mozzarella cheese, and sprinkle with Parmesan cheese. Bake 10 additional minutes. **Yield: 8 to 10 servings.**

Grilled Chicken-Pasta Salad

4 ounces bow tie pasta, uncooked
½ cup Italian salad dressing, divided
2 skinned and boned chicken breast halves
½ small cucumber
1 cup Marinara Sauce, chilled (recipe on
   facing page)

Cook pasta according to package directions, omitting salt; drain.

Combine pasta and 2 tablespoons salad dressing in a bowl, and toss gently. Cover pasta mixture, and chill at least 8 hours.

Place chicken in a shallow dish; drizzle with remaining salad dressing, turning to coat. Cover and chill 2 hours.

Cut cucumber half crosswise into 2 equal portions. Peel and chop 1 portion of cucumber; cut remaining portion into thin strips, and set aside. Stir chopped cucumber into Marinara Sauce, and set aside.

Drain chicken breasts; cook, without grill lid, over hot coals (450° to 500°) for 5 to 7 minutes on each side or until chicken is tender.

Arrange pasta on individual salad plates; spoon sauce over pasta, and top with chicken breasts and cucumber strips. **Yield: 2 servings.**

Italian Tomato Sauce

3 large vine-ripened tomatoes
2 tablespoons extra-virgin olive oil
3 cloves garlic, minced
¼ cup sliced ripe olives
1 tablespoon chopped fresh basil
1 tablespoon chopped fresh parsley
¼ teaspoon salt
¼ teaspoon pepper
4 ounces spaghetti, uncooked
4 ounces mozzarella cheese, cut into cubes

Peel tomatoes; coarsely chop over a medium bowl, reserving juice.

Combine tomato, reserved juice, olive oil, and next 6 ingredients; cover and let stand at room temperature 1 hour.

Cook pasta according to package directions; drain. Serve tomato mixture over pasta, and top with cheese. **Yield: 2 servings.**

Creamy Tomato Sauce

2 cloves garlic, minced
2 tablespoons butter or margarine, melted
6 large tomatoes, peeled, seeded, and chopped
   (about 5 pounds)
½ teaspoon salt
¼ teaspoon freshly ground pepper
½ cup whipping cream
2 tablespoons chopped fresh basil or
   2 teaspoons dried basil
Hot cooked vermicelli

Cook garlic in butter in a large skillet over medium heat, stirring constantly, 1 minute.

Add tomato, salt, and pepper; cook 12 to 15 minutes or until sauce is thickened. Gradually stir in whipping cream and basil, and cook 10 additional minutes.

Serve sauce over vermicelli. **Yield: 4 to 6 servings.**

Dried Tomato Spaghetti Sauce

1 (7-ounce) jar oil-packed dried tomatoes,
    undrained
1 cup chopped onion
1 cup chopped celery
1 cup diced carrot
3 cloves garlic, minced
2 (28-ounce) cans whole tomatoes, undrained
⅔ cup dry white wine
1 teaspoon dried fennel seeds
½ teaspoon pepper

Drain dried tomatoes, reserving ¼ cup oil. Chop tomatoes; set aside.

Heat reserved oil in a Dutch oven; cook onion, celery, carrot, and garlic in hot oil 15 minutes, stirring occasionally.

Stir in dried and canned tomatoes, wine, fennel seeds, and pepper; cook, uncovered, over medium heat 1 hour or to desired consistency, stirring occasionally.

Position knife blade in food processor bowl; add half of sauce mixture. Pulse 4 or 5 times or until mixture is chopped but not smooth. Repeat procedure with remaining half of sauce mixture. Serve over hot pasta. **Yield: 6 cups.**

Spinach Pasta Sauce

2 cloves garlic, sliced
2 tablespoons butter or margarine, melted
2 (9.5-ounce) packages frozen creamed
    spinach, thawed
1 cup half-and-half
⅓ cup grated Parmesan cheese
Hot cooked spaghetti
4 slices bacon, cooked and crumbled

Cook garlic in butter in a medium saucepan over medium heat, stirring constantly, until lightly browned; remove and discard garlic.

Add spinach and half-and-half to butter. Bring to a boil, stirring constantly; reduce heat, and add Parmesan cheese. Cook over low heat, stirring occasionally, 8 to 10 minutes.

Serve sauce over spaghetti; sprinkle with bacon. **Yield: 4 to 6 servings.**

Southwestern Tomato Sauce

3 small vine-ripened tomatoes
2 tablespoons extra-virgin olive oil
3 cloves garlic, minced
1 jalapeño pepper, seeded and finely chopped
3 tablespoons chopped fresh cilantro
1 tablespoon fresh lime juice
½ teaspoon chili powder
¼ teaspoon salt
¼ teaspoon ground white pepper
4 ounces angel hair pasta, uncooked
4 ounces goat cheese, crumbled
2 tablespoons pine nuts, toasted

Peel tomatoes, and coarsely chop over a medium bowl, reserving juice.

Combine chopped tomato, reserved juice, olive oil, and next 7 ingredients; cover and let stand at room temperature 1 hour.

Cook pasta according to package directions; drain. Serve tomato mixture over pasta; top with cheese and pine nuts. **Yield: 2 servings.**

Try Dried Tomatoes

Dried tomatoes add a rich, robust flavor to pasta dishes—especially sauces, salads, and entrées. They come packed either dry or in olive oil. Recipes usually suggest that the dry-pack type be soaked in water or cooked in a liquid before use.

Southwestern Tomato Sauce

Quick Spaghetti Sauce

3⅓ cups Ground Beef Mix
1 (28-ounce) can crushed tomatoes, undrained
½ cup water
¼ cup tomato paste
¼ cup chopped fresh parsley
1 bay leaf
½ teaspoon dried basil
½ teaspoon dried oregano
¼ to ½ teaspoon salt
¼ teaspoon dried thyme
¼ teaspoon pepper
Hot cooked spaghetti

Heat Ground Beef Mix, or cook frozen Ground Beef Mix in a 3-quart saucepan over medium heat until thoroughly heated. Add crushed tomatoes and next 9 ingredients; stir well.

Bring mixture to a boil; reduce heat, and simmer 20 minutes, stirring occasionally. Remove and discard bay leaf. Serve sauce over hot cooked spaghetti. **Yield: 6 cups.**

Ground Beef Mix

3 pounds ground beef
1 large green pepper, finely chopped
3 cloves garlic, minced
1 cup water
1 tablespoon plus 1 teaspoon beef-flavored bouillon granules
2 medium onions, finely chopped
¼ teaspoon pepper

Cook beef, green pepper, and garlic in a large skillet over medium-high heat until meat browns and crumbles. Remove from skillet, and drain well.

Add water and bouillon granules to skillet. Bring to a boil, stirring to dissolve granules.

Add onion; cover, reduce heat to medium, and cook 15 minutes. Uncover and cook 5 to 10 minutes or until liquid evaporates. Stir onion mixture and pepper into beef mixture. **Yield: 10 cups.**

Note: To freeze Ground Beef Mix, spread mixture in a 15- x 10- x 1-inch jellyroll pan; cool. Cover tightly, and freeze at least 4 hours. Crumble frozen mixture into small pieces. Freeze in 3 (1-quart) labeled airtight containers up to 2 months.

Italian Sauce

2 pounds ground beef
1½ cups chopped onion
1 clove garlic, chopped
2 (16-ounce) cans plum tomatoes, undrained and chopped
1 (6-ounce) can tomato paste
1 cup water
2 tablespoons chopped fresh parsley or 2 teaspoons dried parsley flakes
1 tablespoon sugar
1½ teaspoons salt
1 teaspoon dried oregano
1 teaspoon dried basil
½ teaspoon pepper

Cook first 3 ingredients in a large skillet over medium heat, stirring until meat browns and crumbles; drain well. Stir in tomatoes and remaining ingredients.

Bring to a boil over medium heat, stirring occasionally. Reduce heat, and simmer, uncovered, 45 minutes. Serve sauce with spaghetti, lasagna, or manicotti. **Yield: 7½ cups.**

Note: To freeze, prepare recipe as directed, and freeze in 2 (1½-quart) airtight containers or freezer bags up to 2 months.

To defrost and reheat: For **conventional** method, thaw sauce in refrigerator, and cook in saucepan 15 minutes or until thoroughly heated. For **microwave** oven, cover and defrost one container of sauce in a 1½-quart baking dish at MEDIUM (50% power) 20 minutes, rotating dish after 10 minutes. Microwave at HIGH 5 minutes or until thoroughly heated, stirring after 3 minutes.

Easy Spaghetti Meat Sauce

(pictured on page 405)

Servings				Ingredients
For 8	**For 16**	**For 24**	**For 32**	
2 lbs	4 lbs	6 lbs	8 lbs	**Ground beef**
1	2	3	4	**15-ounce can(s) tomato sauce**
2 cups	3 cups	4 cups	5 cups	**Water**
¼ cup	½ cup	¾ cup	1 cup	**Dried onion flakes**
1½ Tbsp	3 Tbsp	¼ cup	⅓ cup	**Worcestershire sauce**
1 tsp	2 tsp	1 Tbsp	1½ Tbsp	**Garlic powder**
½ tsp	1 tsp	1½ tsp	2 tsp	**Pepper**
1	2	3	4	**28-ounce jar(s) spaghetti sauce**
1	2	3	4	**16-ounce package(s) spaghetti, uncooked**
				Grated Parmesan cheese

To serve 24, prepare sauce in an 8-quart Dutch oven.

To serve 32 without the use of institutional cooking equipment, divide the ingredients in half, and cook in 2 Dutch ovens.

Brown ground beef in a large Dutch oven, stirring until beef crumbles and draining once during browning. Drain beef again. Stir in tomato sauce and next 5 ingredients.

Bring to a boil over medium heat. Cover, reduce heat, and simmer 20 minutes, stirring occasionally. Add spaghetti sauce; simmer, uncovered, 20 minutes, stirring occasionally.

Cook spaghetti according to package directions; drain. Spoon meat sauce over cooked spaghetti, and sprinkle with Parmesan cheese.

Note: To make ahead, freeze sauce in an airtight container up to 2 months; thaw in refrigerator. To prepare spaghetti ahead, cook pasta; drain and chill. To reheat cooked pasta, place in a colander, and immerse in boiling water for 1 to 2 minutes; drain. Or microwave at HIGH, stirring occasionally, until pasta is just heated through.

Match Pasta with a Sauce

• Thin sauces, such as marinara sauce or pesto sauce, should be served with thin pasta.
• Thicker, chunkier meat and vegetable sauces go well with tubular and shell pastas that are designed to "trap" the toppings.
• Chunky vegetable or meat sauces should be served with thick pasta: ziti, mostaccioli, rigatoni, or fettuccine.
• Rich, thick, smooth sauces need a flat pasta that won't trap too much of the sauce.

Southern Living.

ALL-TIME FAVORITE

SOUP & STEW
RECIPES

Contents

Versatile
Soups and Stews

Soups and stews can be whatever you want them to be. Simple or
dramatic, warm or chilled, light or robust, soups are enjoyed at all times
of the day. Try a hearty stew for a Sunday night supper or a creamy
soup as an elegant appetizer. These chilies and gumbos will warm
you in winter, while a chilled fruit or vegetable soup will cool
you in the heat of summer.

Soup's On

Soup making does not require much special equipment. A large Dutch oven or stockpot is all you'll need to prepare most of these soups and stews.

Cream soups and purees also require an electric blender or food processor to obtain the right consistency. Soups that simmer with a large number of whole herbs and spices often call for cheesecloth in which to confine spices. Called a bouquet garni, the filled spice bag allows for easy removal of the spices after the soup is cooked.

Bouquet Garni Technique

For a different method, prepare a bouquet garni for stock by wrapping aromatic herbs in leek pieces and tying with string.

Ladle Up the Soup

Our soup yields are given in cup or quart measurements rather than numbers of servings so you can be the judge, depending on how you plan to serve the soup. Allow ¾ to 1 cup soup when offering it as an appetizer. For an entrée, 1¼ to 1¾ cups is usually standard.

Serve a heavy or meaty soup as the main course. Choose a lighter, more delicate soup for an appetizer; it should have just enough taste and body to whet the appetite, especially if the main course will be filling.

Use only the freshest ingredients for savory stocks.

Homemade Made Easy

Soups and stews need not simmer for hours to be good. Several of our soup recipes call for commercially canned soup as the base, with fresh or frozen vegetables, meats, or seasonings added to enhance the flavor. These convenience foods cut preparation time but still give the finished product a "homemade" flavor.

Because some brands of soups are condensed while other similar soups are regular strength, be sure to use the exact name and ounce-size of the soups our recipes specify. If a recipe indicates a condensed soup, the recipe will note if the soup needs diluting.

When our recipes call for chicken or beef broth, you can use our broth or stock recipes or you can substitute commercially canned broth. Just remember that canned varieties are saltier than our homemade versions, so hold

extra seasonings until the end of cooking.

Bouillon cubes, granules, and powdered mixes diluted according to package directions may be used as a soup base, but these, too, are saltier than our homemade broths.

Freezing Soups and Stews

Many soups taste even better when refrigerated a day or so to allow the flavors to blend. Because of this, they are an excellent make-ahead dish for entertaining or for accommodating a busy schedule.

Most soups also freeze well, especially thick gumbos, chilies, and stews, which tend to have a large yield anyway.

• Make a double batch of soup or stew; freeze half. To freeze, cool by dividing into small portions; refrigerate until chilled.

• Use freezer containers with tight-fitting lids or freezer bags. Fill containers to ½ inch from the top to allow room for expansion.

• Select containers with wide openings so soup can be easily removed when partially thawed.

• Freeze single servings in bowls or mugs lined with heavy-duty plastic wrap; after the food is frozen, remove from bowl. Wrap with additional plastic wrap, and place in 1 large freezer bag. Label and store in freezer.

• To keep from having all of your large plastic containers in the freezer, slip a freezer bag into any container; fill with soup, and freeze. Remove the bag of frozen soup, label, and store in freezer.

• Use the frozen soup within 3 or 4 months for optimum flavor.

• Thaw frozen soups in the refrigerator or microwave oven.

Homemade Stocks

Soups and stews are only as good as the stock from which they're made.

Stocks are usually made by slowly simmering meaty bones and vegetables until they have yielded most of their flavor to the water in which they've been cooked.

The liquid is then strained off, and the stock is either served as a hearty broth or used as a delicate background for other flavorings in soups and sauces.

Here are methods for making four basic stocks: beef, chicken, fish, and vegetable. Although they take a long time to make, once preparation has begun they require little supervision. And each batch yields ample quantities that can be refrigerated or frozen in small containers for future use. Each type of homemade stock lends itself to a host of uses.

10 Tips for High-Yield Stocks

When making stock, the goal is to produce a foundation that's clear and distinctly flavored. Follow these cardinal rules when making stock.

• Use a heavyweight stockpot that holds 10 to 20 quarts of liquid.

• To produce a more flavorful stock, cut all vegetables into pieces, remove excess fat from bones, and crack large bones.

Cut vegetables to allow the stock to absorb their flavor and nutrients.

• If making fish stock, use the heads, bones, and trimmings from any mild whitefish; avoid oily, strong-flavored fish, such as salmon and mackerel, as they will yield a milky, bitter-tasting stock.

• When making beef stock, roast bones and vegetables in the oven only until golden brown; overbrowning will damage the stock's flavor and darken its color.

Brown bones for a dark-colored stock.

• To coax maximum flavor from meat, bones, and vegetables, cook these ingredients in a cold liquid. If the ingredients have been browned first, allow them to cool slightly before adding them to the cold cooking liquid.

• It's best to bring stock to a boil slowly; then reduce heat, and simmer gently throughout cooking time. Rapid boiling will produce a murky, unpalatable stock. Gentle simmering, on the other hand, extracts flavors from ingredients and produces a relatively clear, well-flavored stock.

• To achieve a clear stock, it is important to carefully skim the fat and foam from the surface of the mixture as it rises to the top during cooking. To make the skimming easier, vegetables and "aromatics" (seasonings) are best added after about one-fourth of the cooking time has elapsed. Once the vegetables are added, do not skim the fat again unless it is necessary.

After chilling, skim solidified fat from stock.

• As a stock simmers, its flavor becomes more pronounced; therefore, you should add salt only after stock is finished cooking.

• Homemade stock may be refrigerated up to four days. For longer storage, cool and freeze up to four months, with the exception of fish and vegetable stocks, which can be frozen only up to two months.

• Degrease stock before freezing; frozen fat can turn rancid. A fat-off ladle allows you to skim fat from stocks. Ladle the defatted mixture into containers, such as plastic bags or ice-cube trays, for convenient quantities. Each cube yields approximately 2 tablespoons of stock.

Freeze stock in ice-cube trays for convenience.

Beef Stock

5 pounds beef or veal bones
2 large carrots, quartered
2 large onions, quartered
4 stalks celery, quartered
4 quarts water, divided
3 tablespoons tomato paste
6 to 8 sprigs fresh parsley
3 to 4 sprigs fresh thyme
4 whole cloves
½ teaspoon black peppercorns
1 bay leaf
2 cloves garlic, crushed

Place first 4 ingredients in a large roasting pan; bake at 500° for 1 hour, turning mixture occasionally with a large spatula.

Transfer mixture to a large stockpot; set aside. Discard drippings from roasting pan.

Add 1 quart water to roasting pan; bring to a boil over medium-high heat, stirring to loosen pieces. Pour into stockpot; add 3 quarts water and remaining ingredients. Bring to a boil; cover, reduce heat, and simmer 2 hours.

Line a large wire-mesh strainer with a double layer of cheesecloth; place in a large bowl. Pour stock through strainer; discard solids. Cool stock.

Cover and chill stock; remove and discard solidified fat from top of stock. Store stock in refrigerator up to 2 days, or freeze up to 4 months. **Yield: 2 quarts.**

Quick Full-Bodied Stock

2 (14½-ounce) cans ready-to-serve chicken or
    beef broth
1 large carrot, scraped and sliced
1 medium onion, sliced
1 bay leaf
3 or 4 sprigs fresh parsley

Remove solidified fat from top of broth, if necessary, and discard. Combine broth and remaining ingredients in a medium saucepan.

Bring mixture to a boil over medium heat; cover, reduce heat, and simmer 25 minutes.

Pour through a wire-mesh strainer into a bowl; discard solids. Cool stock. Cover; chill up to 2 days, or freeze up to 4 months. **Yield: 2 cups.**

Vegetable Stock

4½ quarts water
3 medium onions, chopped
5 stalks celery, sliced
1 pound carrots, scraped and sliced
1 small bunch parsley
1 medium turnip, chopped
3 cloves garlic, quartered
3 bay leaves
1 teaspoon dried thyme

Combine all ingredients in a stockpot. Bring to a boil; cover, reduce heat, and simmer 1½ to 2 hours. Uncover and continue cooking 2 hours.

Pour mixture through a large wire-mesh strainer into a large bowl, discarding vegetables. Cool stock slightly. Cover and chill up to 2 days, or freeze up to 2 months. **Yield: 1 quart.**

Chicken Stock

4 pounds chicken pieces
1 pound chicken wings
4 quarts water
2 onions, peeled and quartered
4 stalks celery with tops, cut into 2-inch pieces
4 carrots, scraped and cut into 2-inch pieces
1 large bay leaf
6 sprigs fresh parsley
1 tablespoon fresh thyme or 1 teaspoon dried thyme
6 sprigs fresh dill or ½ teaspoon dried dillweed
½ teaspoon black peppercorns

Combine chicken and water in a large stock-pot; bring to a boil, skimming surface to remove excess fat and foam.

Add onion and remaining ingredients. Return to a boil; reduce heat, and simmer, uncovered, 2 hours, skimming surface to remove fat.

Line a large wire-mesh strainer with a double layer of cheesecloth; place in a large bowl. Pour stock through strainer; reserve chicken for other uses, and discard remaining solids. Cool stock.

Cover and chill stock. Remove and discard solidified fat from top of stock. Cover; chill up to 2 days, or freeze up to 4 months. **Yield: 2 quarts.**

Chicken Stock Technique

Strain stock through a colander lined with several layers of moistened cheesecloth.

Fish Stock

2 leeks
6 to 9 sprigs fresh parsley
1 large bay leaf
4 sprigs fresh basil
4 sprigs fresh rosemary
3 sprigs fresh thyme
2 (2- x ½-inch) strips lemon rind
2 (2- x ½-inch) strips orange rind
2 tablespoons margarine
1 medium onion, sliced
½ carrot, sliced
2 stalks celery with leaves, coarsely chopped
3 pounds fish bones and shrimp shells
6 whole peppercorns
2 quarts water
1 cup dry white wine
½ teaspoon salt

Remove roots, outer leaves, and green tops of leeks, reserving 2 pieces of tops. Split white portion in half lengthwise, and wash; set aside. Trim reserved green pieces; place parsley and next 6 ingredients on top of 1 green piece; top with other green piece, and tie with string. (See bouquet garni technique on page 414.) Set bouquet garni aside.

Melt margarine in a stockpot over medium heat. Add leek, onion, carrot, and celery; cook, stirring constantly, until tender. Add bouquet garni, fish bones and shrimp shells, and next 3 ingredients to stockpot. Bring mixture to a boil; cover, reduce heat, and simmer 35 to 45 minutes.

Line a wire-mesh strainer with a double layer of cheesecloth; place in a large bowl. Pour stock through strainer, discarding solids. Stir in salt; cool stock slightly.

Cover and chill stock. Remove and discard solidified fat from top of stock. Cover stock, and chill in the refrigerator up to 2 days, or freeze up to 2 months. **Yield: 1½ quarts.**

Light Soups

When your winter meal needs a warm broth-based soup or your
summer menu calls for a refreshing tomato-based gazpacho,
choose one of these lighter soups.

Egg Drop Soup, Fancy French Onion Soup, Easy Tortilla Soup

Shrimp-Cream Cheese Gazpacho, Summer Garden Soup, Calico Cheese Soup

Southwestern Scallop Broth with Black Beans and Cilantro, Beer-Cheese Soup

Spicy Thai Lobster Soup, Tomato Soup with Herbed Croutons

Tortilla Soup (page 424)

Egg Drop Soup

4 cups hot water
1 (10½-ounce) can condensed chicken broth, undiluted
1 (4-ounce) can sliced mushrooms, drained
2 cloves garlic
1 teaspoon soy sauce
1 teaspoon chicken-flavored bouillon granules
⅛ teaspoon ground white pepper
2 large eggs, beaten
⅓ cup sliced green onions

Combine first 6 ingredients in a deep 3-quart baking dish. Cover with heavy-duty plastic wrap; fold back a small edge of wrap to allow steam to escape. Microwave at HIGH 10 to 12 minutes or until boiling.

Add pepper, stirring well. Gradually pour beaten eggs in a thin stream into soup, stirring constantly. (The eggs form lacy strands as they cook.)

Cover and let stand 3 minutes. Remove garlic; sprinkle with green onions. **Yield: 1½ quarts.**

Egg Drop Soup for Two

1⅓ cups water
1 (10½-ounce) can condensed chicken broth, undiluted
1 teaspoon soy sauce
1 tablespoon cornstarch
2 tablespoons water
1 large egg, beaten
1 tablespoon dry sherry
Thinly sliced green onions

Combine first 3 ingredients in a medium saucepan; bring to a boil.

Combine cornstarch and 2 tablespoons water, stirring well; add to broth mixture. Boil 1 minute over medium heat, stirring occasionally.

Combine egg and sherry; slowly pour egg mixture into boiling soup, stirring constantly. (The egg forms lacy strands as it cooks.) Ladle soup into bowls, and sprinkle with green onions. Serve immediately. **Yield: 2⅔ cups.**

Fancy French Onion Soup

2 large Vidalia or other sweet onions, thinly sliced
1 clove garlic, crushed
¼ cup butter or margarine, melted
1 tablespoon all-purpose flour
2 (10½-ounce) cans condensed beef broth, undiluted
2 cups water
¼ teaspoon pepper
¼ cup Madeira
6 (¾-inch-thick) slices French bread, toasted
1 cup (4 ounces) shredded smoked mozzarella cheese
1 cup (4 ounces) shredded mozzarella cheese
Grated Parmesan cheese

Cook onion and garlic in butter in a Dutch oven over medium heat 10 to 15 minutes or until very tender.

Add flour, stirring until smooth. Gradually add beef broth and water. Bring to a boil; cover, reduce heat, and simmer 15 minutes. Stir in pepper and wine. Remove from heat.

Place 6 ovenproof serving bowls on a baking sheet. Place 1 toasted bread slice in each bowl; ladle soup into bowls.

Sprinkle each serving evenly with mozzarella cheeses; sprinkle with Parmesan cheese. Broil 5½ inches from heat (with electric oven door partially opened) 1 minute or until cheese melts. **Yield: 1½ quarts.**

Fancy French Onion Soup

French Onion Soup

1 tablespoon butter or margarine, softened
    and divided
6 (¾-inch-thick) slices French bread
¾ teaspoon garlic powder, divided
1 tablespoon grated Parmesan cheese, divided
1½ pounds onions, sliced (about 5 cups)
¼ cup butter or margarine, melted
2 (10½-ounce) cans condensed beef broth,
    undiluted
1⅓ cups water
2 teaspoons Worcestershire sauce
⅛ teaspoon cracked pepper
⅛ teaspoon curry powder
Pinch of garlic powder
½ cup (2 ounces) shredded mozzarella cheese

Spread ½ teaspoon softened butter on one side of each slice of bread; sprinkle each slice with ⅛ teaspoon garlic powder.

Place bread on a baking sheet; bake at 300° for 15 to 20 minutes. Sprinkle each bread slice with ½ teaspoon Parmesan cheese. Set aside.

Separate onion into rings; cook in ¼ cup butter in a Dutch oven over medium heat 25 to 30 minutes, stirring frequently. Add beef broth and next 5 ingredients; bring to a boil. Cover, reduce heat, and simmer 30 minutes.

Fill 6 soup bowls with soup. Sprinkle each serving evenly with mozzarella cheese, and top with a bread slice. **Yield: about 1½ quarts.**

Easy Tortilla Soup

½ cup chopped onion
1 clove garlic, minced
1 tablespoon vegetable oil
3 medium zucchini, sliced
1 quart ready-to-serve chicken broth
1 (16-ounce) can stewed tomatoes, undrained
1 (15-ounce) can tomato sauce
1 (12-ounce) can whole kernel corn,
    undrained
1 teaspoon ground cumin
½ teaspoon pepper
Tortilla chips
½ cup (2 ounces) shredded Monterey Jack or
    Cheddar cheese

Cook onion and garlic in oil in a Dutch oven. Add zucchini and next 6 ingredients; bring to a boil. Cover, reduce heat, and simmer 15 to 20 minutes.

Spoon soup into bowls; add tortilla chips and cheese. **Yield: 2¼ quarts.**

Stock Options

- If you don't have time to make homemade stock, give canned broth a flavor boost by simmering it with aromatic vegetables for 30 minutes.
- To defat commercial beef or chicken broth, place the unopened can in the refrigerator at least 1 hour before using. Open the can, and skim off the layer of solidified fat.

Easy Tortilla Soup

Tortilla Soup

(pictured on page 419)

1 dried ancho chile
¼ cup olive oil
4 corn tortillas, cut into 1-inch pieces
1 large onion, coarsely chopped
1 medium-size green pepper, seeded and
    chopped
3 cloves garlic, minced
1 quart ready-to-serve chicken broth
½ teaspoon ground cumin
½ teaspoon freshly ground black pepper
2 tomatoes, unpeeled and chopped
2 tablespoons chopped fresh cilantro
1 tablespoon chopped fresh parsley

Remove stem and seeds from chile; cook chile
in hot oil in a Dutch oven until soft. Remove chile,
and chop, reserving drippings in Dutch oven.

Fry tortilla pieces in drippings until brown.
Remove tortillas, and drain, reserving drippings
in Dutch oven.

Cook onion, green pepper, and garlic in drippings until tender. Add chicken broth, cumin, and
pepper. Bring to a boil; cover, reduce heat, and
simmer 20 minutes.

Stir in reserved chile and tomato; simmer 10
minutes. Before serving, stir in cilantro and parsley.

Place fried tortilla pieces in individual soup
bowls, reserving one-fourth of chips; add soup.
Top with reserved chips. **Yield: 1½ quarts.**

Southwestern Scallop Broth with Black Beans and Cilantro

¼ cup dried black beans
10 cups fish stock, divided
¼ cup olive oil
2 cloves garlic, minced
1 medium jicama, chopped
1 stalk celery, chopped
1 medium onion, chopped
1 carrot, scraped and chopped
1 bay leaf
1½ pounds bay scallops
8 tomatillos, ground
2 teaspoons chopped fresh cilantro
1 tablespoon tequila (optional)
½ teaspoon salt
¼ teaspoon pepper
Corn tortillas (optional)

Sort and wash beans. Cover beans with water;
soak overnight. Drain beans.

Bring 5 cups fish stock to a boil. Add beans;
cover and simmer 2 to 3 hours or until desired
degree of doneness. Remove from heat. Cool
beans in fish stock; set aside.

Heat olive oil in a large Dutch oven over
medium-high heat. Add garlic and next 6 ingredients, and cook until vegetables are transparent.
Add tomatillo, cilantro, and remaining 5 cups fish
stock; bring to a boil.

Strain and rinse black beans; discard stock.
Drain and add to vegetable-broth mixture. Bring
to a boil; add tequila (if desired), salt, and pepper.
Remove bay leaf. **Yield: 3 quarts.**

Note: Broth can be garnished with corn tortillas cut into ⅛-inch strips and deep-fried until
crisp, if desired.

Bacon, Lettuce, and Tomato Soup

Bacon, Lettuce, and Tomato Soup

3 beef-flavored bouillon cubes
3 cups hot water
8 slices bacon, cut into 1-inch pieces
⅓ cup chopped onion
⅓ cup chopped celery
5 ripe tomatoes, peeled and coarsely chopped
1 tablespoon Worcestershire sauce
½ teaspoon garlic salt
½ teaspoon dried parsley flakes
¼ teaspoon dried thyme
¼ teaspoon pepper
Dash of hot sauce
2 cups shredded lettuce
Seasoned croutons

Dissolve bouillon cubes in hot water; set aside.

Cook bacon in a Dutch oven until crisp; remove bacon, reserving 2 tablespoons drippings in Dutch oven. Drain bacon on paper towels.

Add onion and celery to drippings, and cook, stirring frequently, until transparent; drain. Add bouillon, tomato, and next 6 ingredients; bring to a boil. Reduce heat, and simmer, uncovered, 20 to 25 minutes. Add lettuce, and cook 2 minutes or until lettuce wilts.

Top each serving with bacon and croutons. Serve immediately. **Yield: 1¼ quarts.**

Turtle Soup

¼ cup butter or margarine, melted
1 pound ground turtle meat
⅓ pound ground veal
1¼ cups diced onion
1 cup diced celery
3 cloves garlic, minced
1½ teaspoons ground cumin
1 teaspoon dried oregano
½ teaspoon dried thyme
½ teaspoon salt
½ teaspoon pepper
3 bay leaves
1 (16-ounce) can tomato puree
1 quart ready-to-serve beef broth
1 cup butter or margarine
¾ cup all-purpose flour
Condiments: dry sherry, chopped hard-
   cooked eggs

Combine first 3 ingredients in a Dutch oven; cook over medium heat until meat is browned, stirring until it crumbles.

Add onion and next 8 ingredients; cook, stirring often, until vegetables are tender. Stir in tomato puree; cook 10 minutes.

Add beef broth, and bring to a boil; reduce heat, and simmer, uncovered, 1 hour. Remove bay leaves. Remove soup from heat, and set aside.

Melt 1 cup butter in a Dutch oven over medium heat. Add flour; cook, stirring constantly, until mixture is chocolate-colored (about 25 minutes). Add turtle mixture; cook until thickened, stirring often. Serve soup with condiments, if desired. **Yield: about 2 quarts.**

Spicy Thai Lobster Soup

2 fresh lobster tails
1 tablespoon ground ginger
½ teaspoon ground red pepper
1 tablespoon peanut oil
5 cups ready-to-serve chicken broth
1 tablespoon coarsely grated lime rind
⅓ cup long-grain rice, uncooked
1 cup unsweetened coconut milk
6 large fresh mushrooms, sliced
½ cup chopped onion
1 tablespoon chopped fresh cilantro
2 tablespoons lime juice
Garnishes: chopped green onions, fresh
   cilantro sprigs

Remove lobster from shell; slice. Set aside.

Cook ground ginger and red pepper in peanut oil in a large saucepan over medium heat 1 minute. Add chicken broth and lime rind.

Bring to a boil. Stir in rice; cover, reduce heat, and simmer 15 to 20 minutes.

Add coconut milk and next 3 ingredients; cook 5 minutes, stirring occasionally.

Add lobster; cook 3 to 5 minutes. Remove from heat, and stir in lime juice. Spoon into bowls; garnish, if desired. **Yield: 1½ quarts.**

Note: You may substitute 1 pound unpeeled, medium-size fresh shrimp for lobster tails. Peel shrimp, and devein, if desired.

Keep Cilantro Fresh

Extend the life of fresh cilantro, also known as coriander leaves, by placing it, stem down, in a glass jar with a small amount of water. Cover the leaves with a plastic bag, and refrigerate up to one week, changing the water every 2 days.

Summer Garden Soup

Summer Garden Soup

2¼ cups tomato juice
1 medium carrot, scraped and sliced
1 stalk celery, sliced
½ cup seeded, chopped cucumber
2 green onions, chopped
1 (¼-inch-thick) slice lemon
½ teaspoon celery salt
½ teaspoon Worcestershire sauce
⅛ teaspoon hot pepper sauce
Garnish: green onion fans

Combine first 9 ingredients in container of a food processor or an electric blender; process until smooth.

Cover and chill. Ladle soup into individual serving bowls, or store in refrigerator in a tightly covered container up to 3 days. Garnish, if desired. **Yield: 3 cups.**

Tomato Soup with Herbed Croutons

Tomato Soup with Herbed Croutons

½ cup chopped onion
3 tablespoons butter or margarine, melted
3 tablespoons all-purpose flour
1 cup ready-to-serve chicken broth
1 (28-ounce) can Italian-style tomatoes, undrained
3 tablespoons tomato paste
1 tablespoon minced fresh parsley
1 tablespoon sugar
1 teaspoon salt
½ teaspoon dried basil
¼ teaspoon pepper
1 bay leaf
Herbed Croutons
Garnish: fresh basil sprigs

Cook onion in butter in a Dutch oven 3 minutes or until tender. Reduce heat to low; add flour, stirring until smooth. Cook 1 minute, stirring constantly.

Add chicken broth gradually; cook over medium heat, stirring constantly, until thickened and bubbly.

Add tomatoes and next 7 ingredients; stir well. Bring to a boil; cover, reduce heat, and simmer 30 minutes. Remove bay leaf.

Spoon one-third of tomato mixture into container of an electric blender; cover and process until smooth. Repeat procedure twice with remaining tomato mixture.

Ladle soup into individual serving bowls. Top with Herbed Croutons, and garnish, if desired. **Yield: 3½ cups.**

Herbed Croutons

2 slices white bread
1 tablespoon butter or margarine, melted
1 tablespoon grated Parmesan cheese
½ teaspoon dried basil

Trim crust from bread slices; reserve for another use. Brush butter over bread slices; sprinkle evenly with cheese and basil. Cut each slice into 4 squares; cut each square into 2 triangles.

Place on an ungreased baking sheet; bake at 350° for 10 to 12 minutes or until croutons are dry and lightly browned. **Yield: 16 croutons.**

Shrimp-Cream Cheese Gazpacho

5 cups water
1½ pounds unpeeled small fresh shrimp
2 quarts tomato juice
1 bunch green onions, chopped
2 cucumbers, peeled, seeded, and chopped
4 tomatoes, peeled, seeded, and chopped
1 avocado, peeled and chopped
1 (8-ounce) package cream cheese, cubed
¼ cup lemon juice or white wine vinegar
2 tablespoons sugar
½ teaspoon hot sauce
Garnishes: cucumber slices, sour cream, shrimp

Bring water to a boil; add shrimp, and cook 3 to 5 minutes or until shrimp turn pink. Drain well; rinse with cold water. Chill.

Peel shrimp, and devein, if desired. (Set aside about 10 shrimp for garnishing, if desired.)

Combine shrimp, tomato juice, and next 8 ingredients in a large bowl; cover gazpacho, and chill at least 3 hours. Garnish, if desired. **Yield: 3¼ quarts.**

Gazpacho

1 (10¾-ounce) can tomato soup, undiluted
1½ cups tomato juice
1¼ cups water
½ to 1 cup chopped cucumber
½ to 1 cup chopped tomato
½ cup chopped green pepper
½ cup chopped onion
2 tablespoons white wine vinegar
1 tablespoon commercial Italian dressing
1 tablespoon lemon or lime juice
1 clove garlic, minced
¼ teaspoon pepper
¼ teaspoon hot sauce

Combine all ingredients; cover and chill at least 6 hours. **Yield: 1½ quarts.**

Spicy Gazpacho

4 (6-ounce) cans spicy hot tomato juice
1½ cups tomato juice
1 cup chopped tomato
¾ cup chopped cucumber
½ cup minced green pepper
2 tablespoons minced green onions
3 tablespoons white wine vinegar
1 tablespoon lemon juice
¼ teaspoon lemon-pepper seasoning
¼ teaspoon coarsely ground black pepper
Dash of hot sauce
Seasoned Croutons
Additional chopped tomato, green onions, and
    cucumber

Combine first 11 ingredients in a large bowl; stir well. Cover and chill at least 2 hours.

Pour gazpacho into chilled individual soup bowls. Top each serving with Seasoned Croutons and additional chopped tomato, green onions, and cucumber. **Yield: 1½ quarts.**

Seasoned Croutons

¼ cup butter or margarine
2 teaspoons dried Italian seasoning
½ teaspoon garlic salt
4 (¾-inch) slices French bread, cubed

Melt butter in a large skillet; stir in Italian seasoning and garlic salt. Add bread cubes, tossing to coat well. Remove from heat.

Spread bread cubes evenly on an ungreased 15- x 10- x 1-inch jellyroll pan. Bake at 300° for 30 minutes or until crisp; remove from pan, and cool. **Yield: about 2 cups.**

Seasoned Croutons Techniques

Cut French bread slices into ¾-inch cubes.

Stir croutons occasionally during baking.

Spicy Gazpacho

Beer-Cheese Soup

6 cups milk
2 (12-ounce) cans beer, divided
5 (8-ounce) jars process cheese spread
1 (10½-ounce) can condensed chicken broth,
    undiluted
1 teaspoon Worcestershire sauce
3 dashes of hot sauce
⅓ cup cornstarch

Combine milk and 2½ cups beer in a large Dutch oven. Cook over low heat, stirring constantly, until thoroughly heated. Add cheese spread and next 3 ingredients. Cook over low heat, stirring constantly, until heated.

Combine cornstarch and remaining beer. Add to cheese mixture; simmer, stirring constantly, until thickened (do not boil). **Yield: 4 quarts.**

Cheese Velvet Soup

6 ounces Brie cheese
½ cup finely chopped celery
½ cup finely chopped carrot
¼ cup finely chopped onion
½ cup butter or margarine, melted
½ cup all-purpose flour
2 cups ready-to-serve chicken broth
1 teaspoon dried thyme
1 bay leaf
½ cup whipping cream
Garnish: shredded carrot

Cut rind from Brie; set cheese aside.
Cook celery, carrot, and onion in butter in a saucepan over medium heat, stirring constantly, until tender.
Add flour, and cook over low heat 1 minute, stirring constantly. Gradually stir in chicken broth, dried thyme, and bay leaf. Cook, stirring constantly, until mixture is thickened and bubbly.

Add cheese, stirring until smooth. Add whipping cream, and heat thoroughly. Remove bay leaf. Garnish, if desired. **Yield: 3 cups.**

Calico Cheese Soup

½ cup finely chopped carrot
½ cup finely chopped green pepper
½ cup finely chopped sweet red pepper
½ cup finely chopped celery
2 tablespoons minced onion
¼ cup butter or margarine, melted
3 tablespoons all-purpose flour
2 cups milk
2 cups ready-to-serve chicken broth
2 cups (8 ounces) shredded sharp Cheddar
    cheese
Salt and pepper to taste
Commercial seasoned croutons
½ cup (2 ounces) finely shredded sharp
    Cheddar cheese

Combine first 4 ingredients in a medium saucepan; add water to cover. Bring to a boil; cover, reduce heat, and simmer 3 to 5 minutes or until vegetables are tender. Drain and set aside.

Cook onion in butter in a large saucepan over medium heat until tender. Reduce heat to low; add flour, stirring until smooth. Cook 1 minute, stirring constantly. Combine milk and chicken broth; gradually add to flour mixture. Cook over medium heat, stirring constantly, until mixture is slightly thickened. Stir in 2 cups shredded cheese; cook, stirring constantly, until cheese melts. Add reserved vegetables and salt and pepper to taste. Cook until thoroughly heated.

Ladle soup into individual serving bowls. Top with croutons and cheese. **Yield: 1½ quarts.**

Calico Cheese Soup

Vegetable-Cheese Soup

Vegetable-Cheese Soup

2 stalks celery, chopped
2 carrots, scraped and diced
1 medium onion, chopped
1 cup chopped cauliflower
½ cup chopped broccoli
1 clove garlic, minced
½ cup butter or margarine, melted
½ cup all-purpose flour
3 cups ready-to-serve chicken broth
1 tablespoon Worcestershire sauce
½ teaspoon pepper
2½ cups milk
2 cups (8 ounces) shredded sharp Cheddar
     cheese
¼ cup sliced almonds, toasted

Cook first 6 ingredients in butter in a Dutch oven until crisp-tender; add flour, stirring until smooth. Cook 1 minute, stirring constantly.

Add chicken broth gradually; cook over medium heat, stirring constantly, until mixture is thickened and bubbly. Cover, reduce heat, and simmer 20 minutes or until vegetables are tender.

Add Worcestershire sauce and next 3 ingredients. Cook over low heat 10 minutes, stirring occasionally. Top each serving with sliced almonds, and serve immediately. **Yield: 2 quarts.**

Creams and Purees

Let your blender, processor, and soup pot refine vegetables and fruits into their purest, smoothest forms. Serve these soups as elegant appetizers, light lunches, or sweet endings to dinner.

Artichoke Cream Soup, Creamy Asparagus Soup, Cold Dill Soup

Strawberry-Banana Soup

Yellow Squash Soup, Cream Pea Soup, Cantaloupe Soup,

Cream of Broccoli Soup, Chilled Carrot-Mint Soup, Velvety Roquefort Vichyssoise

Baked Potato Soup, Sweet Potato Soup, Watercress-Zucchini Soup

Cream of Roasted Sweet Red Pepper Soup (page 447)

Artichoke Cream Soup

Artichoke Cream Soup

6 artichokes
1 lemon, sliced
1 teaspoon salt
1 quart ready-to-serve chicken broth
½ cup butter or margarine
1 onion, finely chopped
½ cup chopped celery
1 tablespoon minced garlic
2 cups dry white wine
1 quart whipping cream
⅛ teaspoon seasoned salt
¼ teaspoon freshly ground pepper
Pumpernickel Croutons
Garnish: peeled tomato strips

Wash artichokes by plunging them up and down in cold water. Cut off stem end, and trim about ½ inch from top of each artichoke. Remove and discard any loose bottom leaves.

Place artichokes in a large stainless steel Dutch oven; cover with water, and add lemon and 1 teaspoon salt. Bring to a boil; cover, reduce heat, and simmer 35 minutes. Drain well.

Spread leaves apart; remove fuzzy thistle (choke) with a spoon, and discard. Remove all leaves, leaving artichoke bottoms intact; set leaves aside. Finely chop artichoke bottoms, and set aside.

Combine artichoke leaves and chicken broth. Bring to a boil; cover, reduce heat, and simmer 40 minutes.

Pour broth mixture through a large wire-mesh strainer into a container, discarding solids; set artichoke stock aside.

Melt butter in a Dutch oven over medium-high heat; add onion, celery, and garlic, and cook, stirring constantly, 10 minutes or until tender.

Add chopped artichoke bottoms and wine; cook over medium heat about 2 minutes. Add artichoke stock, and cook over low heat 20 minutes, stirring occasionally.

Pour half of broth mixture into container of an electric blender; cover and process until smooth, stopping once to scrape down sides. Pour mixture into a large bowl. Repeat procedure with remaining mixture; return all mixture to Dutch oven.

Add whipping cream, seasoned salt, and pepper; cook over low heat until thoroughly heated. Top each serving with Pumpernickel Croutons. Garnish, if desired. **Yield: 2¼ quarts.**

Pumpernickel Croutons

4 slices dark pumpernickel bread

Cut bread into desired shapes; place on a baking sheet.

Bake at 325° for 20 minutes or until crisp. **Yield: 1 cup.**

Serve with Style

Spark appetites by serving soup in surprising containers.
• Use hollowed-out fruits or vegetables such as peppers, acorn squash, pumpkins, tomatoes, or cantaloupes.
• Make edible bowls by scooping out the center of French rolls or small round bread loaves.
• Serve cold soups from chilled goblets or punch cups.

Creamy Asparagus Soup

½ cup chopped onion
1 cup sliced celery
3 cloves garlic, crushed
3 tablespoons butter or margarine, melted
2 (14.5-ounce) cans cut asparagus, undrained
1 (16-ounce) can sliced potatoes, drained
1 (14½-ounce) can ready-to-serve chicken broth
1 teaspoon white vinegar
1 teaspoon salt
½ teaspoon ground black pepper
¼ teaspoon ground red pepper
½ teaspoon dried basil
1 cup milk
½ cup sour cream (optional)
Garnish: celery leaves

Cook first 3 ingredients in butter in a Dutch oven over medium-high heat, stirring constantly, until tender. Add asparagus and next 7 ingredients.

Bring to a boil, stirring often. Reduce heat, and simmer 10 minutes, stirring often. Cool slightly.

Pour half of mixture into container of an electric blender; cover and process until smooth, stopping once to scrape down sides. Transfer mixture to another container. Repeat procedure.

Return asparagus mixture to Dutch oven. Stir in milk; cook just until thoroughly heated (do not boil). If desired, dollop each serving with sour cream, and garnish. **Yield: 2 quarts.**

Note: You may substitute 2 medium potatoes, cooked, peeled, and sliced, for canned sliced potatoes.

Chilled Avocado Soup

2 ripe avocados, peeled and seeded
1 (14½-ounce) can ready-to-serve chicken broth
1 (8-ounce) carton plain yogurt
2 tablespoons lemon juice, divided
1 ripe avocado, peeled, seeded, and finely chopped
Coarsely ground pepper

Position knife blade in food processor bowl; add 2 avocados. Process until smooth, scraping sides of processor bowl once.

Combine pureed avocado, chicken broth, yogurt, and 1 tablespoon lemon juice in a large bowl. Cover and chill.

Toss chopped avocado with remaining 1 tablespoon lemon juice; set aside. Just before serving soup, stir in chopped avocado and ground pepper. **Yield: 1¼ quarts.**

Borscht

1 (16-ounce) can whole beets, undrained
1 (10½-ounce) can condensed chicken broth, undiluted
1 (8-ounce) carton sour cream
⅛ teaspoon ground white pepper
1½ teaspoons lemon juice
2 tablespoons chopped chives

Combine beets and chicken broth in container of an electric blender or food processor. Cover and process until smooth.

Combine beet puree, sour cream, pepper, and lemon juice; stir well. Cover and chill. Sprinkle each serving of soup with chives. **Yield: 1 quart.**

Cream of Broccoli Soup

2 cups water
1 (16-ounce) package frozen broccoli cuts
½ cup chopped onion
½ cup butter or margarine, melted
½ cup all-purpose flour
6 cups milk
4 chicken-flavored bouillon cubes
1 teaspoon ground white pepper

Bring water to a boil in a medium saucepan; add broccoli. Cover, reduce heat, and simmer 5 minutes. Remove from heat, and set aside.

Cook onion in butter in a Dutch oven over low heat 10 minutes or until tender. Add flour; stir until smooth. Cook 1 minute, stirring constantly.

Add milk and bouillon cubes; cook over medium heat, stirring constantly, until thickened. Add broccoli, cooking water, and pepper. Simmer 20 to 30 minutes, stirring occasionally. **Yield: 2¼ quarts.**

Carrot Cream Soup
(pictured on page 445)

3 cups sliced carrot
1 cup chopped onion
3 cups ready-to-serve chicken broth
¼ teaspoon ground white pepper
1 cup whipping cream
Garnishes: ground nutmeg, carrot curls, fresh chives

Combine first 3 ingredients in a Dutch oven; cover and cook over medium heat 25 minutes.

Spoon half of carrot mixture into a food processor or electric blender; process until smooth. Repeat procedure with remaining mixture.

Stir in white pepper; cover and chill soup thoroughly. Stir in whipping cream; ladle into individual soup bowls. Garnish, if desired. **Yield: 1¼ quarts.**

Chilled Carrot-Mint Soup

Chilled Carrot-Mint Soup

2 **cups sliced carrot**
2 **tablespoons water**
½ **teaspoon onion powder**
2 **cups ready-to-serve chicken broth**
1 **tablespoon sugar**
¼ **to ½ teaspoon salt**
2 **tablespoons minced fresh mint**
1 **cup milk**
**Garnishes: sour cream, fresh mint sprigs,
    carrot curls**

Combine sliced carrot, water, and onion powder in a 1-quart bowl. Cover with heavy-duty plastic wrap; fold back a small edge of wrap to allow steam to escape. Microwave at HIGH 6 to 8 minutes or until carrot is tender.

Spoon carrot mixture into container of an electric blender. Add chicken broth, sugar, salt, and mint; cover and process at high until mixture is smooth. Pour into a bowl; cover and chill.

Stir milk into chilled soup. Spoon into serving bowls. Garnish, if desired. **Yield: 1 quart.**

Creamy Carrot Soup

Creamy Carrot Soup

1 medium onion, chopped
2 tablespoons butter or margarine, melted
2 pounds carrots, scraped and sliced
3 cups ready-to-serve chicken broth, divided
1 cup half-and-half
¼ teaspoon coarsely ground pepper
Pinch of salt
1 (8-ounce) carton plain yogurt
1 tablespoon minced fresh dill or 1 teaspoon
    dried dillweed
Garnish: fresh dill sprigs

Cook onion in butter in a Dutch oven over medium-high heat, stirring constantly, until tender. Add carrot and 1 cup chicken broth; bring to a boil over medium heat. Cover, reduce heat, and simmer 8 minutes or until carrot is tender.

Spoon carrot mixture into container of an electric blender; cover and process until smooth. Return to Dutch oven; add remaining chicken broth, half-and-half, pepper, and salt. Cook over low heat, stirring constantly, until thoroughly heated. Stir in yogurt (at room temperature) and dill with a wire whisk. Serve hot or chilled. Garnish, if desired. **Yield: 2 quarts.**

Microwave Directions:

Place onion and butter in a 3-quart baking dish. Cover with heavy-duty plastic wrap; fold back a small edge of wrap to allow steam to escape. Microwave at HIGH 2 minutes. Stir in carrot; cover and microwave at HIGH 12 minutes or until tender, turning dish after 6 minutes.

Spoon carrot mixture and 1 cup chicken broth into container of an electric blender; cover and process until smooth. Return to baking dish; add remaining chicken broth, half-and-half, pepper, and salt. Microwave at HIGH 8 to 10 minutes.

Stir in yogurt (at room temperature) and dill with a wire whisk. Serve hot or chilled. Garnish, if desired.

Cauliflower Soup

1 cup chopped cauliflower
2 teaspoons minced shallots
3 cups ready-to-serve chicken broth
¼ cup butter or margarine
¼ cup all-purpose flour
½ cup half-and-half
1 tablespoon minced parsley
⅛ teaspoon dried tarragon
⅛ teaspoon pepper

Combine first 3 ingredients in a large saucepan; bring to a boil. Cover, reduce heat, and simmer 15 minutes. Remove from heat, and drain vegetables, reserving liquid. Set both aside.

Melt butter in a heavy saucepan over low heat; add flour, stirring until smooth. Cook 1 minute, stirring constantly. Gradually stir in reserved liquid; cook over medium heat, stirring constantly, until thickened and bubbly.

Stir in reserved vegetables, half-and-half, and remaining ingredients; cook until thoroughly heated. **Yield: 1 quart.**

Hot Soup Tips

• To avoid burns, allow a hot soup mixture to cool slightly before pureeing in a blender.
• To prevent hot soup from curdling when sour cream or yogurt is stirred into it, heat mixture only until it is warm (do not boil).

Favorite Corn Soup

6 medium ears fresh corn
1 large onion, chopped
¼ cup butter or margarine, melted
1 bay leaf
2 whole cloves
Pinch of dried rosemary
Pinch of dried thyme
1½ quarts ready-to-serve chicken broth
Dash of ground nutmeg
Dash of pepper
2 tablespoons cornstarch
1 cup whipping cream
Garnish: fresh parsley sprigs

Cut corn from cob, scraping cob to remove pulp. Set aside.

Cook onion in butter in a Dutch oven until tender. Add 2 cups corn, and cook 3 minutes.

Tie bay leaf, cloves, rosemary, and thyme in a cheesecloth bag. Add cheesecloth bag, chicken broth, nutmeg, and pepper to onion mixture, stirring well. Simmer, uncovered, 45 minutes.

Remove and discard cheesecloth bag. Pour broth mixture through a large wire-mesh strainer into a large container, reserving liquid. Spoon strained vegetables into container of an electric blender; cover and process 30 seconds or until smooth.

Add pureed mixture to strained liquid, and return to Dutch oven. Stir in remaining corn. Bring soup to a boil. Reduce heat, and simmer, uncovered, 10 minutes.

Combine cornstarch and whipping cream; stir into soup. Cook just until thickened. Garnish each serving, if desired. **Yield: 2 quarts.**

Chilled Cucumber-Buttermilk Soup

5 (7- to 8-inch-long) cucumbers (about 2¾ pounds)
½ teaspoon salt
6 green onions, chopped
½ cup chopped fresh parsley
1 tablespoon chopped fresh dill
1 quart buttermilk
1 (16-ounce) carton sour cream
¼ cup lemon juice
¼ teaspoon salt
¼ teaspoon ground white pepper

Peel cucumbers; cut in half lengthwise, and scoop out seeds. Place cucumber shells on a paper towel; sprinkle ½ teaspoon salt evenly over both sides of cucumber. Let stand 30 minutes. Drain; coarsely chop.

Combine cucumber, green onions, and next 7 ingredients. Place one-third of mixture in container of an electric blender; cover and process 1 minute or until smooth. Pour soup into a 3-quart container. Repeat procedure twice with remaining soup. Cover and chill. **Yield: 2¼ quarts.**

Cold Dill Soup

2 cups half-and-half
2 (8-ounce) cartons plain yogurt
2 cucumbers, peeled, seeded, and diced
3 tablespoons minced fresh dill or 1 tablespoon dried dillweed
2 tablespoons lemon juice
1 tablespoon chopped green onions
½ teaspoon salt
⅛ to ¼ teaspoon ground white pepper
Garnishes: cucumber slices, fresh dill sprigs

Combine first 8 ingredients, stirring well; cover and chill thoroughly. Stir well; garnish, if desired. **Yield: 1 quart.**

Creamy Mushroom Soup

4 (10¾-ounce) cans cream of mushroom soup, undiluted
2 cups half-and-half
2 cups milk
1 (8-ounce) carton sour cream
1 (8-ounce) loaf process cheese spread, cubed
⅛ teaspoon ground red pepper
1 pound fresh mushrooms, sliced
¼ cup dry white wine
Garnish: fresh chives

Combine first 6 ingredients in a large Dutch oven; stir well. Cook over low to medium heat, stirring frequently, until cheese melts.

Stir mushrooms into soup; cook over low heat 20 minutes, stirring frequently. Stir wine into soup just before serving. Garnish, if desired. **Yield: about 3½ quarts.**

Creamy Mushroom Soup

Cream of Mustard Greens Soup

Cream of Mustard Greens Soup

1 (1-pound) center-cut ham slice with bone
8 cups water
1 large bunch fresh mustard greens, washed
    and finely chopped (about 4½ cups)
¼ cup butter or margarine
2 cups chopped green onions
2 cups chopped celery
1 cup chopped onion
⅓ cup butter or margarine
⅓ cup all-purpose flour
5 cups half-and-half
½ teaspoon salt
⅛ teaspoon hot sauce

Combine ham and water in a Dutch oven;
bring to a boil. Cover, reduce heat, and simmer 3
hours. Remove ham, leaving liquid in Dutch
oven. (Reserve ham for another use.)

Add mustard greens to Dutch oven, and cook,
uncovered, 1 hour, stirring occasionally. Set aside.

Melt ¼ cup butter in a skillet over medium
heat. Add green onions, celery, and onion; cook,

stirring constantly, until vegetables are tender.
Remove from heat.

Position knife blade in food processor bowl;
add onion mixture. Process onion mixture until
smooth, stopping occasionally to scrape down
sides. Set aside.

Melt ⅓ cup butter in Dutch oven over low
heat; gradually add flour, stirring until smooth.
Cook 1 minute, stirring constantly. Gradually add
half-and-half; cook over medium heat, stirring
constantly, until thickened and bubbly.

Stir in mustard green mixture, pureed vegetables, salt, and hot sauce. Cook just until thoroughly heated (do not boil). **Yield: 2½ quarts.**

Pea and Watercress Soup

3 tablespoons butter or margarine
1 small onion, finely chopped
1 bunch watercress, chopped
½ cup fresh or frozen English peas
2 tablespoons long-grain rice, uncooked
2 cups ready-to-serve chicken broth
1 cup skim milk
¼ teaspoon ground white pepper
Garnish: chopped fresh mint

Melt butter in a large saucepan over medium
heat; add onion, and cook 5 minutes, stirring
constantly. Add watercress; cook 3 minutes, stirring constantly. Add peas and rice; cook 5 minutes, stirring constantly.

Stir in chicken broth; bring to a boil. Cover,
reduce heat, and simmer 20 minutes. Remove
from heat; cool slightly.

Spoon half of mixture into container of an
electric blender; cover and process until smooth.
Pour into a saucepan, and repeat procedure with
remaining mixture.

Stir in milk and white pepper; bring to a boil.
Remove from heat; cool slightly. Cover and chill
thoroughly. Garnish, if desired. **Yield: 2⅓ cups.**

Cream Pea Soup

4 cups shredded lettuce
1 medium onion, chopped
¼ cup butter or margarine, melted
1 tablespoon all-purpose flour
¼ teaspoon ground coriander
2 (10-ounce) packages frozen peas, thawed
   and divided
3 (14½-ounce) cans ready-to-serve chicken
   broth
1 cup milk
Cream sherry (optional)
Garnish: fresh mint sprigs

Cook lettuce and onion in butter in a Dutch oven until onion is tender. Add flour and coriander, and cook 1 minute, stirring constantly.

Set aside ¼ cup peas; gradually add broth and remaining peas to Dutch oven. Cover and cook 15 minutes, stirring often.

Place one-fourth of soup mixture in container of an electric blender; cover and process until smooth. Repeat procedure with remaining mixture, returning pureed mixture to Dutch oven.

Stir in milk and reserved ¼ cup peas, and cook until thoroughly heated. If desired, add cream sherry to individual servings, and garnish. **Yield: 2¼ quarts.**

From left: Cream Pea Soup and Carrot Cream Soup (page 438)

From left: Black Bean Soup (page 484) and Peanut Butter-Carrot Soup

Peanut Butter-Carrot Soup

1 stalk celery, coarsely chopped
1 medium carrot, coarsely chopped
2 tablespoons chopped onion
¾ cup water
2 chicken-flavored or beef-flavored bouillon
     cubes
2 cups water, divided
½ cup creamy peanut butter
¼ teaspoon pepper
1 tablespoon cornstarch
½ cup half-and-half
Garnishes: carrot strips, chopped peanuts

Combine first 4 ingredients in a saucepan; cover and cook over low heat 10 minutes or until tender. Add bouillon cubes and 1½ cups water; cook, uncovered, until bouillon cubes dissolve.

Pour mixture into container of an electric blender, and add peanut butter and pepper; cover and process until smooth. Return mixture to saucepan.

Combine cornstarch and remaining ½ cup water, stirring until blended; stir into soup mixture. Bring to a boil; reduce heat to low, and cook 1 minute.

Stir in half-and-half; cook over low heat, uncovered, stirring constantly, until thoroughly heated. Ladle into individual soup bowls, and garnish, if desired. **Yield: 3 cups.**

Chilled Sweet Red Pepper Soup

½ cup butter or margarine
3 large sweet red peppers, sliced
2 cups chopped leeks
1½ cups ready-to-serve chicken broth
3 cups buttermilk
⅛ teaspoon ground white pepper
Sweet yellow peppers, halved and seeded
Garnish: fresh chives

Melt butter in a large saucepan. Add sweet red pepper slices, leeks, and chicken broth; bring to a boil. Cover, reduce heat, and simmer, stirring occasionally, 30 minutes or until tender.

Pour mixture into container of an electric blender or food processor; cover and process until smooth, stopping once to scrape down sides.

Pour mixture through a wire-mesh strainer, making sure to get 3 cups liquid. Transfer liquid to a large bowl; stir in buttermilk and ground white pepper.

Cover and chill at least 2 hours. Garnish, if desired. **Yield: 1½ quarts.**

Cream of Roasted Sweet Red Pepper Soup

(pictured on page 435)

8 large sweet red peppers
6 cloves garlic, minced
1 small onion, chopped
3 tablespoons butter or margarine, divided
2 (14½-ounce) cans ready-to-serve chicken broth
2 cups dry white wine
1 bay leaf
½ teaspoon salt
¼ teaspoon pepper
2 tablespoons all-purpose flour
1½ cups whipping cream
Garnish: fresh basil, cut into thin strips

Place peppers on an aluminum foil-lined baking sheet; broil 5½ inches from heat (with electric oven door partially opened) about 5 minutes on each side or until peppers look blistered.

Place roasted peppers in a heavy-duty, zip-top plastic bag immediately; seal and let stand 10 minutes. Peel peppers; remove and discard stem and seeds. Set roasted peppers aside.

Cook garlic and onion in 1 tablespoon melted butter in a Dutch oven over medium heat until crisp-tender. Add chicken broth and next 4 ingredients; bring to a boil. Reduce heat, and simmer 30 minutes.

Pour broth mixture through a large wire-mesh strainer into a large container, reserving solids. Remove bay leaf. Set broth mixture aside.

Position knife blade in food processor bowl; add reserved solids and roasted peppers. Process 30 seconds or until mixture is smooth, stopping once to scrape down sides; set roasted pepper puree aside.

Melt remaining 2 tablespoons butter in Dutch oven over low heat; add flour, stirring until smooth. Cook 1 minute, stirring constantly. Gradually add broth mixture; cook over medium heat, stirring constantly, until thickened and bubbly (about 3 minutes).

Stir in pepper puree. Gradually stir in whipping cream. Cook over low heat until thoroughly heated. Garnish, if desired. **Yield: 2 quarts.**

Freezing Roasted Peppers

Roast extra sweet red and yellow peppers, freeze, and use later to add flavor to soups, pastas, pizzas, and salads. To freeze, cut roasted peppers into strips, and place in a single layer on a baking sheet sprayed with cooking spray. Freeze; remove from baking sheet, and place in a heavy-duty, zip-top plastic bag. Return to the freezer, and use as needed.

Red and Yellow Pepper Soup

Red and Yellow Pepper Soup Techniques

Roast peppers by placing them on a baking sheet and broiling. Turn peppers with tongs as they blister and darken.

Seal roasted peppers in a paper bag for 10 minutes; peel. The captured steam loosens pepper skins, making them easier to peel.

Serve soup by steadily and evenly pouring ½ cup of each pureed pepper mixture into a bowl at the same time.

Red and Yellow Pepper Soup

3 large sweet red peppers
3 large sweet yellow peppers
1½ cups chopped onion
1 tablespoon minced garlic
2 tablespoons olive oil
1 quart ready-to-serve chicken broth, divided
2 tablespoons sherry wine vinegar
Salt and pepper to taste
Garnish: fresh chives

Place peppers on a baking sheet. Broil 5½ inches from heat (with electric oven door partially opened), turning with tongs as peppers blister and turn dark on all sides.

Place peppers in a paper bag; seal and let stand 10 minutes to loosen skins. Peel and discard skins; remove and discard seeds from peppers. Set peppers aside.

Cook onion and garlic in olive oil in a large skillet until onion is tender. Remove from heat.

Combine red peppers, half of onion mixture, and 2 cups chicken broth in container of an electric blender; cover and process until smooth. Transfer mixture to a Dutch oven.

Combine yellow peppers, remaining onion mixture, and remaining 2 cups broth in container of electric blender; cover and process until smooth. Transfer yellow pepper mixture to a separate Dutch oven.

Bring pepper mixtures to a boil; cover, reduce heat, and simmer 10 minutes. Add vinegar and salt and pepper to taste to red pepper mixture; stir well.

Pour steadily and evenly ½ cup of each pepper mixture into individual soup bowls at the same time. Serve warm. Garnish, if desired.
Yield: 1¼ quarts.

Crème Vichyssoise

2 cups coarsely chopped leeks with tops or
    onions
3 cups peeled, sliced potato
3 cups water
4 chicken-flavored bouillon cubes
¼ teaspoon ground white pepper
3 tablespoons butter or margarine
2 cups half-and-half or milk
Garnish: chopped chives

Combine first 6 ingredients in a Dutch oven;
cook over medium heat until tender.

Spoon half of mixture into container of an
electric blender; cover and process until smooth.
Pour into a 2-quart container. Repeat procedure
with remaining mixture.

Stir in half-and-half; cover and chill. Garnish,
if desired. **Yield: 1¼ quarts.**

Velvety Roquefort Vichyssoise

2 cups finely chopped onion
¼ cup butter or margarine, melted
1 quart ready-to-serve chicken broth
2 cups diced potato
¼ teaspoon salt
Pinch of ground white pepper
6 ounces Roquefort cheese, divided
½ cup dry white wine
2 cups buttermilk
2 tablespoons minced fresh parsley

Cook onion in butter in a large Dutch oven
over medium heat 10 minutes or until tender and
slightly golden.

Stir in chicken broth, potato, salt, and pepper;
bring to a boil. Reduce heat; simmer, uncovered,
15 minutes or until potato is tender.

Spoon half of potato mixture into container
of an electric blender; cover and process until

smooth. Repeat with remaining mixture. Return
potato mixture to Dutch oven.

Crumble 4 ounces cheese. Add cheese and
wine to potato mixture; cook over low heat, stirring constantly, about 5 minutes or until cheese
melts. Cool; cover and chill about 4 hours. Stir in
buttermilk. Crumble remaining cheese; sprinkle
each serving with cheese and parsley. **Yield: 2
quarts.**

Cucumber Vichyssoise

1 small onion, chopped
2 tablespoons butter or margarine, melted
2 cups ready-to-serve chicken broth
3 medium potatoes, peeled and finely
    chopped
1 teaspoon salt
¼ teaspoon ground white pepper
2 medium cucumbers, peeled, seeded, and
    chopped
2 cups milk
1 cup half-and-half
¼ cup sour cream
Garnish: shreds of cucumber peel

Cook onion in butter in a large saucepan over
medium heat, stirring constantly, until tender.

Add chicken broth and next 3 ingredients.
Bring to a boil; cover, reduce heat, and simmer
12 minutes.

Add chopped cucumber and milk; simmer,
uncovered, 7 minutes.

Stir half-and-half and sour cream into cucumber mixture.

Pour one-third of soup mixture into container
of an electric blender; cover and process until
smooth, stopping once to scrape down sides.
Pour into a large bowl. Repeat procedure twice
with remaining soup mixture.

Cover and chill at least 2 hours. Garnish, if
desired. **Yield: 1¾ quarts.**

Baked Potato Soup

4 large baking potatoes
⅔ cup butter or margarine
⅔ cup all-purpose flour
6 cups milk
¾ teaspoon salt
½ teaspoon pepper
12 slices bacon, cooked, crumbled, and divided
4 green onions, chopped and divided
1½ cups (6 ounces) shredded Cheddar cheese, divided
1 (8-ounce) carton sour cream

Wash potatoes; prick several times with a fork. Bake at 400° for 1 hour or until done; cool.

Cut potatoes in half lengthwise; scoop out and reserve pulp. Discard shells.

Melt butter in a heavy saucepan over low heat; add flour, stirring until smooth. Cook 1 minute, stirring constantly. Gradually add milk; cook over medium heat, stirring constantly, until thickened and bubbly.

Stir in potato, salt, pepper, ½ cup bacon, 2 tablespoons green onions, and 1 cup cheese. Cook until thoroughly heated (do not boil).

Stir in sour cream; cook just until heated (do not boil). Serve with remaining bacon, green onions, and cheese. **Yield: 2½ quarts.**

Sweet Potato Soup

1 (17-ounce) can sweet potatoes, drained
1 cup orange juice
½ cup white wine
¼ cup honey
¼ cup sour cream
1 teaspoon pumpkin pie spice
Garnish: toasted flaked coconut

Combine first 6 ingredients in container of an electric blender or food processor; cover and process until smooth.

Chill. Garnish, if desired. **Yield: 3⅓ cups.**

Pumpkin-Pear Soup

3 ripe pears, peeled and thinly sliced
¼ cup chopped onion
2 tablespoons butter, melted
2 cups canned or cooked, mashed pumpkin
2 (14½-ounce) cans ready-to-serve chicken broth
½ cup water
¼ cup dry white wine
¼ teaspoon salt
1 (3-inch) stick cinnamon
⅓ cup half-and-half
Garnishes: sour cream, green onion strips

Cook pear and onion in butter in a large skillet over medium-high heat, stirring constantly, until tender. Position knife blade in food processor bowl; add pear mixture and pumpkin. Process until smooth.

Transfer pureed pumpkin mixture to a large saucepan; add chicken broth and next 4 ingredients. Bring to a boil. Reduce heat, and simmer, uncovered, 20 minutes; remove cinnamon stick.

Stir in half-and-half, and heat thoroughly (do not boil). Garnish, if desired. **Yield: 1½ quarts.**

Yellow Squash Soup

Yellow Squash Soup

1 medium onion, finely chopped
2 cloves garlic, minced
1 teaspoon chopped fresh thyme
¼ cup butter or margarine, melted
3 pounds yellow squash, thinly sliced
1 quart ready-to-serve chicken broth
1 cup half-and-half
1 teaspoon salt
Garnishes: edible flowers, fresh thyme sprigs

Cook first 3 ingredients in butter in a large Dutch oven until onion is tender.

Add squash and chicken broth. Bring to a boil; cover, reduce heat, and simmer 20 minutes or until squash is tender.

Transfer mixture in batches to container of an electric blender; cover and process until smooth. Return pureed squash mixture to Dutch oven.

Stir in half-and-half and salt. Cook just until thoroughly heated. Serve hot. Garnish, if desired. **Yield: 2¾ quarts.**

Creamed Butternut and Apple Soup

1 (2½-pound) butternut squash, peeled and diced
¾ pound cooking apples, peeled, cored, and quartered
1 quart ready-to-serve chicken broth
1 (1½-inch) stick cinnamon
1 cup half-and-half
¼ cup unsalted butter or margarine, melted
2 tablespoons maple syrup
¼ teaspoon salt
¼ teaspoon ground nutmeg
¼ teaspoon ground ginger
Garnishes: apple slices, ground nutmeg

Combine first 4 ingredients in a Dutch oven. Bring to a boil; cover, reduce heat, and simmer 20 to 30 minutes or until squash is tender. Remove cinnamon stick.

Spoon mixture into container of an electric blender; cover and process until smooth.

Return squash mixture to Dutch oven; stir in half-and-half and next 5 ingredients. Cook over low heat, stirring constantly, until heated. Serve hot. Garnish, if desired. **Yield: 2 quarts.**

Watercress-Zucchini Soup

3 leeks, sliced (about 2 pounds)
1 tablespoon butter or margarine, melted
1½ pounds zucchini, peeled and sliced
1 quart ready-to-serve chicken broth
1 bunch fresh watercress
⅛ teaspoon pepper
⅓ cup whipping cream

Cook leeks in butter in a Dutch oven 3 minutes. Stir in zucchini, and cook 2 minutes, stirring constantly.

Add chicken broth; bring to a boil, reduce heat, and simmer 4 minutes. Add watercress and pepper; simmer 1 minute.

Spoon one-third of soup mixture into container of an electric blender; cover and process until smooth. Pour into a large bowl. Repeat procedure twice until all mixture is pureed. Add to bowl.

Stir in whipping cream; cover and chill. **Yield: 1¾ quarts.**

Zucchini Soup with Cilantro

1 large onion, chopped
3 tablespoons butter or margarine, melted
3 pounds zucchini, chopped
1 (14½-ounce) can ready-to-serve chicken broth
2 cups buttermilk, divided
1 cup fresh cilantro, chopped and divided
3 tablespoons lemon juice
½ teaspoon salt
¼ to ½ teaspoon pepper
Garnishes: zucchini slices, fresh cilantro sprigs

Cook onion in butter in a 3-quart saucepan over medium heat, stirring constantly, until tender; add zucchini and chicken broth. Bring to a boil; reduce heat, and cook 15 to 20 minutes. Remove from heat; cool.

Combine half of zucchini mixture, ½ cup buttermilk, and ½ cup cilantro in container of an electric blender or food processor; cover and process until smooth, stopping once to scrape down sides. Pour into a large bowl.

Repeat procedure with remaining zucchini mixture, ½ cup buttermilk, and remaining cilantro. Add to bowl, and stir in remaining 1 cup buttermilk, lemon juice, salt, and pepper. Cover and chill at least 8 hours. Garnish each serving, if desired. **Yield: 2 quarts.**

Dried Tomato-Cream Soup

¾ cup dried tomatoes
2 cups water
2 cups whipping cream
½ teaspoon salt
¼ teaspoon freshly ground pepper

Combine tomatoes and water in a large saucepan; bring to a boil, and let boil 2 minutes. Remove from heat, and cool in pan 30 minutes.

Pour mixture into container of an electric blender; cover and process until smooth. Return to saucepan, and stir in remaining ingredients. Cook over low heat until thoroughly heated. Do not boil. **Yield: 3½ cups.**

Tomatillo Soup with Crunchy Jicama

½ pound fresh tomatillos
¼ cup chopped onion
2 tablespoons seeded, chopped poblano pepper
1 tablespoon chopped fresh cilantro or parsley
1 tablespoon lime juice
½ teaspoon salt
½ teaspoon ground cumin
¼ teaspoon sugar
1 clove garlic, minced
1 cup half-and-half
1 cup peeled, finely chopped jicama
Garnishes: tomatillo slices, fresh cilantro sprigs

Remove husks from tomatillos, and rinse. Place tomatillos in a saucepan; add water to cover. Bring to a boil; reduce heat, and simmer 6 minutes or until tender. Drain and cool.

Combine tomatillos, onion, and next 7 ingredients in container of an electric blender or food processor; cover and process until smooth, stopping once to scrape down sides.

Transfer mixture to a large bowl; stir in half-and-half and chopped jicama. Cover and chill. Serve in individual bowls; garnish, if desired. **Yield: 3 cups.**

Tomatillo Soup with Crunchy Jicama

Cantaloupe Soup

8 cups cubed cantaloupe, chilled (about 2
    medium)
¾ cup sweet white wine, chilled
¼ cup whipping cream
Garnish: fresh mint sprigs

Place half of cantaloupe in container of an
electric blender; cover and process until smooth.
With blender running, add half each of wine and
whipping cream; process until smooth.

Repeat procedure with remaining cantaloupe,
wine, and whipping cream. Ladle mixture into
individual soup bowls; garnish, if desired. **Yield:
1½ quarts.**

Peach-Plum Soup

½ pound fresh peaches, peeled and sliced
½ pound fresh plums, peeled and sliced
1 cup plus 2 tablespoons sugar
1 (2-inch) stick cinnamon
1¾ cups water
2 cups dry red wine
1 teaspoon arrowroot
¼ cup water
½ cup whipping cream, whipped

Combine first 6 ingredients in a Dutch oven.
Bring to a boil; reduce heat, and simmer 10 minutes or until fruit is tender.

Spoon 2 cups fruit mixture into container of an
electric blender; cover and process until smooth.
Repeat procedure with remaining mixture.

Return fruit to Dutch oven; bring to a boil.
Combine arrowroot and ¼ cup water; stir into
soup, and boil 1 minute, stirring constantly. Ladle
soup into individual serving bowls. Top each
serving with whipped cream. **Yield: 1½ quarts.**

Strawberry-Banana Soup

2 cups fresh strawberries, sliced
1 small banana, thinly sliced
¼ cup sugar, divided
1 (8-ounce) carton sour cream
1 cup whipping cream
¾ cup milk
¼ cup dry white wine
Garnish: fresh strawberry fans

Combine strawberries, banana, and 2 tablespoons sugar; stir gently, and set aside.

Combine sour cream and remaining 2 tablespoons sugar; add whipping cream, milk, and
wine. Whisk until well blended.

Fold strawberry and banana mixture into sour
cream mixture. Cover and chill 2 hours. Garnish,
if desired. **Yield: 1 quart.**

Sherry-Berry Dessert Soup

2 cups fresh strawberries or raspberries
1 (8-ounce) carton sour cream
1 cup half-and-half
¼ cup sugar
2 tablespoons dry sherry
½ teaspoon vanilla extract
Garnish: fresh mint sprigs

Combine first 6 ingredients in container of an
electric blender; cover and process until smooth,
stopping and scraping sides as necessary.

Pour into individual bowls or wine glasses;
garnish, if desired. **Yield: 3½ cups.**

Rosy Berry Soup

Rosy Berry Soup

2 (10-ounce) packages frozen raspberries or
    strawberries, thawed
2 cups dry red wine
2½ cups water
1 (3-inch) stick cinnamon
¼ cup sugar
2 tablespoons cornstarch
Whipping cream

Combine first 5 ingredients in a stainless steel saucepan (mixture will discolor aluminum). Bring to a boil; reduce heat, and simmer 15 minutes.

Press raspberry mixture through a wire-mesh strainer, reserving ¼ cup. Return liquid to saucepan. Discard seeds.

Combine cornstarch and reserved ¼ cup raspberry liquid; stir until smooth. Bring remaining liquid to a boil. Reduce heat to low, and stir in cornstarch mixture. Cook, stirring constantly, until slightly thickened. Pour into a large bowl.

Cover soup mixture, and chill 6 to 8 hours. Just before serving, ladle into individual serving bowls. Drizzle whipping cream in soup, swirling gently with a knife. Yield: 1¼ quarts.

Chilled Strawberry Soup

Chilled Strawberry Soup

5 cups sliced fresh strawberries
2 cups half-and-half
1¼ cups sour cream
¾ cup sifted powdered sugar
¼ cup balsamic vinegar
Garnishes: whipped cream, strawberry slices,
    fresh mint sprigs

Place strawberries in container of an electric blender or food processor; cover and process until smooth.

Transfer puree to a large bowl. Add half-and-half and next 3 ingredients; stir with a wire whisk until smooth. Cover and chill at least 2 hours.

Serve soup in chilled soup bowls. Garnish, if desired. **Yield: 1¾ quarts.**

Cold Fresh Fruit Soup

2 cups coarsely chopped cantaloupe
2½ cups fresh strawberries
¼ cup seedless green grapes
3 cups coarsely chopped cooking apple
¼ cup sugar
2 cups water
¼ cup lemon juice
1¼ cups orange juice
Garnishes: sour cream, orange rind strips

Combine first 7 ingredients in a large Dutch oven; bring to a boil. Reduce heat, and simmer, uncovered, 15 minutes.

Pour half of fruit mixture into container of an electric blender; cover and process until smooth. Repeat procedure with remaining mixture. Stir orange juice into fruit mixture; cover and chill.

Spoon soup into individual serving bowls; garnish, if desired. **Yield: 1¾ quarts.**

Berry-Peach Soup

2 tablespoons cornstarch
1 cup cold water, divided
¾ cup maple-flavored syrup
¾ cup dry white wine
1 teaspoon lemon juice
2 cups sliced fresh peaches, cut into bite-size
    pieces
1 cup sliced strawberries
1 cup fresh blueberries

Combine cornstarch and ¼ cup water in a saucepan; stir until smooth. Add remaining ¾ cup water, syrup, wine, and lemon juice; mix well.

Cook over medium heat, stirring constantly, until mixture comes to a boil. Boil 1 minute. Remove from heat; cool completely.

Stir in fruit; cover soup, and chill thoroughly. **Yield: 1¼ quarts.**

Refreshing Fruit Soup

1 (16-ounce) can applesauce
1 (6-ounce) can unsweetened pineapple juice
1 (8½-ounce) can pear halves, undrained and
    chopped
1 (8-ounce) can pineapple tidbits, undrained
1 cup frozen unsweetened sliced peaches,
    thawed and chopped
2 to 3 tablespoons brandy (optional)
1 teaspoon ground cinnamon
1 cup sliced fresh strawberries

Combine first 7 ingredients in a large bowl; stir gently. Cover and chill several hours.

Stir in strawberries just before serving. **Yield: 1¼ quarts.**

Note: All ingredients may be combined and frozen. Remove from freezer; let stand for 30 minutes. Serve soup while still slushy.

Elegant Chocolate-Apricot Dessert Soup

1 (14½-ounce) can apricot halves in light
   syrup, drained
1 (6-ounce) package semisweet chocolate
   morsels
1 cup milk
1½ cups whipping cream
1 tablespoon apricot-flavored brandy
¼ teaspoon ground cardamom
Whipped cream
Garnish: chocolate strips

Place apricots in container of an electric blender or food processor; cover and process until smooth. Set aside.

Combine chocolate morsels and milk in a deep 2-quart baking dish. Cover with heavy-duty plastic wrap; fold back a small edge of wrap to allow steam to escape. Microwave at MEDIUM HIGH (70% power) 3 to 4 minutes or until chocolate melts. Stir with a wire whisk until mixture is smooth.

Add chocolate mixture to apricot puree in container of electric blender. Add whipping cream, brandy, and cardamom; cover and process until smooth. Cover and chill thoroughly.

Ladle into dessert bowls; top each serving with a dollop of whipped cream, gently swirling with a knife. Garnish, if desired. **Yield: 1 quart.**

Elegant Chocolate-Apricot Dessert Soup

Bisques and Chowders

Stir up a smooth, delicate bisque or a chunky, rich chowder for a satisfying meal-in-a-bowl. Thick with seafood, meat, vegetables, or cheese, these soups offer a tantalizing array of flavors and textures.

Artichoke-Shrimp Bisque, Clam Bisque, Crab and Corn Bisque

Oven-Roasted Vegetable Chowder, Corn Chowder, Mushroom-Potato Chowder

Make-Ahead Tomato-Basil Bisque, Shrimp Bisque, Clam and Sausage Chowder

Chunky Fish Chowder, Creamy Ham Chowder, Harvest Chowder

Mexican Cheddar-Corn Chowder (page 477)

Artichoke-Shrimp Bisque

Artichoke-Shrimp Bisque

2 (10¾-ounce) cans cream of shrimp soup,
   undiluted

3 cups milk

½ (16-ounce) loaf mild Mexican-style process
   cheese spread, cubed

1 (14-ounce) can artichoke hearts, drained
   and chopped

¼ teaspoon seasoned salt

¼ teaspoon ground white pepper

½ teaspoon Beau Monde seasoning (optional)

1 (5-ounce) package frozen cooked small
   shrimp

Garnishes: sweet red pepper slices, fresh
   parsley sprigs

Combine first 7 ingredients in a Dutch oven; cook over low heat, stirring often, until cheese melts and mixture is hot.

Add shrimp; cook, stirring often, 1 minute or until thoroughly heated. Spoon into serving bowls, and garnish, if desired. **Yield: 2 quarts.**

Note: Bisque may be prepared a day ahead, except for adding shrimp. When ready to serve, reheat bisque over low heat, stirring often. Stir in shrimp as directed above.

Make-Ahead Tomato-Basil Bisque

½ pound leeks, finely chopped
1 stalk celery, chopped
2 to 3 cloves garlic, crushed
2 tablespoons olive oil
2 (14½-ounce) cans Italian plum tomatoes,
    undrained and chopped
12 fresh basil leaves
1 (14½-ounce) can ready-to-serve chicken
    broth
¼ teaspoon salt
¼ teaspoon ground white pepper
1 cup whipping cream
Crème fraîche (optional)

Cook first 3 ingredients in olive oil in a Dutch oven over low heat, stirring constantly, 10 to 12 minutes (do not brown).

Add tomato and basil; cook over medium heat 10 minutes, stirring occasionally.

Add chicken broth, salt, and pepper; bring to a boil. Reduce heat, and simmer, uncovered, 1 hour, stirring occasionally. Cool; cover mixture, and chill 2 hours.

Position knife blade in food processor bowl; add tomato mixture. Process until smooth. (If a finer texture is desired, pour mixture through a fine wire-mesh strainer into a 2-quart container, discarding pulp.) Cover and chill at least 1 hour or overnight.

Stir in whipping cream, and spoon bisque into individual bowls. If desired, pipe crème fraîche on top in a design or initial. **Yield: 1¼ quarts.**

Note: To make your own crème fraîche for the garnish, combine 1 cup sour cream and 1 cup whipping cream.

Clam Bisque

½ cup chopped onion
3 tablespoons butter or margarine, melted
2 tablespoons all-purpose flour
3 (6½-ounce) cans minced clams, undrained
1 (8-ounce) bottle clam juice
1 cup evaporated milk
2 tablespoons tomato juice
1 to 2 tablespoons lemon juice
Garnish: chopped fresh parsley

Cook onion in butter in a heavy saucepan over medium heat, stirring constantly, until tender. Add flour, stirring until smooth. Cook 1 minute, stirring constantly.

Add clams and clam juice; cook over medium heat, stirring constantly, until mixture is bubbly. Reduce heat, and simmer, uncovered, 5 minutes, stirring constantly.

Stir in milk and tomato juice; cook over medium heat, stirring constantly, until mixture is heated. Remove from heat; stir in lemon juice. Garnish, if desired. **Yield: 2 quarts.**

Crab Bisque

1 (10¾-ounce) can cream of mushroom soup,
    undiluted
1 (10¾-ounce) can cream of asparagus soup,
    undiluted
2 cups milk
1 cup half-and-half
1 (6-ounce) can crabmeat, drained and flaked
¼ to ⅓ cup dry white wine or sherry

Combine first 4 ingredients in a saucepan; heat thoroughly, stirring occasionally. Gently stir in crabmeat and wine; heat thoroughly. **Yield: 1½ quarts.**

Crab and Corn Bisque

½ cup chopped celery
½ cup chopped green onions
¼ cup chopped green pepper
½ cup butter or margarine, melted
2 (10¾-ounce) cans cream of potato soup, undiluted
1 (17-ounce) can cream-style corn
1½ cups half-and-half
1½ cups milk
2 bay leaves
1 teaspoon dried thyme
½ teaspoon garlic powder
¼ teaspoon ground white pepper
Dash of hot sauce
1 pound fresh lump crabmeat, drained
Garnishes: chopped fresh parsley, lemon slices

Cook first 3 ingredients in butter in a Dutch oven, stirring constantly, until vegetables are tender. Add soup and next 8 ingredients; cook until thoroughly heated.

Stir in crabmeat, and heat thoroughly. Discard bay leaves. Garnish, if desired. **Yield: 2¾ quarts.**

Know Your Soups

Bisque is a thick, creamy soup most often made with chopped or pureed seafood, but it can also contain vegetables or game.

Chowder is a thick, chunky soup rich with seafood, meat, or vegetables. The name chowder comes from the French *chaudière*, a large kettle fishermen used when making their soups or stews.

Shrimp Bisque

1¾ pounds unpeeled medium-size fresh shrimp
¼ cup butter or margarine
3 tablespoons all-purpose flour
¼ cup finely chopped celery
¼ cup finely chopped carrot
¼ cup finely chopped onion
1 (10½-ounce) can condensed chicken broth, undiluted
1 cup water
¼ teaspoon salt
⅛ to ¼ teaspoon ground red pepper
1½ cups half-and-half
½ cup dry white wine
Garnishes: cooked shrimp with tails, chives

Peel shrimp, and devein, if desired; set aside.

Melt butter in a Dutch oven over medium heat. Add flour, stirring until smooth. Cook 1 minute, stirring constantly. Add celery, carrot, and onion; cook 2 minutes, stirring constantly.

Stir in chicken broth and next 3 ingredients. Bring mixture to a boil over medium heat. Add shrimp, and cook 2 to 3 minutes or until shrimp turn pink. Remove from heat.

Strain shrimp mixture; transfer ⅔ cup liquid to container of an electric blender or food processor, and return remaining liquid to Dutch oven. Set aside 1 cup cooked shrimp.

Add remaining shrimp and cooked vegetables to liquid in blender or food processor; cover and process until smooth.

Return pureed mixture to Dutch oven; heat thoroughly. Stir in half-and-half and 1 cup reserved shrimp. Cook over low heat until thoroughly heated. Stir in wine. Remove from heat.

Ladle bisque into individual serving bowls. Garnish, if desired. **Yield: 1¾ quarts.**

Shrimp Bisque

Seafood Bisque

¾ pound unpeeled medium-size fresh shrimp
¼ cup chopped green onions with tops
¼ cup butter or margarine, melted
¼ cup all-purpose flour
1 quart milk
¼ teaspoon hot sauce
¼ teaspoon salt
¼ teaspoon ground white pepper
¾ cup fresh crabmeat, drained and flaked
3 tablespoons chopped parsley

Peel and chop shrimp; set aside.

Cook green onions in butter in a heavy saucepan over medium heat, stirring constantly, until tender. Add flour, stirring until smooth. Cook 1 minute, stirring constantly.

Add milk gradually; cook over medium heat, stirring constantly, until thickened and bubbly. Stir in hot sauce, salt, and pepper. Stir in crab-meat and shrimp; cook over low heat until shrimp turn pink. Stir in parsley. **Yield: 1¼ quarts.**

Chunky Fish Chowder

½ cup chopped onion
1 clove garlic, minced
2 tablespoons butter or margarine, melted
2 cups water
2 medium potatoes, peeled and diced
1 (10-ounce) package frozen baby lima beans
⅓ cup dry white wine
1 pound cod fillets, cut into 1-inch pieces
1 (16-ounce) can whole tomatoes, drained and chopped
1 (10¾-ounce) can cream of mushroom soup
1 (10-ounce) package frozen whole kernel corn
1 teaspoon lemon-pepper seasoning
1 teaspoon Worcestershire sauce
4 drops of hot sauce
1 cup evaporated skimmed milk

Cook onion and garlic in butter in a Dutch oven over medium heat, stirring constantly, until tender.

Add water and next 3 ingredients. Bring to a boil; cover, reduce heat, and simmer 15 minutes, stirring occasionally.

Add fish and next 6 ingredients; cover and simmer 15 minutes, stirring occasionally. Stir in milk; cook 2 minutes or until thoroughly heated. **Yield: 2 quarts.**

New England Clam Chowder

3 cups water
2 chicken-flavored bouillon cubes
4 medium-size round red potatoes, finely diced
2 (6½-ounce) cans minced clams, undrained
4 slices bacon, cut into 1-inch pieces
¾ cup chopped onion
3 tablespoons butter or margarine
¼ cup plus 2 tablespoons all-purpose flour
1 quart milk
¾ teaspoon salt
¼ teaspoon pepper

Combine water and bouillon cubes in a Dutch oven; bring to a boil. Add potato; cover and simmer 10 minutes or until tender. Drain potato, and set aside. Drain clams, reserving juice. Set clams and juice aside.

Cook bacon and onion in a medium skillet over medium-high heat, stirring constantly, until bacon is crisp and onion is tender. Remove bacon and onion, reserving 2 tablespoons drippings. Set bacon and onion aside.

Combine reserved drippings and butter in Dutch oven; cook over low heat until butter melts. Add flour, stirring until smooth. Cook, stir-ring constantly, 1 minute.

Add reserved clam juice and milk gradually; cook over medium heat, stirring constantly, until mixture is thickened and bubbly. Remove mixture from heat; stir in potato, clams, bacon mixture, salt, and pepper. Cook, stirring constantly, until mixture is thoroughly heated (do not boil). **Yield: 2 quarts.**

Clam Chowder

4   slices bacon, chopped
3   (6⅓-ounce) cans whole shelled clams
3   tablespoons butter or margarine
½   cup chopped celery
½   cup chopped onion
2   green onions with tops, chopped
2   cups chopped potato
3   tablespoons all-purpose flour
2   cups milk
2   cups half-and-half
¼   teaspoon hot sauce
½   teaspoon salt
¼   teaspoon ground white pepper
Paprika
Garnish: fresh parsley sprigs

Cook bacon in a Dutch oven until crisp; pour off pan drippings. Set aside.

Drain clams, reserving 1 cup juice; set clams aside. Add clam juice, butter, and next 4 ingredients to bacon in Dutch oven. Bring to a boil; cover, reduce heat, and simmer 15 minutes or until potato is tender.

Chop clams coarsely; set aside.

Combine flour and milk; stir until smooth. Add milk mixture, clams, half-and-half, hot sauce, salt, and pepper to Dutch oven. Cook over medium heat, stirring constantly, until chowder is thoroughly heated.

Sprinkle each serving with paprika, and garnish, if desired. **Yield: 2 quarts.**

Clam and Sausage Chowder

2   dozen fresh clams
2   pounds smoked Polish sausage, thinly sliced
1   medium onion, chopped
2   cloves garlic, minced
2   tablespoons olive oil
1½ pounds potatoes, cubed
1   (10-ounce) package frozen whole kernel
      corn, thawed
4   (8-ounce) bottles clam juice
2   cups water
1   teaspoon fennel seeds, crushed
½   to 1 teaspoon ground red pepper
2   (16-ounce) cans crushed tomatoes,
      undrained
½   cup fresh parsley, chopped

Wash clams thoroughly, discarding any opened shells; set aside.

Brown sausage in a Dutch oven over medium heat; drain on paper towels, and set aside.

Cook onion and garlic in olive oil in a Dutch oven over medium-high heat, stirring constantly, until tender. Add potato and next 5 ingredients.

Bring to a boil; cover, reduce heat, and simmer 15 minutes or until potato is tender. Stir in tomatoes.

Remove 2 cups potato mixture, and pour into container of an electric blender. Cover and process until smooth, stopping once to scrape down sides. Return mixture to Dutch oven.

Bring to a boil. Add clams; cover, reduce heat, and simmer 4 to 5 minutes or until clam shells open. (Discard any unopened shells.)

Stir in sausage and parsley; cook until thoroughly heated. **Yield: 3 quarts.**

Manhattan-Style Seafood Chowder

Manhattan-Style Seafood Chowder

4 medium onions, chopped
1 large green pepper, seeded and chopped
¼ cup vegetable oil
2 tablespoons all-purpose flour
3 (14½-ounce) cans stewed tomatoes, undrained
1 tablespoon celery salt
1 teaspoon garlic powder
1 teaspoon hot sauce
½ teaspoon pepper
2 pounds unpeeled medium-size fresh shrimp
½ pound fresh crabmeat, drained and flaked
½ pound firm white fish fillets, cut into bite-size pieces
1 (12-ounce) container Standard oysters, drained
Garnish: celery leaves

Cook onion and green pepper in oil in a Dutch oven over medium-high heat, stirring constantly, until tender.

Add flour; cook, stirring constantly, 1 minute. Stir in tomatoes and next 4 ingredients. Bring to a boil; cover, reduce heat, and simmer 15 minutes.

Peel shrimp. Add shrimp, crabmeat, fish, and oysters to Dutch oven; cover and simmer 15 minutes. Garnish, if desired. **Yield: 3 quarts.**

Curried Seafood Chowder

1 pound unpeeled medium-size fresh shrimp
3 tablespoons butter or margarine
3 tablespoons all-purpose flour
1 tablespoon curry powder
2 cups ready-to-serve chicken broth
2 (8-ounce) bottles clam juice
2 cups half-and-half
4 medium potatoes, peeled and chopped
1 pound grouper or amberjack fillets, cut into bite-size pieces

Peel shrimp, and devein, if desired; set aside.

Melt butter in a large Dutch oven over medium heat; add flour and curry powder, stirring constantly, until smooth. Cook 1 minute, stirring constantly. Gradually add chicken broth, stirring until smooth.

Stir in clam juice, half-and-half, and potato. Bring to a boil; reduce heat, and simmer 20 minutes or until potato is tender.

Add fish and shrimp; cook 5 minutes or until shrimp turn pink. Serve chowder immediately. **Yield: 3½ quarts.**

Shrimp Chowder

8 slices bacon
1 medium onion, chopped
1 stalk celery, chopped
1 green pepper, seeded and chopped
2 (10¾-ounce) cans cream of potato soup, undiluted
1 (10¾-ounce) can cream of celery soup, undiluted
2 (4¼-ounce) cans small shrimp, drained and rinsed
1 quart milk
¼ teaspoon pepper

Cook bacon in a large Dutch oven until crisp; remove bacon, reserving 1 tablespoon drippings in Dutch oven. Crumble bacon, and set aside.

Cook onion, celery, and green pepper in bacon drippings over medium heat, stirring constantly, until tender.

Add potato soup and next 4 ingredients, stirring well. Cook over medium heat until thoroughly heated. Sprinkle each serving with bacon. **Yield: 2½ quarts.**

Chicken Chowder Sauterne

1 (3½- to 4-pound) broiler-fryer, cut up and
    skinned
1 quart water
1 large carrot, scraped and sliced
1 teaspoon salt
1 cup milk
½ cup chopped green onions
½ cup chopped green pepper
½ cup chopped fresh parsley
½ cup chopped celery
2 tablespoons butter or margarine, melted
3 tablespoons butter or margarine
⅓ cup all-purpose flour
1 egg yolk, beaten
½ cup Sauterne
½ teaspoon salt
¼ teaspoon pepper

Combine first 4 ingredients in a large Dutch
oven; bring to a boil. Cover, reduce heat, and
simmer 35 minutes or until chicken is tender.

Drain chicken, reserving broth. Cool, bone,
and chop chicken; set aside. Strain broth, reserving 3 cups. Add milk to reserved broth; set aside.

Cook green onions and next 3 ingredients in 2
tablespoons butter in a heavy skillet over medium
heat, stirring constantly, until tender; set aside.

Melt 3 tablespoons butter in a heavy Dutch
oven over low heat; add flour, stirring well. Cook
1 minute, stirring constantly.

Add reserved broth mixture gradually; cook
over medium heat, stirring constantly, until thickened and bubbly.

Combine egg yolk and wine; mix well. Stir
into broth mixture. Add chicken, vegetables, ½
teaspoon salt, and pepper; cook, stirring constantly, until thoroughly heated. **Yield: 2 quarts.**

Crowd-Pleasing Turkey Chowder

1 turkey carcass
4 quarts water
1 cup butter or margarine
1 cup all-purpose flour
3 onions, chopped
2 large carrots, diced
2 stalks celery, diced
1 cup long-grain rice, uncooked
2 teaspoons salt
¾ teaspoon pepper
2 cups half-and-half
Garnish: fresh parsley sprigs

Place turkey carcass and water in a large
Dutch oven; bring to a boil. Cover, reduce heat,
and simmer 1 hour.

Remove carcass from broth, and pick meat
from bones. Set meat aside. Measure broth, and
add water, if necessary, to measure 3 quarts; set
broth aside.

Melt butter in Dutch oven; add flour, and cook
over medium heat, stirring constantly, 5 minutes.
(Roux will be a very light color.)

Stir onion, carrot, and celery into roux; cook
over medium heat 10 minutes, stirring often.

Add broth, turkey, rice, salt, and pepper; bring
to a boil. Cover, reduce heat, and simmer 20 minutes or until rice is tender. Add half-and-half, and
cook until thoroughly heated. Garnish, if desired.
Yield: 4½ quarts.

Crowd-Pleasing Turkey Chowder

Turkey Chowder

2 tablespoons butter or margarine
2 tablespoons all-purpose flour
2 cups milk
2 cups cubed process cheese
2 cups chopped cooked turkey
1½ cups sliced cooked potato
1 (10-ounce) package frozen mixed vegetables
1 teaspoon chicken-flavored bouillon granules
½ teaspoon instant minced onion
¼ teaspoon dry mustard
⅛ teaspoon pepper

Melt butter in a large saucepan over low heat; add flour, stirring until smooth. Cook 1 minute, stirring constantly.

Add milk and cheese gradually; cook over medium heat, stirring constantly, until mixture thickens and cheese melts.

Add turkey and remaining ingredients, and mix well. Cook over low heat, stirring occasionally, until vegetables are tender. **Yield: 1¼ quarts.**

Creamy Ham Chowder

1 (8-ounce) package frozen mixed vegetables
1 (18¾-ounce) can creamy chunky mushroom soup, undiluted
1 cup milk
¼ teaspoon dried dillweed
⅛ teaspoon coarsely ground black pepper
1 (6¾-ounce) can chunk ham, drained and broken into chunks
¼ cup (1 ounce) shredded Swiss cheese
¼ to ½ cup plain croutons

Place vegetables in a 2-quart baking dish. Cover tightly with heavy-duty plastic wrap; fold back a small edge of wrap to allow steam to escape. Microwave at HIGH 7 to 9 minutes or until vegetables are crisp-tender.

Uncover and stir in soup; gradually add milk, stirring until blended. Add dillweed and pepper. Microwave at HIGH 3 minutes; stir.

Add ham, and microwave at HIGH 2 to 3 minutes or until thoroughly heated. Let stand 2 minutes. Sprinkle each serving with shredded cheese and croutons. **Yield: 1 quart.**

Sausage-Bean Chowder

2 pounds ground pork sausage
4 cups water
2 (16-ounce) cans kidney beans, undrained
2 (16-ounce) cans whole tomatoes, undrained and chopped
2 medium onions, chopped
2 medium potatoes, peeled and cubed
½ cup chopped green pepper
1 large bay leaf
½ teaspoon salt
½ teaspoon dried thyme
¼ teaspoon garlic powder
¼ teaspoon pepper

Brown sausage in a Dutch oven, stirring until it crumbles; drain off drippings.

Add water and remaining ingredients to Dutch oven; bring to a boil. Cover, reduce heat, and simmer 1 hour. Remove bay leaf before serving. **Yield: 3 quarts.**

Simmering Success

An enameled cast-iron Dutch oven is excellent for cooking bisques and chowders because it allows steady simmering with little risk of scorching. Heavy stainless steel and aluminum pots are also good choices.

Fresh Corn and Bacon Chowder

8 ears fresh corn
4 slices bacon
½ cup finely chopped onion
½ cup thinly sliced celery
1 cup water
2 cups milk, divided
1 teaspoon sugar
1 teaspoon dried thyme
½ teaspoon salt
¼ teaspoon pepper
2 teaspoons cornstarch

Cut off tips of corn kernels into a large bowl; scrape milk and remaining pulp from cob with a paring knife. Set aside.

Cook bacon in a large Dutch oven until crisp; remove bacon, reserving 2 tablespoons drippings in Dutch oven. Crumble bacon, and set aside.

Cook onion and celery in reserved bacon drippings over medium-high heat, stirring constantly, until tender.

Stir in corn and water. Bring to a boil; cover, reduce heat, and simmer 10 minutes, stirring occasionally. Stir in 1½ cups milk and next 4 ingredients.

Combine cornstarch and remaining ½ cup milk; stir until smooth. Gradually add to corn mixture, stirring constantly. Cover and cook 10 minutes, stirring often, until thickened and bubbly. Sprinkle with bacon. **Yield: 1¼ quarts.**

Fresh Corn and Bacon Chowder

Hot Cheese Chowder

½ cup chopped celery
½ cup chopped onion
½ cup chopped green pepper
¼ cup butter or margarine, melted
3 cups chicken broth
1 medium potato, peeled and cubed
½ cup chopped carrot
½ cup all-purpose flour
2 cups milk, divided
12 ounces sharp American cheese, cubed
1 tablespoon chopped fresh parsley

Cook celery, onion, and green pepper in butter in a Dutch oven, stirring constantly, until tender.

Add chicken broth, potato, and carrot; bring to a boil. Cover, reduce heat, and simmer 20 minutes or until vegetables are tender.

Combine flour and ¾ cup milk; stir until smooth. Stir flour mixture, remaining 1¼ cups milk, cheese, and parsley into vegetable mixture. Cook over low heat, stirring constantly, until chowder is thickened and bubbly. Serve immediately. **Yield: 2 quarts.**

Harvest Chowder

4 slices bacon
2 stalks celery, thinly sliced
2 carrots, thinly sliced
2 green onions, sliced
2 cups mashed potatoes
1 (17-ounce) can cream-style corn
½ cup frozen English peas
2 cups milk
½ teaspoon salt
1 cup (4 ounces) shredded sharp Cheddar
   cheese
1 large tomato, peeled and thinly sliced
Seasoned pepper

Cook bacon in a large saucepan until crisp; remove bacon, reserving 1 tablespoon drippings in pan. Crumble bacon, and set aside.

Cook celery, carrot, and green onions in drippings 5 to 8 minutes, stirring constantly. Stir in potatoes and next 5 ingredients. Cook over medium heat, stirring constantly, until cheese melts.

Ladle into individual serving bowls. Top each with a tomato slice, bacon, and a dash of seasoned pepper. **Yield: about 1¾ quarts.**

Corn Chowder

1 cup chopped onion
½ cup chopped celery
2 tablespoons butter or margarine, melted
3 cups fresh corn, cut from cob
1½ cups peeled, cubed potato
1½ cups water
2 chicken-flavored bouillon cubes
1 teaspoon salt
¼ teaspoon pepper
¼ teaspoon dried thyme
2 cups milk
1 cup half-and-half

Cook onion and celery in butter in a large saucepan, stirring constantly, until tender. Stir in corn and next 6 ingredients; cover and simmer 15 minutes.

Add milk and half-and-half; cook chowder, stirring constantly, until thoroughly heated.
Yield: 2 quarts.

Note: You may substitute 3 cups frozen corn for fresh.

Pepper-Cheese Chowder

Pepper-Cheese Chowder

1 **cup chopped sweet red pepper**
1 **cup chopped sweet yellow pepper**
½ **cup chopped carrot**
½ **cup sliced celery**
½ **cup chopped onion**
2 **cloves garlic, minced**
⅓ **cup butter or margarine, melted**
½ **cup all-purpose flour**
1 **quart half-and-half**
2 **(10½-ounce) cans condensed chicken broth**
1 **(12-ounce) can beer**
½ **teaspoon dry mustard**
¼ **teaspoon dried rosemary, crushed**
¼ **teaspoon salt**
¼ **teaspoon ground red pepper**
½ **teaspoon freshly ground black pepper**
2 **cups (8 ounces) shredded sharp Cheddar
     cheese**
**Garnishes: fresh rosemary sprigs, finely
     chopped sweet red and yellow pepper**

Cook first 6 ingredients in butter in a large Dutch oven over medium-high heat, stirring constantly, 5 minutes or until tender.

Add flour, stirring constantly. Cook 1 minute, stirring constantly. Gradually add half-and-half, chicken broth, and beer; cook, stirring constantly, until thickened and bubbly.

Stir in mustard and next 4 ingredients; gradually add cheese, stirring until cheese melts. Ladle into individual serving bowls; garnish, if desired. Serve chowder immediately. **Yield: 2¾ quarts.**

Tortilla-Corn Chowder

Tortilla-Corn Chowder

5 cups ready-to-serve chicken broth
1 large onion, chopped
2 cloves garlic, minced
6 large ears fresh corn
4 (6-inch) corn tortillas, coarsely chopped
1 (4.5 ounce) can chopped green chiles,
    undrained
½ cup sour cream
2 to 3 tablespoons chopped fresh cilantro
¼ teaspoon salt
¼ teaspoon pepper
Garnishes: crushed tortilla chips, sour cream,
    fresh cilantro sprigs

Combine first 3 ingredients in a Dutch oven. Cut corn from cobs, scraping cobs well to remove all milk; add corn to Dutch oven.

Stir in tortilla pieces. Cover and simmer over medium-low heat 1 hour and 15 minutes, stirring occasionally. Remove from heat.

Stir in green chiles and next 4 ingredients; cook until heated. Spoon into individual soup bowls. Garnish, if desired. **Yield: 2 quarts.**

Variation

Cream of Corn Soup: Transfer simmered corn-tortilla mixture to container of an electric blender; cover and process until smooth. Return mixture to Dutch oven. Stir in green chiles and next 4 ingredients; proceed as directed above.

Mexican Cheddar-Corn Chowder

(pictured on page 461)

1 tablespoon butter or margarine
½ cup chopped onion
2 cups peeled and diced potato
1 cup water
½ teaspoon dried basil
2 cups milk
2 (17-ounce) cans cream-style corn
1 (14½-ounce) can whole tomatoes, drained
    and chopped
1 (4.5 ounce) can chopped green chiles,
    undrained
½ cup diced sweet red pepper
½ teaspoon salt
⅛ teaspoon pepper
1 cup (4 ounces) shredded sharp Cheddar
    cheese

Place butter in a deep 3-quart baking dish; microwave, uncovered, at HIGH 35 seconds or until melted. Stir in chopped onion; microwave, uncovered, at HIGH 3 to 4 minutes or until onion is tender.

Add potato, water, and basil. Cover with heavy-duty plastic wrap; fold back a small edge of wrap to allow steam to escape. Microwave at HIGH 12 to 15 minutes or until potato is tender, stirring every 5 minutes.

Stir in milk and next 6 ingredients; cover and microwave at HIGH 5 to 6 minutes or until thoroughly heated, stirring after 3 minutes.

Stir in cheese; reduce to MEDIUM LOW (30% power). Cover and microwave 5 to 6 minutes or until cheese melts, stirring after 3 minutes. Serve immediately. **Yield: 2½ quarts.**

Mushroom-Potato Chowder

1 small onion, chopped
1 stalk celery, chopped
½ small green pepper, seeded and chopped
1 (8-ounce) package sliced fresh mushrooms
2 tablespoons butter or margarine, melted
2 cups peeled and diced red potato
2 cups ready-to-serve chicken broth
½ teaspoon dried thyme or 1½ teaspoons
    minced fresh thyme
2 cups milk, divided
½ teaspoon salt
½ teaspoon pepper
3 tablespoons all-purpose flour
Garnish: fresh thyme sprigs

Cook first 4 ingredients in butter in a large Dutch oven over medium heat, stirring constantly, until tender.

Stir in potato, chicken broth, and thyme. Bring to a boil; reduce heat, and simmer, uncovered, 30 minutes or until potato is tender.

Stir in 1½ cups milk, salt, and pepper. Combine flour and remaining ½ cup milk, stirring until smooth. Stir into chowder, and simmer, uncovered, stirring frequently, until slightly thickened. Garnish, if desired. **Yield: 1½ quarts.**

Mushroom-Potato Chowder

Vegetable-Cheddar Chowder

3 cups water
3 chicken-flavored bouillon cubes
4 medium potatoes, peeled and diced
1 medium onion, sliced
1 cup thinly sliced carrot
½ cup diced green pepper
⅓ cup butter or margarine
⅓ cup all-purpose flour
3½ cups milk
4 cups (16 ounces) shredded sharp Cheddar
    cheese
1 (2-ounce) jar diced pimiento, drained
¼ teaspoon hot sauce (optional)
Garnish: fresh parsley sprigs

Combine water and bouillon cubes in a Dutch oven; bring to a boil. Add vegetables; cover and simmer 12 minutes or until vegetables are tender.

Melt butter in a heavy saucepan over low heat; add flour, stirring until smooth. Cook 1 minute, stirring constantly.

Add milk gradually; cook over medium heat, stirring constantly, until thickened and bubbly. Add cheese, stirring until melted.

Stir cheese sauce, pimiento, and hot sauce, if desired, into vegetable mixture. Cook over low heat until thoroughly heated (do not boil). Garnish each serving, if desired. **Yield: 2½ quarts.**

Oven-Roasted Vegetable Chowder

1½ pounds red potatoes, cut into ½-inch
    cubes
2 large carrots, scraped and cut into ½-inch
    cubes
1 large onion, coarsely chopped
6 plum tomatoes, quartered lengthwise
3 (14½-ounce) cans ready-to-serve chicken
    broth
Dash of salt (optional)
Dash of pepper (optional)

Combine potato and carrot in a lightly greased foil-lined 13- x 9- x 2-inch pan. Bake at 375° for 15 minutes.

Stir in onion. Place tomato at one end of pan, keeping separate from potato mixture. Bake 1 hour, stirring every 15 minutes.

Remove vegetables from oven. Coarsely chop tomato; set aside.

Bring chicken broth to a boil in a large saucepan; add potato mixture. Reduce heat, and simmer 10 to 15 minutes.

Stir in tomato; if desired, add salt and pepper. Serve immediately. **Yield: about 1¾ quarts.**

Keep Garnishes Simple

A garnish should complement the flavors in a soup. Try these for added flavor and texture:
• Thinly sliced carrot or green onions
• Shredded cheese or toasted nuts
• Chopped fresh herbs or sprigs of fresh herbs
• Dollops of sour cream, yogurt, or whipped cream
• Croutons, corn chips, or crackers
• Chopped hard-cooked egg or cooked, crumbled bacon
• Lemon or lime slices or strips of citrus rind

Hearty Vegetable Chowder

1 (10½-ounce) can condensed chicken broth,
    undiluted
⅔ cup water
4 cups frozen mixed vegetables
¼ cup chopped onion
¼ cup chopped green pepper
3 tablespoons butter or margarine, melted
¼ cup all-purpose flour
½ teaspoon paprika
½ teaspoon dry mustard
2 cups milk
⅛ teaspoon pepper
2 cups (8 ounces) shredded Cheddar cheese
Garnishes: carrot curls, fresh parsley sprigs

Combine chicken broth and water in a sauce-pan; bring to a boil. Add mixed vegetables, and cook over medium heat 15 minutes or until vegetables are tender.

Cook onion and green pepper in butter in a Dutch oven, stirring constantly, until tender. Stir in flour, paprika, and mustard.

Add milk, vegetables, and broth to Dutch oven; cook over medium heat, stirring constantly, until mixture comes to a boil.

Remove from heat; add pepper and cheese, and stir until cheese melts. Garnish, if desired.
Yield: 1¾ quarts.

Hearty Soups

Chock-full of vegetables, meat, or seafood, these soups stand
on their own as main dishes. Pair them with a green salad
or crusty bread, and you'll have a substantial meal.

Garden Festival Soup, Black Bean Soup, Spicy Three-Bean Soup

Taco Soup, Beefy Lentil Soup, Italian Spinach Soup with Meatballs, Steak Soup

Chunky Minestrone, French Market Soup Mix, Sausage, Bacon, and Bean Soup

Southern Bouillabaisse, Bean 'n' Ham Soup, Ground Beef Soup

Guadalajara Soup (page 492)

Garden Festival Soup

Garden Festival Soup

3 cups water
1 cup peeled, diced red potato
1 cup scraped, sliced carrot
1½ teaspoons salt
1 (16-ounce) package frozen English peas,
  thawed
1½ cups broccoli flowerets
1 cup cauliflower flowerets
1 cup sliced yellow squash
¼ cup chopped green onions
¼ cup butter or margarine, melted
¼ cup all-purpose flour
2 cups milk
2 cups half-and-half
1 (2-ounce) jar diced pimiento, drained
¼ teaspoon ground white pepper
3 dashes of hot sauce
Garnish: chopped fresh parsley

Combine first 4 ingredients in a large sauce-pan; stir well. Bring to a boil; cover, reduce heat, and simmer 10 minutes.

Stir in peas and next 3 ingredients; cover and simmer 10 minutes or until vegetables are tender. Remove from heat, and set aside.

Cook chopped green onions in butter in a large Dutch oven over medium heat, stirring constantly, until tender.

Add flour, stirring until smooth. Cook 1 minute, stirring constantly. Gradually add milk and half-and-half; cook over medium heat, stirring constantly, until mixture is thickened and bubbly.

Add pimiento, pepper, and hot sauce; stir well. Gradually add reserved vegetables and liquid, stirring well. Cook mixture, uncovered, over medium heat until thoroughly heated, stirring occasionally.

Ladle soup into individual serving bowls. Garnish, if desired. Serve soup immediately. **Yield: 2¼ quarts.**

Garden Vegetable Soup

1 cup thinly sliced carrot
1 cup sliced celery with leaves
1 cup chopped onion
1 clove garlic, crushed
¼ cup butter or margarine, melted
9 medium tomatoes, peeled and chopped
1 teaspoon dried oregano
1 teaspoon dried basil
2 teaspoons salt
¼ teaspoon pepper
1 (14½-ounce) can ready-to-serve beef broth
⅓ pound fresh green beans, washed and cut
  into 1-inch pieces
1 medium zucchini, halved lengthwise and
  sliced
¼ cup chopped fresh parsley
Grated Parmesan cheese (optional)

Cook first 4 ingredients in butter in a large Dutch oven over medium heat, stirring constantly, until onion is tender.

Add tomato and seasonings; bring to a boil. Reduce heat and simmer 15 minutes, stirring occasionally.

Add beef broth and green beans; simmer 20 minutes. Add zucchini and parsley; simmer 10 minutes. Spoon into soup bowls; sprinkle with Parmesan cheese, if desired. **Yield: 2¼ quarts.**

Vegetable Variety

When adding vegetables to home-made soup, remember that not all vegetables cook in the same length of time. Those that take the longest to cook should be cut into uniform pieces and added first. Add frozen vegetables after fresh. Canned vegetables need only to be reheated.

Black Bean Soup

(pictured on page 446)

1 (16-ounce) package dried black beans
7 cups water
2 (14½-ounce) cans ready-to-serve chicken broth
1 small ham hock
1 tablespoon butter or margarine
2 cloves garlic, crushed
1 small hot pepper, chopped
1 medium onion, chopped
1 stalk celery, chopped
1 bay leaf
½ teaspoon salt
½ teaspoon pepper
½ teaspoon dry mustard
¼ cup dry sherry
Feta cheese (optional)

Sort and wash beans; place in a Dutch oven. Add 7 cups water. Bring to a boil; cover beans, and cook 2 minutes. Remove from heat, and let stand 1 hour.

Add chicken broth and next 10 ingredients to beans. Bring to a boil; cover, reduce heat, and simmer 2 to 2½ hours, stirring occasionally. Remove bay leaf.

Remove ham hock; cut off meat, and dice. Discard bone, and set meat aside.

Measure 4 cups soup, and pour into container of an electric blender; cover and process until smooth. Return mixture to Dutch oven.

Add diced ham and sherry. Bring mixture to a boil; reduce heat, and simmer soup 10 minutes. Sprinkle each serving with feta cheese, if desired. Yield: 2¼ quarts.

Note: Seeds in small hot pepper make soup very hot. For a milder soup, remove seeds before chopping pepper.

Three-Bean Soup

2 cups dried navy beans
1 cup dried red beans
1½ cups dried garbanzo beans
3 (10½-ounce) cans condensed chicken broth, undiluted
3⅔ cups water
2 onions, chopped
1 cup sliced carrot
1 cup sliced celery
1 large clove garlic, minced
2 tablespoons parsley flakes
2 teaspoons dried basil
1 teaspoon dried oregano
1 teaspoon salt
½ teaspoon pepper
3 cups chopped fresh spinach (about 4 ounces)
Grated Parmesan cheese (optional)

Sort and wash beans; place in a large Dutch oven. Cover with water 2 inches above beans; let soak 8 hours.

Drain beans, and return to Dutch oven. Add chicken broth and next 10 ingredients. Bring to a boil; cover, reduce heat, and simmer 2 hours or until beans are tender, stirring occasionally.

Add spinach, and cook 10 to 15 minutes, stirring occasionally. Sprinkle each serving with Parmesan cheese, if desired. Yield: 3 quarts.

Three-Bean Soup

French Market Soup Mix

1 pound dried black beans
1 pound dried Great Northern beans
1 pound dried navy beans
1 pound dried pinto beans
1 pound dried red beans
1 pound dried black-eyed peas
1 pound dried green split peas
1 pound dried yellow split peas
1 pound dried lentils
1 pound dried baby limas
1 pound dried large limas
1 pound barley pearls

Combine all ingredients in a very large bowl. Divide mixture into 13 (2-cup) packages to give along with the recipe for French Market Soup. **Yield: 26 cups.**

French Market Soup

1 (2-cup) package French Market Soup Mix
2 quarts water
1 large ham hock
1 (16-ounce) can whole tomatoes, undrained and coarsely chopped
1½ cups chopped onion
3 tablespoons lemon juice
1 chile pepper, coarsely chopped
1 clove garlic, minced
1¼ teaspoons salt
¼ teaspoon pepper

Sort and wash soup mix; place in a Dutch oven. Cover with water 2 inches above soup mix; let soak 8 hours.

Drain soup mix, and return to Dutch oven; add 2 quarts water and ham hock. Bring to a boil; cover, reduce heat, and simmer 1½ hours or until beans are tender.

Stir in tomato and next 4 ingredients. Bring mixture to a boil, reduce heat, and simmer, uncovered, 30 minutes.

Remove ham hock; remove meat from bone. Chop meat, and return to soup. Stir in salt and pepper. **Yield: 3 quarts.**

Black, White, and Red All Over Soup

1 (15.5-ounce) can white hominy, drained and rinsed
1 (15-ounce) can black beans, drained and rinsed
1 (14½-ounce) can chili-style diced tomatoes, undrained
1 (14½-ounce) can ready-to-serve chicken broth
1 teaspoon chopped fresh cilantro
½ teaspoon chili powder
½ teaspoon ground cumin

Combine all ingredients in a large saucepan; cook over medium heat, stirring occasionally, until thoroughly heated. **Yield: 1¼ quarts.**

Soaking Dried Beans

Dried beans require soaking to rehydrate.

For **quick soaking**, add 6 to 8 cups water to 1 pound dried beans. Bring to a boil; cover and cook 2 minutes. Remove from heat, and let stand 1 hour.

For **overnight soaking**, add 6 cups water to 1 pound dried beans. Let stand 8 hours at room temperature. (Beans tend to sour if they are placed in too warm a place.) Beans soaked using this method retain their shape and cook faster.

Chunky Minestrone

Split Pea Soup

1 (16-ounce) package dried green split peas
2 quarts water
1 medium onion, chopped
1 medium carrot, diced
1 stalk celery, diced
1 meaty ham bone
¼ to ½ teaspoon salt
¼ teaspoon pepper
¼ teaspoon dried tarragon

Sort and wash peas; place in a Dutch oven. Add 2 quarts water, and bring to a boil. Cover and cook 2 minutes. Remove from heat, and let stand 1 hour.

Add vegetables, ham bone, and seasonings. Bring to a boil; cover, reduce heat, and simmer 2½ to 3 hours, stirring occasionally.

Remove bone; cut off meat, and dice. Discard bone. Return meat to soup, and simmer 10 additional minutes. **Yield: 2 quarts.**

Chunky Minestrone

1 large onion, chopped
1 medium carrot, halved lengthwise and sliced (about ¾ cup)
1 clove garlic, minced
1 tablespoon olive oil
½ cup long-grain rice, uncooked
2½ cups water
2 (14½-ounce) cans Italian-style stewed tomatoes, undrained and chopped
1 (10½-ounce) can condensed chicken broth, undiluted
1⅓ cups water
2 teaspoons dried Italian seasoning
½ teaspoon salt
¼ teaspoon pepper
1 medium zucchini, halved lengthwise and sliced
1 (15-ounce) can cannellini beans, undrained
1 (10-ounce) package frozen chopped spinach, thawed
⅔ cup grated Parmesan cheese

Cook first 3 ingredients in oil in a large Dutch oven over medium-high heat 3 minutes, stirring constantly.

Add rice and next 7 ingredients. Bring to a boil. Cover, reduce heat, and simmer 20 minutes.

Add zucchini, beans, and spinach; cook 5 additional minutes. Sprinkle each serving with cheese. **Yield: 2 quarts.**

Bean 'n' Ham Soup

Bean 'n' Ham Soup

1 pound dried Great Northern beans
1 quart water
1 (10½-ounce) can beef consommé, undiluted
1 meaty ham hock
6 black peppercorns
3 cloves garlic, halved
2 bay leaves
2 fresh parsley sprigs
2 fresh thyme sprigs
1 cup water
3 large carrots, scraped and sliced
2 cups coarsely chopped cooked ham
1 small onion, finely chopped
4 medium potatoes, peeled and cubed
Dash of hot sauce
Salt and freshly ground pepper to taste

Sort and wash beans; place in a Dutch oven. Cover with water 2 inches above beans; let soak 8 hours.

Drain beans, and return to Dutch oven. Add 1 quart water, consommé, and ham hock; bring to a boil. Place peppercorns and next 4 ingredients on a piece of cheesecloth; tie ends of cheesecloth securely. Add this bouquet garni to bean mixture. Cover, reduce heat, and simmer 1 hour.

Add 1 cup water and next 3 ingredients; cover and simmer 15 minutes. Add potato; cover mixture, and simmer 30 minutes or until vegetables are tender.

Remove ham hock from soup; let cool slightly. Chop meat, and add to soup. Discard ham bone and cheesecloth bag. Add hot sauce, salt, and pepper to soup. Stir well. **Yield: 3½ quarts.**

Bean 'n' Ham Soup Technique

A bouquet garni is a combination of herbs used to flavor soups; the herbs are tied in a cheese-cloth bag for easy removal before serving.

Spicy Three-Bean Soup

2 skinned chicken breast halves
3 cups water
1 (28-ounce) can whole tomatoes, undrained and chopped
1 (10-ounce) package frozen cut green beans
1 (10-ounce) package frozen baby lima beans
1 bay leaf
2 teaspoons Creole seasoning
1 teaspoon chili powder
1 teaspoon paprika
¼ teaspoon garlic powder
¼ teaspoon onion powder
¼ teaspoon ground red pepper
Dash of hot sauce
Dash of soy sauce
Dash of Worcestershire sauce
1 (15-ounce) can black beans, drained

Combine all ingredients, except black beans, in a Dutch oven. Bring to a boil over medium heat. Cover, reduce heat, and simmer 1 hour.

Remove chicken from soup; cool, bone, and cut into bite-size pieces. Return chicken to Dutch oven; add black beans, and heat thoroughly. **Yield 2½ quarts.**

Navy Bean Soup

Navy Bean Soup

1 cup dried navy beans
5 cups water
½ cup chopped celery
½ cup chopped onion
½ cup chopped carrot
1 tablespoon chopped fresh parsley
1 chicken-flavored bouillon cube
½ cup diced cooked ham
1 bay leaf

Sort and wash beans; place in a large Dutch oven. Cover with water 2 inches above beans; let soak 8 hours.

Drain beans, and return to Dutch oven. Add 5 cups water and next 5 ingredients. Bring to a boil; cover, reduce heat, and simmer 45 minutes.

Add ham and bay leaf; cover and simmer 30 additional minutes. Remove bay leaf before serving. **Yield: 1½ quarts.**

Bean and Barley Soup

2 pounds dried Great Northern beans
2 quarts water
1 cup fine barley
1 ham hock
2 cups coarsely chopped ham
1 pound ground beef, cooked and drained
1 large onion, chopped
8 cloves garlic, chopped
6 carrots, sliced
4 (10½-ounce) cans beef consommé, undiluted
1 to 1½ teaspoons salt
1 teaspoon pepper
¼ cup Worcestershire sauce
½ teaspoon hot sauce
2 fresh jalapeño peppers, split and seeded

Sort and wash beans; place in a large Dutch oven. Cover with water 2 inches above beans; let soak 8 hours.

Drain beans, and return to Dutch oven. Add 2 quarts water; bring to a boil. Add barley and remaining ingredients; cover, reduce heat, and simmer 2½ hours, stirring occasionally. **Yield: 5½ quarts.**

Note: Add additional water for a thinner consistency, if desired.

Lentil Soup

1 pound dried lentils
1 pound smoked sausage, thinly sliced
1 stalk celery, chopped
4 cloves garlic, minced
½ to 1 teaspoon salt
½ teaspoon black peppercorns
½ teaspoon ground cumin

Sort and wash lentils; place in a Dutch oven. Cover with water 2 inches above lentils; bring to a boil. Cover, reduce heat, and simmer 40 minutes or until tender.

Brown sausage in a heavy skillet; drain. Add sausage, celery, and remaining ingredients to lentils; simmer 5 minutes. Remove peppercorns before serving. **Yield: 2½ quarts.**

Beefy Lentil Soup

1 cup dried lentils
½ pound round steak, cut into 1-inch cubes
3 medium carrots, sliced
1 large onion, chopped
1 small hot pepper, chopped
1 teaspoon salt
1 teaspoon freshly ground pepper
2 tablespoons olive oil
2 bay leaves
Dash of dried basil
6½ cups water
1 (14½-ounce) can stewed tomatoes, undrained
1 (6-ounce) can tomato juice

Sort and wash dried lentils; place in a Dutch oven. Cover with water 2 inches above lentils; let soak 8 hours.

Drain beans, and return to Dutch oven. Add round steak and next 9 ingredients to beans. Bring to a boil; cover, reduce heat, and simmer 1 hour, stirring occasionally.

Add tomato and tomato juice; cover and simmer 30 additional minutes. Remove bay leaves. **Yield: 2 quarts.**

Guadalajara Soup

(pictured on page 481)

1¼ cups dried pinto beans
3½ to 4 pounds country-style pork ribs
2 tablespoons vegetable oil
1 cup finely chopped onion
2 cloves garlic, minced
4 cups water
2 (14½-ounce) cans ready-to-serve beef broth
2 teaspoons chili powder
1 teaspoon dried oregano
1 teaspoon ground cumin
4 cups thinly sliced carrot
1 (7-ounce) jar baby corn on the cob, drained
½ teaspoon salt
¼ teaspoon pepper
Condiments: sour cream, jalapeño salsa, chopped fresh cilantro (optional)

Sort and wash beans; place in a Dutch oven. Cover with water 2 inches above beans. Cover and bring to a boil; boil 2 minutes. Remove from heat; let stand, covered, 1 hour. Drain beans, and set aside.

Brown short ribs in oil in Dutch oven over medium heat. Remove short ribs, reserving drippings in Dutch oven. Cook onion and garlic in drippings over medium-high heat, stirring constantly, until onion is tender.

Add beans, short ribs, 4 cups water, and next 4 ingredients to Dutch oven. Bring to a boil; cover, reduce heat, and simmer 1½ hours or until short ribs are tender, stirring occasionally.

Remove short ribs; let cool slightly. Remove meat from bones; discard fat and bones. Chop meat. Skim fat from broth mixture.

Add chopped meat, carrot, corn, salt, and pepper to Dutch oven. Bring to a boil; cover, reduce heat, and simmer 30 minutes or until carrot is tender. Serve soup with condiments, if desired. **Yield: about 3 quarts.**

Taco Soup

1½ pounds lean ground beef
1 large onion, chopped
2 large cloves garlic, minced
1 (1.25-ounce) package taco seasoning mix
1 (28-ounce) can whole tomatoes, undrained and chopped
2 (16-ounce) cans red kidney beans, drained
1 (15-ounce) can tomato sauce
1 (10½-ounce) can condensed beef broth, undiluted
2 (4.5-ounce) cans chopped green chiles, drained
3 tablespoons chopped jalapeño pepper
1½ cups water
1 teaspoon ground cumin
1 teaspoon chili powder
Condiments: finely shredded iceberg lettuce, chopped tomato, corn chips, shredded Cheddar cheese

Brown ground beef, onion, and garlic in a Dutch oven, stirring until beef crumbles. Drain well, and return to Dutch oven. Add taco seasoning mix; stir well.

Add tomato and next 8 ingredients. Bring to a boil; cover, reduce heat, and simmer 30 minutes.

Ladle soup into bowls; serve with condiments. **Yield: 3¾ quarts.**

Taco Soup

Sausage, Bacon, and Bean Soup

Sausage, Bacon, and Bean Soup

¾ pound smoked sausage, cut into ¾-inch-thick slices
4 slices thick-sliced peppered bacon, cut into 1-inch pieces
2 medium onions, chopped
1 large green pepper, seeded and chopped
2 cloves garlic, minced
2 (15-ounce) cans kidney beans, drained
1 (28-ounce) can tomatoes, undrained and chopped
1 quart water
1 (8-ounce) can tomato sauce
1 bay leaf
½ teaspoon seasoned salt
½ teaspoon dried thyme
½ teaspoon pepper
2 cups peeled, coarsely chopped potato
¼ cup chopped fresh parsley

Cook sausage in a large skillet until browned; remove from heat, and set aside.

Cook bacon in a Dutch oven until crisp. Remove bacon, and set aside, reserving 1 tablespoon drippings in Dutch oven. Add onion, green pepper, and garlic to Dutch oven; cook 2 minutes, stirring constantly.

Add kidney beans and next 7 ingredients. Bring to a boil; cover, reduce heat, and simmer 30 minutes. Add chopped potato; cover and simmer 30 additional minutes.

Add reserved sausage; cover and simmer 30 to 40 minutes or until vegetables are tender. Remove bay leaf. Add bacon, and sprinkle with parsley before serving. **Yield: 3½ quarts.**

Mexican Pork and Bean Soup

1 pound boneless pork loin chops, cut into cubes
1 tablespoon butter or margarine, melted
1 tablespoon olive oil
2 medium onions, chopped
3 cloves garlic, minced
3 (14½-ounce) cans ready-to-serve chicken broth
3 (16-ounce) cans pinto beans, rinsed and drained
1¼ teaspoons dried oregano
¾ teaspoon cumin seeds
½ teaspoon pepper
Vegetable oil
12 (6-inch) corn tortillas, cut into 2- x ¼-inch strips
2 (3-ounce) packages cream cheese, cut into cubes
Condiments: shredded lettuce, chopped tomato, sliced green onions, chopped fresh cilantro

Cook pork in butter and olive oil in a Dutch oven over medium-high heat until browned. Remove pork with a slotted spoon, reserving drippings in Dutch oven. Drain pork on paper towels; set aside.

Cook onion and garlic in reserved drippings over medium heat, stirring constantly, 3 to 5 minutes or until onion is tender.

Add pork, chicken broth, and next 4 ingredients. Bring to a boil; cover, reduce heat, and simmer 20 to 30 minutes.

Pour oil to depth of 1 inch into a heavy skillet. Fry one-fourth of tortilla strips in hot oil over medium heat until browned. Remove strips; drain on paper towels. Repeat procedure with remaining tortilla strips.

Ladle soup into bowls; top with tortilla strips and cream cheese cubes. Serve with condiments. **Yield: 2¾ quarts.**

Italian Spinach Soup with Meatballs

3 quarts ready-to-serve chicken broth
2 stalks celery, cut into chunks
2 carrots, scraped and cut into chunks
1 large onion, quartered
½ teaspoon salt
1 pound lean ground beef
1½ slices bread, crumbled
1 large egg, lightly beaten
2 tablespoons grated Parmesan cheese
1½ tablespoons chopped fresh parsley
½ teaspoon salt
¼ teaspoon ground white pepper
1 (16-ounce) can crushed Italian-style
    tomatoes, undrained
1 (10-ounce) package frozen chopped spinach,
    thawed and drained
2 tablespoons grated Parmesan cheese
3 tablespoons olive oil
2 tablespoons lemon juice
2 teaspoons dried basil
4 cloves garlic, crushed

Combine first 5 ingredients in a large Dutch oven. Bring to a boil; reduce heat, and simmer, uncovered, 30 minutes. Remove vegetables, and discard. Set broth aside.

Combine ground beef and next 6 ingredients; shape into 1-inch meatballs, and cook in a large nonstick skillet over medium heat until browned. Drain on paper towels.

Bring broth to a boil; add meatballs. Reduce heat, and simmer 10 minutes. Stir in tomatoes and remaining ingredients; simmer 10 to 15 minutes. **Yield: 3 quarts.**

Steak Soup

2 tablespoons vegetable oil
2 pounds lean boneless round steak, cut into
    1-inch cubes
Salt and freshly ground pepper
1 medium onion, chopped
2 cloves garlic, minced
5 cups water
½ cup Worcestershire sauce
1 teaspoon cracked pepper
½ teaspoon paprika
2½ cups medium egg noodles, uncooked
    (about 6 ounces)
2 cups sliced fresh mushrooms
2 cups (8 ounces) shredded Cheddar cheese

Heat oil in a Dutch oven over medium-high heat. Add meat, and sprinkle generously with salt and pepper. Brown meat on all sides, stirring occasionally.

Add onion and garlic; cook 2 minutes, stirring occasionally. Add water and next 3 ingredients. Bring to a boil; cover, reduce heat, and simmer 1 hour and 15 minutes.

Stir in egg noodles and mushrooms. Bring mixture to a boil; cover, reduce heat, and simmer 30 minutes or until meat is tender and noodles are cooked.

Ladle soup into individual serving bowls; top with shredded cheese. **Yield: about 1¾ quarts.**

Steak Soup

Chunky Vegetable-Beef Soup

Chunky Vegetable-Beef Soup

3 pounds beef short ribs
2½ quarts water
3 stalks celery with leaves, thinly sliced
1 large onion, quartered
4 fresh parsley sprigs
1 tablespoon salt
12 black peppercorns
1 bay leaf
2 (28-ounce) cans whole tomatoes, undrained
1 cup shredded cabbage
1 cup thinly sliced leeks
1 medium potato, peeled and chopped
1 medium sweet potato, peeled and chopped
1 turnip, peeled and chopped
¾ cup scraped and thinly sliced carrot
¼ cup chopped fresh parsley
½ (10-ounce) package frozen baby lima beans
½ (10-ounce) package frozen whole kernel corn
½ cup ditalini (small tubular pasta), uncooked
1 medium zucchini, halved lengthwise and thinly sliced
½ (9-ounce) package frozen cut green beans
½ (10-ounce) package frozen English peas
1 tablespoon sugar
1 teaspoon salt
½ teaspoon pepper
½ teaspoon dried basil
½ teaspoon dried oregano

Combine first 8 ingredients in a large Dutch oven. Bring to a boil; cover, reduce heat, and simmer 2 hours. Remove from heat.

Remove short ribs, and let cool. Remove meat from bones; discard fat and bones. Cut meat into ½-inch pieces, and set aside.

Pour soup stock through a large wire-mesh strainer into a large bowl, discarding solids; skim off fat. Return stock to Dutch oven; add meat, tomatoes and next 7 ingredients. Bring to a boil; cover, reduce heat, and simmer 15 minutes.

Stir in lima beans, corn, and pasta; cover and simmer 5 minutes. Add zucchini and remaining ingredients; cover and simmer 10 minutes or until vegetables and pasta are tender. **Yield: 6 quarts.**

Ground Beef Soup

1 pound ground beef
1 cup chopped onion
2 cloves garlic, crushed
1 (30-ounce) jar chunky garden-style spaghetti sauce with mushrooms and peppers
1 (10½-ounce) can condensed beef broth, undiluted
2 cups water
1 cup sliced celery
1 teaspoon sugar
1 teaspoon salt
½ teaspoon freshly ground pepper
1 (10-ounce) can diced tomatoes and green chiles
1 (16-ounce) package frozen mixed vegetables

Cook first 3 ingredients in a large Dutch oven over medium heat until meat is browned, stirring to crumble. Drain and return meat to Dutch oven.

Add spaghetti sauce and next 6 ingredients. Bring to a boil; cover, reduce heat, and simmer 20 minutes, stirring occasionally.

Stir in tomatoes and vegetables; return to a boil. Cover and simmer 10 to 12 minutes or until vegetables are tender. **Yield: 3 quarts.**

Chicken Noodle Soup

1 (3½- to 4-pound) broiler-fryer, halved
2 stalks celery, halved
1 large onion, quartered
1 carrot, scraped and halved
1 turnip, peeled and halved
2 cloves garlic, crushed
1¼ teaspoons salt
¾ teaspoon pepper
¼ teaspoon dried tarragon
4 cups water
3 cups ready-to-serve chicken broth
4 ounces medium egg noodles, uncooked
1 large onion, chopped
2 stalks celery, sliced
2 carrots, scraped and sliced
½ teaspoon salt
½ teaspoon pepper
¼ teaspoon tarragon

Combine first 11 ingredients in a large Dutch oven, and bring mixture to a boil over high heat. Reduce heat, and cook 45 minutes or until chicken is tender.

Remove chicken from broth, reserving broth; set chicken aside to cool slightly.

Pour broth through a wire-mesh strainer into a large bowl; discard vegetables. Remove and discard fat from broth; return broth to Dutch oven.

Cook noodles according to package directions, omitting salt and fat; drain and set aside.

Skin and bone cooked chicken; chop chicken, and set aside.

Add chopped onion, sliced celery, and sliced carrot to chicken broth; bring to a boil over high heat. Reduce heat; simmer 15 minutes.

Stir in chopped chicken and noodles; add ½ teaspoon salt and remaining ingredients. Cook until thoroughly heated. **Yield: 2½ quarts.**

Garden Chicken Noodle Soup

2 (8-ounce) chicken breast halves, skinned
1½ quarts water
1 cup frozen green peas
1 medium-size yellow squash, thinly sliced
½ cup thinly sliced carrot
½ cup chopped celery
½ cup chopped onion
1 tablespoon chicken-flavored bouillon
   granules
1 teaspoon salt
¼ teaspoon pepper
2 cups uncooked medium egg noodles

Arrange chicken in a deep 3-quart baking dish; add water. Stir in green peas and next 7 ingredients.

Cover with heavy-duty plastic wrap; fold back a small edge of wrap to allow steam to escape. Microwave at HIGH 20 to 25 minutes or until boiling.

Stir in noodles. Reduce to MEDIUM (50% power); cover and microwave 20 to 30 minutes or until noodles and chicken are tender, stirring every 10 minutes.

Remove chicken from soup; let cool. Skim excess fat from soup. Bone chicken, and cut meat into bite-size pieces; return chicken to soup.

Cover and microwave at HIGH 5 to 6 minutes or until soup is thoroughly heated. Serve immediately. **Yield: 2 quarts.**

Garden Chicken Noodle Soup

Chicken-Rice Soup

broth. Let chicken cool. Bone chicken; coarsely chop meat, and set aside.

Remove and discard fat from broth. Bring broth to a boil. Add rice and next 7 ingredients; cover and cook 20 minutes or until rice and vegetables are tender, stirring occasionally.

Stir in chicken, and cook until thoroughly heated. **Yield: 2¼ quarts.**

Mexican Chicken Soup

1 (3- to 3½-pound) broiler-fryer
1½ quarts water
3 stalks celery
1 medium onion, sliced
1 teaspoon salt
⅛ teaspoon pepper
1 tablespoon plus 1 teaspoon chicken-flavored bouillon granules
3 medium carrots, thinly sliced
1 medium onion, chopped
1 (16-ounce) can tomatoes, undrained and chopped
1 small zucchini, thinly sliced
1 cup frozen English peas

Combine first 6 ingredients in a Dutch oven; bring to a boil. Cover, reduce heat, and simmer 1 hour or until chicken is tender. Remove chicken from broth; let cool. Bone chicken; cut into bite-size pieces.

Pour broth through a wire-mesh strainer into a large bowl, discarding vegetables. Remove and discard fat from broth; return broth to Dutch oven. Add bouillon granules and next 3 ingredients; cover and simmer 30 minutes.

Add chicken, zucchini, and peas; cover and simmer 10 to 15 additional minutes or until vegetables are tender. **Yield: 1½ quarts.**

Chicken-Rice Soup

1 (2½- to 3-pound) broiler-fryer, cut in half and skinned
2 quarts water
1 cup long-grain rice, uncooked
2 carrots, scraped and sliced
1 stalk celery, chopped
1 medium onion, chopped
2 cloves garlic, crushed
1 tablespoon chicken-flavored bouillon granules
2 teaspoons salt
¼ teaspoon pepper

Combine chicken and water in a Dutch oven; bring to a boil. Cover, reduce heat, and simmer 40 minutes or until chicken is tender.

Remove chicken from Dutch oven, and reserve

Turkey-Rice Soup

¾ pound turkey tenderloin, cut into bite-size
    pieces
1½ quarts water
2 stalks celery, sliced
1 medium onion, chopped
2 chicken-flavored bouillon cubes
1 teaspoon salt
¼ teaspoon poultry seasoning
1 bay leaf
½ cup long-grain rice, uncooked
2 carrots, scraped and sliced

Combine first 8 ingredients in a Dutch oven.
Bring to a boil; cover, reduce heat, and simmer
40 minutes.

Add rice and carrot; cover and simmer 20
additional minutes or until rice is tender. Remove
bay leaf. **Yield: 1½ quarts.**

Turkey-Noodle Soup

1 turkey carcass
4 quarts water
½ cup finely chopped onion
½ cup finely chopped celery
1 teaspoon salt
¼ teaspoon pepper
4 ounces medium egg noodles, uncooked

Place turkey carcass and water in a large
Dutch oven; bring to a boil. Cover, reduce heat,
and simmer 1 hour.

Remove carcass from broth, and pick meat
from bones; set meat aside. Measure 8 cups
broth, and return it to Dutch oven. (Chill remaining broth for other uses.)

Add onion and next 3 ingredients to broth in
Dutch oven. Bring to a boil; cover, reduce heat,
and simmer 1 hour.

Stir in turkey and noodles; simmer, uncovered, 8 minutes or until noodles are tender.
Yield: 2 quarts.

Turkey-Vegetable Soup

1 turkey carcass
4 quarts water
1 small onion, chopped
2 tablespoons butter or margarine, melted
2 medium potatoes, peeled and diced
2 carrots, scraped and diced
½ cup chopped celery
1 teaspoon salt
⅛ teaspoon pepper
2 tablespoons all-purpose flour
2½ cups milk, divided

Place turkey carcass and water in a large
Dutch oven; bring to a boil. Cover, reduce heat,
and simmer 1 hour.

Remove carcass from broth, and pick meat
from bones; set meat aside. Measure and set aside
2 cups turkey broth. (Chill remaining broth for
other uses.)

Cook onion in butter in Dutch oven over
medium heat, stirring constantly, until tender.
Add 2 cups broth, turkey, potato, and next 4
ingredients. Bring mixture to a boil; cover, reduce
heat, and simmer 10 minutes or until vegetables
are tender.

Combine flour and ½ cup milk, stirring until
smooth; add remaining milk, and stir into turkey
mixture. Cook over medium heat until soup is
slightly thickened, stirring occasionally. **Yield:
1¾ quarts.**

Louisiana Oyster and Artichoke Soup

2 (12-ounce) containers fresh Standard
    oysters, undrained
½ cup finely chopped shallots
1 bay leaf
⅛ to ¼ teaspoon ground red pepper
Pinch of dried thyme
3 tablespoons butter or margarine, melted
2 tablespoons all-purpose flour
1 (14½-ounce) can ready-to-serve chicken
    broth
1 (14-ounce) can artichoke hearts, drained
    and cut into eighths
1 tablespoon chopped fresh parsley
½ teaspoon salt
⅛ to ¼ teaspoon hot sauce
½ cup whipping cream

Drain oysters, reserving 1 cup liquid. Cut each oyster into fourths; set oysters and liquid aside.

Cook shallots and next 3 ingredients in butter in a Dutch oven over medium heat, stirring constantly, until shallots are tender.

Add flour, stirring until smooth. Cook, stirring constantly, 1 minute. Gradually add chicken broth and oyster liquid; simmer, stirring occasionally, 15 minutes. Remove bay leaf.

Add oysters, artichoke hearts, and next 3 ingredients; simmer mixture 10 minutes. Stir in whipping cream; cook until thoroughly heated. **Yield: 1½ quarts.**

Microwave Directions:

Drain oysters, reserving 1 cup liquid. Cut each oyster into fourths, and set oysters and reserved liquid aside.

Place chopped shallots, bay leaf, ground red pepper, and thyme in a 3-quart baking dish. Add melted butter, and microwave at HIGH 3 minutes, stirring after 2 minutes.

Add flour, stirring until smooth. Gradually add broth and reserved oyster liquid, stirring well.

Microwave at HIGH 9 to 10 minutes, stirring after 5 minutes. Remove bay leaf.

Add oysters, artichoke hearts, and next 3 ingredients; microwave at HIGH 5 to 8 minutes, stirring mixture after 4 minutes. Stir in whipping cream. Serve immediately.

Artichoke-Seafood Soup

2 (12-ounce) containers fresh Standard
    oysters, undrained
¼ cup butter or margarine
¼ cup all-purpose flour
2 cups milk
1½ cups half-and-half
1¼ cups freshly grated Parmesan cheese,
    divided
1 (14-ounce) can artichoke hearts, drained
    and coarsely chopped
1 (12-ounce) container fresh lump crabmeat
2 tablespoons chopped fresh chives
¼ teaspoon pepper
2 tablespoons Sauterne
Additional chopped fresh chives

Drain oysters, reserving ½ cup liquid; set oysters aside.

Melt butter in a 3-quart saucepan over low heat; add flour, stirring until smooth. Cook, stirring constantly, until golden. Gradually stir in milk and half-and-half.

Add reserved oyster liquid and ¾ cup Parmesan cheese. Cook over medium heat, stirring constantly, until thickened and bubbly.

Add oysters, chopped artichokes, and next 3 ingredients; simmer mixture 4 to 5 minutes or until edges of oysters curl and soup is thoroughly heated. Stir in wine.

Ladle soup into individual serving bowls. Sprinkle with remaining ½ cup Parmesan cheese and chopped fresh chives. **Yield: about 2 quarts.**

Artichoke-Seafood Soup

Southern Bouillabaisse

1 large onion, coarsely chopped
2 cloves garlic, minced
¼ cup butter or margarine, melted
2 tablespoons all-purpose flour
2 cups water
1 cup coarsely chopped fresh tomato
1 (8-ounce) can tomato sauce
½ cup dry sherry
1 bay leaf
1 teaspoon salt
¼ teaspoon ground red pepper
¼ teaspoon dried thyme
⅛ teaspoon ground allspice
Pinch of ground saffron
1 pound unpeeled medium-size fresh shrimp
2 pounds red snapper, skinned and cut into
   large pieces
1 (12-ounce) container fresh Standard oysters,
   undrained
Toasted French bread

Cook onion and garlic in butter in a large
Dutch oven over medium heat, stirring constantly, until tender. Add flour, stirring until smooth.
Cook 1 minute, stirring constantly. Gradually stir
in water.

Add tomato and next 8 ingredients. Bring mixture to a boil; reduce heat, and simmer, uncovered, 30 minutes.

Peel shrimp, and devein, if desired. Add
shrimp, fish, and oysters; simmer 5 minutes or
until shrimp turn pink and fish flakes easily when
tested with a fork. Remove bay leaf. Serve each
portion over a slice of toasted French bread.
Yield: 2½ quarts.

Gulf Coast Cioppino

20 fresh mussels
20 fresh clams
¼ cup butter or margarine
1 tablespoon olive oil
2 cups chopped celery
2 cups chopped green pepper
1 cup chopped green onions
2 cloves garlic, crushed
1 (16-ounce) can crushed tomatoes, undrained
1 (15-ounce) can tomato sauce
1 to 1½ tablespoons dried Italian seasoning
1 to 1½ teaspoons ground red pepper
1½ teaspoons paprika
1 teaspoon sugar
1 teaspoon salt
½ teaspoon ground black pepper
2 (14½-ounce) cans ready-to-serve chicken
   broth
1 pound grouper, amberjack, or sea bass
   fillets, cut into bite-size pieces

Scrub mussels with a brush, removing beards.
Wash clams. Discard any opened mussels and
clams. Set aside.

Melt butter in a large Dutch oven over medium heat. Add olive oil and next 4 ingredients;
cook, stirring constantly, 5 minutes or until vegetables are tender.

Stir in tomatoes and next 7 ingredients; cook
mixture 2 to 3 minutes, stirring occasionally. Stir
in chicken broth.

Bring tomato mixture to a boil; reduce heat,
and simmer 45 minutes, stirring occasionally.

Stir in mussels, clams, and fish; cook 3 to 4
minutes, stirring occasionally. (Mussels and
clams should open during cooking. Discard any
unopened shells.) Serve immediately. **Yield:
about 3 quarts.**

Stews and Burgoos

Seasoned with herbs and spices and simmered to perfection, heart-warming stews and burgoos are nutritious as well as simple to prepare. And most of them require only one pot for cooking.

Irish Stew, White Wine Stew with Dumplings, Mexican Stew Olé

Old-Fashioned Burgoo, Kentucky Burgoo, Virginia Brunswick Stew, Lamb Stew

Hearty Lamb Stew, Beef or Lamb Stew with Popovers, Venison Sausage Stew

Pancho Villa Stew, Holiday Oyster Stew, Bama Brunswick Stew

Burgundy Beef Stew (page 508)

Burgundy Beef Stew

(pictured on page 507)

1 cup Burgundy or other dry red wine
1 (8-ounce) can tomato sauce
2 tablespoons red wine vinegar
2 cloves garlic, crushed
2 bay leaves
½ teaspoon pepper
¼ teaspoon ground allspice
2½ pounds beef stew meat, cut into 1-inch
   cubes
¼ cup olive oil
2 (10½-ounce) cans condensed beef broth,
   undiluted
1 (9-ounce) package frozen green beans
½ pound fresh mushrooms, halved
1 medium onion, coarsely chopped
3 carrots, scraped and diagonally sliced
2 tablespoons all-purpose flour
2 tablespoons water

Combine first 7 ingredients in a large shallow dish; stir well. Add stew meat; cover and marinate in refrigerator 8 hours.

Drain meat, reserving marinade. Remove bay leaves; set marinade aside.

Heat olive oil in a Dutch oven over medium heat; add meat, and cook until browned on all sides. Drain and return meat to Dutch oven.

Add reserved marinade and beef broth to Dutch oven. Bring to a boil; cover, reduce heat, and simmer 1½ hours. Add green beans and next 3 ingredients, stirring well; cover and cook 30 minutes or until vegetables are tender.

Combine flour and water, stirring until smooth. Stir into stew, and cook until slightly thickened. **Yield: 2¼ quarts.**

Irish Stew

1 cup dry red wine
1 clove garlic, minced
2 bay leaves
1 teaspoon salt
½ teaspoon freshly ground pepper
¼ teaspoon dried thyme
3 pounds beef stew meat, cut into 1-inch
   cubes
¼ cup olive oil
2 (10½-ounce) cans condensed beef broth,
   undiluted
6 carrots, scraped and cut into 2-inch slices
12 small boiling onions
6 medium potatoes, peeled and halved

Combine first 6 ingredients in a large shallow dish; stir well. Add stew meat; cover and marinate in refrigerator 8 hours.

Drain meat, reserving marinade. Remove bay leaves; set marinade aside.

Heat oil in a Dutch oven over medium heat; brown beef in oil. Add beef broth and reserved marinade; bring to a boil. Cover, reduce heat, and simmer 1½ hours.

Add carrot, onions, and potato; cover and cook 30 minutes. **Yield: 2½ quarts.**

Meats for Stew

Using stew meat or less tender cuts of beef, lamb, or pork is economical when making stew. The long simmering time of most of these dishes will help tenderize the meat.

Irish Stew

White Wine Stew with Dumplings

White Wine Stew with Dumplings

¼ cup plus 1 tablespoon flour
1 teaspoon salt
½ teaspoon pepper
1¼ pounds boneless beef chuck roast, cut into
    1-inch cubes
3 tablespoons butter or margarine
2 cups water
1½ cups dry white wine
1 cup chopped onion
2 cloves garlic, minced
2 teaspoons beef-flavored bouillon granules

1 bay leaf
⅛ teaspoon dried thyme
2 medium carrots, scraped and sliced
1 large potato, peeled and cubed
1 cup frozen green peas
¼ cup sliced celery
1 cup biscuit mix
1 large egg, beaten
3 tablespoons milk
1 tablespoon plus 1 teaspoon minced fresh
    parsley

Combine first 3 ingredients; dredge beef in flour mixture. Place a 10-inch browning skillet in microwave oven; preheat, uncovered, at HIGH 6 minutes.

Add butter to hot skillet, tilting to coat surface. Add beef to skillet, stirring well. Microwave, uncovered, at HIGH 6 minutes or until beef is browned, stirring after 3 minutes.

Combine beef, water, and next 6 ingredients in a deep 3-quart baking dish. Cover with heavy-duty plastic wrap; fold back a small edge of wrap to allow steam to escape. Microwave at HIGH 5 minutes.

Stir in carrot and next 3 ingredients. Reduce to MEDIUM (50% power); cover and microwave 75 to 80 minutes or until vegetables and beef are tender, stirring every 20 minutes. Remove bay leaf.

Combine biscuit mix and next 3 ingredients, stirring well. Drop mixture by heaping table-spoonfuls on top of stew. Increase to HIGH; cover and microwave 3½ to 4 minutes or until dumplings are set, but still moist. Let stand, covered, 5 minutes. **Yield: 2 quarts.**

Mexican Stew Olé

1½ pounds beef stew meat, cut into 1-inch cubes
¼ cup all-purpose flour
¼ cup vegetable oil
1 large onion, chopped
1 clove garlic, minced
2 (4.5-ounce) cans chopped green chiles, drained
½ teaspoon salt
1 teaspoon coarsely ground pepper
2 tablespoons red wine vinegar
1 cup dry red wine
1 (15-ounce) can tomato sauce
1 cup water

Dredge stew meat in flour; cook in hot oil in a Dutch oven over medium heat until meat is browned.

Add onion and remaining ingredients; stir well. Cover, reduce heat, and simmer1 hour, stirring occasionally. **Yield: 1½ quarts.**

Red Chili Stew

1½ pounds lean beef chuck roast, cut into 1-inch cubes
2 cups water
3 tablespoons ground red chile or chili powder
1 teaspoon salt
1 teaspoon ground oregano
1 clove garlic, crushed
3 large tomatoes, chopped

Combine beef and water in a Dutch oven; bring to a boil over medium-high heat. Cover, reduce heat, and simmer 45 minutes or until tender, stirring occasionally.

Stir in ground chile and remaining ingredients; cook 30 additional minutes. **Yield: 1 quart.**

Flavor Boosters

• Madeira or sherry enhances the flavor of seafood or chicken soups and stews while red wine or beer adds flavor to beef stews.

• Leftover pan juices or cooking liquids from meats and vegetables enrich soups and stews.

• Some fresh herbs lose flavor when cooked a long time. Taste the stew before serving, and add additional herbs, if necessary.

Beef Stew with Popovers

Beef or Lamb Stew with Popovers

1 medium onion, chopped
1 clove garlic, crushed
1 tablespoon olive oil
¼ cup all-purpose flour
2 (14½-ounce) cans ready-to-serve chicken
     broth
½ cup dry white wine
2 tablespoons lemon juice
1 teaspoon salt
¼ teaspoon dried marjoram
¼ teaspoon dried rosemary
⅛ teaspoon pepper
1 bay leaf
12 pearl onions
6 small new potatoes, peeled and thinly sliced
3 carrots, scraped and cut into 1-inch pieces
3 cups cubed cooked beef or lamb
Popovers
Garnish: fresh rosemary sprigs

Cook onion and garlic in olive oil in a Dutch
oven over medium heat, stirring constantly, until
tender. Sprinkle with flour, stirring well.

Stir in chicken broth and next 7 ingredients.
Bring to a boil; cover, reduce heat, and simmer
30 minutes.

Add pearl onions, potato, and carrot; cover
and simmer 20 to 30 minutes or until vegetables
are tender. Remove bay leaf.

Stir in beef or lamb, and cook until thoroughly
heated. Serve with Popovers. Garnish, if desired.
Yield: 1¾ quarts.

Popovers

1 cup all-purpose flour
¼ teaspoon salt
1 cup milk
2 large eggs, lightly beaten

Combine all ingredients; beat at low speed of
an electric mixer just until smooth.

Heat a well-greased 3½-inch muffin pan or
popover pan in a 450° oven 3 minutes or until a
drop of water sizzles when dropped in pan. Remove pan from oven; fill half full with batter.

Bake at 450° for 15 minutes. Reduce heat to
350°, and bake 20 to 25 additional minutes. Serve
immediately. **Yield: 6 popovers.**

Lamb Stew

Juice of 2 lemons
3 pounds boneless lamb shoulder, cubed
6 cups cold water
4 medium potatoes, peeled and quartered
3 medium onions, sliced
3 to 4 cloves garlic, chopped
2 chicken-flavored bouillon cubes
½ teaspoon salt
½ teaspoon freshly ground pepper
6 cups water
8 small boiling onions, sliced
8 small new potatoes, peeled and quartered
8 baby carrots, scraped and cut in half
1½ teaspoons minced fresh thyme or
     ½ teaspoon dried thyme

Drizzle lemon juice over lamb, and let stand 10
minutes. Place lamb in a large Dutch oven; add 6
cups cold water. Bring to a boil; reduce heat, and
simmer 5 minutes. Drain and discard liquid. Rinse
lamb and Dutch oven with cold water.

Return lamb to Dutch oven; add 4 potatoes
and next 6 ingredients. Bring to a boil; reduce
heat, and simmer, uncovered, 1½ hours.

Remove potatoes and onions; place in container of a food processor or blender. Add ¼ cup
cooking liquid, and process until smooth; stir into
lamb mixture.

Add 8 onions and remaining ingredients; cover
and simmer 30 minutes. **Yield: 3½ quarts.**

Hearty Lamb Stew

Hearty Lamb Stew

2 pounds boneless lamb or top round beef
    steak, cut into 1½-inch cubes
¼ cup all-purpose flour
1 clove garlic, crushed
2 tablespoons vegetable oil
3 cups water
1 (8-ounce) can tomato sauce
1 tablespoon beef-flavored bouillon granules
1 teaspoon salt
¼ teaspoon pepper
1 teaspoon dried thyme
1 teaspoon dried parsley flakes
1 bay leaf
4 medium potatoes, peeled and cubed
12 carrots, scraped and sliced
1 (10-ounce) package frozen English peas

Dredge meat in flour. Brown meat and garlic in oil in a large Dutch oven over medium heat, stirring constantly.

Add 3 cups water and remaining ingredients.

Bring to a boil; cover, reduce heat, and simmer 1 hour or until meat is tender. Remove bay leaf. **Yield: 2 quarts.**

Note: Stew may be frozen in an airtight container up to 3 months.

Pancho Villa Stew

½ pound chorizo, casings removed
2 pounds boneless pork loin, cut into 1-inch
    cubes
¼ cup all-purpose flour
2 tablespoons vegetable oil
3 (14½-ounce) cans ready-to-serve chicken
    broth
1 (14½-ounce) can whole tomatoes, drained
    and chopped
3 (4.5-ounce) cans chopped green chiles,
    undrained
1 large purple onion, sliced into rings
3 cloves garlic, crushed
2 teaspoons ground cumin
2 teaspoons cocoa
1 teaspoon dried oregano
¼ teaspoon salt
1 (2-inch) stick cinnamon
2 (15-ounce) cans black beans, rinsed and
    drained
1 (15½-ounce) can white hominy, rinsed and
    drained
1 (10-ounce) package frozen whole kernel
    corn
½ cup beer or tequila
Flour tortillas
Butter or margarine

Brown chorizo in a Dutch oven, stirring until
it crumbles; drain well, and set aside.

Dredge pork in flour. Brown pork in oil in
Dutch oven over medium heat. Stir in chorizo,
chicken broth, and next 9 ingredients. Bring to a
boil; reduce heat, and simmer 1 hour.

Stir in black beans and next 3 ingredients;
cover and simmer 30 minutes. Remove cinnamon
stick. Set stew aside, and keep warm.

Wrap tortillas tightly in aluminum foil; bake
at 350° for 15 minutes or until thoroughly heated.
Spread warm tortillas with butter, and serve with
stew. **Yield: 1 gallon.**

Venison Sausage Stew

2 pounds venison summer sausage, cut into
    ¼-inch slices
1 large onion, chopped
1 green pepper, seeded and chopped
2 tablespoons butter or margarine, melted
2 (14½-ounce) cans stewed tomatoes,
    undrained
2 cups diced carrot
2 cups cubed unpeeled potato
1 teaspoon dried thyme
1 teaspoon dried oregano
1 bay leaf
1 (17-ounce) can whole kernel corn, drained
1 tablespoon all-purpose flour
¼ cup water

Cook first 3 ingredients in butter in a large
Dutch oven until sausage is browned. Drain and
return to Dutch oven.

Add tomatoes and next 5 ingredients. Bring to
a boil; cover, reduce heat, and simmer 30 minutes, stirring occasionally. Add corn; cook until
thoroughly heated.

Combine flour and water, stirring until
smooth; stir into sausage mixture. Cook, stirring
constantly, until thickened. Remove bay leaf.
Yield: 2½ quarts.

Note: You may substitute other types of summer sausage for venison sausage.

What's Chorizo?

Chorizo is a coarsely ground pork
sausage that's seasoned with lots of
garlic and chili powder. It provides a
spicy flavor to many Mexican and
Spanish recipes.

Venison Stew

2 pounds boneless venison, cubed
½ cup all-purpose flour
¼ cup bacon drippings
4 carrots, cut into ½-inch slices
2 (10½-ounce) cans beef broth, undiluted
2 cups dry red wine
2 bay leaves
1 (10½-ounce) can French onion soup,
  undiluted
1 large onion, coarsely chopped
1 large green pepper, seeded and coarsely
  chopped
¼ teaspoon salt
¼ teaspoon pepper
Hot cooked rice or biscuits (optional)

Dredge venison in flour; brown in hot bacon
drippings in a large Dutch oven.

Add carrot and next 8 ingredients; cover,
reduce heat, and simmer 2 hours. Remove bay
leaves. Serve over rice or biscuits, if desired.
Yield: 2½ quarts.

Hunter's Stew

1½ pounds boneless venison, cubed
½ pound smoked sausage, cut into ½-inch
  slices
2 tablespoons vegetable oil
½ cup chopped onion
½ cup chopped celery
2 (28-ounce) cans tomatoes, chopped
1 (12-ounce) can beer
1 teaspoon salt
1 teaspoon sugar
½ teaspoon dried rosemary
½ teaspoon dried basil
½ teaspoon freshly ground pepper
2 carrots, diced
2 medium potatoes, cubed

Brown venison and sausage in oil in a large
Dutch oven. Add onion and celery; cook, stirring
constantly, until onion is tender.

Add tomato and next 6 ingredients; cover,
reduce heat, and simmer 30 minutes. Add carrot;
cook, uncovered, 30 minutes. Add potato, and
cook 30 additional minutes or until tender. **Yield:
about 2 quarts.**

Frogmore Stew

¼ cup Old Bay seasoning
4 pounds small red potatoes
2 pounds kielbasa or hot, smoked link
  sausage, cut into 1½-inch slices
6 ears fresh corn, halved
4 pounds unpeeled large fresh shrimp
Additional Old Bay seasoning
Commercial cocktail sauce

Fill large container of a propane cooker
halfway with water; add ¼ cup Old Bay seasoning. Bring to a boil, following manufacturer's
instructions.

Add potatoes; return to a boil, and cook 10
minutes. Add sausage and corn; return to a boil,
and cook 10 minutes or until potatoes are tender.

Add shrimp; cook 3 to 5 minutes or until
shrimp turn pink.

Remove potatoes, sausage, corn, and shrimp
with a slotted spoon onto a serving platter or
newspaper-lined table. Serve with additional Old
Bay seasoning and cocktail sauce. **Yield: 12
servings.**

Note: Frogmore Stew, a hallmark of Low-
country hospitality, is a casual way to entertain a
crowd. It may be cooked indoors in a large Dutch
oven on a cooktop over high heat, if desired.

Potato-Oyster Stew

1 (12-ounce) container fresh Standard oysters,
    undrained
1 medium-size red potato,
    peeled and cubed
3 cups water
½ teaspoon salt
1 medium onion, chopped
1 stalk celery, chopped
⅓ cup butter or margarine, melted
¼ cup all-purpose flour
2 cups half-and-half
¼ teaspoon garlic powder
¼ teaspoon pepper
2 teaspoons chopped fresh parsley
Garnish: chopped fresh parsley

Drain oysters, reserving liquid. Using kitchen shears, cut through oysters 6 to 8 times. Set aside.

Combine potato, water, and salt in a medium saucepan. Bring to a boil; cover, reduce heat, and simmer 15 minutes or until tender. Drain, reserving liquid and potato.

Cook onion and celery in butter in a 3-quart saucepan until tender. Stir in flour, and cook 1 minute, stirring constantly.

Add reserved potato liquid and half-and-half gradually; cook over medium heat, stirring constantly, until mixture slightly thickens.

Stir in potato, oysters, reserved oyster liquid, garlic powder, and next 2 ingredients. Simmer 8 to 10 minutes or until edges of oysters curl. Garnish, if desired. **Yield: 1½ quarts.**

Potato-Oyster Stew

Black-Eyed Pea Stew

Holiday Oyster Stew

2 tablespoons butter or margarine
1½ tablespoons all-purpose flour
3 cups milk
1 cup half-and-half
1 (12-ounce) container fresh Standard oysters, undrained
2 tablespoons butter or margarine
1½ teaspoons salt
Dash of hot sauce

Melt 2 tablespoons butter in a heavy saucepan over low heat; add flour, stirring until smooth. Cook 1 minute, stirring constantly.

Add milk and half-and-half gradually; cook over medium heat, stirring constantly, until mixture is bubbly.

Add oysters with liquid and remaining ingredients. Reduce heat, and simmer, stirring constantly, 5 to 8 minutes or until edges of oysters curl. **Yield: about 1¼ quarts.**

Black-Eyed Pea Stew

1 (16-ounce) package dried black-eyed peas
1 meaty ham hock
1 (10½-ounce) can beef consommé, undiluted
2 bay leaves
6 cups water, divided
3 stalks celery, chopped
1 large onion, chopped
1 large green pepper, seeded and chopped
2 cups chopped cooked ham
2 tablespoons ketchup
1 tablespoon Worcestershire sauce
1 cup thinly sliced green onions
½ teaspoon pepper
¼ teaspoon hot sauce

Sort and wash peas. Combine peas, ham hock, consommé, bay leaves, and 4 cups water in a Dutch oven. Bring to a boil; cover, reduce heat, and simmer 1 hour, stirring occasionally.

Add remaining 2 cups water, celery, and next 5 ingredients to pea mixture. Cover, reduce heat, and simmer 1 hour and 15 minutes or until peas and vegetables are tender.

Remove ham hock from stew; cool slightly. Remove meat from bone; discard fat and bone. Chop meat, and return to stew. Remove bay leaves.

Stir in green onions, pepper, and hot sauce; cook until thoroughly heated. **Yield: about 3 quarts.**

Minestrone

3 large potatoes, peeled and cut into cubes
2 small onions, chopped
6 carrots, scraped and cut into chunks
1 small zucchini, cut into chunks
2 cloves garlic, minced
1 (10-ounce) package frozen chopped spinach
2 cups rotini (corkscrew pasta)
1½ quarts water
1 (18-ounce) can tomato paste
1 cup water
1 (15-ounce) can red kidney beans, undrained
1 (8-ounce) can cut green beans, undrained
1 (8½-ounce) can English peas, undrained
1½ to 2 teaspoons dried oregano
1 teaspoon dried basil
½ teaspoon dried tarragon
½ teaspoon dried thyme
1 bay leaf
Grated Parmesan cheese

Combine first 8 ingredients in a large Dutch oven; bring to a boil. Cover, reduce heat, and simmer 10 minutes or until potatoes are tender.

Stir tomato paste and 1 cup water into potato mixture. Add kidney beans and next 7 ingredients; simmer 5 minutes.

Remove bay leaf. Sprinkle each serving with Parmesan cheese. **Yield: 5 quarts.**

Bama Brunswick Stew

1 (2½- to 3-pound) broiler-fryer
1 (2- to 2½-pound) boneless pork loin roast
1 (2-pound) beef chuck roast
2½ quarts water
3 large potatoes, peeled and finely chopped
3 large onions, finely chopped
1 (28-ounce) can tomatoes, undrained and
    chopped
1 (17-ounce) can cream-style corn
1 (14-ounce) bottle ketchup
1 small hot pepper
¼ cup dry red wine
2 to 3 tablespoons lemon juice
2 tablespoons dry sherry
1½ teaspoons paprika
1 teaspoon brown sugar
1 teaspoon black pepper
½ teaspoon ground red pepper
½ teaspoon dried red pepper flakes

Combine first 4 ingredients in a large Dutch oven; cover and bring to a boil. Reduce heat, and simmer 1 hour or until meat is tender.

Remove meat from broth, reserving broth. Cool meat completely. Remove meat from bones. Grind meat in food processor or food grinder. Skim fat from broth.

Add potato and onion to broth; cook over medium heat 20 to 25 minutes or until tender.

Add meat, tomato, and remaining ingredients; bring mixture to a boil. Reduce heat; simmer, uncovered, 2½ hours, stirring often. Add additional water for a thinner consistency, if desired. **Yield: 1½ gallons.**

Georgia Brunswick Stew

½ cup butter or margarine
3 cups chopped cooked chicken
3 cups chopped potato
2 cups chopped smoked pork (½ pound)
1 cup chopped onion
2 (14½-ounce) cans ready-to-serve chicken
    broth
2 (14½-ounce) cans stewed tomatoes
1 (16-ounce) can lima beans, drained
1 (17-ounce) can cream-style corn
1 (8½-ounce) can English peas, drained
¼ cup liquid smoke
Barbecue Sauce

Melt butter in a large Dutch oven. Stir in chicken and next 4 ingredients; bring to a boil. Reduce heat, and simmer, uncovered, 20 minutes.

Add tomatoes and remaining ingredients to Dutch oven; bring mixture to a boil. Reduce heat, and simmer, uncovered, 2 hours, stirring occasionally. **Yield: 3 quarts.**

Barbecue Sauce

¼ cup butter or margarine, melted
1¾ cups ketchup
¼ cup firmly packed brown sugar
¼ cup prepared mustard
¼ cup white vinegar
2 tablespoons Worcestershire sauce
1 to 2 tablespoons hot sauce
1 tablespoon liquid smoke
1½ teaspoons lemon juice
1½ teaspoons minced garlic
1 teaspoon coarsely ground black pepper
½ teaspoon crushed red pepper

Combine all ingredients in a large heavy saucepan. Cook over low heat 25 to 30 minutes, stirring often. **Yield: 1½ cups.**

Georgia Brunswick Stew

Virginia Brunswick Stew

Virginia Brunswick Stew

1 (3-pound) broiler-fryer
2 stalks celery, cut into 1-inch pieces
1 small onion, quartered
7 cups water, divided
2 (10-ounce) packages frozen baby lima beans
2 (10-ounce) packages frozen whole kernel corn
1 cup chopped onion
2 (28-ounce) cans whole tomatoes, undrained and chopped
1 (8-ounce) can whole tomatoes, undrained and chopped
3 medium potatoes, peeled and diced
2 tablespoons butter or margarine
1 tablespoon salt
1 to 1½ teaspoons black pepper
½ to 1 teaspoon ground red pepper
10 saltine crackers, crumbled

Combine broiler-fryer, celery, onion, and 5 cups water in a large Dutch oven or stockpot; bring to a boil. Cover, reduce heat, and simmer mixture 1 hour.

Remove chicken, celery, and onion from broth, reserving broth in Dutch oven; discard celery and onion. Cool chicken; skin, bone, and coarsely chop meat. Skim fat from broth.

Add chicken, lima beans, and next 9 ingredients to broth; bring to a boil. Reduce heat, and simmer, uncovered, about 4½ hours or until desired consistency, stirring often.

Add remaining 2 cups water as needed. Add cracker crumbs, and cook 15 additional minutes. **Yield: 3½ quarts.**

Brunswick Chicken Stew

1 (2½- to 3-pound) broiler-fryer
1 tablespoon salt
2 quarts water
¼ pound cooked pork or ham, cut into cubes
2 large onions, chopped
1 green pepper, seeded and chopped
2 tablespoons chopped fresh parsley
1 (16-ounce) can tomatoes, undrained and chopped
1 (16-ounce) can whole kernel corn, drained
1 (10-ounce) package frozen lima beans
1 (10-ounce) package frozen sliced okra
1 teaspoon salt
½ teaspoon black pepper
½ teaspoon dried thyme
1 bay leaf
1¼ teaspoons hot sauce

Combine first 3 ingredients in a large Dutch oven; bring to a boil. Cover, reduce heat, and simmer 1 hour.

Remove chicken from broth, reserving broth. Cool chicken; skin, bone, and coarsely chop meat. Skim fat from broth.

Combine 2 quarts reserved broth, chicken, pork, and remaining ingredients in a large Dutch oven. Cover and simmer 2 hours or until desired consistency, stirring often. Add broth or water for a thinner consistency, if desired. Remove bay leaf. **Yield: 1 gallon.**

Old-Fashioned Burgoo

Old-Fashioned Burgoo

1 cup dried Great Northern beans
¾ cup dried baby lima beans
¼ cup dried split peas
8 slices bacon, cut into 1-inch pieces
1 pound meaty beef or ham bones or 1 pound
   beef short ribs
1 (3-pound) broiler-fryer
1½ quarts water
2 large potatoes, peeled and chopped
1 large onion, chopped
1 large cooking apple, peeled and chopped
5 stalks celery with leaves, sliced
3 large carrots, scraped and sliced
2 large turnips, peeled and chopped
1 large green pepper, seeded and chopped
1 medium-size hot pepper, seeded
½ cup sliced okra
1 cup shredded cabbage
½ cup chopped fresh parsley
1 (8½-ounce) can English peas, undrained
1 (17-ounce) can whole kernel corn
3 (16-ounce) cans whole tomatoes, chopped
2 teaspoons salt
1 teaspoon pepper
¼ teaspoon ground red pepper
¼ teaspoon chili powder

Sort and wash beans and peas; place in a medium bowl. Cover with water 2 inches above beans; soak 8 hours.

Cook bacon in a large Dutch oven until crisp; remove bacon, and set aside. Drain pan drippings. Add soup bones, chicken, and water to Dutch oven. Bring to a boil; cover, reduce heat, and simmer 2 hours.

Remove chicken and soup bones from broth, reserving broth; cool meat completely. Bone and coarsely chop meat; set aside. Skim fat from broth.

Drain beans, and add to broth. Cover and cook over medium heat 30 minutes or until beans are almost tender.

Add chicken, bacon, potato, and remaining ingredients. Cover, reduce heat, and simmer 2 to 3 hours, stirring often. Add water for a thinner consistency, if desired. **Yield: about 1½ gallons.**

Burgoo for a Crowd

1 (2- to 2½-pound) pork loin roast
1 (2- to 2½-pound) broiler-fryer
3 quarts water
4 pounds ground beef
6 cups frozen whole kernel corn
5 cups frozen purple hull peas
5 cups frozen lima beans
3 cups chopped cabbage
2 medium potatoes, peeled and cubed
2 medium onions, chopped
1 (46-ounce) can tomato juice
1 (16-ounce) can whole tomatoes, undrained
   and chopped
2 cups frozen cut okra
1 pound carrots, scraped and diced
1 green pepper, seeded and chopped
¾ cup chopped celery
¼ cup chopped fresh parsley
1 to 2 tablespoons crushed red pepper
1 tablespoon salt
1 tablespoon celery salt
1½ teaspoons pepper

Combine first 3 ingredients in a large Dutch oven; bring to a boil. Cover, reduce heat, and simmer 2 hours.

Drain meat, reserving broth. Remove bone, and shred pork. Skin, bone, and shred chicken. Skim fat from broth. Return meat to broth.

Brown ground beef in a large skillet, stirring until it crumbles; drain. Add ground beef, corn, and remaining ingredients to broth; bring to a boil. Reduce heat, and simmer, uncovered, 2 hours; stir often. Add additional water for a thinner consistency, if desired. **Yield: 2½ gallons.**

Kentucky Burgoo

Kentucky Burgoo

1 (3- to 3½-pound) broiler-fryer
1 pound boneless beef
1 pound boneless veal
1 pound boneless pork
1 gallon water
3 medium potatoes, peeled and cubed
3 medium carrots, scraped and sliced
1 large onion, chopped
1 large green pepper, seeded and chopped
1 cup frozen cut okra
1 cup shredded cabbage
1 cup frozen whole kernel corn
1 cup frozen lima beans
1 cup chopped fresh parsley
½ cup finely chopped celery
1 hot red pepper
2 cups tomato puree
2 tablespoons salt
1 teaspoon red pepper
1 to 1½ teaspoons hot sauce

Combine broiler-fryer, beef, veal, pork, and water in a large Dutch oven; bring to a boil. Cover, reduce heat, and simmer 2 hours or until chicken and meat are tender.

Remove chicken and meat from broth, reserving broth; cool completely. Skin, bone, and chop chicken; discard skin. Coarsely chop meat, and set aside.

Skim fat from surface of broth. Measure broth, and return 3 quarts to Dutch oven.

Add chicken, meats, potato, and remaining ingredients; bring to a boil. Reduce heat, and simmer, uncovered, 4 hours, stirring often.

Add additional reserved broth and water, if necessary, to make desired consistency. Discard red pepper pod. **Yield: 5 quarts.**

Chilies, Gumbos, and Jambalayas

Warm up the menu and stir up some fun with chilies, gumbos, and jambalayas. This collection of classic cold-weather specialties runs the gamut in ingredients and flavors.

Friday Night Chili, Five-Ingredient Chili, Hearty Kielbasa Chili

Spicy Seafood Gumbo, Savannah Snapper Gumbo, Creole Shrimp Jambalaya

Black Bean Chili Marsala, Bodacious Chili, Spicy Lamb and Black Bean Chili

Chicken-White Bean Chili, Vegetarian Chili, Microwave Gumbo

Cook-Off Chili (page 529)

Friday Night Chili

Friday Night Chili

2 pounds ground chuck
2 large onions, chopped
3 large cloves garlic, minced
2 (16-ounce) cans kidney beans, undrained
1 (16-ounce) can whole tomatoes, undrained
  and chopped
1 (8-ounce) can tomato sauce
2 cups water
1½ to 2 tablespoons chili powder
2 teaspoons garlic salt
1½ teaspoons ground cumin
1 teaspoon dried oregano
1 teaspoon black pepper
½ teaspoon ground red pepper
¼ teaspoon hot sauce
Condiments: corn chips, shredded sharp
  Cheddar cheese, sliced green onions

Cook first 3 ingredients in a Dutch oven over medium-high heat until meat is browned and onion is tender, stirring until meat crumbles. Drain well.

Stir in beans and next 10 ingredients. Bring to a boil; reduce heat, and simmer, uncovered, 1 hour, stirring occasionally. Serve chili with desired condiments. **Yield: 2¼ quarts.**

Chili Heritage

Chili owes much of its popularity to the introduction of chili powder in the 1890s by a Texan named William Gebhardt.

Five-Ingredient Chili

2 pounds ground chuck
1 medium onion, chopped
4 (16-ounce) cans chili-hot beans, undrained
2 (1¾-ounce) packages chili seasoning mix
1 (46-ounce) can tomato juice

Cook ground chuck and onion in a Dutch oven, stirring until meat crumbles; drain. Stir in beans and remaining ingredients.

Bring mixture to a boil; reduce heat, and simmer, uncovered, stirring occasionally, 2 hours. **Yield: 3½ quarts.**

Cook-Off Chili

(pictured on page 527)

2 pounds ground beef
½ teaspoon chili powder
¼ teaspoon ground cumin
2 large onions, chopped
4 cloves garlic, minced
1 jalapeño pepper, seeded and chopped
2 tablespoons vegetable oil
2 (15-ounce) cans tomato sauce
1 (15½-ounce) can Mexican-style chili beans, undrained
1½ cups water
1 (6-ounce) can tomato paste
½ cup green chile salsa or jalapeño salsa
3 to 4 tablespoons chili powder
1 (16-ounce) can red kidney beans, drained
1 (12-ounce) can beer
1 (2¼-ounce) can sliced ripe olives, drained
½ teaspoon ground cumin
Salt and pepper to taste
Hot sauce to taste
Condiments: shredded Cheddar cheese, sour cream, sliced ripe olives, tortilla chips

Cook first 3 ingredients in a Dutch oven, stirring until meat crumbles and browns. Drain and set aside.

Cook chopped onion, garlic, and jalapeño pepper in oil until tender. Stir in ground beef mixture, tomato sauce, and next 5 ingredients. Cover and simmer 20 minutes.

Add kidney beans and next 5 ingredients, stirring well; simmer 15 minutes. Serve chili with desired condiments. **Yield: 3½ quarts.**

Cook-Off Chili Techniques

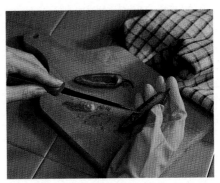

Gloves are recommended when handling hot peppers. Capsaicin, the oil in the seeds and veins, is dangerously hot.

Simmer kidney beans gently over low heat since a rolling boil may cause them to lose their shape and texture.

Now, Thatsa Chili

2 pounds lean ground beef
1 pound hot Italian link sausage, casings
    removed
1 large onion, chopped
½ cup sliced fresh mushrooms
1½ tablespoons minced fresh garlic
¼ cup chili powder
2 to 3 tablespoons ground cumin
2 (16-ounce) cans Italian-style tomatoes,
    undrained and chopped
1 (16-ounce) can kidney beans, drained
1 (6-ounce) can tomato paste
⅔ cup beer
¼ cup chopped fresh parsley
¼ cup dry red wine
¼ cup Dijon mustard
1 tablespoon dried oregano
1 tablespoon dried basil
1 teaspoon salt
1 teaspoon pepper
2 tablespoons lemon juice
Condiments: shredded cheese, chopped green
    onions, commercial salsa, sour cream

Cook ground beef and sausage in a large
Dutch oven, stirring until meat crumbles and
browns. Drain; return to Dutch oven.

Add onion, mushrooms, and garlic; cook
about 3 minutes, stirring constantly. Stir in chili
powder and next 13 ingredients.

Bring to a boil; reduce heat, and simmer 1 to
2 hours, stirring occasionally. Serve with desired
condiments. **Yield: 2¾ quarts.**

Hearty Kielbasa Chili

1 pound ground beef
½ pound kielbasa, cut into ½-inch slices
2 medium onions, chopped
2 cloves garlic, minced
1 (29-ounce) can tomato sauce
2 (15-ounce) cans red kidney beans,
    undrained
½ cup water
2 teaspoons chili powder
¼ teaspoon seasoned pepper
¼ teaspoon freshly ground black pepper

Cook first 4 ingredients in a Dutch oven, stirring until meat crumbles and browns; drain.

Stir in tomato sauce and remaining ingredients. Bring mixture to a boil; cover, reduce heat,
and simmer chili 1 hour, stirring occasionally.
Yield: 2 quarts.

Black Bean Chili Marsala

1 large onion, chopped
2 cloves garlic, minced
3 tablespoons vegetable oil
1 (2½-pound) boneless beef chuck roast,
    trimmed and chopped
1 (29-ounce) can tomato sauce
2 (6-ounce) cans tomato paste
1 cup Marsala wine
1 cup water
2 or 3 (4-ounce) cans sliced mushrooms,
    drained
3 to 4 tablespoons chili powder
2 teaspoons seasoned salt
1 teaspoon freshly ground pepper
2 (15-ounce) cans black beans, undrained
Hot cooked rice
Garnish: strips of lime rind or cilantro sprigs

Cook onion and garlic in vegetable oil in a Dutch oven over medium-high heat, stirring constantly, until tender.

Add chopped roast and next 8 ingredients. Bring to a boil. Cover, reduce heat, and simmer 1 hour, stirring occasionally.

Add beans, and cook until thoroughly heated. Serve chili over hot cooked rice. Garnish, if desired. **Yield: 3 quarts.**

Note: You may substitute 1 cup dry white wine plus 1½ tablespoons brandy for Marsala wine.

Black Bean Chili Marsala

Chili con Carne

16 **large dried red chiles**
2½ **quarts water**
2 **pounds round steak, cut into ½-inch cubes**
3 **tablespoons vegetable oil**
1 **large onion, chopped**
2 **cups water**
2 **cloves garlic, crushed**
2 **tablespoons chili powder**
1 **tablespoon ground cumin**
1 **teaspoon dried oregano**
½ **teaspoon salt**
2 **(16-ounce) cans ranch-style beans, undrained**

Wash chiles, and place in a large Dutch oven; add 2½ quarts water. Cover and bring to a boil. Remove from heat, and let stand, covered, 45 minutes or until softened.

Drain chiles, reserving ½ cup soaking liquid. Wearing rubber gloves, pull off stems, slit chiles open, and rinse away seeds under running water.

Place half of chiles and ¼ cup soaking liquid in blender or food processor; cover and process until smooth. Repeat with remaining chiles and remaining ¼ cup soaking liquid. Press pureed mixture through a wire-mesh strainer, using the back of a spoon; set puree aside.

Brown steak in oil in Dutch oven. Add pureed mixture, onion, and next 6 ingredients. Cover and simmer 1½ hours. Add beans, and cook until heated thoroughly. **Yield: 1¾ quarts.**

From top: Chili Verde and Bodacious Chili

Chili Verde

¾ **pound beef chuck roast, cut into 1-inch cubes**
¾ **pound pork loin or shoulder roast, cubed**
1 **large onion, chopped**
1 **large green pepper, seeded and chopped**
1 **clove garlic, minced**
2 **tablespoons olive oil, divided**
2 **(16-ounce) cans whole tomatoes, undrained and chopped**
2 **(4.5-ounce) cans chopped green chiles**
1 **cup dry red wine**
1 **cup commercial salsa**
¼ **cup chopped fresh cilantro**
2 **beef bouillon cubes**
1 **tablespoon brown sugar**
3 **tablespoons lemon juice**
Hot cooked rice
Garnish: fresh cilantro sprigs

Combine first 5 ingredients. Cook half of mixture in 1 tablespoon olive oil in a large Dutch oven over medium-high heat, stirring constantly, until meat browns. Remove from Dutch oven; set aside. Repeat procedure with remaining meat mixture and 1 tablespoon olive oil.

Combine meat mixture, tomato, and next 7 ingredients. Bring to a boil; cover, reduce heat, and simmer 1 hour or until meat is tender, stirring occasionally. Serve over rice, and garnish, if desired. **Yield: 2¾ quarts.**

Bodacious Chili

2 pounds boneless beef chuck roast, cut into
    1-inch cubes
2 large onions, chopped
3 stalks celery, cut into 1-inch pieces
1 large green pepper, seeded and coarsely
    chopped
1 large sweet red pepper, seeded and coarsely
    chopped
1 cup sliced fresh mushrooms
2 jalapeño peppers, seeded and chopped
4 cloves garlic, minced
3 tablespoons olive oil
2 tablespoons cocoa
2 tablespoons chili powder
1 teaspoon ground cumin
1 teaspoon dried oregano
1 teaspoon paprika
1 teaspoon ground turmeric
½ teaspoon salt
½ teaspoon ground cardamom
¼ teaspoon pepper
1 tablespoon molasses
½ cup dry red wine
2 (16-ounce) cans whole tomatoes, undrained
    and chopped
1 (16-ounce) can kidney beans, drained
1 (16-ounce) can chick peas (garbanzo beans),
    drained
Spicy Sour Cream Topping
Shredded Cheddar cheese

Cook first 8 ingredients in olive oil in a large
Dutch oven over medium-high heat, stirring constantly, until meat browns. Drain and return meat
mixture to Dutch oven.

Stir in cocoa and next 13 ingredients. Bring
mixture to a boil; cover, reduce heat, and simmer
1½ hours, stirring occasionally.

Serve chili with Spicy Sour Cream Topping
and shredded Cheddar cheese. **Yield: 3 quarts.**

Spicy Sour Cream Topping

1 (8-ounce) carton sour cream
⅓ cup commercial salsa
2 tablespoons mayonnaise
1 teaspoon chili powder
½ teaspoon onion powder
½ teaspoon curry powder
Dash of ground red pepper
1 tablespoon lemon juice
1 teaspoon Dijon mustard

Combine all ingredients; cover and chill.
Serve with chili. **Yield: 1⅔ cups.**

Venison Chili

½ pound salt pork, quartered
2 pounds ground venison
2 medium onions, chopped
1 clove garlic, minced
1 (16-ounce) can whole tomatoes, undrained
    and coarsely chopped
1 cup water
¾ cup dry red wine
2 or 3 large green chiles, diced
3 tablespoons chili powder
¾ teaspoon dried oregano
½ teaspoon cumin seeds, crushed

Brown salt pork in a Dutch oven over medium
heat. Add venison, onion, and garlic; cook, stirring frequently, until venison crumbles and
browns. Drain.

Stir in tomato and remaining ingredients.
Bring to a boil; reduce heat, and simmer, uncovered, 1 hour, stirring occasionally. Remove salt
pork before serving. **Yield: 1½ quarts.**

Chicken-White Bean Chili

Chicken-White Bean Chili

1 pound dried navy beans
4 (14½-ounce) cans ready-to-serve chicken
　broth
1 large onion, chopped
2 cloves garlic, crushed
1 tablespoon pepper
1 tablespoon dried oregano
1 tablespoon ground cumin
1 teaspoon salt
5 cups chopped cooked chicken
1 (4.5-ounce) can chopped green chiles,
　drained
1 cup water
8 (8-inch) flour tortillas (optional)
Condiments: commercial salsa, sour cream,
　sliced green onions

Sort and wash beans; place in a large Dutch oven. Cover with water 2 inches above beans. Soak 8 hours. Drain beans, and return to Dutch oven.

Add chicken broth and next 6 ingredients. Bring to a boil. Cover, reduce heat, and simmer 2 hours or until beans are tender, stirring occasionally.

Add chicken, green chiles, and 1 cup water. Cover and simmer 1 hour, stirring occasionally.

Make 4 cuts in each tortilla toward, but not through, center with kitchen shears. If desired, line serving bowls with tortillas, overlapping cut edges. Serve chili with desired condiments. **Yield: 3 quarts.**

Spicy Lamb and Black Bean Chili

1 pound ground lamb or turkey
½ cup chopped onion
Vegetable cooking spray
3 (8-ounce) cans no-salt-added tomato sauce
2 (15-ounce) cans black beans, drained
1 (14.5-ounce) can no-salt-added whole
　tomatoes, undrained and chopped
1 (16-ounce) can ready-to-serve chicken broth
2 (4.5-ounce) cans chopped green chiles,
　undrained
1½ tablespoons chili powder
2 teaspoons ground cumin
¼ teaspoon salt
¼ to ½ teaspoon ground red pepper

Cook meat and onion in a large Dutch oven coated with cooking spray over medium-high heat, stirring until meat crumbles and browns.

Add tomato sauce and remaining ingredients. Bring to a boil; reduce heat, and simmer 15 minutes, stirring occasionally. **Yield: 2 quarts.**

Turkey-Bean Chili

1 pound ground turkey
1 cup chopped onion
1 clove garlic, crushed
1 (15-ounce) can tomato sauce
1 (15½-ounce) can Mexican-style chili beans,
    undrained
¼ teaspoon salt
⅛ teaspoon pepper
2 tablespoons chili powder
1 tablespoon ground cumin
Condiments: commercial sour cream, chopped
    green onions, tortilla chips (optional)

Combine first 3 ingredients in a 3-quart baking dish. Cover and microwave at HIGH 5 to 6 minutes or until meat is no longer pink, stirring once; drain.

Add tomato sauce and next 5 ingredients. Cover and microwave at HIGH 10 to 12 minutes, stirring after 6 minutes. Serve with condiments, if desired. **Yield: 1¼ quarts.**

Turkey-Bean Chili

Turkey-Bean Chili Technique

To absorb fat and eliminate draining ground meat when microwaving, layer four white paper towels in a bowl. Microwave meat at HIGH; discard paper towels.

Vegetarian Chili

1 cup dried pinto beans
4 cups water
1 (17-ounce) can whole kernel corn,
    undrained
1 (15-ounce) can tomato sauce
1 large onion, chopped
1 (4.5-ounce) can chopped green chiles,
    drained
1 clove garlic, minced
1 teaspoon salt
2 teaspoons chili powder
1 teaspoon dried oregano
1 bay leaf
1 cup (4 ounces) shredded Monterey Jack
    cheese (optional)

Sort and wash beans; place in a Dutch oven. Cover with water 2 inches above beans; soak 8 hours. Drain beans, and return to Dutch oven.

Add 4 cups water and next 9 ingredients to Dutch oven. Bring to a boil; cover, reduce heat, and simmer 2½ hours or until beans are tender. Remove bay leaf. Serve with cheese, if desired. **Yield: about 2 quarts.**

Spicy Seafood Gumbo

1 cup vegetable oil
1 cup all-purpose flour
4 medium onions, chopped
8 stalks celery, chopped
3 cloves garlic, minced
4 (14½-ounce) cans ready-to-serve chicken
    broth
2 (28-ounce) cans whole tomatoes, undrained
    and chopped
2 (10-ounce) packages frozen sliced okra,
    thawed
1 pound crab claws
¼ cup Worcestershire sauce
1 tablespoon hot sauce
5 bay leaves
½ cup minced fresh parsley
2 teaspoons dried thyme
2 teaspoons dried basil
2 teaspoons dried oregano
2 teaspoons rubbed sage
1 teaspoon pepper
2 pounds unpeeled medium-size fresh shrimp
2 (12-ounce) containers Standard oysters,
    undrained
1 pound fresh crabmeat, drained and flaked
1 pound firm white fish fillets, cut into 1-inch
    cubes
Hot cooked rice
Gumbo filé (optional)

Combine oil and flour in a cast-iron skillet; cook over medium heat, stirring constantly, until roux is chocolate colored (about 20 minutes).

Stir in onion, celery, and garlic; cook 10 minutes, stirring frequently. Transfer mixture to a Dutch oven.

Add chicken broth and next 12 ingredients. Bring to a boil; reduce heat, and simmer, uncovered, 2 hours, stirring occasionally.

Peel shrimp, and devein, if desired. Add shrimp, oysters, crabmeat, and fish to Dutch

oven. Bring to a boil; reduce heat, and simmer, uncovered, 10 minutes or until seafood is done. Remove bay leaves.

Serve gumbo over hot rice; sprinkle with gumbo filé, if desired. **Yield: 7 quarts.**

Spicy Seafood Gumbo Techniques

To make a roux, first whisk flour into oil.

Stir constantly until mixture becomes a light caramel color.

More cooking produces a rich, dark chocolate-colored roux.

Spicy Seafood Gumbo

Creole Gumbo

Creole Gumbo

1 cup vegetable oil
1 cup all-purpose flour
3 medium onions, chopped
3 green onions, chopped
2 large green peppers, seeded and chopped
2 stalks celery, sliced
4 cloves garlic, chopped
2 (16-ounce) cans Italian-style tomatoes, undrained and chopped
2 (10-ounce) packages frozen sliced okra, thawed
1 pound fully cooked Polish sausage, sliced
1 (6-ounce) can tomato paste
2 quarts water
4 bay leaves
3 tablespoons lemon juice
2 teaspoons dried thyme
1 teaspoon salt
¾ teaspoon pepper
½ teaspoon Creole seasoning
½ teaspoon ground red pepper
2 pounds unpeeled medium-size fresh shrimp
1 pound fresh crabmeat, drained and flaked
1 (12-ounce) container Standard oysters, undrained
⅓ cup chopped fresh parsley
Hot cooked rice

Combine oil and flour in a large Dutch oven; cook over medium heat, stirring constantly, until roux is chocolate colored (about 25 minutes).

Stir in onion, green onions, and next 3 ingredients; cook 3 to 5 minutes, stirring frequently.

Add tomato and next 11 ingredients. Bring to a boil; cover, reduce heat, and simmer 1½ hours, stirring occasionally. Remove bay leaves.

Peel shrimp, and devein, if desired. Stir in shrimp, crabmeat, oysters, and parsley; simmer 5 to 10 minutes or until shrimp turn pink and edges of oysters begin to curl.

Serve over hot cooked rice. **Yield: 6½ quarts.**

Microwave Gumbo

⅔ cup vegetable oil
⅔ cup all-purpose flour
2 cups sliced okra
1 cup chopped onion
1 cup chopped celery
½ cup chopped green pepper
2 cloves garlic, minced
2 (10½-ounce) cans condensed chicken broth
1½ cups water
1 (16-ounce) can whole tomatoes, drained and chopped
2 tablespoons Worcestershire sauce
1 to 2 teaspoons hot sauce
½ teaspoon paprika
½ teaspoon dried thyme
¼ teaspoon ground mace
1 pound unpeeled medium-size fresh shrimp
2 cups chopped cooked chicken or turkey
1 (12-ounce) container Standard oysters, drained
Hot cooked rice

Combine oil and flour in a deep 3-quart baking dish; stir well. Microwave, uncovered, at HIGH 6 minutes, stirring after 3 minutes. Stir well. Microwave, uncovered, at HIGH 2 to 4 minutes or until caramel colored, stirring every 30 seconds.

Stir in okra and next 4 ingredients. Cover with heavy-duty plastic wrap; fold back a small edge of wrap to allow steam to escape. Microwave at HIGH 4 to 5 minutes or until tender.

Stir in chicken broth and next 7 ingredients. Cover and microwave at HIGH 13 to 15 minutes or until boiling, stirring after 8 minutes.

Peel shrimp. Add shrimp, chicken, and oysters. Reduce to MEDIUM HIGH (70% power); cover and microwave 8 to 10 minutes or until shrimp turn pink and edges of oysters begin to curl.

Serve gumbo over hot cooked rice. **Yield: about 3 quarts.**

Southern Seafood Gumbo

½ cup vegetable oil
½ cup all-purpose flour
4 stalks celery, chopped
2 medium onions, chopped
1 small green pepper, seeded and chopped
1 clove garlic, minced
½ pound okra, sliced
1 tablespoon vegetable oil
1 quart ready-to-serve chicken broth
1 quart water
¼ cup Worcestershire sauce
1 teaspoon hot sauce
¼ cup ketchup
1 small tomato, chopped
1 teaspoon salt
2 slices bacon or 1 small ham slice, chopped
1 bay leaf
¼ teaspoon dried thyme
¼ teaspoon dried rosemary
¼ teaspoon red pepper flakes
2 pounds unpeeled medium-size fresh shrimp
2 cups chopped cooked chicken
1 pound fresh crabmeat, drained and flaked
1 (12-ounce) container Standard oysters,
    undrained (optional)
Hot cooked rice
Gumbo filé (optional)

Combine ½ cup oil and flour in a large Dutch oven; cook over medium heat, stirring constantly, until roux is caramel colored (15 to 20 minutes). Stir in celery and next 3 ingredients; cook 45 minutes, stirring occasionally.

Fry okra in 1 tablespoon hot oil until browned. Add to gumbo, and stir well over low heat for a few minutes. (At this stage, the mixture may be cooled, packaged, and frozen or refrigerated for later use.)

Add chicken broth and next 11 ingredients. Bring to a boil; reduce heat, and simmer, uncovered, 2½ hours, stirring occasionally.

Peel shrimp, and devein, if desired. Add shrimp, chicken, crabmeat, and oysters, if desired, during last 10 minutes of simmering period. Remove bay leaf.

Serve over rice. Sprinkle with gumbo filé, if desired. **Yield: 3½ quarts.**

Make a Roux

You can prepare a roux using the traditional procedure (pictured on page 536), or you can eliminate the fat from the roux by using the conventional oven method. A third and quicker method is to prepare the roux in your microwave.

To make an oven roux:
Place ¾ cup all-purpose flour in a 13- x 9- x 2-inch pan. Bake at 400° for 15 to 20 minutes, stirring every 4 minutes. Flour will be the color of caramel. Yield: enough roux for 1 gallon gumbo.

To make a microwave roux:
Combine ¾ cup vegetable oil and ¾ cup all-purpose flour in a 4-cup glass measure, stirring until mixture is blended. Microwave at HIGH 6 minutes; stir and microwave at HIGH 2 minutes. Stir mixture, and continue microwaving at HIGH 1 to 3 minutes, stirring at 1-minute intervals until mixture turns the color of caramel or chocolate. (Roux continues to brown as it cools; do not overcook.) Yield: enough roux for 1 gallon gumbo.

Catfish Gumbo

reduce heat, and simmer 30 minutes, stirring occasionally.

Cut catfish into 1-inch pieces; add to gumbo, and simmer 10 minutes. Stir in okra; cook 5 minutes. Remove bay leaf.

Serve gumbo over hot cooked rice. **Yield: about 3½ quarts.**

Catfish Gumbo

1 cup chopped green pepper
1 cup chopped celery
1 cup chopped onion
2 cloves garlic, minced
¼ cup vegetable oil
2 (14½-ounce) cans ready-to-serve beef broth
1 (16-ounce) can whole tomatoes, undrained and chopped
1 teaspoon salt
½ teaspoon dried oregano
½ teaspoon dried thyme
½ teaspoon red pepper
1 bay leaf
2 pounds farm-raised catfish fillets
1 (10-ounce) package frozen sliced okra, thawed
Hot cooked rice

Cook first 4 ingredients in oil in a Dutch oven, stirring constantly, until tender. Stir in beef broth and next 6 ingredients. Bring to a boil; cover,

Savannah Snapper Gumbo

3 tablespoons vegetable oil
2 tablespoons all-purpose flour
1 medium-size green pepper, seeded and chopped
1 stalk celery, chopped
1 medium onion, chopped
1 (14½-ounce) can stewed tomatoes
1 (14½-ounce) can ready-to-serve chicken broth
1 (10-ounce) package frozen sliced okra
1 (10-ounce) package frozen whole kernel corn
1 cup water
1 tablespoon Worcestershire sauce
½ teaspoon salt
¼ teaspoon ground red pepper
⅛ teaspoon dried thyme
1 bay leaf
12 ounces fresh red snapper fillets, cubed
Hot cooked rice

Combine oil and flour with a wire whisk in a Dutch oven; cook over medium heat, stirring constantly, until caramel colored (10 to 15 minutes).

Stir in green pepper, celery, and onion. Cook over medium heat, stirring occasionally, about 10 minutes or until vegetables are tender.

Add tomatoes and next 9 ingredients. Bring to a boil; reduce heat, and simmer 10 minutes.

Stir in red snapper, and cook 5 minutes. Remove bay leaf.

Serve over hot cooked rice. **Yield: 2 quarts.**

Chicken and Sausage Gumbo

1½ pounds smoked sausage or andouille
1 (3½- to 4-pound) broiler-fryer, cut up and
   skinned
¼ cup vegetable oil
½ cup all-purpose flour
2 large onions, minced
1 large green pepper, seeded and minced
1 cup minced celery
3 cloves garlic, minced
2 quarts water
2 teaspoons Creole seasoning
⅛ teaspoon hot sauce
½ cup chopped green onions
¼ cup minced fresh parsley
Hot cooked rice

Cut sausage lengthwise into 4 pieces; cut pieces into ½-inch slices. Brown in a Dutch oven. Drain; reserve drippings in pan. Set sausage aside. Brown chicken in drippings; drain and set aside.

Combine oil and flour in Dutch oven; cook over medium heat, stirring constantly, until roux is chocolate colored (25 to 30 minutes).

Add onion and next 3 ingredients; cook until vegetables are tender. Add water; bring to a boil. Reduce heat, and simmer, uncovered, 45 minutes.

Add chicken, Creole seasoning, and hot sauce; cook, uncovered, 1 hour.

Remove chicken, and set aside to cool. Add green onions and parsley to gumbo. Bone chicken, and coarsely chop. Add chicken and sausage to gumbo; heat thoroughly.

Ladle gumbo into bowls. Pack hot cooked rice into greased custard cups; invert into bowls of gumbo, or serve gumbo over hot cooked rice.
Yield: about 3 quarts.

Note: To remove fat from surface, cover and chill 8 hours. Remove fat; reheat gumbo, and serve. For a more traditional gumbo, leave chicken pieces intact.

Duck, Oyster, and Sausage Gumbo

2 large wild ducks, cleaned
2 stalks celery with leaves, cut into 2-inch
    pieces
1 medium onion, sliced
1 tablespoon salt
Chicken broth
1 pound hot smoked sausage, cut into 1-inch
    pieces
½ cup vegetable oil
½ cup all-purpose flour
¾ cup finely chopped celery
1 large onion, finely chopped
1 green pepper, seeded and finely chopped
Salt and pepper to taste
6 green onions with tops, finely chopped
2 tablespoons chopped fresh parsley
1 (12-ounce) container Standard oysters,
    undrained
Hot cooked rice
Gumbo filé

Combine first 4 ingredients in a large Dutch oven; cover with water. Bring to a boil; cover, reduce heat, and simmer about 1 hour or until ducks are tender.

Remove ducks from stock, reserving stock. Let ducks cool; remove meat from bones, and cut into bite-size pieces. Set aside.

Return skin and bones to stock; cover and simmer 1 hour. Pour stock through a wire-mesh strainer into a large bowl, discarding solids. Add enough chicken broth to make 2½ quarts liquid; set aside.

Cook sausage in a skillet over medium heat about 5 minutes, stirring occasionally. Drain on paper towels, and set aside.

Heat oil in a 5-quart heavy cast-iron pot or Dutch oven; stir in flour. Cook over medium heat, stirring constantly, until roux is chocolate colored (about 25 minutes).

Add chopped celery, chopped onion, and green pepper; cook over medium heat 10 minutes, stirring constantly.

Remove from heat, and gradually stir in reserved hot stock. Bring mixture to a boil; reduce heat, and simmer 20 minutes.

Add duck, sausage, salt, and pepper to stock mixture; simmer 20 minutes. Stir in green onions and parsley; simmer 20 minutes. Add oysters; simmer 10 minutes.

Serve gumbo over hot cooked rice. Sprinkle with gumbo filé. **Yield: 8 to 10 servings.**

Note: Gumbo is best when made a day ahead, chilled, and reheated.

Turkey and Sausage Gumbo

1 pound smoked sausage, cut into ½-inch
    slices
¼ cup vegetable oil
¼ cup all-purpose flour
3 stalks celery, chopped
2 medium onions, chopped
2 cups cubed cooked turkey
3 cups water
½ teaspoon salt
¼ teaspoon pepper
Hot cooked rice
Gumbo filé

Brown sausage in a large skillet over medium heat; drain and set aside.

Combine oil and flour in a Dutch oven; cook over medium heat, stirring constantly, until roux is caramel colored (about 10 minutes). Add celery and onion; cook until tender, stirring frequently.

Add sausage, turkey, and water. Bring to a boil; reduce heat, and simmer, uncovered, 2 hours, stirring occasionally. Stir in salt and pepper.

Serve gumbo over rice; sprinkle with gumbo filé, if desired. **Yield: 1½ quarts.**

Wild Game Gumbo

2 quarts water
1 (2½- to 3-pound) broiler-fryer
1½ teaspoons salt
8 dove breasts (about 1 pound)
1 pound venison roast, cut into 1-inch cubes
1 squirrel, dressed and cut into pieces (optional)
1 rabbit, dressed and quartered (about 2 pounds)
2 quail, dressed
1 small onion
1 stalk celery
1 bay leaf
1 tablespoon salt
¼ teaspoon red pepper
1½ pounds smoked link sausage, cut into ½-inch slices
¼ cup bacon drippings
½ cup all-purpose flour
1 cup chopped onion
1 cup chopped celery
2 to 3 teaspoons pepper
1 teaspoon hot sauce
½ teaspoon ground red pepper
1 teaspoon Worcestershire sauce
Hot cooked rice

Combine first 3 ingredients in a large Dutch oven. Bring to a boil; cover, reduce heat, and simmer 1 hour or until tender.

Remove chicken from broth. Chill broth; remove fat from broth. Skin, bone, and coarsely chop chicken. Set aside.

Combine dove breasts and next 8 ingredients (or 9, if you add squirrel) in large Dutch oven; add water to cover. Bring to a boil; cover, reduce heat, and simmer 2 hours.

Remove meat from broth; strain broth. Set aside. Remove meat from bones, and chop into bite-size pieces. Set aside.

Brown sausage in a large heavy skillet over medium heat. Drain on paper towels, leaving drippings in skillet.

Add bacon drippings to skillet. Heat over medium heat until hot. Add flour, and cook, stirring constantly, until roux is caramel colored (15 to 20 minutes.) Add chopped onion, celery, and pepper; cook 10 minutes.

Combine roux and reserved chicken broth in large Dutch oven; cover and simmer 30 minutes. Add game, sausage, chicken, hot sauce, red pepper, and Worcestershire sauce.

Add reserved stock from game if additional liquid is desired; simmer, uncovered, 2 hours, stirring occasionally. Serve over hot cooked rice. **Yield: 4½ quarts.**

Dove and Sausage Gumbo

15 dove breasts
1 (10½-ounce) can beef consommé, undiluted
1 beef-flavored bouillon cube
½ cup vegetable oil
½ cup all-purpose flour
1½ cups finely chopped onion
1 cup finely chopped celery
2 cloves garlic, minced
1 or 2 bay leaves
2 tablespoons Worcestershire sauce
½ teaspoon dried basil
¼ teaspoon poultry seasoning
¼ teaspoon freshly ground black pepper
⅛ teaspoon ground red pepper
⅛ teaspoon ground allspice
⅛ teaspoon ground cloves
¾ pound smoked sausage, cut into ¼-inch slices
¼ cup dry red wine
⅛ teaspoon hot sauce
Hot cooked rice
Gumbo filé (optional)

Place dove breasts in a Dutch oven; add water to cover. Bring to a boil; cover, reduce heat, and simmer 10 minutes.

Remove dove from broth, reserving broth. Let dove cool. Bone and coarsely chop dove; set aside. Add enough water to reserved broth to measure 3 cups, if necessary.

Combine broth, consommé, and bouillon cube in a medium saucepan; cook over medium heat until bouillon cube dissolves. Set aside.

Brown dove in oil in Dutch oven over medium heat. Remove dove, reserving drippings in Dutch oven; add flour to drippings. Cook over medium heat, stirring constantly, until roux is caramel colored (about 15 minutes).

Add 1½ cups broth gradually; cook over medium heat, stirring constantly, until mixture is thickened and bubbly.

Add onion and celery to roux mixture; cook 5 minutes or until vegetables are tender, stirring occasionally. Add remaining broth, garlic, and next 8 ingredients; stir well.

Brown sausage in a large skillet over medium heat. Add sausage and dove to roux mixture. Bring to a boil; cover, reduce heat, and simmer 1½ hours, stirring occasionally.

Stir in wine and hot sauce. Remove bay leaves. Serve gumbo over rice; sprinkle with gumbo filé, if desired. **Yield: 1¼ quarts.**

Okra Gumbo

1 **large onion, chopped**
1 **large green pepper, seeded and chopped**
2 **tablespoons vegetable oil or bacon drippings**
4 **cups sliced fresh okra**
3 **ripe tomatoes, peeled and chopped**
1 **cup corn cut from cob (about 2 ears)**
1 **tablespoon white vinegar**
½ **teaspoon salt**
¼ **teaspoon black pepper**
⅛ **teaspoon ground red pepper**

Cook onion and green pepper in oil in a Dutch oven, stirring constantly, until tender. Add okra and remaining ingredients, and cook over medium heat 15 minutes, stirring frequently. Serve immediately. **Yield: 1½ quarts.**

Ground Beef Gumbo

1½ **pounds ground beef**
⅔ **cup chopped onion**
⅔ **cup chopped celery**
⅔ **cup chopped green pepper**
2 **or 3 cloves garlic, minced**
1 **(16-ounce) can whole tomatoes, undrained and chopped**
1 **(15-ounce) can tomato sauce**
2 **(6-ounce) cans tomato paste**
1 **(6-ounce) jar sliced mushrooms, drained**
2½ **cups frozen sliced okra**
2 **bay leaves**
1½ **tablespoons dried parsley flakes**
2½ **teaspoons Italian seasoning**
1½ **teaspoons dried basil**
1 **teaspoon dried oregano**
1 **teaspoon chili powder**
1 **teaspoon onion powder**
½ **teaspoon cumin powder**
Salt and pepper to taste
½ **cup water**
2 **tablespoons dry red wine**
Hot cooked rice

Cook first 5 ingredients in a heavy Dutch oven over medium heat, stirring until meat crumbles and browns; drain.

Stir in tomato and next 15 ingredients. Bring to a boil; reduce heat, and simmer, uncovered, 1 hour. Remove bay leaves. Serve over hot cooked rice. **Yield: 1¼ quarts.**

Creole Jambalaya

1½ pounds unpeeled medium-size fresh
   shrimp
¾ cup chopped onion
½ cup chopped celery
¼ cup chopped green pepper
1 tablespoon minced fresh parsley
1 clove garlic, minced
2 tablespoons butter or margarine, melted
1 (28-ounce) can whole tomatoes, undrained
   and chopped
1 (10½-ounce) can condensed beef broth,
   undiluted
1¼ cups water
½ teaspoon dried thyme
½ teaspoon chili powder
¼ teaspoon pepper
2 cups cubed cooked ham
1 cup long-grain rice, uncooked

Peel shrimp, and devein, if desired. Set aside.

Cook onion and next 4 ingredients in butter in a Dutch oven over medium-high heat, stirring constantly, until vegetables are tender.

Stir in tomato and next 6 ingredients. Bring to a boil; stir in rice. Cover, reduce heat, and simmer 25 minutes.

Add shrimp to rice mixture. Bring to a boil; cover, reduce heat, and simmer 10 minutes or until shrimp turn pink. **Yield: 6 servings.**

Hearty Fare

Gumbos and jambalayas may contain one or more kinds of seafood, chicken or other poultry, or combinations of pork, seafood, and sausage. Gumbos are served over rice; jambalayas have rice as an ingredient.

Creole Shrimp Jambalaya

1½ pounds unpeeled medium-size fresh
   shrimp
2 tablespoons vegetable oil
1 cup chopped onion
½ cup chopped green pepper
1 carrot, scraped and cut into thin strips
½ cup chopped celery
3 cloves garlic, minced
1 (8-ounce) can tomato sauce
1 (16-ounce) can whole tomatoes, undrained
   and chopped
1 (14½-ounce) can ready-to-serve chicken
   broth
1¼ cups water
1 cup long-grain rice, uncooked
1 teaspoon salt
½ teaspoon dried thyme
½ teaspoon red pepper
¼ teaspoon chili powder
¼ teaspoon sugar
½ cup chopped fresh parsley
⅛ teaspoon hot sauce (optional)

Peel shrimp, and devein, if desired. Cook shrimp in oil in a small Dutch oven over medium heat, stirring constantly, 5 minutes or until shrimp turn pink. Remove shrimp with a slotted spoon; cover and chill.

Add onion and next 4 ingredients to Dutch oven; cook over medium heat 3 minutes.

Stir in tomato sauce and next 9 ingredients. Bring to a boil; cover, reduce heat, and simmer, stirring frequently, 45 minutes or until rice is tender and most of liquid is absorbed.

Stir in parsley and shrimp; cook about 10 minutes or until thoroughly heated. Add hot sauce, if desired. **Yield: 4 servings.**

Black-Eyed Pea Jambalaya

Black-Eyed Pea Jambalaya

1½ cups dried black-eyed peas
4 (10½-ounce) cans condensed chicken broth, undiluted
2 medium tomatoes, chopped
2 cloves garlic, minced
1 medium-size green pepper, seeded and chopped
1 small onion, chopped
1 stalk celery, chopped
1 bay leaf
1 cup cubed cooked ham
½ teaspoon salt
¼ teaspoon dried thyme
⅛ teaspoon ground cloves
1½ cups long-grain rice, uncooked
½ cup sliced green onions
1½ teaspoons hot sauce
Garnish: fresh thyme sprigs

Sort and wash peas; place in a 6-quart pressure cooker. Add water to chicken broth to make 5 cups.

Add broth, tomato, and next 9 ingredients to peas; stir well. Close lid securely. According to manufacturer's directions, bring to high pressure over high heat (about 10 to 12 minutes). Reduce

heat to medium or level needed to maintain high pressure; cook 15 minutes.

Remove from heat; run cold water over cooker to reduce pressure rapidly. Remove lid so that steam escapes away from you.

Drain pea mixture, reserving 3 cups liquid. Remove bay leaf. Remove pea mixture from cooker; set aside, and keep warm.

Add rice and reserved liquid to cooker; stir gently. Close lid securely; bring to high pressure over high heat (about 5 minutes). Reduce heat to medium or level needed to maintain high pressure; cook 5 minutes.

Remove from heat; run cold water over cooker to reduce pressure rapidly. Remove lid so that steam escapes away from you.

Stir in pea mixture, green onions, and hot sauce. Garnish, if desired. **Yield: 6 servings.**

Good Luck Jambalaya

½ cup salt pork strips
2 cloves garlic, minced
1 large onion, chopped
1 medium-size green pepper, seeded and chopped
2 (16-ounce) cans black-eyed peas with jalapeño peppers, undrained
⅔ cup Bloody Mary mix
⅓ cup long-grain rice, uncooked
1 pound unpeeled medium-size fresh shrimp

Cook salt pork in a large skillet, stirring constantly, until golden. Add garlic, onion, and green pepper, and cook, stirring constantly, until tender.

Add peas, Bloody Mary mix, and rice. Bring to a boil over medium heat; cover, reduce heat, and simmer 20 minutes.

Peel shrimp, and devein, if desired. Add shrimp; cover jambalaya, and cook 5 minutes or until shrimp turn pink.

Serve immediately. **Yield: 6 to 8 servings.**

Southern Living®

ALL-TIME FAVORITE

DESSERT
RECIPES

Contents

Bring on Dessert!

Sweet endings have been mealtime essentials for generations.
From cakes to pies, mousses to meringues, and fruits to frosty favorites,
you'll find something here to dazzle family and friends.

Make Dessert Special

Whether they're simple or elegant, desserts make the meal complete. To achieve perfect cakes, pastries, and other sweets, you must measure accurately and mix ingredients properly. Use the following tips to ensure your success in making desserts guaranteed to satisfy the most discriminating sweet tooth.

Blue-Ribbon Cakes

• Position oven rack in center of oven, and preheat oven.

• Use the correct pan size.

• Grease cakepans with solid shortening; do not use oil, butter, or margarine. Lightly dust pans with flour. Do not grease pans for sponge-type cakes.

• Let butter or margarine reach room temperature before mixing.

• Do not sift all-purpose flour unless specified. Always sift cake flour before measuring.

• Beat butter or shortening until creamy. Gradually add sugar, and beat well. (Beating may take up to 7 minutes with a standard mixer and longer with a portable mixer.)

• Add only one egg at a time, and beat after each addition just until yellow disappears.

• Add dry and liquid ingredients alternately to creamed mixture, beginning and ending with dry ingredients. Beat after each addition but only until batter is smooth; do not overbeat.

• Use a rubber spatula to scrape the sides and bottom of the bowl often during mixing.

• Arrange cakepans so that they do not touch each other or the sides of the oven. If placed on separate racks, the pans should be staggered to allow air to circulate.

• Keep oven door closed until the minimum baking time has elapsed.

• Test cake for doneness before removing it from the oven. The cake is done when a wooden pick inserted in the center comes out clean or if the cake springs back when lightly touched.

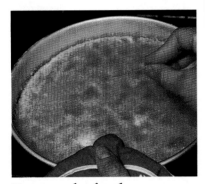

Testing cake for doneness

• Cool layer cakes in pans 10 minutes and tube cakes in pans 15 minutes. Invert cakes onto wire racks to cool completely.

• Cool cake completely before adding filling and frosting. Lightly brush cake to remove loose crumbs.

• Keep frosting off the serving plate by arranging several strips of wax paper around edges of plate before stacking cake layers.

Placing wax paper under cake before frosting

• Place bottom cake layer upside-down on serving plate.

Spread frosting on top of bottom layer, and smooth to sides of cake with a metal spatula. Place top layer of cake right side up.

• Spread sides of cake with a liberal amount of frosting, making decorative swirls. Spread remaining frosting on top of cake, joining frosting at top and sides; again make decorative swirls.

Frosting cake layers

Cake Problems and Causes

If cake falls:
Oven not hot enough
Undermixing
Insufficient baking
Opening oven door during baking
Too much leavening, liquid, or sugar

If cake peaks in center:
Oven too hot at start of baking
Too much flour
Not enough liquid

If cake sticks to pan:
Cooled in pan too long
Pan not greased and floured properly

If cake cracks and falls apart:
Removed from pan too soon
Too much shortening, leavening, or sugar

If crust is sticky:
Insufficient baking
Oven not hot enough
Too much sugar

If texture is coarse:
Inadequate mixing or creaming
Oven not hot enough
Too much leavening

If texture is dry:
Overbaking
Overbeaten egg whites
Too much flour or leavening
Not enough shortening or sugar

Picture-Perfect Pies

• Cut shortening into flour using a pastry blender or two knives until mixture resembles coarse crumbs.

Cutting shortening into flour with a pastry blender

• Sprinkle cold water, one tablespoon at a time, over flour mixture; stir with a fork just enough to moisten dry ingredients. Add the minimum amount of water that will moisten flour mixture; too much can make pastry tough and soggy.

• Once water is added to flour mixture, don't overwork the dough—the more you handle it, the more gluten will develop, toughening the pastry.

• Shape dough into a ball, cover with plastic wrap, and chill at least 1 hour. Chilling makes dough easier to handle and helps prevent crust from being soggy.

• Roll dough on a lightly floured surface or pastry cloth, using a floured rolling pin cover on the rolling pin. Place chilled dough in the center of the floured surface; flatten dough with the side of your hand. Carefully roll dough from the center to outer edges; do not roll back and forth across dough, as this will stretch it and cause it to shrink during baking.

Rolling dough with a cloth-covered rolling pin

• Roll dough to ⅛-inch thickness and about two inches larger in diameter than the pieplate.

• To transfer pastry to pieplate, carefully fold dough in half and then into quarters. Place point of fold in center of pieplate, and carefully unfold. Try not to pull at dough, as it will stretch.

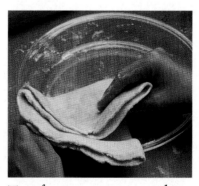

Transferring pastry to pieplate

• Trim edges of dough, leaving about ½-inch overhang. (Kitchen shears or scissors are easier to use than a knife.) Fold overhanging dough under, pressing firmly against pieplate edge to seal. Flute as desired (see Creative Finishes).

• For best results, use an ovenproof glass pieplate or a dull metal piepan. Shiny metal pans reflect heat and prevent crust from browning.

• When baking a pastry shell without a filling, prick bottom and sides generously before baking. Do not prick shell if it is to be filled.

Pricking bottom of pastry shell

• Cool baked pastries on a wire rack; this will help keep crusts from becoming soggy.

Creative Finishes

Make a spiral fluted crust design by pinching pastry at an angle between your thumb and index finger.

Cut a scalloped edge for pastry shell by rolling the tip of a teaspoon around edge of pastry.

Give pastry a forked design by gently pressing a fork around edge. Dip fork in flour to keep it from sticking to pastry.

Press a twirled rope around edge of pastry shell. Cut pastry strips about ½ inch wide. Moisten edge of shell; twist rope with one hand, while pressing rope with other hand where it joins pastry.

To apply cutouts, moisten edge of pastry shell, and gently press small cutouts around edge; overlap slightly.

To weave a lattice crust, place strips across pie in one direction. Repeat process of alternately folding back every other strip and laying a strip perpendicular to the original strips.

Pastry Problems and Causes

Tough pastry:
Too little fat
Too much water
Too much flour
Overmixing
Kneading the dough

Crumbly crust:
Too little water
Too much fat
Self-rising flour used
Insufficient mixing

Soggy lower crust:
Filling too moist
Oven not hot enough
Too much liquid in pastry

Crust shrinks:
Too much handling
Pastry stretched in pan
Dough uneven in thickness
Rolling dough back and forth
    with rolling pin

Perfect Ice Cream

• Start with the freshest ingredients possible when making the base for ice cream. If recipe contains eggs, be sure to cook the custard over medium heat, stirring constantly, until mixture reaches 160°.

Cooking custard ingredients

• For a creamier texture, chill ice cream mixture at least 4 hours before freezing it. A chilled mixture also will freeze faster.

• Check the manufacturer's instructions for your ice cream machine. Freezers are made of different materials, making a difference in the ice-salt ratio recommended. Most 1-gallon freezers use 3 to 4 cups rock salt and 20 pounds crushed ice (1 cup salt to 6 cups ice).

• Fill freezer container no more than two-thirds full to allow room for expansion. For electric freezers, let the motor run about one minute before adding ice and salt in layers. Hand-turned freezers should be turned about 1 minute to stir the mixture before freezing.

• Do not skimp on ice and salt; both are essential for freezing ice cream. The ice cream freezes because the ice and salt absorb its heat. Ice alone will not freeze ice cream.

• Use the amount of salt called for by the manufacturer. If you use too little salt, the brine will not get cold enough to thoroughly freeze ice cream. If you use too much salt, the ice cream will freeze too quickly, causing large ice crystals to form. Rock salt is usually preferred over table salt because table salt dissolves rapidly.

• When alternately adding ice and salt, make four thick layers of ice and four thin layers of salt, beginning with ice and ending with salt. Add leftover ice and salt as ice melts and when "ripening" ice cream.

• When ice cream is frozen, the crank barely turns (an electric freezer usually shuts off but needs to be unplugged immediately). Churning takes 25 to 35 minutes.

• Before opening ice cream canister, drain water, and remove ice below level of lid. Wipe canister lid, open, and remove the dasher. Pack ice cream down with a spoon. Cover with plastic wrap or foil, and replace lid.

• Let ice cream ripen to harden and blend flavors. Pack freezer bucket with ice and salt using 4 parts ice to 1 part salt. (You need more salt here to harden the ice cream.) Wrap well with a towel or newspaper, and let stand 1 to 2 hours.

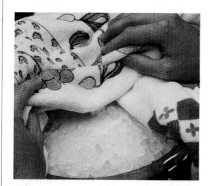

Allowing ice cream to ripen

Ice Cream Shapes

• Freeze commercial or homemade ice cream in special shapes. Select molds with clean lines and simple designs as they are easier to unmold than ones with intricate designs.
• Metal molds conduct cold quickly; this allows for complete freezing and easy unmolding.
• Lightly oil ice cream molds for easy unmolding, or line one-piece molds with plastic wrap.
• Let ice cream soften at room temperature a few minutes before unmolding, or speed up the process by patting the mold with a warm, damp cloth.

Cakes—Plain and Fancy

Birthdays and holidays almost always call for a special cake. Make your
next celebration memorable with an easy-to-assemble
shortcake, a rich roulage, or a heavenly angel food cake.

Tart Lemon-Cheese Cake, Italian Cream Cake, Devil's Food Cake

Lady Baltimore Cake, Apple Cake with Brown Sugar Glaze, Old South Fruitcake

Lemon-Coconut Cake, Creamy Chocolate Cake, Whipping Cream Pound Cake

Chocolate-Sour Cream Pound Cake, Old-Fashioned Carrot Cake

Banana-Nut Layer Cake (page 568)

White Cake

¾ cup shortening
1½ cups sugar
2¼ cups sifted cake flour
1 tablespoon baking powder
¾ teaspoon salt
1 cup milk
1½ teaspoons vanilla extract
5 egg whites
Favorite Caramel Frosting

Beat shortening at medium speed of an electric mixer until fluffy; gradually add sugar, beating well.

Combine flour, baking powder, and salt; add to shortening mixture alternately with milk, beginning and ending with flour mixture. Beat at low speed until blended after each addition. Stir in vanilla.

Beat egg whites in a large mixing bowl at high speed until stiff peaks form; gently fold into batter. Pour batter into 2 greased and floured 9-inch round cakepans.

Bake at 350° for 25 to 30 minutes or until a wooden pick inserted in center comes out clean. Cool in pans on wire racks 10 minutes; remove from pans, and cool completely on wire racks.

Spread Favorite Caramel Frosting between layers and on sides and top of cake, or frost as desired. **Yield: one 2-layer cake.**

Favorite Caramel Frosting
3 cups sugar, divided
¾ cup milk
1 large egg, beaten
Pinch of salt
½ cup butter or margarine, cut up

Sprinkle ½ cup sugar in a heavy saucepan; place over medium heat. Cook, stirring constantly, until sugar melts and turns a light golden brown.

Combine remaining 2½ cups sugar, milk, egg, and salt, stirring well; stir in butter. Stir into hot caramelized sugar. (Mixture will tend to lump, becoming smooth with further cooking.)

Cook over medium heat, stirring frequently, until a candy thermometer registers 230° (about 15 to 20 minutes). Cool 5 minutes. Beat with a wooden spoon to almost spreading consistency (about 5 minutes), and spread on cooled cake. **Yield: about 2½ cups.**

Yellow Cake

1 cup shortening
2 cups sugar
4 large eggs
3 cups sifted cake flour
2½ teaspoons baking powder
½ teaspoon salt
1 cup milk
1 teaspoon almond extract
1 teaspoon vanilla extract
Pineapple Filling
Seven-Minute Frosting

Beat shortening at medium speed of an electric mixer until fluffy; gradually add sugar, beating well. Add eggs, one at a time, beating until blended after each addition.

Combine flour, baking powder, and salt; add to shortening mixture alternately with milk, beginning and ending with flour mixture. Beat at low speed until blended after each addition. Stir in flavorings. Pour batter into 3 greased and floured 9-inch round cakepans.

Bake at 375° for 20 to 25 minutes or until a wooden pick inserted in center comes out clean. Cool in pans on wire racks 10 minutes; remove from pans, and cool completely on wire racks.

Spread Pineapple Filling between layers; spread Seven-Minute Frosting on sides and top of cake. **Yield: one 3-layer cake.**

Pineapple Filling

3 tablespoons all-purpose flour
½ cup sugar
1 (20-ounce) can crushed pineapple
2 tablespoons butter or margarine

Combine flour and sugar in a small saucepan; add undrained pineapple and butter. Cook over medium heat, stirring constantly, until thickened. Cool. **Yield: 2⅔ cups.**

Seven-Minute Frosting

1½ cups sugar
¼ cup plus 1 tablespoon warm water
2 egg whites
1 tablespoon light corn syrup
Dash of salt
1 teaspoon vanilla extract

Combine first 5 ingredients in top of a large double boiler. Beat at low speed of an electric mixer 30 seconds or just until blended.

Place over boiling water; beat constantly at high speed 7 to 9 minutes or until stiff peaks form and temperature reaches 160°. Remove from heat. Add vanilla; beat 2 minutes or until thick enough to spread. **Yield: 4¼ cups.**

Devil's Food Cake

¾ cup butter or margarine, softened
2 cups sugar
2 large eggs
4 (1-ounce) squares unsweetened chocolate, melted
1 teaspoon vanilla extract
2 cups all-purpose flour
2 teaspoons baking powder
½ teaspoon salt
⅛ teaspoon ground cinnamon (optional)
1½ cups milk
Chocolate Frosting

Beat softened butter at medium speed of an electric mixer until creamy; gradually add sugar, beating well.

Add eggs, one at a time, beating until blended after each addition. Stir in melted chocolate and vanilla.

Combine flour, baking powder, salt, and, if desired, cinnamon; add to chocolate mixture alternately with milk, beginning and ending with flour mixture. Beat at low speed until blended after each addition. Pour batter into 2 greased and floured 9-inch round cakepans.

Bake at 350° for 25 to 30 minutes or until a wooden pick inserted in center comes out clean. Cool in pans on wire racks 10 minutes; remove from pans, and cool completely on wire racks.

Spread Chocolate Frosting between layers and on sides and top of cake. **Yield: one 2-layer cake.**

Chocolate Frosting

4½ (1-ounce) squares unsweetened chocolate
½ cup butter or margarine
5⅔ cups sifted powdered sugar
½ cup milk
1 teaspoon vanilla extract

Combine chocolate and butter in a heavy saucepan; cook over low heat until chocolate melts. Remove from heat, and cool.

Add powdered sugar and milk; beat at low speed of an electric mixer until smooth. Stir in vanilla. **Yield: 3 cups.**

Creamy Chocolate Cake

Creamy Chocolate Cake

1 (4-ounce) package sweet baking chocolate
½ cup boiling water
1 cup butter or margarine, softened
2 cups sugar
4 large eggs
1 teaspoon baking soda
1 cup buttermilk
3¾ cups sifted cake flour
½ teaspoon salt
2 teaspoons vanilla extract
Buttercream Filling
Creamy Frosting
1 cup finely chopped pecans
Garnish: pecan halves

Grease three 9-inch round cakepans, and line with wax paper; grease and flour paper. Set aside.

Combine chocolate and boiling water; stir until chocolate melts. Set aside.

Beat butter at medium speed of an electric mixer until creamy. Add sugar; beat 5 minutes. Add eggs, one at a time, beating after each addition.

Dissolve soda in buttermilk. Combine flour and salt; add to butter mixture alternately with buttermilk mixture, beginning and ending with flour mixture. Beat at low speed until blended after each addition. Stir in chocolate and vanilla. Pour batter into prepared pans.

Bake at 350° for 30 minutes or until a wooden pick inserted in center comes out clean. Remove from pans. Remove wax paper; cool on wire racks.

Spread filling between layers; spread frosting on sides and top of cake. Decorate top of cake, using a cake comb, if desired. Press chopped pecans into frosting on sides of cake. Garnish, if desired. **Yield: one 3-layer cake.**

Buttercream Filling
⅓ cup unsalted butter, softened
2¼ cups sifted powdered sugar
2 to 3 tablespoons half-and-half

Beat butter at medium speed of an electric mixer until creamy; gradually add sugar, beating well. Add half-and-half, 1 tablespoon at a time, beating until spreading consistency. **Yield: 1⅓ cups.**

Creamy Frosting
¾ cup sugar
⅓ cup water
3 egg yolks
1 cup unsalted butter, softened
2 (1-ounce) squares unsweetened chocolate, melted and cooled
2 (1-ounce) squares semisweet chocolate, melted and cooled
1 teaspoon chocolate extract

Combine sugar and water in a medium saucepan. Bring to a boil; cook over medium heat, without stirring, until mixture reaches soft ball stage (240°).

Beat egg yolks at high speed of an electric mixer until thick and pale; continue beating, adding 240° syrup in a heavy stream. Beat until mixture thickens and cools.

Add butter, 3 tablespoons at a time, beating until smooth. Stir in melted chocolate and extract. Chill to spreadable consistency. **Yield: 2 cups.**

Creamy Chocolate Cake Technique

Add texture to a frosted cake by decorating with a frosting comb (available in kitchen shops).

Lemon-Coconut Cake

1 cup butter, softened
2 cups sugar
3¼ cups sifted cake flour
2½ teaspoons baking powder
½ teaspoon salt
1 cup milk
¾ teaspoon coconut extract
½ teaspoon lemon extract
6 egg whites
¾ teaspoon cream of tartar
Lemon-Coconut Filling
Fluffy Lemon Frosting
1½ to 2 cups flaked coconut
Garnish: lemon rind curls

Beat softened butter at medium speed of an electric mixer until creamy; gradually add sugar, beating well.

Combine flour, baking powder, and salt; add to butter mixture alternately with milk, beginning and ending with flour mixture. Beat mixture at low speed until blended after each addition. Stir in flavorings.

Beat egg whites in a large mixing bowl at high speed until foamy. Add cream of tartar; beat until stiff peaks form. Gently fold one-third of egg whites into batter; fold in remaining egg whites. Pour batter into 3 greased and floured 9-inch round cakepans.

Bake at 350° for 20 to 25 minutes or until a wooden pick inserted in center comes out clean. Cool in pans on wire racks 10 minutes; remove from pans, and cool completely on wire racks.

Spread Lemon-Coconut Filling between layers; spread Fluffy Lemon Frosting on sides and top of cake. Gently press coconut into frosting. Garnish, if desired. **Yield: one 3-layer cake.**

Lemon-Coconut Filling

1 cup sugar
3 tablespoons cornstarch
⅛ teaspoon salt
1 tablespoon grated lemon rind
⅔ cup lemon juice
⅓ cup water
5 egg yolks, beaten
½ cup butter or margarine
½ cup flaked coconut

Combine first 3 ingredients in a heavy saucepan; stir well.

Stir in lemon rind, juice, and water. Cook over medium heat, stirring constantly, until mixture thickens and comes to a boil. Boil 1 minute, stirring constantly.

Stir half of hot mixture gradually into egg yolks; add to remaining hot mixture, stirring constantly. Cook 1 minute, stirring constantly.

Remove from heat; add butter and coconut, stirring until butter melts. Cool completely. **Yield: 2½ cups.**

Fluffy Lemon Frosting

1 cup sugar
⅓ cup water
2 tablespoons light corn syrup
2 egg whites
¼ cup sifted powdered sugar
1 teaspoon grated lemon rind
½ teaspoon lemon extract

Combine first 3 ingredients in a heavy saucepan. Cook over medium heat, stirring constantly, until clear. Cook, without stirring, until candy thermometer registers 232°.

Beat egg whites at high speed of an electric mixer until soft peaks form; continue to beat, adding hot syrup mixture. Add powdered sugar, lemon rind, and lemon extract; continue beating until stiff peaks form and frosting is spreading consistency. **Yield: about 3 cups.**

Lemon-Coconut Cake

Tart Lemon-Cheese Cake

1 cup butter, softened
2 cups sugar
¾ cup water
¼ cup milk
3¼ cups sifted cake flour
2¾ teaspoons baking powder
½ teaspoon salt
½ teaspoon rum flavoring or 1 teaspoon
    vanilla extract
6 egg whites
Lemon-Cheese Filling
Lemony White Frosting

Beat butter at medium speed of an electric mixer until creamy; gradually add sugar, beating well.

Combine water and milk; set aside.

Combine flour, baking powder, and salt; add to butter mixture alternately with milk mixture, beginning and ending with flour mixture. Stir in rum flavoring.

Beat egg whites in a large mixing bowl at high speed until stiff peaks form; fold into batter. Pour batter into 3 greased and floured 9-inch round cakepans.

Bake at 350° for 20 to 25 minutes or until a wooden pick inserted in center comes out clean. Cool in pans on wire racks 10 minutes; remove from pans, and cool completely on wire racks.

Spread Lemon-Cheese Filling between layers and on top of cake. Spread Lemony White Frosting on sides. **Yield: one 3-layer cake.**

Lemon-Cheese Filling

1 cup sugar
3 tablespoons cornstarch
⅛ teaspoon salt
2 tablespoons grated lemon rind
1 cup lemon juice
6 egg yolks, beaten
⅓ cup butter or margarine

Combine first 3 ingredients in a heavy saucepan; stir well. Add lemon rind and juice; cook over medium heat, stirring constantly, until mixture thickens and comes to a boil. Boil 1 minute, stirring constantly.

Stir half of hot mixture gradually into egg yolks; add to remaining hot mixture, stirring constantly. Cook, stirring constantly, about 1 minute or until mixture is thoroughly heated.

Remove from heat. Add butter, stirring until butter melts; cool. **Yield: 2 cups.**

Lemony White Frosting

1 cup sugar
⅓ cup water
2 tablespoons light corn syrup
2 egg whites
¼ cup sifted powdered sugar
½ teaspoon lemon extract

Combine first 3 ingredients in a heavy saucepan. Cook over medium heat, stirring constantly, until clear. Cook, without stirring, until candy thermometer registers 232°.

Beat egg whites at high speed of an electric mixer until soft peaks form; continue to beat, adding hot syrup mixture.

Add powdered sugar and lemon extract; continue beating until stiff peaks form and frosting is spreading consistency. **Yield: about 3 cups.**

Why Use Cake Flour?

Cake flour is a soft wheat flour with a high starch content. It makes very tender, fine-textured cakes but should be sifted before measuring. The substitution for 1 cup cake flour is 1 cup all-purpose flour minus 2 tablespoons.

Italian Cream Cake

Italian Cream Cake

1 cup butter or margarine, softened
2 cups sugar
5 large eggs, separated
2½ cups all-purpose flour
1 teaspoon baking soda
1 cup milk
⅔ cup finely chopped pecans
1 (3½-ounce) can flaked coconut
1 teaspoon vanilla extract
½ teaspoon cream of tartar
3 tablespoons light rum
Cream Cheese Frosting

Grease three 9-inch round cakepans, and line with wax paper; grease and flour paper. Set aside.

Beat butter at medium speed of an electric mixer until creamy; add sugar, beating well. Add egg yolks, one at a time, beating until blended after each addition.

Combine flour and baking soda; add to butter mixture alternately with milk, beginning and ending with flour mixture. Beat at low speed after each addition. Stir in chopped pecans, coconut, and vanilla.

Beat egg whites in a large mixing bowl at high speed until foamy. Add cream of tartar; beat until stiff peaks form. Gently fold one-third of egg whites into batter; fold in remaining egg whites. Pour batter into prepared pans.

Bake at 350° for 25 to 30 minutes or until a wooden pick inserted in center comes out clean. Cool in pans on wire racks 10 minutes. Remove from pans; peel off wax paper, and cool completely on wire racks.

Sprinkle each layer with 1 tablespoon light rum. Let stand 10 minutes. Spread Cream Cheese Frosting between layers and on sides and top of cake. **Yield: one 3-layer cake.**

Cream Cheese Frosting

1 (8-ounce) package cream cheese, softened
½ cup butter, softened
1 (16-ounce) package powdered sugar, sifted
1 cup chopped pecans
2 teaspoons vanilla extract

Combine cream cheese and butter, beating until smooth. Gradually add powdered sugar, and beat until light and fluffy. Stir in pecans and vanilla. **Yield: 4 cups.**

From left: Lady Baltimore Cake and Lord Baltimore Cake

Lord Baltimore Cake

¾ cup shortening
2¼ cups sugar
8 egg yolks
3¾ cups sifted cake flour
1½ tablespoons baking powder
½ teaspoon salt
1¾ cups milk
½ teaspoon almond extract
½ teaspoon vanilla extract
Frosting
1 cup chopped mixed candied fruit
1 cup chopped pecans or walnuts
½ cup macaroon crumbs
1 teaspoon vanilla extract
½ teaspoon almond extract
Garnish: candied cherries

Beat shortening at medium speed of an electric mixer until fluffy; gradually add sugar, beating well. Add egg yolks, one at a time, beating until blended after each addition.

Combine flour, baking powder, and salt; add to shortening mixture alternately with milk, beginning and ending with flour mixture. Beat at low speed until blended after each addition. Stir in ½ teaspoon each of almond and vanilla extract. Pour batter into 3 greased and floured 9-inch round cakepans.

Bake at 350° for 20 to 25 minutes or until a wooden pick inserted in center comes out clean. Cool in pans on wire racks 10 minutes. Remove from pans, and cool completely on wire racks.

Combine 2 cups Frosting, candied fruit, and

next 4 ingredients; spread between layers. Spread remaining Frosting on sides and top of cake. Garnish, if desired. **Yield: one 3-layer cake.**

Frosting

1½ cups sugar
½ cup water
1 tablespoon light corn syrup
4 egg whites

Combine first 3 ingredients in a heavy saucepan; cook over low heat until mixture reaches soft ball stage (240°).

Beat egg whites in a large mixing bowl at high speed until soft peaks form; continue beating, adding 240° syrup mixture. Beat 1 minute. **Yield: 7 cups.**

Lady Baltimore Cake

1 cup butter or margarine, softened
2 cups sugar
½ cup water
½ cup milk
3 cups sifted cake flour
2¾ teaspoons baking powder
½ teaspoon salt
½ teaspoon almond extract
6 egg whites
1 cup chopped raisins or currants
1 cup chopped dried figs
1 cup chopped almonds or walnuts
½ cup sherry or brandy
Boiled Frosting
Garnish: whole roasted almonds

Beat softened butter at medium speed of an electric mixer until creamy; gradually add sugar, beating well.

Combine water and milk; set aside.

Combine flour, baking powder, and salt; add to butter mixture alternately with milk mixture,

beginning and ending with flour mixture. Beat at low speed until blended after each addition. Stir in almond extract.

Beat egg whites in a large mixing bowl at high speed until stiff peaks form; fold into batter. Pour batter into 3 greased and floured 9-inch round cakepans.

Bake at 350° for 25 minutes or until a wooden pick inserted in center comes out clean. Cool in pans on wire racks 10 minutes; remove from pans, and cool completely on wire racks.

Combine raisins, figs, almonds, and sherry; let stand 30 minutes. Drain well, discarding sherry; set fruit aside.

Combine 2 cups Boiled Frosting and fruit mixture; spread between layers. Spread remaining frosting on sides and top of cake. Garnish, if desired. **Yield: one 3-layer cake.**

Boiled Frosting

1½ cups sugar
½ teaspoon cream of tartar
⅛ teaspoon salt
½ cup water
4 egg whites
½ teaspoon almond extract
½ teaspoon vanilla extract

Combine first 4 ingredients in a heavy saucepan. Cook over medium heat, stirring constantly, until clear. Cook, without stirring, to soft ball stage (240°).

Beat egg whites in a large mixing bowl at high speed until soft peaks form; continue beating, adding 240° syrup mixture. Add flavorings; beat until stiff peaks form and frosting is spreading consistency. **Yield: 7 cups.**

Apple Cake with Brown Sugar Glaze

2 cups sugar
1 cup vegetable oil
3 large eggs
3 cups all-purpose flour
1 teaspoon baking soda
½ teaspoon salt
1 teaspoon ground cinnamon
3 cups peeled, finely chopped cooking apple
½ cup chopped pecans
Brown Sugar Glaze

Beat first 3 ingredients at medium speed of an electric mixer until creamy.

Combine flour and next 3 ingredients; add to sugar mixture, beating well. Stir in apple and pecans. Spoon batter into a greased and floured 12-cup Bundt pan.

Bake at 350° for 1 hour and 20 minutes or until a wooden pick inserted in center comes out clean. Cool in pan on a wire rack 10 to 15 minutes; remove from pan, and cool completely on wire rack.

Drizzle Brown Sugar Glaze over cake. **Yield: one 10-inch cake.**

Brown Sugar Glaze
½ cup firmly packed brown sugar
¼ cup butter or margarine
2 tablespoons evaporated milk

Combine all ingredients in a small saucepan; cook over high heat, stirring constantly, 2 minutes or until butter melts. Cool to lukewarm. **Yield: ½ cup.**

Favorite Stack Cake

½ cup butter or margarine, softened
1 cup sugar
½ cup buttermilk
1 large egg
1 teaspoon vanilla extract
3½ cups all-purpose flour
1½ teaspoons baking powder
½ teaspoon baking soda
½ teaspoon salt
¼ cup butter or margarine, melted
Dried Apple Filling
Sifted powdered sugar (optional)

Beat butter at medium speed of an electric mixer until creamy; add sugar, beating well. Add buttermilk, egg, and vanilla; beat until blended.

Combine flour, baking powder, soda, and salt; gradually add to butter mixture, beating until blended.

Divide dough into 6 equal portions; pat each into the bottom of a lightly greased 9-inch round cakepan. Prick dough several times with a fork.

Bake at 400° for 10 minutes or until lightly browned. Remove layers to a wire rack; cool.

Stack cake layers, spreading melted butter and Dried Apple Filling between each layer. Cover and chill 8 hours before serving. Sprinkle with powdered sugar, if desired. **Yield: one 9-inch cake.**

Dried Apple Filling
2 (8-ounce) packages dried apples
4 cups water
¾ cup sugar
1 teaspoon ground cinnamon
½ teaspoon pumpkin pie spice

Combine apples and water in a large saucepan. Bring to a boil; cover, reduce heat, and simmer 30 minutes or until tender. Add sugar and spices; stir well. **Yield: about 3½ cups.**

Hummingbird Cake

Hummingbird Cake

3 cups all-purpose flour
1 teaspoon baking soda
½ teaspoon salt
2 cups sugar
1 teaspoon ground cinnamon
3 large eggs, lightly beaten
¾ cup vegetable oil
1½ teaspoons vanilla extract
1 (8-ounce) can crushed pineapple, undrained
1 cup chopped pecans
1¾ cups mashed banana
Cream Cheese Frosting
Garnish: fresh rose petals

Combine first 5 ingredients in a large bowl; add eggs and oil, stirring until dry ingredients are moistened. (Do not beat.)

Stir in vanilla and next 3 ingredients. Pour batter into 3 greased and floured 9-inch round cakepans.

Bake at 350° for 23 to 28 minutes or until a wooden pick inserted in center comes out clean. Cool in pans on wire racks 10 minutes; remove from pans, and cool completely on wire racks.

Spread Cream Cheese Frosting between layers and on sides and top of cake. Store in refrigerator up to 3 days, or freeze up to 3 months. Garnish, if desired. **Yield: one 3-layer cake.**

Cream Cheese Frosting
½ cup butter or margarine, softened
1 (8-ounce) package cream cheese, softened
1 (16-ounce) package powdered sugar, sifted
1 teaspoon vanilla extract

Beat butter and cream cheese at medium speed of an electric mixer until creamy. Gradually add powdered sugar, beating until light and fluffy. Stir in vanilla. **Yield: about 3 cups.**

Note: Store cake in the refrigerator.

Banana-Nut Layer Cake

(pictured on page 555)

½ cup butter or margarine, softened
¾ cup sugar
¾ cup firmly packed brown sugar
2 large eggs, separated
1 teaspoon baking soda
⅓ cup buttermilk
2 cups all-purpose flour
½ teaspoon ground allspice
½ teaspoon instant coffee granules
3 ripe bananas, mashed
1 cup chopped pecans, toasted
1 teaspoon vanilla extract
Vanilla Buttercream Frosting
Garnish: toasted sliced almonds

Beat butter at medium speed of an electric mixer until creamy; gradually add sugars, beating well. Add egg yolks, beating until blended.

Dissolve soda in buttermilk. Combine flour, allspice, and coffee granules; add to butter mixture alternately with buttermilk mixture, beginning and ending with flour mixture. Beat at low speed until blended after each addition. Stir in mashed banana, pecans, and vanilla.

Beat egg whites at high speed until stiff peaks form; gently fold into batter, one-third at a time. Pour batter into 2 greased and floured 8-inch round cakepans.

Bake at 350° for 30 minutes or until a wooden pick inserted in center comes out clean. Cool in pans on wire racks 10 minutes; remove from pans, and cool completely on wire racks.

Split cake layers in half horizontally to make 4 layers. Set aside 1½ cups Vanilla Buttercream Frosting. Spread remaining 3 cups frosting between layers and on sides and top of cake.

Spoon 1 cup reserved frosting into a decorating bag fitted with a No. 2B tip. Pipe frosting in a lattice design across top of cake. Spoon remaining ½ cup reserved frosting into a bag fitted with a No. 21 tip, and pipe frosting around top edge of cake. Garnish, if desired. **Yield: one 4-layer cake.**

Vanilla Buttercream Frosting

2¼ cups butter or margarine, softened
6 cups sifted powdered sugar
3 tablespoons milk
1½ teaspoons vanilla extract
¾ teaspoon ground allspice

Beat butter at medium speed of an electric mixer until creamy; add sugar, beating until light and fluffy. Add milk; beat until spreading consistency. Stir in vanilla and allspice. **Yield: 4½ cups.**

Special Spice Cake

1 cup butter or margarine, softened
2 cups firmly packed light brown sugar
3 large eggs
1 teaspoon baking soda
1 cup buttermilk
2 cups all-purpose flour
2 teaspoons ground cinnamon
1 teaspoon vanilla extract
½ cup golden raisins
½ cup raisins
1 cup chopped pecans
Chocolate-Coffee Frosting

Beat butter at medium speed of an electric mixer until creamy; gradually add sugar, beating well. Add eggs, one at a time, beating until blended after each addition.

Dissolve soda in buttermilk. Combine flour and cinnamon; add to butter mixture alternately with buttermilk mixture, beginning and ending with flour mixture. Beat at low speed until blended after each addition. Stir in vanilla, raisins, and pecans. Pour batter into 3 greased and floured 9-inch round cakepans.

Bake at 325° for 25 to 27 minutes or until a

wooden pick inserted in center comes out clean. Cool in pans on wire racks 10 minutes; remove from pans, and cool completely on wire racks.

Spread Chocolate-Coffee Frosting between layers and on sides and top of cake. **Yield: one 3-layer cake.**

Chocolate-Coffee Frosting

1 teaspoon instant coffee granules
½ cup boiling water
7 cups sifted powdered sugar
⅔ cup cocoa
½ cup butter or margarine, softened
1 teaspoon vanilla extract

Dissolve coffee granules in boiling water, and set aside.

Combine powdered sugar and cocoa; mix well. Set aside.

Beat butter at medium speed of an electric mixer until creamy; add sugar mixture and vanilla. Gradually add coffee mixture, beating at high speed to desired spreading consistency. **Yield: enough for one 3-layer cake.**

Old-Fashioned Carrot Cake

3 cups shredded carrot
2 cups all-purpose flour
1 teaspoon baking soda
1 teaspoon baking powder
½ teaspoon salt
2 cups sugar
1 teaspoon ground cinnamon
4 large eggs, beaten
¾ cup vegetable oil
1 teaspoon vanilla extract
Cream Cheese Frosting
Garnish: chopped pecans

Grease three 9-inch round cakepans; line with wax paper. Grease and flour paper. Set aside.

Combine first 7 ingredients in a large bowl; add eggs, oil, and vanilla, stirring until blended. Pour into prepared pans.

Bake at 350° for 25 minutes or until a wooden pick inserted in center comes out clean. Cool in pans on wire racks 10 minutes; remove from pans, and cool completely on wire racks.

Spread Cream Cheese Frosting between layers and on sides and top of cake. Garnish, if desired, and chill. Freeze up to 3 months, if desired. **Yield: one 3-layer cake.**

Cream Cheese Frosting

1 (8-ounce) package cream cheese, softened
½ cup butter or margarine, softened
1 (16-ounce) package powdered sugar, sifted
1 teaspoon vanilla extract

Beat cream cheese and butter at medium speed of an electric mixer until creamy. Gradually add powdered sugar, beating until light and fluffy. Stir in vanilla. **Yield: about 3 cups.**

Old-Fashioned Carrot Cake

Old South Fruitcake

Old South Fruitcake

1½ cups butter, softened
1¼ cups firmly packed brown sugar
⅓ cup molasses
7 large eggs, separated
3 cups all-purpose flour
1½ pounds yellow, green, and red candied
    pineapple, chopped (about 3¾ cups)
1 pound red and green candied cherries,
    halved (about 2½ cups)
3 cups pecan halves, lightly toasted
1 cup walnuts, coarsely chopped
¾ cup golden raisins
¾ cup raisins
½ cup all-purpose flour
1 teaspoon ground allspice
¼ cup brandy
1 tablespoon powdered sugar
Additional brandy (optional)

Draw a circle with a 10-inch diameter on a piece of brown paper, using a tube pan as a guide. (Do not use recycled paper.) Cut out circle; set tube pan insert in center, and draw around inside tube. Cut out smaller circle. Grease paper, and set aside.

Grease heavily and flour 10-inch tube pan, and set aside.

Beat butter at medium speed of an electric mixer; gradually add brown sugar, beating well. Stir in molasses.

Beat egg yolks; alternately add yolks and 3 cups flour to butter mixture. Beat until blended. (Batter will be very thick.)

Combine pineapple, cherries, nuts, and raisins in a bowl; sprinkle with ½ cup flour and allspice, stirring to coat well. Stir mixture into batter.

Beat egg whites in a large bowl at high speed until stiff peaks form; gradually fold into batter.

Spoon batter into prepared pan. Cover pan with 10-inch paper circle, greased side down.

Bake at 250° for 4 hours or until a wooden pick inserted in center comes out clean. Remove from oven; discard paper cover. Loosen cake from sides of pan, using a narrow metal spatula; invert pan, and remove cake. Invert cake again onto a wire rack.

Combine ¼ cup brandy and powdered sugar; stir well. Slowly pour brandy evenly over cake; cool completely on wire rack.

Wrap cake in brandy-soaked cheesecloth. Store in an airtight container in a cool place 3 weeks. Pour a small amount of brandy over cake each week, if desired. **Yield: one 10-inch cake.**

Note: Refrigerate Old South Fruitcake for longer storage. Refrigeration also makes slicing the cake neater and easier.

Variation

Old South Fruitcake Loaves: Spoon batter into 3 greased and floured 8½- x 4½- x 3-inch loafpans or 6 greased and floured 6- x 3½- x 2¼-inch miniature loafpans. Bake at 250° for 2½ hours or until cakes test done.

Old South Fruitcake Technique

Soak cheesecloth in brandy; wring out excess moisture. Wrap fruitcake in cheesecloth to keep it moist and flavorful.

Smoothest Southern Pound Cake

1 cup butter or margarine, softened
3 cups sugar
3 cups sifted cake flour
¼ teaspoon baking soda
6 large eggs, separated
1 (8-ounce) carton sour cream
1 teaspoon vanilla extract

Beat butter at medium speed of an electric mixer (not a handheld one) 2 minutes or until butter is creamy. Gradually add sugar, beating 5 to 7 minutes.

Combine flour and soda; add to butter mixture 1 cup at a time. (Batter will be extremely thick.)

Add egg yolks to batter, and mix well. Stir in sour cream and vanilla. Beat egg whites in a large mixing bowl at high speed until stiff; fold into batter. Spoon batter into a greased and floured 10-inch Bundt or tube pan.

Bake at 300° for 2 hours or until a wooden pick inserted in center comes out clean. (You may also spoon batter into two 9- x 5- x 3-inch loaf-pans, and bake at 300° for 1½ hours or until a wooden pick inserted in center comes out clean.)

Cool in pan on a wire rack 10 to 15 minutes; remove from pan, and cool completely on wire rack. **Yield: one 10-inch cake or two loaves.**

Variation

If you prefer to use a handheld mixer or prefer not to separate the eggs, try this procedure.

Beat butter at medium speed of an electric mixer about 2 minutes or until creamy. Gradually add sugar, beating 7 minutes. Add eggs, one at a time, beating just until yellow disappears.

Combine flour and soda; add to butter mixture alternately with sour cream, beginning and ending with flour mixture. Beat at low speed just until blended after each addition. Stir in vanilla.

Bake as directed.

Whipping Cream Pound Cake

1 cup butter or margarine, softened
3 cups sugar
6 large eggs
3 cups sifted cake flour
1 cup whipping cream
2 teaspoons vanilla extract
Powdered sugar
Garnish: fresh strawberries, mint sprigs

Beat butter at medium speed of an electric mixer 2 minutes or until creamy. Gradually add 3 cups sugar, beating 5 to 7 minutes.

Add eggs, one at a time, beating just until yellow disappears.

Add flour to butter mixture alternately with whipping cream, beginning and ending with flour. Beat at low speed just until blended after each addition. Stir in vanilla. Spoon batter into a greased and floured 10-inch Bundt pan.

Bake at 325° for 1 hour or until a wooden pick inserted in center comes out clean. Cool in pan on a wire rack 10 minutes; remove from pan, and cool completely on wire rack.

Sift powdered sugar over cake. Garnish, if desired. **Yield: one 10-inch cake.**

Whipping Cream Pound Cake Technique

Sift powdered sugar over cooled pound cake; place wax paper underneath wire rack to catch excess sugar.

Whipping Cream Pound Cake

Cream Cheese Pound Cake

1½ cups butter, softened
1 (8-ounce) package cream cheese, softened
3 cups sugar
6 large eggs
1½ teaspoons vanilla extract
3 cups all-purpose flour
⅛ teaspoon salt

Beat butter and cream cheese at medium speed of an electric mixer 2 minutes or until mixture is creamy. Gradually add sugar, beating 5 to 7 minutes.

Add eggs, one at a time, beating just until yellow disappears. Add vanilla, mixing well.

Combine flour and salt; gradually add to butter mixture, beating at low speed just until blended after each addition. Spoon batter into a greased and floured 10-inch tube pan.

Fill a 2-cup, ovenproof measuring cup with water, and place in oven with tube pan.

Bake at 300° for 1 hour and 45 minutes or until a wooden pick inserted in center comes out clean. Cool in pan on a wire rack 10 to 15 minutes; remove from pan, and cool completely on wire rack. **Yield: one 10-inch cake.**

Chocolate-Sour Cream Pound Cake

1 cup butter or margarine, softened
2 cups sugar
1 cup firmly packed brown sugar
6 large eggs
2½ cups all-purpose flour
¼ teaspoon baking soda
½ cup cocoa
1 (8-ounce) carton sour cream
2 teaspoons vanilla extract
Powdered sugar (optional)

Beat butter at medium speed of an electric mixer 2 minutes or until creamy. Gradually add sugars, beating 5 to 7 minutes.

Add eggs, one at a time, beating just until yellow disappears.

Combine flour, baking soda, and cocoa; add to butter mixture alternately with sour cream, beginning and ending with flour mixture. Beat at low speed just until blended after each addition. Stir in vanilla. Spoon batter into a greased and floured 10-inch tube pan.

Bake at 325° for 1 hour and 20 minutes or until a wooden pick inserted in center comes out clean. Cool in pan on a wire rack 10 to 15 minutes; remove from pan, and cool completely on wire rack. Sprinkle with powdered sugar, if desired. **Yield: one 10-inch cake.**

Chocolate-Sour Cream Pound Cake

Orange-Pecan Pound Cake

1 cup butter or margarine, softened
1 cup sugar
3 large eggs
1½ teaspoons grated orange rind
½ teaspoon grated lemon rind
¼ teaspoon orange extract
½ cup finely chopped pecans
2 cups all-purpose flour, divided
½ teaspoon baking powder
⅛ teaspoon salt
⅓ cup milk

Beat butter at medium speed of an electric mixer 2 minutes or until creamy. Gradually add sugar, beating 5 to 7 minutes.

Add eggs, one at a time, beating just until yellow disappears. Stir in rinds and orange extract.

Combine pecans and ¼ cup flour; set aside.

Combine remaining 1¾ cups flour, baking powder, and salt; add to butter mixture alternately with milk, beginning and ending with flour mixture. Beat at low speed just until blended after each addition.

Stir in floured pecans. Spoon batter into a greased and floured 9- x 5- x 3-inch loafpan.

Bake at 325° for 1 hour and 5 minutes or until a wooden pick inserted in center comes out clean. Cool in pan on a wire rack 10 to 15 minutes; remove from pan, and cool completely on wire rack. **Yield: 1 loaf.**

Peach Brandy Pound Cake

1 cup butter or margarine, softened
3 cups sugar
6 large eggs
3 cups all-purpose flour
¼ teaspoon baking soda
⅛ teaspoon salt
1 (8-ounce) carton sour cream
½ cup peach brandy
2 teaspoons rum
1 teaspoon orange extract
1 teaspoon vanilla extract
½ teaspoon lemon extract
¼ teaspoon almond extract

Beat butter at medium speed of an electric mixer 2 minutes or until creamy. Gradually add sugar, beating 5 minutes.

Add eggs, one at a time, beating just until yellow disappears.

Combine flour, soda, and salt; add to butter mixture alternately with sour cream, beginning and ending with flour mixture. Beat at low speed just until blended after each addition. Stir in brandy and remaining ingredients. Spoon batter into a greased and floured 10-inch tube pan.

Bake at 325° for 1½ hours or until a wooden pick inserted in center comes out clean. Cool in pan on a wire rack 10 to 15 minutes; remove from pan, and cool completely on wire rack. **Yield: one 10-inch cake.**

Pound Cake Pointers

- Use the correct pan size. Recipes suitable for a 10-inch tube pan, which holds 16 cups, won't always fit in a 12- or 13-cup Bundt pan.
- Grease pan with solid shortening; do not substitute butter, margarine, or vegetable cooking spray. Flour the greased pan.
- Beat butter and sugar 5 to 7 minutes or until mixture is a fluffy consistency.
- Keep oven door closed until minimum baking time has elapsed.

Angel Food Cake

12 egg whites
1½ teaspoons cream of tartar
¼ teaspoon salt
1½ cups sugar
1 cup sifted cake flour
1½ teaspoons vanilla extract

Beat egg whites in a large mixing bowl at high speed of an electric mixer until foamy. Add cream of tartar and salt; beat until soft peaks form. Add sugar, 2 tablespoons at a time, beating until stiff peaks form.

Sprinkle flour over egg white mixture, ¼ cup at a time; fold in carefully. Fold in vanilla. Spoon batter into an ungreased 10-inch tube pan, spreading evenly.

Bake at 375° for 30 to 35 minutes or until cake springs back when lightly touched. Invert pan, and cool 40 minutes. Loosen cake from sides of pan using a narrow metal spatula; remove from pan. **Yield: one 10-inch cake.**

Variation

Chocolate Angel Food Cake: For a chocolate version, sift ¼ cup cocoa with flour.

Angel Cake Surprise

1 (10-inch) angel food cake
½ cup semisweet chocolate morsels
3 cups whipping cream, divided
1 tablespoon Chambord or other raspberry-
    flavored liqueur
¼ cup sifted powdered sugar
Garnishes: grated chocolate, fresh raspberries

Slice off top one-third of cake; set aside. Using a sharp knife, hollow out center of remaining cake, leaving a 1-inch shell; reserve cake pieces for another use. Place cake shell on serving plate, and set aside.

Melt chocolate morsels in a heavy saucepan over low heat, stirring occasionally, until smooth; remove from heat, and cool.

Beat 1 cup whipping cream at medium speed of an electric mixer until firm peaks form; fold in liqueur and melted chocolate. Spoon into cake shell; place top one-third of cake over filling, pressing firmly.

Beat remaining 2 cups whipping cream at medium speed until foamy; add powdered sugar, beating until firm peaks form. Spread over sides and top of cake; chill up to 8 hours. Garnish, if desired. **Yield: one 10-inch cake.**

Note: You may substitute 1 tablespoon Cointreau or other orange-flavored liqueur for Chambord.

Triple Mint Ice Cream Angel Dessert

1 (10-inch) angel food cake
4 cups chocolate-mint ice cream, slightly
    softened and divided
2 cups pink peppermint ice cream, slightly
    softened
Whipped Cream Frosting
Chocolate-Mint Sauce

Split cake horizontally into 4 equal layers. Place bottom layer on a serving plate; spread top of layer with half of chocolate-mint ice cream to within ½ inch from edge. Top with second cake layer; cover and freeze 45 minutes or until firm.

Spread second cake layer with pink peppermint ice cream. Add third cake layer; cover and freeze 45 minutes or until firm.

Spread third layer with remaining chocolate-mint ice cream, and top with remaining cake layer; cover and freeze until firm.

Triple Mint Ice Cream Angel Dessert

Spread Whipped Cream Frosting on sides and top of cake. Cover and freeze up to 12 hours, if desired; let stand at room temperature 15 to 20 minutes before serving. Serve with Chocolate-Mint Sauce. **Yield: one 10-inch cake.**

Whipped Cream Frosting
3 cups whipping cream
3 tablespoons powdered sugar
1½ teaspoons vanilla extract

Beat whipping cream at low speed of an electric mixer until thickened; add sugar and vanilla, beating until firm peaks form. **Yield: 6 cups.**

Chocolate-Mint Sauce
¾ cup half-and-half
1 (10-ounce) package mint chocolate morsels
1½ cups miniature marshmallows
¼ teaspoon salt
1 teaspoon vanilla extract

Heat half-and-half in a heavy saucepan over low heat. Stir in chocolate morsels, marshmallows, and salt; cook, stirring constantly, until chocolate and marshmallows melt. Remove from heat; stir in vanilla. **Yield: 1½ cups.**

Note: Dip knife in hot water to make cutting cake easier.

Daffodil Sponge Cake

Daffodil Sponge Cake

1 cup sifted cake flour
½ cup sugar
4 egg yolks
½ teaspoon lemon extract
10 egg whites
1 teaspoon cream of tartar
½ teaspoon salt
¾ cup sugar
½ teaspoon vanilla extract
Lemon Glaze
Garnishes: lemon roses, fresh lemon balm
  leaves

Sift flour and ½ cup sugar together 3 times; set aside.

Beat egg yolks at high speed of an electric mixer 4 minutes or until thick and pale. Add lemon extract; beat at medium speed 5 minutes or until thick. Set aside.

Beat egg whites, cream of tartar, and salt at high speed just until foamy. Gradually add ¾ cup sugar, 2 tablespoons at a time, beating until stiff peaks form and sugar dissolves (2 to 4 minutes).

Sprinkle one-fourth of flour mixture over beaten egg whites; gently fold in, using a rubber spatula. Repeat procedure with remaining flour mixture, adding one-fourth of mixture at a time. Divide egg white mixture in half.

Fold vanilla into half of egg white mixture. Gently fold beaten egg yolk mixture into remaining egg white mixture.

Drop batters alternately by spoonfuls into an ungreased 10-inch tube pan. Gently swirl batters with a knife to create a marbled effect.

Bake at 350° for 45 to 50 minutes or until cake springs back when lightly touched. Invert pan, and cool 40 minutes. Loosen cake from sides of pan using a narrow metal spatula; remove from pan. Place on a serving plate.

Drizzle cake with Lemon Glaze. Garnish, if desired. **Yield: one 10-inch cake.**

Lemon Glaze

1½ cups sifted powdered sugar
1 teaspoon grated lemon rind
⅛ teaspoon lemon extract
2 to 3 tablespoons lemon juice

Combine all ingredients in a small bowl, stirring until smooth. **Yield: about ½ cup.**

Orange Chiffon Cake

2¼ cups sifted cake flour
1 tablespoon baking powder
½ teaspoon salt
1½ cups sugar
½ cup vegetable oil
5 egg yolks
2 teaspoons grated orange rind
¾ cup orange juice
1 teaspoon vanilla extract
8 egg whites
½ teaspoon cream of tartar

Combine first 4 ingredients in a mixing bowl; make a well in center. Add oil and next 4 ingredients; beat at medium speed of an electric mixer until smooth.

Beat egg whites and cream of tartar in a large mixing bowl at high speed until soft peaks form. Pour egg yolk mixture in a thin, steady stream over egg whites; gently fold yolks into whites. Pour batter into an ungreased 10-inch tube pan, spreading evenly.

Bake at 325° for 1 hour or until cake springs back when lightly touched. Invert pan; cool 40 minutes. Loosen cake from sides of pan using a narrow metal spatula; remove from pan. **Yield: one 10-inch cake.**

Peanut Butter Surprise Cake

Peanut Butter Surprise Cake

10 (6-ounce) peanut butter cup candies
1 cup creamy peanut butter
¾ cup butter or margarine, softened
1 cup sugar
¾ cup firmly packed brown sugar
3 large eggs
2 cups all-purpose flour
2 teaspoons baking powder
½ teaspoon salt
1 cup milk
Chocolate-Peanut Butter Frosting
¼ cup chopped roasted peanuts

Freeze peanut butter cup candies. Beat peanut butter and butter at medium speed of an electric mixer until creamy.

Add sugars, beating until light and fluffy. Add eggs, one at a time, beating until blended after each addition.

Combine flour, baking powder, and salt; add to butter mixture alternately with milk, beginning and ending with flour mixture. Beat at low speed until blended after each addition. Coarsely chop frozen candies, and fold into batter.

Pour batter into a greased and floured 13- x 9- x 2-inch pan.

Bake at 350° for 55 minutes to 1 hour or until a wooden pick inserted in center comes out clean. Cool in pan on a wire rack. (Cake may sink slightly in center.)

Spread Chocolate-Peanut Butter Frosting over top of cake. Sprinkle with peanuts. **Yield: 15 servings.**

Chocolate-Peanut Butter Frosting
1 (6-ounce) package semisweet chocolate
    morsels
1⅓ cups creamy peanut butter
½ cup butter or margarine, softened
½ cup sifted powdered sugar

Melt chocolate morsels in a small saucepan over low heat; set aside.

Combine peanut butter, butter, and powdered sugar in a mixing bowl; beat at medium speed of an electric mixer until smooth. Add melted chocolate; beat until smooth. Chill 30 minutes or until spreading consistency. **Yield: 2½ cups.**

Old-Fashioned Gingerbread

½ cup butter or margarine, softened
½ cup sugar
1 large egg
1 cup molasses
2½ cups all-purpose flour
1½ teaspoons baking soda
½ teaspoon salt
1 teaspoon ground cinnamon
1 teaspoon ground cloves
1 teaspoon ground ginger
1 cup hot water
Sweetened whipped cream

Beat butter at medium speed of an electric mixer until creamy; gradually add sugar, beating well. Add egg and molasses, mixing well.

Combine flour and next 5 ingredients; add to butter mixture alternately with water, beginning and ending with flour mixture. Beat at low speed until blended after each addition.

Pour batter into a lightly greased and floured 9-inch square pan.

Bake at 350° for 35 to 40 minutes or until a wooden pick inserted in center comes out clean. Serve with a dollop of whipped cream. **Yield: 9 servings.**

Quick Chocolate-Cola Cake

1 (18.25-ounce) package devil's food cake mix
    without pudding
1 (3.9-ounce) package chocolate instant
    pudding mix
4 large eggs
½ cup vegetable oil
1 (10-ounce) bottle cola-flavored carbonated
    beverage (1¼ cups)
Chocolate-Cola Frosting

Combine first 4 ingredients in a large mixing bowl; beat at low speed of an electric mixer until blended, and set aside.

Bring cola to a boil in a small saucepan over medium heat. With mixer on low speed, gradually pour hot cola into cake batter. Increase speed to medium; beat 2 minutes.

Pour batter into a greased and floured 13- x 9- x 2-inch pan.

Bake at 350° for 30 minutes or until a wooden pick inserted in center comes out clean. Cool in pan on a wire rack 10 minutes.

Spread Chocolate-Cola Frosting over top of warm cake; cool cake completely on wire rack.
Yield: 15 servings.

Chocolate-Cola Frosting

½ cup butter or margarine
¼ cup plus 2 tablespoons cola-flavored
    carbonated beverage
3 tablespoons cocoa
1 (16-ounce) package powdered sugar, sifted
1 teaspoon vanilla extract
1 cup chopped pecans

Combine first 3 ingredients in a large saucepan; cook over medium heat, stirring constantly, until butter melts. (Do not boil.)

Remove from heat; add powdered sugar and vanilla, stirring until smooth. Stir in pecans.
Yield: about 2¼ cups.

Pineapple Upside-Down Cake

½ cup butter or margarine
1 cup firmly packed brown sugar
3 (8¼-ounce) cans pineapple slices, undrained
10 pecan halves
11 maraschino cherries, halved
2 large eggs, separated
1 egg yolk
1 cup sugar
1 cup all-purpose flour
1 teaspoon baking powder
½ teaspoon ground cinnamon
¼ teaspoon salt
1 teaspoon vanilla extract
¼ teaspoon cream of tartar

Melt butter in a 10-inch cast-iron skillet over low heat. Sprinkle brown sugar in skillet. Remove from heat.

Drain pineapple, reserving ¼ cup juice. Cut pineapple slices in half, reserving 1 whole slice.

Place whole pineapple slice in center of skillet. Arrange 10 pineapple pieces in a spoke fashion around whole slice in center of skillet.

Place a pecan half and a cherry half between each piece of pineapple. Place a cherry half in center of whole pineapple slice. Arrange remaining pineapple pieces, cut side up, around sides of skillet. Place a cherry half in center of each piece of pineapple around sides of skillet.

Beat 3 egg yolks at medium speed of an electric mixer until thick and pale; gradually add 1 cup sugar, beating well.

Combine flour and next 3 ingredients; stir well. Add to yolk mixture alternately with reserved pineapple juice. Stir in vanilla.

Beat egg whites and cream of tartar at high speed until stiff peaks form; fold into batter. Spoon batter evenly over pineapple in skillet.

Bake at 350° for 45 to 50 minutes or until set. Invert onto a serving plate immediately. Cut into wedges to serve. **Yield: one 10-inch cake.**

Pineapple Upside-Down Cake

Strawberry Shortcake

1 quart strawberries, sliced
¼ to ½ cup sugar
½ cup butter or margarine, softened and
    divided
2 cups all-purpose flour
1 tablespoon plus 1 teaspoon baking powder
¼ teaspoon salt
¼ cup sugar
Dash of ground nutmeg
½ cup milk
2 large eggs, separated
¼ cup sugar
1 cup whipping cream
¼ cup sifted powdered sugar
Whole strawberries

Combine sliced strawberries and ¼ to ½ cup sugar; stir gently. Cover and chill 1 to 2 hours. Drain.

Butter two 9-inch round cakepans each with ½ tablespoon butter; set aside.

Combine flour and next 4 ingredients in a large mixing bowl; cut in remaining butter with a pastry blender until mixture is crumbly.

Combine milk and egg yolks; beat well. Add to flour mixture; stir with a fork until a soft dough forms. Pat dough out evenly into cakepans. (Dough will be sticky; moisten fingers with water as necessary.)

Beat egg whites at high speed of an electric mixer until stiff but not dry. Gently brush surface of dough with beaten egg whites; sprinkle evenly with ¼ cup sugar.

Bake at 450° for 8 to 10 minutes or until layers are golden. Remove from pans, and cool completely on wire racks. (Layers will be thin.)

Beat whipping cream until foamy; gradually add powdered sugar, beating until soft peaks form.

Place 1 cake layer on a serving plate. Spread half of whipped cream over layer, and arrange half of sliced strawberries on top.

Repeat procedure with remaining layer, whipped cream, and strawberries, reserving a small amount of whipped cream. Garnish cake with remaining whipped cream and whole strawberries. **Yield: one 2-layer cake.**

Orange-Strawberry Shortcake

2 pints fresh strawberries, sliced
2 (11-ounce) cans mandarin oranges, drained
½ cup sugar
1½ tablespoons Triple Sec or other orange-
    flavored liqueur
2 cups biscuit mix
⅔ cup milk
1 tablespoon sugar
1½ teaspoons ground cinnamon
2 cups whipping cream
½ cup sifted powdered sugar
¼ cup sour cream

Combine first 4 ingredients, stirring until sugar dissolves. Cover and chill 2 hours.

Combine biscuit mix and next 3 ingredients; stir with a fork until dry ingredients are moistened. Turn out onto a floured surface; knead 4 or 5 times. Place dough on a lightly greased baking sheet; press into a 7- x ¾-inch round.

Bake at 425° for 15 minutes or until done. Carefully remove from pan; cool on a wire rack.

Beat whipping cream at medium speed of an electric mixer until foamy; gradually add powdered sugar, beating until soft peaks form. Add sour cream, and beat until firm peaks form.

Split biscuit round in half horizontally. Place bottom half on a serving plate.

Drain fruit, reserving 2 tablespoons liquid. Spoon two-thirds of fruit on bottom round; drizzle with reserved liquid. Spoon half of whipped cream mixture over fruit. Add top biscuit round. Top with remaining fruit and whipped cream. **Yield: 8 servings.**

Orange-Strawberry Shortcake

Chocolate-Raspberry Shortcake

Chocolate-Raspberry Shortcake

½ cup butter or margarine, softened
1¼ cups sugar
2 large eggs, separated
1¼ cups sifted cake flour
2 teaspoons baking powder
¼ teaspoon salt
⅓ cup cocoa
⅔ cup milk
1 teaspoon vanilla extract
2 tablespoons seedless raspberry jam
2 tablespoons Chambord or other raspberry-
    flavored liqueur
2 cups whipping cream
¼ cup sifted powdered sugar
3 cups fresh raspberries
Garnish: fresh mint sprigs

Grease two 9-inch round cakepans; line with wax paper, and grease wax paper. Set aside.

Beat butter at medium speed of an electric mixer 2 minutes or until creamy; gradually add sugar, beating well. Add egg yolks, one at a time, beating until blended after each addition.

Combine flour and next 3 ingredients; add to butter mixture alternately with milk, beginning and ending with flour mixture. Beat at low speed until blended after each addition. Stir in vanilla.

Beat egg whites at high speed until stiff peaks form; fold into batter. Pour batter into pans.

Bake at 350° for 18 minutes or until a wooden pick inserted in center comes out clean. Cool in pans on wire racks 10 minutes. Remove from pans; cool completely on wire racks.

Cook jam in a small saucepan over low heat until melted; stir in liqueur. Set jam mixture aside.

Beat whipping cream at medium speed until foamy; gradually add powdered sugar, beating until soft peaks form.

Place one cake layer on a serving plate; brush with half of jam mixture. Arrange half of raspberries over jam. Spread half of whipped cream over raspberries.

Top with second cake layer; brush with remaining jam mixture. Spread remaining whipped cream over jam mixture; arrange remaining raspberries on top. Garnish, if desired. **Yield: one 9-inch shortcake.**

Pumpkin Roll

(pictured on page 643)

3 large eggs
1 cup sugar
⅔ cup mashed, cooked pumpkin
1 teaspoon lemon juice
¾ cup all-purpose flour
1 teaspoon baking powder
¼ teaspoon salt
1 teaspoon ground cinnamon
1 teaspoon pumpkin pie spice
¼ teaspoon ground nutmeg
1 cup chopped pecans
1 to 2 tablespoons powdered sugar
1 (8-ounce) package cream cheese, softened
⅓ cup butter or margarine, softened
1 cup sifted powdered sugar
1 teaspoon vanilla extract
Garnishes: sweetened whipped cream,
    chopped pecans

Grease and flour a 15- x 10- x 1-inch jellyroll pan; set aside.

Beat eggs in a large bowl at high speed of an electric mixer until thick; gradually add sugar,

and beat 5 additional minutes. Stir in pumpkin and lemon juice.

Combine flour and next 5 ingredients; gradually stir into pumpkin mixture. Spread batter evenly in prepared pan; sprinkle with 1 cup pecans, gently pressing into batter.

Bake at 375° for 12 to 15 minutes.

Sift 1 to 2 tablespoons powdered sugar in a 15-x 10-inch rectangle on a cloth towel. When cake is done, immediately loosen from sides of pan, and turn cake out onto sugared towel. Starting at narrow end, roll up cake and towel together; cool on a wire rack, seam side down.

Beat cream cheese and butter at high speed; gradually add 1 cup powdered sugar and vanilla, beating until blended.

Unroll cake; spread with cream cheese mixture, and carefully reroll. Place cake on a serving plate, seam side down. Garnish, if desired. **Yield: 10 servings.**

Roll Up a Perfect Roulage

Don't let the fancy name roulage fool you. This classic rolled cake has its beginning in a jellyroll pan.

• Prepare jellyroll pan according to recipe directions.

• Avoid overbaking; check oven at the lower range of baking time.

• When cake is done, immediately loosen from sides of pan and turn out onto a cloth towel dusted with powdered sugar or cocoa.

• While cake is warm, roll up cake and towel together, beginning at narrow end. Cool cake on a wire rack, seam side down.

• Gently unroll cooled cake, and spread with filling.

• Reroll cake without towel; place on serving plate, seam side down.

Mint-Chocolate Roulage

Vegetable cooking spray
4 large eggs
½ cup water
1 (18.25- or 18.5-ounce) package Swiss
    chocolate, devil's food, or fudge cake mix
2 to 4 tablespoons cocoa
2 cups whipping cream
5 to 6 tablespoons green crème de menthe,
    divided
Cocoa
Chocolate Sauce
Garnish: fresh mint sprigs

Coat two 15- x 10- x 1-inch jellyroll pans with cooking spray; line with wax paper, and coat with cooking spray. Set aside.

Beat eggs in a large mixing bowl at medium-high speed of an electric mixer 5 minutes. Add water, beating at low speed to blend.

Add cake mix gradually, beating at low speed until moistened. Beat at medium-high speed 2 minutes. Divide batter in half, and spread batter evenly into prepared pans. (Layers will be thin.)

Bake each cake at 350° on the middle rack in separate ovens for 13 minutes or until cake springs back when lightly touched in center. (If you don't have a double oven, set 1 pan aside.)

Sift 1 to 2 tablespoons cocoa in a 15- x 10-inch rectangle on a cloth towel; repeat with second towel. When cakes are done, immediately loosen from sides of pans, and turn each out onto a prepared towel.

Peel off wax paper. Starting at narrow end, roll up each cake and towel together; place cakes, seam side down, on wire racks. Cool cakes completely.

Beat whipping cream at medium speed until soft peaks form. Fold in 2 to 3 tablespoons crème de menthe; set aside.

Unroll cake rolls; brush each lightly with 1½ tablespoons crème de menthe. Spread each cake with half of whipped cream mixture. Reroll cakes

without towels; place, seam side down, on a baking sheet. Cover and freeze at least 1 hour or up to 3 months.

Dust cakes with cocoa, and drizzle with 2 tablespoons Chocolate Sauce; garnish, if desired. Cut cakes into slices, and serve with remaining Chocolate Sauce. **Yield: 2 filled cake rolls (8 servings each).**

Chocolate Sauce

¾ cup half-and-half
1½ cups semisweet chocolate morsels
1½ cups miniature marshmallows
¼ teaspoon salt
1 teaspoon vanilla extract

Heat half-and-half in a heavy saucepan over low heat. Stir in chocolate morsels, marshmallows, and salt; cook over low heat, stirring constantly, until chocolate and marshmallows melt. Remove from heat, and stir in vanilla. **Yield: 1½ cups.**

Note: You may substitute 1½ teaspoons mint extract and 5 drops of green food coloring for green crème de menthe. Omit brushing cake rolls.

Mint-Chocolate Roulage Technique

While cakes are warm, roll up each cake and towel together, beginning at narrow end.

Cheesecakes and Tortes

These lavish desserts taste as good as they look. And the good news is that all of them in this collection are simple to make and most can be made ahead of time.

Chocolate Praline Torte, Lemon Cheesecake, Apricot Praline Torte

Amaretto-Irish Cream Cheesecake, Chocolate-Glazed Triple Layer Cheesecake

Boston Cream Pie, Chocolate-Mint Baked Alaska Cheesecake, Mocha-Pecan Torte

Lemon Meringue Cream Cups, Blueberries 'n' Cream Cheesecake

Rich White Chocolate Cheesecake (page 594)

From left: Creamy Vanilla, Chocolate Marble, Black Forest, Crème de Menthe, and Praline cheesecakes

Creamy Vanilla Cheesecake

5 (8-ounce) packages cream cheese, softened
1½ cups sugar
3 large eggs
2½ teaspoons vanilla extract
Graham Cracker Crust
Garnish: strawberry fans

Beat cream cheese at high speed of an electric mixer until fluffy; gradually add sugar, beating well. Add eggs, one at a time, beating after each addition. Stir in vanilla. Pour into Graham Cracker Crust.

Bake at 350° for 40 minutes; turn oven off, and partially open oven door. Leave cheesecake in oven 30 minutes. Remove from oven, and cool on a wire rack in a draft-free place.

Cover and chill at least 8 hours. Garnish, if desired. **Yield: 10 to 12 servings.**

Variations

Black Forest Cheesecake: Use Graham Cracker Crust or Chocolate Wafer Crust. Prepare basic cheesecake mixture; stir in 6 ounces melted semisweet chocolate. Pour half of chocolate mixture into crust; top with 1 cup canned dark, sweet, pitted cherries, drained and patted dry. Spoon remaining chocolate mixture evenly over cherries. Bake at 350° for 45 minutes. Garnish with whipped cream and additional cherries, if desired.

Brown Sugar and Spice Cheesecake: Use Gingersnap Crust. For cheesecake mixture, substitute brown sugar for white sugar, and add 1 teaspoon ground cinnamon, ½ teaspoon ground cloves, and ½ teaspoon ground nutmeg when sugar is added. Bake at 350° for 45 minutes. Garnish with whipped cream, and sprinkle with nutmeg, if desired.

Chocolate Marble Cheesecake: Use Chocolate Wafer Crust. Prepare basic cheesecake mixture, and divide in half. Stir 6 ounces melted semisweet chocolate into half of cheesecake mixture. Pour half of plain cheesecake mixture into prepared crust; top with half of chocolate mixture. Repeat layers to use all of mixture. Gently swirl batter with a knife to create a marbled effect. Bake at 350° for 40 minutes. Garnish with mint sprigs, if desired.

Crème de Menthe Cheesecake: Use Chocolate Wafer Crust. Stir ¼ cup green crème de menthe into cheesecake mixture when vanilla is added. Bake at 350° for 45 minutes. Garnish with chocolate leaves, if desired.

Praline Cheesecake: Use Graham Cracker Crust. Substitute dark brown sugar for white sugar in cheesecake mixture. Sauté 1 cup chopped pecans in 3 tablespoons melted butter or margarine; drain pecans on paper towel. Fold into cheesecake mixture when vanilla is added. Bake at 350° for 45 minutes. Garnish with toasted pecan halves, if desired.

Graham Cracker Crust

1⅔ cups graham cracker crumbs
⅓ cup butter or margarine, melted

Combine crumbs and butter; press onto bottom and 1 inch up sides of a 10-inch springform pan. Bake at 350° for 5 minutes. **Yield: one 10-inch crust.**

Variations

Chocolate Wafer Crust: Substitute 1⅔ cups chocolate wafer crumbs for graham cracker crumbs.

Gingersnap Crust: Substitute 1⅔ cups gingersnap crumbs for graham cracker crumbs.

Amaretto-Irish Cream Cheesecake

1½ cups vanilla wafer crumbs
½ cup blanched whole almonds, toasted and finely chopped
¼ cup butter or margarine, melted
1 tablespoon amaretto
3 (8-ounce) packages cream cheese, softened
1 cup sugar
4 large eggs
⅓ cup whipping cream
⅓ cup blanched whole almonds, toasted and ground
¼ cup Irish Cream liqueur
¼ cup amaretto
1½ cups sour cream
1 tablespoon sugar
½ teaspoon vanilla extract
¼ cup sliced almonds

Combine first 4 ingredients; press onto bottom of a lightly greased 10-inch springform pan.

Bake at 350° for 10 minutes. Cool.

Beat cream cheese at high speed of an electric mixer until fluffy; gradually add 1 cup sugar, beating well. Add eggs, one at a time, beating after each addition. Stir in whipping cream and next 3 ingredients; pour into prepared crust.

Bake at 350° for 50 minutes; turn oven off, and leave cheesecake in oven 30 minutes.

Combine sour cream and next 2 ingredients; stir and spoon over cheesecake. Sprinkle ¼ cup sliced almonds around edge.

Bake at 500° for 5 minutes. Cool; cover and chill at least 8 hours. **Yield: 10 to 12 servings.**

Blueberries 'n' Cream Cheesecake

2½ cups fresh blueberries
1 tablespoon cornstarch
3 (8-ounce) packages cream cheese, softened
1 cup sugar
5 large eggs
2 tablespoons cornstarch
¼ teaspoon salt
1½ cups sour cream
2 tablespoons sugar
½ teaspoon vanilla extract
¼ cup sugar
¼ cup water
1 cup fresh blueberries

Combine 2½ cups blueberries and 1 tablespoon cornstarch in container of an electric blender; cover and process until smooth. Cook puree in saucepan over medium-high heat about 15 minutes or until slightly thickened, stirring constantly. Set aside to cool. Reserve ½ cup puree for glaze.

Beat cream cheese at medium speed of an electric mixer until fluffy. Gradually add 1 cup sugar, mixing well. Add eggs, one at a time, beating after each addition. Stir in 2 tablespoons cornstarch and salt.

Pour batter into a greased 9-inch springform pan. Pour puree over cheesecake batter; gently swirl with a knife.

Bake at 325° for 45 minutes or until set. Remove from oven; cool on a wire rack 20 minutes.

Combine sour cream, 2 tablespoons sugar, and vanilla in a small bowl; spread over cheesecake.

Bake at 325° for 10 additional minutes. Cool on wire rack. Cover and chill 8 hours.

Combine reserved ½ cup puree, ¼ cup sugar, and water in a small saucepan; cook over medium heat, stirring constantly, until thickened. Gently fold in 1 cup blueberries; cool.

Remove sides of springform pan, and spoon blueberry glaze on cheesecake. **Yield: 10 to 12 servings.**

Chocolate-Glazed Triple Layer Cheesecake

1 (9-ounce) package chocolate wafer cookies, crushed (about 2 cups)
¾ cup sugar, divided
¼ cup plus 1 tablespoon butter or margarine, melted
2 (8-ounce) packages cream cheese, softened and divided
3 large eggs, divided
¼ teaspoon vanilla extract
2 (1-ounce) squares semisweet chocolate, melted
1⅓ cups sour cream, divided
⅓ cup firmly packed dark brown sugar
1 tablespoon all-purpose flour
½ teaspoon vanilla extract
¼ cup chopped pecans
5 ounces cream cheese, softened
¼ teaspoon vanilla extract
¼ teaspoon almond extract
Chocolate Glaze
Garnish: chocolate leaves

Combine cookie crumbs, ¼ cup sugar, and butter; press onto bottom and 2 inches up sides of a 9-inch springform pan. Set aside.

Beat 1 (8-ounce) package cream cheese at medium speed of an electric mixer until fluffy; gradually add ¼ cup sugar, beating well. Add 1 egg and ¼ teaspoon vanilla; mix well. Stir in melted chocolate and ⅓ cup sour cream. Spoon over prepared crust.

Beat remaining 1 (8-ounce) package cream cheese until fluffy; gradually add brown sugar and flour, beating well. Add 1 egg and ½ teaspoon vanilla; mix well. Stir in pecans. Spoon gently over chocolate layer.

Beat 5 ounces cream cheese and remaining ¼ cup sugar until fluffy. Add 1 egg; mix well. Stir in remaining 1 cup sour cream, ¼ teaspoon vanilla, and almond extract. Spoon gently over praline layer.

Chocolate-Glazed Triple Layer Cheesecake

Bake at 325° for 1 hour. Turn oven off; leave cheesecake in oven, with oven door closed, 30 minutes. Partially open door; leave cheesecake in oven 30 additional minutes. Cool. Cover and chill 8 hours. Remove sides of springform pan.

Spread Chocolate Glaze over cheesecake. Garnish, if desired. **Yield: 10 to 12 servings.**

Chocolate Glaze
6 (1-ounce) squares semisweet chocolate
¼ cup butter or margarine
¾ cup sifted powdered sugar
2 tablespoons water
1 teaspoon vanilla extract

Melt chocolate and butter in a heavy saucepan over low heat, stirring occasionally. Remove from heat; stir in sugar, water, and vanilla.

Spread over cheesecake while glaze is warm. **Yield: enough for one 9-inch cheesecake.**

Rich White Chocolate Cheesecake

(pictured on page 589)

2 cups chocolate wafer crumbs
2 tablespoons sugar
¼ cup plus 2 tablespoons butter or
    margarine, melted
4 (8-ounce) packages cream cheese, softened
1 cup sugar
4 large eggs
½ cup Irish Cream liqueur
1 tablespoon vanilla extract
½ pound premium white chocolate, chopped
Garnish: marbled chocolate curls

Combine first 3 ingredients in a medium bowl; press onto bottom and 2 inches up sides of a 10-inch springform pan. Bake at 325° for 6 to 8 minutes. Set aside, and cool.

Beat cream cheese at medium speed of an electric mixer until fluffy; gradually add 1 cup sugar, beating well. Add eggs, one at a time, beating after each addition. Stir in liqueur and vanilla. Add chopped white chocolate; stir. Pour into crust.

Bake at 325° for 50 to 60 minutes or until set. Turn oven off, and partially open oven door; leave cheesecake in oven 1 hour. Remove cheesecake from oven, and cool in pan on a wire rack. Cover and chill thoroughly.

Remove sides of springform pan. Garnish, if desired. **Yield: 10 to 12 servings.**

Note: To make marbled chocolate curls, pour 12 ounces melted semisweet chocolate onto a smooth surface, such as marble or an aluminum foil-lined cookie sheet. Pour 12 ounces melted white chocolate over semisweet chocolate layer. Using a small spatula, swirl chocolates to create a marbled effect, covering about a 12- x 9-inch area. Let stand at room temperature until chocolate feels slightly tacky but not firm. (If chocolate is too hard, curls will break; if too soft, chocolate will not curl.) Pull a cheese plane across chocolate to form curls.

Chocolate-Mint Baked Alaska Cheesecake

1 cup chocolate wafer crumbs
2 tablespoons sugar
3 tablespoons butter or margarine, melted
1 cup mint chocolate morsels
3 (8-ounce) packages cream cheese, softened
⅔ cup sugar
3 large eggs
1 teaspoon vanilla extract
3 egg whites
1 (7-ounce) jar marshmallow cream

Combine first 3 ingredients; press onto bottom of a 9-inch springform pan.

Bake at 350° for 10 minutes; set aside.

Melt chocolate morsels in a small heavy saucepan over low heat, stirring constantly. Set aside.

Beat cream cheese at medium speed of an electric mixer until fluffy; gradually add ⅔ cup sugar, beating well. Add eggs, one at a time, beating after each addition. Stir in melted chocolate and vanilla. Pour into prepared crust.

Bake at 350° for 50 minutes.

Remove from oven; immediately run a knife around sides of cheesecake to loosen, and cool completely in pan on a wire rack. Cover and chill 8 hours.

Beat egg whites at high speed of an electric mixer until soft peaks form. Gradually add marshmallow cream, beating until stiff peaks form. Remove sides of springform pan. Carefully spread egg white mixture over top and sides of cake.

Bake at 325° for 25 to 30 minutes or until golden. Serve immediately. **Yield: 10 to 12 servings.**

Lemon Cheesecake

¾ cup graham cracker crumbs
2 tablespoons sugar
1 tablespoon ground cinnamon
1 tablespoon butter or margarine, softened
5 (8-ounce) packages cream cheese, softened
1⅔ cups sugar
5 large eggs
⅛ teaspoon salt
1½ teaspoons vanilla extract
¼ cup lemon juice

Combine first 3 ingredients; stir well, and set aside. Grease bottom and sides of a 10-inch springform pan with butter. Add crumb mixture; tilt pan to coat sides and bottom. Chill.

Beat cream cheese at medium speed of an electric mixer until fluffy; gradually add 1⅔ cups sugar, beating well. Add eggs, one at a time, beating after each addition. Stir in salt, vanilla, and lemon juice; pour into prepared crust.

Bake at 300° for 1 hour and 20 minutes. (Center may be soft but will set when chilled.) Cool on a wire rack; cover and chill 8 hours. **Yield: 10 to 12 servings.**

Sour Cream-Almond Dessert

¾ cup butter or margarine, softened
1½ cups all-purpose flour
½ cup chopped almonds
2 tablespoons sugar
¾ to 1 cup almond paste, broken into small
    pieces
4 large eggs
1 cup sugar
2 tablespoons cornstarch
1 (16-ounce) carton sour cream
1 pint whipping cream
3 tablespoons powdered sugar
¼ cup sliced almonds, toasted

Combine first 4 ingredients in a large mixing bowl; beat at medium speed of an electric mixer until blended. Spread mixture onto bottom and 1½ inches up sides of an ungreased 9-inch springform pan.

Bake at 400° for 10 minutes or until lightly browned; set aside.

Combine almond paste, eggs, and 1 cup sugar; beat at medium speed of an electric mixer until blended (about 4 minutes). Combine cornstarch and sour cream; stir into almond paste mixture, and pour into prepared crust.

Bake at 325° for 1 hour or until lightly browned (center will be a little soft). Cool on a wire rack; cover and chill at least 8 hours.

Remove sides of springform pan. Beat whipping cream until foamy; gradually add powdered sugar, beating until soft peaks form. Set aside 1 cup whipped cream, and spread remaining whipped cream on top of dessert. Pipe or dollop reserved whipped cream around outer edges, and sprinkle with toasted almonds. **Yield: 8 to 10 servings.**

Sour Cream-Almond Dessert

Boston Cream Pie

Boston Cream Pie

½ cup butter or margarine, softened
1 cup sugar
3 large eggs
2 cups sifted cake flour
2 teaspoons baking powder
¼ teaspoon salt
½ cup milk
2 teaspoons vanilla extract
Cream Filling
Chocolate Glaze

Beat butter at medium speed of an electric mixer until creamy; gradually add sugar, beating well. Add eggs, one at a time, beating after each addition.

Combine flour, baking powder, and salt; add to butter mixture alternately with milk, beginning and ending with flour mixture. Mix after each addition. Stir in vanilla.

Pour batter into 2 greased and floured 9-inch round cakepans.

Bake at 350° for 20 to 25 minutes or until a wooden pick inserted in center comes out clean. Cool in pans on wire racks 10 minutes; remove from pans, and cool completely on wire racks.

Spread Cream Filling between cake layers. Spread Chocolate Glaze over top of cake, letting excess drip down sides of cake. Chill until ready to serve. **Yield: 8 to 10 servings.**

Cream Filling

½ cup sugar
¼ cup cornstarch
¼ teaspoon salt
2 cups milk
4 egg yolks, lightly beaten
1 teaspoon vanilla extract

Combine first 3 ingredients in a heavy saucepan. Add milk and egg yolks, stirring with a wire whisk until blended.

Cook over medium heat, stirring constantly, until mixture comes to a boil. Boil 1 minute or until thickened, stirring constantly; remove from heat. Stir in vanilla; cool. **Yield: 2½ cups.**

Chocolate Glaze

2 tablespoons butter or margarine
1 (1-ounce) square unsweetened chocolate
1 cup sifted powdered sugar
2 tablespoons boiling water

Melt butter and chocolate in a saucepan, stirring constantly. Cool slightly. Add powdered sugar and water; beat until smooth. **Yield: ½ cup.**

Chocolate Praline Torte

1½ cups chopped walnuts
1½ cups vanilla wafer crumbs
1 cup firmly packed brown sugar
1 cup butter or margarine, melted
1 (18.5-ounce) package devil's food cake mix without pudding
1½ cups whipping cream
3 tablespoons sifted powdered sugar
1 teaspoon vanilla extract

Combine first 4 ingredients. Sprinkle about ¾ cup of walnut mixture in each of 4 ungreased 9-inch round cakepans, pressing lightly into pans.

Prepare cake mix according to package directions; pour over walnut mixture in pans.

Bake at 350° for 15 to 20 minutes or until a wooden pick inserted in center comes out clean. Remove from pans, and cool on wire racks.

Beat whipping cream at medium speed of an electric mixer until foamy; gradually add powdered sugar, beating until firm peaks form. Stir in vanilla.

Place 1 layer, nut side up, on a serving plate. Spread ¾ cup whipped cream over layer. Repeat with remaining 3 layers, ending with whipped cream; chill. **Yield: one 9-inch torte.**

Apricot Praline Torte

1 (16-ounce) loaf pound cake
1 cup apricot preserves
Praline Buttercream
Sifted powdered sugar

Cut pound cake loaf horizontally into 3 layers.
Melt apricot preserves in a small saucepan over low heat. Spread half of preserves over bottom layer of cake. Spread half of Praline Buttercream over preserves, and place second layer of cake on buttercream.
Repeat procedure with remaining preserves and buttercream; top with remaining layer of cake. Sprinkle cake lightly with sifted powdered sugar. **Yield: 10 to 12 servings.**

Praline Buttercream

½ cup unsalted butter, softened
2½ cups sifted powdered sugar
2 to 3 tablespoons whipping cream
½ cup Praline Powder
1 teaspoon vanilla extract

Beat butter at medium speed of an electric mixer until creamy; gradually add sugar, beating well. Beat in whipping cream; fold in Praline Powder and vanilla. **Yield: 2 cups.**

Praline Powder

2 tablespoons butter
¼ cup sugar
¾ cup almonds, chopped and toasted

Cook butter and sugar in a saucepan over medium heat until sugar melts and turns a light caramel color (mixture will separate), stirring occasionally. Remove from heat; stir in almonds.
Pour onto a greased aluminum foil-lined baking sheet; cool. Break into chunks. Position knife blade in food processor bowl; add chunks of praline. Process until finely crushed. **Yield: 1 cup.**

Toffee Meringue Torte

6 egg whites
¾ teaspoon cream of tartar
1 cup superfine sugar
8 (1.4-ounce) English toffee-flavored candy bars, frozen and crushed
2½ cups whipping cream, whipped
Toffee Sauce

Line 2 baking sheets with parchment paper. Trace a 9-inch circle on each, using a 9-inch cakepan as a guide. Turn paper over; set aside.
Beat egg whites at high speed of an electric mixer until foamy; add cream of tartar, beating until soft peaks form. Add sugar, 2 tablespoons at a time, beating until stiff peaks form. Spoon meringue mixture evenly inside circles on baking sheets. Form each into a smooth circle.
Bake at 275° for 2 hours. Turn oven off; cool slightly. Remove from oven; peel off paper. Dry meringues on wire racks, away from drafts.
Reserve 2 tablespoons crushed candy for garnish. Fold remaining crushed candy into whipped cream. Chill or freeze until firm, but spreadable.
Spread whipped cream mixture between layers of meringue and on top and sides. Garnish with reserved candy. Place torte in an airtight cake cover; freeze at least 8 hours. Cut into wedges; serve with Toffee Sauce. **Yield: 8 to 10 servings.**

Toffee Sauce

1½ cups firmly packed brown sugar
½ cup light corn syrup
⅓ cup butter
⅔ cup whipping cream
1 teaspoon butter flavoring

Combine first 3 ingredients in a saucepan. Cook over medium heat until mixture comes to a full boil, stirring frequently. Remove from heat; cool 5 minutes. Stir in whipping cream and flavoring. Serve warm with torte. **Yield: 2 cups.**

Toffee Meringue Torte

Mocha-Pecan Torte

Mocha-Pecan Torte

8 eggs, separated
⅔ cup sifted powdered sugar
1 teaspoon baking powder
⅓ cup cocoa
⅓ cup soft breadcrumbs
1 teaspoon vanilla extract
2 cups ground pecans
Mocha Buttercream Frosting
Chocolate candy sprinkles

Line the bottom of 4 (8-inch) round cakepans with wax paper. Grease and flour paper; set aside.

Combine egg yolks, sugar, and baking powder; beat at high speed of an electric mixer 2 to 3 minutes or until mixture is thick and pale.

Combine cocoa and breadcrumbs; stir into egg yolk mixture. Stir in vanilla; fold in pecans.

Beat egg whites in a mixing bowl until stiff peaks form; fold one-fourth of egg whites into yolk mixture. Fold remaining egg whites into yolk mixture. Pour into pans; spread tops to smooth.

Bake at 350° for 15 minutes or until layers spring back when lightly touched. Cool in pans on wire racks 5 minutes. Invert layers onto wire racks; peel off wax paper. (Layers will be thin.) Cool.

Set aside 1½ cups frosting. Spread 3 cups frosting between layers and on sides and top of torte. Pat sprinkles onto sides. Score frosting on top of torte into 12 wedges. Spoon reserved frosting into a decorating bag fitted with a No. 2F metal tip. Pipe 12 rosettes around top edge; sprinkle rosettes with sprinkles. Chill. **Yield: one 8-inch torte.**

Mocha Buttercream Frosting

2½ teaspoons instant coffee granules
2 tablespoons water
¾ cup plus 2 tablespoons butter, softened
1 tablespoon plus 2 teaspoons cocoa
7 cups sifted powdered sugar
⅓ cup half-and-half
1 teaspoon vanilla extract

Dissolve coffee granules in water; set aside. Beat butter at medium speed of an electric mixer until creamy. Add coffee mixture and cocoa; beat well. Add sugar alternately with half-and-half; beat until fluffy. Stir in vanilla. **Yield: 4½ cups.**

Lemon Meringue Cream Cups

2 egg whites
Pinch of salt
1 teaspoon lemon juice
½ cup sugar
Lemon Cream Filling
Garnishes: whipped cream, grated lemon rind

Beat first 3 ingredients at high speed of an electric mixer until foamy. Add sugar, 1 tablespoon at a time, beating until stiff peaks form. (Do not underbeat.)

Line a baking sheet with parchment paper. Spoon meringue into 6 equal portions on paper. Shape meringue into circles about 3 inches in diameter; shape each circle into a shell (sides should be about 1 to 1½ inches high).

Bake at 275° for 1 hour. Turn oven off; cool in oven several hours.

Peel off paper. Spoon Lemon Cream Filling into shells. Garnish, if desired. **Yield: 6 servings.**

Lemon Cream Filling
3 large eggs
½ cup sugar
3 tablespoons lemon juice
1½ teaspoons grated lemon rind
½ cup whipping cream, whipped

Beat eggs until thick and pale. Add sugar and lemon juice; beat well. Stir in lemon rind.

Cook over low heat, stirring constantly, until mixture thickens and reaches 160°. Cool thoroughly. Fold whipped cream into cooled mixture. **Yield: about 1½ cups.**

Coffee Meringues with Butterscotch Mousse

3 egg whites
1 teaspoon instant coffee granules
¼ teaspoon cream of tartar
1 cup sugar
Butterscotch Mousse

Beat first 3 ingredients at high speed of an electric mixer until foamy. Add sugar, 1 tablespoon at a time, beating until stiff peaks form.

Line baking sheets with unglazed brown paper or parchment paper. (Do not use recycled paper.) Spoon meringue by rounded teaspoonfuls onto paper. Make an indentation in center of each with back of a spoon.

Bake at 225° for 1 hour and 15 minutes; turn oven off, and cool in oven 2 hours or overnight.

Remove meringues from paper; store in an airtight container up to 1 week. Just before serving, spoon Butterscotch Mousse into each meringue. **Yield: 4½ dozen.**

Butterscotch Mousse

1 cup butterscotch morsels
3 tablespoons butter or margarine
1 tablespoon instant coffee granules
3 tablespoons water
1 large egg, lightly beaten
1 cup whipping cream, whipped

Combine first 4 ingredients in a heavy saucepan; cook over low heat, stirring constantly, until morsels and butter melt.

Stir about one-fourth of hot mixture into egg; add to remaining hot mixture, stirring constantly. Cook over medium heat, stirring constantly, 1 minute. Remove from heat, and cool to room temperature.

Fold in whipped cream. Cover and chill 8 hours. **Yield: 2⅔ cups.**

Pavlova

1 teaspoon cornstarch
4 egg whites
1 cup sugar
1 teaspoon white vinegar
1 teaspoon vanilla extract
1½ cups whipping cream
2 tablespoons strawberry jam
1 tablespoon water
1 banana
Lemon juice
2 kiwifruit, peeled and sliced
1 pint strawberries, halved
Garnish: strawberry fans

Mark an 11- x 7-inch rectangle on wax paper; place on baking sheet. Grease wax paper, and dust with cornstarch. Set aside.

Beat egg whites at high speed of an electric mixer until foamy. Gradually add sugar, ¼ cup at a time, beating until stiff peaks form (2 to 4 minutes). Beat in vinegar and vanilla. Spread meringue onto rectangle.

Bake at 275° for 45 minutes. Carefully remove meringue from baking sheet, and cool on a wire rack. Carefully turn meringue over, and remove wax paper. Place meringue, right side up, on a platter.

Beat whipping cream at medium speed until soft peaks form. Set aside 1 cup whipped cream.

Spread remaining whipped cream over meringue, leaving a 1-inch border. Pipe or dollop reserved whipped cream around edges.

Combine jam and water in a small saucepan; heat just until jam melts, stirring constantly. Pour mixture through a wire-mesh strainer into a bowl, discarding seeds; set liquid aside to cool.

Slice banana, and sprinkle with lemon juice. Arrange banana, kiwifruit, and strawberry halves on whipped cream. Brush strawberries with strawberry liquid. Garnish, if desired. Serve immediately. **Yield: 10 to 12 servings.**

Frozen Favorites

Don't wait for summer to enjoy these frosty favorites. Use your freezer to churn out ice creams, sherbets, and sorbets any time of year. Or start with commercial ice cream to create a tempting treat.

Strawberries and Cream, Piña Colada Ice Cream, Champagne Ice

Frozen Viennese Torte, Brownie Baked Alaska, Chocolate Ice Cream Brownies

Pineapple-Orange Sherbet, Watermelon Sherbet, Blackberry Sorbet, Praline Freeze

Caramel-Toffee Bombe, Spumoni Charlotte, Frozen Almond Crunch

Fresh Peach Ice Cream (page 607)

Basic Vanilla Ice Cream

2 (14-ounce) cans sweetened condensed milk
1 quart half-and-half
1 tablespoon plus 1 teaspoon vanilla extract

Combine all ingredients, mixing well. Pour mixture into freezer container of a 1-gallon hand-turned or electric freezer.

Freeze according to manufacturer's instructions. Pack freezer with additional ice and rock salt, and let stand 1 hour. **Yield: 2½ quarts.**

Variations

Black Forest Ice Cream: Stir in ½ cup chocolate syrup and 1 (16½-ounce) can pitted Bing cherries, drained and halved, before freezing.

Blueberry Ice Cream: Stir in 2 cups fresh or frozen blueberries before freezing.

Butter Pecan Ice Cream: Stir in 1 tablespoon butter flavoring and 2 cups coarsely chopped toasted pecans before freezing.

Cherry-Pecan Ice Cream: Substitute 1 teaspoon almond extract for vanilla, and add ⅓ cup maraschino cherry juice to ice cream mixture; freeze as directed. Stir in ¾ cup quartered maraschino cherries and ¾ cup chopped pecans.

Chocolate-Covered Peanut Ice Cream: Stir in ½ cup chocolate syrup and 2 (7-ounce) packages chocolate-covered peanuts before freezing.

Coffee Ice Cream: Combine ⅔ cup hot water and 1 tablespoon instant coffee granules, stirring until granules dissolve. Cool slightly. Stir in before freezing.

Cookies and Cream Ice Cream: Break 15 cream-filled chocolate sandwich cookies into small pieces; stir in before freezing.

Double Chocolate Ice Cream: Stir in ½ cup chocolate syrup and 1 (6-ounce) package semisweet chocolate mini-morsels before freezing.

Lemonade Ice Cream: Stir in 1 (6-ounce) can frozen lemonade concentrate, thawed and undiluted, before freezing.

Mint-Chocolate Chip Ice Cream: Stir in ½ cup green crème de menthe and 1 (6-ounce) package semisweet chocolate mini-morsels before freezing.

Mocha Ice Cream: Combine 1 cup hot water and 1 tablespoon instant coffee granules, stirring until granules dissolve. Cool slightly. Stir in coffee mixture and ½ cup chocolate syrup before freezing.

Peanut Butter Ice Cream: Stir in ¾ cup chunky peanut butter before freezing. Serve with chocolate syrup, if desired.

Rainbow Candy Ice Cream: Stir in 1½ cups candy-coated milk chocolate pieces before freezing.

Strawberry-Banana-Nut Ice Cream: Stir in 3 bananas, mashed; 1 pint strawberries, coarsely chopped; and ¾ cup chopped pecans before freezing.

Toffee Ice Cream: Stir in 1 (6-ounce) package toffee-flavored candy pieces before freezing.

Butter Crisp Ice Cream

2 cups finely crushed cornflakes cereal
2 cups chopped pecans
1 cup firmly packed brown sugar
½ cup butter or margarine, melted
4 envelopes unflavored gelatin
2 cups sugar
¼ teaspoon salt
6 cups milk, divided
6 large eggs, lightly beaten
1 quart whipping cream
2 tablespoons vanilla extract

Combine first 3 ingredients; stir in butter. Spoon mixture into a 15- x 10- x 1-inch jellyroll pan. Bake at 350° for 25 minutes, stirring occasionally; cool. Set aside.

Combine gelatin, sugar, and salt in a large saucepan; stir in 2 cups milk. Let stand 1 minute.

Cook over low heat, stirring until gelatin dissolves (about 5 minutes).

Stir a small amount of hot milk mixture gradually into eggs; add to remaining hot milk mixture, stirring constantly. Cook over medium heat, stirring often, until thermometer registers 160° (3 to 5 minutes). Add remaining 4 cups milk, whipping cream, and vanilla.

Pour mixture into freezer container of a 5-quart hand-turned or electric freezer. Freeze according to manufacturer's instructions.

Spoon ice cream into a large airtight container, and stir in reserved cornflakes mixture. Cover and freeze. **Yield: 1 gallon.**

Strawberries and Cream

1 **quart milk**
1 **pint half-and-half**
2 **(14-ounce) cans sweetened condensed milk**
2 **teaspoons vanilla extract**
⅛ **to ¼ teaspoon almond extract**
1 **quart fresh strawberries, sliced**

Combine first 5 ingredients in a large bowl. Pour mixture into freezer container of a 5-quart hand-turned or electric freezer.

Freeze according to manufacturer's instructions. Pack freezer with additional ice and rock salt, and let stand 1 hour before serving. Serve with sliced strawberries. **Yield: 3 quarts.**

From left: Butter Crisp Ice Cream, Peanut Ice Cream (page 609), and Strawberries and Cream

Honey-Vanilla Ice Cream

Honey-Vanilla Ice Cream

2 cups sugar
⅓ cup all-purpose flour
¼ teaspoon salt
4 cups milk
5 large eggs, beaten
5 cups half-and-half
1 tablespoon vanilla extract
½ cup honey

Combine first 3 ingredients; stir well, and set sugar mixture aside.

Heat milk in a heavy 3-quart saucepan over low heat just until hot. Gradually add sugar mixture, stirring until blended. Cook over medium heat, stirring constantly, 10 minutes or until thickened.

Stir about one-fourth of hot milk mixture gradually into beaten eggs; add to remaining hot milk mixture, stirring constantly. Cook 1 minute, stirring constantly. Remove from heat, and cool. Cover and chill at least 2 hours.

Stir half-and-half and vanilla into chilled custard mixture. Pour into freezer container of a 1-gallon hand-turned or electric freezer.

Freeze according to manufacturer's instructions. Remove dasher, and stir in honey. Pack freezer with additional ice and rock salt, and let stand 1 hour before serving. **Yield: 3 quarts.**

Honey-Vanilla Ice Cream Technique

Remove dasher from frozen ice cream, and stir in honey. Let ice cream ripen 1 hour.

Fresh Peach Ice Cream

(pictured on page 603)

1⅓ cups sugar
¼ cup all-purpose flour
¼ teaspoon salt
3⅓ cups milk
3 large eggs, beaten
4 cups peeled, mashed fresh peaches
⅔ cup sugar
1⅔ cups half-and-half
1 cup whipping cream
2 teaspoons vanilla extract
1 teaspoon almond extract
Garnish: toasted sliced almonds

Combine first 3 ingredients; stir well, and set sugar mixture aside.

Heat milk in a heavy 3-quart saucepan over low heat just until hot. Gradually add sugar mixture, stirring until blended. Cook over medium heat, stirring constantly, 10 minutes or until thickened.

Stir about one-fourth of hot milk mixture gradually into beaten eggs; add to remaining hot milk mixture, stirring constantly. Cook 1 minute, stirring constantly. Remove from heat, and cool. Cover and chill at least 2 hours.

Combine mashed peaches and ⅔ cup sugar; stir well, and set aside.

Combine half-and-half and next 3 ingredients in a large bowl; stir well. Add chilled custard mixture, stirring with a wire whisk. Stir in reserved peach mixture. Pour into freezer container of a 1-gallon hand-turned or electric freezer.

Freeze according to manufacturer's instructions. Pack freezer with additional ice and rock salt, and let stand 1½ to 2 hours before serving. Garnish each serving, if desired. **Yield: 3 quarts.**

Piña Colada Ice Cream

6 **large eggs, beaten**
1½ **cups sugar**
5 **cups milk**
2 **cups half-and-half**
1 **cup whipping cream**
1 **(10-ounce) can frozen piña colada tropical**
   fruit mixer, thawed and undiluted
½ **cup light rum**
Garnish: toasted coconut

Combine eggs and sugar in a large heavy saucepan; gradually add milk, beating well. Cook mixture over medium heat, stirring constantly, until thermometer registers 160°. Remove from heat, and cool.

Stir in half-and-half and next 3 ingredients.

Pour mixture into container of a 1-gallon hand-turned or electric freezer.

Freeze according to manufacturer's instructions. Pack freezer with additional ice and rock salt, and let stand 1 hour before serving (ice cream will be soft). Garnish each serving, if desired. **Yield: about 1 gallon.**

Note: To scoop ice cream into balls as shown in photograph, spoon into an airtight container after standing time. Cover; freeze at least 8 hours.

Piña Colada Ice Cream

Frangelica Cream

⅔ cup hazelnuts or slivered almonds
¾ cup sugar
1¾ cups milk
½ cup sugar, divided
5 egg yolks
¼ cup Frangelica or other hazelnut-flavored
   liqueur
1 cup whipping cream

Place hazelnuts in a shallow pan, and bake at 350° for 15 minutes; cool. Remove loose skins by rubbing nuts together. Chop nuts, and set aside.

Cook ¾ cup sugar in a heavy saucepan over medium heat, stirring occasionally, until caramelized (sugar melts and turns golden). Remove from heat; add nuts, and stir. Immediately pour into a buttered jellyroll pan. Cool 1 hour. Break brittle into small pieces.

Combine milk and 2 tablespoons sugar in a heavy saucepan; cook over medium heat until mixture boils.

Beat egg yolks and remaining 6 tablespoons sugar at medium speed of an electric mixer until thick and pale. Gradually stir about one-fourth of milk mixture into yolks; add to remaining milk mixture, stirring constantly.

Add Frangelica, and cook over low heat 5 minutes or until mixture reaches 160° (it does not thicken). Do not boil. Cover and chill. Add whipping cream and brittle.

Pour mixture into freezer container of a 2-quart hand-turned or electric freezer.

Freeze according to manufacturer's instructions. Pack freezer with additional ice and rock salt, and let stand 1 hour before serving. **Yield: about 1½ quarts.**

Peanut Ice Cream

(pictured on page 605)

6 large eggs, lightly beaten
1 cup firmly packed brown sugar
3 cups milk
⅔ cup creamy peanut butter
3 cups whipping cream
2 cups unsalted peanuts, coarsely chopped
Commercial hot fudge sauce
Garnish: chopped peanuts

Combine eggs and brown sugar; set aside.

Heat milk in a large heavy saucepan over medium heat until hot. Gradually stir a small amount of hot milk into egg mixture; add to remaining hot milk, stirring constantly. Cook over medium heat, stirring often, until thermometer registers 160° (3 to 5 minutes).

Remove from heat; stir in peanut butter, and cool. Stir in whipping cream and peanuts.

Pour mixture into freezer container of a 1-gallon hand-turned or electric freezer.

Freeze according to manufacturer's instructions. Pack freezer with additional ice and rock salt, and let stand 1 hour. Serve with hot fudge sauce. Garnish, if desired. **Yield: 2½ quarts.**

Champagne Ice

1½ cups sugar
3 cups water
1½ tablespoons grated lemon rind
⅓ cup fresh lemon juice
2 (750-milliliter) bottles champagne

Combine all ingredients in freezer container of a 1-gallon hand-turned or electric freezer; stir mixture well.

Freeze according to manufacturer's instructions. Pack freezer with additional ice and rock salt, and let stand 1 hour. **Yield: 2½ quarts.**

Apricot Sherbet

2 (16-ounce) cans apricot halves in light
    syrup, drained
2 cups sugar
1 quart milk
¼ cup lemon juice

Place apricots in container of an electric blender; cover and process until smooth, stopping once to scrape down sides.

Combine apricot puree, sugar, milk, and lemon juice. Pour into freezer container of a 1-gallon hand-turned or electric freezer.

Freeze according to manufacturer's instructions. Pack freezer with additional ice and rock salt, and let stand 1 hour. **Yield: 2 quarts.**

Pineapple-Orange Sherbet

1 (8-ounce) can crushed pineapple, undrained
2 (14-ounce) cans sweetened condensed milk
6 (12-ounce) cans orange carbonated beverage

Combine pineapple and condensed milk in freezer container of a 1-gallon hand-turned or electric freezer; stir well. Add orange beverage, stirring well.

Freeze according to manufacturer's instructions. Pack freezer with additional ice and rock salt, and let stand 1 hour. **Yield: 1 gallon.**

Watermelon Sherbet

4 cups diced and seeded watermelon
¾ to 1 cup sugar
3 tablespoons lemon juice
Dash of salt
1 envelope unflavored gelatin
¼ cup cold water
1 cup whipping cream

Combine first 4 ingredients in a large bowl; cover and chill 30 minutes.

Spoon mixture into container of an electric blender; cover and process until smooth. Return to bowl.

Sprinkle gelatin over cold water in a saucepan; let stand 1 minute. Cook over low heat until gelatin dissolves; add to watermelon mixture, stirring well.

Add whipping cream; beat at medium speed of an electric mixer until fluffy. Pour into freezer container of a 1-gallon hand-turned or electric freezer.

Freeze according to manufacturer's instructions. Serve immediately as mixture does not need ripening. **Yield: 1 quart.**

Blackberry Sorbet

1 cup sugar
1 cup water
2 (16-ounce) packages frozen blackberries,
    thawed and divided
3 large ripe pears, peeled, cored, and chopped
¼ cup plus 2 tablespoons orange juice

Combine sugar and water in a medium saucepan; cook over medium heat until sugar dissolves, stirring constantly. Cool slightly; transfer to a large bowl. Cover and chill 1 hour.

Place 1 package of blackberries and pears in container of an electric blender; cover and process until smooth. Add remaining package of blackberries; process until smooth. Press puree through a fine wire-mesh strainer to remove seeds; discard seeds. Add puree and orange juice to sugar mixture; stir well.

Pour blackberry mixture into freezer container of a 1-gallon hand-turned or electric freezer.

Freeze according to manufacturer's instructions. Pack freezer with additional ice and rock salt, and let stand 1 hour. **Yield: 7½ cups.**

Blackberry Sorbet

Praline Freeze

Pralines

1½ cups sugar
¾ cup firmly packed brown sugar
¼ cup plus 2 tablespoons butter or margarine
½ cup half-and-half
2 cups pecan halves

Combine all ingredients in a large heavy saucepan. Cook over low heat, stirring gently, until sugar dissolves. Cover and cook over medium heat 2 to 3 minutes to wash sugar crystals from sides of pan.

Uncover and cook to soft ball stage (235°), stirring constantly.

Remove from heat, and beat with a wooden spoon just until mixture begins to thicken. Working rapidly, drop by tablespoonfuls onto greased wax paper; let stand until firm. **Yield: 1½ dozen.**

Praline Freeze

½ gallon vanilla ice cream, slightly softened
½ cup praline liqueur
1 cup whipping cream
2 tablespoons sugar
Pralines

Combine ice cream and liqueur in a large bowl. Spoon mixture into a 13- x 9- x 2-inch pan, and freeze.

Beat whipping cream at medium speed of an electric mixer until foamy; gradually add sugar, beating until soft peaks form.

Scoop ice cream mixture into individual compotes; sprinkle with crumbled pralines, and top with whipped cream mixture and praline pieces. **Yield: 8 servings.**

Royal Mocha Freeze

1 pint whipping cream
½ cup chocolate syrup
⅓ cup brandy
1 quart coffee ice cream, slightly softened
1 (6-ounce) package semisweet chocolate morsels
¾ cup chopped almonds, toasted
Garnishes: whipped cream, chocolate leaves, maraschino cherries

Beat first 3 ingredients at medium speed of an electric mixer until thickened. Place ice cream in a large plastic or metal freezer container; fold chocolate mixture into ice cream. Stir in chocolate morsels and almonds. Freeze, uncovered, about 3 hours.

Remove from freezer, and stir well. Cover and freeze.

Spoon mixture into parfait glasses, and garnish, if desired. **Yield: 8 servings.**

Frozen Fruit Cream

1 envelope unflavored gelatin
3 cups sugar
2 cups pineapple juice
2 cups orange juice
⅓ cup lemon juice
2 (8-ounce) packages cream cheese, softened
1 pint whipping cream, whipped
1 teaspoon almond extract
Fresh Plum Sauce

Combine first 3 ingredients in a saucepan; cook over medium heat, stirring constantly, until gelatin dissolves (about 2 minutes). Pour into a large bowl. Add orange juice and lemon juice, and set aside.

Beat cream cheese at high speed of an electric mixer until creamy. Gradually stir about one-fourth of juice mixture into cream cheese; add to remaining juice mixture, stirring constantly.

Fold whipped cream and almond extract into juice mixture.

Pour mixture into freezer container of a 1-gallon hand-turned or electric freezer.

Freeze according to manufacturer's instructions. Pack freezer with additional ice and rock salt, and let stand 1 hour. Top each serving with Fresh Plum Sauce. **Yield: 3 quarts.**

Fresh Plum Sauce

1 pound ripe plums, pitted and quartered
   (about 4 plums)
½ cup water
3 tablespoons sugar
¼ teaspoon ground cinnamon
3 tablespoons port or other sweet red wine

Combine first 4 ingredients in a small saucepan; bring to a boil. Reduce heat, and simmer 15 minutes or until plums are soft.

Pour mixture through a fine wire-mesh strainer into a small bowl, pressing mixture against sides of strainer with back of spoon; discard solids, and cool.

Stir in port; cover and chill. **Yield: 1¼ cups.**

Frozen Fruit Cream

Creamy Bombe with Raspberry Sauce

Creamy Bombe with Raspberry Sauce

1 (16-ounce) package frozen unsweetened
   sliced peaches, thawed and drained
1 (8-ounce) carton sour cream
½ cup grenadine
½ gallon vanilla ice cream, slightly softened
Vegetable cooking spray
Garnishes: fresh raspberries, fresh mint sprigs
Raspberry Sauce

Position knife blade in food processor bowl;
add peaches, and process until smooth. Add sour
cream and grenadine; process until well blended.

Combine peach mixture and ice cream; beat
at low speed of an electric mixer until blended.

Pour mixture into an 11-cup mold coated with
cooking spray; cover and freeze 8 hours or until
mixture is firm.

Loosen edges of ice cream from mold two
hours before serving, using tip of a knife. Invert
mold onto a chilled serving plate. Wrap a warm
towel around mold for 30 seconds. Remove
towel, and firmly hold plate and mold together.
Shake gently, and slowly lift off mold. Immediately return bombe to freezer. Remove from
freezer just before serving.

Garnish, if desired. To serve, cut bombe into
slices, and top with Raspberry Sauce. Yield: 12
servings.

Raspberry Sauce

1 (16-ounce) package frozen unsweetened
   raspberries, thawed and undrained
¾ cup light corn syrup
¼ cup Grand Marnier

Place raspberries in container of a food processor or electric blender. Process 1 minute or
until smooth.

Press raspberry puree through a wire-mesh
strainer; discard seeds. Stir syrup and Grand
Marnier into puree. **Yield: 2 cups.**

Caramel-Toffee Bombe

1⅓ cups gingersnap cookie crumbs (about 20
   cookies)
¼ cup butter or margarine, melted
1 quart vanilla ice cream, slightly softened
4 (1.4-ounce) English toffee-flavored candy
   bars, crushed
Praline Sauce

Line a 2-quart bowl with heavy-duty plastic
wrap. Set aside.

Combine cookie crumbs and butter; press
mixture into prepared bowl. Combine ice cream
and crushed candy; spoon into bowl. Cover and
freeze at least 8 hours.

Let bowl stand at room temperature 5 minutes
before serving; invert onto a chilled serving plate.
Carefully remove bowl and plastic wrap. Cut
bombe into wedges, and serve immediately with
warm Praline Sauce. **Yield: 10 to 12 servings.**

Praline Sauce

½ cup firmly packed brown sugar
½ cup half-and-half
¼ cup butter or margarine
¼ cup slivered almonds, toasted and chopped
1 teaspoon vanilla extract

Combine first 3 ingredients in a small saucepan; bring to a boil over medium heat, stirring
occasionally. Boil 2 minutes, stirring occasionally.

Remove mixture from heat; stir in almonds
and vanilla. **Yield: 1 cup.**

Spumoni Charlotte

20 ladyfingers, split
¼ cup amaretto
⅔ cup chocolate wafer crumbs
1 quart vanilla ice cream, slightly softened
1 tablespoon rum
1 (6-ounce) jar maraschino cherries, drained
1 quart pistachio ice cream, slightly softened
1 cup whipping cream
½ cup sifted powdered sugar
1 tablespoon rum
Garnish: maraschino cherries

Brush cut side of ladyfingers with amaretto;
roll lightly in chocolate crumbs. Line bottom and
sides of a 9-inch springform pan with ladyfingers.

Combine vanilla ice cream and 1 tablespoon
rum; spoon into pan, spreading to sides. Place
cherries over ice cream; press cherries gently.
Freeze until firm.

Spoon pistachio ice cream over cherries;
spread to sides. Freeze until firm.

Combine whipping cream, sugar, and 1 tablespoon rum in a mixing bowl; beat at high speed
of an electric mixer until soft peaks form. Spoon
cream mixture into a decorating bag fitted with
large metal tip No. 2110. Remove sides of springform pan. Pipe rosettes over top and around bottom edge.

Return to freezer until ready to serve.
Garnish, if desired. **Yield: 10 to 12 servings.**

Layered Sherbet Dessert

Layered Sherbet Dessert

2⅔ cups chocolate wafer crumbs, divided
½ cup butter or margarine, melted
1 quart orange sherbet, slightly softened
1 quart rainbow sherbet, slightly softened
1 quart lime sherbet, slightly softened
Raspberry-Orange Sauce
Garnishes: chocolate curls, orange rind curls,
    fresh mint sprigs

Combine 1⅔ cups chocolate crumbs and butter; press onto bottom of a 10-inch springform pan. Freeze until firm.

Spread orange sherbet evenly over frozen crust. Sprinkle with ½ cup chocolate crumbs; freeze until firm. Repeat procedure with rainbow sherbet and remaining crumbs; freeze until firm.

Spread lime sherbet over frozen crumb layer. Cover and freeze at least 8 hours.

Remove sides of springform pan. Spoon 2 to 3 tablespoons Raspberry-Orange Sauce onto each serving plate. Place wedge of sherbet dessert over sauce. Garnish, if desired. **Yield: 12 to 14 servings.**

Raspberry-Orange Sauce

2 (10-ounce) packages frozen raspberries in
    light syrup, thawed
2 tablespoons frozen orange juice concentrate,
    thawed and undiluted
1 tablespoon plus 1 teaspoon cornstarch

Place raspberries in container of a food processor or electric blender. Process 1 minute or until smooth.

Press raspberry puree through a wire-mesh strainer; discard seeds. Set puree aside.

Combine orange juice concentrate and cornstarch in a saucepan; add puree, and stir well. Cook over medium heat, stirring constantly, until mixture comes to a boil. Cook 1 minute, stirring constantly. Pour sauce into a bowl. Cover and chill. **Yield: 2⅓ cups.**

Frozen Almond Crunch

⅔ cup sliced almonds
½ cup sugar
½ cup butter or margarine
1 tablespoon all-purpose flour
2 tablespoons milk
½ gallon vanilla ice cream, slightly softened
Dark Chocolate Sauce

Combine first 5 ingredients in a heavy saucepan; bring to a boil over medium heat, stirring constantly. Remove from heat, and set aside.

Line a 15- x 10- x 1-inch jellyroll pan with aluminum foil; spread almond mixture onto foil.

Bake mixture at 350° for 7 minutes or until light golden. Cool; remove from foil, and crumble.

Sprinkle half of almond mixture in a 10-inch springform pan. Spoon ice cream evenly on top; gently press remaining almond mixture on top.

Freeze 8 hours or until firm. Serve with Dark Chocolate Sauce. **Yield: 12 servings.**

Dark Chocolate Sauce

½ cup butter or margarine
4 (1-ounce) squares unsweetened chocolate
1½ cups sugar
½ cup cocoa
Pinch of salt
1 cup milk
1 teaspoon vanilla extract

Melt butter and chocolate in a heavy saucepan over low heat, stirring often.

Combine sugar, cocoa, and salt; stir sugar mixture and milk into chocolate mixture.

Bring just to a boil over medium heat, stirring constantly; remove from heat, and stir in vanilla. Cool, stirring occasionally. Sauce may be refrigerated up to 1 week. **Yield: 2½ cups.**

Note: Sauce thickens when refrigerated. To serve, microwave at HIGH, stirring at 30-second intervals, until drizzling consistency.

Frozen Viennese Torte

18 large cinnamon graham crackers
2 (2-ounce) packages slivered almonds
⅓ cup butter or margarine, cut into small
    pieces
1 quart chocolate ice cream, slightly softened
1 quart coffee ice cream, slightly softened
1 quart vanilla ice cream, slightly softened
2½ teaspoons ground cinnamon
1 (2-ounce) package slivered almonds, toasted
Amaretto-Cinnamon Sauce

Position knife blade in food processor bowl;
add graham crackers and 2 packages almonds.
Process until crushed. Add butter, processing
until blended.

Press mixture onto bottom and 1 inch up sides
of a 10-inch springform pan. Bake at 375° for 10
minutes. Cool on a wire rack.

Spread chocolate ice cream onto bottom and 1
inch up sides of crust; freeze until firm.

Spread coffee ice cream over chocolate ice
cream; freeze until firm.

Beat vanilla ice cream and cinnamon at low
speed of an electric mixer until blended; spread
over coffee ice cream, and freeze 8 hours.

Sprinkle each serving with toasted almonds,
and drizzle with Amaretto-Cinnamon Sauce.
Yield: 12 to 14 servings.

Amaretto-Cinnamon Sauce

¾ cup amaretto or other almond-flavored
    liqueur
¾ cup honey
¼ teaspoon ground cinnamon

Combine all ingredients in a small saucepan;
cook over medium heat until thoroughly heated,
stirring often.

Remove from heat, and cool to room temperature. **Yield: 1½ cups.**

Chocolate Ice Cream Brownies

1 (23.6-ounce) package fudge brownie mix
½ gallon vanilla ice cream, slightly softened
2 cups sifted powdered sugar
⅔ cup semisweet chocolate morsels
1½ cups evaporated milk
½ cup butter or margarine
1 teaspoon vanilla extract
1½ cups chopped pecans or walnuts

Prepare brownie mix according to package
directions in a lightly greased 13- x 9- x 2-inch
pan. Cool in pan on a wire rack.

Spread ice cream over brownies; freeze until
ice cream is firm.

Combine sugar and next 3 ingredients in a
saucepan. Bring to a boil; reduce heat to medium,
and cook 8 minutes. Remove from heat, and stir
in vanilla and pecans. Cool. Spread frosting over
ice cream. Freeze.

Remove from freezer 5 to 10 minutes before
serving. Cut into squares. **Yield: 15 servings.**

Frosty Findings

• Avoid purchasing a sticky carton
of sherbet or ice cream as it has
likely thawed and been refrozen.
• After opening a carton of ice
cream, press a sheet of plastic wrap
over the unused portion before clos-
ing the carton. This helps keep ice
crystals from forming.
• If ice cream is too hard to scoop,
use an electric knife to cut blocks of
ice cream into slices.
• To soften a quart of ice cream,
microwave at MEDIUM-LOW
(30% power) about 30 seconds.

Mint-Chocolate Chip Ice Cream Squares

Mint-Chocolate Chip Ice Cream Squares

3 cups cream-filled chocolate sandwich cookie crumbs (about 30 cookies, crushed)
¼ cup butter or margarine, melted
½ gallon mint-chocolate chip ice cream, slightly softened
1 (5-ounce) can evaporated milk
½ cup sugar
1½ (1-ounce) squares unsweetened chocolate
1 tablespoon butter or margarine
1 (12-ounce) carton frozen whipped topping, thawed
1 cup chopped pecans, toasted
Garnish: fresh mint sprigs

Combine cookie crumbs and ¼ cup butter. Press mixture into a lightly greased 13- x 9- x 2-inch pan; freeze until firm.

Spread ice cream evenly over crust; freeze until firm.

Combine evaporated milk and next 3 ingredients in a small heavy saucepan. Bring to a boil over low heat, stirring constantly with a wire whisk. Cook, stirring constantly, 3 to 4 minutes or until mixture thickens. Cool mixture to room temperature.

Spread chocolate mixture over ice cream; top with whipped topping, and sprinkle with pecans. Freeze until firm.

Let stand 10 minutes at room temperature before serving. Cut into squares, and garnish, if desired. **Yield: 15 servings.**

Brownie Baked Alaska

Brownie Baked Alaska

1 quart strawberry or vanilla ice cream
½ cup butter or margarine, softened
2 cups sugar, divided
2 large eggs
1 cup all-purpose flour
½ teaspoon baking powder
¼ teaspoon salt
2 tablespoons cocoa
1 teaspoon vanilla extract
5 egg whites
½ teaspoon cream of tartar
Strawberry halves

Line a 1-quart freezerproof bowl (about 7 inches in diameter) with wax paper, leaving an overhang around edges. Pack ice cream into bowl, and freeze until very firm.

Beat butter at medium speed of an electric mixer until creamy. Add 1 cup sugar; beat well. Add 2 eggs, one at a time; beat after each addition.

Combine flour and next 3 ingredients. Add to butter mixture; mix well. Stir in vanilla. Pour into a greased and floured 8-inch round cakepan.

Bake at 350° for 25 to 30 minutes or until a wooden pick inserted in center comes out clean. Cool in pan on a wire rack 10 minutes. Remove from pan, and cool completely on wire rack.

Place cake on an ovenproof wooden board or serving dish. Invert ice cream onto cake, leaving wax paper intact; remove bowl. Place ice cream-topped cake in freezer.

Combine egg whites, remaining 1 cup sugar, and cream of tartar in top of a double boiler. Place over simmering water. Cook, stirring constantly with a wire whisk, 5 minutes or until mixture reaches 160°. Remove from heat. Beat at high speed 5 minutes or until soft peaks form.

Remove ice cream-topped cake from freezer, and peel off wax paper. Quickly spread meringue over entire surface, making sure edges are sealed.

Bake at 500° for 2 minutes or until meringue peaks are lightly browned. Arrange strawberry halves around edges, and serve immediately.
Yield: 10 to 12 servings.

Note: After meringue is sealed, dessert can be frozen up to 1 week; bake just before serving.

Brownie Baked Alaska Technique

Pack ice cream into a freezerproof bowl for Brownie Baked Alaska; freeze until very firm.

Fruit Finales

Fruit desserts make a spectacular presentation and, best of all, are not difficult to prepare. Most recipes take advantage of the natural beauty of fresh fruit by calling for only a few additional ingredients.

Caramel Brie with Fresh Fruit, Fantastic Ambrosia, Peach Frost

Bananas Foster, Fresh Peach Crêpes, Peaches and Cream, Blueberry Buckle

Blueberry-Lemon Napoleons, Baked Pears à la Mode, Hot Cranberry Bake

Strawberries Jamaica, Poached Pears with Dark Chocolate Sauce

Ruby Poached Pears (page 638)

Caramel Brie with Fresh Fruit

1 (15-ounce) mini Brie
2 tablespoons butter or margarine
¾ cup firmly packed brown sugar
¼ cup light corn syrup
1½ tablespoons all-purpose flour
¼ cup milk
½ cup coarsely chopped pecans, toasted
1 tablespoon lemon juice
¼ cup water
Pear and apple wedges
Grapes

Place Brie on a large serving plate.

Melt butter in a saucepan; add brown sugar, corn syrup, and flour, stirring well. Bring mixture to a boil; reduce heat, and simmer 5 minutes, stirring constantly.

Remove from heat; cool to lukewarm. Gradually stir in milk.

Pour caramel over Brie, allowing excess to drip down sides; sprinkle with pecans.

Combine lemon juice and water; toss with fruit wedges. Drain. Arrange fruit around Brie. Serve immediately. **Yield: 14 servings.**

Festive Fruit Compote

2 cups cantaloupe or honeydew melon balls
2 cups fresh strawberries, halved
2 cups fresh blueberries
3 medium bananas, sliced
1½ cups sliced fresh peaches
1 (25.4-ounce) bottle sparkling white grape
  juice, chilled

Layer first 3 ingredients in a bowl or compote; cover and chill until serving time.

Top with sliced bananas and peaches; pour white grape juice over top. Serve with a slotted spoon. **Yield: 8 to 10 servings.**

Layered Ambrosia

1 (6-ounce) can pineapple juice
½ cup orange juice
¼ cup sifted powdered sugar
7 large oranges
3 medium-size pink grapefruit
5 medium bananas
1 small fresh pineapple, peeled and cored
1 (3½-ounce) can flaked coconut
Garnish: maraschino cherries with stems

Combine first 3 ingredients; stir well, and set juice mixture aside.

Peel oranges; cut crosswise into ½-inch slices. Peel and section grapefruit, catching juice in a bowl.

Peel bananas, and cut diagonally into ½-inch slices. Dip banana slices in pineapple juice mixture to prevent browning, using a slotted spoon.

Cut pineapple into 1-inch chunks.

Arrange half of orange slices in a 3-quart serving bowl. Top with sliced bananas, grapefruit, half of coconut, and pineapple chunks. Top with remaining orange slices.

Pour grapefruit juice and pineapple juice mixture over fruit. Cover and chill thoroughly.

Sprinkle with remaining coconut, and garnish, if desired. **Yield: 12 servings.**

Layered Ambrosia Technique

Prepare pineapple by cutting off the leafy green top. Then trim the eyes, and remove the hard core.

Layered Ambrosia

Fantastic Ambrosia

4 bananas, sliced
¼ cup orange juice
2 cups orange sections
1 cup fresh strawberries, halved
¼ cup salad dressing or mayonnaise
1 tablespoon sugar
½ cup whipping cream, whipped
2 tablespoons flaked coconut, toasted

Toss bananas in orange juice; drain and reserve juice. Layer orange sections, bananas, and strawberries in a serving bowl; cover and chill.

Combine salad dressing, sugar, and reserved orange juice; fold in whipped cream. Spoon mixture over fruit, and sprinkle with coconut. **Yield: 6 to 8 servings.**

Bananas Foster

4 bananas
1 tablespoon lemon juice
½ cup firmly packed brown sugar
¼ cup butter or margarine
Dash of ground cinnamon
⅓ cup light rum
Coffee or vanilla ice cream

Cut bananas in half lengthwise, and toss in lemon juice; set aside.

Combine brown sugar and butter in a large skillet; cook over low heat 2 minutes, stirring constantly, until sugar melts. Add bananas; stir gently, and cook 1 to 2 minutes or until mixture is thoroughly heated. Remove from heat, and sprinkle with cinnamon.

Heat rum in a small, long-handled saucepan over medium heat (do not boil). Remove from heat. Ignite rum with a long match, and pour over banana mixture. Let flames die down. Spoon immediately over ice cream. **Yield: 4 servings.**

Blueberry-Lemon Napoleons

1 (17¼-ounce) package frozen puff pastry
    sheets, thawed
Blueberry Sauce
Lemon Filling

Unfold pastry sheets, and cut into 9 (3-inch) rounds. Place on an ungreased baking sheet.

Bake at 400° for 10 minutes or until lightly browned. Remove to a wire rack to cool. Split each round in half crosswise, forming 18 rounds.

Spoon Blueberry Sauce evenly onto 6 plates; place 1 pastry round in center of each. Spoon or pipe half of Lemon Filling evenly onto pastry rounds; top each with a second pastry round and remaining filling. Top with remaining rounds. Serve immediately. **Yield: 6 servings.**

Blueberry Sauce
2 cups fresh blueberries
¼ cup sifted powdered sugar

Position knife blade in food processor bowl; add blueberries and sugar. Process until pureed.

Pour through a wire-mesh strainer, discarding solids. **Yield: about 1 cup.**

Lemon Filling
1 (14-ounce) can sweetened condensed milk
1 (8-ounce) package cream cheese, softened
¼ cup lemon juice
½ teaspoon vanilla extract

Combine all ingredients in a small mixing bowl; beat at medium speed of an electric mixer until smooth.

Cover and chill 1 hour or until thickened. **Yield: 1¾ cups.**

Flaming Cranberry Jubilee

1 cup sugar
1 cup water
⅛ teaspoon ground cinnamon
2 cups fresh cranberries
⅓ cup chopped pecans
3 tablespoons rum
Vanilla ice cream

Combine first 3 ingredients in a saucepan. Bring mixture to a boil, stirring occasionally; boil 5 minutes.

Add cranberries, and return to a boil; cook 5 minutes, stirring occasionally. Stir in pecans. Remove from heat.

Heat rum in a small, long-handled saucepan over medium heat (do not boil). Remove from heat. Ignite rum with a long match, and pour over cranberries. Let flames die down. Spoon immediately over ice cream. **Yield: 4 to 6 servings.**

Oranges Grand Marnier

12 medium navel oranges
⅓ to ½ cup Grand Marnier or other orange-
    flavored liqueur
1½ quarts orange sherbet, slightly softened

Cut a ½-inch slice from the stem end of each orange. Scoop out pulp, removing membrane and seeds; reserve orange shells. Chop pulp, and drain well.

Combine orange pulp, Grand Marnier, and sherbet; stir until blended. Spoon into orange shells, and place in muffin pans. Freeze 8 hours.

Remove from freezer 20 to 30 minutes before serving. **Yield: 12 servings.**

Peaches Foster

2 tablespoons butter or margarine
¼ cup firmly packed brown sugar
4 medium peaches, peeled and sliced
Dash of ground cinnamon
2 tablespoons rum
Vanilla ice cream

Melt butter in a medium skillet; add brown sugar, and cook over medium heat until bubbly. Add peaches; heat 3 to 4 minutes, basting constantly with syrup. Stir in cinnamon.

Heat rum in a small, long-handled saucepan over medium heat (do not boil). Remove from heat. Ignite rum with a long match, and pour over peaches. Let flames die down. Spoon rum and peaches immediately over ice cream. **Yield: 6 servings.**

Peach Frost

(pictured on page 635)

3 ripe peaches, pitted, and quartered (about
    1 pound)
¼ to ½ cup light corn syrup
¼ teaspoon ground ginger
1 cup pineapple or lemon sherbet
1 cup vanilla ice cream
½ cup ginger ale
Garnishes: peach slices, peach leaves

Combine first 3 ingredients in container of an electric blender; cover and process until smooth.

Add sherbet and ice cream; cover and process until smooth. Add ginger ale; blend 30 seconds. Garnish, if desired. **Yield: 4 servings.**

Berry Napoleons

Strawberries Jamaica

1 (3-ounce) package cream cheese, softened
½ cup firmly packed brown sugar
1½ cups sour cream
2 tablespoons Grand Marnier or other orange-
    flavored liqueur
1 quart fresh strawberries

Beat cream cheese at medium speed of an electric mixer until smooth. Add sugar, sour cream, and Grand Marnier; beat 1 minute or until smooth. Cover and chill. Serve as a dip with strawberries. **Yield: about 10 to 12 servings.**

Berry Napoleons

Vegetable cooking spray
1½ cups quick-cooking oats, uncooked
½ cup butter or margarine, melted
¾ cup sugar
1 teaspoon all-purpose flour
1 teaspoon baking powder
1 large egg, lightly beaten
½ cup chopped pecans
1 teaspoon vanilla extract
¾ cup semisweet chocolate morsels
1½ tablespoons Chambord or other
    raspberry-flavored liqueur
1 tablespoon butter or margarine
2 cups whipping cream
¼ cup sifted powdered sugar
1 pint fresh raspberries or blackberries
Garnish: fresh berries

Cover baking sheets with aluminum foil, and coat with cooking spray. Set aside.

Combine oats and ½ cup melted butter in a bowl; stir in sugar, flour, and baking powder. Add egg, pecans, and vanilla, stirring until blended.

Drop by rounded teaspoonfuls 2 inches apart into 36 mounds onto prepared baking sheets.

Bake at 325° for 12 minutes or until lightly browned. Cool completely on baking sheets. Remove from foil, and place on wax paper.

Combine chocolate morsels, liqueur, and 1 tablespoon butter in a small saucepan; cook mixture over low heat, stirring constantly, until chocolate melts.

Spoon mixture into a heavy-duty, zip-top plastic bag; seal. Snip a tiny hole in 1 corner of bag, and gently squeeze bag to drizzle chocolate over cooled cookies. Let stand until chocolate is firm.

Beat whipping cream until foamy; gradually add powdered sugar, beating until soft peaks form. Set aside ¾ cup whipped cream.

Place 1 cookie on each serving plate. Pipe or dollop ½-inch layer of whipped cream onto each cookie, and top with berries. Top each with a second cookie, and repeat procedure. Top with remaining cookies. Pipe or dollop with reserved ¾ cup whipped cream; top each with a berry. Garnish, if desired. **Yield: 12 servings.**

Apple Crisp

6 large cooking apples, peeled, cored, and
    sliced
½ cup sugar
¼ teaspoon ground nutmeg
¼ teaspoon ground cinnamon
1 cup all-purpose flour
1 cup firmly packed brown sugar
½ cup butter or margarine
Vanilla ice cream (optional)

Place apple slices in a lightly greased 13- x 9- x 2-inch baking dish. Combine ½ cup sugar, nutmeg, and cinnamon; sprinkle over apple.

Combine flour and brown sugar; cut in butter with a pastry blender until mixture is crumbly. Sprinkle over apple.

Bake, uncovered, at 300° for 1 hour. Serve warm with ice cream, if desired. **Yield: 8 servings.**

Sugar-Crusted Apples in Walnut-Phyllo Baskets

Sugar-Crusted Apples in Walnut-Phyllo Baskets

¼ cup lemon juice
2 cups water
6 large Granny Smith apples, peeled and
    cored
⅔ cup sugar
⅓ cup all-purpose flour
½ teaspoon ground cinnamon
⅓ cup butter or margarine
1 large egg, lightly beaten
1¼ to 1½ cups orange juice, divided
Walnut-Phyllo Baskets
Sifted powdered sugar
Garnish: fresh mint leaves

Combine lemon juice and water in a large bowl; add apples, tossing to coat well, and set aside.

Combine sugar, flour, and cinnamon; cut in butter with a pastry blender until mixture is crumbly.

Drain apples; pat dry. Brush top half of each apple with egg, and dredge in sugar mixture; place in a lightly greased 13- x 9- x 2-inch baking dish.

Spoon remaining sugar mixture into apple cavities. Pour ¾ cup orange juice over apples.

Bake at 350° for 1 hour or until tender. Remove apples; reserve pan drippings in baking dish. Place each apple in a Walnut-Phyllo Basket.

Add enough of remaining ½ to ¾ cup orange juice to pan drippings, stirring constantly, until sauce is desired consistency; spoon over apples. Sprinkle with powdered sugar, and garnish, if desired. Serve immediately. **Yield: 6 servings.**

Walnut-Phyllo Baskets

1¼ cups finely chopped walnuts
⅓ cup sugar
1¼ teaspoons grated lemon rind
1 teaspoon ground cinnamon
12 sheets frozen phyllo pastry, thawed
Vegetable cooking spray

Combine first 4 ingredients in a small bowl; set aside.

Place phyllo sheets on a damp towel. Using kitchen shears, cut phyllo lengthwise in half, and cut each portion crosswise in half, forming 48 rectangles. Place rectangles on a damp towel. (Keep phyllo covered with a damp towel.)

Spray 6 rectangles with cooking spray, and place 1 rectangle in each lightly greased 10-ounce custard cup. Repeat procedure 3 times, placing each rectangle at alternating angles.

Spoon about 1½ tablespoons walnut mixture into each shell; top each with 2 phyllo rectangles coated with cooking spray, alternating angles. Repeat procedure with remaining walnut mixture and phyllo rectangles.

Bake at 350° for 20 to 25 minutes or until golden. Gently remove shells from custard cups, and cool on wire racks. **Yield: 6 baskets.**

Note: To store any leftover thawed phyllo, wrap phyllo sheets in plastic wrap, and place in an airtight container; refreeze.

Pick an Apple

• Choose apples that have good color and smooth skin without bruises.
• For cooking or baking, select one of the following apple varieties: Granny Smith, McIntosh, Rome Beauty, Stayman, Winesap, or York Imperial.

Blueberry Buckle

½ cup shortening
¼ cup sugar
1 large egg
1 cup all-purpose flour
2 teaspoons baking powder
¼ teaspoon salt
½ cup milk
1 (16-ounce) package frozen blueberries,
    thawed and drained
2 teaspoons lemon juice
½ cup all-purpose flour
¼ cup sugar
½ teaspoon ground cinnamon
¼ cup butter or margarine

Beat shortening and ¼ cup sugar at medium speed of an electric mixer until fluffy; add egg, and beat well.

Combine 1 cup flour, baking powder, and salt; add to shortening mixture alternately with milk, beginning and ending with flour mixture. Beat until blended after each addition. Spread batter into a greased 9-inch square pan.

Combine blueberries and lemon juice; sprinkle over batter.

Combine ½ cup flour, ¼ cup sugar, and cinnamon; cut in butter with a pastry blender until mixture is crumbly. Sprinkle over blueberries.

Bake at 350° for 45 to 55 minutes or until a wooden pick inserted in center comes out clean. Serve warm. **Yield: 9 servings.**

Hot Cranberry Bake

4 cups peeled chopped cooking apple
2 cups fresh cranberries
1½ teaspoons lemon juice
1 cup sugar
1⅓ cups quick-cooking oats, uncooked
1 cup chopped walnuts
⅓ cup firmly packed brown sugar
½ cup butter or margarine, melted
Vanilla ice cream

Layer apple and cranberries in a lightly greased 2-quart baking dish. Sprinkle with lemon juice; spoon sugar over fruit. Set aside.

Combine oats and next 3 ingredients; stir just until dry ingredients are moistened and mixture is crumbly. Sprinkle over fruit.

Bake, uncovered, at 325° for 1 hour. Serve warm with ice cream. **Yield: 8 servings.**

Cranberry Criteria

• Select fresh cranberries ranging from light to dark red. A 12-ounce bag equals 3 cups berries.
• Store cranberries in original airtight package in refrigerator up to 2 weeks; freeze up to 1 year.
• Rinse frozen cranberries in cold water and drain. Stir frozen cranberries into any recipe; do not thaw berries before using.

Hot Cranberry Bake

Crêpes Suzette

Crêpes Suzette

1 cup all-purpose flour
1 teaspoon sugar
⅛ teaspoon salt
1¼ cups milk
½ teaspoon vanilla extract
2 large eggs
1 tablespoon butter or margarine, melted
Vegetable oil
2 cups orange juice
2 tablespoons cornstarch
¼ cup orange marmalade
1 tablespoon butter or margarine
1 tablespoon grated orange rind
2 medium oranges, peeled and sectioned
¼ cup Grand Marnier or other orange-
   flavored liqueur
2 tablespoons light rum
Powdered sugar (optional)

Combine first 5 ingredients in a medium bowl, beating at medium speed of an electric mixer until smooth. Add eggs, and beat well; stir in 1 tablespoon melted butter. Cover and chill batter 1 hour. (This allows flour particles to swell and soften so crêpes are light in texture.)

Brush bottom of a 6-inch crêpe pan or heavy skillet with oil; place over medium heat just until hot, not smoking.

Pour 2 tablespoons batter into pan; quickly tilt pan in all directions so batter covers bottom of pan. Cook 1 minute or until crêpe can be shaken loose from pan. Turn crêpe over, and cook about 30 seconds. (This side is usually spotty brown.)

Place crêpe on a towel to cool. Repeat with remaining batter.

Stack crêpes between sheets of wax paper to prevent sticking.

Combine orange juice and cornstarch, stirring well; pour into a chafing dish or large skillet. Add orange marmalade, 1 tablespoon butter, and orange rind; stir well.

Cook over medium heat until mixture comes to a boil, stirring constantly; boil 1 minute. Gently stir in orange sections, and cool slightly.

Dip both sides of each crêpe in orange sauce; fold in half, and then in half again. Arrange crêpes in any remaining sauce; cook over low heat until thoroughly heated.

Heat liqueur and rum in a small saucepan over medium heat (do not boil). Quickly pour over crêpes, and immediately ignite with a long match. Serve after flames die down. Sprinkle each serving with powdered sugar, if desired. **Yield: 8 servings.**

Crêpes Suzette Techniques

Lift edges to test crêpes for doneness. Crêpes are ready for turning when they can be shaken loose from pan.

Dip both sides of crêpes in orange sauce; fold crêpes in half, and then in half again. Arrange crêpes in sauce.

Fresh Peach Crêpes

2 (8-ounce) packages cream cheese, softened
½ cup sugar
2 teaspoons vanilla extract
Crêpes
6 large ripe peaches, peeled and sliced
½ cup butter or margarine, softened
½ cup firmly packed light brown sugar
1 cup whipping cream
2 tablespoons powdered sugar

Beat first 3 ingredients at medium speed of an electric mixer until smooth. Spread about 3 tablespoons mixture over each crêpe. Place peaches down center of each crêpe.

Dot peaches in each crêpe with 1 tablespoon butter, and sprinkle with 1 tablespoon brown sugar. Roll up crêpes, and place in a 13- x 9- x 2-inch baking dish; bake at 325° for 8 to 10 minutes.

Beat whipping cream and powdered sugar at medium speed until firm peaks form. Place crêpes on serving dishes; top with whipped cream. Serve immediately. **Yield: 8 servings.**

Crêpes
¾ cup all-purpose flour
¾ cup milk
2 large eggs
1 tablespoon light brown sugar
1 tablespoon vegetable oil
Dash of ground cinnamon
Dash of ground nutmeg
Dash of ground ginger
Vegetable oil

Combine first 8 ingredients in container of an electric blender; process 1 minute, stopping once to scrape down sides. Process 15 additional seconds. Cover; chill batter 1 hour.

Brush bottom of an 8-inch crêpe pan or nonstick skillet with oil; place over medium heat until hot, not smoking.

Pour about 3 tablespoons batter into pan; quickly tilt in all directions so batter covers bottom. Cook 1 minute or until crêpe can be shaken loose. Turn crêpe over; cook about 30 seconds.

Place crêpe on a towel to cool. Repeat with remaining batter. Stack crêpes between sheets of wax paper to prevent sticking. **Yield: 8 crêpes.**

Peach Cardinale

4 fresh peaches
3 cups water
1 cup sugar
1 tablespoon vanilla extract
1 (10-ounce) package frozen raspberries, thawed
1 tablespoon sugar
2 teaspoons cornstarch
¼ cup water
½ cup whipping cream, whipped
Garnish: fresh mint leaves

Place peaches in boiling water for 20 seconds. Remove peaches, and plunge into ice water. Remove skins. Cut peaches in half.

Combine 3 cups water and 1 cup sugar in a Dutch oven; bring to a boil, and cook 3 minutes, stirring occasionally. Reduce heat to low; add peach halves and vanilla.

Simmer, uncovered, 10 to 15 minutes or until tender. Chill in syrup 1 hour or up to 2 days.

Puree raspberries. Press pureed raspberries through a fine wire-mesh strainer; discard seeds.

Combine 1 tablespoon sugar and cornstarch; stir in ¼ cup water. Add to puree, stirring well.

Cook over medium heat until mixture boils. Boil 1 minute, stirring constantly. Cover; chill.

Spoon whipped cream into 4 dessert dishes. Put 2 peach halves together; place on top of cream in each dish. Pour about ¼ cup sauce around each peach. Garnish, if desired. **Yield: 4 servings.**

From front: Peach Cardinale and Peach Frost (page 625)

Peaches and Cream

1½ cups all-purpose flour
2 tablespoons sugar
½ teaspoon baking powder
½ teaspoon salt
½ cup butter or margarine
6 peaches, peeled and halved
1 cup sugar
1 teaspoon ground cinnamon
2 egg yolks
1 cup whipping cream
Vanilla ice cream

Combine first 4 ingredients; cut in butter with a pastry blender until mixture is crumbly. Press into bottom and 1 inch up sides of an 8-inch square pan.

Arrange peaches, cut side down, over crust. Combine 1 cup sugar and 1 teaspoon ground cinnamon; sprinkle over peaches.

Bake at 400° for 15 minutes.

Combine egg yolks and whipping cream; pour over peaches. Bake 30 additional minutes. Serve warm with ice cream. **Yield: 6 servings.**

Baked Pears à la Mode

2 (16-ounce) cans pear halves, drained
½ cup honey
½ cup butter or margarine, melted
1 cup crumbled almond or coconut
     macaroons or amaretto cookies
Vanilla ice cream

Arrange pears in an 11- x 7- x 1½-inch baking dish. Set aside.

Combine honey and butter; pour over pears.

Bake at 350° for 20 minutes. Sprinkle cookie crumbs over pears; bake 10 additional minutes. Serve warm with ice cream. **Yield: 6 servings.**

Poached Pears
with Dark Chocolate Sauce

½ cup water
¼ cup brandy
¼ cup sugar
1 tablespoon grated orange rind
2 tablespoons grated fresh gingerroot
4 whole black peppercorns
4 firm ripe pears with stems
⅓ cup lemon juice
2 (1-ounce) squares semisweet chocolate
2 tablespoons whipping cream
1 tablespoon light corn syrup
1 tablespoon Grand Marnier or brandy
½ teaspoon vanilla extract

Combine first 6 ingredients in a 3-quart baking dish. Microwave at HIGH 1 to 2 minutes or until sugar dissolves.

Peel pears; core from the bottom, cutting to, but not through, the stem end, leaving stems intact. Baste pears with lemon juice.

Place pears, on their sides, in brandy mixture. Cover tightly with heavy-duty plastic wrap; fold back a small edge of wrap to allow steam to escape. Microwave at HIGH 4 minutes.

Uncover, baste pears with brandy mixture, and turn them over. Cover and microwave at HIGH 3 to 5 minutes or until tender. (A sharp knife should pierce the fruit as it would room-temperature butter, yet fruit should retain its shape.)

Cool pears in liquid, turning and basting once. Place pears in serving dishes.

Place chocolate in a 1-quart glass bowl. Microwave at MEDIUM (50% power) 2 to 3 minutes or until melted, stirring every minute. Cool slightly.

Add whipping cream and next 3 ingredients, stirring until smooth. Spoon sauce over pears. **Yield: 4 servings.**

Poached Pears with Dark Chocolate Sauce

Ruby Poached Pears

(pictured on page 621)

4 large, ripe pears with stems
Lemon juice
2 cups water
½ cup grenadine syrup
½ cup sugar
½ (10-ounce) package frozen raspberries,
   thawed
Custard Sauce
Garnish: fresh mint sprigs

Peel pears; core from the bottom, cutting to, but not through, the stem end, leaving stems intact. Brush pears with lemon juice.

Combine water, grenadine, and sugar in a large saucepan; bring to a boil. Add pears, standing them upright; cover, reduce heat, and simmer 15 to 20 minutes or until pears are tender, basting often with syrup. Remove from heat.

Transfer cooked pears and syrup to a medium bowl. Cover and chill thoroughly, turning pears occasionally.

Puree raspberries. Press pureed raspberries through a fine wire-mesh strainer; discard seeds.

Spoon ¼ cup Custard Sauce onto each of 4 dessert plates. Place a chilled pear in sauce on each plate. Discard syrup.

Spoon raspberry puree in small circles over custard around each pear. Pull a wooden pick or the tip of a knife continuously through raspberry circles surrounding each pear. Garnish, if desired. **Yield: 4 servings.**

Custard Sauce

¾ cup half-and-half
½ cup milk
1 vanilla bean, split lengthwise
⅓ cup sugar
3 egg yolks
½ teaspoon cornstarch
⅛ teaspoon salt

Combine first 3 ingredients in a heavy saucepan, and simmer over medium heat. Remove and discard vanilla bean.

Beat sugar and egg yolks until thick and pale. Stir in cornstarch. Gradually add one-fourth of hot milk mixture to yolk mixture, stirring constantly. Add to remaining hot mixture, stirring constantly.

Cook mixture over medium-low heat, stirring constantly, until thickened (about 10 minutes). Remove from heat, and stir in salt. Cover and chill custard thoroughly. **Yield: 1 cup.**

Note: You may substitute vanilla extract for vanilla bean. Stir 1 teaspoon vanilla extract into custard when adding salt.

Ruby Poached Pears Techniques

Puree thawed raspberries; press pureed raspberries through a small strainer, reserving thin puree. Discard raspberry seeds.

Spoon circles of raspberry mixture over custard, using a tiny spoon. Pull a knife through the circles to create a design.

Custards and Puddings

Light and airy or smooth and creamy, these rich-tasting treats belie their humble origins. You'll be surprised at how the simplest of ingredients can be combined to create family favorites or dazzling company desserts.

Bavarian Cream with Raspberry Sauce, Orange Chiffon Dessert

Apple-Nut Rice Pudding, Buttermilk Bread Pudding with Butter-Rum Sauce

Chocolate Mousse au Grand Marnier, Charlotte Russe with Strawberry Sauce

Pineapple Angel Food Trifle, Soufflé au Chocolate Cointreau

Grand Marnier Soufflés (page 654)

Butterscotch Mousse

Bavarian Cream
with Raspberry Sauce

1½ cups sugar
2 envelopes unflavored gelatin
1 cup cold water
1 pint whipping cream
3 (8-ounce) cartons sour cream
2 teaspoons vanilla extract
Raspberry Sauce

Combine sugar and gelatin in a saucepan; add water, and stir well. Let stand 1 minute. Cook over medium heat, stirring constantly, until gelatin dissolves. Stir in whipping cream, and set aside.

Combine sour cream and vanilla in a large bowl. Whisk in whipping cream mixture until blended. Pour into a lightly oiled 7-cup mold. Cover; chill 8 hours. Unmold onto serving dish; spoon sauce over top. **Yield: 12 servings.**

Raspberry Sauce
1 (10-ounce) package frozen raspberries, thawed
2 tablespoons sugar
1 tablespoon raspberry-flavored liqueur

Combine all ingredients in container of an electric blender; cover, and process until smooth. Press mixture through a fine wire-mesh strainer; discard seeds. **Yield: ¾ cup.**

Butterscotch Mousse

2½ cups butterscotch morsels
1 tablespoon shortening
½ cup sugar
¼ cup water
4 egg whites
1 pint whipping cream
1 teaspoon vanilla extract
Garnish: white chocolate and chocolate curls

Melt butterscotch morsels and shortening in a heavy saucepan over low heat, stirring frequently. Remove from heat; set aside, and keep warm.

Combine sugar and water in a small saucepan; cook over medium heat, stirring gently, until sugar dissolves. Cook, without stirring, to soft ball stage (240°). Remove from heat.

Beat egg whites in a large mixing bowl at high speed of an electric mixer until soft peaks form. Pour hot sugar mixture in a heavy stream over egg whites, beating constantly at high speed until thickened.

Fold in butterscotch mixture. Cool to room temperature.

Beat whipping cream at medium speed until soft peaks form; gently fold whipped cream into butterscotch mixture. Fold in vanilla.

Spoon mousse into dessert dishes. Cover and chill. Garnish, if desired. **Yield: 8 servings.**

Chocolate Mousse
au Grand Marnier

1 (4-ounce) package sweet baking chocolate
4 (1-ounce) squares semisweet chocolate
¼ cup Grand Marnier or other orange-flavored liqueur
1 pint whipping cream
½ cup sifted powdered sugar
Garnish: chocolate curls

Combine first 3 ingredients in a heavy saucepan; cook over low heat until chocolate melts, stirring constantly. Remove from heat, and cool to lukewarm.

Beat whipping cream at medium speed of an electric mixer until foamy; gradually add powdered sugar, beating until soft peaks form. Gently fold about one-fourth of whipped cream into chocolate; fold in remaining whipped cream.

Spoon into individual serving dishes. Cover; chill. Garnish, if desired. **Yield: 6 servings.**

Almond Cream
with Fresh Strawberries

1 quart fresh strawberries
⅓ cup amaretto
⅔ cup water
2 to 2½ dozen ladyfingers
1 cup butter or margarine, softened
1 cup sugar
½ cup amaretto
¼ teaspoon almond extract
1⅓ cups finely chopped almonds, toasted
1 pint whipping cream
Strawberry Sauce

Wash and hull strawberries; drain well. Set aside.

Line bottom and sides of a 3-quart glass bowl or mold with wax paper. Combine ⅓ cup amaretto and ⅔ cup water in a small bowl; mix well. Brush over ladyfingers.

Beat butter and sugar at high speed of an electric mixer until fluffy. Add ½ cup amaretto and almond extract, mixing well. Fold in almonds.

Beat whipping cream at medium speed until soft peaks form; fold into butter mixture.

Line bottom and sides of bowl or mold with ladyfingers. Arrange about 10 strawberries between ladyfingers. Layer half each of whipped cream mixture, strawberries, and ladyfingers. Repeat layers. Cover bowl with wax paper. Place a plate over bowl; chill 8 hours or overnight.

Unmold and remove wax paper; serve with Strawberry Sauce. **Yield: 12 servings.**

Strawberry Sauce

2 cups fresh strawberries
¼ to ⅓ cup sugar
1½ tablespoons kirsch
½ teaspoon lemon juice

Wash and hull strawberries; drain well. Puree strawberries in blender. Add remaining ingredients; mix well. **Yield: 1¾ cups.**

Island Trifle

6 large eggs, beaten
¾ cup sugar
6 cups half-and-half
1½ teaspoons vanilla extract
1 (16-ounce) frozen pound cake, thawed and cut into ½-inch cubes
3 to 4 tablespoons bourbon, divided
2 Red Delicious apples, unpeeled, cored, and chopped
2 cups seedless green grapes, halved

Combine eggs and sugar in a heavy saucepan; gradually stir in half-and-half. Cook over medium heat, stirring constantly with a wire whisk, until mixture thickens and coats a spoon (about 30 minutes). Stir in vanilla.

Place half of cake in bottom of a 16-cup trifle bowl; sprinkle with 1½ tablespoons bourbon. Pour half of custard over cake. Repeat procedure with remaining cake, bourbon, and custard. Cover and chill 3 to 4 hours.

Combine chopped apple and grapes; serve with trifle. **Yield: 12 to 15 servings.**

Apricot Mousse

20 ladyfingers
3 (16-ounce) cans apricot halves, undrained
2 envelopes unflavored gelatin
5 egg yolks
1¼ cups sugar, divided
⅛ teaspoon salt
1 cup milk
2 tablespoons apricot brandy or light rum
1 (2-ounce) package slivered almonds
2¼ cups whipping cream, divided
2 tablespoons powdered sugar
⅛ teaspoon almond extract

Apricot Mousse and Pumpkin Roll (page 587)

Cut a 30- x 3-inch strip of wax paper; line sides of a 9-inch springform pan with strip. Split ladyfingers in half lengthwise; line sides and bottom of pan with ladyfingers.

Drain apricots, reserving ½ cup juice. Set aside 4 apricots for garnish. Place knife blade in food processor bowl; add remaining apricots, and process 1 minute. Set aside.

Sprinkle gelatin over reserved ½ cup apricot juice. Set aside.

Combine egg yolks, ¾ cup sugar, and salt in a saucepan. Gradually add milk; cook over medium heat, stirring constantly, about 4 minutes or until mixture thickens and thermometer registers 160°.

Add softened gelatin, stirring mixture until gelatin dissolves. Stir in pureed apricots, brandy, and slivered almonds. Chill mixture until the consistency of unbeaten egg white (about 30 minutes).

Beat 1½ cups whipping cream at medium speed of an electric mixer until foamy; gradually add remaining ½ cup sugar, beating until soft peaks form. Fold whipped cream into apricot mixture; spoon into springform pan. Cover and chill 8 hours.

Remove sides of springform pan; remove wax paper. Beat remaining ¾ cup whipping cream until foamy; gradually add powdered sugar and almond extract, beating until soft peaks form. Pipe or dollop on top of mousse.

Slice reserved apricots; arrange on whipped cream. **Yield: 8 to 10 servings.**

Charlotte Russe
with Strawberry Sauce

2 envelopes unflavored gelatin
¼ cup cold water
⅔ cup sugar
4 egg yolks
1⅓ cups milk
1 teaspoon vanilla extract
½ cup sour cream
⅓ cup chopped almonds, toasted
1 cup whipping cream, whipped
16 ladyfingers, split
Strawberry Sauce

Sprinkle gelatin over cold water; let stand 1 minute. Set aside.

Combine sugar and egg yolks in a heavy saucepan; beat at medium speed of an electric mixer until thick and pale. Add milk, and cook over medium heat, stirring constantly, until thermometer registers 160° (about 5 minutes).

Add reserved gelatin mixture, stirring until gelatin dissolves. Stir in vanilla, sour cream, and almonds; cool slightly. Fold in whipped cream.

Line a 2-quart mold with 20- x 2-inch strips of wax paper, slightly overlapping. Line sides and bottom of mold with ladyfingers. Spoon cream mixture over ladyfingers. Arrange remaining ladyfingers over cream mixture. Cover and chill at least 8 hours. Invert mold, and remove dessert. Carefully peel off wax paper. Serve with Strawberry Sauce. **Yield: 8 to 10 servings.**

Strawberry Sauce
1 pint fresh strawberries
1 tablespoon lemon juice
½ cup sugar
2 tablespoons framboise or other raspberry brandy

Wash and hull strawberries; drain well. Put in container of an electric blender. Cover; process until smooth. Add lemon juice and remaining ingredients; blend until smooth. **Yield: 1⅓ cups.**

Orange Chiffon Dessert

2 (3-ounce) packages ladyfingers
3 to 4 tablespoons Grand Marnier or other orange-flavored liqueur
3 envelopes unflavored gelatin
1¾ cups cold water, divided
1 cup sugar
3 oranges, peeled, seeded, and sectioned
1 tablespoon grated orange rind
1¾ cups fresh orange juice
2 tablespoons fresh lemon juice
1¾ cups whipping cream
¾ cup miniature marshmallows
¼ cup chopped pecans, toasted
Garnishes: orange sections, fresh mint leaves

Cut a 30- x 3-inch strip of wax paper; line sides of a 9-inch springform pan with strip. Split ladyfingers in half lengthwise; line sides and bottom of pan with ladyfingers. Brush ladyfingers with liqueur. Set aside.

Sprinkle gelatin over ¾ cup cold water; stir and let stand 1 minute.

Combine remaining 1 cup water and sugar in a saucepan; bring to a boil, stirring until sugar dissolves. Add gelatin, stirring until it dissolves.

Chop orange sections; drain on paper towels. Stir oranges and next 3 ingredients into gelatin mixture. Chill until consistency of unbeaten egg white (about 30 minutes).

Beat whipping cream at medium speed of an electric mixer until soft peaks form. Fold whipped cream and marshmallows into orange mixture. Spoon into prepared pan, and sprinkle with pecans. Cover and chill 8 hours.

Remove sides of springform pan; remove wax paper. Place on serving plate, and garnish, if desired. **Yield: 10 to 12 servings.**

Orange Chiffon Dessert

Special Strawberry Trifle

Pineapple Angel Food Trifle

1 (16-ounce) can pineapple tidbits, undrained
2 (3.4-ounce) packages vanilla instant
   pudding mix
3 cups milk
1 (8-ounce) carton sour cream
1 (10-inch) angel food cake, cut into 1-inch
   cubes
1 (8-ounce) carton frozen whipped topping,
   thawed
Garnishes: mint leaves, pineapple slices

Drain pineapple tidbits, reserving 1 cup juice;
set aside.

Combine pudding mix, ½ cup reserved juice,
and milk in a mixing bowl; beat at low speed of
an electric mixer 2 minutes or until thickened.
Fold in sour cream and pineapple tidbits.

Place one-third of cake cubes in bottom of a
16-cup trifle bowl; drizzle with 2 to 3 tablespoons
remaining reserved pineapple juice. Spoon one-
third of pudding mixture over cake. Repeat procedure twice, ending with pudding mixture.
Cover and chill at least 3 hours.

Spread top with whipped topping just before
serving. Garnish, if desired. **Yield: 12 servings.**

Special Strawberry Trifle

5 cups sliced fresh strawberries, divided
2 (10¾-ounce) loaves angel food cake, cut into
   1-inch cubes
¼ cup plus 2 tablespoons strawberry-flavored
   liqueur, divided
Custard
½ cup strawberry preserves
1 pint whipping cream
¼ cup sifted powdered sugar
2 teaspoons strawberry-flavored liqueur
Garnishes: strawberry fans, toasted slivered
   almonds

Arrange enough strawberry slices, cut side
down, to line the lower edge of a 14-cup trifle
bowl. Arrange half of cake cubes in bowl.
Sprinkle with 2 tablespoons liqueur.

Combine remaining strawberry slices and 2
tablespoons liqueur; let stand 30 minutes. Drain,
reserving 2 tablespoons liquid.

Top cake with half of strawberry slices. Spoon
2 cups chilled Custard over strawberries. Top
with remaining cake cubes; sprinkle with remaining 2 tablespoons liqueur. Spoon remaining
strawberry slices over cake cubes.

Combine preserves and reserved strawberry
liquid, stirring well; spread over strawberries.
Spoon remaining Custard over preserves.

Beat whipping cream at medium speed of an
electric mixer until foamy; gradually add powdered sugar, beating until soft peaks form. Add 2
teaspoons liqueur, and beat well; spread sweetened whipped cream over trifle. Garnish, if
desired. Serve immediately. **Yield: 14 servings.**

Custard
1¾ cups milk, divided
¼ cup plus 2 teaspoons cornstarch
2 cups half-and-half
4 egg yolks
¾ cup sugar
2 teaspoons vanilla extract

Combine ½ cup milk and cornstarch in a large
saucepan; stir well. Add remaining 1¼ cups milk
and half-and-half. Cook over medium heat until
thickened, stirring constantly. Set aside.

Beat egg yolks and sugar at medium speed of
an electric mixer until thickened. Gradually stir
about one-fourth of hot mixture into yolk mixture; add to remaining hot mixture, stirring constantly. Cook over low heat, stirring constantly, 1
to 2 minutes or until mixture thickens.

Remove from heat; stir in vanilla. Cool; cover
and chill thoroughly. **Yield: 4 cups.**

Apple-Nut Rice Pudding

1 cup short-grain rice, uncooked
1 teaspoon salt
1 teaspoon butter or margarine
2 cups hot water
½ cup firmly packed brown sugar
2 tablespoons cornstarch
½ teaspoon ground cinnamon
2 cups milk
½ cup raisins
1 teaspoon vanilla extract
½ teaspoon grated lemon rind
2 egg yolks, lightly beaten
Apple-Nut Sauce

Combine rice, salt, and butter in a 2-quart baking dish; stir in hot water. Cover and microwave at HIGH 5 minutes; stir well. Cover and microwave at MEDIUM (50% power) 13 to 15 minutes or until water is absorbed; set aside.

Combine brown sugar, cornstarch, and cinnamon in a 1½-quart baking dish. Stir in milk and next 3 ingredients. Add reserved rice; stir well.

Cover; microwave at HIGH 6 minutes or until slightly thickened, stirring every 1½ minutes. Stir about 3 tablespoons of hot mixture into yolks; add to remaining hot mixture, stirring constantly.

Cover and microwave at HIGH 6 minutes or until thickened, stirring after every minute. Let stand, covered, 2 minutes.

Spoon into individual dessert bowls. Top each with warm Apple-Nut Sauce. **Yield: 6 servings.**

Apple-Nut Sauce
1 (20-ounce) can sliced cooking apples
½ cup firmly packed brown sugar
1½ tablespoons cornstarch
1 teaspoon ground cinnamon
⅛ teaspoon salt
⅓ cup chopped pecans, toasted
⅓ cup raisins
1 tablespoon butter or margarine, melted

Drain apples, reserving liquid. Add water to liquid to measure ¾ cup. Set aside.

Combine sugar and next 3 ingredients in a 4-cup glass measure; stir well. Stir in reserved liquid. Microwave, uncovered, at HIGH 5 minutes or until thickened, stirring after every minute.

Add apples, pecans, raisins, and butter; stir well. Microwave, uncovered, at HIGH 2 minutes or until mixture is thoroughly heated, stirring after every minute. **Yield: 3½ cups.**

Banana Pudding

⅔ cup sugar
3½ tablespoons all-purpose flour
Dash of salt
1 (14-ounce) can sweetened condensed milk
2½ cups milk
4 large eggs, separated
2 teaspoons vanilla extract
1 (12-ounce) package vanilla wafers
6 large bananas
¼ cup plus 2 tablespoons sugar
½ teaspoon banana or vanilla extract

Combine first 3 ingredients in a saucepan. Combine milks and yolks; add to dry ingredients.

Cook over medium heat, stirring constantly, until smooth and thickened. Remove from heat; stir in 2 teaspoons vanilla.

Arrange one-third of wafers in bottom of a 3-quart baking dish. Slice 2 bananas, and layer over wafers. Pour one-third of pudding mixture over bananas. Repeat layers twice, arranging remaining wafers around outside edge of dish.

Beat egg whites at high speed of an electric mixer until soft peaks form. Add ¼ cup plus 2 tablespoons sugar, 1 tablespoon at a time, beating until stiff peaks form and sugar dissolves. Fold in ½ teaspoon extract. Spread over pudding, sealing to edge of dish. Bake at 325° for 25 minutes or until meringue is golden. **Yield: 8 to 10 servings.**

Banana Pudding

Tennessee Bread Pudding with Bourbon Sauce

2 cups hot water
1½ cups sugar
1 (12-ounce) can evaporated milk
4 large eggs
1 cup flaked coconut
½ cup crushed pineapple, drained
½ cup raisins
⅓ cup butter or margarine, melted
1 teaspoon vanilla extract
½ teaspoon ground nutmeg
9 slices white bread with crust, cut into
    ½-inch cubes
Bourbon Sauce

Combine water and sugar in a bowl, stirring until sugar dissolves. Add milk and eggs, stirring with a wire whisk until blended.

Stir in coconut and next 5 ingredients. Add bread cubes; let mixture stand 30 minutes, stirring occasionally. Pour into a greased 13- x 9- x 2-inch pan.

Bake at 350° for 45 minutes or until a knife inserted in center comes out clean. Serve warm with Bourbon Sauce. **Yield: 12 servings.**

Bourbon Sauce

1 cup light corn syrup
¼ cup butter or margarine
¼ cup bourbon
½ teaspoon vanilla extract

Bring corn syrup to a boil in a saucepan. Remove from heat, and cool slightly.

Stir in butter, bourbon, and vanilla with a wire whisk. Serve warm. **Yield: 1½ cups.**

Tennessee Bread Pudding with Bourbon Sauce

Bread Pudding with Whiskey Sauce

1 (1-pound) loaf French bread
2 cups half-and-half
2 cups milk
3 large eggs, lightly beaten
2 cups sugar
½ cup chopped pecans
½ cup raisins
¼ cup shredded coconut
1 tablespoon plus 1 teaspoon vanilla extract
½ teaspoon orange extract
1½ teaspoons ground cinnamon
2 tablespoons butter or margarine, melted
½ cup shredded coconut
½ cup chopped pecans
Whiskey Sauce

Break bread into small pieces, and place in a shallow bowl. Add half-and-half and milk, and let stand 10 minutes. Crush mixture with hands until blended. Add eggs and next 7 ingredients, stirring well.

Pour melted butter into a 13- x 9- x 2-inch baking dish; tilt dish to coat evenly. Spoon pudding mixture into dish.

Bake at 325° for 40 to 45 minutes or until pudding is very firm. Remove from oven. Cool.

Combine ½ cup coconut and ½ cup pecans; stir well.

Cut pudding into squares to serve. Place each square in an ovenproof dish. Place dishes on baking sheet.

Pour Whiskey Sauce evenly over squares, and sprinkle with coconut mixture. Broil 5½ inches from heat (with electric oven door partially opened) until sauce is bubbly and coconut is lightly browned. **Yield: 15 servings.**

Whiskey Sauce

1 cup butter
2 cups sifted powdered sugar
3 tablespoons bourbon
2 large eggs, beaten

Place butter in top of a double boiler; bring water to a boil. Reduce heat to low; cook until butter melts. Add sugar and bourbon, stirring until sugar dissolves.

Stir about one-fourth of hot mixture into eggs; add to remaining hot mixture in pan, stirring constantly. Cook, stirring constantly, 5 minutes or until mixture thickens. **Yield: about 2 cups.**

Buttermilk Bread Pudding with Butter-Rum Sauce

1 (16-ounce) loaf unsliced French bread
¼ cup butter or margarine
1 quart buttermilk
1 cup raisins
2 large eggs, lightly beaten
1⅓ cups firmly packed light brown sugar
1 tablespoon vanilla extract
Butter-Rum Sauce

Tear bread into 1-inch pieces; reserve 7½ cups. Set aside remaining bread for other uses.

Melt ¼ cup butter in a 13- x 9- x 2-inch pan in 350° oven.

Combine reserved bread pieces, buttermilk, and raisins in a large bowl; set aside.

Combine eggs, brown sugar, and vanilla, whisking well. Add to bread mixture, stirring gently. Pour into pan of melted butter.

Bake at 350° for 1 hour. Serve pudding warm or cold with Butter-Rum Sauce. **Yield: 10 to 12 servings.**

Butter-Rum Sauce

½ cup butter or margarine
½ cup sugar
1 egg yolk
¼ cup water
3 tablespoons rum

Combine first 4 ingredients in a small saucepan, stirring well.

Cook over medium heat, stirring constantly, until sugar dissolves and sauce begins to thicken (about 10 minutes). Stir in rum. **Yield: ¾ cup.**

Hot Chocolate Soufflé

Hot Chocolate Soufflé

Butter or margarine
2 teaspoons sugar
2 tablespoons butter or margarine
2 tablespoons all-purpose flour
1 cup half-and-half
2 teaspoons instant coffee granules
2 (1-ounce) squares unsweetened chocolate
1 (1-ounce) square semisweet chocolate
4 large eggs, separated
1 teaspoon vanilla extract
4 egg whites
½ teaspoon cream of tartar
⅔ cup sugar
Vanilla ice cream
Velvet Ganache Sauce

Butter bottom of a 2-quart soufflé dish; sprinkle with 2 teaspoons sugar. Cut a piece of aluminum foil long enough to fit around soufflé dish, allowing a 1-inch overlap; fold foil lengthwise into thirds. Lightly butter one side of foil. Wrap foil around outside of dish, buttered side against dish, allowing it to extend 3 inches above rim to form a collar; secure with string. Set aside.

Melt 2 tablespoons butter in a heavy saucepan over low heat; add flour, stirring until smooth. Cook 1 minute, stirring constantly.

Add half-and-half gradually; cook over medium heat, stirring constantly, until thickened and bubbly. Remove from heat. Add coffee granules, stirring to dissolve.

Melt chocolate in a heavy saucepan over low heat; stir into coffee mixture.

Beat egg yolks. Stir one-fourth of hot mixture into yolks; add to remaining hot mixture, stirring constantly. Add vanilla. Transfer to a large bowl.

Beat 8 egg whites in a large mixing bowl at high speed of an electric mixer until foamy. Add cream of tartar, and beat until soft peaks form. Add ⅔ cup sugar, 1 tablespoon at a time, beating until stiff peaks form and sugar dissolves.

Stir 2 tablespoons beaten egg whites into chocolate mixture. Fold remaining beaten egg whites into chocolate mixture, one-third at a time. Spoon into prepared dish.

Make a groove 1½ inches deep around the top in a circle (about 1¼ inches from edge of dish), using a large spoon handle.

Bake at 350° for 50 to 60 minutes or until puffed and set. Remove collar. Serve soufflé immediately with ice cream. Drizzle with warm Velvet Ganache Sauce. **Yield: 8 servings.**

Velvet Ganache Sauce

1 cup whipping cream
1 (6-ounce) package semisweet chocolate morsels

Bring whipping cream to a simmer in a heavy saucepan. Remove from heat; pour over chocolate morsels. Let stand 1 minute. Stir until chocolate melts. **Yield: 1½ cups.**

Hot Chocolate Soufflé Technique

If desired, create a puffy top hat by dragging a spoon handle through batter before baking soufflé.

Soufflé au Chocolate Cointreau

Butter or margarine
2 tablespoons sugar
¼ cup butter or margarine
1 (12-ounce) package semisweet chocolate
    morsels
¼ cup Cointreau or other orange-flavored
    liqueur
12 large eggs, separated
1½ cups sifted powdered sugar
1 teaspoon ground cinnamon
1 teaspoon cream of tartar
Powdered sugar
Chocolate Cream

Butter a 2¾-quart soufflé dish. Cut a piece of aluminum foil long enough to fit around soufflé dish, allowing a 1-inch overlap; fold foil lengthwise into thirds. Lightly butter one side of foil. Wrap foil around outside of dish, buttered side against dish, allowing it to extend 3 inches above rim to form a collar; secure with string or masking tape. Add 2 tablespoons sugar, tilting prepared dish to coat sides. Set aside.

Melt ¼ cup butter and chocolate morsels in a heavy saucepan over low heat, stirring often. Cool 5 minutes; stir in Cointreau. Set aside.

Beat egg yolks; gradually add 1½ cups powdered sugar, beating until mixture is thick and pale. Stir in cinnamon and chocolate mixture. Set aside.

Beat egg whites and cream of tartar in a large mixing bowl at high speed of an electric mixer until stiff peaks form.

Stir 1½ cups egg white mixture into chocolate mixture. Fold remaining egg white mixture into chocolate mixture. Spoon into prepared dish.

Bake at 375° for 50 to 55 minutes. Sprinkle with powdered sugar, and remove collar. Serve immediately with Chocolate Cream. **Yield: 12 servings.**

Chocolate Cream
1 cup whipping cream
1 tablespoon powdered sugar
1½ teaspoons cocoa

Beat all ingredients at medium speed until soft peaks form. **Yield: 2 cups.**

Grand Marnier Soufflés
(pictured on page 639)

Butter
1 tablespoon sugar
¼ cup butter
¼ cup all-purpose flour
1 cup milk
4 egg yolks
2 tablespoons Grand Marnier or other
    orange-flavored liqueur
¾ cup sugar
2 tablespoons cornstarch
5 egg whites
1 tablespoon sugar
Custard Sauce

Butter six 6-ounce custard cups; coat bottom and sides with 1 tablespoon sugar. Set aside.

Melt ¼ cup butter in a large saucepan over low heat; add flour, stirring until smooth. Cook, stirring constantly, 1 minute. Gradually stir in milk, and cook, stirring constantly, until mixture thickens and begins to leave sides of pan.

Remove from heat, and cool 15 minutes. Add egg yolks, one at a time, beating after each addition. Stir in Grand Marnier; set aside.

Combine ¾ cup sugar and cornstarch; set aside.

Beat egg whites until foamy. Add sugar mixture, beating until stiff peaks form and sugar dissolves (2 to 4 minutes). Stir one-fourth of egg white mixture into egg yolk mixture; fold in remaining egg whites. Spoon into prepared custard cups; sprinkle evenly with 1 tablespoon sugar.

Place custard cups in a shallow pan. Add hot water to pan to depth of 1 inch.

Bake at 400° for 10 minutes.

Reduce temperature to 350°, and bake 20 to 25 additional minutes or until golden. Remove custard cups from water. Serve immediately with Custard Sauce. **Yield: 6 servings.**

Custard Sauce

½ cup sugar
2 tablespoons cornstarch
4 egg yolks
1 cup milk
2 tablespoons Grand Marnier or other
    orange-flavored liqueur
½ cup half-and-half
½ cup whipping cream, whipped

Combine sugar and cornstarch in a medium saucepan; add egg yolks, stirring until smooth. Add milk, stirring until smooth.

Cook over medium heat, stirring constantly, 10 minutes or until mixture thickens and thermometer registers 160°. Remove from heat, and cool.

Stir in Grand Marnier and half-and-half. Fold in whipped cream. Cover; chill. **Yield: 1¾ cups.**

Lemon Soufflé

Butter or margarine
2 tablespoons sugar
2 envelopes unflavored gelatin
½ cup cold water
1 teaspoon sugar
1 tablespoon grated lemon rind
¾ cup lemon juice
⅓ cup meringue powder
1½ cups sugar, divided
1 cup water
1 pint whipping cream
1 (2-ounce) package slivered almonds, toasted
    and chopped

Butter a 2-quart soufflé dish. Cut a piece of wax paper long enough to fit around soufflé dish, allowing a 1-inch overlap; fold paper lengthwise into thirds. Lightly butter one side of paper. Wrap paper around outside of dish, buttered side against dish, allowing it to extend 3 inches above rim to form a collar; secure with masking tape. Sprinkle sides of dish with 2 tablespoons sugar. Set aside.

Sprinkle gelatin over cold water in a saucepan; let stand 1 minute. Add 1 teaspoon sugar; cook over low heat, stirring until gelatin dissolves. Stir in lemon rind and juice. Set aside.

Combine meringue powder, 1 cup sugar, and water in a large bowl. Beat at high speed of an electric mixer 5 minutes. Gradually add remaining ½ cup sugar, and beat at high speed 5 minutes or until stiff peaks form. Fold in gelatin mixture.

Beat whipping cream at medium speed until soft peaks form; fold into gelatin mixture.

Pour into prepared dish, and chill 8 hours.

Remove collar, and gently pat chopped almonds around sides. **Yield: 8 to 10 servings.**

Lemon Soufflé

Old-Fashioned Stirred Custard

3 large eggs
½ cup sugar
2 tablespoons all-purpose flour
¼ teaspoon salt
3 cups milk
¾ teaspoon vanilla extract

Place eggs in top of a double boiler; beat at medium speed of an electric mixer until frothy. Combine sugar, flour, and salt; gradually add to eggs, beating until thick.

Pour milk into a medium saucepan; cook over low heat until thoroughly heated (do not boil). Gradually stir about one-fourth of hot milk into egg mixture; add remaining hot milk, stirring constantly.

Bring water in bottom of double boiler to a boil. Reduce heat to low; cook, stirring constantly, 20 to 25 minutes or until mixture thickens and coats a metal spoon.

Stir in vanilla. Serve warm, or cover and chill thoroughly. **Yield: 4 cups.**

Variations

Coffee Custard: Add 1 tablespoon instant coffee granules to milk; cook over low heat until thoroughly heated and granules dissolve. Reduce vanilla extract to ¼ teaspoon. **Yield: 4 cups.**

Orange Custard: Omit vanilla extract. Gently stir 1 teaspoon orange extract into prepared custard mixture. **Yield: 4 cups.**

Peppermint Custard: Increase flour to 2½ tablespoons. Add ¼ cup finely crushed peppermint candy to milk; cook over low heat until thoroughly heated and candy dissolves. Omit vanilla extract. **Yield: 4 cups.**

Rum Custard: Reduce vanilla extract to ½ teaspoon. Gently stir 1 teaspoon rum extract into prepared custard mixture. **Yield: 4 cups.**

Sabayon Glacé

6 egg yolks
Dash of salt
⅔ cup sugar
1 cup whipping cream
½ cup dry white wine
⅔ cup Chambord or other raspberry-flavored liqueur
1 pint whipping cream, whipped
3 to 4 kiwifruit, peeled and sliced
Garnishes: kiwifruit slices, fresh raspberries, fresh mint sprigs

Combine egg yolks and salt in a large bowl; beat at high speed of an electric mixer until blended. Add sugar, 1 tablespoon at a time, beating until mixture is thick and pale (about 5 minutes).

Heat 1 cup whipping cream, white wine, and Chambord until hot, but not boiling. With mixer running on low speed, slowly pour hot cream mixture into beaten egg mixture.

Transfer mixture to top of a double boiler; place over boiling water, and cook, stirring constantly, 20 minutes. (Mixture will thicken only slightly.) Remove from heat.

Place top of double boiler with mixture over ice water, and stir until mixture is completely cold. Fold in whipped cream. Cover and chill thoroughly. Fold glacé gently at least 4 hours before serving.

Arrange sliced kiwifruit around sides of compotes; spoon glacé into compotes. Chill desserts until ready to serve. Garnish, if desired. **Yield: 8 servings.**

Sabayon Glacé

Caramel-Crowned Flans

Caramel-Crowned Flans

¾ **cup sugar**
1 **(14-ounce) can sweetened condensed milk**
⅔ **cup milk**
2 **large eggs**
2 **egg yolks**
1 **teaspoon vanilla extract**
1 **cup sugar**
4 **to 6 drops of hot water**

Place ¾ cup sugar in a heavy saucepan; cook over medium heat, stirring constantly, until sugar melts and turns light golden.

Remove from heat; pour hot caramelized sugar evenly into 4 (10-ounce) custard cups. Cool.

Combine sweetened condensed milk and next 4 ingredients in container of an electric blender; cover and process at high speed 15 seconds. Pour evenly into custard cups.

Place custard cups in a 13- x 9- x 2-inch pan; add hot water to pan to depth of 1 inch, and cover pan with aluminum foil.

Bake at 350° for 30 minutes or until a knife inserted near center comes out clean. Remove cups from water, and cool. Cover and chill at least 8 hours.

Loosen edge of custard with a spatula; invert onto individual plates, letting caramel drizzle over the top. Set aside.

Place 1 cup sugar in a heavy saucepan; cook over medium heat, stirring constantly, until sugar melts and syrup is light golden. Stir in drops of hot water; let stand 1 minute or until syrup spins a thread when drizzled from a spoon.

Drizzle syrup, quickly wrapping threads around and over flans until a delicate web is formed. (If sugar hardens before webs are formed, place saucepan over medium heat until mixture softens.)

Chill flans, uncovered, up to 45 minutes before serving. **Yield: 4 servings.**

Note: If spiced flans are desired, add ¼ teaspoon ground cinnamon, ⅛ teaspoon ground ginger, and ⅛ teaspoon ground nutmeg to egg mixture in blender. Spices will float to the top as mixture bakes.

Caramel-Crowned Flans Technique

Cook ¾ cup sugar until melted and caramel colored; pour into custard cups, and cool. Prepare and bake mixture in custard cups as directed.

Pies and Pastries

Spectacular pies and pastries are a hallmark of Southern cooking. Whether it's a pecan tart, peach cobbler, or a meringue-topped chocolate pie, these desserts tingle the taste buds.

American Apple Pie, Blackberry and Peach Pie, Fried Apricot Pies

Pecan Tart with Praline Cream, Vanilla Cream Pie, Raspberry-Sour Cream Pie

Lemony Cherry Pie, Strawberry-Chocolate Truffle Pie, Berry Good Lemon Tarts

Peanut Butter Pie, Carolina Sweet Potato Pie, Coffee Cream Pie

Double Pecan Pie (page 666)

American Apple Pie

2 cups all-purpose flour
1 cup firmly packed brown sugar
½ cup regular oats, uncooked
½ teaspoon salt
⅓ cup chopped pecans
¾ cup butter or margarine, melted
4 cups peeled, sliced cooking apples
¾ cup sugar
1 tablespoon cornstarch
¼ teaspoon salt
½ cup water
½ teaspoon vanilla extract
Vanilla ice cream

Combine first 5 ingredients in a large bowl; add butter, and stir until blended. Measure 1 cup firmly packed mixture; set aside for pie topping.

Press remaining oats mixture in bottom and up sides of a 9-inch deep-dish pieplate. Arrange apple slices in pieplate; set aside.

Combine ¾ cup sugar, cornstarch, and salt in a saucepan; stir in water. Cook over medium heat until mixture boils. Stir in vanilla.

Pour hot mixture evenly over apples; crumble reserved topping mixture evenly over pie.

Bake at 375° for 40 minutes, covering with foil the last 15 minutes, if necessary. Serve with ice cream. **Yield: one 9-inch pie.**

Fried Apricot Pies

1 (6-ounce) package dried apricot halves, chopped
1¼ cups water
½ cup sugar
½ teaspoon ground cinnamon
½ teaspoon ground nutmeg
1 tablespoon lemon or orange juice
1 (15-ounce) package refrigerated piecrusts
Vegetable oil
Powdered sugar

Combine apricots and 1¼ cups water in a saucepan; bring to a boil. Cover, reduce heat, and simmer 20 minutes or until tender. Drain.

Mash apricots. Stir in sugar and next 3 ingredients; set aside.

Unfold 1 piecrust, and press out fold lines. Roll piecrust to ⅛-inch thickness on a lightly floured surface. Cut into five 5-inch circles; stack circles between wax paper. Repeat procedure.

Spoon 2 tablespoons apricot mixture on half of each circle. Moisten edges with water; fold dough over apricot mixture, pressing edges to seal. Crimp edges with a fork.

Pour oil to depth of 1 inch into a heavy skillet. Fry pies in hot oil (375°) 2 minutes or until golden, turning once. Drain on paper towels. Sprinkle with powdered sugar. **Yield: 10 pies.**

Berry Basics

- Check the bottom of the container when you buy packaged berries. It should be free of stains and any mashed or moldy berries.
- Wash berries just before eating.
- To store, spread berries in a single layer in a paper towel-lined container; cover with an airtight lid or plastic wrap. Refrigerate blueberries up to 10 days, strawberries up to 3 days, and raspberries and blackberries up to 2 days.
- To freeze, place berries in a single layer on a baking sheet, and freeze until firm. Pack lightly in freezer containers; label and date them. Freeze up to 9 months.

From left: Chilled Blueberry Pie (page 677), Blackberry and Peach Pie, Juicy Blackberry Cobbler (page 682)

Blackberry and Peach Pie

⅔ cup sugar
1½ tablespoons quick-cooking tapioca
Pinch of salt
1 teaspoon grated orange rind
2 cups fresh blackberries
2 cups sliced fresh peaches
Cream Cheese Pastry

Combine first 4 ingredients in a large bowl, mixing well. Add blackberries and peaches, tossing gently. Set aside.

Roll half of Cream Cheese Pastry to ⅛-inch thickness on a lightly floured surface. Fit into a 9-inch pieplate; trim off excess pastry along edges. Fold edges under, and flute. Spoon filling into pastry shell.

Roll remaining pastry to ⅛-inch thickness; cut pastry into ½-inch-wide strips. Twist each strip several times, and place on pie in a spiral design.

Bake at 425° for 35 to 40 minutes or until crust is browned. **Yield: one 9-inch pie.**

Cream Cheese Pastry
2 cups all-purpose flour
½ teaspoon salt
½ cup shortening
2 (3-ounce) packages cream cheese
5 to 6 tablespoons cold water

Combine flour and salt; cut in shortening and cream cheese with a pastry blender until mixture is crumbly.

Sprinkle cold water, 1 tablespoon at a time, evenly over surface; stir with a fork until moistened. Shape into a ball; cover and chill. **Yield: pastry for one double-crust pie.**

Lemony Cherry Pie

2 (16-ounce) cans tart, red pitted cherries,
   undrained
1 cup sugar
3 tablespoons cornstarch
2 tablespoons butter or margarine
1 tablespoon lemon juice
⅛ teaspoon liquid red food coloring (optional)
1 (15-ounce) package refrigerated piecrusts
1 teaspoon all-purpose flour

Drain cherries, reserving ½ cup juice. Set both aside.

Combine sugar and cornstarch in a large saucepan; stir in reserved cherry juice. Cook over medium heat, stirring constantly, until mixture comes to a boil; boil 1 minute, stirring constantly.

Remove sugar mixture from heat, and stir in cherries, butter, lemon juice, and, if desired, food coloring; cool.

Unfold 1 piecrust, and press out fold lines; sprinkle with flour, spreading over surface. Place piecrust, floured side down, in a 9-inch pieplate; trim off excess pastry along edges. Spoon filling into pastry shell.

Roll remaining piecrust to press out fold lines. Cut into ½-inch strips. Arrange in lattice design over filling; trim strips even with edge.

Cut remaining pastry into shapes with a 1-inch cutter, if desired. Moisten edge of piecrust with water, and gently press cutouts around edge.

Bake at 375° for 30 to 35 minutes. **Yield: one 9-inch pie.**

662   Pies and Pastries

Peachy Keen Tarts

(pictured on page 665)

Tart Pastry
1 (3-ounce) package cream cheese, softened
2 tablespoons powdered sugar
½ teaspoon grated orange rind
2 teaspoons orange juice
3 large fresh peaches
¾ cup apricot preserves
2 tablespoons Cointreau

Roll each portion of pastry to ⅛-inch thickness on a floured surface. Fit pastry into six 4-inch shallow tart pans or quiche pans. Roll over top of tart pans with a rolling pin to trim excess pastry. Prick bottom of pastry with a fork.

Bake at 450° for 10 minutes or until lightly browned. Cool.

Beat cream cheese and next 3 ingredients at medium speed of an electric mixer until blended. Spoon mixture evenly into 6 tart pans, spreading to edges.

Dip peaches in boiling water 10 seconds; drain and cool slightly. Carefully peel peaches, and cut in half lengthwise; remove pit.

Cut peaches into ⅛-inch-thick lengthwise slices, keeping slices in order as they are cut. Arrange slices over cream cheese mixture in the shape of peach halves, letting slices fan out slightly.

Heat preserves over low heat until melted. Press preserves through a wire-mesh strainer to remove lumps. Stir Cointreau into preserves, and brush liberally over peaches. **Yield: 6 servings.**

Tart Pastry
1½ cups all-purpose flour
½ teaspoon baking powder
½ teaspoon salt
¼ cup butter or margarine
¼ cup shortening
4 to 6 tablespoons milk

Combine first 3 ingredients; cut in butter and shortening with a pastry blender until mixture is crumbly.

Sprinkle milk, 1 tablespoon at a time, evenly over surface; stir with a fork until dry ingredients are moistened. Divide into 6 equal portions. Wrap in plastic wrap; cover and chill. **Yield: pastry for six 4-inch tarts.**

Strawberry-Chocolate Truffle Pie

1 (6-ounce) package semisweet chocolate morsels
1 (8-ounce) package cream cheese, cubed
2 tablespoons butter or margarine
¼ cup sifted powdered sugar
3 tablespoons Triple Sec or orange juice
1 baked 9-inch pastry shell
3 to 4 cups fresh strawberries, hulled
¼ cup red currant jelly, melted
½ cup whipping cream
2 tablespoons powdered sugar
½ teaspoon grated orange rind
Garnish: fresh mint leaves

Combine first 3 ingredients in top of a double boiler; place over boiling water. Cook, stirring constantly, until melted.

Remove from heat, and stir in ¼ cup powdered sugar and Triple Sec. Spread mixture in pastry shell. Cool.

Place strawberries, stem side down, over chocolate mixture; brush with jelly. Chill pie 2 to 3 hours.

Beat whipping cream and 2 tablespoons powdered sugar at medium speed of an electric mixer until soft peaks form. Fold in orange rind.

Slice pie, and top each serving with a dollop of whipped cream mixture. Garnish, if desired. **Yield: one 9-inch pie.**

Fancy Fruit Tart

Sugar Cookie Pastry
Lemon Cream
½ cup fresh blueberries
½ cup fresh blackberries
½ cup grape halves
⅔ cup fresh raspberries
1 cup halved strawberries
1 peach, peeled and sliced
1 cup peach preserves

Roll Sugar Cookie Pastry into a rectangle of ⅛-inch thickness between two sheets of wax paper; chill. Remove one sheet of paper, and invert pastry into an 11- x 7½- x 1-inch tart pan, paper side up. Carefully peel away paper, and press pastry into pan.

Roll over top of tart pan with a rolling pin to trim excess pastry. (Sugar Cookie Pastry is fragile; patch with pastry trimmings, if necessary.)

Line pastry with aluminum foil, and fill foil with pastry weights or dried beans.

Bake at 375° for 15 minutes. Carefully remove foil and weights, and bake 7 additional minutes or until browned. Cool on a wire rack.

Spoon Lemon Cream into baked pastry. Arrange fruit over Lemon Cream.

Heat preserves over low heat until melted. Press preserves through a wire-mesh strainer to remove lumps. Brush strained preserves lightly over fruit. **Yield: one 11- x 7½-inch tart.**

Sugar Cookie Pastry

1¼ cups all-purpose flour
1½ tablespoons sugar
½ cup butter or margarine
3 to 4 tablespoons ice water
1 egg yolk, lightly beaten

Combine flour and sugar; cut in butter with a pastry blender until mixture is crumbly. Combine water and egg yolk; sprinkle, 1 tablespoon at a time, evenly over dry ingredients. Stir with a fork until dry ingredients are moistened.

Shape into a ball; cover and chill at least 1 hour. **Yield: pastry for one 11- x 7½-inch tart.**

Lemon Cream

4 egg yolks
⅔ cup sugar
¼ cup lemon juice
⅓ cup butter or margarine
3 tablespoons half-and-half

Combine all ingredients in a heavy saucepan, beating well. Cook mixture over medium-low heat 10 minutes or until mixture thickens, stirring constantly. Remove from heat, and cool. **Yield: 1¼ cups.**

Berry Good Lemon Tarts

½ (15-ounce) package refrigerated piecrusts
3 egg yolks
⅔ cup sugar
¼ cup lemon juice
⅓ cup butter or margarine
2 teaspoons grated lemon rind
Garnishes: blueberries, blackberries, raspberries, or strawberries

Unfold piecrust, and divide into 18 equal portions; press each portion into a 2-inch tart pan. Prick bottom of pastry generously with a fork.

Bake at 375° for 12 to 15 minutes or until lightly browned.

Combine egg yolks, sugar, and lemon juice in a small heavy saucepan, stirring until blended. Cook over low heat, stirring constantly, 5 minutes or until mixture thickens.

Remove from heat, and stir in butter and lemon rind; cool. Spoon filling evenly into tart shells. Cover and chill thoroughly. Garnish, if desired. **Yield: 1½ dozen.**

From front: Berry Good Lemon Tarts, Peachy Keen Tarts (page 663), Fancy Fruit Tart

Pecan Tart with Praline Cream

Pastry for 9-inch pie
⅓ cup butter or margarine, melted
1 cup sugar
1 cup light corn syrup
4 large eggs, beaten
1 teaspoon vanilla extract
¼ teaspoon salt
1 cup pecan halves
¼ cup semisweet chocolate morsels
½ cup whipping cream
½ teaspoon vanilla extract
1 teaspoon praline liqueur
2 tablespoons powdered sugar

Press pastry into a 9-inch tart pan with removable bottom; set aside.

Combine butter, sugar, and corn syrup in a medium saucepan; cook over low heat, stirring constantly, until sugar dissolves. Cool slightly.

Add eggs, 1 teaspoon vanilla, and salt; stir well. Pour filling into prepared pastry shell, and top with pecan halves.

Bake at 325° for 50 to 55 minutes.

Place chocolate morsels in a heavy-duty, zip-top plastic bag; seal. Submerge bag in boiling water until chocolate morsels melt. Cut a small hole in corner of bag; drizzle chocolate thinly over pecan pie.

Beat whipping cream, ½ teaspoon vanilla, and praline liqueur at medium speed of an electric mixer until foamy. Gradually add powdered sugar, beating until soft peaks form.

Spoon about 2 tablespoons whipped cream mixture onto each dessert plate. Place a slice of pie on top of cream, and serve immediately. **Yield: one 9-inch pie.**

Pecan Tart with Praline Cream

Double Pecan Pie

(pictured on page 659)

1 cup light corn syrup
¾ cup sugar
3 large eggs
3 tablespoons butter or margarine, melted
1 tablespoon brandy
1 teaspoon vanilla extract
¼ teaspoon salt
1 cup pecan pieces
Pecan Pastry
1 cup pecan halves

Combine first 7 ingredients in a medium bowl. Beat at medium speed of an electric mixer just until blended. Stir in pecan pieces.

Pour mixture into Pecan Pastry. Top with pecan halves.

Bake at 350° for 50 to 60 minutes or until set. Cover edges of pastry with aluminum foil, if necessary, to prevent excessive browning. **Yield: one 9-inch pie.**

Pecan Pastry

1 cup all-purpose flour
¼ cup ground pecans
¼ teaspoon salt
¼ cup plus 2 tablespoons butter or margarine
1 tablespoon brandy
1 to 2 tablespoons cold water

Combine first 3 ingredients in a medium bowl; cut in butter with a pastry blender until mixture is crumbly.

Sprinkle brandy over mixture, stirring with a fork. Add water, stirring just until dry ingredients are moistened. Shape pastry into a ball; cover and chill 30 minutes.

Roll pastry to ⅛-inch thickness on a lightly floured surface. Place in a 9-inch pieplate; flute edges. **Yield: pastry for one 9-inch pie.**

Peanut Butter Pie

1 (8-ounce) package cream cheese, softened
1 cup sifted powdered sugar
1 cup chunky peanut butter
½ cup milk
1 (8-ounce) container frozen whipped topping, thawed
1 (9-inch) graham cracker crust
¼ cup coarsely chopped peanuts

Combine first 4 ingredients in a large mixing bowl; beat at medium speed of an electric mixer until well blended.

Fold in whipped topping; spoon into crust, and sprinkle with peanuts. Chill 8 hours. **Yield: one 9-inch pie.**

Spirited Mince Pie

¾ cup raisins
3 tablespoons brandy
1 (15-ounce) package refrigerated piecrusts
1 teaspoon all-purpose flour
1 (27-ounce) jar mincemeat
1 large cooking apple, cored and finely chopped
1 cup chopped walnuts
¼ cup firmly packed brown sugar
1 teaspoon grated lemon or orange rind
1 tablespoon lemon juice

Combine raisins and brandy in a large bowl; let stand 2 hours.

Unfold 1 piecrust, and press out fold lines; sprinkle with flour, spreading over surface. Place, floured side down, in a 9-inch pieplate; fold edges under, and flute. Set aside.

Combine raisin mixture, mincemeat, and next 5 ingredients; spoon into pastry shell.

Roll remaining piecrust on a lightly floured surface to press out fold lines; cut with a 3¼-inch leaf-shaped cutter, and mark veins using a pastry wheel or knife. Roll pastry scraps into small balls representing berries. Arrange pastry on top of filling as desired.

Bake at 375° for 10 minutes; shield edges with aluminum foil, and bake 25 additional minutes. Cool on a wire rack. **Yield: one 9-inch pie.**

Note: You may substitute orange juice for brandy.

Harvest Pumpkin Pie

Harvest Pumpkin Pie

Pastry for double-crust 10-inch pie
3 cups cooked, mashed pumpkin
1 (12-ounce) can evaporated milk
2 large eggs, lightly beaten
1 cup sugar
¼ cup all-purpose flour
1 teaspoon vanilla extract
½ teaspoon salt
½ teaspoon ground allspice
½ teaspoon ground cinnamon
½ teaspoon ground ginger
¼ teaspoon ground cloves
¼ teaspoon ground nutmeg
1 cup whipping cream
2 tablespoons honey
2 tablespoons finely chopped pecans, toasted

Roll half of pastry to ⅛-inch thickness on a lightly floured surface. Fit into a 10-inch pieplate; trim off excess pastry along edges.

Roll remaining pastry to ⅛-inch thickness; cut leaf shapes in pastry, and mark veins using a pastry wheel or knife. Arrange leaves around edge of pieplate, reserving 6 small leaves for garnish. Set aside.

Combine pumpkin and next 11 ingredients; stir well with a wire whisk. Pour into pastry shell.

Bake at 425° for 15 minutes. Reduce heat to 350°, and bake 35 to 45 additional minutes or until a knife inserted near center comes out clean. Shield pastry leaves with strips of aluminum foil to prevent excessive browning, if necessary. Remove pie from oven, and cool completely.

Place reserved pastry leaves on an ungreased baking sheet. Bake at 450° for 6 to 8 minutes or until lightly browned. Remove to a wire rack, and cool.

Beat whipping cream at medium speed of an electric mixer until soft peaks form; fold in honey. Top pie with dollops of whipped cream; sprinkle pecans over whipped cream. Garnish with small pastry leaves. **Yield: one 10-inch pie.**

Carolina Sweet Potato Pie

1 (17-ounce) can sweet potatoes, drained and mashed
1 cup firmly packed brown sugar
⅔ cup milk
⅔ cup whipping cream
3 large eggs
3 tablespoons bourbon
1 tablespoon butter or margarine, melted
1 teaspoon ground cinnamon
½ teaspoon ground nutmeg
½ teaspoon ground ginger
¼ teaspoon salt
1 unbaked 9-inch pastry shell

Combine first 4 ingredients in a large bowl; beat at low speed of an electric mixer until smooth. Add eggs one at a time; beat after each addition. Add bourbon and next 5 ingredients; beat just until blended. Pour into pastry shell.

Bake at 375° for 50 to 55 minutes or until filling is set. Cool. **Yield: one 9-inch pie.**

Easy Lemon Chess Pie

1¾ cups sugar
2 tablespoons yellow cornmeal
¼ teaspoon salt
⅓ cup butter or margarine, melted
¼ cup evaporated milk
3 tablespoons lemon juice
4 large eggs
1 unbaked 9-inch pastry shell

Combine first 3 ingredients in a medium bowl, stirring well. Add butter, milk, and lemon juice; stir well.

Add eggs, one at a time, beating after each addition. Pour filling into pastry shell.

Bake at 350° for 45 minutes or until pie is set. Cool on a wire rack. **Yield: one 9-inch pie.**

Chocolate Dream Pie

Chocolate Dream Pie

¾ cup sugar
¼ cup cornstarch
1 tablespoon cocoa
¼ teaspoon salt
2½ cups milk
1 cup half-and-half
3 egg yolks
1 (6-ounce) package semisweet chocolate
    morsels, melted
1 teaspoon vanilla extract
Chocolate Pastry Shell
1 cup whipping cream
2 tablespoons powdered sugar
Grated semisweet chocolate

Combine first 4 ingredients in a saucepan. Add milk and half-and-half; cook over medium heat, stirring constantly, until thickened and bubbly.

Beat egg yolks at medium speed of an electric mixer until thick and pale. Gradually add one-fourth of hot mixture to yolks; add to remaining hot mixture, stirring constantly. Cook over low heat, stirring constantly, until mixture thickens. Remove from heat.

Stir in melted chocolate and vanilla. Cool completely. Pour filling into Chocolate Pastry Shell. Cover loosely; chill several hours.

Beat whipping cream at medium speed until foamy. Add powdered sugar, and beat until soft peaks form; spoon over pie. Sprinkle with grated chocolate. Garnish with pastry cutouts, if desired. **Yield: one 9-inch pie.**

Chocolate Pastry Shell

1½ cups all-purpose flour
¼ cup plus 2 tablespoons firmly packed
    brown sugar
3 tablespoons cocoa
¼ teaspoon salt
½ cup shortening
5 to 6 tablespoons cold water

Combine first 4 ingredients; cut in shortening with a pastry blender until mixture is crumbly.

Sprinkle cold water, 1 tablespoon at a time, over surface; stir with a fork until moistened. Shape into a ball; cover and chill 1 hour.

Pinch off ¼ cup pastry, and set aside to make decorative cutouts, if desired. Roll remaining pastry to ⅛-inch thickness on a floured surface. Fit into a greased 9-inch pieplate; fold edges under, and flute. Freeze 10 minutes.

Prick bottom and sides of pastry with a fork; bake at 450° for 6 to 8 minutes or until done.

Roll reserved ¼ cup pastry to ¼-inch thickness. Cut into decorative shapes, using small cookie cutters. Place on a baking sheet. Bake at 450° for 5 to 6 minutes. Cool. **Yield: enough for one 9-inch pastry shell and pastry cutouts.**

Sweetheart Fudge Pie

½ cup butter or margarine, softened
¾ cup firmly packed brown sugar
3 large eggs
1 (12-ounce) package semisweet chocolate
    morsels, melted
2 teaspoons instant coffee granules
1 teaspoon rum extract
½ cup all-purpose flour
1 cup coarsely chopped walnuts
1 unbaked 9-inch pastry shell
Garnishes: piped whipped cream, chopped
    walnuts

Beat butter at medium speed of an electric mixer until creamy; gradually add brown sugar, beating well. Add eggs, one at a time, beating after each addition.

Add melted chocolate, coffee granules, and rum extract; mix well. Stir in flour and walnuts. Spoon mixture into pastry shell.

Bake at 375° for 25 minutes; cool completely. Chill. Garnish, if desired. **Yield: 9-inch pie.**

Coffee Cream Pie

(pictured on page 548)

¼ cup butter or margarine
⅔ cup semisweet chocolate morsels
1⅓ cups graham cracker crumbs
½ cup sugar
3 tablespoons cornstarch
1 teaspoon instant coffee granules
¼ cup boiling water
1¼ cups milk
5 egg yolks, lightly beaten
1¾ cups whipping cream
¼ cup sifted powdered sugar
Garnish: chocolate-covered coffee beans

Melt butter and chocolate morsels in a heavy saucepan over low heat; stir in graham cracker crumbs. Press into a lightly greased 9-inch pieplate.

Bake at 375° for 8 minutes. Cool pie shell completely on a wire rack.

Combine ½ cup sugar and cornstarch in a large heavy saucepan; set aside.

Combine coffee granules and boiling water; stir until coffee granules dissolve. Gradually stir coffee, milk, and egg yolks into sugar mixture.

Cook over medium heat, stirring constantly, until mixture thickens and boils. Boil 1 minute, stirring constantly. Remove from heat; whisk until smooth. Place plastic wrap directly on surface of mixture; chill 1 hour.

Beat whipping cream at medium speed of an electric mixer until foamy; gradually add powdered sugar, beating until soft peaks form.

Fold 1½ cups whipped cream into coffee mixture, reserving remaining whipped cream for topping. Spoon filling into baked pie shell.

Pipe or dollop remaining cream on top of pie. Chill up to 8 hours. Garnish, if desired. **Yield: one 9-inch pie.**

Vanilla Cream Pie

¾ cup sugar
¼ cup plus 2 teaspoons cornstarch
⅛ teaspoon salt
3 egg yolks, beaten
3 cups milk
1½ tablespoons butter or margarine
1½ teaspoons vanilla extract
1 baked 9-inch pastry shell
¾ cup whipping cream
⅓ cup sifted powdered sugar

Combine first 3 ingredients in a heavy saucepan; stir well. Combine egg yolks and milk; gradually stir into sugar mixture. Cook over medium heat, stirring constantly, until mixture thickens and boils. Boil 1 minute, stirring mixture constantly.

Remove from heat; stir in butter and vanilla. Immediately pour into pastry shell. Cover filling with wax paper. Cool 30 minutes; chill until firm.

Beat whipping cream at medium speed of an electric mixer until foamy; gradually add powdered sugar, beating until soft peaks form. Spread over filling. Chill. **Yield: one 9-inch pie.**

Variations

Banana Cream Pie: Slice 2 small bananas into pastry shell before adding filling.

Butterscotch Cream Pie: Substitute ¾ cup firmly packed dark brown sugar for ¾ cup sugar; reduce vanilla to ¾ teaspoon and add ¾ teaspoon butter flavoring.

Chocolate Cream Pie: Add ¼ cup cocoa when combining sugar and cornstarch.

Coconut Cream Pie: Add ½ cup flaked coconut with vanilla. Sprinkle ¼ cup toasted flaked coconut over whipped cream.

Vanilla Cream Pie (Coconut Cream Pie variation)

Best-Ever Lemon Meringue Pie

(pictured on page 548)

1½ cups sugar
⅓ cup cornstarch
⅛ teaspoon salt
4 egg yolks
1¾ cups water
½ cup lemon juice
3 tablespoons butter or margarine
1 teaspoon grated lemon rind
1 baked 9-inch pastry shell
Meringue

Combine first 3 ingredients in a heavy saucepan; set aside.

Combine egg yolks, water, and lemon juice; stir into sugar mixture.

Cook over medium heat, stirring constantly, until mixture thickens and boils. Boil 1 minute, stirring constantly. Remove from heat.

Stir in butter and grated lemon rind. Spoon hot filling into pastry shell. Spread Meringue over hot filling, sealing to edge of pastry.

Bake at 325° for 25 to 28 minutes. **Yield: one 9-inch pie.**

Meringue

4 egg whites
½ teaspoon cream of tartar
¼ cup plus 2 tablespoons sugar
½ teaspoon vanilla extract

Beat egg whites and cream of tartar at high speed of an electric mixer until foamy. Gradually add sugar, 1 tablespoon at a time, beating until stiff peaks form and sugar dissolves (2 to 4 minutes). Beat in vanilla. **Yield: enough for one 9-inch pie.**

Lemon-Lime Meringue Pie

1⅓ cups sugar
½ cup cornstarch
⅛ teaspoon salt
1¾ cups cold water
4 large eggs, separated
3 tablespoons butter or margarine
2½ teaspoons grated lemon rind
1 teaspoon grated lime rind
2 tablespoons lime juice
2 tablespoons lemon juice
1 baked 9-inch pastry shell
½ teaspoon cream of tartar
⅓ cup sifted powdered sugar

Combine first 3 ingredients in a heavy saucepan. Gradually add water, stirring until smooth. Cook over medium heat, stirring constantly, until mixture thickens and comes to a boil. Boil 1 minute, stirring constantly. Remove from heat.

Beat egg yolks at high speed of an electric mixer until thick and pale. Gradually stir about one-fourth of hot mixture into egg yolks; add to remaining hot mixture, stirring constantly. Cook over medium heat, stirring constantly, 2 to 3 minutes.

Remove from heat. Add butter and next 4 ingredients, stirring until butter melts. Spoon hot filling into pastry shell.

Beat egg whites and cream of tartar in a large bowl at high speed 1 minute. Gradually add powdered sugar, 1 tablespoon at a time, beating until stiff peaks form and powdered sugar dissolves (2 to 4 minutes).

Spread meringue immediately over filling, sealing to edge of pastry. Bake at 325° for 25 minutes or until browned and set. Cool pie completely several hours before slicing and serving. **Yield: one 9-inch pie.**

674   Pies and Pastries

Lemon-Lime Meringue Pie

From left: Florida Orange Pie and Key Lime Pie

Key Lime Pie

4 large eggs, separated
1 (14-ounce) can sweetened condensed milk
⅓ cup Key lime juice
½ teaspoon cream of tartar
⅓ cup sugar
1 baked 9-inch pastry shell

Combine egg yolks, condensed milk, and Key lime juice in a heavy saucepan. Cook over low heat, stirring constantly, until mixture reaches 160° (about 10 minutes).

Beat egg whites and cream of tartar at high speed of an electric mixer until foamy. Gradually add sugar, 1 tablespoon at a time, beating until stiff peaks form and sugar dissolves (2 to 4 minutes).

Pour hot filling into pastry shell. Immediately spread meringue over filling, sealing to edge.

Bake at 325° for 25 to 28 minutes. **Yield: one 9-inch pie.**

Florida Orange Pie

3 egg yolks
½ cup sugar
1 cup orange juice, divided
1 envelope unflavored gelatin
2 tablespoons grated orange rind
1 teaspoon grated lemon rind
1 pint whipping cream, divided
⅔ cup powdered sugar
⅛ teaspoon salt
½ cup flaked coconut
1 cup diced orange sections, drained
1 baked 9-inch pastry shell
3 tablespoons powdered sugar
Garnishes: toasted flaked coconut, orange
    sections, fresh mint

Beat egg yolks slightly. Combine yolks, ½ cup sugar, and ½ cup orange juice in a heavy saucepan.

Cook over low heat, stirring constantly, 10 to 12 minutes or until mixture reaches 160°. Remove from heat.

Sprinkle gelatin over remaining ½ cup orange juice; stir and let stand 1 minute. Add gelatin mixture and rinds to yolk mixture. Chill until consistency of unbeaten egg white.

Beat ½ cup whipping cream, ⅔ cup powdered sugar, and salt at medium speed of an electric mixer until soft peaks form.

Fold in gelatin mixture; then fold in coconut and diced orange sections. Spoon into pastry shell; chill until firm.

Beat remaining 1½ cups whipping cream until foamy; gradually add 3 tablespoons powdered sugar, beating until soft peaks form.

Spread about half of whipped cream over pie. Dollop or pipe remaining whipped cream around outer edge of pie. Garnish, if desired. **Yield: one 9-inch pie.**

Chilled Blueberry Pie

(pictured on page 661)

4 cups blueberries, divided
2 tablespoons cornstarch
2 tablespoons water
½ cup light corn syrup
2 teaspoons lemon juice
1 cup whipping cream
2 tablespoons powdered sugar (optional)
1 (9-inch) graham cracker crust
Garnishes: lemon slices, mint leaves

Puree 1 cup blueberries in an electric blender or food processor; set aside.

Combine cornstarch and water in a medium saucepan, stirring until blended. Add corn syrup, lemon juice, and blueberry puree. Bring to a boil over medium heat, stirring constantly; boil 1 minute. Cool 1 hour.

Fold remaining 3 cups blueberries into blueberry mixture. Set aside.

Beat whipping cream at medium speed of an electric mixer until foamy; gradually add powdered sugar, if desired, beating until soft peaks form. Spread in bottom and on sides of piecrust, forming a 1-inch-thick shell.

Spoon blueberry mixture into whipped cream shell. Chill at least 4 hours. Garnish, if desired. **Yield: one 9-inch pie.**

Raspberry-Sour Cream Pie

1 cup sugar
⅓ cup all-purpose flour
2 large eggs, lightly beaten
1⅓ cups sour cream
1 teaspoon vanilla extract
3 cups fresh raspberries
1 unbaked 9-inch pastry shell
⅓ cup all-purpose flour
⅓ cup firmly packed brown sugar
⅓ cup chopped pecans
3 tablespoons butter, softened

Combine first 5 ingredients in a large bowl, stirring until smooth. Gradually fold in raspberries. Spoon into pastry shell.

Bake at 400° for 30 to 35 minutes or until center is set.

Combine ⅓ cup flour and next 3 ingredients; sprinkle over hot pie.

Bake at 400° for 10 minutes or until golden. Cool pie before slicing and serving. **Yield: one 9-inch pie.**

Ice Cream Pie Spectacular

1 cup graham cracker crumbs
½ cup chopped walnuts
¼ cup butter or margarine, melted
1 pint coffee ice cream, slightly softened
1 pint vanilla ice cream, slightly softened
Brown Sugar Sauce

Combine first 3 ingredients; press into a buttered 9-inch pieplate. Bake at 375° for 8 to 10 minutes; cool.

Spoon coffee ice cream evenly into cooled crust; freeze until almost firm.

Spread vanilla ice cream over coffee ice cream, and freeze until firm.

Spoon warm Brown Sugar Sauce over slices. **Yield: one 9-inch pie.**

Brown Sugar Sauce
3 tablespoons butter or margarine
1 cup firmly packed brown sugar
½ cup half-and-half
1 cup chopped walnuts
1 teaspoon vanilla extract

Melt butter in a heavy saucepan over low heat; add brown sugar. Cook 5 to 6 minutes, stirring constantly.

Remove from heat, and gradually stir in half-and-half. Return to heat, and cook 1 minute.

Remove from heat, and stir in walnuts and vanilla. **Yield: about 1½ cups.**

Peppermint Ice Cream Pie

2 (1-ounce) squares semisweet chocolate
½ cup butter or margarine
2 large eggs
1 cup sugar
½ cup all-purpose flour
⅛ teaspoon salt
1 quart peppermint ice cream, slightly softened
½ cup hot fudge sauce
2 cups whipping cream
½ cup finely crushed peppermint candy
Peppermint candy pieces

Combine chocolate and butter in a small saucepan; cook over medium-low heat, stirring occasionally, until chocolate and butter melt. Remove from heat; cool.

Beat eggs at medium speed of an electric mixer until thick and pale; gradually add sugar, beating well.

Combine flour and salt, stirring well.

Add flour and chocolate mixtures to egg mixture, beating just until blended. Heavily grease and flour the bottom of a 10-inch pieplate. Spread batter evenly in prepared pieplate.

Bake at 350° for 30 to 40 minutes or until done. Cool completely.

Spoon ice cream over cooled crust; freeze 1 hour. Drizzle fudge sauce over ice cream; swirl fudge gently into ice cream with a knife. Freeze several hours or until firm.

Beat whipping cream at medium speed until soft peaks form. Gently fold in crushed peppermint candy. Pipe or spoon whipped cream in a decorative design over top of frozen pie. Freeze 30 minutes.

Decorate top of pie with peppermint candy pieces. Let pie stand at room temperature 5 to 10 minutes before slicing and serving. **Yield: one 10-inch pie.**

Peppermint Ice Cream Pie

Grasshopper Pie

Grasshopper Pie

1¼ cups chocolate wafer crumbs (about 32 wafers)
⅓ cup butter or margarine, melted
1 (6-ounce) package chocolate-covered mint wafer candies
4 cups miniature marshmallows
¼ cup sugar
2 tablespoons butter or margarine
⅓ cup green crème de menthe
1½ cups whipping cream, whipped

Combine chocolate crumbs and melted butter; press evenly over bottom and sides of a greased 9-inch pieplate.

Bake at 350° for 6 to 8 minutes. Cool crust completely.

Cut 3 mint candies diagonally in half; set aside. Reserve 10 whole candies for garnish. Chop remaining candies; set aside.

Combine marshmallows, sugar, and 2 table-spoons butter in top of a double boiler. Bring water to a boil. Reduce heat to low; cook until marshmallows melt, stirring frequently.

Remove from heat. Stir in crème de menthe. Cool mixture to room temperature. Fold in chopped mint candies and whipped cream.

Spread mixture evenly into prepared crust. Arrange reserved candy halves in a circle in center of pie; freeze until firm.

Pull a vegetable peeler down sides of reserved whole candies to make tiny shavings. Garnish pie with candy shavings. **Yield: one 9-inch pie.**

Frozen Chocolate Pie with Pecan Crust

6 (1-ounce) squares semisweet chocolate
½ teaspoon instant coffee granules
2 large eggs, beaten
3 tablespoons Kahlúa
¼ cup powdered sugar
¾ cup whipping cream
1 teaspoon vanilla extract
Pecan Crust
¾ cup whipping cream
1 tablespoon Kahlúa
Grated chocolate

Combine chocolate squares and coffee granules in a saucepan over low heat; cook, stirring constantly, until melted. Stir one-fourth of melted chocolate into eggs; mix well. Add to remaining chocolate. Stir in 3 tablespoons Kahlúa and sugar.

Cook, stirring constantly, until mixture reaches 160°. Cool to room temperature.

Beat ¾ cup whipping cream at medium speed of an electric mixer until soft peaks form; fold into chocolate mixture. Stir in vanilla.

Spoon into cooled Pecan Crust. Cover; freeze. Transfer pie to refrigerator 1 hour before serving.

Beat ¾ cup whipping cream at medium speed until foamy; gradually add 1 tablespoon Kahlúa, beating until soft peaks form. Pipe or dollop whipped cream around edge of pie. Sprinkle with grated chocolate. **Yield: one 9-inch pie.**

Pecan Crust
2 cups coarsely chopped pecans
⅓ cup firmly packed brown sugar
3 tablespoons butter or margarine, melted
2 teaspoons Kahlúa

Combine all ingredients; press evenly over bottom and up sides of a 9-inch pieplate.

Bake at 350° for 10 to 12 minutes. Press sides with back of spoon. Cool. **Yield: one 9-inch crust.**

Apple Cobbler à la Mode

6 cups peeled, sliced cooking apples
1 cup chopped walnuts
½ cup firmly packed brown sugar
1 teaspoon ground cinnamon
1 cup all-purpose flour
1 teaspoon baking powder
¼ teaspoon salt
1 cup sugar
¼ teaspoon ground ginger
1 large egg, beaten
½ cup half-and-half
½ cup butter or margarine, melted
½ cup chopped walnuts
Vanilla ice cream

Combine first 4 ingredients; toss gently. Spread in a greased 11- x 7- x 1½-inch baking dish.

Combine flour and next 4 ingredients in a bowl; stir well. Combine egg, half-and-half, and butter. Add to flour mixture; stir just until blended. Pour over apple mixture; sprinkle with ½ cup walnuts.

Bake at 350° for 45 minutes to 1 hour or until lightly browned. Spoon warm cobbler into serving bowls, and top with ice cream. **Yield: 8 servings.**

Juicy Blackberry Cobbler

(pictured on page 661)

4 cups fresh blackberries or 2 (16-ounce)
    packages frozen blackberries, thawed
1 cup sugar
½ cup water
Pastry
2 tablespoons butter, melted and divided
2 tablespoons sugar, divided

Combine first 3 ingredients in a saucepan. Cook over medium heat 10 minutes; stir gently.

Pour half of berry mixture into a greased 12- x 8- x 2-inch baking dish.

Roll pastry to ⅛-inch thickness on a floured surface. Cut into 1-inch strips; arrange half of strips in a lattice design over berry mixture. Brush with 1 tablespoon melted butter; sprinkle with 1 tablespoon sugar. Bake at 375° for 10 to 12 minutes or until pastry is lightly browned.

Pour remaining berry mixture over baked pastry. Arrange remaining strips in lattice design over berries. Brush with remaining butter; sprinkle with remaining sugar. Bake at 375° for 20 minutes or until pastry is golden. **Yield: 6 servings.**

Pastry

1½ cups all-purpose flour
¾ teaspoon salt
½ cup shortening
5 tablespoons cold water

Combine flour and salt; cut in shortening with a pastry blender until mixture is crumbly.

Sprinkle water, 1 tablespoon at a time, evenly over surface; stir with a fork until dry ingredients are moistened. Shape into a ball; cover and chill. **Yield: pastry for 1 cobbler.**

Strawberry-Rhubarb Cobbler

2 cups cubed rhubarb (about 1 pound)
2 cups halved strawberries
1 cup sugar
1½ tablespoons quick-cooking tapioca
⅛ teaspoon salt
2 tablespoons butter or margarine
Pastry for 8-inch pie

Combine first 5 ingredients; toss. Spoon into a greased 8-inch square baking dish. Dot with butter.

Roll pastry to ⅛-inch thickness on a lightly floured surface; cut into ½-inch strips, and arrange in a lattice design over rhubarb mixture.

Bake at 375° for 40 to 45 minutes or until pastry is golden. **Yield: 6 servings.**

Crusty Peach Cobbler

Crusty Peach Cobbler

7 to 7½ cups sliced fresh peaches
1½ to 2 cups sugar
2 to 4 tablespoons all-purpose flour
½ teaspoon ground nutmeg
1 teaspoon almond or vanilla extract
⅓ cup butter or margarine
Pastry for double-crust pie
Vanilla ice cream

Combine first 4 ingredients in a Dutch oven; set aside until syrup forms.

Bring peach mixture to a boil; reduce heat to low, and cook 10 minutes or until peaches are tender. Remove from heat; stir in almond extract and butter.

Roll half of pastry to ⅛-inch thickness on a lightly floured surface; cut into a 9-inch square. Spoon half of peach mixture into a lightly buttered 9-inch square dish; top with pastry square.

Bake at 425° for 14 minutes or until lightly browned. Spoon remaining peach mixture over baked pastry square.

Roll remaining pastry to ⅛-inch thickness, and cut into 1-inch strips; arrange in lattice design over peach mixture.

Bake at 425° for 15 to 18 minutes or until browned. Spoon into serving bowls, and top with ice cream. **Yield: 8 servings.**

Peach Cobbler with Praline Biscuits

1½ cups sugar
2 tablespoons cornstarch
1 teaspoon ground cinnamon
1 cup water
8 cups sliced fresh peaches (about 5½ pounds)
3 tablespoons butter or margarine, melted
¼ cup firmly packed dark brown sugar
1 cup chopped pecans
2 cups self-rising flour
2 teaspoons sugar
½ cup shortening
¾ cup buttermilk

Combine first 3 ingredients in a Dutch oven. Gradually stir in water; add peaches. Bring to a boil, and cook 1 minute, stirring often.

Remove from heat. Pour into a lightly greased 13- x 9- x 2-inch baking dish; set aside.

Combine butter, brown sugar, and pecans; set mixture aside.

Combine flour and 2 teaspoons sugar; cut in shortening with a pastry blender until mixture is crumbly. Add buttermilk, stirring just until dry ingredients are moistened. Turn dough out onto a floured surface, and knead 3 or 4 times.

Roll dough to a 12- x 8-inch rectangle; spread with reserved pecan mixture, leaving a ½-inch border. Starting with long side, roll up jellyroll fashion. Cut into ½-inch slices; arrange slices over peach mixture.

Bake at 400° for 25 to 30 minutes or until lightly browned. **Yield: 12 servings.**

Southern Living

ALL-TIME FAVORITE
LOW-FAT
RECIPES

Contents

Low-Fat Basics

Low-fat eating isn't just for people who are trying to lose weight. Today everyone can benefit from keeping dietary fat to 30 percent or less of total daily calories. Research studies show that decreasing your fat intake can also reduce risks of heart disease, diabetes, and some types of cancer.

How Much Fat?

The current dietary recommendation to reduce fat intake to no more than 30 percent of total calories refers to the fat intake for the entire day. If you have a high-fat item at one meal, you can balance it with low-fat choices for the rest of the day and still remain within the recommended percentage. The goal of fat reduction need not be to eliminate fat from the diet. Some fat is necessary each day to transport fat-soluble vitamins and maintain other normal body functions.

To achieve a diet with 30 percent or less of total calories from fat, first establish a fat budget for the day based on the total number of daily calories needed. Estimate your daily calorie requirements by multiplying your current weight by 15. (This is only a rough guide because calorie requirements vary by age, body size, and level of physical activity.) Once you determine your personal daily calorie requirement, use the Daily Fat Limits chart (right) to figure the maximum amount of fat grams allowed each day for you to stay within the recommended percentages. For example, if you are consuming 1,800 calories per day, you should eat no more than 60 grams of fat per day.

Daily Fat Limits		
Calories Per Day	30 Percent of Calories	Grams of Fat
1,200	360	40
1,500	450	50
1,800	540	60
2,000	600	67
2,200	660	73
2,500	750	83
2,800	840	93

Nutritional Analysis

Southern Living® All-Time Favorite Low-Fat Recipes has a realistic approach to trimming fat from your diet. While each recipe has been kitchen-tested by a staff of home economists, registered dietitians have determined the nutritional information using a computer system that analyzes each ingredient.

The nutrient grid following each recipe includes calories per serving and the percentage of calories from fat. Also, the grid lists the grams of total fat, saturated fat, protein, and carbohydrate, and the milligrams of cholesterol and sodium per serving. The nutrient values are as accurate as possible and are based on these assumptions:

• All meats are trimmed of fat and skin before cooking.

• When the recipe calls for cooked pasta, rice, or noodles, the analysis is based on cooking without additional salt or fat.

• Fruits and vegetables listed in the ingredients are not peeled unless specified.

• When a range is given for an ingredient, the lesser amount is calculated.

• A percentage of alcohol calories evaporates when heated; this reduction is reflected in the calculations.

• When a marinade is used, only the amount of marinade absorbed is calculated.

• Garnishes and optional ingredients are not calculated.

Low-Fat Cooking Tips

These cooking techniques are basic to low-fat cooking. Apply these techniques to your own recipes to turn high-fat standbys into healthy favorites.

• Buy only the leanest cuts of beef, pork, lamb, and veal. Select cuts such as beef tenderloin, beef round, beef sirloin, pork tenderloin, pork loin chops, leg of lamb, lamb loin chops, and veal cutlets. Trim meat of all visible fat before cooking.

• Trim fat and remove the skin of chicken and turkey before or after cooking.

• Brown ground meat in a nonstick skillet or in a skillet coated with vegetable cooking spray. In addition to lean ground beef, try ground turkey breast or ground chicken breast.

After cooking the meat, place it in a colander to drain excess fat. To further reduce the fat, pat the cooked meat dry with paper towels after draining, and wipe drippings from the skillet with a paper towel before continuing to cook.

Draining meat in a colander

• Roast meats and poultry on a rack in a broiler pan so fat can drip away. For easy cleanup, coat broiler pan with vegetable cooking spray before cooking.

• Marinate lean meats, fish, and poultry in fat-free or low-fat marinades to enhance their flavors. Reduce or omit oil from marinade recipes by substituting water or broth. Other low-fat ingredients for marinades include citrus juices, wines, and flavored vinegars.

• Cook pasta, rice, grains, and green and starchy vegetables with little or no added fat. Steaming, sautéing, and stir-frying are best for cooking vegetables because these require a minimum of fat while preserving nutrients. Use a nonstick skillet or wok or a skillet coated with vegetable cooking spray for sautéing and stir-frying.

Sautéing in a nonstick skillet

• Coat baking dishes, pans, and casseroles with vegetable cooking spray instead of butter, oil, or shortening. To add more flavor to foods, use olive oil-flavored or butter-flavored cooking spray.

• Make soups, stews, stocks, or broths ahead of time, and chill overnight in the refrigerator. After the soup has chilled, skim off the hardened fat with a spoon, and discard the fat; then reheat.

If there is no time to chill the soup, skim off as much fat as possible, and add several ice cubes to the warm liquid. The fat will cling to the ice cubes, which can then be removed and discarded.

Skimming fat from soup

• Use herbs, spices, and salt-free seasoning blends to flavor vegetables, meats, fish, and poultry. Citrus juices, flavored vinegars, and wines can also help bring out the natural flavor of foods. To substitute dried herbs for fresh, use approximately one-third of the fresh amount.

• Substitute fat-free milk when a recipe calls for cream or whole milk. And if the recipe doesn't look creamy enough, add nonfat dry milk 1 tablespoon at a time until desired consistency is reached.

• Use whipped evaporated fat-free milk in place of fat-laden whipping cream or whipped topping mixes. Place evaporated fat-free milk in a mixing bowl; place the mixing

bowl and the beaters in the freezer for 30 minutes or until small ice crystals form around the top of the bowl. Remove the bowl and the beaters from the freezer, and beat milk at high speed until soft peaks form.

Whipping evaporated fat-free milk

• Use reduced-fat cheese and nonfat sour cream and yogurt. Since many of the reduced-fat cheeses are still over 50 percent fat, try to substitute a strong-flavored cheese and use less of it. You'll get the cheese flavor without all the fat.

When cooking with yogurt, keep temperature low and heating time short to prevent separation.

• Decrease butter, margarine, vegetable oil, and shortening. When fat is decreased, you may need to add a liquid such as water, fruit juice, or fat-free milk to make up for moisture loss.

Although margarine and vegetable oils contain about the same number of fat grams and calories as butter, they are lower in saturated fat and cholesterol.

Use reduced-fat margarine for some recipes but not baked

goods unless specified; the water that is whipped into reduced-calorie margarine may cause sogginess.

• Use egg whites or an egg substitute in place of whole eggs. Instead of one whole egg, use two egg whites or one-fourth cup egg substitute. Egg whites and egg substitutes should be cooked over low heat, or they will toughen and become dry.

Low-Fat Cooking Methods

Low fat doesn't have to mean low flavor. These cooking methods will help you achieve the fullest flavor possible while keeping the fat content low.

• *Bake or roast.* Cooking in an oven where the food is surrounded by dry heat is known as baking or roasting. Baked meats and poultry are generally covered and may have liquid added to help keep them moist. Roasted meats and poultry are cooked uncovered, without the addition of liquid, until they have a well-browned exterior and moist interior.

To prevent lean meats from drying out, marinate in a low-fat marinade before roasting, or baste with a low-fat liquid while cooking. Baking works well for lean meats and poultry, and roasting requires fairly tender cuts of meat or poultry.

• *Braise or stew.* Cooking food slowly in a small amount of liquid in a tightly covered pot is known as braising or stewing. Use either of these methods to develop the flavor of the food and to tenderize tough cuts of meat. Unlike stewing, braising requires that meat be browned before it is covered with liquid and simmered. Coat the pan with cooking spray or a small amount of vegetable oil when browning meat. Stewing usually requires more liquid than braising and uses smaller pieces of meat.

• *Broil or grill.* Cooking food directly over or under a heat source is known as broiling or grilling. The cooking temperature is regulated by the distance between the food and the heat source. To broil foods, place meats, fish, and poultry on a rack in a broiler pan to allow fat to drip away from the food.

When grilling, coat the grill rack with vegetable cooking spray before placing over the coals. The cooking spray helps keep the food from sticking.

Broiling fish on a rack

• *Oven-fry.* Baking foods on a rack to give all sides equal exposure to the heat is known as oven-frying. The food is often breaded, and the result is a crisp outer coating and juicy interior similar to that of deep-fat fried foods. Oven-frying is a low-fat cooking method often used for pork chops, chicken, and fish.

• *Poach.* Cooking food gently in water or other liquid held just below the boiling point is called poaching. No added fat is required, and the food retains its flavor, shape, and texture. Poultry, firm fish, and firm fruits such as pears and apples are examples of foods suitable for poaching.

Poaching chicken in seasoned liquid

• *Steam.* Cooking food over, not in, boiling water is called steaming. Food is placed on a rack or in a steamer basket and covered. If you don't have a steamer basket, you can place a colander or strainer in a large saucepan and cover it tightly. Food can also be steamed in the oven without any liquid in a parchment paper package (*en papillote*) or in a package made from heavy-duty aluminum foil.

No added fat is needed for steaming, and the food retains its shape, texture, and flavor. Fish, shellfish, poultry, and vegetables are ideal foods for steaming.

Steaming vegetables in a steamer basket

• *Stir-fry or sauté.* Cooking food quickly in a wok or skillet over high heat in a small amount of fat is known as stir-frying or sautéing. Coating a nonstick skillet or wok with vegetable cooking spray or cooking in a small amount of broth, wine, vinegar, or water can eliminate the need for added fat. The ingredients are stirred in the pan constantly during cooking so that they cook evenly. Because it is deep and has sloping sides, a wok requires less fat than does a skillet.

Low-Fat Cooking Tools

Use these kitchen tools to make low-fat cooking easier.

• A colander or strainer allows you to drain fat from cooked ground meats as well as drain liquid from other foods.

Spoon cooked ground meat into the colander, let the fat drain, and discard fat.

• An egg separator easily separates the low-fat egg white from the higher-fat yolk. It holds the yolk in the saucer and allows the white to slide through the slots.

• A fat-off ladle allows you to skim fat from meat stocks, soups, and stews. When the ladle is lowered into the liquid, the fat flows through slots around the edge of the ladle and collects in the bowl. When the ladle is full, pour off fat from the opposite end.

• A gravy strainer or a fat-separating cup looks like a measuring cup with a spout. The spout, attached near the bottom of the cup, allows liquid to be poured out while the fat floats to the top.

Skimming fat from liquids with a gravy strainer

• Kitchen shears make easy work of trimming excess fat from meats and poultry, cutting fins off fish, cutting poultry into pieces, snipping fresh herbs, and performing a variety of other kitchen tasks.

• Nonstick baking pans, baking sheets, and muffin pans allow baking without having to heavily grease the pan. This decreases the amount of fat.

• A nonstick skillet helps keep fat to a minimum because foods that already contain fat, such as meat and poultry, can be cooked without adding additional fat. And fruits, vegetables, and other foods with almost no fat can be cooked successfully with just a little vegetable cooking spray.

• A steam basket or steamer allows food to cook without the addition of fat. Because the food is not cooked in water, vitamin loss is minimal. Many varieties of steamers are available, from metal baskets to stackable bamboo baskets. A simple rack or folding steam basket that prevents food from touching the water will work for most recipes.

Cooking fresh vegetables in a folding steam basket

• A wire grilling basket prevents tender fish steaks, fillets, and vegetables from falling

through the grill rack. To prevent sticking and to aid in cleanup, coat the basket with vegetable cooking spray before adding the food.

• A wok is the favored cooking utensil for stir-frying because its sloping sides allow for even distribution of heat, quick cooking, and the use of very little oil. The traditional wok has a round bottom for cooking over a gas flame. Flat-bottomed woks and stir-fry pans are for cooking on electric cooktops. Nonstick woks and stir-fry pans can eliminate the need for added fat.

Stir-frying fresh vegetables in a wok

• A ruler is helpful for measuring the dimensions and thicknesses of foods that are called for in some recipes.

• Scales help determine portion sizes; this is important because the cooked weight of food will vary from the uncooked weight. Look for a model that has a sturdy base, gives measurements in ounces, and is easy to read and clean.

Appetizers and Beverages

From simple snacks to fancy hors d'oeuvres, these light-and-healthy appetizers are something to cheer about. We've also included tasty sippers that are satisfying yet low in fat and calories.

Skinny Ranch Dip, Pita Chips, Bagel Chips, Sweet Potato Chips

Spiced Pineapple Sparkle, Spicy Virgin Mary, Snack Mix, White Grape Punch

Garbanzo Dip, Chicken Wontons, Baked Wonton Chips, Parmesan Pita Chips

Potato Skin Snack, Mock Black Russian, Whole Wheat Pretzels

Clockwise from top: Festive Crab Dip (page 692), Chicken Wontons (page 699), Apricot-Orange Bread (page 705), and Tortellini with Rosemary-Parmesan Sauce (page 699)

Festive Crab Dip

(pictured on page 691)

1 (4¼-ounce) can lump crabmeat, drained
1 cup nonfat mayonnaise
¼ cup plain nonfat yogurt
¼ cup nonfat sour cream
1 tablespoon chopped fresh parsley
1 tablespoon diced pimiento, drained
1 tablespoon dry sherry
1 teaspoon lemon juice
¼ teaspoon celery seeds
⅛ teaspoon pepper

Combine all ingredients; cover and chill thoroughly. Serve with assorted fresh vegetables. **Yield: 2 cups.**

PER TABLESPOON: 13 CALORIES (7% FROM FAT)
FAT 0.1G (SATURATED FAT 0.0G)
PROTEIN 1.0G CARBOHYDRATE 1.9G
CHOLESTEROL 3MG SODIUM 110MG

Skinny Ranch Dip

1 (24-ounce) carton nonfat cottage cheese
1 (1.1-ounce) envelope reduced-calorie
   Ranch-style salad dressing mix
½ cup fat-free milk
1 tablespoon white vinegar

Combine all ingredients in container of an electric blender; cover and process until smooth, stopping once to scrape down sides. Serve with assorted fresh vegetables. **Yield: 3 cups.**

PER TABLESPOON: 12 CALORIES (0% FROM FAT)
FAT 0.0G (SATURATED FAT 0.0G)
PROTEIN 1.9G CARBOHYDRATE 1.2G
CHOLESTEROL 1MG SODIUM 117MG

Garbanzo Dip

1 (19-ounce) can chickpeas (garbanzo beans),
   drained
½ cup commercial oil-free Italian dressing
1 tablespoon fresh lemon juice
1 clove garlic

Combine all ingredients in container of an electric blender; cover and process until smooth, stopping once to scrape down sides. Chill. Serve with fresh vegetables. **Yield: 1¾ cups.**

PER TABLESPOON: 23 CALORIES (12% FROM FAT)
FAT 0.3G (SATURATED FAT 0.0G)
PROTEIN 1.1G CARBOHYDRATE 4.1G
CHOLESTEROL 0MG SODIUM 71MG

Mock Guacamole

2 (10½-ounce) cans cut asparagus, drained
1 cup finely chopped tomato
¼ cup finely chopped onion
2 tablespoons lemon juice
1 tablespoon reduced-calorie mayonnaise
½ teaspoon garlic salt
½ teaspoon chili powder
¼ teaspoon hot sauce

Position knife blade in food processor bowl, and add asparagus. Process until smooth, and transfer to a large mixing bowl.

Stir in tomato and remaining ingredients. Place in a paper towel-lined wire-mesh strainer or colander, and let drain 1 hour.

Cover and chill at least 3 hours before serving with fresh vegetables. **Yield: 2 cups.**

PER TABLESPOON: 6 CALORIES (30% FROM FAT)
FAT 0.2G (SATURATED FAT 0.0G)
PROTEIN 0.3G CARBOHYDRATE 0.9G
CHOLESTEROL 0MG SODIUM 63MG

Artichoke-Parmesan Spread

Artichoke-Parmesan Spread

1 cup soft breadcrumbs
1 cup nonfat mayonnaise
½ cup freshly grated Parmesan cheese
¼ teaspoon reduced-sodium Worcestershire
     sauce
¼ teaspoon hot sauce
⅛ teaspoon garlic powder
2 (14-ounce) cans artichoke hearts, drained
     and chopped
Vegetable cooking spray

Combine first 6 ingredients; gently fold in
artichokes. Spoon into a 1-quart casserole coated
with cooking spray.

Cover and bake at 350° for 20 minutes or
until thoroughly heated. Serve with assorted raw
vegetables or low-fat crackers. **Yield: 3¼ cups.**

Microwave Directions

Combine first 6 ingredients; gently fold in
artichokes. Spoon into a 1-quart casserole coated
with cooking spray.

Cover with wax paper, and microwave at
MEDIUM (50% power) 12 to 14 minutes, stirring twice.

PER TABLESPOON: 15 CALORIES (18% FROM FAT)
FAT 0.3G (SATURATED FAT 0.2G)
PROTEIN 0.8G CARBOHYDRATE 2.4G
CHOLESTEROL 1MG SODIUM 112MG

From left: Baked Wonton Chips (page 696), Sweet Potato Chips, Tortilla Chips (page 696), Pita Chips, and Bagel Chips

Pita Chips

3 (6-inch) whole wheat pita bread rounds
Butter-flavored vegetable cooking spray
1½ teaspoons lemon juice
1 clove garlic, crushed
1 tablespoon minced fresh parsley
1½ teaspoons minced fresh chives
¼ teaspoon salt
⅛ teaspoon pepper

Separate each pita bread into 2 rounds; cut each into 8 wedges to make 48 triangles. Arrange in a single layer on an ungreased baking sheet, cut side up. Coat with cooking spray.

Combine lemon juice and garlic; lightly brush over each triangle. Combine parsley and remaining ingredients; sprinkle evenly over triangles.

Bake at 350° for 15 minutes or until crisp and lightly browned. Let cool. Yield: 4 dozen.

PER CHIP: 11 CALORIES (8% FROM FAT)
FAT 0.1G (SATURATED FAT 0.0G)
PROTEIN 0.2G CARBOHYDRATE 2.0G
CHOLESTEROL 0MG SODIUM 22MG

Bagel Chips

6 plain bagels
Butter-flavored vegetable cooking spray

Cut each bagel horizontally into 6 (¼-inch) slices using an electric slicer or serrated knife. Arrange slices in a single layer on wire racks; place racks on baking sheets. Coat slices with cooking spray.

Bake at 325° for 12 to 15 minutes or until crisp and lightly browned. Remove bagels from oven, and let cool. Store in an airtight container. **Yield: 3 dozen.**

PER CHIP: 26 CALORIES (7% FROM FAT)
FAT 0.2G (SATURATED FAT 0.0G)
PROTEIN 1.0G CARBOHYDRATE 5.1G
CHOLESTEROL 0MG SODIUM 51MG

Variations

Parmesan Cheese Bagel Chips: Sprinkle 2 teaspoons grated Parmesan cheese evenly over bagel chips coated with cooking spray. Bake as directed. **Yield: 3 dozen.**

PER CHIP: 27 CALORIES (7% FROM FAT)
FAT 0.2G (SATURATED FAT 0.0G)
PROTEIN 1.0G CARBOHYDRATE 5.1G
CHOLESTEROL 0MG SODIUM 52MG

Lemon-and-Herb Bagel Chips: Sprinkle 2 teaspoons salt-free lemon-and-herb spice blend evenly over bagel chips coated with cooking spray. Bake as directed. **Yield: 3 dozen.**

PER CHIP: 27 CALORIES (7% FROM FAT)
FAT 0.2G (SATURATED FAT 0.0G)
PROTEIN 1.0G CARBOHYDRATE 5.3G
CHOLESTEROL 0MG SODIUM 51MG

Garlic Bagel Chips: Sprinkle 1 teaspoon garlic powder evenly over bagel chips coated with cooking spray. Bake as directed. **Yield: 3 dozen.**

PER CHIP: 27 CALORIES (7% FROM FAT)
FAT 0.2G (SATURATED FAT 0.0G)
PROTEIN 1.0G CARBOHYDRATE 5.1G
CHOLESTEROL 0MG SODIUM 51MG

Cinnamon-and-Sugar Bagel Chips: Combine ¼ teaspoon ground cinnamon and 1½ teaspoons sugar; sprinkle mixture evenly over bagel chips coated with cooking spray. Bake as directed. **Yield: 3 dozen.**

PER CHIP: 27 CALORIES (7% FROM FAT)
FAT 0.2G (SATURATED FAT 0.0G)
PROTEIN 1.0G CARBOHYDRATE 5.3G
CHOLESTEROL 0MG SODIUM 51MG

Sweet Potato Chips

1 (½-pound) sweet potato, peeled
Vegetable cooking spray
¼ teaspoon salt

Slice sweet potato crosswise into ⅛-inch slices using a very sharp knife or vegetable cutter. Arrange in a single layer on baking sheets coated with cooking spray. Spray slices with cooking spray.

Bake at 325° for 14 minutes or until crisp. Remove chips from baking sheet as they begin to brown; cool. Sprinkle with salt. Store in an airtight container. **Yield: 3 dozen.**

PER CHIP: 5 CALORIES (18% FROM FAT)
FAT 0.1G (SATURATED FAT 0.0G)
PROTEIN 0.1G CARBOHYDRATE 1.1G
CHOLESTEROL 0MG SODIUM 17MG

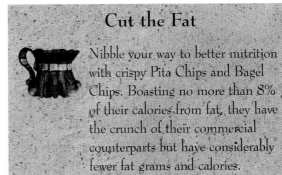

Cut the Fat

Nibble your way to better nutrition with crispy Pita Chips and Bagel Chips. Boasting no more than 8% of their calories from fat, they have the crunch of their commercial counterparts but have considerably fewer fat grams and calories.

Tortilla Chips

(pictured on page 694)

12 (6-inch) corn tortillas
½ cup lime juice
¼ cup water
½ teaspoon garlic powder
¼ teaspoon salt
⅛ teaspoon ground cumin
⅛ teaspoon ground red pepper

Cut 3 (2-inch) rounds from each tortilla using a cookie cutter or kitchen shears. Combine lime juice and water in a small bowl; set aside. Combine garlic powder and remaining ingredients.

Dip tortillas in lime juice mixture; drain on paper towels. Arrange tortillas in a single layer on an ungreased baking sheet; sprinkle evenly with garlic powder mixture.

Bake at 350° for 10 to 12 minutes or until chips are crisp. Cool; store in airtight containers. **Yield: 3 dozen.**

PER CHIP: 6 CALORIES (15% FROM FAT)
FAT 0.1G (SATURATED FAT 0.0G)
PROTEIN 0.2G CARBOHYDRATE 1.4G
CHOLESTEROL 0MG SODIUM 20MG

Baked Wonton Chips

(pictured on page 694)

56 (2-inch-square) wonton skins
Water

Cut wonton skins in half diagonally. Arrange in a single layer on ungreased baking sheets. Spray lightly with water.

Bake at 375° for 8 minutes or until lightly browned. Serve warm or cold. **Yield: 112 chips.**

PER CHIP: 10 CALORIES (9% FROM FAT)
FAT 0.1G (SATURATED FAT 0.0G)
PROTEIN 0.3G CARBOHYDRATE 2.1G
CHOLESTEROL 0MG SODIUM 20MG

Variations

Parmesan Cheese Wonton Chips: Sprinkle 2 teaspoons grated Parmesan cheese evenly over wonton chips sprayed with water. Bake as directed. **Yield: 112 chips.**

PER CHIP: 10 CALORIES (9% FROM FAT)
FAT 0.1G (SATURATED FAT 0.0G)
PROTEIN 0.4G CARBOHYDRATE 2.1G
CHOLESTEROL 0MG SODIUM 21MG

Lemon-and-Herb Wonton Chips: Sprinkle 2 teaspoons salt-free lemon-and-herb spice blend evenly over wonton chips sprayed with water. Bake as directed. **Yield: 112 chips.**

PER CHIP: 11 CALORIES (8% FROM FAT)
FAT 0.1G (SATURATED FAT 0.0G)
PROTEIN 0.4G CARBOHYDRATE 2.1G
CHOLESTEROL 0MG SODIUM 20MG

Garlic Wonton Chips: Sprinkle 1½ teaspoons garlic powder evenly over wonton chips sprayed with water. Bake as directed. **Yield: 112 chips.**

PER CHIP: 10 CALORIES (9% FROM FAT)
FAT 0.1G (SATURATED FAT 0.0G)
PROTEIN 0.4G CARBOHYDRATE 2.1G
CHOLESTEROL 0MG SODIUM 20MG

Cinnamon-and-Sugar Wonton Chips: Combine ¼ teaspoon ground cinnamon and 1½ teaspoons sugar. Sprinkle cinnamon-sugar mixture evenly over wonton chips sprayed with water. Bake as directed. **Yield: 112 chips.**

PER CHIP: 11 CALORIES (8% FROM FAT)
FAT 0.1G (SATURATED FAT 0.0G)
PROTEIN 0.3G CARBOHYDRATE 2.1G
CHOLESTEROL 0MG SODIUM 20MG

From left: Parmesan Pita Chips, Whole Wheat Pretzels (page 698), Snack Mix, and Pita Pizzas (page 698)

Parmesan Pita Chips

4 (6-inch) whole wheat pita bread rounds
⅓ cup commercial oil-free Italian salad
    dressing
½ cup grated Parmesan cheese
1½ tablespoons sesame seeds

Separate each pita bread into 2 rounds; cut each into 8 wedges to make 64 triangles. Brush inside of each triangle with dressing. Place on ungreased baking sheets, dressing side up.

Combine Parmesan cheese and sesame seeds; sprinkle evenly over triangles.

Bake at 425° for 10 minutes or until lightly browned. Cool on wire racks. Store in an airtight container. **Yield: 64 chips.**

PER CHIP: 15 CALORIES (24% FROM FAT)
FAT 0.4G (SATURATED FAT 0.1G)
PROTEIN 0.5G CARBOHYDRATE 2.2G
CHOLESTEROL 0MG SODIUM 48MG

Snack Mix

2 cups toasted oat cereal
2 cups bite-size crispy wheat squares
2 cups bite-size crispy rice squares
2 cups stick pretzels
1½ cups bite-size shredded whole wheat
    cereal biscuits
Butter-flavored vegetable cooking spray
1½ teaspoons onion powder
1 teaspoon garlic powder
1 teaspoon ground celery seeds
1½ tablespoons reduced-sodium
    Worcestershire sauce
1 teaspoon hot sauce

Combine first 5 ingredients in a large roasting pan; spray thoroughly with cooking spray.

Combine onion powder and remaining ingredients; distribute over cereal mixture, tossing to coat well.

Bake at 250° for 2 hours, stirring and spraying with cooking spray every 15 minutes. Cool; store in airtight containers. **Yield: 18 (½-cup) servings.**

PER SERVING: 74 CALORIES (10% FROM FAT)
FAT 0.8G (SATURATED FAT 0.2G)
PROTEIN 1.8G CARBOHYDRATE 15.2G
CHOLESTEROL 0MG SODIUM 149MG

Snack Smart

Instead of high-fat snacks, try one of these low-fat alternatives; each has less than 5 grams of total fat.

1 apple	2 fig bars
1 bagel	3 gingersnaps
1 banana	1 orange
8 carrot sticks	20 pretzel sticks
½ cup dried fruit	2 rice cakes
1 English muffin	5 vanilla wafers

Pita Pizzas

(pictured on page 697)

1 cup thinly sliced zucchini
¾ cup sliced fresh mushrooms
½ cup sliced green onions
½ cup chopped green pepper
1 cup pizza sauce
8 (6-inch) whole wheat pita bread rounds
Vegetable cooking spray
3 tablespoons grated Parmesan cheese

Combine first 5 ingredients in a medium bowl; toss gently. Place pita rounds on baking sheets coated with cooking spray. Spread ¼ cup zucchini mixture on each pita round; sprinkle evenly with Parmesan cheese.

Bake at 400° for 10 minutes. Cut each round into 8 wedges. Serve hot. **Yield: 64 wedges.**

PER WEDGE: 25 CALORIES (11% FROM FAT)
FAT 0.3G (SATURATED FAT 0.1G)
PROTEIN 0.6G CARBOHYDRATE 4.5G
CHOLESTEROL 0MG SODIUM 61MG

Potato Skin Snack

2 (6¾-ounce) baking potatoes
Vegetable cooking spray
2 tablespoons commercial oil-free Italian salad dressing
2 teaspoons salt-free herb-and-seasoning blend (regular or spicy)

Scrub potatoes, and coat with cooking spray. Bake at 400° for 1 hour or until done. Allow potatoes to cool.

Cut potatoes in half lengthwise; carefully scoop out pulp, leaving a ¼-inch shell. (Pulp may be reserved for other uses.)

Cut shells into 5 (½-inch-wide) strips. Place strips, skin side down, on a baking sheet. Brush with salad dressing; sprinkle with seasoning blend. Broil 6 inches from heat (with electric oven door partially opened) 5 minutes or until browned. Serve warm. **Yield: 20 appetizers.**

PER APPETIZER: 7 CALORIES (2% FROM FAT)
FAT 0.0G (SATURATED FAT 0.0G)
PROTEIN 0.2G CARBOHYDRATE 1.6G
CHOLESTEROL 0MG SODIUM 17MG

Whole Wheat Pretzels

(pictured on page 697)

1 package active dry yeast
1 tablespoon sugar
¾ teaspoon salt
1½ cups warm water (105° to 115°)
2¼ cups all-purpose flour
1½ cups whole wheat flour
1 cup (4 ounces) shredded sharp Cheddar cheese
Vegetable cooking spray
1 egg white
2 tablespoons water

Dissolve yeast, sugar, and salt in 1½ cups warm water; let yeast mixture stand 5 minutes.

Combine flours and cheese in a large mixing bowl. Add yeast mixture; beat at low speed of an electric mixer until mixture is well blended. Turn dough out onto a lightly floured surface, and knead until smooth (about 5 minutes).

Cut dough into 32 pieces using kitchen shears dipped in flour; shape each piece into a ball. Roll each ball on a lightly floured surface to form a rope 14 inches long. Twist each into a pretzel shape; place on baking sheets coated with cooking spray.

Combine egg white and 2 tablespoons water; mix well. Brush each pretzel with egg white mixture.

Bake at 425° for 12 to 15 minutes or until lightly browned. **Yield: 32 pretzels.**

PER PRETZEL: 70 CALORIES (18% FROM FAT)
FAT 1.4G (SATURATED FAT 0.8G)
PROTEIN 2.8G CARBOHYDRATE 11.7G
CHOLESTEROL 4MG SODIUM 79MG

Chicken Wontons

(pictured on page 691)

2 (4-ounce) skinned and boned chicken breast
    halves, cut into ¼-inch strips
1 clove garlic, minced
½ cup shredded carrot
¼ cup finely chopped celery
1 tablespoon low-sodium soy sauce
1 tablespoon dry sherry
1 tablespoon fresh lime juice
2 teaspoons cornstarch
1 teaspoon ground ginger
½ (16-ounce) package wonton wrappers
    (32 wrappers)
Butter-flavored vegetable cooking spray

Position knife blade in food processor bowl;
add chicken. Process 1 minute or until ground.
Cook chicken and garlic in a nonstick skillet over
medium heat, stirring constantly, until chicken is
no longer pink; drain.

Combine chicken, shredded carrot, and next 6
ingredients.

Spoon 1 rounded teaspoon of chicken mixture
into center of each wonton wrapper; moisten
edges with water. Carefully bring 2 opposite
points of wrapper to center over filling; pinch
points together. Bring two remaining opposite
points to center, and pinch together.

Place filled wontons on a baking sheet coated
with cooking spray. Lightly coat each wonton
with cooking spray.

Bake at 375° for 8 to 10 minutes or until lightly browned. **Yield: 32 wontons.**

PER WONTON: 33 CALORIES (11% FROM FAT)
FAT 0.4G (SATURATED FAT 0.1G)
PROTEIN 2.3G CARBOHYDRATE 4.6G
CHOLESTEROL 5MG SODIUM 58MG

Tortellini with Rosemary-Parmesan Sauce

(pictured on page 691)

2½ tablespoons nonfat dry milk powder
⅔ cup fat-free milk
1⅔ cups nonfat cottage cheese
¼ cup grated Parmesan cheese
¼ cup chopped fresh chives
1 tablespoon lemon juice
1¾ teaspoons chopped fresh rosemary
¼ teaspoon pepper
¼ teaspoon salt
1 (9-ounce) package refrigerated cheese-filled
    tortellini, cooked without salt or fat
1 (9-ounce) package refrigerated cheese-filled
    spinach tortellini, cooked without salt
    or fat
Garnish: fresh chives

Position knife blade in food processor bowl;
add dry milk and fat-free milk. Process 10 seconds or until blended.

Add cottage cheese and next 6 ingredients;
process 1 minute, stopping once to scrape down
sides of bowl.

Cover and chill thoroughly. Serve sauce with
tortellini and garnish, if desired. **Yield: 20 servings.**

PER SERVING: 92 CALORIES (23% FROM FAT)
FAT 2.4G (SATURATED FAT 0.7G)
PROTEIN 7.3G CARBOHYDRATE 10.4G
CHOLESTEROL 16MG SODIUM 209MG

Special-Occasion Appetizer

Pair cheese-filled tortellini with
Rosemary-Parmesan Sauce.
Refrigerated tortellini can be stored
in the refrigerator up to 5 days or
frozen up to 4 months. Cooking
time is less than 10 minutes.

Clockwise from top: Spiced Pineapple Sparkle, Mock Black Russian, Mock Eggnog with Orange and Nutmeg, and Spicy Virgin Mary (page 702)

Spiced Pineapple Sparkle

1½ cups water
6 (3-inch) sticks cinnamon
12 whole cloves
½ cup sugar
1 (46-ounce) can unsweetened pineapple juice, chilled
1½ cups unsweetened orange juice, chilled
½ cup lemon juice, chilled
3 (12-ounce) bottles lemon-lime carbonated beverage, chilled
Garnishes: orange slices, maraschino cherries

Combine first 3 ingredients in a saucepan; bring to a boil. Cover, reduce heat, and simmer 15 minutes. Remove from heat, and stir in sugar; let cool.

Pour mixture through a large, wire-mesh strainer into a punch bowl, discarding spices; stir in juices and lemon-lime beverage. Garnish, if desired. **Yield: 12 (1-cup) servings.**

PER SERVING: 147 CALORIES (1% FROM FAT)
FAT 0.1G (SATURATED FAT 0.0G)
PROTEIN 0.6G CARBOHYDRATE 37.0G
CHOLESTEROL 0MG SODIUM 2MG

Mock Black Russian

1½ tablespoons instant coffee granules
1 cup boiling water
1 quart low-fat vanilla ice cream, divided
½ cup chocolate syrup, divided
2 teaspoons vanilla extract
2 teaspoons semisweet chocolate shavings

Dissolve coffee granules in boiling water; let coffee cool.

Place half of ice cream and half of chocolate syrup in container of an electric blender; cover and process until smooth, stopping to scrape down sides. Pour into a large bowl or pitcher.

Repeat with remaining ice cream and syrup, and add to bowl. Add coffee and vanilla; stir with a wire whisk.

Pour into glasses; sprinkle each with ¼ teaspoon chocolate shavings. Serve immediately. **Yield: 8 (5-ounce) servings.**

PER SERVING: 150 CALORIES (20% FROM FAT)
FAT 3.4G (SATURATED FAT 1.9G)
PROTEIN 3.3G CARBOHYDRATE 27.1G
CHOLESTEROL 9MG SODIUM 69MG

Mock Eggnog with Orange and Nutmeg

2 tablespoons sugar
2 tablespoons cornstarch
1 quart fat-free milk
1 teaspoon vanilla extract
½ teaspoon rum extract
½ teaspoon grated orange rind
⅛ teaspoon salt
⅓ cup sugar, divided
1 tablespoon meringue powder
½ cup cold water
Ground nutmeg (optional)

Combine sugar and cornstarch in a medium saucepan; stir in milk. Bring to a boil over medium heat, stirring constantly. Boil mixture, stirring constantly, 1 minute. Remove from heat.

Stir in vanilla and next 3 ingredients; cover and chill.

Combine 3 tablespoons sugar, meringue powder, and water in a large mixing bowl just before serving. Beat at high speed of an electric mixer 5 minutes; gradually add remaining 2⅓ tablespoons sugar, beating until soft peaks form.

Fold into milk mixture. Sprinkle with nutmeg, if desired. **Yield: 7 (¾-cup) servings.**

PER SERVING: 115 CALORIES (2% FROM FAT)
FAT 0.2G (SATURATED FAT 0.2G)
PROTEIN 5.6G CARBOHYDRATE 22.1G
CHOLESTEROL 3MG SODIUM 127MG

Spicy Virgin Mary

(pictured on page 700)

1 (48-ounce) can low-sodium tomato juice
1 (14.25-ounce) can ready-to-serve, no-salt-added beef broth
¼ cup low-sodium Worcestershire sauce
3 tablespoons lime juice
1½ teaspoons seasoned salt
1 teaspoon celery seeds
½ teaspoon onion powder
½ teaspoon freshly ground pepper
⅛ teaspoon garlic powder
¼ teaspoon hot sauce
Ice cubes
Garnish: celery stalks

Combine first 10 ingredients; chill. Serve over ice and garnish, if desired. **Yield: 8 (1-cup) servings.**

PER SERVING: 49 CALORIES (2% FROM FAT)
FAT 0.1G (SATURATED FAT 0.0G)
PROTEIN 1.9G CARBOHYDRATE 11.4G
CHOLESTEROL 0MG SODIUM 437MG

White Grape Punch

1 (48-ounce) bottle apple juice
1 (24-ounce) bottle white grape juice
1 (12-ounce) can frozen lemonade concentrate, thawed and undiluted
1 (33.8-ounce) bottle club soda, chilled

Combine first 3 ingredients; chill well. Stir in club soda just before serving. **Yield: 14 (1-cup) servings.**

PER SERVING: 127 CALORIES (1% FROM FAT)
FAT 0.2G (SATURATED FAT 0.0G)
PROTEIN 0.1G CARBOHYDRATE 32.4G
CHOLESTEROL 0MG SODIUM 21MG

Bourbon Blizzard

½ gallon low-fat vanilla ice cream, divided
½ gallon 1% low-fat milk, divided
¾ cup bourbon
¼ cup vanilla extract
1 tablespoon ground nutmeg
Additional ground nutmeg

Combine 2 cups ice cream, 2 cups milk, bourbon, vanilla, and 1 tablespoon nutmeg in container of an electric blender; cover and process until smooth. Pour into a large bowl.

Add one-third each of remaining ice cream and milk to blender; cover and process until smooth, stopping once to scrape down sides. Add to bowl. Repeat procedure twice with remaining ice cream and milk. Stir with a wire whisk. Cover; chill.

Pour into punch cups, and sprinkle with additional nutmeg. **Yield: 26 (½-cup) servings.**

PER SERVING: 138 CALORIES (23% FROM FAT)
FAT 3.5G (SATURATED FAT 2.2G)
PROTEIN 4.7G CARBOHYDRATE 17.7G
CHOLESTEROL 11MG SODIUM 89MG

Sugar-Free Spiced Tea Mix

1 (3.3-ounce) jar sugar-free, caffeine-free iced tea mix with lemon
2 (1.8-ounce) packages sugar-free orange breakfast drink mix
1 tablespoon plus 1 teaspoon ground cinnamon
2 teaspoons ground cloves

Combine all ingredients, and store in an airtight container. To serve, stir 1½ teaspoons mix into 1 cup hot water. **Yield: 96 (1-cup) servings.**

PER SERVING: 6 CALORIES (3% FROM FAT)
FAT 0.0G (SATURATED FAT 0.0G)
PROTEIN 0.1G CARBOHYDRATE 1.1G
CHOLESTEROL 0MG SODIUM 6MG

Breads

Freshly baked biscuits, cornbread, and yeast breads can remain dinnertime staples. It will be hard to tell the difference between these lightened-up recipes and their original counterparts.

Whole Wheat Biscuits, Granola Muffins, Oatmeal-Bran Muffins

Old-Fashioned Cinnamon Rolls, Herbed Bread, English Muffin Bread, Spoonbread

Fruity Banana Bread, Cinnamon-Oat Bread, Honey Pancakes, Cornmeal Muffins

Jalapeño Cornbread, Yogurt Crescent Rolls, Parsley-Garlic Rolls

Mini Swiss Cheese Loaves (page 712)

Whole Wheat Biscuits

Whole Wheat Biscuits

1½ cups all-purpose flour
½ cup whole wheat flour
1 tablespoon baking powder
½ teaspoon salt
3 tablespoons reduced-calorie margarine
¾ cup evaporated fat-free milk
Vegetable cooking spray

Combine flours, baking powder, and salt; cut in margarine with a pastry blender until mixture is crumbly.

Add milk, stirring until dry ingredients are moistened. Turn dough out onto a lightly floured surface, and knead about 1 minute.

Shape dough into 12 balls; place balls in an 8-inch square pan coated with cooking spray.

Flatten dough slightly. Bake at 450° for 10 to 12 minutes or until golden. **Yield: 1 dozen.**

PER BISCUIT: 105 CALORIES (19% FROM FAT)
FAT 2.2G (SATURATED FAT 0.3G)
PROTEIN 3.6G CARBOHYDRATE 18.2G
CHOLESTEROL 1MG SODIUM 144MG

Granola Muffins

1½ cups reduced-fat biscuit mix
1 cup firmly packed brown sugar
1 teaspoon ground cinnamon
1 cup oats and honey granola cereal with
   almonds
½ cup raisins
1 large egg, lightly beaten
¾ cup fat-free milk
1 tablespoon vegetable oil
Vegetable cooking spray

Combine first 3 ingredients in a bowl; stir in cereal and raisins. Make a well in center; set flour mixture aside.

Combine egg, milk, and oil; add to flour mixture, stirring just until dry ingredients are moistened. (Batter will be thin.)

Coat muffin cups with cooking spray; spoon batter into cups, filling three-fourths full.

Bake at 375° for 15 to 20 minutes or until golden. **Yield: 16 muffins.**

PER MUFFIN: 140 CALORIES (21% FROM FAT)
FAT 3.3G (SATURATED FAT 0.7G)
PROTEIN 2.5G CARBOHYDRATE 25.1G
CHOLESTEROL 14MG SODIUM 153MG

Oatmeal-Bran Muffins

¾ cup morsels of wheat bran cereal
¾ cup regular oats, uncooked
1¼ cups fat-free milk
1 egg or ¼ cup egg substitute
¼ cup vegetable oil
½ cup raisins
1¼ cups all-purpose flour
1 tablespoon baking powder
½ teaspoon salt
½ cup sugar
Vegetable cooking spray

Combine first 3 ingredients in a bowl; let stand 5 minutes. Stir in egg, oil, and raisins.

Combine flour, baking powder, salt, and sugar; make a well in center of mixture. Add bran mixture, stirring just until moistened.

Spoon batter into muffin pans coated with cooking spray, filling three-fourths full. Bake at 400° for 20 to 25 minutes. **Yield: 1½ dozen.**

PER MUFFIN: 127 CALORIES (28% FROM FAT)
FAT 4.0G (SATURATED FAT 0.7G)
PROTEIN 3.0G CARBOHYDRATE 21.4G
CHOLESTEROL 13MG SODIUM 100MG

Apricot-Orange Bread
(pictured on page 691)

1 (6-ounce) package dried apricots, diced
¾ cup firmly packed brown sugar
1 cup nonfat buttermilk
½ cup egg substitute
3 tablespoons vegetable oil
1 tablespoon grated orange rind
1¼ teaspoons vanilla extract
¼ teaspoon almond extract
1½ cups all-purpose flour
¾ cup whole wheat flour
1½ teaspoons baking powder
1 teaspoon baking soda
½ teaspoon salt
Vegetable cooking spray
Garnishes: dried apricots, orange rind strips, cinnamon sticks, grape leaves

Combine first 8 ingredients; let stand 5 minutes. Combine all-purpose flour and next 4 ingredients in a large bowl; make a well in center of mixture. Add apricot mixture to dry ingredients, stirring just until moistened.

Coat either a 6-cup Bundt pan or 9- x 5- x 3-inch loafpan with cooking spray. Spoon batter into pan.

Bake at 350° for 35 minutes or until a wooden pick inserted in center comes out clean. Cool in pan on a wire rack 10 minutes; remove from pan, and cool on wire rack. Garnish, if desired. **Yield: 21 slices.**

PER SLICE: 111 CALORIES (19% FROM FAT)
FAT 2.3G (SATURATED FAT 0.4G)
PROTEIN 2.8G CARBOHYDRATE 20.6G
CHOLESTEROL 0MG SODIUM 145MG

Fruity Banana Bread

Vegetable cooking spray
⅓ cup margarine, softened
¾ cup sugar
½ cup egg substitute
1¾ cups all-purpose flour
2¾ teaspoons baking powder
1 cup mashed banana
¾ cup coarsely chopped mixed dried fruit

Coat an 8½- x 4½- x 3-inch loafpan with cooking spray; set aside.

Beat margarine at medium speed of an electric mixer until creamy; gradually add ¾ cup sugar, beating well. Add egg substitute, beating until blended.

Combine all-purpose flour and baking powder; add to margarine mixture. Beat at low speed until blended. Stir in mashed banana and dried fruit. Pour batter into prepared loafpan.

Bake at 350° for 1 hour or until a wooden pick inserted in center of loaf comes out clean. Cool in pan on a wire rack 10 minutes; remove from pan, and cool completely on wire rack. **Yield: 16 (½-inch) slices.**

PER SLICE: 149 CALORIES (23% FROM FAT)
FAT 3.8G (SATURATED FAT 0.7G)
PROTEIN 2.3G CARBOHYDRATE 27.3G
CHOLESTEROL 0MG SODIUM 54MG

Waffles

1¾ cups all-purpose flour
1¼ teaspoons baking powder
2 tablespoons sugar
1 large egg, separated
1 cup fat-free milk
2 tablespoons plus 2 teaspoons reduced-calorie stick margarine, melted
1 egg white
Vegetable cooking spray

Combine first 3 ingredients in a medium bowl; make a well in center of mixture.

Beat egg yolk in a small bowl; add milk and margarine, stirring well. Add liquid mixture to dry ingredients, stirring until smooth.

Beat 2 egg whites at high speed of an electric mixer until stiff peaks form; fold beaten egg whites into batter.

Coat waffle iron with cooking spray; allow waffle iron to preheat. For each waffle, pour ½ cup batter onto hot waffle iron, spreading batter to edges. Bake 4 to 5 minutes or until steaming stops. Repeat procedure with remaining batter. **Yield: 20 (3-inch) waffles.**

PER WAFFLE: 63 CALORIES (21% FROM FAT)
FAT 1.5G (SATURATED FAT 0.2G)
PROTEIN 2.0G CARBOHYDRATE 10.3G
CHOLESTEROL 11MG SODIUM 27MG

Honey Pancakes

3 cups all-purpose flour
2 tablespoons baking powder
½ teaspoon salt
3 cups fat-free milk
½ cup egg substitute
¼ cup honey
¼ cup vegetable oil
Vegetable cooking spray

Combine first 3 ingredients in a large bowl. Combine milk and next 3 ingredients; add to flour mixture, stirring until smooth.

Pour about ¼ cup batter for each pancake onto a hot griddle coated with cooking spray. Turn pancakes when tops are covered with bubbles and edges look cooked. **Yield: 28 (4-inch) pancakes.**

PER PANCAKE: 88 CALORIES (23% FROM FAT)
FAT 2.2G (SATURATED FAT 0.4G)
PROTEIN 2.7G CARBOHYDRATE 14.3G
CHOLESTEROL 1MG SODIUM 62MG

Honey Pancakes

Cornmeal Muffins

Cornmeal Muffins

1 cup yellow cornmeal
1 cup all-purpose flour
2 teaspoons baking powder
1 teaspoon baking soda
½ teaspoon salt
1 teaspoon sugar
¼ cup egg substitute or 2 egg whites
1¼ cups plain nonfat yogurt
2½ tablespoons vegetable oil
Vegetable cooking spray

Combine first 6 ingredients in a large bowl; make a well in center of mixture. Combine egg substitute, yogurt, and oil; add to dry ingredients, stirring just until moistened.

Spoon mixture into muffin pans coated with cooking spray, filling three-fourths full.

Bake at 425° for 12 to 14 minutes or until golden. Remove muffins from pans immediately. **Yield: 1½ dozen.**

PER MUFFIN: 80 CALORIES (28% FROM FAT)
FAT 2.5G (SATURATED FAT 0.4G)
PROTEIN 2.5G CARBOHYDRATE 12.1G
CHOLESTEROL 0MG SODIUM 155MG

Jalapeño Cornbread

1 cup cornmeal
2 teaspoons baking powder
¼ teaspoon salt
2 large eggs
3 tablespoons nonfat sour cream
1½ teaspoons vegetable oil
1 (8¾-ounce) can cream-style corn
1 (4.25-ounce) jar pickled, chopped jalapeño
    peppers, drained
Vegetable cooking spray

Heat an 8-inch cast-iron skillet in a 400° oven for 5 minutes.

Combine first 3 ingredients in a large bowl; make a well in center of mixture. Set aside.

Combine eggs and next 4 ingredients; add to dry ingredients, stirring until moistened.

Remove skillet from oven, and coat with cooking spray; pour batter into hot skillet.

Bake at 400° for 20 minutes or until golden. **Yield: 8 servings.**

Note: For best results use whole eggs, not egg substitute.

PER SERVING: 178 CALORIES (21% FROM FAT)
FAT 4.1G (SATURATED FAT 0.8G)
PROTEIN 6.8G CARBOHYDRATE 28.4G
CHOLESTEROL 74MG SODIUM 684MG

Spoonbread

1 cup white cornmeal
2 cups evaporated fat-free milk
1 cup water
2 tablespoons reduced-calorie margarine
½ teaspoon salt
2 egg whites
½ cup egg substitute
Vegetable cooking spray

Combine first 5 ingredients; cook mixture over medium heat, stirring constantly, 5 minutes or until thickened. Remove from heat.

Beat egg whites at medium speed of an electric mixer until stiff. With mixer running, slowly add egg substitute. Gradually stir about one-third of hot mixture into egg mixture; add to remaining hot mixture, stirring constantly. Pour into a 1½-quart casserole coated with cooking spray.

Bake at 350° for 35 minutes or until a knife inserted in center comes out clean. **Yield: 9 (½-cup) servings.**

PER SERVING: 118 CALORIES (18% FROM FAT)
FAT 2.3G (SATURATED FAT 0.4G)
PROTEIN 7.5G CARBOHYDRATE 17.2G
CHOLESTEROL 2MG SODIUM 256MG

Old-Fashioned Cinnamon Rolls

Old-Fashioned Cinnamon Rolls

⅓ cup fat-free milk
⅓ cup reduced-calorie margarine
¼ cup firmly packed brown sugar
1 teaspoon salt
1 package active dry yeast
½ cup warm water (105° to 115°)
½ cup egg substitute
3½ cups bread flour, divided
¾ cup quick-cooking oats, uncooked
Vegetable cooking spray
¼ cup reduced-calorie margarine, softened
¾ cup firmly packed brown sugar
¼ cup raisins
2 teaspoons ground cinnamon
1 cup sifted powdered sugar
2 tablespoons water

Combine first 4 ingredients in a saucepan; heat until margarine melts, stirring occasionally. Cool mixture to 105° to 115°.

Combine yeast and warm water; let stand 5 minutes. Combine yeast mixture, milk mixture, egg substitute, 1 cup flour, and oats in a large mixing bowl, mixing well. Gradually stir in enough remaining flour to make a soft dough.

Turn dough out onto a lightly floured surface; knead until smooth and elastic (about 8 minutes). Place dough in a large bowl coated with cooking spray, turning to grease top.

Cover and let rise in a warm place (85°), free from drafts, 1 hour or until doubled in bulk.

Punch dough down. Cover; let rest 10 minutes. Divide in half; roll each half into a 12-inch square. Spread each with 2 tablespoons margarine.

Combine ¾ cup brown sugar, raisins, and cinnamon; sprinkle over each square. Roll up jelly-roll fashion; pinch seam to seal. Cut each roll into 1-inch slices; place, cut side down, in two 8-inch square pans coated with cooking spray.

Cover; let rise in a warm place, free from drafts, 30 minutes or until almost doubled in bulk.

Bake at 375° for 15 to 20 minutes or until golden. Combine powdered sugar and 2 tablespoons water; drizzle over warm rolls. **Yield: 2 dozen.**

PER ROLL: 159 CALORIES (19% FROM FAT)
FAT 3.4G (SATURATED FAT 0.5G)
PROTEIN 3.6G CARBOHYDRATE 29.0G
CHOLESTEROL 0MG SODIUM 153MG

Yogurt Crescent Rolls

⅓ cup vegetable oil
1 (8-ounce) carton plain low-fat yogurt
½ cup sugar
2 packages active dry yeast
½ cup warm water (105° to 115°)
1 large egg
1 egg white
4 cups all-purpose flour
1 teaspoon salt
Butter-flavored vegetable cooking spray

Combine first 3 ingredients in a large bowl.

Combine yeast and warm water; let stand 5 minutes. Stir yeast mixture, egg, and egg white into yogurt mixture.

Combine flour and salt. Stir 2 cups flour mixture into yogurt mixture; beat at medium speed of an electric mixer until smooth. Gradually stir in remaining flour mixture. Cover and chill 8 hours.

Punch dough down, and divide into 4 equal portions. Roll each portion to a 10-inch circle on a floured surface; coat with cooking spray. Cut each circle into 12 wedges; roll up each wedge, beginning at wide end. Place on baking sheets coated with cooking spray, point side down.

Cover and let rise in a warm place (85°), free from drafts, 45 minutes or until doubled in bulk.

Bake at 375° for 10 to 12 minutes or until rolls are golden. **Yield: 4 dozen.**

PER ROLL: 66 CALORIES (25% FROM FAT)
FAT 1.8G (SATURATED FAT 0.4G)
PROTEIN 1.7G CARBOHYDRATE 10.6G
CHOLESTEROL 5MG SODIUM 55MG

Parsley-Garlic Rolls

2 tablespoons reduced-calorie margarine,
   melted
2 cloves garlic, crushed
1 (16-ounce) loaf frozen bread dough, thawed
1 tablespoon chopped fresh parsley
Vegetable cooking spray

   Combine margarine and garlic; set aside.
   Cut bread dough crosswise into 6 even portions with kitchen shears; cut portions in half
crosswise. Roll each half to ¼-inch thickness on
a lightly floured surface; brush with margarine
mixture, and sprinkle with parsley. Roll each
piece of dough, jellyroll fashion, and place,
swirled side down, in muffin pans coated with
cooking spray.
   Cover and let rise in a warm place (85°), free
from drafts, 1 hour or until doubled in bulk. Bake
at 400° for 10 to 12 minutes. Serve immediately.
Yield: 1 dozen.

PER ROLL: 97 CALORIES (20% FROM FAT)
FAT 2.2G (SATURATED FAT 0.2G)
PROTEIN 3.0G CARBOHYDRATE 16.1G
CHOLESTEROL 0MG SODIUM 196MG

Mini Swiss Cheese Loaves

(pictured on page 703)

1 package active dry yeast
¼ cup warm water (105° to 115°)
2⅓ cups all-purpose flour, divided
1 teaspoon salt
¼ teaspoon baking soda
2 tablespoons sugar
1 (8-ounce) carton plain nonfat yogurt
1 large egg
1 cup (4 ounces) shredded reduced-fat Swiss
   cheese
Vegetable cooking spray
2 teaspoons sesame seeds, toasted

   Combine yeast and warm water in a 1-cup
liquid measuring cup; let stand 5 minutes.
   Combine yeast mixture, 1 cup flour, and next
5 ingredients in a large mixing bowl.
   Beat at low speed of an electric mixer 30 seconds. Beat at high speed 2 minutes, scraping
bowl occasionally.
   Stir in remaining 1⅓ cups flour and cheese,
mixing well.
   Divide batter evenly among 8 (5- x 3- x 2-
inch) loafpans coated with cooking spray; sprinkle evenly with sesame seeds.
   Cover and let rise in a warm place (85°),
free from drafts, 1 hour. (Batter may not double
in bulk.)
   Bake at 350° for 25 minutes or until golden.
Remove from pans; serve warm, or cool on wire
racks. **Yield: 16 (½-loaf) servings.**
   Note: For reduced-fat Swiss cheese, we used
Alpine Lace.

PER SERVING: 113 CALORIES (20% FROM FAT)
FAT 2.5G (SATURATED FAT 1.1G)
PROTEIN 5.3G CARBOHYDRATE 17.1G
CHOLESTEROL 19MG SODIUM 190MG

Cinnamon-Oat Bread

1⅔ cups bread flour
1 cup regular oats, uncooked
½ cup unprocessed oat bran
1½ teaspoons salt
3 packages active dry yeast
1¾ cups water
½ cup honey
½ cup vegetable oil
½ cup egg substitute
2½ cups whole wheat flour
1¾ cups bread flour, divided
Butter-flavored vegetable cooking spray
1 tablespoon sugar
2 teaspoons ground cinnamon

Cinnamon-Oat Bread

Combine first 5 ingredients in a large mixing bowl. Combine water, honey, and oil in a medium saucepan; heat to 120° to 130°.

Add liquid mixture and egg substitute gradually to flour mixture; beat at low speed of an electric mixer until blended. Beat 3 additional minutes at medium speed. Gradually stir in wheat flour and ¼ cup bread flour to form a soft dough.

Turn dough out onto a lightly floured surface. Knead until smooth and elastic (about 10 minutes); add enough of remaining 1½ cups bread flour to prevent dough from sticking to hands.

Place dough in a large bowl coated with cooking spray, turning to coat top. Cover and let rise in a warm place (85°), free from drafts, 1 hour or until doubled in bulk.

Punch dough down; let rest 15 minutes. Divide in half. Roll each portion to a 15- x 7-inch rectangle on a lightly floured surface. Coat dough with butter-flavored cooking spray. Combine sugar and cinnamon; sprinkle over dough.

Roll up dough, jellyroll fashion, starting with narrow end. Place, seam side down, in 2 (9- x 5- x 3-inch) loafpans coated with cooking spray. Let dough rise in a warm place, free from drafts, 30 minutes or until loaves are doubled in bulk.

Bake at 375° for 35 minutes or until loaves sound hollow when tapped. (Cover loaves loosely with aluminum foil for the last 20 minutes of baking to prevent overbrowning, if necessary.) Remove from pans immediately; cool. **Yield: 2 loaves or 36 (½-inch) slices.**

PER SLICE: 137 CALORIES (24% FROM FAT)
FAT 3.7G (SATURATED FAT 0.6G)
PROTEIN 3.9G CARBOHYDRATE 22.8G
CHOLESTEROL 0MG SODIUM 104MG

Herbed Bread

¼ cup margarine
1¼ cups water
2 cups whole wheat flour
1 package active dry yeast
1 teaspoon onion powder
¼ teaspoon salt
¼ teaspoon white pepper
2 tablespoons instant nonfat dry milk powder
2 tablespoons honey
1¾ cups all-purpose flour, divided
Vegetable cooking spray
1 tablespoon margarine, melted
¼ cup minced fresh parsley
1 tablespoon minced fresh thyme
¾ teaspoon minced fresh sage
¾ teaspoon minced fresh rosemary

Combine ¼ cup margarine and water in a saucepan; heat to 120° to 130°. Set aside.

Combine whole wheat flour and next 6 ingredients in a large mixing bowl; add margarine mixture. Beat at medium speed of an electric mixer until smooth. Stir in 1½ cups all-purpose flour. Turn dough out onto a lightly floured surface. Knead dough 5 minutes, using remaining ¼ cup flour.

Place dough in a bowl coated with cooking spray, turning dough to coat top. Cover and let rise in a warm place (85°), free from drafts, 1 hour or until doubled in bulk.

Punch dough down; turn out onto a lightly floured surface. Roll into a 15- x 9-inch rectangle; brush with melted margarine.

Combine parsley and remaining herbs; stir well. Sprinkle over dough. Roll up, jellyroll fashion, starting with narrow end. Place, seam side down, in a 9- x 5- x 3-inch loafpan coated with cooking spray. Let rise in a warm place (85°), free from drafts, 45 minutes or until doubled in bulk.

Bake at 350° for 45 minutes or until golden.

Remove loaf from pan, and cool slightly on a wire rack. **Yield: 18 (½-inch) slices.**

PER SLICE: 134 CALORIES (24% FROM FAT)
FAT 3.6G (SATURATED FAT 0.7G)
PROTEIN 3.7G CARBOHYDRATE 22.4G
CHOLESTEROL 0MG SODIUM 76MG

English Muffin Bread

3½ to 3¾ cups all-purpose flour, divided
1 cup whole wheat flour
½ cup oat bran
2 teaspoons salt
1 package rapid-rise yeast
1 cup fat-free milk
1 cup water
3 tablespoons reduced-calorie margarine
Vegetable cooking spray
2 tablespoons cornmeal

Combine 1½ cups all-purpose flour and next 4 ingredients in a large bowl; set aside.

Combine fat-free milk, water, and margarine in a 4-cup liquid measuring cup. Microwave at HIGH 2 minutes; pour over flour mixture.

Beat mixture at medium speed of an electric mixer 2 minutes. Stir in 2 cups all-purpose flour. Turn dough out onto a lightly floured surface; if dough is sticky, knead in remaining ¼ cup flour. Cover with a large bowl; let stand 10 minutes.

Coat 2 (8½- x 4½- x 3-inch) loafpans with cooking spray; sprinkle evenly with cornmeal. Divide dough in half; shape each portion into a loaf, and place in pan.

Cover; let rise in a warm place (85°), free from drafts, 1 hour or until doubled in bulk.

Bake at 400° for 25 minutes. Remove loaves from pans, and cool on wire racks. **Yield: 2 loaves or 32 (½-inch) slices.**

PER SLICE: 77 CALORIES (10% FROM FAT)
FAT 0.9G (SATURATED FAT 0.1G)
PROTEIN 2.5G CARBOHYDRATE 14.6G
CHOLESTEROL 0MG SODIUM 154MG

Desserts

These dazzling light desserts will please the eye as well as the palate. Each one conquers the myth that dessert must be high in calories, fat, and sugar to be delicious.

Angel Food Trifle, Peach Sherbet, Raspberry-Cherry Cobbler

Oatmeal-Raisin Cookies, Chocolate-Hazelnut Biscotti, Flaky Apple Turnovers

Banana-Coconut Cake, Frosted Carrot Cake, Strawberry Shortcake, Buttermilk Pie

Old-Fashioned Banana Pudding, Orange-Coconut Angel Food Cake

Pound Cake (page 719), Buttermilk Pie (page 726), and Fresh Strawberry Ice Milk (page 730)

Orange-Coconut Angel Food Cake

1 (16-ounce) package angel food cake mix
1 cup water
⅓ cup freshly squeezed orange juice
2 teaspoons orange extract, divided
1 (3-ounce) package vanilla pudding mix
2 cups fat-free milk
1 tablespoon grated orange rind
2 cups flaked coconut, divided
2½ cups reduced-fat frozen whipped topping,
   thawed and divided

Prepare cake mix according to package directions, using 1 cup water and ⅓ cup orange juice instead of liquid called for on package. Stir in 1 teaspoon orange extract. Spoon evenly into an ungreased 10-inch tube pan.

Bake at 375° on lowest oven rack for 30 minutes or until cake springs back when lightly touched. Invert pan; cool completely. Loosen cake from sides of pan, using a narrow metal spatula; remove from pan, and slice horizontally into 4 equal layers. Set aside.

Combine pudding mix and fat-free milk in a large saucepan; bring to a boil over medium heat, stirring constantly. Remove from heat, and stir in remaining 1 teaspoon orange extract and orange rind. Cool mixture. Fold in 1 cup coconut and 1 cup whipped topping.

Place bottom cake layer on a serving plate; spread top of layer with one-third of pudding mixture. Repeat procedure with remaining cake layers and pudding mixture, ending with top cake layer.

Spread remaining 1½ cups whipped topping on top and sides of cake; sprinkle with remaining 1 cup coconut. Store in refrigerator. **Yield: 16 servings.**

PER SERVING: 193 CALORIES (21% FROM FAT)
FAT 4.5G (SATURATED FAT 2.5G)
PROTEIN 4.0G CARBOHYDRATE 33.8G
CHOLESTEROL 1MG SODIUM 301MG

Angel Food Trifle

1 (16-ounce) package angel food cake mix
⅓ cup sugar
¼ cup cornstarch
¼ teaspoon salt
2 cups fat-free milk
¼ cup egg substitute
1 teaspoon grated lemon rind
¼ cup lemon juice
2 (8-ounce) cartons vanilla low-fat yogurt
2 cups sliced strawberries
3 kiwifruit, sliced
3 strawberry fans

Prepare cake mix according to package directions. Cut into bite-size cubes; set aside.

Combine sugar, cornstarch, and salt in a saucepan; gradually add milk, stirring well. Cook over medium heat until mixture begins to thicken, stirring constantly.

Remove mixture from heat; gradually add egg substitute, stirring constantly with a wire whisk. Cook over medium-low heat 2 minutes, stirring constantly.

Remove from heat; cool slightly. Stir in lemon rind and lemon juice; chill. Fold yogurt into custard mixture; set aside.

Place one-third of cake in bottom of a 16-cup trifle bowl. Spoon one-third of custard over cake; arrange half each of strawberry slices and kiwi slices around lower edge of bowl and over custard. Repeat process with remaining ingredients, ending with strawberry fans on top.

Cover and chill 3 to 4 hours. **Yield: 15 (⅔-cup) servings.**

PER SERVING: 193 CALORIES (3% FROM FAT)
FAT 0.7G (SATURATED FAT 0.3G)
PROTEIN 6.0G CARBOHYDRATE 41.5G
CHOLESTEROL 2MG SODIUM 305MG

Angel Food Trifle

Lemon Angel Rolls

Lemon Angel Rolls

1 angel food cake loaf
¼ cup Key Largo liqueur
1 (11¼-ounce) jar lemon curd
Sifted powdered sugar
Raspberry Sauce
Garnishes: lemon twist, fresh mint sprigs

Remove crust from cake. Cut cake horizontally into 8 slices; flatten each slice slightly with a rolling pin. Brush with liqueur. Spread each cake slice with 1½ tablespoons lemon curd. Starting from the narrow end, roll up cake jellyroll fashion.

Wrap filled cake rolls in wax paper; chill. Cut each into thirds; sprinkle with sugar.

Spoon 1½ tablespoons Raspberry Sauce onto each dessert plate; arrange 3 cake roll slices on sauce. Garnish, if desired. **Yield: 8 servings.**

Raspberry Sauce

1 (10-ounce) package frozen raspberries in
    light syrup, thawed
2 teaspoons cornstarch

Place raspberries in container of an electric blender; process until smooth. Pour mixture through a wire-mesh strainer into a small saucepan. Stir in cornstarch; place over medium heat, stirring constantly, until mixture thickens and boils. Boil 1 minute, stirring constantly. Remove from heat, and let cool. **Yield: ¾ cup.**

PER SERVING: 331 CALORIES (19% FROM FAT)
FAT 6.9G (SATURATED FAT 1.5G)
PROTEIN 4.3G CARBOHYDRATE 60.7G
CHOLESTEROL 65MG SODIUM 168MG

Banana-Coconut Cake

1¾ cups all-purpose flour
½ teaspoon baking soda
¼ teaspoon salt
⅓ cup sugar
1¼ teaspoons cream of tartar
¾ cup mashed ripe banana
¼ cup egg substitute
¼ cup fat-free milk
¼ cup margarine, melted
1 teaspoon vanilla extract
1 tablespoon flaked coconut
¼ teaspoon ground cinnamon
Vegetable cooking spray

Combine first 5 ingredients in a large bowl; make a well in center of mixture. Combine banana and next 4 ingredients; add to dry mixture, stirring until moistened. Combine coconut and cinnamon; set aside.

Coat an 8-inch square pan with cooking spray. Spoon batter into pan; sprinkle with coconut mixture.

Bake at 350° for 20 to 25 minutes or until a wooden pick inserted in center comes out clean. Cool in pan on a wire rack 5 minutes. Remove from pan; let cool on wire rack. **Yield: 8 servings.**

PER SERVING: 230 CALORIES (25% FROM FAT)
FAT 6.5G (SATURATED FAT 1.5G)
PROTEIN 4.3G CARBOHYDRATE 39.3G
CHOLESTEROL 0MG SODIUM 241MG

Frosted Carrot Cake

1½ cups all-purpose flour
⅔ cup whole wheat flour
2 teaspoons baking soda
2 teaspoons ground cinnamon
¼ teaspoon salt
1 cup firmly packed brown sugar
¾ cup egg substitute
¾ cup nonfat buttermilk
1 (8-ounce) can crushed pineapple in juice,
    drained
2 cups grated carrot
⅓ cup raisins
3 tablespoons vegetable oil
2 teaspoons vanilla extract
Vegetable cooking spray
Orange-Cream Cheese Frosting

Combine first 5 ingredients; set aside. Combine brown sugar and next 7 ingredients in a large mixing bowl; stir in dry ingredients, and beat at medium speed of an electric mixer until well blended.

Pour batter into a 13- x 9- x 2-inch pan coated with cooking spray.

Bake at 350° for 30 to 35 minutes or until a wooden pick inserted in center comes out clean. Cool cake completely in pan on a wire rack. Spread Orange-Cream Cheese Frosting over top of cake. Cover and chill. **Yield: 18 servings.**

Orange-Cream Cheese Frosting

½ cup 1% low-fat cottage cheese
2 teaspoons vanilla extract
1 (8-ounce) package light cream cheese,
    softened
1 teaspoon grated orange rind
1 cup sifted powdered sugar

Position knife blade in food processor bowl; add cottage cheese. Process about 1 minute or until smooth. Add vanilla, cream cheese, and orange rind; process until smooth. Add powdered sugar; pulse 3 to 5 times until mixture is smooth. **Yield: 1½ cups.**

PER SERVING: 207 CALORIES (21% FROM FAT)
FAT 4.8G (SATURATED FAT 1.8G)
PROTEIN 5.4G CARBOHYDRATE 36.1G
CHOLESTEROL 8MG SODIUM 304MG

Pound Cake

(pictured on page 715)

Vegetable cooking spray
½ cup margarine, softened
1 cup sugar
⅓ cup egg substitute
2½ cups sifted cake flour
½ teaspoon baking powder
¼ teaspoon baking soda
¼ teaspoon salt
1 (8-ounce) carton low-fat vanilla yogurt
1 tablespoon vanilla extract
¾ teaspoon almond extract

Coat the bottom of a 9- x 5- x 3-inch loafpan with cooking spray; dust with flour, and set aside.

Beat margarine at medium speed of an electric mixer until fluffy. Gradually add sugar; beat well. Add egg substitute; beat until blended.

Combine flour and next 3 ingredients; add to creamed mixture alternately with yogurt, beginning and ending with flour mixture. Mix just until blended after each addition. Stir in flavorings.

Spoon batter into prepared pan. Bake at 350° for 1 hour and 5 minutes or until a wooden pick inserted in center comes out clean. Cool in pan on a wire rack 10 minutes; remove from pan, and let cool on wire rack. Serve with ½ cup chopped or sliced fruit. **Yield: 18 (½-inch) servings.**

PER SERVING: 159 CALORIES (30% FROM FAT)
FAT 5.4G (SATURATED FAT 1.1G)
PROTEIN 2.4G CARBOHYDRATE 24.9G
CHOLESTEROL 1MG SODIUM 125MG

Strawberry Shortcake

Strawberry Shortcake

4 cups sliced fresh strawberries
¼ cup sugar
Vegetable cooking spray
¼ cup margarine, softened
⅓ cup sugar
1 large egg, separated
1¾ cups all-purpose flour
1½ teaspoons baking powder
¼ teaspoon salt
¾ cup fat-free milk
½ teaspoon vanilla extract
1 egg white
2 tablespoons sugar
1½ cups frozen reduced-calorie whipped
      topping, thawed
Garnish: strawberry fan

Combine strawberries and ¼ cup sugar; cover and chill 2 to 3 hours, stirring occasionally.

Coat a 9-inch round cakepan with vegetable cooking spray; dust with flour, and set aside.

Beat margarine at medium speed of an electric mixer until soft; add ⅓ cup sugar, beating well. Add egg yolk, beating just until blended.

Combine flour, baking powder, and salt in a small bowl; add to creamed mixture alternately with milk, beginning and ending with flour mixture. Mix after each addition. Stir in vanilla.

Beat 2 egg whites until foamy. Gradually add 2 tablespoons sugar, one at a time, beating until stiff peaks form. Stir about ½ cup beaten egg white into batter; fold in remaining egg white. Spoon batter into prepared pan.

Bake at 350° for 30 minutes or until a wooden pick inserted in center comes out clean. Let cool in pan on a wire rack 10 minutes. Remove cake from pan; let cool completely on wire rack.

Slice shortcake in half horizontally. Place bottom half, cut side up, on a serving plate.

Drain strawberries, reserving juice; drizzle half of juice over bottom layer. Set aside 1 table-spoon whipped topping. Spread ¾ cup topping over cake layer; arrange half of strawberries over topping. Top with remaining layer, cut side down. Repeat procedure. Dollop with reserved 1 table-spoon whipped topping and garnish, if desired. **Yield: 9 servings.**

PER SERVING: 260 CALORIES (27% FROM FAT)
FAT 7.9G (SATURATED FAT 1.2G)
PROTEIN 5.1G CARBOHYDRATE 42.9G
CHOLESTEROL 25MG SODIUM 157MG

Chocolate Mint Torte

Vegetable cooking spray
1 (18.5-ounce) package 97% fat-free devil's
      food cake mix
3 egg whites
1¾ cups water
1 (2.6-ounce) package whipped topping mix
⅔ cup fat-free milk
2 tablespoons green crème de menthe

Coat a 15- x 10- x 1-inch jellyroll pan with cooking spray; line with wax paper, and coat with cooking spray.

Combine cake mix, egg whites, and water in a large mixing bowl; beat at high speed of an electric mixer 2 minutes. Pour batter into prepared pan.

Bake at 350° for 18 to 20 minutes or until a wooden pick inserted in center comes out clean.

Cool in pan on a wire rack 10 minutes. Invert onto wire rack. Remove wax paper carefully; cool completely. Cut cake crosswise into thirds.

Combine whipped topping mix, milk, and crème de menthe; beat at high speed of an electric mixer 4 minutes or until stiff peaks form.

Spread topping between layers, reserving ½ cup. Pipe reserved topping on top of cake. Chill at least 2 hours or freeze. **Yield: 12 servings.**

PER SERVING: 204 CALORIES (13% FROM FAT)
FAT 3.0G (SATURATED FAT 0.0G)
PROTEIN 4.7G CARBOHYDRATE 38.0G
CHOLESTEROL 0MG SODIUM 319MG

Lemon Cheesecake

Lemon Cheesecake

3 cups nonfat yogurt
1 envelope unflavored gelatin
⅓ cup lemon juice
¾ cup sugar
1½ cups 1% low-fat cottage cheese
½ cup light cream cheese
2 teaspoons grated lemon rind
Graham Cracker Crust
Garnishes: lemon rind curls, fresh mint sprigs

Place colander in a large bowl. Line with 2 layers of cheesecloth or a coffee filter. Spoon yogurt into colander. Cover loosely; chill 24 hours. Discard liquid. Cover; chill yogurt cheese.

Sprinkle gelatin over lemon juice in a small saucepan; let stand 1 minute. Add sugar; cook over low heat, stirring until gelatin dissolves.

Remove from heat, and place in container of a food processor or electric blender. Add cottage cheese; cover and process until smooth. Add

cream cheese and grated lemon rind; process until smooth.

Add yogurt cheese, and process until smooth; pour mixture into crust. Cover and chill 8 hours. Garnish, if desired. **Yield: 10 servings.**

Graham Cracker Crust

¾ cup graham cracker crumbs
3 tablespoons reduced-calorie margarine, melted
¼ cup sugar

Combine all ingredients; mix well, and press mixture firmly into a 9-inch springform pan. Bake at 350° for 8 to 10 minutes. Cool. **Yield: one 9-inch crust.**

PER SLICE: 218 CALORIES (22% FROM FAT)
FAT 5.3G (SATURATED FAT 1.9G)
PROTEIN 10.4G CARBOHYDRATE 33.2G
CHOLESTEROL 9MG SODIUM 334MG

Black Forest Cheesecake

¾ cup teddy bear-shaped chocolate graham
    cracker cookies, crushed
Butter-flavored cooking spray
3 (8-ounce) packages nonfat cream cheese,
    softened
1½ cups sugar
¾ cup egg substitute
1 (6-ounce) package semisweet chocolate
    morsels, melted
¼ cup unsweetened cocoa
1½ teaspoons vanilla extract
1 (8-ounce) carton nonfat sour cream
1 (21-ounce) can reduced-calorie cherry pie
    filling
½ cup reduced-calorie frozen whipped
    topping, thawed
Garnishes: fresh cherries, mint sprig

Spread cookie crumbs on bottom of a 9-inch springform pan coated with cooking spray; set aside.

Beat cream cheese at high speed of an electric mixer until fluffy; add sugar, beating well. Add egg substitute, mixing well. Add melted chocolate, cocoa, and vanilla, mixing until blended. Stir in sour cream. Pour into prepared pan.

Bake at 300° for 1 hour and 40 minutes. Remove from oven; run a knife around edge of pan to release sides. Let cool completely on a wire rack; cover and chill at least 8 hours.

Remove sides of pan; spread cheesecake with cherry pie filling. Spoon whipped topping in center. Garnish, if desired. **Yield: 12 servings.**

Note: For a creamy-textured cheesecake, bake at 300° for 1 hour and 20 minutes.

PER SLICE: 302 CALORIES (18% FROM FAT)
FAT 6.0G (SATURATED FAT 2.8G)
PROTEIN 12.5G CARBOHYDRATE 47.1G
CHOLESTEROL 13MG SODIUM 406MG

Chocolate-Hazelnut Biscotti

2 large eggs
⅔ cup sugar
1 tablespoon Frangelico or other hazelnut-
    flavored liqueur
2 cups sifted cake flour
1½ teaspoons baking powder
¼ teaspoon salt
1½ tablespoons cocoa
⅔ cup hazelnuts, chopped and toasted
Vegetable cooking spray

Beat eggs at medium speed of an electric mixer until foamy. Gradually add sugar, beating at high speed until mixture is thick and pale. Add liqueur, beating until blended.

Combine flour and next 3 ingredients; fold into egg mixture. Fold in nuts. Cover and chill 30 minutes.

Coat a large cookie sheet with cooking spray. Divide dough into 3 portions, and spoon portions onto cookie sheet 2 inches apart. Shape each portion into an 8- x 1½-inch strip. Cover and chill 30 minutes; reshape, if necessary.

Bake at 375° for 20 minutes or until lightly browned. Remove to wire racks to cool. Cut diagonally into ½-inch-thick slices. Lay slices flat on cookie sheet. Bake at 375° for 5 minutes; turn slices over, and bake 5 additional minutes. Remove to wire racks to cool. **Yield: 3½ dozen.**

PER COOKIE: 47 CALORIES (26% FROM FAT)
FAT 1.4G (SATURATED FAT 0.2G)
PROTEIN 1.0G CARBOHYDRATE 7.8G
CHOLESTEROL 11MG SODIUM 17MG

Oatmeal-Raisin Cookies

Oatmeal-Raisin Cookies

¼ cup margarine, softened
½ cup sugar
½ cup firmly packed brown sugar
½ cup egg substitute
2 teaspoons vanilla extract
¾ cup all-purpose flour
¼ teaspoon baking soda
⅛ teaspoon salt
1½ cups quick-cooking oats, uncooked
½ cup raisins
Vegetable cooking spray

Beat margarine at medium speed of an electric mixer. Gradually add sugars, beating well. Add egg substitute and vanilla; mix well.

Combine flour and next 3 ingredients. Gradually add to margarine mixture, mixing well. Stir in raisins.

Drop dough by 2 teaspoonfuls onto cookie sheets coated with cooking spray.

Bake at 350° for 10 to 12 minutes or until lightly browned. Remove to wire racks to cool. **Yield: 3 dozen.**

PER COOKIE: 65 CALORIES (21% FROM FAT)
FAT 1.5G (SATURATED FAT 0.3G)
PROTEIN 1.2G CARBOHYDRATE 11.7G
CHOLESTEROL 0MG SODIUM 27MG

Lighten Up Cookies

When making cookies with regular or reduced-calorie margarine, be sure to use stick-type margarine, not a spread. If you are using 100 percent corn oil margarine, the dough may be softer than with other margarines and may need to be chilled if the cookies will be sliced or shaped.

Raspberry-Cherry Cobbler

1 (16-ounce) package frozen unsweetened raspberries, thawed
1 (16-ounce) package frozen no-sugar-added pitted dark sweet cherries, thawed
1 cup sugar
¼ cup all-purpose flour
1 tablespoon lemon juice
⅛ teaspoon ground cinnamon
Vegetable cooking spray
2 cups all-purpose flour
1 tablespoon baking powder
1 teaspoon baking soda
1 teaspoon salt
2 tablespoons sugar
¼ cup reduced-calorie margarine
¾ cup plain nonfat yogurt
¼ cup evaporated fat-free milk

Combine first 6 ingredients, and spoon into an 11- x 7- x 1½-inch baking dish coated with cooking spray.

Combine 2 cups flour and next 4 ingredients in a large bowl; cut in margarine with a pastry blender until mixture is crumbly. Add yogurt and milk, stirring with a fork until dry ingredients are moistened.

Turn dough out onto a lightly floured surface, and knead about 10 times. Roll dough to ½-inch thickness; cut 12 rounds using a 2-inch cutter. Cut 6 diamonds from remaining dough.

Arrange rounds and diamond shapes on top of fruit mixture.

Bake at 425° for 20 to 25 minutes or until bubbly and golden. Remove from oven; lightly coat each biscuit with cooking spray. **Yield: 12 servings.**

PER SERVING: 225 CALORIES (11% FROM FAT)
FAT 2.7G (SATURATED FAT 0.4G)
PROTEIN 4.4G CARBOHYDRATE 47.1G
CHOLESTEROL 0MG SODIUM 403MG

Buttermilk Pie

(pictured on page 715)

⅔ cup sugar
¼ cup cornstarch
2½ cups nonfat buttermilk
3 tablespoons light cream cheese
⅔ cup egg substitute
1 teaspoon grated lemon rind
2 tablespoons lemon juice
½ teaspoon lemon extract
Light Pastry
3 egg whites
½ teaspoon cream of tartar
1 tablespoon sugar
⅛ teaspoon lemon extract
Garnishes: lemon rind curls, fresh mint sprigs

Combine ⅔ cup sugar and cornstarch in a heavy saucepan; gradually stir in buttermilk. Add cream cheese, and cook over medium heat, stirring constantly, until mixture thickens and comes to a boil. Boil, stirring constantly, 1 minute.

Stir about one-fourth of hot mixture gradually into egg substitute; add to remaining hot mixture, stirring constantly. Cook over low heat, stirring constantly, 2 minutes.

Remove from heat; stir in lemon rind, juice, and ½ teaspoon lemon extract. Spoon into baked pastry shell.

Beat egg whites and cream of tartar at medium speed of an electric mixer until foamy. Gradually add 1 tablespoon sugar, beating until stiff peaks form. Stir in ⅛ teaspoon lemon extract. Spread meringue over filling, sealing to edge.

Bake at 325° for 25 to 28 minutes. Garnish, if desired. **Yield: 8 servings.**

Light Pastry

1¼ cups all-purpose flour
⅓ cup margarine
3 tablespoons cold water

Place flour in a bowl; cut in margarine with a pastry blender until mixture is crumbly. Sprinkle cold water (1 tablespoon at a time) evenly over surface; stir with a fork until dry ingredients are moistened.

Shape dough into a ball; gently press between 2 sheets of heavy-duty plastic wrap into a 4-inch circle. Chill 15 minutes.

Roll dough into an 11-inch circle; freeze 5 minutes. Remove top sheet of plastic wrap, and invert into a 9-inch pieplate. Remove plastic wrap. Fold edges under and crimp; prick bottom and sides with a fork.

Bake at 425° for 15 minutes or until golden. Cool on a wire rack. **Yield: one (9-inch) pastry shell.**

PER SERVING: 285 CALORIES (28% FROM FAT)
FAT 8.9G (SATURATED FAT 2.3G)
PROTEIN 8.8G CARBOHYDRATE 42.0G
CHOLESTEROL 6MG SODIUM 253MG

Treat Yourself to Dessert

• Fresh fruit, loaded with vitamins, minerals, and fiber, is always a good dessert choice.
• Angel food cake contains no fat and is a smart selection for healthy eating.
• Frozen fruit sorbet or nonfat frozen yogurt is a delicious substitution for ice cream.

Flaky Apple Turnovers

Flaky Apple Turnovers

2¼ cups peeled, chopped cooking apples
  (¾ pound)
1½ teaspoons lemon juice
¼ cup sugar
1 tablespoon all-purpose flour
½ teaspoon ground cinnamon
⅛ teaspoon salt
⅛ teaspoon ground nutmeg
7 sheets frozen phyllo pastry, thawed
Vegetable cooking spray

Combine apples and lemon juice in a bowl; toss gently. Add sugar and next 4 ingredients; toss well, and set mixture aside.

Keep phyllo covered with a slightly damp towel until ready for use. Working with 1 phyllo sheet at a time, cut each sheet lengthwise into 4 (3½-inch-wide) strips; lightly spray with cooking spray. Stack 2 strips, one on top of the other.

Spoon 1 tablespoon apple mixture onto each stack; spread to within 1 inch of each end. Fold left bottom corner over mixture, forming a triangle. Keep folding back and forth into a triangle to end of stack. Repeat with remaining ingredients.

Place triangles, seam side down, on a baking sheet coated with cooking spray. Lightly spray tops of triangles with cooking spray.

Bake at 400° for 15 minutes or until golden. Serve warm. **Yield: 14 turnovers.**

PER TURNOVER: 60 CALORIES (18% FROM FAT)
FAT 1.2G (SATURATED FAT 0.1G)
PROTEIN 0.8G CARBOHYDRATE 11.7G
CHOLESTEROL 0MG SODIUM 67MG

Old-Fashioned Banana Pudding

½ cup sugar
3 tablespoons cornstarch
⅓ cup water
1 (12-ounce) can evaporated fat-free milk
⅓ cup egg substitute
½ cup nonfat sour cream
1 teaspoon vanilla extract
22 vanilla wafers
3 medium bananas, sliced
3 egg whites
¼ teaspoon cream of tartar
1 tablespoon sugar

Combine ½ cup sugar and cornstarch in a heavy saucepan; stir in next 3 ingredients. Cook over medium heat, stirring constantly, until mixture boils. Boil, stirring constantly, 1 minute. Remove from heat; fold in sour cream and vanilla.

Place a layer of wafers in bottom of a 1½-quart baking dish. Spoon one-third of pudding over wafers; top with half of bananas. Repeat layers, ending with pudding; place wafers around edge.

Beat egg whites and cream of tartar at medium speed of an electric mixer until foamy. Gradually add 1 tablespoon sugar; beat until stiff peaks form. Spread meringue over pudding, sealing to edge.

Bake at 325° for 25 to 28 minutes. **Yield: 10 (½-cup) servings.**

PER SERVING: 172 CALORIES (12% FROM FAT)
FAT 2.2G (SATURATED FAT 0.1G)
PROTEIN 6.0G CARBOHYDRATE 32.2G
CHOLESTEROL 1MG SODIUM 112MG

Peach Sherbet

1 (8-ounce) carton plain low-fat yogurt
½ cup orange juice
⅓ cup honey
2 cups peeled, sliced ripe peaches or 2 cups frozen peaches, partially thawed

Combine all ingredients in container of an electric blender or food processor. Cover; process until peaches are finely chopped. Pour into an 8-inch square pan; freeze until almost firm.

Remove from freezer; break into chunks, and place in blender container. Process until fluffy but not thawed. Return mixture to pan; freeze until firm. Let stand at room temperature 10 minutes before serving. **Yield: 6 (½-cup) servings.**

PER SERVING: 115 CALORIES (5% FROM FAT)
FAT 0.6G (SATURATED FAT 0.4G)
PROTEIN 2.6G CARBOHYDRATE 26.7G
CHOLESTEROL 2MG SODIUM 27MG

Banana Yogurt Ice Milk

1 envelope unflavored gelatin
3 tablespoons water
1 cup mashed ripe banana
1 cup evaporated fat-free milk
1 (8-ounce) carton plain low-fat yogurt
3 tablespoons honey
1 kiwifruit, peeled and thinly sliced
¼ cup blueberries
¼ cup raspberries

Sprinkle gelatin over water in a saucepan; let stand 1 minute. Cook over medium heat, stirring until gelatin dissolves; remove from heat.

Combine banana and next 3 ingredients. Stir into gelatin. Spoon into an 8-inch square pan; freeze until firm.

Remove from freezer; break frozen mixture into chunks. Spoon into a bowl; beat at medium speed of an electric mixer until smooth. Return mixture to pan; freeze until firm. Let stand at room temperature 10 minutes.

Serve with kiwifruit, blueberries, and raspberries. **Yield: 7 (½-cup) servings.**

PER SERVING: 120 CALORIES (6% FROM FAT)
FAT 0.8G (SATURATED FAT 0.4G)
PROTEIN 5.9G CARBOHYDRATE 23.8G
CHOLESTEROL 3MG SODIUM 67MG

Banana Yogurt Ice Milk

Fresh Strawberry Ice Milk

(pictured on page 715)

4 cups fresh strawberries
1½ cups sugar, divided
3 cups fat-free milk
2 envelopes unflavored gelatin
½ cup egg substitute
2 (12-ounce) cans evaporated fat-free milk
1½ tablespoons vanilla extract
3 drops of red food coloring
Garnish: 16 whole fresh strawberries

Place strawberries in container of an electric blender or food processor, and process just until chopped. Sprinkle strawberries with ½ cup sugar, and set aside.

Combine remaining 1 cup sugar and fat-free milk in a saucepan; sprinkle gelatin over mixture, and let stand 1 minute. Cook mixture over medium heat, stirring constantly, until sugar and gelatin dissolve. Gradually stir in egg substitute; cook mixture 1 minute. Remove mixture from heat and chill.

Stir in chopped strawberries, evaporated fat-free milk, vanilla, and food coloring. Pour into container of a 1-gallon hand-turned or electric freezer.

Freeze according to manufacturer's instructions. Pack ice milk with additional ice and rock salt; let stand 1 hour before serving (ice milk will be soft). Garnish, if desired. **Yield: 16 (1-cup) servings.**

PER SERVING: 143 CALORIES (2% FROM FAT)
FAT 0.3G (SATURATED FAT 0.1G)
PROTEIN 6.5G CARBOHYDRATE 28.7G
CHOLESTEROL 3MG SODIUM 86MG

Cranberries Jubilee

Cranberries Jubilee

1 (12-ounce) package fresh cranberries
1 (10.25-ounce) jar reduced-sugar strawberry jam
1 teaspoon grated orange rind
⅓ cup brandy
2 tablespoons brandy
7 cups vanilla low-fat frozen yogurt

Combine first 4 ingredients in a saucepan. Bring to a boil over medium heat; cook 5 minutes, stirring constantly, or until cranberries pop and sauce begins to thicken (do not overcook). Remove from heat, and let cool slightly.

Place 2 tablespoons brandy in a small, long-handled saucepan; heat just until warm (do not boil). Remove from heat. Ignite brandy, and pour over cranberries; stir until flames die down. Serve immediately over frozen yogurt. **Yield: 14 (½-cup) servings.**

PER SERVING: 124 CALORIES (12% FROM FAT)
FAT 1.7G (SATURATED FAT 1.2G)
PROTEIN 2.6G CARBOHYDRATE 25.4G
CHOLESTEROL 8MG SODIUM 30MG

Fish and Shellfish

Low in fat and calories and rich in protein, fish and shellfish offer many tasty and healthful options. And for an added bonus—they're easy to prepare and quick to cook.

Crab Cakes, Breaded Catfish with Creole Sauce, Fillets Tomatillo

Crab-and-Mushroom Casserole, Crab-and-Shrimp Étouffée, Baked Oysters Italiano

Steamed Fish and Vegetables, Poached Fish with Greek Sauce, Barbecued Shrimp

Blackened Red Snapper, Peppered Snapper with Creamy Dill Sauce

Grilled Marinated Grouper (page 733)

Breaded Catfish with Creole Sauce

Breaded Catfish with Creole Sauce

½ cup yellow cornmeal
¼ teaspoon pepper
2 tablespoons evaporated fat-free milk
4 (4-ounce) farm-raised catfish fillets
Olive oil-flavored vegetable cooking spray
Creole Sauce

Combine cornmeal and pepper; set aside. Pour milk into a shallow dish. Dip fillets in milk; dredge in cornmeal mixture.

Place fish on a baking sheet coated with cooking spray. Spray each fillet lightly with cooking spray.

Bake at 425° for 10 minutes or until fish flakes easily when tested with a fork. Broil fish 3 inches from heat (with electric oven door partially opened) 1 minute or until browned. Serve fish with Creole Sauce. **Yield: 4 servings.**

Creole Sauce

Olive oil-flavored vegetable cooking spray
1 teaspoon reduced-calorie margarine
¾ cup chopped onion
½ cup chopped celery
2 cloves garlic, minced
1 cup coarsely chopped tomato
1 cup sliced fresh okra
½ cup chopped green pepper
½ teaspoon dried basil
½ teaspoon dried oregano
½ teaspoon dried thyme
¼ teaspoon salt
¼ teaspoon ground red pepper
¼ teaspoon freshly ground black pepper
1¼ cups ready-to-serve, no-salt-added
    chicken broth
1 (8-ounce) can no-salt-added tomato sauce
Dash of hot sauce

Coat a large nonstick skillet with cooking spray; place skillet over medium-high heat. Add margarine, onion, celery, and garlic; cook, stirring

constantly, until vegetables are tender. Add tomato and remaining ingredients; bring to a boil. Reduce heat, and simmer, uncovered, 20 minutes, stirring occasionally. **Yield: 3 cups.**

PER SERVING: 267 CALORIES (23% FROM FAT)
FAT 6.8G (SATURATED FAT 1.3G)
PROTEIN 25.0G CARBOHYDRATE 26.3G
CHOLESTEROL 66MG SODIUM 275MG

Grilled Marinated Grouper

(pictured on page 731)

1 teaspoon grated lemon rind
⅓ cup fresh lemon juice
2 teaspoons prepared horseradish
1 teaspoon dried Italian seasoning
½ teaspoon salt
¼ teaspoon pepper
1 clove garlic, halved
1 pound grouper fillet or other lean white fish,
    cut into 4 pieces
Vegetable cooking spray

Combine first 7 ingredients in container of an electric blender or food processor; cover and process 20 seconds. Arrange fish in a 13- x 9- x 2-inch baking dish. Pour marinade over fish, turning to coat both sides; cover and marinate in refrigerator 4 hours.

Place fish in a wire basket coated with cooking spray. Cook, covered with grill lid, over medium-hot coals (350° to 400°) 7 to 8 minutes on each side or until fish flakes easily when tested with a fork. **Yield: 4 servings.**

PER SERVING: 111 CALORIES (11% FROM FAT)
FAT 1.3G (SATURATED FAT 0.3G)
PROTEIN 21.4G CARBOHYDRATE 2.8G
CHOLESTEROL 40MG SODIUM 341MG

Steamed Fish and Vegetables

Steamed Fish and Vegetables

4 small round red potatoes
2 (4-ounce) grouper fillets or other lean
      white fish
2 small yellow squash
8 medium okra
½ pound fresh or frozen green beans
1 cup sweet red pepper slices
½ cup sliced onion
1 tablespoon reduced-calorie margarine
½ teaspoon salt-free herb-and-spice blend

Place potatoes in a vegetable steamer over boiling water; cover and steam 10 minutes. Add fish and next 3 ingredients; cover and steam 10 minutes. Add red pepper slices and onion.

Dot with margarine, and sprinkle with herb-and-spice blend; cover and steam 5 minutes.
Yield: 2 servings.

PER SERVING: 316 CALORIES (16% FROM FAT)
FAT 5.5G (SATURATED FAT 0.9G)
PROTEIN 29.2G CARBOHYDRATE 40.1G
CHOLESTEROL 41MG SODIUM 126MG

Poached Fish with Greek Sauce

2 tablespoons chopped onion
2 sprigs fresh parsley
½ bay leaf
⅛ teaspoon salt
4 whole peppercorns
½ cup Chablis or other dry white wine
½ cup water
4 (4-ounce) skinned flounder fillets or other lean white fish
Greek Sauce

Combine first 7 ingredients in an 11- x 7- x 1½-inch baking dish. Cover with heavy-duty plastic wrap; fold back a small corner of wrap for steam to escape.

Microwave at HIGH 5 minutes or until boiling. Uncover; arrange fillets in liquid with thickest portion to outside of dish.

Cover and microwave at HIGH 4 minutes, giving dish a half-turn after 2 minutes. Cook until fish turns opaque. Let stand, covered, 3 to 5 minutes. Fish is done if it flakes easily when tested with a fork. Remove bay leaf.

Remove to a serving dish, reserving liquid. Serve with Greek Sauce. **Yield: 4 servings.**

Greek Sauce

¼ cup reduced-fat mayonnaise
¼ cup plain low-fat yogurt
¼ cup minced fresh parsley
2 tablespoons lemon juice
⅛ teaspoon fresh ground pepper
⅛ teaspoon garlic powder
2 tablespoons reserved poaching liquid

Combine all ingredients in a small bowl; stir well. **Yield: ¾ cup.**

PER SERVING: 138 CALORIES (17% FROM FAT)
FAT 2.6G (SATURATED FAT 0.5G)
PROTEIN 21.5G CARBOHYDRATE 6.2G
CHOLESTEROL 59MG SODIUM 279MG

Fillets Tomatillo

1 cup finely chopped fresh tomatillo (4 large tomatillos)
¼ cup finely chopped onion
¼ cup finely chopped celery
2 tablespoons chopped green pepper
1 clove garlic, minced
2 teaspoons olive oil
¼ cup clam juice or chicken broth
2 tablespoons canned chopped green chiles
2 tablespoons lime juice
½ teaspoon chopped fresh cilantro
½ teaspoon ground cumin
¼ teaspoon dried oregano
⅛ teaspoon salt
⅛ teaspoon ground red pepper
4 (4-ounce) orange roughy fillets
Vegetable cooking spray

Cook first 5 ingredients in olive oil in a medium skillet over medium-high heat, stirring constantly, 5 minutes.

Add clam juice and next 7 ingredients; cover, reduce heat, and simmer 15 minutes, stirring occasionally. Remove from heat, and keep warm.

Arrange fish in a grill basket coated with cooking spray. Cook, covered with grill lid, over medium-hot coals (350° to 400°) 7 to 8 minutes on each side or until fish flakes easily when tested with a fork. Serve fillets with tomatillo mixture. **Yield: 4 servings.**

PER SERVING: 124 CALORIES (27% FROM FAT)
FAT 3.7G (SATURATED FAT 0.3G)
PROTEIN 17.4G CARBOHYDRATE 4.8G
CHOLESTEROL 23MG SODIUM 193MG

Blackened Red Snapper

Vegetable cooking spray
1 tablespoon olive oil
¼ cup minced onion
2 cloves garlic, minced
½ tablespoon paprika
¼ teaspoon ground white pepper
¼ teaspoon ground red pepper
¼ teaspoon black pepper
¼ teaspoon dried oregano
4 (5-ounce) skinned red snapper fillets

Coat a nonstick skillet with cooking spray; place over medium-high heat until hot. Add olive oil, onion, and garlic; cook, stirring constantly, until onion is tender.

Stir in paprika and next 4 ingredients; set aside to cool. Spread cooled spice mixture on both sides of fish fillets.

Place fish on rack coated with cooking spray; place rack in a broiler pan. Broil 3 inches from heat (with electric oven door partially opened) 7 to 9 minutes or until fish flakes easily when tested with a fork (fish will be lightly charred). **Yield: 4 servings.**

PER SERVING: 183 CALORIES (28% FROM FAT)
FAT 5.6G (SATURATED FAT 0.9G)
PROTEIN 29.5G CARBOHYDRATE 2.2G
CHOLESTEROL 52MG SODIUM 64MG

Peppered Snapper with Creamy Dill Sauce

4 (4-ounce) red snapper fillets
2 teaspoons olive oil, divided
2 tablespoons coarsely ground pepper
Vegetable cooking spray
2 cups hot cooked rice (cooked without salt or fat)
Creamy Dill Sauce

Brush snapper on both sides with 1 teaspoon olive oil; sprinkle with pepper, and gently press into fish. Cover and let stand 15 minutes.

Coat a large nonstick skillet with cooking spray; add remaining 1 teaspoon olive oil, and place over medium heat. Cook fillets on both sides 3 to 5 minutes or until fish flakes easily when tested with a fork. Remove from heat; keep warm.

Spoon rice evenly onto serving plates; top each with a fillet and Creamy Dill Sauce. Serve immediately. **Yield: 4 servings.**

Creamy Dill Sauce

1 (10-ounce) container refrigerated reduced-calorie Alfredo sauce
2 tablespoons Chablis or other dry white wine
1 teaspoon dried dill

Combine all ingredients in a small heavy saucepan; cook, stirring constantly, over medium heat until thoroughly heated. Remove from heat; keep warm. **Yield: 1 cup.**

PER SERVING: 389 CALORIES (28% FROM FAT)
FAT 11.9G (SATURATED FAT 6.8G)
PROTEIN 31.7G CARBOHYDRATE 33.9G
CHOLESTEROL 72MG SODIUM 1825MG

Red Snapper Veracruz

Vegetable cooking spray
½ cup chopped green pepper
¼ cup chopped onion
2 cloves garlic, minced
1½ cups chopped, peeled tomato (about 2)
2 tablespoons chopped green chiles, drained
1 tablespoon chopped fresh cilantro or parsley
¼ teaspoon salt
¼ teaspoon hot sauce
Dash of ground white pepper
4 (4-ounce) red snapper fillets
2 teaspoons margarine, melted

Coat a nonstick skillet with cooking spray; place over medium-high heat until hot. Add green pepper, onion, and garlic; cook, stirring constantly, until tender.

Stir in tomato and next 5 ingredients; cook, stirring frequently, until thoroughly heated.

Brush fish with margarine; place in a grill basket coated with cooking spray. Cook, covered with grill lid, over medium-hot coals (350° to 400°) 5 minutes on each side or until fish flakes easily when tested with a fork. Serve fish with tomato mixture. **Yield: 4 servings.**

PER SERVING: 154 CALORIES (23% FROM FAT)
FAT 4.0G (SATURATED FAT 0.7G)
PROTEIN 23.4G CARBOHYDRATE 5.7G
CHOLESTEROL 40MG SODIUM 226MG

Poached Salmon with Horseradish Sauce

4 cups water
1 lemon, sliced
1 carrot, sliced
1 stalk celery, sliced
1 teaspoon peppercorns
4 (4-ounce) salmon steaks
Horseradish Sauce

Combine first 5 ingredients in a large skillet; bring to a boil over medium-high heat. Cover, reduce heat, and simmer 10 minutes.

Add salmon steaks; cover and simmer 10 minutes. Remove skillet from heat; let stand 8 minutes. Remove salmon steaks to serving plate; serve with Horseradish Sauce. **Yield: 4 servings.**

Horseradish Sauce

¼ cup nonfat mayonnaise
¼ cup plain nonfat yogurt
2 teaspoons prepared horseradish
1½ teaspoons lemon juice
1½ teaspoons chopped fresh chives

Combine all ingredients in a small bowl; cover and chill. **Yield: ½ cup.**

Note: Because salmon is high in omega-3 fatty acid (a polyunsaturated fat in fish with dark, moist flesh), this recipe derives more than 30 percent of total calories per serving from fat.

PER SERVING: 205 CALORIES (41% FROM FAT)
FAT 9.4G (SATURATED FAT 1.7G)
PROTEIN 24.1G CARBOHYDRATE 4.5G
CHOLESTEROL 74MG SODIUM 259MG

Salmon-Pesto Vermicelli

1 cup firmly packed fresh basil leaves
¼ cup commercial oil-free Italian dressing
2 tablespoons water
3 cloves garlic, crushed
1 (1-pound) salmon fillet
¼ teaspoon cracked pepper
Vegetable cooking spray
4 cups cooked vermicelli (cooked without salt or fat)
6 lemon wedges (optional)

Combine first 4 ingredients in food processor bowl fitted with knife blade. Process 2 minutes, scraping sides of bowl occasionally. Set aside.

Sprinkle fish with pepper, and place, skin side down, on a broiler pan coated with cooking spray. Broil 6 inches from heat (with electric oven door partially opened) 5 minutes.

Turn fish over carefully, and broil (with electric oven door partially opened) 4 minutes or until fish flakes easily when tested with a fork. Remove from pan; cool. Remove and discard skin; break fish into bite-size pieces.

Combine fish, basil mixture, and vermicelli in a large bowl; toss gently. Serve with lemon wedges, if desired. **Yield: 6 servings.**

PER SERVING: 265 CALORIES (24% FROM FAT)
FAT 7.0G (SATURATED FAT 1.2G)
PROTEIN 20.3G CARBOHYDRATE 28.5G
CHOLESTEROL 49MG SODIUM 146MG

Seared Tuna Steaks on Mixed Greens with Lemon-Basil Vinaigrette

4 (4-ounce) tuna steaks
1 tablespoon reduced-sodium Cajun seasoning
Vegetable cooking spray
8 cups mixed salad greens
Lemon-Basil Vinaigrette
Garnish: finely chopped sweet red pepper

Sprinkle tuna evenly with seasoning.

Coat food rack with cooking spray; place rack on grill over medium-hot coals (350° to 400°). Place tuna on rack.

Cook, covered with grill lid, 5 minutes on each side or until done.

Cover and chill at least 8 hours.

Combine salad greens and half of Lemon-Basil Vinaigrette; arrange on 4 plates. Top each with a tuna steak, and drizzle evenly with remaining vinaigrette. Garnish, if desired. **Yield: 4 servings.**

Lemon-Basil Vinaigrette

2 lemons, peeled, sectioned, and finely chopped
2 tablespoons white wine vinegar
1 tablespoon vegetable oil
1 tablespoon fresh basil, finely chopped
¼ teaspoon cracked black pepper
¼ teaspoon hot sauce

Combine all ingredients in a jar. Cover tightly, and shake vigorously. **Yield: ½ cup.**

PER SERVING: 189 CALORIES (24% FROM FAT)
FAT 5.1G (SATURATED FAT 0.3G)
PROTEIN 28.4G CARBOHYDRATE 7.7G
CHOLESTEROL 51MG SODIUM 59MG

Crab Cakes

2 egg whites, lightly beaten
2 tablespoons reduced-calorie mayonnaise
2 teaspoons chopped fresh parsley
1¼ teaspoons Old Bay seasoning
1 teaspoon reduced-sodium Worcestershire sauce
1 teaspoon dry mustard
¼ teaspoon pepper
½ cup soft breadcrumbs
1 pound fresh, lump crabmeat, drained
Olive oil-flavored vegetable cooking spray

Combine first 7 ingredients. Stir in soft breadcrumbs and crabmeat, and shape into 8 (2½-inch) patties. Place on a baking sheet lined with wax paper; chill 30 minutes.

Coat a large nonstick skillet with cooking spray; place over medium-high heat until hot. Add crab cakes, and cook 3 minutes on each side or until browned. **Yield: 4 servings.**

Note: The crab cakes may be broiled on a nonstick baking sheet coated with cooking spray. Broil on one side for 5 minutes or until golden.

PER SERVING: 166 CALORIES (25% FROM FAT)
FAT 4.6G (SATURATED FAT 0.6G)
PROTEIN 25.4G CARBOHYDRATE 4.2G
CHOLESTEROL 116MG SODIUM 613MG

Preparing Fish

• Cook seafood within 24 hours of purchase. If a fish smells "fishy" or like ammonia, don't buy it.
• To keep grilled fish from sticking, spray the grill basket or rack with vegetable cooking spray before grilling.
• The amount of grilling time depends on the kind of fish and its thickness. A good guide is to allow 6 to 12 minutes per inch of thickness.

Crab Cakes

Crab-and-Mushroom Casserole

¼ cup finely chopped onion
¼ cup finely chopped celery
¼ cup finely chopped green pepper
2 tablespoons reduced-calorie margarine,
    melted
1 pound fresh mushrooms, sliced
¼ cup all-purpose flour
2 cups low-sodium chicken broth
½ cup egg substitute
1 pound fresh crabmeat, drained and flaked
1 tablespoon salt-free herb-and-spice blend
¾ teaspoon salt
⅛ teaspoon ground ginger
Vegetable cooking spray
¼ cup (1 ounce) shredded reduced-fat sharp
    Cheddar cheese

Cook onion, celery, and green pepper in margarine in a large skillet, stirring constantly, until tender. Add mushrooms, and cook 10 minutes.

Add flour, stirring until smooth. Cook 1 minute, stirring constantly. Gradually add chicken broth; cook over medium heat, stirring constantly, until mixture is thickened and bubbly.

Stir one-fourth of hot mixture into egg substitute; add to remaining hot mixture, stirring constantly. Stir in crabmeat and next 3 ingredients.

Spoon mixture into an 11- x 7- x 1½-inch baking dish coated with cooking spray.

Bake at 350° for 35 minutes; sprinkle with cheese, and bake 5 additional minutes. **Yield: 6 servings.**

Per Serving: 179 Calories (28% from Fat)
Fat 5.6g (Saturated Fat 1.3g)
Protein 21.0g Carbohydrate 11.6g
Cholesterol 74mg Sodium 628mg

Crab-and-Shrimp Étouffée

2 pounds unpeeled medium-size fresh shrimp
⅔ cup chopped onion
¼ cup chopped green pepper
¼ cup chopped celery
3 cloves garlic, minced
2 tablespoons reduced-calorie margarine,
    melted
⅔ cup no-salt-added chicken broth
⅓ cup white wine
1 tablespoon no-salt-added tomato paste
¼ cup chopped green onions
2 tablespoons chopped fresh parsley
2 teaspoons low-sodium Worcestershire sauce
¼ teaspoon salt
¼ teaspoon pepper
⅛ teaspoon hot sauce
1½ tablespoons cornstarch
⅓ cup no-salt-added chicken broth
12 ounces fresh crabmeat, drained and flaked
2 cups hot cooked rice (cooked without salt
    or fat)

Peel and devein shrimp; set aside. Cook ⅔ cup chopped onion and next 3 ingredients in margarine in a large skillet until tender.

Stir in ⅔ cup chicken broth and next 8 ingredients. Add shrimp; cover and simmer 5 minutes, stirring occasionally.

Combine cornstarch and ⅓ cup chicken broth; add to shrimp mixture. Cook, stirring constantly, until mixture boils; boil 1 minute, stirring constantly.

Stir in crabmeat, and cook until thoroughly heated. Serve over hot cooked rice. **Yield: 6 servings**.

Per Serving: 297 Calories (17% from Fat)
Fat 5.5g (Saturated Fat 0.8g)
Protein 35.6g Carbohydrate 23.7g
Cholesterol 224mg Sodium 464mg

Baked Oysters Italiano

Baked Oysters Italiano

Rock salt
3 tablespoons commercial oil-free Italian
     dressing
2 teaspoons lemon juice
¼ teaspoon hot sauce
2 tablespoons Italian-seasoned
     breadcrumbs
1 tablespoon grated Parmesan cheese
⅛ teaspoon garlic powder
⅛ teaspoon dried Italian seasoning
12 medium-size fresh raw oysters on the
      half shell
1 tablespoon minced fresh parsley

Sprinkle a thin layer of rock salt in a shallow baking pan.

Combine Italian dressing, lemon juice, and hot sauce; set aside. Combine breadcrumbs and next 3 ingredients; set aside.

Place oysters (in shells) over rock salt. Sprinkle each oyster evenly with Italian dressing mixture and breadcrumb mixture.

Bake at 425° for 6 to 8 minutes or until edges of oysters begin to curl. Sprinkle with fresh parsley. **Yield: 12 oysters.**

PER OYSTER: 18 CALORIES (25% FROM FAT)
FAT 0.5G (SATURATED FAT 0.2G)
PROTEIN 1.4G CARBOHYDRATE 2.0G
CHOLESTEROL 8MG SODIUM 98MG

Grilled Orange Scallops with Cilantro-Lime Vinaigrette

Grilled Orange Scallops with Cilantro-Lime Vinaigrette

1 cup orange juice
3 tablespoons chopped fresh basil
18 sea scallops
1 head Bibb lettuce
4 cups mixed baby lettuces
Cilantro-Lime Vinaigrette
30 yellow pear-shaped cherry tomatoes
30 red pear-shaped cherry tomatoes
2 cucumbers, cut into thin strips
Garnishes: fresh basil sprigs, thin orange rind strips

Combine orange juice and basil in a shallow dish; add scallops, tossing to coat.

Cover dish, and chill about 1 hour. Uncover and drain, discarding marinade.

Cook scallops, covered with grill lid, over hot coals (400° to 500°) 3 to 5 minutes on each side or until done.

Combine lettuces in a bowl; drizzle with Cilantro-Lime Vinaigrette, and toss gently.

Arrange lettuces on individual plates, and top with scallops, tomatoes, and cucumber. Garnish, if desired. Serve immediately. **Yield: 6 servings.**

Cilantro-Lime Vinaigrette

¼ cup sugar
¼ cup extra-virgin olive oil
2 tablespoons lime juice
2 tablespoons rice wine vinegar
1 clove garlic, minced
1 shallot, minced
1½ teaspoons fresh cilantro leaves, finely chopped

Combine all ingredients in a jar. Cover tightly, and shake mixture vigorously. **Yield: ¾ cup.**

Note: Scallops may be grilled directly on grill rack or, if rack openings are too large, in a grill basket or threaded on skewers.

PER SERVING: 268 CALORIES (29% FROM FAT)
FAT 8.5G (SATURATED FAT 1.1G)
PROTEIN 25.4G CARBOHYDRATE 23.7G
CHOLESTEROL 45MG SODIUM 240MG

Broiled Marinated Shrimp

2 tablespoons sliced green onions
2 cloves garlic, minced
Vegetable cooking spray
¾ cup ready-to-serve, no-salt-added chicken broth
3 tablespoons reduced-fat creamy peanut butter spread
1 tablespoon reduced-sodium soy sauce
1 tablespoon lemon juice
1 teaspoon chili powder
1 teaspoon brown sugar
½ teaspoon ground ginger
1 pound unpeeled large fresh shrimp

Cook green onions and garlic in a skillet coated with cooking spray over medium heat, stirring constantly, about 3 minutes.

Add chicken broth and next 6 ingredients, stirring until smooth. Reduce heat; simmer 10 minutes, stirring often. Remove from heat; cool.

Peel and devein shrimp, leaving tails attached. Place shrimp in sauce; turn to coat. Cover and chill 1 hour. Remove from sauce; discard sauce. Thread shrimp onto skewers.

Broil 6 inches from heat (with electric oven door partially opened) 5 minutes on each side or until shrimp turn pink. **Yield: 4 servings.**

PER SERVING: 106 CALORIES (27% FROM FAT)
FAT 3.2G (SATURATED FAT 0.6G)
PROTEIN 15.1G CARBOHYDRATE 4.3G
CHOLESTEROL 124MG SODIUM 234MG

Barbecued Shrimp

Barbecued Shrimp

Olive oil-flavored vegetable cooking spray
¼ **cup diced onion**
1 **tablespoon brown sugar**
1 **tablespoon dry mustard**
¼ **teaspoon garlic powder**
1 **tablespoon white vinegar**
½ **cup reduced-calorie ketchup**
Dash of hot sauce
2 **tablespoons fresh rosemary, chopped**
24 **unpeeled jumbo fresh shrimp**
1 **lemon, cut into wedges**

Coat a nonstick skillet with cooking spray; place over medium-high heat until hot. Add onion, and cook, stirring constantly, until tender; remove from heat.

Add brown sugar and next 6 ingredients; stir until well blended. Let stand 2 to 3 hours.

Peel and devein shrimp; place in a shallow dish. Pour marinade over shrimp, turning to coat both sides. Cover and chill 1 hour.

Soak 4 (8-inch) wooden skewers in water 30 minutes. Thread tail and neck of six shrimp on each skewer so shrimp will lie flat.

Cook shrimp, covered with grill lid, over medium-hot coals (350° to 400°) 3 minutes on each side or until shrimp turn pink. Squeeze lemon over shrimp and serve. **Yield: 4 servings.**

PER SERVING: 191 CALORIES (11% FROM FAT)
FAT 2.3G (SATURATED FAT 0.5G)
PROTEIN 35.9G CARBOHYDRATE 4.2G
CHOLESTEROL 332MG SODIUM 385MG

Meatless Main Dishes

Enjoy our best bean, pasta, and cheese entrées.
These dishes prove that eating meatless meals doesn't mean
settling for less taste or less nutrition.

Black Bean-and-Barley Salad, Mamma Mia Pasta, Artichoke Quiche

Mediterranean Ravioli, Roasted Chiles Rellenos with Tomatillo Sauce, Fiesta Quiche

Vegetable-Cheese Enchiladas, Fettuccine Primavera, Light Chiles Rellenos

Lentil Spaghetti Sauce, Three-Bean Enchiladas, Vegetable Burritos

Vegetable Pizzas (page 750)

Black Bean-and-Barley Salad

Black Bean-and-Barley Salad

¾ cup barley, uncooked
¼ cup lime juice
2 tablespoons water
1 tablespoon vegetable oil
1 teaspoon sugar
½ teaspoon garlic powder
¼ teaspoon salt
¼ teaspoon ground black pepper
¼ teaspoon ground cumin
¼ teaspoon ground red pepper
1 (15-ounce) can black beans, drained and
    rinsed
Leaf lettuce
1 cup chopped tomato
¼ cup (2 ounces) shredded reduced-fat
    Cheddar cheese
¼ cup sliced green onions

Cook barley according to package directions; drain and set aside.

Combine lime juice and next 8 ingredients in a jar. Cover tightly, and shake vigorously.

Pour half of dressing over barley; cover and chill 8 hours, stirring mixture occasionally.

Combine beans and remaining dressing; cover and chill 8 hours, stirring occasionally.

Spoon barley mixture evenly onto lettuce-lined plates. Top evenly with black beans, tomato, cheese, and green onions. **Yield: 4 servings**.

PER SERVING: 342 CALORIES (20% FROM FAT)
FAT 7.6G (SATURATED FAT 0.3G)
PROTEIN 17.4G CARBOHYDRATE 53.7G
CHOLESTEROL 10MG SODIUM 260MG

Black Bean Terrine with Fresh Tomato Coulis and Jalapeño Sauce

3 (15-ounce) cans black beans, drained and
   rinsed
⅓ cup egg substitute
1½ teaspoons salt-free, extra-spicy herb-and-
   spice blend
1½ teaspoons ground cumin
¼ teaspoon freshly ground pepper
Vegetable cooking spray
Fresh Tomato Coulis
Jalapeño Sauce

Position knife blade in food processor bowl; add first 5 ingredients, and process until smooth, stopping occasionally to scrape down sides.

Pack bean mixture into an 8½- x 4½- x 3-inch loafpan coated with cooking spray. Cover with aluminum foil, and place in a large, shallow pan. Add hot water to large pan to depth of 1 inch. Bake at 350° for 55 to 60 minutes or until a knife inserted in center comes out clean.

Remove loafpan from water, and place a small weight on top of bean mixture; cover and chill 8 hours. Cut into 16 (½-inch) slices; serve each slice with 1½ tablespoons Fresh Tomato Coulis and 1 tablespoon Jalapeño Sauce. Yield: 16 slices.

Note: For salt-free, extra-spicy herb-and-spice blend, we used extra-spicy Mrs. Dash.

Fresh Tomato Coulis

4 medium to large tomatoes, peeled and
   seeded
1 clove garlic, halved
3 tablespoons chopped fresh cilantro
2 tablespoons rice wine vinegar
1 teaspoon dried thyme
1 teaspoon freshly ground pepper

Place tomatoes in container of an electric blender; process until smooth. Set puree aside.

Place colander in a large bowl; line colander with 2 layers of cheesecloth or a coffee filter. Pour puree into colander; cover loosely with plastic wrap, and chill 24 hours. Discard liquid in bowl.

Combine puree, garlic, and remaining ingredients in container of an electric blender; process until smooth. Yield: 1½ cups.

Jalapeño Sauce

¾ cup plain nonfat yogurt
1 clove garlic, minced
¼ cup seeded and chopped jalapeño peppers
¼ cup chopped fresh cilantro
1 teaspoon frozen unsweetened orange juice
   concentrate, thawed
½ teaspoon ground cumin
¼ teaspoon salt

Combine all ingredients in a small bowl. Yield: 1 cup.

PER SERVING: 136 CALORIES (6% FROM FAT)
FAT 0.9G (SATURATED FAT 0.1G)
PROTEIN 9.3G CARBOHYDRATE 24.5G
CHOLESTEROL 0MG SODIUM 289MG

What are Legumes?

Legumes are plants that produce pods containing edible seeds.
• The best known legumes are black beans, black-eyed peas, chickpeas, kidney beans, lentils, split peas, pinto beans, and white beans.
• Legumes are loaded with complex carbohydrates, fiber, vitamins, minerals, and protein.
• For an added bonus, legumes have no cholesterol and are very low in fat and sodium.

Fettuccine Primavera

1 small onion, chopped
Vegetable cooking spray
1 (10-ounce) package frozen snow pea pods,
     thawed
1 sweet red pepper, cut into thin strips
1 cup fresh broccoli flowerets
½ cup sliced fresh mushrooms
Alfredo Sauce
1 (12-ounce) package fettuccine, cooked
     without salt or fat

Cook onion in a large nonstick skillet coated
with cooking spray over medium heat, stirring
constantly, until tender. Add snow peas and next
3 ingredients; cook, stirring constantly, until vegetables are crisp-tender.
  Stir in Alfredo Sauce; add fettuccine, and toss
gently. Serve immediately. **Yield: 6 servings**.

Alfredo Sauce

2 cups nonfat cottage cheese
3 tablespoons grated Parmesan cheese
2 tablespoons butter-flavored granules
½ cup evaporated fat-free milk
½ teaspoon chicken-flavored bouillon
     granules
½ teaspoon dried basil
¼ teaspoon ground black pepper
Dash of ground red pepper

Combine all ingredients in container of an
electric blender; process until smooth, stopping
once to scrape down sides.
  Pour into a small saucepan; cook sauce over
low heat, stirring constantly, until thoroughly
heated. **Yield: 2¾ cups**.

PER SERVING: 339 CALORIES (6% FROM FAT)
FAT 2.1G (SATURATED FAT 0.7G)
PROTEIN 23.3G CARBOHYDRATE 57.1G
CHOLESTEROL 6MG SODIUM 509MG

Mamma Mia Pasta

6 ounces wheel-shaped (rotelle) pasta,
     uncooked
4 cloves garlic, minced
1 medium onion, finely chopped
2 teaspoons olive oil
1 (14½-ounce) can no-salt-added whole
     tomatoes, undrained and chopped
1 tablespoon tomato paste
2 teaspoons sugar
2 teaspoons dried oregano
1 teaspoon dried basil
¼ teaspoon salt
¼ teaspoon freshly ground pepper
¼ cup freshly grated Parmesan cheese
½ cup (2 ounces) shredded part-skim
     mozzarella cheese, divided

Cook pasta according to package directions,
omitting salt and oil; drain pasta, and set aside.
  Cook garlic and onion in olive oil in a large
skillet over medium heat until tender. Add tomatoes and next 6 ingredients; cook 5 minutes.
  Add Parmesan cheese and ¼ cup mozzarella
cheese, stirring until cheese melts. Pour over
cooked pasta. Sprinkle with remaining ¼ cup
mozzarella cheese. **Yield: 3 servings**.

PER SERVING: 389 CALORIES (22% FROM FAT)
FAT 9.6G (SATURATED FAT 2.8G)
PROTEIN 17.4G CARBOHYDRATE 59.2G
CHOLESTEROL 16MG SODIUM 479MG

Pasta Fasta

Save time by cooking extra pasta for
another meal. Toss it with a small
amount of olive oil, and store in a
covered container in the refrigerator
up to 3 days.
  To reheat, place pasta in a colander, and pour hot water over it.

Mediterranean Ravioli

Mediterranean Ravioli

Vegetable cooking spray
2 teaspoons olive oil
½ pound eggplant, peeled and cut into
    ½-inch cubes
1 cup chopped onion
2 cloves garlic, minced
1 (15-ounce) container refrigerated light
    chunky tomato sauce
2 tablespoons sliced ripe olives
1 tablespoon balsamic vinegar
1 teaspoon dried thyme
1 (9-ounce) package refrigerated
    cheese-filled ravioli, uncooked
3 tablespoons grated Parmesan cheese

Coat a large nonstick skillet with cooking
spray. Add olive oil; place over medium-high heat.

Add eggplant, onion, and garlic; cook, stirring
constantly, 5 minutes or until tender. Stir in
tomato sauce and next 3 ingredients; remove
from heat.

Cook ravioli according to package directions;
drain. Rinse and drain. Toss with vegetables;
place in a 1½-quart shallow baking dish coated
with cooking spray. Sprinkle with cheese.

Bake at 350° for 30 minutes. **Yield: 4 servings**.

Per Serving: 288 Calories (25% from Fat)
Fat 7.9g (Saturated Fat 2.6g)
Protein 14.1g Carbohydrate 40.0g
Cholesterol 44mg Sodium 771mg

Lentil Spaghetti Sauce

Vegetable cooking spray
¾ cup chopped onion
2 cloves garlic, minced
4 cups water
1½ cups dried lentils, uncooked
1 teaspoon dried crushed red pepper
¾ teaspoon salt
½ teaspoon pepper
1 (14½-ounce) can no-salt-added whole
    tomatoes, undrained and chopped
1 (6-ounce) can no-salt-added tomato paste
1 tablespoon white vinegar
2 beef-flavored bouillon cubes
½ teaspoon dried basil
½ teaspoon dried oregano
8 cups hot cooked spaghetti (cooked without
    salt or fat)

Coat a Dutch oven with cooking spray. Add
onion and garlic; cook until tender, stirring constantly. Add next 5 ingredients. Bring to a boil;
cover, reduce heat, and simmer 30 minutes.

Add tomatoes and next 5 ingredients. Bring to a
boil; reduce heat, and simmer 45 minutes to 1 hour
or to desired thickness, stirring often. Serve over
hot cooked spaghetti. **Yield: 8 servings**.

Per Serving: 357 Calories (4% from Fat)
Fat 1.6g (Saturated Fat 0.2g)
Protein 18.3g Carbohydrate 68.6g
Cholesterol 0mg Sodium 347mg

Vegetable Pizzas

(pictured on page 745)

6 (8-inch) Skillet Pizza Crusts
1½ cups commercial reduced-fat pasta sauce
1 cup sliced fresh mushrooms
1 cup (4 ounces) shredded part-skim
    mozzarella cheese
¾ cup chopped green pepper
½ cup chopped onion
¼ cup sliced ripe olives

Place pizza crusts on baking sheets. Spread each crust with ¼ cup pasta sauce, and sprinkle evenly with remaining ingredients.

Bake at 425° for 12 to 15 minutes or until edges are lightly browned and cheese melts. Cut into wedges. **Yield: 6 servings.**

Skillet Pizza Crusts

3 packages active dry yeast
1 teaspoon sugar
¾ cup warm water (105° to 115°)
3 cups all-purpose flour
1 teaspoon salt
½ cup warm water (105° to 115°)
2 tablespoons olive oil
Vegetable cooking spray

Combine first 3 ingredients in a 2-cup liquid measuring cup; let stand 5 minutes.

Combine yeast mixture, flour, and next 3 ingredients in a large bowl, stirring until well blended.

Turn dough out onto a lightly floured surface, and knead 5 minutes. Place in a bowl coated with cooking spray, turning to grease top.

Cover and let rise in a warm place (85°), free from drafts, 30 minutes or until doubled in bulk.

Punch dough down, and knead lightly 4 or 5 times. Divide dough into 6 equal portions; roll each into an 8-inch circle.

Cook each round on one side in an 8-inch nonstick skillet coated with cooking spray over medium heat about 2 minutes or until lightly browned. **Yield: 6 (8-inch) pizza crusts.**

Note: Cooled crusts may be frozen in an airtight container up to 6 months.

PER SERVING: 391 CALORIES (24% FROM FAT)
FAT 10.3G (SATURATED FAT 2.8G)
PROTEIN 14.3G CARBOHYDRATE 59.9G
CHOLESTEROL 11MG SODIUM 607MG

Artichoke Quiche

2 cups cooked rice (cooked without salt or fat)
¾ cup (3 ounces) shredded farmer cheese,
    divided
¾ cup egg substitute, divided
1 teaspoon dried dill
Vegetable cooking spray
1 (14-ounce) can artichoke hearts, drained
    and quartered
¾ cup fat-free milk
¼ cup thinly sliced green onions
2 teaspoons Dijon mustard
¼ teaspoon ground white pepper

Combine rice, ¼ cup cheese, ¼ cup egg substitute, and dill; press mixture into a 9-inch pieplate coated with cooking spray. Bake at 350° for 5 minutes.

Arrange artichokes in rice crust; sprinkle with remaining ½ cup cheese. Combine remaining ½ cup egg substitute, fat-free milk, and remaining ingredients; pour over cheese.

Bake at 350° for 50 minutes or until set. Let stand 5 minutes; serve warm. **Yield: 6 servings.**

PER SERVING: 163 CALORIES (18% FROM FAT)
FAT 3.5G (SATURATED FAT 0.1G)
PROTEIN 11.3G CARBOHYDRATE 23.8G
CHOLESTEROL 1MG SODIUM 163MG

Artichoke Quiche

Fiesta Quiche

Fiesta Quiche

Vegetable cooking spray
4 (8½-inch) flour tortillas
½ cup (2 ounces) shredded reduced-fat
    Cheddar cheese
1 (4.5-ounce) can chopped green chiles,
    drained
¼ cup sliced green onions
½ cup picante sauce
1 cup egg substitute
⅓ cup fat-free milk
½ teaspoon chili powder
¼ teaspoon cracked black pepper
6 tomato slices
2 tablespoons plain nonfat yogurt
Fresh cilantro

Coat a 12-inch quiche dish with cooking spray; layer tortillas in dish. Sprinkle cheese, chiles, and green onions over tortillas; dollop with picante sauce.

Combine egg substitute and next 3 ingredients; pour into quiche dish.

Bake at 350° for 30 to 35 minutes. Remove from oven, and arrange tomato slices around edge of quiche; top each tomato slice with 1 teaspoon yogurt and a sprig of cilantro. Cut into wedges. **Yield: 6 servings.**

PER SERVING: 238 CALORIES (22% FROM FAT)
FAT 5.7G (SATURATED FAT 1.7G)
PROTEIN 12.6G CARBOHYDRATE 33.7G
CHOLESTEROL 6MG SODIUM 675MG

Three-Bean Enchiladas

½ cup dried kidney beans
½ cup dried navy beans
½ cup dried pinto beans
6 cups water
½ teaspoon salt
½ cup chopped onion
2 cloves garlic
1 teaspoon chili powder
1 teaspoon ground cumin
¼ teaspoon salt
1 (4.5-ounce) can chopped green chiles,
    undrained
12 (6-inch) corn tortillas
Vegetable cooking spray
1 (10-ounce) can enchilada sauce
1 cup (4 ounces) shredded reduced-fat
    Monterey Jack cheese

Sort and wash beans; place in a Dutch oven.
Cover with water 2 inches above beans, and
bring to a boil; cover and cook 2 minutes. Remove from heat, and let stand 1 hour. Drain
beans; return to Dutch oven.

Add 6 cups water and ½ teaspoon salt to
beans. Bring to a boil; cover, reduce heat, and
simmer 1 hour or until beans are tender. Drain,
reserving ¼ cup liquid (add water, if necessary,
to make ¼ cup).

Place beans in container of an electric blender;
add reserved ¼ cup liquid, onion, and next 5
ingredients. Process 5 seconds or until chunky.

Brush tortillas with water. Divide bean mixture among tortillas. Roll up; place, seam side
down, in a 13- x 9- x 2-inch baking dish coated
with cooking spray. Top with enchilada sauce.

Cover and bake at 350° for 20 minutes. Top
with cheese, and bake, uncovered, 5 minutes.
Yield: 6 servings.

PER SERVING: 373 CALORIES (16% FROM FAT)
FAT 6.6G (SATURATED FAT 2.4G)
PROTEIN 20.5G CARBOHYDRATE 61.1G
CHOLESTEROL 12MG SODIUM 700MG

Vegetable-Cheese Enchiladas

8 (6-inch) corn tortillas
1 medium zucchini, cut into ½-inch cubes
1 cup (4 ounces) shredded reduced-fat
    Monterey Jack cheese, divided
1 cup cooked brown rice (cooked without salt
    or fat)
¼ cup chopped green onions
⅓ cup low-fat sour cream
¼ teaspoon salt
¼ teaspoon pepper
Vegetable cooking spray
2 (10-ounce) cans chopped tomatoes and
    green chiles, undrained

Wrap tortillas in aluminum foil, and bake at
350° for 7 minutes.

Cook zucchini in boiling water to cover 2
minutes; drain and pat dry with paper towels.

Combine zucchini, half of cheese, and next
5 ingredients. Spoon mixture evenly down center
of each tortilla; fold opposite sides over filling,
and roll up tortillas. Place, seam side down, in an
11- x 7- x 1½-inch baking dish coated with cooking spray.

Pour chopped tomatoes and green chiles over
tortillas.

Bake at 350° for 15 minutes; sprinkle with
remaining cheese, and bake 5 additional minutes.
Yield: 4 servings.

PER SERVING: 343 CALORIES (26% FROM FAT)
FAT 9.9G (SATURATED FAT 4.9G)
PROTEIN 14.1G CARBOHYDRATE 47.3G
CHOLESTEROL 26MG SODIUM 1031MG

Vegetable Burritos

Vegetable Burritos

4½ cups sliced fresh mushrooms (1 pound)
1 cup chopped onion
1 cup chopped green pepper
2 cloves garlic, crushed
2 teaspoons olive oil
1 (15-ounce) can kidney beans, drained
2 tablespoons finely chopped ripe olives
¼ teaspoon pepper
8 (8-inch) flour tortillas
½ cup nonfat sour cream
1 cup commercial chunky salsa, divided
¾ cup (3 ounces) shredded reduced-fat sharp
 Cheddar cheese
Vegetable cooking spray
Garnish: fresh cilantro

Cook first 4 ingredients in olive oil in a large, nonstick skillet over medium-high heat, stirring constantly, until tender. Remove from heat; drain. Combine cooked vegetables, kidney beans, olives, and pepper.

Spoon about ½ cup bean mixture evenly down center of each tortilla. Top with 1 tablespoon sour cream, 1 tablespoon salsa, and 1½ tablespoons cheese; fold opposite sides over filling.

Coat a large nonstick skillet or griddle with cooking spray. Place over medium-high heat until hot. Cook tortillas, seam side down, 1 minute on each side or until thoroughly heated. Top each tortilla with 1 tablespoon salsa. Garnish, if desired. **Yield: 8 servings.**

PER SERVING: 316 CALORIES (22% FROM FAT)
FAT 7.6G (SATURATED FAT 2.0G)
PROTEIN 15.0G CARBOHYDRATE 47.9G
CHOLESTEROL 7MG SODIUM 528MG

Light Chiles Rellenos

6 ounces reduced-fat Monterey Jack cheese
3 (4-ounce) cans whole green chiles, drained
¼ cup egg substitute
⅛ teaspoon salt
⅛ teaspoon pepper
4 egg whites
Vegetable cooking spray
½ cup all-purpose flour
1 (14½-ounce) can no-salt-added stewed
 tomatoes, undrained and chopped

Cut cheese into 9 (2- x ½- x ½-inch) pieces; place 1 piece inside each chile. (Cheese pieces may need trimming slightly to fit chiles.) Set chiles aside.

Combine egg substitute, salt, and pepper in a large bowl. Beat egg whites until stiff peaks form; fold into egg substitute mixture.

Place a large nonstick skillet coated with cooking spray over medium heat. Quickly dredge cheese-filled chiles in flour, and coat each generously with egg white mixture. Place coated chiles in skillet, and brown on both sides.

Transfer browned chiles to a 13- x 9- x 2-inch baking dish coated with cooking spray. Pour tomatoes over chiles, and bake at 350° for 30 minutes. **Yield: 3 servings.**

PER SERVING: 384 CALORIES (30% FROM FAT)
FAT 13.0G (SATURATED FAT 7.0G)
PROTEIN 31.2G CARBOHYDRATE 36.5G
CHOLESTEROL 42MG SODIUM 653MG

Low-Fat Secrets

Here are tips for reducing the fat in traditional Chiles Rellenos.
• Substitute reduced-fat Monterey Jack for regular cheese.
• Use an equivalent amount of egg substitute in place of an egg yolk.

Roasted Chiles Rellenos with Tomatillo Sauce

8 Anaheim chile peppers
10 tomatillos, husked
1 small onion, sliced
2 cloves garlic, minced
¼ teaspoon salt
¼ teaspoon pepper
¼ teaspoon ground cumin
2 tablespoons chopped fresh cilantro
¾ cup canned black beans, drained and
   rinsed
1 cup (4 ounces) shredded reduced-fat
   Monterey Jack cheese
1 egg white
¼ cup egg substitute
¾ cup all-purpose flour
1 teaspoon vegetable oil
Vegetable cooking spray

Place chile peppers, tomatillos, and onion on food rack of grill. Cook, covered with grill lid, over hot coals (400° to 500°) about 5 minutes on each side or until peppers look blistered, and tomatillos and onion are lightly browned.

Place peppers immediately in a heavy-duty, zip-top plastic bag; seal and chill at least 8 hours.

Place grilled vegetables in an airtight container; chill at least 8 hours.

Peel peppers, and remove seeds; set aside.

Combine tomatillos, onion, garlic, and next 3 ingredients in container of an electric blender. Process until smooth. Stir in cilantro; set tomatillo sauce aside.

Combine black beans and cheese; spoon into peppers (some peppers may split). Set aside.

Beat egg white at high speed of an electric mixer until stiff peaks form; gradually beat in egg substitute. Set aside.

Coat stuffed peppers with flour; dip in egg white mixture. Lightly recoat peppers with flour.

Add oil to a large nonstick skillet coated with cooking spray. Cook chiles in hot oil on both sides until lightly browned. Serve immediately with tomatillo sauce. **Yield: 4 servings.**

PER SERVING: 311 CALORIES (24% FROM FAT)
FAT 8.3G (SATURATED FAT 3.2G)
PROTEIN 18.9G CARBOHYDRATE 42.8G
CHOLESTEROL 19MG SODIUM 523MG

Low-Fat Ingredient Substitutions

Item	Substitution	Item	Substitution
DAIRY PRODUCTS			**FATS AND OILS**
Cheeses	Cheeses with 5 grams of fat or less per ounce (American, Cheddar, colby, edam, Monterey Jack, mozzarella, Swiss)	Butter or Margarine	Reduced-calorie margarine or margarine with liquid polyunsaturated or monounsaturated oil listed as the first ingredient; also, polyunsaturated or monounsaturated oil
Cottage cheese	Nonfat or 1% low-fat cottage cheese		
Cream cheese	Nonfat or light cream cheese, Neufchâtel cheese	Chocolate, unsweetened	3 tablespoons unsweetened cocoa plus 1 tablespoon polyunsaturated oil or margarine
Ricotta cheese	Nonfat, light, or part-skim ricotta cheese	Mayonnaise	Nonfat or reduced-calorie mayonnaise
Ice cream	Nonfat or low-fat frozen yogurt, low-fat frozen dairy dessert, low-fat ice cream, sherbet, sorbet	Oil	Polyunsaturated or monounsaturated oil in reduced amount
Milk, whole or 2%	Fat-free milk, 1% low-fat milk, evaporated fat-free milk diluted equally with water	Salad dressing	Nonfat or oil-free salad dressing
Sour cream	Nonfat sour cream, light sour cream, low-fat or nonfat yogurt	Shortening	Polyunsaturated or monounsaturated oil in amount reduced by one-third
Whipping cream	Chilled evaporated fat-free milk, whipped		

Meats

With today's beef and pork being leaner than ever before, make these juicy meats part of your low-fat eating plan. Select entrées for any occasion—from casual suppers to elegant dinners.

American Steakhouse Beef, Mustard Marinated Sirloin, Lemon Veal

Stewed Lamb with Five Spices, Barbecued Pork Loin Roast, Chile-Beef Kabobs

Beef and Cauliflower over Rice, French-Style Beef Roast, Cornbread-Tamale Pie

Hopping John with Grilled Pork Medaillons, Country Sausage

Steak au Poivre (page 760)

French-Style Beef Roast

French-Style Beef Roast

1 (3-pound) boneless beef rump roast
1 large clove garlic, quartered
1 teaspoon dried thyme
½ teaspoon pepper
1 bay leaf
4 cups water
1 pound turnips, peeled and quartered
¾ pound onions, quartered
2 cups (2-inch pieces) carrot
1 cup (2-inch pieces) celery
Garnish: fresh parsley sprig

   Trim all visible fat from roast. Place roast in a large Dutch oven; add garlic and next 4 ingredients. Bring to a boil. Cover, reduce heat, and simmer 2½ hours.
   Add turnip, onion, carrot, and celery to roast. Cover and cook an additional 30 minutes or until vegetables are tender.
   Remove roast to a serving platter; let roast stand 10 minutes before slicing. Arrange vegetables around roast. Strain broth, and serve with roast. Garnish, if desired. **Yield: 10 servings.**

PER SERVING: 187 CALORIES (23% FROM FAT)
FAT 4.7G (SATURATED FAT 1.7G)
PROTEIN 26.5G CARBOHYDRATE 8.7G
CHOLESTEROL 64MG SODIUM 104MG

Lean Meats

   The recipes included here call for the leanest cuts of meats with little, if any, added fat.
   Although most of our dishes derive 30 percent or less of their calories from fat, some cuts of meat are naturally higher in fat content.

Marinated Sauerbraten Beef

1 pound trimmed top round roast
Vegetable cooking spray
2 cups water
1 cup Burgundy or other dry red wine
2 small onions, thinly sliced
2 tablespoons pickling spice
2 tablespoons brown sugar
1 teaspoon salt
10 black peppercorns, crushed
2 bay leaves
Sauerbraten Sauce

   Brown roast in a Dutch oven coated with cooking spray. Combine water and next 7 ingredients; reserve 1 cup mixture for Sauerbraten Sauce. Pour remaining mixture over roast. Cover; chill 8 hours.
   Remove Dutch oven from refrigerator; uncover and place over medium heat. Bring to a boil; cover, reduce heat, and simmer 45 minutes or until tender. Drain. Remove and discard bay leaves. Slice roast, and serve with Sauerbraten Sauce. **Yield: 3 servings.**

Sauerbraten Sauce

1 cup reserved marinade
¼ cup gingersnap crumbs
¼ cup nonfat sour cream

   Combine first 2 ingredients in a heavy saucepan; cook over medium heat, stirring constantly, until thickened. Reduce heat; stir in sour cream, and cook over low heat until thoroughly heated. (Do not boil.) **Yield: 1 cup.**

PER SERVING: 319 CALORIES (24% FROM FAT)
FAT 8.6G (SATURATED FAT 2.6G)
PROTEIN 33.3G CARBOHYDRATE 19.3G
CHOLESTEROL 84MG SODIUM 563MG

Steak au Poivre

(pictured on page 757)

6 (4-ounce) beef tenderloin steaks
1 clove garlic, crushed
1 teaspoon crushed black peppercorns
Vegetable cooking spray
⅓ cup chopped onion
1 cup green pepper strips
1 cup sweet red pepper strips
1 cup sweet yellow pepper strips
1 clove garlic, minced
½ teaspoon beef-flavored bouillon granules
½ teaspoon paprika
½ teaspoon crushed black peppercorns
½ cup water
½ cup evaporated fat-free milk
3 tablespoons brandy

Trim fat from steaks. Combine crushed garlic and 1 teaspoon peppercorns; press mixture into each side of steaks. Coat a nonstick skillet with cooking spray; place over medium heat until hot.

Arrange steaks in skillet, and cook to desired degree of doneness, turning once. Remove steaks to a serving platter, and keep steaks warm.

Wipe skillet with paper towels; coat with cooking spray, and place over medium heat until hot. Add onion and next 4 ingredients; cook, stirring constantly, until vegetables are crisp-tender. Spoon pepper mixture over steaks, and keep warm.

Combine bouillon granules and next 4 ingredients in a small bowl; stir well. Pour into skillet, and cook over medium heat, stirring often, until mixture is reduced to ⅔ cup.

Place brandy in a long-handled saucepan; heat until warm. Remove from heat. Ignite with a long match. Pour into sauce mixture; stir until flames die down. Spoon over each steak. **Yield: 6 servings.**

PER SERVING: 182 CALORIES (35% FROM FAT)
FAT 7.0G (SATURATED FAT 2.7G)
PROTEIN 22.2G CARBOHYDRATE 6.7G
CHOLESTEROL 60MG SODIUM 150MG

Mustard Marinated Sirloin

2 tablespoons Dijon mustard
2 tablespoons Burgundy or other dry red wine
1 teaspoon coarsely ground pepper
2 cloves garlic, minced
1 pound lean, boneless sirloin steak, trimmed
Vegetable cooking spray
1 cup sliced fresh mushrooms
1½ tablespoons all-purpose flour
1 cup reduced-sodium, fat-free beef broth
½ cup Burgundy or other dry red wine
¼ teaspoon salt
¼ teaspoon pepper

Combine first 4 ingredients. Coat steak on both sides with mustard mixture, and place in a shallow dish. Cover and chill 8 hours.

Place steak on a rack coated with cooking spray; place rack in a broiler pan. Broil 3 inches from heat (with electric oven door partially opened) 4 to 5 minutes on each side or until desired degree of doneness. Let stand 5 minutes. Thinly slice steak diagonally across grain; keep steak warm.

Coat a nonstick skillet with cooking spray; add mushrooms, and cook, stirring constantly, over medium heat until tender.

Add flour; cook 1 minute, stirring constantly. Gradually add beef broth and ½ cup Burgundy; cook, stirring constantly, until thickened. Stir in salt and pepper. Spoon sauce evenly over meat.
Yield: 4 servings.

PER SERVING: 213 CALORIES (29% FROM FAT)
FAT 6.8G (SATURATED FAT 2.4G)
PROTEIN 28.2G CARBOHYDRATE 6.5G
CHOLESTEROL 80MG SODIUM 435MG

Mustard Marinated Sirloin

American Steakhouse Beef

1 (1½-pound) trimmed lean boneless top
    sirloin steak
⅓ cup low-sodium soy sauce
⅓ cup unsweetened pineapple juice
⅓ cup dry sherry
¼ cup cider vinegar

Place steak in a large, shallow dish. Combine soy sauce and remaining ingredients; pour over steak. Cover and chill 4 hours, turning steak occasionally. Drain, discarding marinade.

Cook over hot coals (400° to 500°) 10 to 15 minutes on each side or to desired degree of doneness. To serve, slice across grain into thin slices. **Yield: 7 servings.**

PER SERVING: 210 CALORIES (33% FROM FAT)
FAT 7.8G (SATURATED FAT 3.2G)
PROTEIN 27.4G CARBOHYDRATE 0.3G
CHOLESTEROL 80MG SODIUM 96MG

Steak Kabobs

1½ pounds sirloin tip, trimmed
¼ cup low-sodium soy sauce
2 tablespoons brown sugar
½ teaspoon ground ginger
2 teaspoons dry sherry
1½ teaspoons vegetable oil
1 (15¼-ounce) can unsweetened pineapple
    chunks
4½ cups hot cooked rice (cooked without salt
    or fat)

Cut meat into ½-inch cubes; place in a shallow dish or a heavy-duty, zip-top plastic bag, and set aside.

Combine soy sauce and next 4 ingredients; pour over meat and cover or seal. Chill at least 3 hours. Drain meat, discarding marinade.

Drain pineapple, reserving juice for another use. Alternate meat and pineapple on 14-inch skewers.

Cook over medium-hot coals (350° to 400°) 8 minutes or until desired degree of doneness, turning often. Serve with rice. **Yield: 6 servings.**

PER SERVING: 382 CALORIES (18% FROM FAT)
FAT 7.5G (SATURATED FAT 2.7G)
PROTEIN 30.8G CARBOHYDRATE 45.2G
CHOLESTEROL 81MG SODIUM 191MG

Chile-Beef Kabobs

16 (1½-inch) boiling onions
1 pound lean boneless sirloin, cut into
    16 pieces
16 medium-size fresh mushrooms
2 sweet red peppers, each cut into 8 pieces
2 sweet yellow peppers, each cut into 8 pieces
1 cup Red Chile Sauce, divided
½ cup Burgundy or other dry red wine
1 cup nonfat sour cream
Garnishes: jalapeño peppers, kale leaves

Cook onions in boiling water to cover 8 minutes; drain.

Alternate meat, onions, mushrooms, and peppers on 8 (14-inch) skewers; place skewers in a shallow dish.

Combine ½ cup Red Chile Sauce and wine. Pour over kabobs, turning to coat. Cover and chill 4 hours.

Remove kabobs from marinade, discarding marinade. Place kabobs on a rack; place rack in broiler pan.

Broil 5½ inches from heat (with electric oven door partially opened) 8 to 10 minutes, turning occasionally.

Combine sour cream and remaining ½ cup Red Chile Sauce. Serve with kabobs. Garnish, if desired. **Yield: 4 servings.**

Chile-Beef Kabobs

Red Chile Sauce

4 ounces dried Anaheim chile peppers
2 cloves garlic, minced
1 tablespoon vegetable oil
2 tablespoons all-purpose flour
2 cups water
1½ teaspoons ground cumin
¾ teaspoon salt

Remove pepper stems and seeds. (Wear rubber gloves when handling peppers.) Cover peppers with boiling water; let stand 30 minutes. Drain, reserving 1 cup liquid.

Position knife blade in food processor bowl; add peppers and reserved liquid. Process until smooth, stopping twice to scrape down sides. Set pepper mixture aside.

Cook garlic in oil in a heavy saucepan until tender. Gradually stir in flour, and cook over medium heat, stirring constantly, until mixture is the color of caramel. Gradually add 2 cups water, stirring constantly. Stir in pepper mixture, and cook until slightly thickened.

Pour mixture through a wire-mesh strainer into a bowl, discarding solids remaining in strainer. Return to saucepan; add cumin and salt, and cook over medium heat until thickened. Sauce may be refrigerated up to 3 days or frozen up to 3 months. **Yield: 2¾ cups.**

Note: The Red Chile Sauce and sour cream mixture makes a spicy dip for raw vegetables or baked tortilla chips.

PER SERVING: 372 CALORIES (22% FROM FAT)
FAT 8.5G (SATURATED FAT 2.6G)
PROTEIN 36.8G CARBOHYDRATE 32.6G
CHOLESTEROL 80MG SODIUM 244MG

Beef and Cauliflower over Rice

1 pound boneless top round steak
3 tablespoons reduced-sodium soy sauce
Vegetable cooking spray
3 cups cauliflower flowerets
¾ cup coarsely chopped sweet red pepper
2 cloves garlic, minced
1 tablespoon cornstarch
¼ teaspoon beef-flavored bouillon granules
½ to 1 teaspoon dried crushed red pepper
½ teaspoon sugar
1 cup water
1 cup sliced green onions
2 cups hot cooked rice

Trim fat from steak. Slice diagonally across grain into thin strips; place in a shallow dish. Coat with soy sauce; cover. Chill 30 minutes.

Coat a Dutch oven with cooking spray; place over medium heat until hot. Add meat and cook, stirring until browned. Reduce heat; cover and cook 10 minutes. Stir in cauliflower, sweet red pepper, and garlic; cover and cook 5 minutes.

Combine cornstarch and next 4 ingredients, stirring until smooth; stir into meat. Add green onions; bring to a boil. Cook, stirring constantly, 1 minute. Serve over rice. **Yield: 4 servings.**

PER SERVING: 305 CALORIES (14% FROM FAT)
FAT 4.9G (SATURATED FAT 1.8G)
PROTEIN 29.1G CARBOHYDRATE 35.1G
CHOLESTEROL 61MG SODIUM 506MG

Beef Hash

1 cup cubed cooked lean beef
1 cup peeled, cubed potato
½ cup chopped onion
1 tablespoon chopped fresh parsley
¼ teaspoon salt
¼ teaspoon pepper
2 teaspoons vegetable oil
⅓ cup fat-free milk

Combine first 6 ingredients; cook in hot oil in a large nonstick skillet over medium-high heat, stirring occasionally, 10 minutes or until mixture is browned and tender. Stir in milk; cover, reduce heat, and simmer 5 minutes. **Yield: 2 servings.**

PER SERVING: 282 CALORIES (30% FROM FAT)
FAT 9.4G (SATURATED FAT 1.7G)
PROTEIN 26.9G CARBOHYDRATE 21.5G
CHOLESTEROL 63MG SODIUM 366MG

Deli-Style Roast Beef

1 (4-pound) eye of round roast, trimmed
5 cloves garlic, halved
1 (8-ounce) can tomato sauce
1 cup Burgundy or other dry red wine
¼ cup Worcestershire sauce
¼ cup lemon juice
¼ cup Creole mustard
2 tablespoons hot sauce
2 tablespoons prepared horseradish
2 teaspoons onion powder
2 bay leaves
Vegetable cooking spray

Cut 10 slits in roast; insert garlic halves into slits. Place in a heavy-duty, zip-top plastic bag.

Combine tomato sauce and next 8 ingredients; reserve ⅓ cup marinade. Pour remaining marinade over roast; seal bag. Chill 8 hours.

Remove roast from marinade, discarding marinade. Place on a rack in a roasting pan coated with cooking spray; insert meat thermometer.

Bake at 325° for 1 hour and 30 minutes or until thermometer registers 145° (medium-rare), basting 3 times with ⅓ cup reserved marinade. Remove from oven; wrap roast securely in plastic wrap to retain moisture. Chill roast several hours before slicing. **Yield: 15 servings.**

PER SERVING: 171 CALORIES (29% FROM FAT)
FAT 5.6G (SATURATED FAT 2.1G)
PROTEIN 24.5G CARBOHYDRATE 1.9G
CHOLESTEROL 57MG SODIUM 169MG

Cornbread-Tamale Pie

Vegetable cooking spray
1 pound ground round
1 cup chopped onion
1 cup chopped green pepper
1 clove garlic, minced
2 (8-ounce) cans no-salt-added tomato sauce
1 (12-ounce) can no-salt-added whole kernel corn, drained
10 ripe olives, sliced
1 tablespoon sugar
1 tablespoon chili powder
⅛ teaspoon salt
¼ teaspoon pepper
¾ cup (3 ounces) shredded, reduced-fat sharp Cheddar cheese
¾ cup yellow cornmeal
½ teaspoon salt
2 cups water
1 tablespoon reduced-calorie margarine

Coat a large, nonstick skillet with cooking spray; place over medium heat. Add ground round; cook until browned, stirring until it crumbles. Drain and pat dry with paper towels. Wipe pan drippings from skillet with a paper towel.

Coat skillet with cooking spray. Add onion, green pepper, and garlic; cook until vegetables are tender.

Stir in ground round, tomato sauce, and next 6 ingredients. Simmer, uncovered, 15 to 20 minutes.

Add Cheddar cheese, stirring until cheese melts. Spoon into an 8-inch square baking dish coated with cooking spray.

Combine cornmeal, ½ teaspoon salt, and water in a saucepan; bring to a boil, stirring constantly. Reduce heat, and cook, stirring constantly, until mixture thickens (about 3 minutes). Stir in margarine.

Spoon over meat mixture to within 1 inch of edge. Bake at 375° for 40 minutes or until topping is golden. **Yield: 6 servings.**

Note: Freeze pie before topping with cornmeal mixture. Thaw in refrigerator 24 hours. Remove from refrigerator, and let stand at room temperature 30 minutes; proceed as directed, baking 45 to 50 minutes.

PER SERVING: 325 CALORIES (29% FROM FAT)
FAT 10.4G (SATURATED FAT 3.6G)
PROTEIN 24.1G CARBOHYDRATE 33.7G
CHOLESTEROL 56MG SODIUM 491MG

Lemon Veal

1 tablespoon all-purpose flour
1 teaspoon beef-flavored bouillon granules
½ teaspoon paprika
½ teaspoon chopped fresh parsley
¼ teaspoon dried rosemary
⅛ teaspoon pepper
½ pound boneless round rump veal, trimmed and cut into 1-inch cubes
Vegetable cooking spray
2 medium carrots, scraped and cut into thin strips
¼ cup dry white wine
¼ cup water
1 tablespoon lemon juice
2 cups hot cooked rice (cooked without salt or fat)

Combine first 6 ingredients in a heavy-duty, zip-top plastic bag; add veal, seal bag, and shake to coat.

Coat a nonstick skillet with cooking spray; place over medium heat until hot. Add veal, and cook, stirring constantly, until lightly browned.

Add carrot and next 3 ingredients; bring to a boil, stirring constantly. Cover, reduce heat, and simmer 40 minutes. Serve over rice. **Yield: 2 servings.**

PER SERVING: 472 CALORIES (14% FROM FAT)
FAT 7.3G (SATURATED FAT 1.8G)
PROTEIN 32.5G CARBOHYDRATE 61.3G
CHOLESTEROL 100MG SODIUM 577MG

Stewed Lamb with Five Spices

Stewed Lamb with Five Spices

1 (3½-pound) leg of lamb
Vegetable cooking spray
2 cups chopped onion
4 cloves garlic, minced
1 teaspoon ground coriander
¼ teaspoon salt
½ teaspoon paprika
½ teaspoon ground cumin
½ teaspoon ground ginger
⅛ teaspoon ground turmeric
1 (16-ounce) can no-salt-added tomatoes, undrained and chopped
1 lemon, sliced into wedges
12 pimiento-stuffed olives, sliced
½ cup chopped fresh parsley
3 cups hot cooked rice (cooked without salt or fat)

Trim fat from lamb; bone and cut lamb into bite-size pieces. Set aside 1½ pounds of lamb; reserve remainder for another use.

Coat a nonstick skillet with cooking spray; place over medium-high heat until hot. Add lamb; cook until browned. Drain well.

Return lamb to skillet; add onion and garlic, and cook until onion is transparent. Stir in coriander and next 6 ingredients.

Transfer lamb mixture to a 3-quart baking dish; cover and bake at 375° for 1 to 1½ hours or until lamb is tender. Squeeze juice of lemon wedges into casserole; stir in lemon wedges, olives, and parsley.

Return to oven, and cook 5 minutes or until thoroughly heated. Serve over rice. **Yield: 6 servings.**

PER SERVING: 310 CALORIES (19% FROM FAT)
FAT 6.4G (SATURATED FAT 1.9G)
PROTEIN 27.1G CARBOHYDRATE 35.2G
CHOLESTEROL 73MG SODIUM 763MG

Barbecued Pork Loin Roast

1 (2¼-pound) boneless pork loin roast,
    trimmed
¾ cup no-salt-added ketchup
¾ cup finely chopped onion
1 tablespoon honey
1½ teaspoons unsweetened cocoa
1½ teaspoons brown sugar
2¼ teaspoons lemon juice
1½ teaspoons liquid smoke
⅛ teaspoon pepper
1 clove garlic, minced
Dash of ground mace
Vegetable cooking spray

Butterfly roast by making a lengthwise cut
down center of one flat side, cutting to within ½
inch of other side. From bottom of cut, slice horizontally to within ½ inch from left side; repeat
procedure to right side. Open roast. Place in a
shallow dish; set aside.

Combine ketchup and next 9 ingredients;
spread half of marinade mixture on roast, reserving remaining marinade.

Cover roast, and chill 8 hours. Cover and chill
reserved marinade.

Remove roast from marinade, discarding marinade. Coat a grill rack with cooking spray; place
rack on grill, and place roast on rack. Cook over
medium-hot coals (350° to 400°) 10 minutes on
each side or until meat thermometer inserted in
thickest portion registers 160°. Remove roast
from grill, and wrap in heavy-duty plastic wrap.

Cook reserved marinade in a heavy saucepan
over medium-low heat 15 minutes, stirring often.
Cut meat into thin slices, and serve with sauce.
Yield: 9 servings.

PER SERVING: 178 CALORIES (21% FROM FAT)
FAT 4.2G (SATURATED FAT 1.4G)
PROTEIN 24.8G CARBOHYDRATE 9.4G
CHOLESTEROL 79MG SODIUM 66MG

Grilled Pork Tenderloin with Brown Sauce

8 cloves garlic, crushed
½ teaspoon pepper
¼ cup lime juice
1 tablespoon minced fresh oregano or
    1 teaspoon dried oregano
2 (¾-pound) pork tenderloins
Brown Sauce

Combine first 4 ingredients; set aside.

Trim excess fat from tenderloins, and place
pork in a large, shallow dish. Spread lime mixture over tenderloins; cover and chill 3 hours,
turning occasionally.

Remove tenderloins from marinade, reserving
marinade. Boil marinade in a small saucepan 1
minute. Cook meat, covered with grill lid, over
medium-hot coals (350° to 400°) 30 minutes,
turning occasionally and basting with reserved
marinade. Meat is done when meat thermometer
inserted in thickest part of tenderloin registers
160°. Serve tenderloins with Brown Sauce.
Yield: 6 servings.

Brown Sauce

2 tablespoons cornstarch
¾ teaspoon ground ginger
1½ cups canned low-sodium chicken broth
1½ tablespoons dry sherry
1½ tablespoons low-sodium soy sauce
½ teaspoon browning-and-seasoning sauce

Combine all ingredients in a heavy saucepan.
Bring to a boil over medium heat; boil 1 minute,
stirring constantly. **Yield: 1½ cups.**

PER SERVING: 181 CALORIES (24% FROM FAT)
FAT 4.8G (SATURATED FAT 1.6G)
PROTEIN 26.7G CARBOHYDRATE 6.1G
CHOLESTEROL 83MG SODIUM 179MG

Hopping John with Grilled Pork Medaillons

Hopping John with Grilled Pork Medaillons

¾ cup chopped onion
½ cup chopped celery
1 teaspoon olive oil
2 (15.75-ounce) cans ready-to-serve, reduced-sodium, fat-free chicken broth
1 teaspoon dried thyme
½ cup wild rice, uncooked
1 cup frozen black-eyed peas
½ cup long-grain rice, uncooked
¾ cup chopped tomato
2 teaspoons lemon juice
2 tablespoons chopped fresh parsley
½ teaspoon salt
¼ teaspoon ground red pepper
¼ teaspoon freshly ground black pepper
Grilled Pork Medaillons
1 Red Delicious apple, cut into 12 wedges
Garnish: fresh thyme sprig

Cook onion and celery in olive oil in a large saucepan over medium heat, stirring constantly, until tender. Add chicken broth and dried thyme; bring mixture to a boil. Add wild rice. Cover, reduce heat, and cook 30 minutes.

Add black-eyed peas and next 7 ingredients; cover and cook 20 minutes or until rice is tender.

Serve with medaillons and apple wedges. Garnish, if desired. **Yield: 4 (1¼-cup) servings.**

Grilled Pork Medaillons

¼ cup lemon juice
2 tablespoons reduced-sodium soy sauce
2 cloves garlic, pressed
1 (¾-pound) pork tenderloin, trimmed
Vegetable cooking spray

Combine first 3 ingredients in a shallow container or a large heavy-duty, zip-top plastic bag. Add tenderloin; cover or seal and chill 8 hours.

Remove tenderloin from marinade, discarding marinade. Coat food rack with cooking spray; place rack on grill, and place tenderloin on rack.

Cook, covered with grill lid, over medium-hot coals (350° to 400°), 12 minutes on each side or until a meat thermometer registers 160°. Cut into 12 slices. **Yield: 4 servings.**

PER SERVING: 410 CALORIES (12% FROM FAT)
FAT 5.4G (SATURATED FAT 1.5G)
PROTEIN 29.7G CARBOHYDRATE 58.6G
CHOLESTEROL 63MG SODIUM 609MG

Fruit-Topped Pork Chops

1 tablespoon reduced-calorie margarine
¼ cup chopped celery
2 tablespoons chopped onion
1 cup herb-seasoned stuffing mix
3 (0.9-ounce) packages mixed dried fruit
2 tablespoons raisins
6 (4-ounce) lean, boneless center-cut loin pork chops (¾ inch thick)
¼ teaspoon salt
¼ teaspoon pepper
¼ cup all-purpose flour
Vegetable cooking spray
½ cup Chablis or other dry white wine

Melt margarine in a large skillet; add celery and onion. Cook, stirring constantly, until tender. Add stuffing mix, dried fruit, and raisins; toss.

Sprinkle pork chops with salt and pepper; dredge in flour. Coat a large nonstick skillet with cooking spray; add chops, and brown on both sides over medium heat.

Arrange chops in an 11- x 7- x 1½-inch baking dish coated with cooking spray; top with fruit mixture. Add wine to dish. Cover; bake at 350° for 40 to 45 minutes. **Yield: 6 servings.**

PER SERVING: 302 CALORIES (27% FROM FAT)
FAT 9.1G (SATURATED FAT 2.8G)
PROTEIN 28.2G CARBOHYDRATE 26.0G
CHOLESTEROL 80MG SODIUM 346MG

Creole-Style Pork Chops

4 (4-ounce) lean, boneless top loin pork chops
Vegetable cooking spray
½ cup chopped onion
½ cup chopped celery
½ cup chopped green pepper
½ cup chopped sweet red pepper
3 large cloves garlic, crushed
1 cup whole tomatoes, undrained and
    chopped
½ teaspoon hot sauce
¼ teaspoon pepper
2 cups hot cooked rice (cooked without salt
    or fat)
1 teaspoon cornstarch
¼ cup ready-to-serve, no-salt-added chicken
    broth

    Trim fat from chops. Coat a nonstick skillet with cooking spray; place over medium-high heat until hot. Add pork chops, and brown on all sides. Remove from skillet.

    Coat a nonstick skillet with cooking spray; place over medium-high heat until hot. Add onion and next 4 ingredients; cook until tender, stirring constantly. Remove ½ cup vegetable mixture from skillet; set aside.

    Add tomato, hot sauce, and pepper to skillet. Return pork chops to skillet; cover and cook 15 minutes, turning pork chops once.

    Stir reserved ½ cup vegetable mixture into rice; spoon onto a serving plate. Arrange pork chops on top of rice.

    Combine cornstarch and chicken broth; add to vegetable mixture in skillet. Cook over medium heat, stirring constantly, until mixture begins to boil; boil 1 minute, stirring constantly, until thickened. Spoon over chops. **Yield: 4 servings.**

PER SERVING: 307 CALORIES (24% FROM FAT)
FAT 8.1G (SATURATED FAT 2.6G)
PROTEIN 24.0G CARBOHYDRATE 33.2G
CHOLESTEROL 60MG SODIUM 303MG

Black-Eyed Pea Jambalaya

1½ cups dried black-eyed peas
3 (15.75-ounce) cans ready-to-serve, reduced-
    sodium, fat-free chicken broth
2 cups chopped tomato
1½ cups cubed lean cooked ham
1 cup chopped onion
¾ cup chopped green pepper
¼ cup chopped celery
2 cloves garlic, minced
1 bay leaf
½ teaspoon salt
¼ teaspoon dried thyme
⅛ teaspoon ground cloves
1½ cups long-grain rice, uncooked
1½ teaspoons hot sauce
½ cup sliced green onions

    Sort and wash peas; place in a 5- or 6-quart pressure cooker. Add next 11 ingredients; stir well.

    Close lid securely; according to manufacturer's directions, bring to high pressure over high heat (about 10 to 12 minutes). Reduce heat to medium-low or level needed to maintain high pressure; cook 15 minutes.

    Remove from heat; run cold water over pressure cooker to reduce pressure instantly. Remove lid so that steam escapes away from you. Drain, reserving 3 cups liquid. Remove pea mixture from cooker, and keep warm. Discard bay leaf.

    Add rice and reserved liquid to cooker. Close lid; bring to high pressure over high heat (about 5 minutes). Reduce heat to medium-low or level needed to maintain high pressure; cook 5 minutes.

    Remove from heat; let stand 10 minutes or until pressure drops. Remove lid. Add pea mixture, hot sauce, and green onions; toss. **Yield: 8 servings.**

PER SERVING: 228 CALORIES (8% FROM FAT)
FAT 2.0G (SATURATED FAT 0.6G)
PROTEIN 11.1G CARBOHYDRATE 40.2G
CHOLESTEROL 12MG SODIUM 538MG

Ham-and-Asparagus Fettuccine

1 pound fresh asparagus
2 cups chopped, reduced-fat, low-salt lean ham
Vegetable cooking spray
Alfredo Sauce
1 (12-ounce) package fettuccine, cooked
    without salt or fat

Snap off tough ends of asparagus. Remove scales from stalks with a knife or vegetable peeler, if desired. Cut diagonally into ½-inch slices.

Cook asparagus in a small amount of boiling water 3 minutes. Drain well, and set aside.

Cook ham over medium heat in a large non-stick skillet coated with cooking spray, stirring constantly, until thoroughly heated.

Stir in Alfredo Sauce; add fettuccine and asparagus, and toss gently before serving. **Yield: 6 servings.**

Alfredo Sauce

2 cups nonfat cottage cheese
3 tablespoons grated Parmesan cheese
2 tablespoons butter-flavored granules
½ cup evaporated fat-free milk
½ teaspoon chicken-flavored bouillon granules
½ teaspoon dried basil
¼ teaspoon ground black pepper
Dash of ground red pepper

Combine all ingredients in container of an electric blender; cover and process until smooth, stopping once to scrape down sides.

Pour into a small saucepan; cook sauce over low heat, stirring constantly, until thoroughly heated. **Yield: 2¾ cups.**

PER SERVING: 370 CALORIES (11% FROM FAT)
FAT 4.6G (SATURATED FAT 1.5G)
PROTEIN 30.4G CARBOHYDRATE 52.0G
CHOLESTEROL 33MG SODIUM 917MG

Ham-and-Asparagus Fettuccine

From left: Country Sausage, Chorizo, and Basic Meat Mixture

Basic Meat Mixture

4 pounds boneless, skinless turkey breast
2 pounds boneless pork loin
2 tablespoons browning-and-seasoning sauce
1 teaspoon salt

Position knife blade in food processor bowl; add half of turkey, pork, and seasonings. Process until smooth. Repeat procedure with remaining ingredients. **Yield: 6 pounds.**

PER POUND: 599 CALORIES (24% FROM FAT)
FAT 16.0G (SATURATED FAT 5.5G)
PROTEIN 102.4G CARBOHYDRATE 3.0G
CHOLESTEROL 272MG SODIUM 688MG

Country Sausage

1 pound Basic Meat Mixture
1 teaspoon rubbed sage
½ teaspoon black pepper
¼ teaspoon dried crushed red pepper
Vegetable cooking spray

Combine first 4 ingredients; shape into eight (2-ounce) patties. Coat a nonstick skillet with cooking spray; place over medium heat until hot.
Cook sausage patties 3 minutes on each side or until browned. **Yield: 4 servings.**

PER SERVING: 153 CALORIES (25% FROM FAT)
FAT 4.2G (SATURATED FAT 1.4G)
PROTEIN 25.7G CARBOHYDRATE 1.1G
CHOLESTEROL 68MG SODIUM 173MG

Chorizo

1 pound Basic Meat Mixture
¼ cup white vinegar
1 tablespoon dry sherry
2 teaspoons paprika
2 teaspoons chili powder
½ teaspoon dried oregano
½ teaspoon ground cumin
¼ teaspoon pepper
⅛ teaspoon ground cinnamon
⅛ teaspoon ground cloves
Pinch of ground coriander
Pinch of ground ginger
½ teaspoon browning-and-seasoning sauce
2 cloves garlic, crushed
1 yard sausage casing
½ cup water

Combine first 14 ingredients; divide into four (4-ounce) portions. Cut casing into four (8-inch) pieces; slip one end of each casing over sausage funnel tip. Force a portion through funnel into each casing; twist ends.
Bring water to a boil in a nonstick skillet; add sausage. Cover, reduce heat, and simmer 10 minutes. Uncover and cook over medium heat 5 minutes or until browned, turning occasionally. **Yield: 4 servings.**

PER SERVING: 166 CALORIES (24% FROM FAT)
FAT 4.5G (SATURATED FAT 1.4G)
PROTEIN 26.1G CARBOHYDRATE 4.3G
CHOLESTEROL 68MG SODIUM 188MG

Poultry

Poultry is no longer reserved just for Sunday dinner. High in protein and low in fat and calories, poultry is a versatile, delicious, and smart choice any day of the week.

Lemon-Roasted Chicken, Old-Fashioned Chicken and Dumplings

Sherried Chicken with Artichokes, Grilled Lime Chicken with Black Bean Sauce

Poached Chicken Breast in Wine, Basil-Stuffed Chicken with Tomato-Basil Pasta

Tarragon Roasted Cornish Hens with Vegetables, Turkey Lasagna

Oven-Fried Chicken (page 774)

Lemon-Roasted Chicken

1½ teaspoons salt
2 teaspoons freshly ground pepper
2 to 3 teaspoons dried rosemary, crushed
1 (3-pound) broiler-fryer
1 medium lemon, cut in half

Combine first 3 ingredients; set aside.
Loosen skin from chicken breast by running fingers between the two; rub about 1 teaspoon seasoning mixture under skin. Rub remaining seasoning mixture over outside of chicken. Place chicken in a heavy-duty, zip-top plastic bag; seal and chill 8 hours.
Remove chicken from bag. Insert lemon halves in cavity; tie ends of legs together with string. Lift wing tips up and over back, and tuck under bird. Place chicken, breast side down, in a lightly greased shallow pan.
Bake at 450°, turning over every 15 minutes, for 50 minutes or until a meat thermometer registers 180°. Let chicken stand 10 minutes. Remove skin before serving. **Yield: 6 servings.**

PER SERVING: 172 CALORIES (35% FROM FAT)
FAT 6.6G (SATURATED FAT 1.8G)
PROTEIN 25.7G CARBOHYDRATE 1.0G
CHOLESTEROL 79MG SODIUM 662MG

Oven-Fried Chicken
(pictured on page 773)

½ cup crisp rice cereal crumbs
½ teaspoon pepper
½ teaspoon paprika
¼ teaspoon salt
4 (6-ounce) skinned chicken breast halves
Butter-flavored cooking spray

Combine first 4 ingredients in a shallow dish. Coat chicken with cooking spray; dredge in rice cereal mixture.

Place chicken on a baking sheet coated with cooking spray, and coat chicken again with cooking spray. Bake at 350° for 50 minutes or until done. **Yield: 4 servings.**

PER SERVING: 170 CALORIES (21% FROM FAT)
FAT 3.9G (SATURATED FAT 0.9G)
PROTEIN 28.3G CARBOHYDRATE 3.4G
CHOLESTEROL 77MG SODIUM 256MG

Poached Chicken Breast in Wine

4 (4-ounce) skinned and boned chicken breast
    halves
¾ cup Chablis or other dry white wine
2½ cups sliced fresh mushrooms
2 tablespoons chopped fresh parsley
½ teaspoon dried tarragon
½ teaspoon salt
¼ teaspoon pepper
1 tablespoon cornstarch
2 teaspoons water

Place chicken between two sheets of heavy-duty plastic wrap; flatten to ¼-inch thickness, using a meat mallet or rolling pin. Set aside.
Combine Chablis and next 5 ingredients in a large skillet; bring to a boil over high heat. Arrange chicken in a single layer in skillet; cover, reduce heat, and simmer 15 minutes or until chicken is tender. Remove chicken to a platter; keep warm.
Combine cornstarch and water; stir into skillet. Bring mixture to a boil; boil 1 minute, stirring constantly. Pour sauce over chicken. **Yield: 4 servings.**

PER SERVING: 147 CALORIES (10% FROM FAT)
FAT 1.6G (SATURATED FAT 0.4G)
PROTEIN 27.3G CARBOHYDRATE 4.8G
CHOLESTEROL 66MG SODIUM 373MG

Dante's Chicken

Dante's Chicken

½ teaspoon ground ginger
½ teaspoon curry powder
⅛ teaspoon ground red pepper
4 (4-ounce) skinned and boned chicken breast halves
Vegetable cooking spray
2 cloves garlic, minced
3 tablespoons minced shallots
¼ cup sliced celery
½ cup sweet red pepper strips
½ cup canned chicken broth
½ cup Chablis or other dry white wine
¼ teaspoon ground ginger
Garnish: celery leaves

Combine first 3 ingredients; rub spice mixture on chicken. Set aside.

Coat a large nonstick skillet with cooking spray; place over medium-high heat until hot. Add garlic, shallots, celery, and red pepper strips; sauté 1 minute, stirring constantly. Remove from skillet.

Place chicken in skillet; cook until lightly browned, turning once. Return vegetables to skillet. Combine broth, Chablis, and ¼ teaspoon ginger; stir well. Pour over chicken. Cover, reduce heat, and simmer 15 minutes.

Arrange chicken and vegetables on a platter; garnish, if desired. **Yield: 4 servings.**

PER SERVING: 147 CALORIES (12% FROM FAT)
FAT 1.9G (SATURATED FAT 0.5G)
PROTEIN 27.4G CARBOHYDRATE 3.6G
CHOLESTEROL 66MG SODIUM 181MG

Chicken and Vegetables with Ginger-Soy Sauce

2 (4-ounce) skinned and boned chicken breast halves
¾ cup onion wedges
1 cup whole fresh mushrooms
¼ teaspoon onion powder
¼ teaspoon garlic powder
2 cups broccoli flowerets
1½ cups hot cooked rice (cooked without salt or fat)
Ginger-Soy Sauce

Layer chicken, onion, and mushrooms in a steamer basket over boiling water. Sprinkle with onion powder and garlic powder. Cover and steam 10 minutes.

Add broccoli; cover and steam 10 additional minutes or until chicken is tender.

Serve chicken and vegetables over rice; top with Ginger-Soy Sauce. **Yield: 2 servings.**

Ginger-Soy Sauce

1 teaspoon sugar
1 tablespoon cornstarch
1 teaspoon chicken bouillon granules
¼ teaspoon ground ginger
1 cup water
1 tablespoon reduced-sodium soy sauce
1 tablespoon dry sherry

Combine all ingredients in a heavy saucepan. Place over medium heat, and bring to a boil; boil 1 minute, stirring constantly. **Yield: 1 cup.**

PER SERVING: 400 CALORIES (10% FROM FAT)
FAT 4.3G (SATURATED FAT 1.1G)
PROTEIN 34.3G CARBOHYDRATE 56.2G
CHOLESTEROL 72MG SODIUM 743MG

Chicken with Mole Sauce

2½ cups no-salt-added chicken broth, divided
½ cup onion slices, separated into rings
1 clove garlic, sliced
½ cup raisins
¼ cup slivered almonds
3 tablespoons chili powder
2 tablespoons sesame seeds
1 tablespoon unsweetened cocoa
1 tablespoon sugar
½ teaspoon ground allspice
¼ teaspoon salt
¼ teaspoon pepper
1 tablespoon cornmeal
Vegetable cooking spray
8 (4-ounce) skinned and boned chicken breast halves

Combine 2 cups chicken broth, onion, and garlic in a saucepan; cook over medium heat 10 minutes or until onion is tender. Pour into container of an electric blender; add raisins and next 8 ingredients.

Process until smooth, stopping once to scrape down sides. Return mixture to saucepan; stir in cornmeal. Cook over medium heat, stirring constantly, until thickened and bubbly. Remove from heat, and keep sauce warm.

Coat a large nonstick skillet with cooking spray; place over high heat until hot. Add chicken; brown quickly on both sides. Reduce heat; add remaining ½ cup chicken broth, and cook 15 minutes or until chicken is tender.

Spoon ¼ cup sauce onto each plate; place a chicken breast over sauce. **Yield: 8 servings.**

PER SERVING: 232 CALORIES (25% FROM FAT)
FAT 6.5G (SATURATED FAT 1.3G)
PROTEIN 28.6G CARBOHYDRATE 14.1G
CHOLESTEROL 72MG SODIUM 169MG

Chicken-Fried Wild Rice

1 pound skinned and boned chicken breasts
¼ cup low-sodium teriyaki sauce
¼ cup low-sodium soy sauce
¼ cup Chablis or other dry white wine
2 cloves garlic, minced
½ teaspoon grated fresh ginger
¼ teaspoon Chinese five-spice powder
1 (4-ounce) package wild rice
1 teaspoon vegetable oil
1 cup sliced green pepper
⅔ cup sliced carrot
⅔ cup chopped onion
⅔ cup sliced fresh mushrooms
½ cup frozen English peas, thawed
Vegetable cooking spray
2 tablespoons slivered almonds, toasted

Cut chicken into 1-inch pieces; place in a bowl. Add teriyaki sauce and next 5 ingredients;

stir well. Cover and marinate in refrigerator at least 1 hour.

Cook rice according to package directions, omitting salt; keep warm.

Add oil to a wok or heavy skillet, and heat to medium-high (375°) for 1 minute. Add green pepper, carrot, and onion; stir-fry 3 minutes. Add mushrooms and peas; stir-fry 2 minutes. Stir into rice; set aside.

Coat wok with cooking spray; place over medium-high heat until hot. Add chicken and marinade to wok; stir-fry 4 minutes or until done. Add rice and vegetables; stir-fry 1 to 2 minutes or until heated. Sprinkle with almonds. **Yield: 4 servings.**

PER SERVING: 317 CALORIES (14% FROM FAT)
FAT 4.9G (SATURATED FAT 0.8G)
PROTEIN 33.6G CARBOHYDRATE 33.4G
CHOLESTEROL 66MG SODIUM 526MG

Chicken-Fried Wild Rice

Chinese Chicken Stir-Fry

1 egg white
1 tablespoon dry sherry
1 teaspoon cornstarch
4 (3-ounce) skinned and boned chicken breast
    halves
3 tablespoons reduced-sodium soy sauce
2 tablespoons water
1 tablespoon rice wine
1½ teaspoons cornstarch
¼ teaspoon salt
2 teaspoons sesame oil
Vegetable cooking spray
2 tablespoons vegetable oil
1 (16-ounce) package frozen broccoli, green
    beans, pearl onions, and red peppers
1 (8-ounce) can bamboo shoots, drained
1 (6-ounce) package frozen snow pea pods
3 cups hot cooked rice (cooked without salt
    or fat)

Combine first 3 ingredients; beat with a wire whisk until frothy. Add chicken; cover and let stand at least 15 minutes.

Combine soy sauce and next 5 ingredients; beat with wire whisk. Set aside.

Coat a wok or heavy skillet with cooking spray; add vegetable oil, and heat to medium-high (375°) for 2 minutes. Add chicken; stir-fry 2 to 3 minutes. Remove chicken from wok.

Add mixed vegetables, bamboo shoots, and snow peas to wok; stir-fry 3 to 4 minutes.

Add chicken and soy sauce mixture; stir-fry until vegetables are crisp-tender. Serve over rice. **Yield: 4 servings.**

Per Serving: 469 Calories (22% from Fat)
Fat 11.4g (Saturated Fat 2.0g)
Protein 29.9g Carbohydrate 60.1g
Cholesterol 49mg Sodium 635mg

Grilled Lime Chicken with Black Bean Sauce

4 (4-ounce) skinned and boned chicken breast
    halves
¼ cup lime juice
2 tablespoons vegetable oil
½ teaspoon ground red pepper
6 cloves garlic, minced
½ cup finely chopped sweet red pepper
1 tablespoon finely chopped purple onion
1 cup canned black beans, rinsed
½ cup orange juice
2 tablespoons balsamic vinegar
¼ teaspoon salt
⅛ teaspoon freshly ground black pepper
1 clove garlic, minced

Place chicken in a shallow dish; set aside.

Combine lime juice and next 3 ingredients; divide mixture in half. Cover one portion and chill; pour remaining portion over chicken, turning to coat.

Cover chicken, and chill 1 hour.

Combine sweet red pepper and onion in a 9-inch microwave-safe pieplate; cover with wax paper. Microwave at HIGH 1 minute; set aside.

Position knife blade in food processor bowl; add black beans and remaining ingredients. Process 1 minute or until smooth.

Pour black bean mixture into a heavy saucepan, and cook over medium heat until mixture is hot. Keep warm.

Uncover chicken; drain, discarding marinade. Cook chicken, without grill lid, over medium-hot coals (350° to 400°) about 5 minutes on each side or until done, basting with chilled marinade.

Serve chicken with black bean sauce and sweet red pepper mixture. **Yield: 4 servings.**

Per Serving: 255 Calories (24% from Fat)
Fat 6.8g (Saturated Fat 1.5g)
Protein 30.4g Carbohydrate 17.5g
Cholesterol 70mg Sodium 334mg

Basil-Stuffed Chicken with Tomato-Basil Pasta

4 (4-ounce) skinned and boned chicken breast
    halves
¼ teaspoon salt
¼ teaspoon garlic powder
2 bunches fresh basil (about 20 large basil
    leaves)
Tomato-Basil Pasta
Garnish: fresh basil sprigs

Place chicken between 2 sheets of heavy-duty plastic wrap; flatten to ¼-inch thickness, using a meat mallet or rolling pin.

Sprinkle evenly with salt and garlic powder.

Arrange basil leaves in a single layer over chicken. Starting at short end, roll up 2 chicken breasts. Place each roll on top of a remaining chicken breast, and roll up, forming two larger rolls. Secure chicken with wooden picks.

Cook, covered with grill lid, over medium-hot coals (350° to 400°) 18 to 20 minutes, turning once. Wrap chicken rolls in aluminum foil; chill at least 8 hours.

Unwrap chicken rolls, and place on a microwave-safe plate; cover with wax paper.

Microwave at MEDIUM-HIGH (70% power) 1½ minutes, turning once. Remove wooden picks.

Cut each chicken roll into thin slices. Serve slices with Tomato-Basil Pasta. Garnish, if desired. **Yield: 4 servings.**

Tomato-Basil Pasta

1 tablespoon reduced-calorie margarine
2 cloves garlic, minced
¼ cup lemon juice
¼ cup Chablis or other dry white wine
¼ cup chopped fresh basil
1 cup peeled, seeded, and finely chopped
    tomato
8 ounces thin spaghetti, cooked without salt
    or fat

Melt margarine in a large saucepan over medium heat; add minced garlic, and cook 1 minute, stirring constantly. Add lemon juice and remaining ingredients; toss gently. **Yield: 4 servings.**

PER SERVING: 387 CALORIES (13% FROM FAT)
FAT 5.4G (SATURATED FAT 1.2G)
PROTEIN 33.7G CARBOHYDRATE 46.7G
CHOLESTEROL 70MG SODIUM 252MG

Sherried Chicken with Artichokes

6 (4-ounce) skinned and boned chicken breast
    halves
½ teaspoon pepper
1 teaspoon paprika
Vegetable cooking spray
1 (14-ounce) can artichoke hearts, drained
1⅓ cups sliced fresh mushrooms
3 tablespoons thinly sliced green onions
1 tablespoon cornstarch
1 teaspoon chicken-flavored bouillon granules
⅔ cup water
¼ cup dry sherry
½ teaspoon dried rosemary, crushed

Sprinkle chicken with pepper and paprika; set aside. Coat a large nonstick skillet with cooking spray; heat skillet. Add chicken, and cook 5 minutes or until browned, turning once.

Place chicken in a 13- x 9- x 2-inch baking dish coated with cooking spray. Arrange artichoke hearts around chicken; set aside.

Combine mushrooms and green onions in a skillet; cook 5 minutes or until vegetables are tender.

Combine cornstarch and remaining ingredients; stir well. Pour into skillet, and bring to a boil; boil 1 minute, stirring constantly. Pour over chicken mixture. Cover and bake at 375° for 30 minutes. **Yield: 6 servings.**

PER SERVING: 161 CALORIES (11% FROM FAT)
FAT 1.9G (SATURATED FAT 0.5G)
PROTEIN 28.1G CARBOHYDRATE 7.5G
CHOLESTEROL 66MG SODIUM 348MG

Chicken Breasts with Fruited Rice Pilaf

½ cup unsweetened apple juice
½ cup no-salt-added chicken broth
1 cup chopped dried apricots
¼ cup raisins
Butter-flavored cooking spray
1 cup chopped onion
½ cup chopped celery
½ cup chopped fresh parsley
2 cups cooked brown rice (cooked without salt or fat)
½ teaspoon salt
½ teaspoon pepper
½ teaspoon rubbed sage
¼ teaspoon poultry seasoning
4 (6-ounce) skinned chicken breast halves
¼ teaspoon pepper

Combine juice and broth in a saucepan; bring to a boil. Stir in apricots and raisins; remove from heat. Cover and let stand 1 hour. (Do not drain.)

Coat a nonstick skillet with cooking spray; place over medium-high heat until hot. Add onion, celery, and parsley; cook, stirring constantly, until tender. Remove from heat; stir in apricot mixture, rice, and next 4 ingredients.

Place chicken in an 11- x 7- x 1½-inch baking dish coated with cooking spray; sprinkle with ¼ teaspoon pepper. Spoon rice around chicken.

Cover and bake at 350° for 35 minutes; uncover and bake 10 minutes or until chicken is tender. **Yield: 4 servings.**

PER SERVING: 401 CALORIES (7% FROM FAT)
FAT 3.1G (SATURATED FAT 0.6G)
PROTEIN 31.4G CARBOHYDRATE 63.6G
CHOLESTEROL 66MG SODIUM 423MG

Old-Fashioned Chicken and Dumplings

1 (3½-pound) broiler-fryer, cut up and skinned
1 stalk celery, cut into thirds
1 medium onion, quartered
2 quarts water
1 teaspoon salt
½ teaspoon pepper
2 cups all-purpose flour
½ teaspoon baking soda
½ teaspoon salt
3 tablespoons margarine
2 tablespoons chopped fresh parsley
¾ cup nonfat buttermilk

Combine first 5 ingredients in a Dutch oven; bring to a boil. Cover, reduce heat, and simmer 1 hour or until chicken is tender. Remove chicken, reserving broth in Dutch oven; discard vegetables. Let chicken and broth cool.

Bone and cut chicken into bite-size pieces. Place chicken and broth in separate containers; cover and chill 8 hours. Remove fat from broth; bring to a boil, and add pepper.

Combine flour, soda, and ½ teaspoon salt; cut in margarine with a pastry blender until mixture is crumbly. Add parsley and buttermilk, stirring with a fork until dry ingredients are moistened.

Turn dough out onto a heavily floured surface, and knead lightly 4 or 5 times. Pat dough to ¼-inch thickness. Pinch off 1½-inch pieces, and drop into boiling broth. Add chicken. Reduce heat to medium-low, and cook 8 to 10 minutes, stirring occasionally. **Yield: 8 servings.**

PER SERVING: 283 CALORIES (27% FROM FAT)
FAT 8.5G (SATURATED FAT 1.3G)
PROTEIN 20.6G CARBOHYDRATE 26.8G
CHOLESTEROL 50MG SODIUM 613MG

Chicken à la King

Chicken à la King

1 tablespoon reduced-calorie margarine

3 (4-ounce) skinned and boned chicken breast
    halves, cut into bite-size pieces

¼ cup chopped onion

¼ cup sliced fresh mushrooms

¼ cup all-purpose flour

2 cups fat-free milk

¼ cup frozen English peas, thawed

1 (2-ounce) jar diced pimiento, drained

½ teaspoon salt

½ teaspoon pepper

4 slices whole wheat bread, trimmed and
    toasted

¼ teaspoon paprika

Melt margarine in a large nonstick skillet over medium heat. Add chicken and onion; cook, stirring constantly, 3 to 5 minutes or until chicken is browned. Add mushrooms; cook 1 minute.

Stir in flour, and cook, stirring constantly, 1 minute. Gradually add milk and next 4 ingredients; cook over medium heat, stirring constantly, until mixture is thickened and bubbly.

Cut each slice of bread into 4 triangles. Serve chicken mixture with toast triangles; sprinkle with paprika. **Yield: 4 servings.**

PER SERVING: 254 CALORIES (14% FROM FAT)
FAT 4.0G (SATURATED FAT 0.6G)
PROTEIN 28.0G CARBOHYDRATE 26.4G
CHOLESTEROL 53MG SODIUM 573MG

Chicken Pot Pie

1 (3½-pound) broiler-fryer
2 quarts water
½ teaspoon salt
½ teaspoon pepper
1 stalk celery, cut into 2-inch pieces
1 medium onion, quartered
1 bay leaf
3½ cups peeled and cubed potato
    (1½ pounds)
1 (16-ounce) package frozen mixed vegetables
½ cup all-purpose flour
1 cup fat-free milk
¾ teaspoon salt
1 teaspoon pepper
½ teaspoon poultry seasoning
Butter-flavored cooking spray
5 sheets frozen phyllo pastry, thawed

Combine first 7 ingredients in a large Dutch oven; bring to a boil. Cover, reduce heat, and simmer 1 hour or until chicken is tender.

Remove chicken, reserving broth in Dutch oven; discard vegetables and bay leaf. Let chicken cool; skin, bone, and cut into bite-size pieces.

Remove fat (oily liquid) from chicken broth, reserving 3½ cups broth.

Bring reserved broth to a boil in Dutch oven. Add potato and mixed vegetables; return to a boil. Cover, reduce heat, and simmer 8 minutes or until vegetables are tender.

Combine flour and milk in a jar; cover tightly, and shake vigorously. Gradually add to broth mixture in a slow, steady stream, stirring constantly. Cook, stirring constantly, 1 minute or until thickened. Stir in ¾ teaspoon salt, 1 teaspoon pepper, poultry seasoning, and chicken.

Spoon mixture into a 13- x 9- x 2-inch baking dish coated with cooking spray; set aside.

Place 1 phyllo sheet horizontally on a flat surface, keeping remaining sheets covered with a slightly damp towel until ready for use. Coat sheet with cooking spray. Layer remaining 4 sheets on first sheet, coating each with cooking spray. Place on top of baking dish, loosely crushing edges around the dish.

Bake pot pie at 400° for 20 minutes. **Yield: 8 servings.**

Note: Remove fat by chilling broth and removing congealed fat, or by pouring broth through a large fat separator.

Per Serving: 249 Calories (20% from Fat)
Fat 5.5g (Saturated Fat 1.0g)
Protein 21.5g Carbohydrate 25.9g
Cholesterol 50mg Sodium 465mg

Game Hens with Chutney-Mustard Glaze

1 (1¼-pound) Cornish hen, skinned and split
Vegetable cooking spray
2 tablespoons chopped mango chutney
2 teaspoons Dijon mustard

Place hen halves, cut side down, on a rack coated with cooking spray; place rack in a broiler pan. Combine chutney and mustard, and brush about one-third of chutney mixture over hen.

Bake, uncovered, at 325° for 50 to 60 minutes, brushing twice with chutney mixture. **Yield: 2 servings.**

Per Serving: 288 Calories (30% from Fat)
Fat 9.6g (Saturated Fat 4.3g)
Protein 37.0g Carbohydrate 11.0g
Cholesterol 113mg Sodium 209mg

Lean Tips for Poultry

• Trim away all visible fat.
• Remove skin either before cooking or before serving.
• Remember that white meat generally contains less fat than dark meat.

Tarragon Roasted Cornish Hens with Vegetables

2 (1¼-pound) Cornish hens, skinned and split
1 teaspoon olive oil
1 tablespoon minced garlic
3 to 4 tablespoons chopped fresh tarragon
1 tablespoon cracked black pepper
½ teaspoon salt
8 Roma tomatoes, halved
4 carrots, cut into 2-inch slices
2 medium onions, quartered
¾ pound fresh mushrooms
1 teaspoon olive oil
½ teaspoon ground white pepper
1 cup Chablis or other dry white wine
1 cup fat-free, reduced-sodium chicken broth
1 teaspoon reduced-sodium Worcestershire
    sauce
2 dashes of hot sauce

Rub hens with 1 teaspoon olive oil and minced garlic. Place hens in a large roasting pan; set aside.

Combine tarragon, black pepper, and salt; sprinkle over hens.

Combine tomato and next 5 ingredients; toss mixture gently, and place in roasting pan.

Bake hens and vegetables at 350° for 45 minutes; keep warm.

Combine pan juices, wine, and remaining ingredients; bring mixture to a boil. Reduce heat, and simmer 20 minutes or until mixture is reduced to 1 cup.

Transfer hens and vegetables to individual serving plates. Serve sauce with hen halves and vegetables. **Yield: 4 servings.**

PER SERVING: 335 CALORIES (20% FROM FAT)
FAT 7.4G (SATURATED FAT 1.7G)
PROTEIN 41.0G CARBOHYDRATE 27.1G
CHOLESTEROL 117MG SODIUM 474MG

Turkey Lasagna

Vegetable cooking spray
1½ pounds freshly ground raw turkey
1¼ cups chopped onion
1 cup chopped green pepper
2 cloves garlic, chopped
½ teaspoon dried Italian seasoning
¼ cup chopped fresh parsley
2 (6-ounce) cans tomato paste
1 (10-ounce) can diced tomatoes and green
    chiles, undrained
1½ cups water
2 egg whites, lightly beaten
2 cups 1% low-fat cottage cheese
2 tablespoons chopped fresh parsley
10 lasagna noodles, cooked without salt or fat
½ cup grated Parmesan cheese
1 cup (4 ounces) shredded part-skim
    mozzarella cheese

Coat a large, nonstick skillet with cooking spray; place over medium-high heat until hot. Add ground turkey and next 3 ingredients; cook until meat is browned and vegetables are tender, stirring to crumble meat. Drain and pat dry with paper towels. Wipe drippings from skillet.

Return mixture to skillet; add Italian seasoning and next 4 ingredients. Cover and cook over medium heat 30 minutes, stirring often; set aside. Combine egg whites and next 2 ingredients; set aside.

Coat a 13- x 9- x 2-inch baking dish with cooking spray. Place 5 cooked noodles in bottom of dish. Top with half each of turkey mixture and cottage cheese mixture. Repeat layers.

Cover and bake at 350° for 25 minutes. Uncover and sprinkle with cheeses; bake, uncovered, 5 minutes or until cheese melts. Let stand 10 minutes. **Yield: 8 servings.**

PER SERVING: 369 CALORIES (21% FROM FAT)
FAT 8.5G (SATURATED FAT 3.9G)
PROTEIN 37.6G CARBOHYDRATE 35.1G
CHOLESTEROL 62MG SODIUM 594MG

Turkey-Vegetable Pizza

Turkey-Vegetable Pizza

½ cup no-salt-added tomato sauce
1 (6-ounce) can tomato paste
2 tablespoons grated Parmesan cheese
¾ teaspoon dried Italian seasoning
½ teaspoon dried basil
¼ teaspoon garlic powder
1 teaspoon sugar
⅛ teaspoon ground black pepper
½ pound freshly ground raw turkey
Dash of ground red pepper
¼ teaspoon fennel seeds, crushed
Special Pizza Crust
1 (4-ounce) can sliced mushrooms, drained
¼ cup thinly sliced onion
1 green pepper, cut into strips
1 cup thinly sliced fresh broccoli
1 cup (4 ounces) shredded part-skim
    mozzarella cheese

Combine first 8 ingredients in a bowl; stir well. Let stand 1 hour.

Cook ground turkey, red pepper, and fennel seeds in a nonstick skillet, stirring constantly to crumble meat; drain.

Spread sauce over Special Pizza Crust. Sprinkle turkey mixture over sauce. Top with mushrooms, onion, green pepper, and broccoli.

Bake at 425° for 15 minutes. Top with cheese; bake 5 minutes. **Yield: 8 servings.**

Special Pizza Crust

½ package active dry yeast
2 tablespoons warm water (105°-115°)
½ cup whole wheat flour
½ cup all-purpose flour
⅛ teaspoon salt
1½ teaspoons olive oil
¼ to ⅓ cup warm water (105°-115°)
Vegetable cooking spray

Dissolve yeast in 2 tablespoons warm water in a small bowl; let stand 5 minutes. Combine flours and salt in a large bowl; stir in yeast mixture and oil. Add enough warm water to make a moderately stiff dough; stir well. Cover; let stand 15 minutes.

Turn dough out onto a lightly floured surface. Knead 5 to 8 times.

Roll dough into a 12-inch circle; place on a 12-inch pizza pan coated with cooking spray.

Bake at 425° for 5 minutes. **Yield: 1 (12-inch) pizza crust.**

PER SERVING: 169 CALORIES (24% FROM FAT)
FAT 4.7G (SATURATED FAT 2.1G)
PROTEIN 12.6G CARBOHYDRATE 20.6G
CHOLESTEROL 23MG SODIUM 164MG

Oven-Fried Turkey Cutlets

1 large egg
2 teaspoons vegetable oil
½ cup Italian-seasoned breadcrumbs
2 tablespoons grated Parmesan cheese
1 pound turkey breast cutlets
Vegetable cooking spray
½ cup commercial marinara sauce

Combine egg and oil in a shallow dish; beat well, and set aside.

Combine breadcrumbs and Parmesan cheese in a shallow dish. Dip turkey in egg mixture; dredge in breadcrumb mixture.

Place turkey on a baking sheet coated with cooking spray. Spray cutlets lightly with cooking spray.

Bake at 350° for 8 to 10 minutes or until done. Serve turkey with marinara sauce. **Yield: 4 servings.**

PER SERVING: 260 CALORIES (27% FROM FAT)
FAT 7.8G (SATURATED FAT 2.2G)
PROTEIN 32.0G CARBOHYDRATE 14.1G
CHOLESTEROL 125MG SODIUM 747MG

Turkey-and-Shrimp Florentine Casserole

1 pound unpeeled medium-size fresh shrimp
1 pound turkey breast fillets
¼ teaspoon garlic powder
¼ teaspoon pepper
¼ cup Chablis or other dry white wine
2 (10-ounce) packages frozen chopped
    spinach
1 (8-ounce) container light cream cheese
1 (10¾-ounce) can 98% fat-free cream of
    mushroom soup, undiluted
3 tablespoons Parmesan cheese
Vegetable cooking spray
2 tablespoons fine, dry breadcrumbs

Peel and devein shrimp; set aside. Sprinkle turkey with garlic powder and pepper; set aside.

Place wine in a large, nonstick skillet; add turkey, and bring to a boil. Add shrimp; cover, reduce heat, and cook 3 to 5 minutes or until shrimp turn pink. Remove from heat; cool slightly. Drain pan juices, and set aside. Cut turkey into bite-size pieces, and set turkey and shrimp aside.

Cook spinach according to package directions, omitting salt; drain well between layers of paper towels.

Place cream cheese in a large saucepan; cook over low heat, stirring constantly, until cheese melts. Remove from heat; stir in reserved pan juices, mushroom soup, Parmesan cheese, and spinach. Gently stir in turkey and shrimp.

Spoon mixture into an 11- x 7- x 1½-inch baking dish coated with cooking spray; sprinkle with breadcrumbs.

Bake at 350° for 35 to 45 minutes or until bubbly. **Yield: 6 servings.**

Note: Cover and freeze casserole before sprinkling with breadcrumbs. Thaw in refrigerator 24 hours; let stand at room temperature 30 minutes.

Sprinkle with breadcrumbs, and bake at 350° for 35 to 45 minutes or until bubbly.

PER SERVING: 296 CALORIES (31% FROM FAT)
FAT 10.3G (SATURATED FAT 4.8G)
PROTEIN 37.3G CARBOHYDRATE 12.7G
CHOLESTEROL 157MG SODIUM 664MG

Lazy Day Turkey

1½ tablespoons butter-flavored granules
¼ cup water
½ cup chopped onion
½ cup chopped green pepper
½ cup sliced fresh mushrooms
1 clove garlic, minced
2 cups cubed, cooked turkey breast
1 (10¾-ounce) can ready-to-serve, reduced-fat
    cream of chicken soup
½ cup fat-free milk
2 tablespoons no-sugar-added apricot spread
1 tablespoon dry white wine
¼ teaspoon salt
¼ teaspoon ground nutmeg
¼ teaspoon pepper
4 cups hot cooked rice or pasta (cooked
    without salt or fat)

Combine butter-flavored mix and water, stirring until mix dissolves. Pour into a large skillet; add onion and next 3 ingredients. Cook over medium heat, stirring constantly, until vegetables are tender.

Stir in turkey and next 7 ingredients; bring mixture to a boil over medium heat. Reduce heat, and simmer, uncovered, 10 to 15 minutes, stirring occasionally.

Serve over rice or pasta. **Yield: 4 servings.**

PER SERVING: 386 CALORIES (6% FROM FAT)
FAT 2.6G (SATURATED FAT 0.3G)
PROTEIN 27.6G CARBOHYDRATE 58.7G
CHOLESTEROL 63MG SODIUM 660MG

Salads

These salads will help make meals appetizing as well as nutritious. We begin with side salads followed by protein-rich treasures substantial enough for a main dish.

Apple-Apricot Salad, Frozen Strawberry Salad, Rice-Shrimp Salad

Asparagus Salad, Sunburst Chicken-and-Walnut Salad, Crab-and-Asparagus Salad

Creamy Potato Salad, Minted Marinated Fruit, Marinated Black-Eyed Pea Salad

Citrus Spinach Salad, Green Beans with Creamy Tarragon Dressing

Three-Layer Aspic (page 788)

Three-Layer Aspic

(pictured on page 787)

1 envelope unflavored gelatin
¼ cup water
1 tablespoon lemon juice
1 (8-ounce) carton plain low-fat yogurt
Vegetable cooking spray
1 envelope unflavored gelatin
1 cup water
1 tablespoon lemon juice
1 teaspoon reduced-sodium Worcestershire
    sauce
1 cup diced green pepper
1 (14½-ounce) can stewed tomatoes,
    undrained
1 (12-ounce) can vegetable cocktail juice
1 tablespoon sugar
1 teaspoon celery salt
1 teaspoon reduced-sodium Worcestershire
    sauce
¼ teaspoon hot sauce
2 tablespoons lemon juice
1 bay leaf
2 envelopes unflavored gelatin
1 cup thinly sliced celery
Lettuce leaves
Garnish: lemon slices

Sprinkle 1 envelope gelatin over ¼ cup water in a small saucepan; let stand 1 minute. Cook over medium heat, stirring constantly, until gelatin dissolves; remove from heat.

Stir in 1 tablespoon lemon juice and yogurt. Pour into a 6-cup mold that has been coated with cooking spray; cover and chill until firm.

Sprinkle 1 envelope gelatin over 1 cup water in a small saucepan; let stand 1 minute. Cook over medium heat, stirring constantly, until gelatin dissolves; remove from heat.

Stir in 1 tablespoon lemon juice and 1 teaspoon Worcestershire sauce; chill until the consistency of unbeaten egg white. Stir in green pepper. Spoon over yogurt layer. Cover; chill.

Drain tomatoes, reserving liquid; chop tomatoes. Combine liquid, tomatoes, vegetable juice, and next 6 ingredients in a saucepan. Cook over low heat 30 minutes; remove from heat.

Remove bay leaf. Sprinkle 2 envelopes gelatin over hot mixture; stir until gelatin dissolves.

Chill until the consistency of unbeaten egg white. Stir in celery; spoon over green pepper layer. Cover; chill. Unmold onto lettuce leaves. Garnish, if desired. **Yield: 12 (½-cup) servings.**

PER SERVING: 50 CALORIES (11% FROM FAT)
FAT 0.6G (SATURATED FAT 0.2G)
PROTEIN 4.0G CARBOHYDRATE 7.9G
CHOLESTEROL 1MG SODIUM 396MG

Apple-Apricot Salad

1 envelope unflavored gelatin
2 cups unsweetened apple juice, divided
2 teaspoons lemon juice
1½ cups chopped apple
8 canned apricot halves in extra-light syrup,
    drained and chopped
Vegetable cooking spray
Lettuce leaves
Garnish: apple wedges

Sprinkle gelatin over 1 cup apple juice in a small saucepan; let stand 1 minute. Cook over medium heat, stirring constantly, until gelatin dissolves; remove from heat.

Add remaining apple juice and lemon juice. Chill until the consistency of unbeaten egg white.

Fold in apple and apricot; spoon into 7 (½-cup) molds coated with cooking spray. Cover and chill until firm.

Unmold onto lettuce-lined plates. Garnish, if desired. **Yield: 7 (½-cup) servings.**

PER SERVING: 77 CALORIES (5% FROM FAT)
FAT 0.4G (SATURATED FAT 0.0G)
PROTEIN 1.4G CARBOHYDRATE 17.9G
CHOLESTEROL 0MG SODIUM 7MG

Apple-Apricot Salad

Frozen Strawberry Salad

1 (8-ounce) package nonfat cream cheese, softened
½ cup sugar
1 (8-ounce) container reduced-fat frozen whipped topping, thawed
2 cups frozen no-sugar-added whole strawberries, thawed and halved
1 (15¼-ounce) can unsweetened crushed pineapple, undrained
1½ cups sliced banana (2 medium)

Beat cream cheese at medium speed of an electric mixer until creamy; gradually add sugar, beating until smooth.

Fold in whipped topping and remaining ingredients; spoon into a 13- x 9- x 2-inch dish.

Cover and freeze until firm. **Yield: 12 servings.**

PER SERVING: 138 CALORIES (17% FROM FAT)
FAT 2.6G (SATURATED FAT 0.0G)
PROTEIN 3.7G CARBOHYDRATE 25.9G
CHOLESTEROL 4MG SODIUM 128MG

Minted Marinated Fruit

1 (20-ounce) can unsweetened pineapple chunks, undrained
1½ cups unpeeled, chopped red apple
1½ cups unpeeled, chopped green apple
1 cup unpeeled, chopped pear
1 cup sliced banana
½ cup orange juice
2 tablespoons chopped fresh mint
1 tablespoon honey

Drain pineapple chunks, reserving juice. Combine fruit in an 11- x 7- x 1½-inch dish.

Combine reserved pineapple juice, orange juice, and remaining ingredients; pour over fruit. Cover and chill 3 hours, stirring occasionally. **Yield: 7 (1-cup) servings.**

PER SERVING: 129 CALORIES (3% FROM FAT)
FAT 0.4G (SATURATED FAT 0.1G)
PROTEIN 0.5G CARBOHYDRATE 32.6G
CHOLESTEROL 0MG SODIUM 1MG

Cabbage-Pineapple Slaw

1 (8-ounce) can unsweetened pineapple tidbits, undrained
3 cups finely shredded cabbage
1½ cups unpeeled, chopped Red Delicious apple
½ cup chopped celery
¼ cup golden raisins
¼ cup reduced-calorie mayonnaise
Lettuce leaves
Garnishes: apple wedges, celery leaves

Drain pineapple, reserving 3 tablespoons juice. Combine pineapple, cabbage, and next 3 ingredients in a large bowl.

Combine reserved pineapple juice and mayonnaise; add to cabbage mixture, tossing gently. Cover and chill. Spoon into a lettuce-lined bowl and garnish, if desired. **Yield: 5 (1-cup) servings.**

PER SERVING: 115 CALORIES (27% FROM FAT)
FAT 3.5G (SATURATED FAT 0.5G)
PROTEIN 1.3G CARBOHYDRATE 21.3G
CHOLESTEROL 4MG SODIUM 110MG

Cleaning Greens

• Wash and dry salad greens before using or storing them. (A salad spinner is useful.)
• Loosely wrap clean greens in paper towels, and store in an airtight container in crisper drawer of the refrigerator. Tear, rather than cut, for salads.

Cabbage-Pineapple Slaw and Parmesan-Stuffed Tomatoes (page 816)

Marinated Black-Eyed Pea Salad and Green Beans with Creamy Tarragon Dressing

Green Beans with Creamy Tarragon Dressing

1½ pounds fresh green beans
1 cup nonfat mayonnaise
⅓ cup chopped fresh parsley
¼ cup chopped onion
¼ cup 1% low-fat cottage cheese
3 tablespoons tarragon vinegar
2 tablespoons fat-free milk
1½ teaspoons lemon juice
½ teaspoon anchovy paste
Belgian endive, sliced

Wash beans; trim ends, if desired, and remove strings. Arrange beans in a steamer basket, and place over boiling water. Cover and steam 12 minutes or until crisp-tender. Remove beans, and plunge into ice water. Drain; cover and chill.

Position knife blade in food processor bowl; add mayonnaise and next 7 ingredients. Process 1 minute or until smooth, stopping once to scrape down sides. Cover and chill at least 1 hour.

Arrange endive on individual plates; place beans in center of plates, and top each serving with ½ tablespoon dressing. Yield: 6 servings.

Note: When preparing young, tender green beans, trim the stem end only, leaving the pointed end of beans on to enhance the appearance and fiber content of the salad.

PER SERVING: 84 CALORIES (4% FROM FAT)
FAT 0.4G (SATURATED FAT 0.1G)
PROTEIN 3.9G CARBOHYDRATE 18.0G
CHOLESTEROL 0MG SODIUM 615MG

Marinated Black-Eyed Pea Salad

1½ cups water
1 medium onion, halved
½ teaspoon salt
½ teaspoon dried crushed red pepper
⅛ teaspoon hickory-flavored liquid smoke
1 (16-ounce) package frozen black-eyed peas
½ cup raspberry wine vinegar
¼ cup water
3 tablespoons chopped fresh parsley
1 clove garlic, minced
1 teaspoon olive oil
¼ teaspoon salt
¼ teaspoon freshly ground pepper
½ cup chopped sweet red pepper
⅓ cup small purple onion rings
Leaf lettuce
¾ cup croutons

  Combine first 5 ingredients in a saucepan; bring to a boil. Add peas; return to a boil. Cover, reduce heat, and simmer 40 to 45 minutes or until peas are tender. Remove and discard onion; drain. Rinse with cold water; drain. Place in a bowl; set aside.
  Combine vinegar and next 7 ingredients. Pour over peas; toss to coat. Cover; chill 8 hours, stirring occasionally. Stir in purple onion. Serve on lettuce-lined plates. Sprinkle with croutons.
Yield: 5 (¾-cup) servings.

PER SERVING: 188 CALORIES (14% FROM FAT)
FAT 3.0G (SATURATED FAT 0.3G)
PROTEIN 9.5G CARBOHYDRATE 31.8G
CHOLESTEROL 0MG SODIUM 257MG

Asparagus Salad

1 pound fresh asparagus spears
¼ cup lemon juice
2 tablespoons honey
2 teaspoons vegetable oil
8 lettuce leaves

  Snap off tough ends of asparagus. Remove scales from stalks, if desired. Arrange asparagus in a steamer basket; place over boiling water. Cover and steam 6 minutes or until crisp-tender.
  Plunge asparagus into ice water to stop the cooking process; drain and chill.
  Combine lemon juice, honey, and oil in a jar; cover tightly, and shake vigorously. Chill.
  Arrange lettuce leaves on individual plates; top with asparagus, and drizzle with dressing.
Yield: 4 servings.

PER SERVING: 75 CALORIES (30% FROM FAT)
FAT 2.5G (SATURATED FAT 0.5G)
PROTEIN 1.9G CARBOHYDRATE 13.6G
CHOLESTEROL 0MG SODIUM 5MG

Citrus Spinach Salad

2 tablespoons orange juice
2 tablespoons rice vinegar
2½ teaspoons vegetable oil
1 tablespoon honey
¼ teaspoon grated orange rind
6 cups torn spinach
2 oranges, peeled, seeded, and sectioned
¾ medium-size purple onion, sliced and
    separated into rings

  Combine first 5 ingredients in a jar; cover tightly, and shake vigorously. Chill thoroughly. Combine spinach, orange sections, and onion rings in a salad bowl.
  Drizzle dressing over spinach mixture; toss gently. **Yield: 6 (1-cup) servings.**

PER SERVING: 73 CALORIES (27% FROM FAT)
FAT 2.2G (SATURATED FAT 0.4G)
PROTEIN 2.3G CARBOHYDRATE 13.1G
CHOLESTEROL 0MG SODIUM 45MG

Creamy Potato Salad

2 pounds unpeeled red potatoes (about 6 medium)
¼ cup chopped green onions
1 (2-ounce) jar diced pimiento, drained
⅓ cup nonfat mayonnaise
¼ cup plain low-fat yogurt
1½ tablespoons prepared mustard
1 tablespoon sugar
1 tablespoon white wine vinegar
½ teaspoon salt
½ teaspoon celery seeds
¼ teaspoon pepper
⅛ teaspoon garlic powder

Place potatoes in a medium saucepan; cover with water, and bring to a boil. Cover, reduce heat, and simmer 25 minutes or until tender; drain and let cool.

Peel potatoes, and cut into ½-inch cubes. Combine potato, green onions, and pimiento in a large bowl.

Combine mayonnaise and remaining ingredients; stir into potato mixture, and toss gently. Cover and chill. **Yield: 10 (½-cup) servings.**

PER SERVING: 86 CALORIES (3% FROM FAT)
FAT 0.3G (SATURATED FAT 0.1G)
PROTEIN 2.5G CARBOHYDRATE 18.9G
CHOLESTEROL 0MG SODIUM 260MG

Lighten Up Potato Salad

Nonfat mayonnaise and low-fat yogurt replace eggs and cream in Creamy Potato Salad. This recipe has less than 1 gram of fat and no cholesterol. For additional fiber, leave the skin on the potatoes.

Sunburst Chicken-and-Walnut Salad

1½ cups water
1 medium onion, halved
1 stalk celery, halved
4 black peppercorns
4 (4-ounce) skinned and boned chicken breast halves
2 tablespoons cider vinegar
2½ teaspoons vegetable oil
2 teaspoons honey
½ teaspoon dry mustard
½ teaspoon dried tarragon
½ teaspoon grated orange rind
2 oranges, peeled and sectioned
8 lettuce leaves
1½ tablespoons chopped walnuts, toasted

Combine first 4 ingredients in a large skillet, and bring to a boil. Cover, reduce heat, and simmer 10 minutes. Place chicken in skillet; cover and simmer 10 minutes or until tender.

Remove chicken, and let cool (discard vegetables, and reserve broth for another use). Cut chicken into strips; set aside.

Combine vinegar and next 5 ingredients in a medium bowl, stirring with a wire whisk. Add orange sections; set aside.

Line each salad plate with 2 lettuce leaves. Remove orange sections from dressing, and divide evenly among plates. Place chicken strips in dressing, and toss gently; divide strips evenly among plates. Drizzle remaining dressing evenly over salads; sprinkle evenly with walnuts. **Yield: 4 servings.**

PER SERVING: 237 CALORIES (30% FROM FAT)
FAT 7.8G (SATURATED FAT 1.5G)
PROTEIN 28.3G CARBOHYDRATE 13.5G
CHOLESTEROL 72MG SODIUM 67MG

Sunburst Chicken-and-Walnut Salad

Crab-and-Asparagus Salad

18 fresh asparagus spears (¾ pound)
¼ cup nonfat mayonnaise
1 tablespoon lemon juice
1 teaspoon chopped capers
½ teaspoon prepared mustard
½ teaspoon white wine Worcestershire sauce
12 large lettuce leaves
¾ pound fresh lump crabmeat, drained
⅛ teaspoon paprika

Snap off tough ends of asparagus. Remove scales from stalks with a vegetable peeler or knife, if desired. Arrange asparagus in a steamer basket over boiling water. Cover and steam 6 minutes or until crisp-tender.

Plunge asparagus into ice water to stop the cooking process; drain and chill.

Combine mayonnaise and next 4 ingredients. Arrange lettuce leaves on individual serving plates; top with equal amounts of asparagus and crabmeat. Serve each salad with 1 tablespoon mayonnaise mixture, and sprinkle with paprika. **Yield: 6 servings.**

PER SERVING: 75 CALORIES (13% FROM FAT)
FAT 1.1G (SATURATED FAT 0.2G)
PROTEIN 11.7G CARBOHYDRATE 4.6G
CHOLESTEROL 52MG SODIUM 323MG

Cooking Shrimp

• Shrimp cooked in its shell is more flavorful than shrimp peeled before cooking. Avoid overcooking shrimp, or it will become tough and rubbery.
• To devein shrimp, cut a shallow slit down the middle of the outside curve. Remove dark vein, and rinse with cold water.

Rice-Shrimp Salad

2 unpeeled, medium tomatoes (¾ pound)
3 cups water
1 pound unpeeled medium-size fresh shrimp
2 cups cooked rice (cooked without salt or fat)
1 cup unpeeled, chopped apple
¾ cup chopped green pepper
½ cup sliced celery
¼ cup chopped green onions
1 tablespoon chopped fresh parsley
3 tablespoons white wine vinegar
1 tablespoon olive oil
½ teaspoon salt
¼ teaspoon pepper
2 cloves garlic, minced
6 red cabbage leaves (optional)
6 lemon wedges (optional)

Cut tomatoes in half. Carefully squeeze each half over a small bowl to remove seeds; pour juice through a wire-mesh strainer into a small bowl, discarding seeds. Reserve 2 tablespoons juice. Chop tomatoes.

Bring water to a boil; add shrimp, and cook 3 to 5 minutes. Drain well, and rinse with cold water. Peel and devein shrimp.

Combine chopped tomato, shrimp, rice, and next 5 ingredients in a large bowl; set aside.

Combine reserved tomato juice, vinegar, and next 4 ingredients; stir with a wire whisk until blended. Pour over shrimp mixture, and toss gently; chill.

Spoon salad over cabbage leaves, and serve with a lemon wedge, if desired. **Yield: 6 (1¼-cup) servings.**

PER SERVING: 170 CALORIES (16% FROM FAT)
FAT 3.1G (SATURATED FAT 0.5G)
PROTEIN 11.2G CARBOHYDRATE 24.1G
CHOLESTEROL 83MG SODIUM 307MG

Rice-Shrimp Salad

Shrimp-and-Rice Salad

(pictured on page 684)

3 cups water
1 pound unpeeled medium-size fresh shrimp
2 cups cooked rice (cooked without salt or fat)
½ cup chopped celery
½ cup chopped green pepper
¼ cup sliced pimiento-stuffed olives
¼ cup chopped onion
2 tablespoons diced pimiento
3 tablespoons commercial oil-free Italian dressing
2 tablespoons reduced-calorie mayonnaise
2 tablespoons prepared mustard
1 tablespoon lemon juice
1 teaspoon salt-free lemon-pepper seasoning
⅛ teaspoon pepper
Lettuce leaves
Garnishes: fresh parsley sprig, cooked shrimp, pimiento-stuffed olive

Bring water to a boil; add shrimp, and cook 3 to 5 minutes or until shrimp turn pink. Drain well; rinse with cold water. Chill. Peel and devein shrimp.

Combine shrimp, rice, and next 5 ingredients in a medium bowl. Combine Italian dressing and next 5 ingredients, stirring until well blended. Pour over shrimp mixture, and toss gently to coat.

Cover; chill 3 to 4 hours. Line a serving plate with lettuce leaves. Spoon salad onto plate and garnish, if desired. **Yield: 5 (1-cup) servings.**

PER SERVING: 188 CALORIES (15% FROM FAT)
FAT 3.1G (SATURATED FAT 0.5G)
PROTEIN 13.5G CARBOHYDRATE 25.8G
CHOLESTEROL 101MG SODIUM 410MG

Asian Pork Salad

(pictured on cover)

¾ cup orange juice, divided
¼ cup low-sodium teriyaki sauce, divided
1 tablespoon rice vinegar
1 tablespoon mirin (sweet rice wine)
2 teaspoons hoisin sauce
1 teaspoon sesame oil
1 garlic clove, minced
3 tablespoons brown sugar
2 tablespoons bourbon
¼ teaspoon dried crushed red pepper
1 (1-pound) pork tenderloin
Vegetable cooking spray
8 cups gourmet salad greens
½ cup sliced purple onion, separated into rings
1 (11-ounce) can mandarin oranges in light syrup, drained
1 (8-ounce) can sliced water chesnuts, drained
1 large sweet red pepper, sliced into rings
2 tablespoons sesame seeds, toasted

Combine ½ cup plus 2 tablespoons orange juice, 2 tablespoons teriyaki sauce, vinegar, and next 4 ingredients; stir well. Cover and chill.

Combine 2 tablespoons orange juice, 2 tablespoons teriyaki sauce, brown sugar, bourbon, and dried crushed red pepper in a large zip-top plastic bag. Trim fat from pork; slice pork into 3-x ½-inch strips. Add pork to bag. Seal; toss to coat. Marinate in refrigerator 15 minutes.

Heat a large nonstick skillet coated with cooking spray over medium-high heat. Add pork and marinade; cook 8 minutes or until pork is done and liquid almost evaporates. Remove from heat.

Divide greens, onion, oranges, water chestnuts, and red pepper rings evenly among 4 plates. Top each with 1 cup pork mixture; drizzle ¼ cup orange juice mixture over each salad. Sprinkle evenly with sesame seeds. **Yield: 4 servings.**

PER SERVING: 322 CALORIES (19% FROM FAT)
FAT 6.8G (SATURATED FAT 1.5G)
PROTEIN 28G CARBOHYDRATE 37.3G
CHOLESTEROL 74MG SODIUM 382MG

Soups and Sandwiches

Let homemade soups and hearty sandwiches solve the what-to-serve dilemma. Use the nutrient grids to help you mix and match recipes to create balanced, light meals.

Light Cream of Broccoli Soup, Corn Chowder, French Onion Soup

Healthy Heroes, Salmon Burgers, Open-Faced Breakfast Sandwiches, Fiesta Burgers

Split Pea Soup, Seafood Chowder, Spicy Ham-and-Bean Soup, Catfish Gumbo

Hot Venison Chili, Smoked Turkey-Roasted Pepper Sandwiches

Beef Stew (page 803)

Light Cream of Broccoli Soup

Light Cream of Broccoli Soup

1 (15.75-ounce) can ready-to-serve, reduced-
    sodium, fat-free chicken broth
⅓ cup instant nonfat dry milk powder
3 tablespoons cornstarch
½ teaspoon dried onion flakes
¼ teaspoon salt
¼ teaspoon dried basil
¼ teaspoon dried thyme
¼ teaspoon pepper
1 (10-ounce) package frozen chopped
    broccoli, thawed and drained
1½ cups fat-free milk
⅓ cup (1.3 ounces) shredded reduced-fat
    Cheddar cheese
1 tablespoon butter-flavored granules
Garnish: shredded reduced-fat Cheddar
    cheese

Combine first 8 ingredients in a large saucepan; bring to a boil, stirring constantly. Cook,
stirring constantly, 1 minute.

Add broccoli and next 3 ingredients; cook
until cheese melts and mixture is thoroughly
heated. Garnish individual servings with ½ teaspoon shredded Cheddar cheese, if desired.
Yield: 4 (1-cup) servings.

PER SERVING: 155 CALORIES (13% FROM FAT)
FAT 2.2G (SATURATED FAT 1.2G)
PROTEIN 11.8G CARBOHYDRATE 21.5G
CHOLESTEROL 10MG SODIUM 396MG

Corn Chowder

½ cup chopped onion
½ cup chopped celery
2 tablespoons reduced-calorie margarine,
    melted
1 tablespoon all-purpose flour
4 cups fat-free milk
1 (17-ounce) can no-salt-added yellow
    cream-style corn
¼ teaspoon salt
¼ teaspoon ground white pepper
¼ teaspoon dried thyme
⅛ teaspoon paprika

Cook onion and celery in margarine in a
Dutch oven until tender, stirring constantly. Add
flour, and cook 1 minute, stirring constantly.
Gradually add milk, stirring until mixture boils.

Stir in corn and next 3 ingredients. Reduce
heat; simmer 20 minutes, stirring occasionally.

Spoon chowder into bowls; sprinkle evenly
with paprika. **Yield: 3 (1⅔-cup) servings.**

PER SERVING: 295 CALORIES (19% FROM FAT)
FAT 6.2G (SATURATED FAT 1.2G)
PROTEIN 14.6G CARBOHYDRATE 49.0G
CHOLESTEROL 7MG SODIUM 462MG

French Onion Soup

2 tablespoons margarine
Vegetable cooking spray
6 large onions, thinly sliced (3 pounds)
2 (10½-ounce) cans beef consommé, undiluted
1 (14.25-ounce) can ready-to-serve, no-salt-added, fat-free beef-flavored broth
1⅓ cups water
¼ cup Chablis or other dry white wine
¼ teaspoon freshly ground pepper
7 (1-inch-thick) slices French bread
¼ cup grated Parmesan cheese

Melt margarine in a Dutch oven coated with cooking spray. Add onion, and cook over medium heat, 5 minutes, stirring often. Add 1 can beef consommé; cook over low heat 30 minutes.

Add remaining beef consommé and next 4 ingredients; bring to a boil, reduce heat, and simmer 10 minutes.

Place bread slices on a baking sheet; sprinkle with Parmesan cheese. Broil 6 inches from heat (with electric oven door partially opened) until cheese is golden. Ladle soup into serving bowls, and top each with a toasted bread slice. **Yield: 7 (1-cup) servings.**

PER SERVING: 247 CALORIES (19% FROM FAT)
FAT 5.2G (SATURATED FAT 1.5G)
PROTEIN 10.3G CARBOHYDRATE 39.0G
CHOLESTEROL 19MG SODIUM 860MG

Split Pea Soup

1 (16-ounce) package dried green split peas
8 cups water
2 bay leaves
1½ teaspoons salt
1 teaspoon dried thyme
3 cloves garlic, minced
¼ cup Chablis or other dry white wine
2 cups sliced carrot
1½ cups diced potato
1 cup chopped celery
¾ cup chopped onion
2 tablespoons dried parsley flakes
2 tablespoons lemon juice

Combine first 6 ingredients in a Dutch oven. Bring mixture to a boil; reduce heat, and simmer, uncovered, 1 hour.

Add wine and remaining ingredients to Dutch oven; cook 30 minutes or until peas are tender. Remove bay leaves.

Spoon mixture into container of an electric blender or food processor; cover and process until mixture is smooth. **Yield: 11 (1-cup) servings.**

PER SERVING: 175 CALORIES (3% FROM FAT)
FAT 0.6G (SATURATED FAT 0.1G)
PROTEIN 11.1G CARBOHYDRATE 32.8G
CHOLESTEROL 0MG SODIUM 345MG

French Onion Soup

Seafood Chowder

1½ pounds unpeeled medium-size fresh shrimp
Vegetable cooking spray
1 teaspoon olive oil
1 cup chopped onion
1 cup chopped celery
1 cup diced sweet red pepper
3 cloves garlic, minced
½ cup all-purpose flour
2½ cups ready-to-serve , no-salt-added
    chicken broth
1½ cups water
3 cups peeled, diced red potato
1 cup diced carrot
½ teaspoon ground white pepper
½ teaspoon dried thyme
2 bay leaves
2 (12-ounce) cans evaporated fat-free milk
2 (8¾-ounce) cans no-salt-added, cream-style
    corn
1 teaspoon hot sauce
1 pound fresh crabmeat, drained and flaked

Peel and devein shrimp; set aside. Coat a Dutch oven with cooking spray; add oil, and place over medium-high heat until hot. Add onion and next 3 ingredients; cook until tender.

Add flour, and cook, stirring constantly, 1 minute. Gradually stir in chicken broth, water, and next 5 ingredients. Bring to a boil; reduce heat, and simmer, uncovered, 20 minutes or until potato is tender, stirring often.

Stir in milk, corn, and hot sauce; return to a boil. Add reserved shrimp and crabmeat; cook 5 minutes or until shrimp turn pink, stirring constantly. Remove and discard bay leaves. **Yield: 10 (1½-cup) servings.**

Note: Freeze in airtight containers. Thaw in refrigerator 24 hours. Place in a saucepan, and cook over low heat until heated.

PER SERVING: 278 CALORIES (9% FROM FAT)
FAT 2.7G (SATURATED FAT 0.5G)
PROTEIN 27.1G CARBOHYDRATE 35.6G
CHOLESTEROL 123MG SODIUM 296MG

Spicy Ham-and-Bean Soup

1 pound dried Great Northern beans
4 quarts water
1 pound reduced-salt lean ham, trimmed and
    cubed
2 stalks celery, chopped
2 carrots, scraped and chopped
2 medium-size red potatoes, finely chopped
1 large onion, finely chopped
1 tablespoon chopped pickled jalapeño
    pepper
1 tablespoon pickled jalapeño pepper juice
1 (6-ounce) can spicy tomato-vegetable juice
1 (4.5-ounce) can chopped green chiles,
    undrained
1 tablespoon Worcestershire sauce
½ teaspoon chili powder
½ teaspoon garlic powder

Sort and wash beans; place in a Dutch oven. Add water, and let stand 2 hours. Bring to a boil; reduce heat, and simmer 1 hour.

Add ham and next 4 ingredients; simmer 1 additional hour.

Add jalapeño pepper and remaining ingredients; simmer 1 hour or until beans are tender and soup is thickened. **Yield: 9 (1½-cup) servings.**

PER SERVING: 297 CALORIES (10% FROM FAT)
FAT 3.2G (SATURATED FAT 0.9G)
PROTEIN 21.9G CARBOHYDRATE 46.8G
CHOLESTEROL 25MG SODIUM 528MG

Beef Stew

(pictured on page 799)

1 pound boneless top round steak
¼ cup all-purpose flour
¼ teaspoon pepper
¾ cup chopped onion
1 tablespoon vegetable oil
3 cups water
½ cup finely chopped carrot
¼ cup finely chopped celery
2 tablespoons minced fresh parsley
½ teaspoon salt
⅛ teaspoon dried thyme
2 cups cubed potato
1 cup sliced carrot
1 cup chopped onion
1 cup frozen green peas, thawed

Trim fat from steak; cut into 1-inch cubes. Combine flour and pepper; dredge meat in flour mixture, reserving excess flour mixture.

Cook meat, ¾ cup onion, and reserved flour mixture in oil in a Dutch oven over low heat until meat is lightly browned.

Add water and next 5 ingredients. Cover, reduce heat, and simmer 1½ hours.

Stir in potato, 1 cup carrot, and 1 cup onion; cover and simmer 20 minutes. Add green peas, and cook 10 additional minutes. **Yield: 4 (1½-cup) servings.**

PER SERVING: 338 CALORIES (21% FROM FAT)
FAT 8.0G (SATURATED FAT 2.2G)
PROTEIN 29.7G CARBOHYDRATE 35.4G
CHOLESTEROL 60MG SODIUM 419MG

Freezing Soups

Most soups, stews, chilis, and gumbos freeze well, which is a bonus when you make a large quantity. When freezing soups, use airtight plastic containers or heavy-duty, zip-top plastic bags; label and date the item, and use within three or four months for optimum flavor.

Catfish Gumbo

Vegetable cooking spray
1 cup chopped celery
1 cup chopped onion
1 cup chopped green pepper
2 cloves garlic, minced
3¾ cups ready-to-serve , no-salt-added
   chicken broth
 2 (14½-ounce) cans no-salt-added tomatoes,
   undrained and chopped
1 (6-ounce) can low-sodium cocktail
   vegetable juice
2 bay leaves
1½ teaspoons salt
½ teaspoon pepper
½ teaspoon dried thyme
½ teaspoon hot sauce
1½ pounds farm-raised catfish fillets, cut into
   1½-inch pieces
2 (10-ounce) packages frozen sliced okra,
   thawed
4 cups hot cooked rice (cooked without salt
   or fat)

Coat a Dutch oven with cooking spray; place
over medium-high heat until hot. Add celery and
next 3 ingredients, stirring constantly until crisp-
tender.

Add chicken broth and next 7 ingredients.
Bring mixture to a boil; cover, reduce heat, and
simmer 30 minutes. Stir in fish and okra; cover
and simmer 15 minutes.

Remove and discard bay leaves. Serve gumbo
over ½ cup hot cooked rice. **Yield: 8 (1⅓-cup)
servings.**

PER SERVING: 283 CALORIES (13% FROM FAT)
FAT 4.2G (SATURATED FAT 0.9G)
PROTEIN 20.6G CARBOHYDRATE 39.6G
CHOLESTEROL 49MG SODIUM 531MG

White Chili

1 cup dried navy beans
3¾ cups ready-to-serve , no-salt-added
   chicken broth
1 cup water
1¼ cups chopped onion
1 clove garlic, minced
¼ teaspoon salt
2 cups chopped cooked chicken breasts
   (skinned before cooking and cooked
   without salt)
1 (4.5-ounce) can chopped green chiles
1 teaspoon ground cumin
¾ teaspoon dried oregano
¼ teaspoon ground red pepper
⅛ teaspoon ground cloves
¾ cup (3 ounces) shredded reduced-fat
   Monterey Jack cheese

Sort and wash beans; place in a Dutch oven.
Cover with water 2 inches above beans; let soak
8 hours. Drain beans, and return to Dutch oven.

Add broth and next 4 ingredients to Dutch
oven. Bring to a boil; cover, reduce heat, and
simmer 2 hours, stirring occasionally.

Add chicken and next 5 ingredients; cover and
cook 30 minutes. Spoon into serving bowls; top
each with cheese. **Yield: 6 (1-cup) servings.**

PER SERVING: 269 CALORIES (17% FROM FAT)
FAT 5.2G (SATURATED FAT 2.3G)
PROTEIN 26.2G CARBOHYDRATE 27.7G
CHOLESTEROL 46MG SODIUM 304MG

Defat Chicken Broth

To defat commercial chicken
broth, place the unopened can in
the refrigerator at least 1 hour
before using. Open the can, and
skim off the layer of solidified fat.

South-of-the-Border Chili

1 pound lean boneless top round steak, trimmed
Vegetable cooking spray
½ cup chopped onion
1 clove garlic, minced
2 tablespoons chili powder
1 tablespoon cocoa
1 teaspoon dried oregano
½ teaspoon salt
½ teaspoon ground cumin
1 (8-ounce) can no-salt-added tomato sauce
2 cups water
2 cups hot cooked rice (cooked without salt or fat)

Partially freeze top round steak; cut into ½-inch cubes, and set aside.

Coat a Dutch oven with cooking spray; place over medium-high heat until hot. Add onion and garlic; cook until tender, stirring constantly.

Add meat, and cook until meat browns, stirring often. Stir in chili powder and next 6 ingredients; bring to a boil.

Cover, reduce heat, and simmer 1 hour, stirring often. Serve over rice. **Yield: 4 (¾-cup) servings.**

PER SERVING: 314 CALORIES (17% FROM FAT)
FAT 5.8G (SATURATED FAT 1.9G)
PROTEIN 29.7G CARBOHYDRATE 34.5G
CHOLESTEROL 65MG SODIUM 404MG

Lower the Fat

For the health-conscious, ground chuck, top round, and venison are good lean choices for chili. Ground or chopped chicken or turkey breast may replace red meat in many recipes.

Hot Venison Chili

2 pounds lean venison stew meat, diced
1 tablespoon olive oil
1¾ cups chopped onion
1 cup diced celery
3 cloves garlic, crushed
3 cups water
3 (14½-ounce) cans no-salt-added tomatoes, undrained and chopped
2 (10-ounce) cans diced tomatoes with green chiles, undrained
2 tablespoons chili powder
1½ tablespoons reduced-sodium Worcestershire sauce
¼ teaspoon dried thyme
¼ teaspoon dried oregano
¼ teaspoon ground cumin
¼ teaspoon salt
1 (16-ounce) can no-salt-added kidney beans, undrained
2 cups finely shredded iceberg lettuce
½ cup (2 ounces) shredded reduced-fat sharp Cheddar cheese
½ cup diced tomato

Brown venison in hot oil in a Dutch oven, stirring constantly. Stir in onion, celery, and garlic; cook until tender.

Add water and next 8 ingredients; bring to a boil. Reduce heat, and simmer, uncovered, 2 hours, stirring occasionally. Add beans, and cook 30 minutes.

Ladle chili into individual bowls. Top each serving with ¼ cup lettuce, 1 tablespoon cheese, and 1 tablespoon tomato. **Yield: 8 (1½-cup) servings.**

PER SERVING: 287 CALORIES (20% FROM FAT)
FAT 6.4G (SATURATED FAT 2.2G)
PROTEIN 33.6G CARBOHYDRATE 23.9G
CHOLESTEROL 101MG SODIUM 289MG

Healthy Heroes

Healthy Heroes

¾ cup thinly sliced fresh mushrooms
½ cup seeded and chopped cucumber
1 tablespoon sliced green onions
1 clove garlic, minced
2 tablespoons balsamic vinegar
⅛ teaspoon freshly ground pepper
1 (2-ounce) hoagie bun
2 lettuce leaves
2 ounces thinly sliced lean ham
2 ounces thinly sliced turkey breast
4 slices tomato
¼ cup (1 ounce) shredded part-skim
   mozzarella cheese

Combine first 6 ingredients in a small bowl; let mixture stand 30 minutes.

Slice bun in half lengthwise; pull out soft inside of top and bottom, leaving a shell (reserve crumbs for another use).

Spoon mushroom mixture into each half of bun; cover with a lettuce leaf. Top with ham, turkey, tomato, and cheese. Cut in half to serve. **Yield: 2 servings.**

PER SERVING: 206 CALORIES (29% FROM FAT)
FAT 6.6G (SATURATED FAT 3.0G)
PROTEIN 20.2G CARBOHYDRATE 16.0G
CHOLESTEROL 52MG SODIUM 546MG

Open-Faced Breakfast Sandwiches

½ cup light cream cheese
4 whole wheat English muffins, split and
    toasted
½ cup low-sugar orange marmalade
8 (1-ounce) slices lean Canadian bacon
1 cup alfalfa sprouts
32 mandarin orange segments

Spread 1 tablespoon cream cheese on cut side of each muffin half; spread 1 tablespoon orange marmalade over cream cheese. Top with Canadian bacon; place on a baking sheet.

Broil 5 inches from heat (with electric oven door partially opened) 3 minutes or until hot. Remove from oven; top each with 2 tablespoons alfalfa sprouts and 4 orange segments. Serve immediately. **Yield: 8 servings.**

PER SERVING: 171 CALORIES (26% FROM FAT)
FAT 5.0G (SATURATED FAT 2.3G)
PROTEIN 10.2G CARBOHYDRATE 20.8G
CHOLESTEROL 22MG SODIUM 650MG

Turkey-in-the-Slaw Sandwich

1 cup shredded green cabbage
1 cup shredded red cabbage
½ cup shredded carrot
¼ cup reduced-calorie mayonnaise
¼ cup plain nonfat yogurt
1½ teaspoons sugar
¼ teaspoon ground white pepper
8 slices whole wheat bread
1 tablespoon commercial reduced-calorie
    Thousand Island salad dressing
¾ pound thinly sliced cooked turkey

Combine first 7 ingredients in a large bowl; cover and chill.

Spread 4 slices of bread equally with dressing. Place 3 ounces sliced turkey and one-fourth

of slaw on each slice of bread; top with remaining bread slices. Cut each sandwich in half, and secure with wooden picks. **Yield: 4 servings.**

PER SERVING: 330 CALORIES (24% FROM FAT)
FAT 8.8G (SATURATED FAT 1.8G)
PROTEIN 32.1G CARBOHYDRATE 31.6G
CHOLESTEROL 66MG SODIUM 488MG

Smoked Turkey-Roasted Pepper Sandwiches

2 tablespoons nonfat cream cheese, softened
1 tablespoon reduced-fat mayonnaise
1 tablespoon spicy brown mustard
⅛ teaspoon pepper
¼ cup chopped commercial roasted red
    peppers, drained
2 tablespoons sliced green onions
8 slices pumpernickel bread
¾ pound sliced smoked turkey breast
¼ cup alfalfa sprouts

Combine first 4 ingredients; stir in red peppers and green onions.

Spread mixture evenly on one side of bread slices. Layer turkey and alfalfa sprouts on 4 slices of bread; top with remaining bread slices. Cut each sandwich in half.

Serve immediately, or wrap each sandwich in heavy-duty plastic wrap and refrigerate. **Yield: 4 servings.**

Note: Smoked turkey breast is soaked in a salt solution before smoking, increasing its sodium content. If you're watching your sodium, substitute roasted turkey breast for the smoked.

PER SERVING: 280 CALORIES (9% FROM FAT)
FAT 2.9G (SATURATED FAT 0.1G)
PROTEIN 29.1G CARBOHYDRATE 36.3G
CHOLESTEROL 44MG SODIUM 1057MG

Fiesta Burgers

Fiesta Burgers

1⅓ cups seeded, chopped unpeeled tomato
¼ cup finely chopped onion
¼ cup taco sauce
1 (4.5-ounce) can chopped green chiles, drained
2 pounds 93% or 96% low-fat ground beef
2 tablespoons Worcestershire sauce
½ teaspoon ground cumin
¼ teaspoon onion powder
¼ teaspoon garlic powder
Vegetable cooking spray
8 (1½-ounce) hamburger buns
8 lettuce leaves

Combine first 4 ingredients in a bowl; cover and chill 30 minutes.

Combine beef and next 4 ingredients; divide into 8 equal portions, shaping each into a ½-inch-thick patty. Place on rack of a broiler pan coated with cooking spray.

Broil 4 inches from heat (with electric oven door partially opened) 8 minutes on each side. Line bottom half of buns with a lettuce leaf; top each with 2 tablespoons tomato mixture, a

hamburger patty, 2 tablespoons tomato mixture, and top half of bun. **Yield: 8 servings.**

PER SERVING: 340 CALORIES (29% FROM FAT)
FAT 10.8G (SATURATED FAT 3.1G)
PROTEIN 28.4G CARBOHYDRATE 30.4G
CHOLESTEROL 84MG SODIUM 313MG

Salmon Burgers

1 (15-ounce) can pink salmon, undrained
1 large egg, lightly beaten
½ cup unsalted saltine cracker crumbs
¼ cup finely chopped onion
¼ cup finely chopped celery
½ teaspoon baking powder
Vegetable cooking spray
½ cup nonfat mayonnaise
2 tablespoons lemon juice
½ teaspoon dried dillweed
¼ teaspoon pepper
¼ teaspoon hot sauce
6 onion sandwich rolls, split
6 tomato slices
1 cup shredded lettuce

Drain salmon, reserving liquid; remove and discard skin and bones. Flake salmon with a fork.

Combine salmon and next 5 ingredients. Add 1 to 2 tablespoons reserved liquid, stirring until mixture sticks together. Shape into 6 patties; set aside.

Coat a large nonstick skillet with cooking spray; add salmon patties, and cook over medium heat about 4 minutes on each side or until lightly browned. Keep warm.

Combine mayonnaise and next 4 ingredients; spread on cut sides of rolls. Place a salmon patty on bottom half of each roll; top each with a tomato slice, lettuce, and top half of bun. **Yield: 6 servings.**

PER SERVING: 322 CALORIES (22% FROM FAT)
FAT 7.9G (SATURATED FAT 1.5G)
PROTEIN 21.6G CARBOHYDRATE 41.7G
CHOLESTEROL 84MG SODIUM 793MG

Vegetables

Indulge in the crisp textures and bright colors of these
favorite vegetables—all cooked in light ways
to preserve nutrients and flavors.

Southern-Style Creamed Corn, Oven-Fried Okra, Lemon Broccoli

Butterbeans, Parmesan-Stuffed Tomatoes, Grilled Sweet Potatoes, Pretty Pepper Kabobs

Roasted Red Pepper Corn, Italian Green Beans, Fresh Corn Pudding, Black-Eyed Peas

Mexican-Stuffed Potatoes, Stuffed Vidalia Onions, Oven French Fries

From front: Herbed Potatoes (page 815), Honey Rutabaga (page 816),
and Rosemary Carrots (page 811)

Butterbeans

Lemon Broccoli

2 tablespoons grated lemon rind
¼ teaspoon salt
¼ teaspoon freshly ground pepper
1½ pounds fresh broccoli
2 tablespoons lemon juice

Combine first 3 ingredients; set aside.

Remove broccoli leaves, and discard tough ends of stalks; cut into spears.

Arrange broccoli in a steamer basket over boiling water. Cover and steam 5 minutes or until crisp-tender.

Arrange broccoli on a serving platter. Sprinkle with lemon rind mixture and lemon juice. **Yield: 6 servings.**

PER SERVING: 33 CALORIES (11% FROM FAT)
FAT 0.4G (SATURATED FAT 0.0G)
PROTEIN 3.4G CARBOHYDRATE 6.7G
CHOLESTEROL 0MG SODIUM 128MG

Butterbeans

2 cups water
1 ounce chopped lean ham
2 cups shelled fresh butterbeans or lima beans
   (about 1¾ pounds)
¼ teaspoon salt
⅛ teaspoon pepper

Combine water and ham in a saucepan; bring to a boil, and cook 5 to 10 minutes. Add beans, salt, and pepper; bring to a boil.

Cover, reduce heat, and simmer 45 minutes or until beans are tender. **Yield: 4 (½-cup) servings.**

PER SERVING: 104 CALORIES (16% FROM FAT)
FAT 1.8G (SATURATED FAT 0.3G)
PROTEIN 6.5G CARBOHYDRATE 16.0G
CHOLESTEROL 4MG SODIUM 247MG

Roasted Red Pepper Corn

4 medium ears fresh corn
Butter-flavored cooking spray
¼ cup diced sweet red pepper

Remove husks and silks from corn. Place each ear on a piece of heavy-duty aluminum foil, and coat with cooking spray. Sprinkle 1 tablespoon sweet red pepper on each ear of corn.

Roll foil lengthwise around corn, and twist foil at each end. Bake at 500° for 20 minutes. **Yield: 4 servings.**

PER SERVING: 87 CALORIES (14% FROM FAT)
FAT 1.4G (SATURATED FAT 0.2G)
PROTEIN 2.5G CARBOHYDRATE 19.3G
CHOLESTEROL 0MG SODIUM 13MG

Rosemary Carrots

(pictured on page 809)

2¼ cups thinly sliced carrots
½ cup water
1 tablespoon brown sugar
1 tablespoon chopped chives
1 teaspoon chicken-flavored bouillon granules
½ teaspoon fresh rosemary
⅛ teaspoon pepper

Combine carrots and water in a saucepan; bring to a boil. Cover, reduce heat, and simmer 7 minutes or until carrots are crisp-tender. Drain, reserving 2 tablespoons liquid.

Combine reserved liquid, brown sugar, and remaining ingredients in a saucepan.

Bring mixture to a boil over medium heat, stirring constantly; pour over carrots and toss. **Yield: 4 (½-cup) servings.**

PER SERVING: 38 CALORIES (9% FROM FAT)
FAT 0.4G (SATURATED FAT 0.1G)
PROTEIN 0.8G CARBOHYDRATE 8.7G
CHOLESTEROL 0MG SODIUM 227MG

Italian Green Beans

Italian Green Beans

1 pound fresh green beans
1 medium onion, sliced and separated into rings
3 cloves garlic
1 teaspoon vegetable oil
2 tablespoons water
1 teaspoon sugar
1 teaspoon dried basil
¼ teaspoon salt
2 tablespoons grated Parmesan cheese

Wash green beans; trim ends, and remove strings.

Add water to depth of 1 inch in a large skillet; bring to a boil, and add beans. Cover, reduce heat, and cook 6 to 8 minutes. Drain and immediately place in ice water. Let stand 5 minutes; drain well.

Cook onion and garlic in oil in a large skillet over medium-high heat, stirring constantly, until tender. Add green beans; cook 1 minute, stirring constantly.

Add 2 tablespoons water, sugar, basil, and salt; cook 1 to 2 minutes, stirring constantly. Remove and discard garlic; sprinkle with Parmesan cheese. **Yield: 3 (1-cup) servings.**

PER SERVING: 98 CALORIES (26% FROM FAT)
FAT 2.8G (SATURATED FAT 1.0G)
PROTEIN 4.6G CARBOHYDRATE 16.2G
CHOLESTEROL 3MG SODIUM 267MG

Cooking Vegetables

The most nutritious vegetables are those that aren't overcooked. Steaming, stir-frying, sautéing, and grilling are great ways to cook vegetables to bring out their natural flavors. Try adding herbs or spices to further enhance the taste.

Fresh Corn Pudding

Southern-Style Creamed Corn

6 medium ears fresh corn
1 cup 1% low-fat milk, divided
2 teaspoons cornstarch
2 (½-inch thick) onion slices
¼ teaspoon salt
¼ teaspoon ground white or black pepper

Cut off tips of kernels into a large bowl; scrape milk and remaining pulp from cob, using a small paring knife. Set aside.

Combine ¼ cup milk and cornstarch; set mixture aside.

Combine remaining ¾ cup milk and onion in a heavy saucepan; bring to a boil over medium heat. Cover, reduce heat, and simmer 5 minutes; remove and discard onion.

Add corn; cook over medium heat, stirring frequently, 5 minutes. Gradually stir in cornstarch mixture, salt, and pepper. Cook, stirring constantly, until thickened and bubbly (about 3 minutes). **Yield: 6 (½-cup) servings.**

PER SERVING: 103 CALORIES (12% FROM FAT)
FAT 1.4G (SATURATED FAT 0.4G)
PROTEIN 3.8G CARBOHYDRATE 22.0G
CHOLESTEROL 2MG SODIUM 131MG

Fresh Corn Pudding

2 cups corn cut from cob (about 4 medium ears)
1 tablespoon minced green pepper
1½ tablespoons all-purpose flour
2 teaspoons sugar
¼ teaspoon salt
¼ teaspoon ground mace
Dash of ground red pepper
½ cup egg substitute
1 cup evaporated fat-free milk
Vegetable cooking spray

Combine first 7 ingredients, stirring well. Combine egg substitute and evaporated milk; add to corn mixture.

Spoon mixture into a 1-quart baking dish coated with cooking spray. Place dish in a large shallow pan; add water to pan to a depth of 1 inch.

Bake at 350° for 1 hour or until a knife inserted in center comes out clean. **Yield: 6 (½-cup) servings.**

PER SERVING: 102 CALORIES (7% FROM FAT)
FAT 0.8G (SATURATED FAT 0.2G)
PROTEIN 7.1G CARBOHYDRATE 18.0G
CHOLESTEROL 2MG SODIUM 185MG

Stuffed Vidalia Onions

4 **medium Vidalia onions (about 1½ pounds)**
2 **tablespoons oil-free Italian**
    dressing
½ **cup diced sweet red pepper**
1 **cup diced zucchini**
½ **cup soft breadcrumbs**
½ **cup (2 ounces) shredded part-skim**
    mozzarella cheese
2 **tablespoons minced fresh parsley**
¼ **teaspoon dried oregano**
Dash of hot sauce
Vegetable cooking spray
Garnishes: paprika, fresh parsley sprigs

Peel onions, and cut a slice from top and bottom; chop slices, and set aside.

Cook onions in boiling water 15 to 20 minutes or until tender but not mushy. Cool. Remove center of onions, leaving shells intact; reserve onion centers for another use. Set onion shells aside.

Heat Italian dressing in a medium skillet until hot; add chopped onion, red pepper, and zucchini, and cook until tender, stirring constantly. Remove from heat; stir in breadcrumbs and next 4 ingredients.

Fill each onion shell with ½ cup vegetable mixture; place filled shells in an 8-inch square baking dish coated with cooking spray.

Cover and bake at 350° for 20 minutes. Uncover and bake 5 additional minutes. Garnish, if desired. **Yield: 4 servings.**

PER SERVING: 111 CALORIES (24% FROM FAT)
FAT 3.0G (SATURATED FAT 1.5G)
PROTEIN 5.9G CARBOHYDRATE 16.2G
CHOLESTEROL 8MG SODIUM 182MG

Oven-Fried Okra

1 **pound fresh okra**
¼ **cup egg substitute**
¼ **cup nonfat buttermilk**
⅔ **cup cornmeal**
⅓ **cup all-purpose flour**
1 **teaspoon baking powder**
½ **teaspoon salt**
1 **tablespoon vegetable oil**
Vegetable cooking spray

Wash okra and drain. Remove tips and stem ends; cut okra crosswise into ½-inch slices.

Combine egg substitute and buttermilk; add okra, stirring to coat well. Let stand 10 minutes.

Combine cornmeal and next 3 ingredients in a zip-top plastic bag. Drain okra, small portions at a time, using a slotted spoon; place okra in bag with cornmeal mixture, shaking gently to coat.

Brush oil on a 15- x 10- x 1-inch jellyroll pan; add okra in a single layer.

Coat okra with cooking spray, and bake at 450° for 8 minutes. Stir well, and spray with cooking spray again; bake 7 to 8 additional minutes. After last baking, broil 4 inches from heat (with electric oven door partially opened) 4 to 5 minutes or until browned, stirring occasionally. **Yield: 7 (½-cup) servings.**

PER SERVING: 113 CALORIES (23% FROM FAT)
FAT 2.9G (SATURATED FAT 0.5G)
PROTEIN 3.9G CARBOHYDRATE 18.6G
CHOLESTEROL 0MG SODIUM 198MG

Black-Eyed Peas

Deviled Purple Hull Peas

3 cups shelled fresh purple hull peas or
   black-eyed peas (1 pound)
2 cups water
½ teaspoon salt
2 tablespoons cider vinegar
1 teaspoon dry mustard
¼ teaspoon sugar
¼ teaspoon pepper
1 clove garlic, minced
1 tablespoon chopped fresh parsley

Combine first 3 ingredients in a large sauce-pan; bring to a boil. Cover, reduce heat, and sim-mer 30 minutes or until tender; drain, reserving ½ cup liquid.

Combine reserved liquid, vinegar, and next 4 ingredients in saucepan. Add peas, and cook, stir-ring occasionally, over medium heat 5 minutes or until thoroughly heated. Spoon into a serving bowl; top with parsley. **Yield: 6 (½-cup) servings.**

PER SERVING: 115 CALORIES (5% FROM FAT)
FAT 0.6G (SATURATED FAT 0.2G)
PROTEIN 7.3G CARBOHYDRATE 20.9G
CHOLESTEROL 0MG SODIUM 201MG

Black-Eyed Peas

6 cups fresh black-eyed peas
3 (14.25-ounce) cans ready-to-serve, reduced-
   sodium, fat-free chicken broth
2 teaspoons Creole seasoning
1 teaspoon olive oil
¼ teaspoon hot sauce

Combine all ingredients in a Dutch oven; bring to a boil. Cover, reduce heat, and simmer 45 minutes or until tender, stirring occasionally. Serve with a slotted spoon. **Yield: 6 (1-cup) servings.**

Note: 2 (16-ounce) packages frozen black-eyed peas may be substituted for 6 cups fresh black-eyed peas.

PER SERVING: 259 CALORIES (11% FROM FAT)
FAT 3.1G (SATURATED FAT 0.4G)
PROTEIN 16.5G CARBOHYDRATE 42.7G
CHOLESTEROL 0MG SODIUM 193MG

Pretty Pepper Kabobs

12 (6-inch) wooden skewers
1 large onion, cut into wedges
1 large sweet yellow pepper, cubed
1 large sweet red pepper, cubed
1 large green pepper, cubed
Olive oil-flavored cooking spray

Soak wooden skewers in water at least 30 minutes.

Alternate vegetables on skewers; spray each kabob with cooking spray.

Cook, covered with grill lid, over medium-hot coals (350° to 400°) 8 to 10 minutes or until done, turning frequently. **Yield: 8 servings.**

PER SERVING: 22 CALORIES (20% FROM FAT)
FAT 0.5G (SATURATED FAT 0.0G)
PROTEIN 0.7G CARBOHYDRATE 4.5G
CHOLESTEROL 0MG SODIUM 2MG

Grilled Sweet Potatoes

2 pounds sweet potatoes, peeled and cut into wedges
3 tablespoons reduced-sodium soy sauce
2 tablespoons dry sherry
2 tablespoons honey
2 tablespoons water
1 clove garlic, minced
Vegetable cooking spray
1 tablespoon sesame oil

Arrange sweet potato in a steamer basket; place over boiling water. Cover and steam 5 to 7 minutes.

Combine soy sauce and next 4 ingredients in a shallow dish; add sweet potato, and toss gently.

Drain sweet potato, reserving soy sauce mixture. Arrange sweet potato in a single layer in a grill basket coated with cooking spray; brush wedges with sesame oil.

Cook, covered with grill lid, over medium coals (300° to 350°) 15 minutes, basting with reserved soy sauce mixture and turning several times. **Yield: 6 servings.**

PER SERVING: 167 CALORIES (15% FROM FAT)
FAT 2.7G (SATURATED FAT 0.4G)
PROTEIN 2.3G CARBOHYDRATE 34.3G
CHOLESTEROL 0MG SODIUM 257MG

Oven French Fries

½ cup grated Parmesan cheese
2 teaspoons dried oregano
2 (8-ounce) baking potatoes, unpeeled
1 egg white, beaten
Vegetable cooking spray

Combine Parmesan cheese and oregano, and set aside.

Cut each potato lengthwise into 8 wedges; dip wedges into egg white, and dredge in Parmesan cheese mixture.

Place fries on a baking sheet coated with cooking spray. Bake at 425° for 25 minutes. **Yield: 4 (4-wedge) servings.**

PER SERVING: 137 CALORIES (22% FROM FAT)
FAT 3.4G (SATURATED FAT 2.0G)
PROTEIN 7.6G CARBOHYDRATE 19.8G
CHOLESTEROL 8MG SODIUM 207MG

Herbed Potatoes

(pictured on page 809)

Vegetable cooking spray
4 medium baking potatoes, cut into ¼-inch slices (1½ pounds)
2 medium-size white onions, cut into ¼-inch slices (12 ounces)
5 plum tomatoes, sliced (1 pound)
½ teaspoon salt
1 teaspoon dried thyme
¾ teaspoon dried rosemary, crushed
1 tablespoon olive oil
2 tablespoons chopped fresh parsley

Coat a 13- x 9- x 2-inch baking dish with cooking spray. Layer half each of potato, onion, and tomato in dish; sprinkle with half each of salt, thyme, and rosemary. Repeat layers, and drizzle evenly with olive oil.

Cover and bake at 425° for 35 to 40 minutes or until tender. Sprinkle with parsley. **Yield: 8 (¾-cup) servings.**

PER SERVING: 108 CALORIES (18% FROM FAT)
FAT 2.1G (SATURATED FAT 0.3G)
PROTEIN 2.9G CARBOHYDRATE 20.7G
CHOLESTEROL 0MG SODIUM 159MG

Mexican-Stuffed Potatoes

4 medium baking potatoes (1½ pounds)
1 (8-ounce) carton plain low-fat yogurt
¼ cup fat-free milk
⅛ teaspoon pepper
1 (4.5-ounce) can chopped green chiles,
    drained
1 (2-ounce) jar diced pimiento, drained
4 large, pitted ripe olives, chopped
½ cup (2 ounces) shredded reduced fat sharp
    Cheddar cheese, divided

Wash potatoes; prick several times with a fork. Bake at 400° for 1 hour or until done. Let cool to touch. Cut potatoes in half lengthwise; carefully scoop out pulp, leaving shells intact. Set aside.

Combine potato pulp, yogurt, milk, and pepper; mash until light and fluffy.

Stir chiles, pimiento, olives, and half of Cheddar cheese into potato mixture. Stuff shells with potato mixture; place on an ungreased baking sheet.

Bake at 375° for 10 minutes. Sprinkle evenly with remaining cheese, and bake 2 additional minutes. **Yield: 8 servings.**

PER SERVING: 111 CALORIES (17% FROM FAT)
FAT 2.1G (SATURATED FAT 1.1G)
PROTEIN 5.9G CARBOHYDRATE 17.9G
CHOLESTEROL 7MG SODIUM 136MG

Honey Rutabaga

(pictured on page 809)

½ cup dry white wine
1 tablespoon brown sugar
2 tablespoons honey
2 teaspoons reduced-calorie margarine
4 cups cubed, uncooked rutabaga

Combine all ingredients in a large saucepan. Bring to a boil; cover, reduce heat, and simmer 40 to 45 minutes. **Yield: 5 (¾-cup) servings.**

PER SERVING: 82 CALORIES (13% FROM FAT)
FAT 1.2G (SATURATED FAT 0.2G)
PROTEIN 1.4G CARBOHYDRATE 18.2G
CHOLESTEROL 0MG SODIUM 40MG

Parmesan-Stuffed Tomatoes

(pictured on page 791)

4 medium tomatoes (2½ pounds)
3 tablespoons chopped green onions
2 tablespoons chopped green pepper
1 teaspoon reduced-calorie margarine, melted
¼ cup Italian-seasoned breadcrumbs
2 tablespoons chopped fresh parsley
⅛ teaspoon dried oregano
⅛ teaspoon ground red pepper
⅛ teaspoon black pepper
Vegetable cooking spray
2 tablespoons grated Parmesan cheese

Slice off top of each tomato, and carefully scoop out pulp. Set tomato shells and pulp aside.

Cook green onions and green pepper in margarine in a large skillet over medium-high heat, stirring constantly, until tender. Remove from heat.

Stir in tomato pulp, breadcrumbs, and next 4 ingredients. Spoon into shells, and place in an 8-inch square baking dish coated with cooking spray.

Cover and bake at 350° for 25 minutes. Sprinkle with cheese, and broil 5 inches from heat (with electric oven door partially opened) 3 minutes or until golden. **Yield: 4 servings.**

PER SERVING: 106 CALORIES (23% FROM FAT)
FAT 2.7G (SATURATED FAT 0.8G)
PROTEIN 4.6G CARBOHYDRATE 18.6G
CHOLESTEROL 2MG SODIUM 281MG

METRIC EQUIVALENTS

The recipes that appear in this cookbook use the standard United States
method for measuring liquid and dry or solid ingredients (teaspoons, tablespoons,
and cups). The information on this chart is provided to help cooks outside
the U.S. successfully use these recipes. All equivalents are approximate.

METRIC EQUIVALENTS FOR DIFFERENT TYPES OF INGREDIENTS

A standard cup measure of a dry or solid ingredient will
vary in weight depending on the type of ingredient.
A standard cup of liquid is the same volume for any type of
liquid. Use the following chart when converting standard cup
measures to grams (weight) or milliliters (volume).

Standard Cup	Fine Powder (ex. flour)	Grain (ex. rice)	Granular (ex. sugar)	Liquid Solids (ex. butter)	Liquid (ex. milk)
1	140 g	150 g	190 g	200 g	240 ml
¾	105 g	113 g	143 g	150 g	180 ml
⅔	93 g	100 g	125 g	133 g	160 ml
½	70 g	75 g	95 g	100 g	120 ml
⅓	47 g	50 g	63 g	67 g	80 ml
¼	35 g	38 g	48 g	50 g	60 ml
⅛	18 g	19 g	24 g	25 g	30 ml

USEFUL EQUIVALENTS FOR DRY INGREDIENTS BY WEIGHT

(To convert ounces to grams, multiply
the number of ounces by 30.)

1 oz	=	¹⁄₁₆ lb	=	30 g
4 oz	=	¼ lb	=	120 g
8 oz	=	½ lb	=	240 g
12 oz	=	¾ lb	=	360 g
16 oz	=	1 lb	=	480 g

USEFUL EQUIVALENTS FOR LENGTH

(To convert inches to centimeters,
multiply the number of inches by 2.5.)

1 in			=	2.5 cm			
6 in	=	½ ft	=	15 cm			
12 in	=	1 ft	=	30 cm			
36 in	=	3 ft	=	1 yd	=	90 cm	
40 in			=	100 cm	=	1 m	

USEFUL EQUIVALENTS FOR LIQUID INGREDIENTS BY VOLUME

¼ tsp						=	1 ml		
½ tsp						=	2 ml		
1 tsp						=	5 ml		
3 tsp	=	1 tbls			=	½ fl oz	=	15 ml	
		2 tbls	=	⅛ cup	=	1 fl oz	=	30 ml	
		4 tbls	=	¼ cup	=	2 fl oz	=	60 ml	
		5⅓ tbls	=	⅓ cup	=	3 fl oz	=	80 ml	
		8 tbls	=	½ cup	=	4 fl oz	=	120 ml	
		10⅔ tbls	=	⅔ cup	=	5 fl oz	=	160 ml	
		12 tbls	=	¾ cup	=	6 fl oz	=	180 ml	
		16 tbls	=	1 cup	=	8 fl oz	=	240 ml	
1 pt			=	2 cups	=	16 fl oz	=	480 ml	
1 qt			=	4 cups	=	32 fl oz	=	960 ml	
						33 fl oz	=	1000 ml	= 1 l

USEFUL EQUIVALENTS FOR COOKING/OVEN TEMPERATURES

	Fahrenheit	Celsius	Gas Mark
Freeze Water	32° F	0° C	
Room Temperature	68° F	20° C	
Boil Water	212° F	100° C	
Bake	325° F	160° C	3
	350° F	180° C	4
	375° F	190° C	5
	400° F	200° C	6
	425° F	220° C	7
	450° F	230° C	8
Broil			Grill

Index

818

ICE CREAMS AND SHERBETS

Almond Crunch, Frozen, 617
Almond Ice Cream Balls, 118
Apricot Sherbet, 610
Banana Yogurt Ice Milk, 728
Blackberry Sorbet, 610
Black Russian, Mock, 701
Blueberry Ice Cream, 604
Bombe, Caramel-Toffee, 615
Bombe with Raspberry Sauce,
    Creamy, 614
Bourbon Blizzard, 702
Butter Crisp Ice Cream, 604
Butter Pecan Ice Cream, 604
Champagne Ice, 609
Cherry-Pecan Ice Cream, 604
Chocolate
    Alaska, Brownie Baked, 620
    Black Forest Ice Cream, 604
    Brownies, Chocolate Ice Cream, 618
    Double Chocolate Ice Cream, 604
    Mint-Chocolate Chip Ice Cream, 604
    Mint-Chocolate Chip Ice Cream
        Squares, 619
    Mocha Ice Cream, 604
    Mocha Freeze, Royal, 612
    Peanut Ice Cream, Chocolate-
        Covered, 604
    Sundaes, Chocolate-Mint, 25
Coffee Ice Cream, 604
Cookies and Cream Ice Cream, 604
Floats, Root Beer, 85
Frangelica Cream, 609
Fruit Cream, Frozen, 613
Honey-Vanilla Ice Cream, 607
Layered Sherbet Dessert, 617
Lemonade Ice Cream, 604
Lemon Ice Cream Tarts, 81
Peach Ice Cream, Fresh, 607
Peach Sherbet, 728
Peachy Sherbet Cooler, 125
Peanut Butter Ice Cream, 604
Peanut Ice Cream, 609
Peppermint Ice Cream Pie, 678
Pie, Double-Delight Ice Cream, 133
Pie, Spectacular Ice Cream, 678
Piña Colada Ice Cream, 608
Pineapple-Orange Sherbet, 610
Praline Freeze, 612
Rainbow Candy Ice Cream, 604
Santa's Hats, 89
Sodas, Old-Fashioned Strawberry, 91
Spumoni, Charlotte, 615
Strawberries and Cream, 605
Strawberry-Banana-Nut Ice Cream, 604
Strawberry Ice Milk, Fresh, 730
Toffee Ice Cream, 604
Triple Mint Ice Cream Angel
    Dessert, 576
Vanilla Ice Cream, Basic, 604
Viennese Torte, Frozen, 618
Watermelon Sherbet, 610

JAMBALAYAS

Black-Eyed Pea Jambalaya, 547, 770
Creole Jambalaya, 546
Good Luck Jambalaya, 547
Shrimp Jambalaya, Creole, 546

LAMB

Chili, Spicy Lamb and Black Bean, 534
Stewed Lamb with Five Spices, 766
Stew, Hearty Lamb, 514
Stew, Lamb, 513
Stew with Popovers, Beef or Lamb, 513

LASAGNA

Cheese Lasagna, Cream, 295
Chicken Lasagna, 234, 330
Chicken Lasagna Florentine, 327
Crawfish Lasagna, 338
Florentine, Lasagna, 362
One-Step Lasagna, 295
Pizza, Lasagna, 312
Sausage-Pepperoni Lasagna, 312
Shrimp-and-Fish Lasagna, 348
Specialty Lasagna, 297
Spinach-Stuffed Lasagna Ruffles, 364
Turkey Lasagna, 783
Vegetable Lasagna, 360

LEMON. *See also* FILLINGS; FROSTINGS.

Broccoli, Lemon, 810
Cake, Daffodil Sponge, 579
Cake, Lemon-Coconut, 560
Cake, Tart Lemon-Cheese, 562
Cheesecake, Lemon, 595, 722
Chicken and Vegetables, Lemon, 245
Chicken, Baked Lemon, 201
Chicken, Lemon-Roasted, 774
Chicken Sauté, Lemon-Dill, 125
Corn on the Cob, Lemony, 19
Dressing, Creamy Lemon, 399
Frappé, Lemon, 113
Glaze, Lemon, 579
Ice Cream, Lemonade, 604
Meringue Cream Cups, Lemon, 601
Pasta, Lemon-Garlic, 371
Pie, Best-Ever Lemon Meringue, 674
Pie, Easy Lemon Chess, 669
Pie, Lemon-Lime Meringue, 674
Pie, Lemony Cherry, 662
Pie, Tart Lemon, 43
Rolls, Lemon Angel, 718
Soufflé, Lemon, 655
Tarts, Berry Good Lemon, 664
Tarts, Lemon Ice Cream, 81
Veal, Lemon, 765
Vermicelli, Lemon, 371
Vinaigrette, Lemon-Basil, 738

LENTILS

Soup, Beefy Lentil, 491
Soup, Lentil, 491
Spaghetti Sauce, Lentil, 749

LIME

Chicken, Grilled Lime-Jalapeño, 261
Chicken Thighs, Soy-Lime Grilled, 267
Chicken with Black Bean Sauce, Grilled
    Lime, 778
Pie, Key Lime, 676
Pie, Lemon-Lime Meringue, 674
Soup, Lime, 250
Stir-Fry, Lime-Ginger Beef, 37
Turkey Tenderloins, Lime-Buttered, 129
Vinaigrette, Cilantro-Lime, 743

LINGUINE

Artichoke-and-Shrimp Linguine, 347
Basil Pasta, Fresh Tomato Sauce over, 368
Chicken, Italian, 318
Chicken, Taste-of-Texas Pasta and, 319
Clam Linguine, 336
Clam Sauce, Linguine with, 53
Clam Sauce, Linguine with Red, 334
Green Peas and Pasta, 371
Grilled Vegetables, Linguine with, 358
Mussels Linguine, 339
Pesto and Linguine, Traditional, 373
Primavera, Pasta, 357
Sauce, Linguine with Clam, 336
Shrimp, Garlic-Buttered, 346
Whole Wheat Linguine, 287

LOBSTER

Soup, Spicy Thai Lobster, 426

MACARONI. *See also* SHELL PASTA.

Casserole, Pizza, 301
Cheese
    Blue Cheese, Macaroni and, 379
    Creamy Macaroni and Cheese, 379
    Deluxe Macaroni and Cheese, 311
    Jack-in-the-Macaroni Bake, 379
    Macaroni and Cheese, 377
    Mushroom-Macaroni Casserole, 380
    Old-Fashioned Macaroni and Cheese, 377
Pasticcio, 301

MANICOTTI

Chicken Manicotti, 233
Saucy Manicotti, 305
Seafood Manicotti, 337
Stuffed Manicotti, Spinach-, 363

MAYONNAISE

Garlic-Basil Mayonnaise, 74

MELONS

Compotes, Mellowed-Out Melon, 40
Salad, Cantaloupe, 13
Salad, Cantaloupe Cooler, 37
Sherbet, Watermelon, 610
Soup, Cantaloupe, 456

MERINGUES

Coffee Meringues with Butterscotch
    Mousse, 602
Lemon Meringue Cream Cups, 601
Meringue, 674
Pavlova, 602
Torte, Toffee Meringue, 598

MOUSSES

Apricot Mousse, 642
Butterscotch Mousse, 602, 641
Chocolate Mousse au Grand Marnier, 641